The
International Critical Commentary

on the Holy Scriptures of the Old and
New Testaments.

A CRITICAL AND EXEGETICAL COMMENTARY

ON THE

SECOND EPISTLE OF ST PAUL TO THE CORINTHIANS

BY THE

Rev. ALFRED PLUMMER, M.A., D.D.

PRINTED IN GREAT BRITAIN BY
MORRISON AND GIBB LIMITED
FOR
T. & T. CLARK, EDINBURGH
NEW YORK: CHARLES SCRIBNER'S SONS

A CRITICAL AND EXEGETICAL COMMENTARY

ON THE

SECOND EPISTLE OF ST PAUL
TO THE CORINTHIANS

BY THE

Rev. ALFRED PLUMMER, M.A., D.D.

LATE MASTER OF UNIVERSITY COLLEGE, DURHAM
FORMERLY FELLOW AND TUTOR OF TRINITY COLLEGE, OXFORD

EDINBURGH
T. & T. CLARK, 38 GEORGE STREET

FIRST PRINTED 1915
Latest Reprint 1966

PREFACE

———

SINCE the volume on the First Epistle of St Paul to the Corinthians appeared, circumstances have arisen, some of which have affected the present volume, while others must affect volumes in this series which still remain un-published.

The increase of episcopal work which had fallen to the lot of the Bishop of Exeter, and the ill-health from which he suffered for a considerable time, convinced the present writer that, in the interests of the Diocese and of the Bishop himself, he ought to offer to free the Bishop from the promise which he had kindly given of sharing with his former colleague the work of producing the present volume. This offer the Bishop, after much consideration, reluctantly accepted, and the commentary has been written without the advantage of his co-operation. The loss is great, but it is not quite total. The writer who has been left to do the work single-handed knows the Bishop's mind about most of the important questions which are raised by this perplexing Epistle, and more-over he has had his article on it in Hastings' *Dictionary of the Bible* (i. pp. 491–498) to aid him. Readers who miss in the present volume qualities which they valued in its predecessor may find in the above statement an explanation of the difference.

The changes of circumstances which must affect the remaining volumes of this series are more grave. The deaths of Dr. Briggs in June 1913 and of Dr. Driver in February 1914 are a loss, not only to these commentaries, but to Christendom. Wherever learning, acute criticism, and sound judgment are appreciated, the loss of two such scholars within less than a year will be deeply deplored; and it is impossible for their surviving colleague among the original editors of the International Critical Commentary adequately to express his own personal loss. Dr. Briggs and he were almost exactly the same age, and a year or two ago Dr. Briggs expressed to him a doubt whether either of them would live to see the series completed. As regards one of the two persons concerned that doubt has been shown to be only too well grounded.

The survivor must leave it to others to decide whether there is room for any such commentary as the present volume, and (if there is) whether the volume in any particulars fills it. He has no new solutions to offer for any of the numerous problems which this Epistle presents. But he has endeavoured to show that in some cases there is one solution which is so reasonable in itself, and so much more probable than any other, that students who have no time to investigate every point for themselves may be allowed, without discussion, to assume this solution as the right one. There must, however, always remain a considerable number of questions to which no certain answer can be given, because certainty requires a knowledge of details respecting the Church of Corinth which we do not possess and are not likely to acquire. It is hoped that no difficulty of importance has been passed over in silence, and that no untenable explanation of a difficulty has been adopted.

Readers will do well to study the paraphrases prefixed to the sections before consulting the notes. No translation, however accurate, can give the full meaning of any Pauline Epistle, and this is specially true of 2 Corinthians. The only adequate method is to paraphrase; and great pains have been taken in both these volumes to make the paraphrases as luminous and exact as possible.

A. PLUMMER.

CONTENTS

—✦—

INTRODUCTION:

ix

INTRODUCTION

——◆——

§ I. AUTHENTICITY.

THE evidence, both external and internal, for the genuineness of 2 Corinthians is so strong that a commentator might be excused for assuming it without discussion. In the present state of criticism there is no need to spend time in examining the captious and speculative objections which have been, during the last sixty years, urged against this and others of the four great Epistles of St Paul by a very small group of eccentric critics,* and various recent commentators not only abstain from doing so, but do not even think it worth while to give so much as a summary of the evidence in favour of the genuineness.

The external evidence does not begin quite so early as that for 1 Corinthians; for we may regard it as certain that the Second Epistle was unknown to Clement of Rome, who was so well acquainted with the First. Much of the Second would have served his purpose much better than the First Epistle; yet, frequently as he quotes the First, he nowhere exhibits any knowledge of the Second, for none of the five or six passages, in which some writers have thought that there may be an echo of something in 2 Corinthians, can be relied upon as showing this. Those who care to verify this statement may compare 2 Cor. i. 5, viii. 9, x. 3, 4, x. 13, 15, 16, x. 17, x. 18 respectively with Clem. ii. 1, xvi. 2, xxxvii. 1, i. 3, xiii. 1, xxx. 6. Clement is writing on behalf of the Church of Rome to rebuke the Corinthians for rebelling against authority, and he tells them to "take up *the* Epistle of the blessed Paul the Apostle" and see how he rebukes them for *party spirit.* It would have been far more to the point to have referred to the Second Epistle in which St Paul rebukes them far more severely for *rebellion.* "Yet in the sixty-five chapters of Clement's epistle there is not a single sentence which indicates that he had ever heard that the

* Bruno Bauer, Bruins, Havet, Loman, Mayborn, Naber, Pierson, Steck, Van Manen.

Corinthians had before his own time rebelled against those set over them, or that they had ever repented of their rebellion, though he tells the Corinthians that he has handled every argument" (Kennedy, *The Second and Third Epistles to the Corinthians*, p. 147). The absence of any clear quotation may be regarded as conclusive. "In the whole field of literature it would hardly be possible to adduce a stronger case of proof" (Rendall, *The Epistles of St Paul to the Corinthians*, p. 91). The inference is that 2 Corinthians in A.D. 96 was not known in the Church of Rome; it had not yet been circulated through the Churches.

On the other hand, Polycarp seems to show knowledge of both letters. See on 2 Cor. iii. 2, iv. 14, viii. 21. Irenaeus quotes from chapters ii., iii., iv., v., xiii., sometimes by name; *in epistola secunda ad Corinthios* (iv. xxviii. 3). Athenagoras and Theophilus of Antioch show knowledge of the Epistle. Clement of Alexandria, Tertullian, and Cyprian quote it very frequently. It is named in the Muratorian Fragment, and Marcion accepted it.

Nearly all critics regard the internal evidence as conclusive. Even if the outside testimony were defective, the contents of the letter would completely reassure us.* It is so natural and so vivid; it so evidently deals with a number of details, well known to the writer and to the Corinthians, but not well known, and (in some cases) not particularly interesting, to outsiders; and so much of it refers to a temporary crisis, that it is utterly unlike the artificial product of a forger. What motive could there be for constructing such a fiction? And here one of the great obstacles to a clear understanding of the writer's meaning becomes an argument for the genuineness of the letter; a forger would at least have taken pains to make his meaning clear to those whom he wished to have as readers. The obscure allusions and insinuations are natural enough, if they were written by one who knew all the circumstances, and knew that they were equally well known to those to whom he was writing. They are quite out of place in the composition of one who was imagining what the Apostle might have said to his Corinthian converts. The items of autobiography, which are among the most precious details in the Epistle, ring true and are not at all like fiction. Moreover, there are frequent links with the other three great Epistles of St Paul, and it would be beyond the skill of any inventor to forge all these, to say nothing of the general agreement with the characteristic ideas of the Apostle. There is no letter which enables us to see so deeply into the workings of the writer's mind and heart. Thankfulness, affection, anxiety, entreaty, and indignation come to the surface in successive waves, and the last

* Bachmann, p. 6.

of these is expressed with a severity and bitterness which can be best understood when we keep in mind his repeated assertion that the attacks on his character and authority have compelled him to break out in what must look like a hateful indulgence in self-praise and self-assertion (x. 12, xi. 1, 16, xii. 1, 11). It is strange criticism that can see in all this the imagination of an anonymous inventor. See Bishop Robertson, Hastings, *DB*. i. p. 492 ; Massie, *1 and 2 Corinthians* in *The Century Bible*, pp 4, 5 ; Knowling, *The Witness of the Epistles*, ch. iii., and *The Testimony of St Paul to Christ*, lect. xxiv. and *passim* (see Index). With regard to the four great Epistles and 1 Thessalonians, B. W. Bacon says ; "No doubt exists to-day among scientific critics regarding the authenticity of any one of them, for indeed 1 Corinthians is referred to in 96 A.D. as written by Paul to Corinth, and this and others of the group can be traced even further back as employed by Hebrews, 1 Peter, and James. Moreover, the impression of vivid feeling, of intense and close relation to objective fact, produced by the writings themselves is corroborated by the largely contemporary tradition of Acts, which shows just such combination of agreement in essentials and discrepancy in detail as we expect from honest witnesses " (*Introd. to N.T.* p. 56 ; see also p. 80).

§ II. Occasion, Problems, and Probabilities.

The familar comparison of the transition from the region of 1 Corinthians to that of 2 Corinthians, to the passage from the somewhat intricate paths of a carefully laid-out park to the obscurity of a pathless forest, gives one a fairly correct idea of the difference between the two Epistles. But it needs to be supplemented, and to some extent corrected. The forest is not only obscure, it is thick with roots which trip one up, and with "wait-a-bit" thorns, which continually arrest one's progress. Moreover, it is not altogether pathless. Three main divisions (i.–vii., viii. and ix., x.–xiii.) are as clear as any divisions in the First Epistle. It is when we endeavour to interpret numerous details in the main divisions, and to get them into an intelligible and consistent relation to one another and to the First Epistle, that we stumble and stick fast. Over and over again the Apostle seems to be alluding to something which his readers can understand ; but we are not always certain that there is any allusion, and we can rarely be certain what the allusion is. For instance, he often states that he is not in the habit of doing, or that he has not done, such and such things. In some cases this may be a mere statement of fact ; he takes the Corinthians into his confidence and acquaints them with his personal conduct. But in some cases he may be alluding to the fact that, although *he* does *not*, yet his opponents *do*, act in this particular way; *e.g.* i. 12, 19, ii. 17, iii. 3, 5, v. 16, x. 2, 4, 8, 12, 15. In others he may be alluding to the fact that he has been accused of doing these things; *e.g.* i. 17, 24, iv. 5, v. 13, vii. 2, xi. 7, 9, 16, xiii. 6. Or there may be allusion to both these points; *e.g.* iv. 2, x. 15.

The immediate occasion of this perplexing, but most instructive letter is plain enough. Since the writing of 1 Corinthians, St Paul had had to deal with a very serious crisis in the Church of Corinth, in which his Apostolic authority had been opposed, questioned, and by some scornfully denied, and he had sent Titus to Corinth to deal with the difficulty and reduce the rebellious persons to submission (ii. 13, vii. 6, 7, 13–15). About the success of this enterprise of Titus the Apostle was intensely anxious. He left Ephesus for Troas, hoping that Titus would return from Corinth and meet him there, and in Troas he found an opening for missionary work. The suspense at last became so intolerable that he threw up his work in Troas and crossed over to Macedonia, in order to meet Titus the sooner. Here he did meet Titus, whose report of the result of his mission to Corinth was so unexpectedly favourable that St Paul, in a fervour of thankfulness and affection, at once begins to dictate this letter, in order to make the reconciliation between himself and his Corinthian converts complete (i.–vii.), and stir them up to increased sympathy with their fellow-Christians in Palestine (viii., ix.).*

Thus far we are upon sure ground; but there are at least a dozen questions arising out of this Epistle, or connected with it, respecting which great diversity of opinion exists. With regard to a few of them a decided answer may with confidence be given, in spite of diversity of view; but with regard to the remainder we can do no more than adopt what seems to us to be probable, while admitting that there is room for doubt. Not all of the questions are of equal importance, but hardly any of them can be set aside as trivial.

1. Did Timothy, who had been sent to Corinth before 1 Corinthians was written (see on 1 Cor. xvi. 10), and was with St Paul when 2 Corinthians was written (2 Cor. i. 1.), reach Corinth and was unsuccessful there? Or did he return to St Paul without having reached Corinth? If he reached Corinth, did he leave before 1 Corinthians arrived?

---

* The whole letter, as Bengel remarks, resembles an itinerary, interwoven with noble instruction. The main points of narrative are found i. 8, 15, 16, ii. 1, 12, 13, vii. 5, 6, viii. 1, 6, ix. 1, 2.

2. How long an interval was there between 1 Corinthians and 2 Corinthians? See on 2 Cor. viii. 10, ix. 2.

3. Did the Apostle pay a visit, short and distressing, to Corinth before 2 Corinthians was written? If so,

4. Did this visit take place before or after 1 Corinthians?

5. Was there a letter (other than 1 Corinthians and the letter mentioned in 1 Cor. v. 9) written by St Paul to Corinth before 2 Corinthians? In other words, Does the severe letter mentioned in 2 Cor. ii. 3, 4 and vii. 8, 9 refer to 1 Corinthians? If it does not refer to 1 Corinthians but to some other letter, two questions arise;—

6. Was this severe letter before or after 1 Corinthians?

7. Is this letter wholly lost, or does part of it survive in 2 Cor. x.–xiii.?

8. Is the offender mentioned in 2 Cor. ii. 5–10 and vii. 12 to be identified with the incestuous person of 1 Cor. v. 1 f.? If not,

9. Who was the offender, and whom did he offend?

10. This offender was punished, not in accordance with a vote of the whole Church of Corinth, but only of a majority of the members (2 Cor. ii. 6). What was the punishment? and was it more severe, or less severe, than that which the minority proposed?

11. What was the nature of the opposition to St Paul at Corinth? Did it come from those who thought that he paid too much regard to the Law, or from those who thought that he paid too little?

12. Does part of the letter mentioned in 1 Cor. v. 9 survive in 2 Cor. vi. 14–vii. 1, or is it wholly lost?

At least two of these questions can be answered with certainty; two others can be answered with confidence, if not with absolute certainty; and in the case of two others the probability is very decidedly on one side. With regard to the remaining six the probabilities are more evenly balanced. In each case the reader is referred to the notes on the passages in question for a discussion of the arguments 'for' and 'against.'

5. It ought to be regarded as certain that 1 Corinthians cannot be the severe letter alluded to in 2 Cor. ii. 3, 4 and vii. 8, 9.* Therefore St Paul wrote two letters to the Church of Corinth in addition to the two which have come down to us, viz. the one mentioned in 1 Cor. v. 9 and this severe letter.

8. The offender mentioned in 2 Cor. ii. 5–10 and vii. 12 is not the incestuous person of 1 Cor. v. 1 f. The identification is untenable, and, like the identification of the sinner in Lk.

---

* It is little use to point to 1 Cor. iv. 8–13, 18–21, v. 1–7. It is of the letter as a whole that St Paul writes in 2 Cor. ii. 34 and vii. 8, 9.

b

vii. 37–39 with Mary Magdalen, it ought to be generally abandoned.*

3. It is almost certain that St Paul did pay a short and distressing visit to Corinth between his first stay there and the writing of 2 Corinthians (ii. 1, xii. 14, xiii. 1).

9. It is almost certain that the offender in 2 Cor. v. 5–10 and vii. 12 is some one who had behaved in an outrageous manner to the Apostle. But, if Timothy reached Corinth, it is possible that he was the person who was outrageously treated.

7. It is probable that part of the severe letter of 2 Cor. ii. 3, 4 and vii. 8, 9 survives in 2 Cor. x.–xiii.

12. It is probable that the letter mentioned in 1 Cor. v. 9 is wholly lost.

But it is not easy to determine

1. Whether Timothy failed to reach Corinth or reached Corinth and failed to effect any good there.

2. Whether the interval between 1 and 2 Corinthians was somewhat less than a year or somewhat less than two years.

4. Whether the distressing visit took place after or before 1 Corinthians.

6. Whether the severe letter was written after or before 1 Corinthians.

10. Whether the minority wished the offender to receive a more or a less severe punishment than that which was inflicted by the majority, and whether that punishment was excommunication.

11. Whether St Paul was opposed for having too little or too much regard for the Law.

In all these six cases the balance is *perhaps* in favour of the alternative which is stated first; but it is more easy to adopt a decided opinion than to convince others that it is right; *e.g.* in the volume on 1 Corinthians (pp. xxi–xxiv) reasons have been given for believing that the *second* visit of St Paul to Corinth † is an historical fact, and that it took place before the writing of 1 Corinthians; but Professor K. Lake (*Earlier Epistles of St Paul*, p. 152) has given strong reasons for believing that it took place between 1 and 2 Corinthians, an arrangement which has mani-

---

* "To identify this offender (ἀδικήσας)—who had not, as Paul insists, caused him personal sorrow (ii. 5)—with the incestuous person of 1 Cor. v. would be almost as monstrous, when we consider the mildness with which Paul treats him, as to identify the First Epistle with the stern letter described in the Second" (Jülicher, *Intr. N.T.* p. 91). After writing 1 Cor. v. 5 how could the Apostle say that he had not written 'for his cause that did the wrong'?

† Sometimes called "the intermediate visit," *i.e.* intermediate between the first visit, during which he founded the Church, and the visit which followed soon after the writing of 2 Corinthians.

fest advantages. How greatly opinions are divided on the subject will be seen from the following statement.

This intermediate visit is *doubted or denied* by Baur, Davidson, De Wette, Farrar, G. H. Gilbert, Heinrici, Hilgenfeld, Lange, Lewin, Lias, Paley, Ramsay, A. Robertson, Stanley.

It is *placed before 1 Corinthians*, and in most cases before the lost letter of 1 Cor. v. 9, by Alford, Beet, J. H. Bernard, Bleek, Conybeare and Howson, Cornely, Denney, Findlay, Klöpper, Hausrath, Lightfoot, McFadyen, Olshausen, Otto, Räbiger, Redlich, Reuss, Sanday, Schmiedel, Waite, B. Weiss, Wieseler, Zahn.

It is placed *after 1 Corinthians*, and before the severe letter of 2 Cor. ii. 3, 4 and vii. 8, 9, by Adeney, Bachmann, Barth, Bousset, Cone, Drescher, Ewald, Eylau, Godet, Hagge, Jacquier, Jülicher, Kennedy, Krenkel, Lake, Mangold, Massie, Menzies, Moffatt, Pfleiderer, Rendall, Sabatier, Weiffenbach, Weizsäcker. Allen and Grensted incline to this alternative, but doubtfully; so also D. Walker. Belser and Schäfer place the intermediate visit after 1 Corinthians, but they omit the intermediate letter, identifying the severe letter with 1 Corinthians. Völter regards the intermediate visit as a return to Corinth after a missionary excursion during the Apostle's first stay in the city. His elaborate dissection of both Epistles, as consisting of Pauline material very freely edited on doctrinal grounds, does not merit consideration.

The problems respecting the intermediate letter will be most conveniently studied when the question respecting the integrity of the Epistle is discussed.

The following scheme as to the sequence of events connected with these two great Epistles covers the whole period of the Apostle's work at Corinth. It is tentative, as all such schemes must be, and the more conjectural items are placed in square brackets. From what has been already stated it follows that no scheme which identifies the severe letter (ii. 3, 4, vii. 8, 9) with 1 Corinthians, and which identifies the great offender (ii. 5–10, vii. 12) with the incestuous man (1 Cor. v. 1), can be right. St Paul wrote four letters to the Corinthian Church, two of which have come down to us, while two have partly or wholly perished; and there were two great offenders whom he required the Church to punish. This much may be treated as too firmly established to be open to reasonable doubt. A good deal of the accompanying scheme is generally admitted to be correct.

Possible Sequence of Events.

1. St Paul spends 'a year and six months' at Corinth, 'teaching the word of God' (Acts xviii. 11).

2. He leaves Corinth with Aquila and Priscilla and settles at Ephesus (Acts xviii. 18, 19).

3. Apollos continues the work at Corinth, ' powerfully confuting the Jews' (Acts xviii. 27, 28, xix. 1), and returns to St Paul at Ephesus (1 Cor. xvi. 12).

4. St Paul sends a letter [by Titus], now [wholly] lost, to Corinth condemning fornicators (1 Cor. v. 9) [and announcing the plan mentioned 2 Cor. i. 5, 16]. [A collection for the poor at Jerusalem is started by Titus.]

5. Bad news is brought from Corinth to Ephesus by members of Chloe's household (1 Cor. i. 11) [and also by Apollos (1 Cor. xvi. 12)].

6. Timothy starts from Ephesus for Macedonia and Corinth, and reaches Macedonia (1 Cor. iv. 17, xvi. 10; Acts xix. 22; 2 Cor. i. 1).

7. Letter of the Corinthians to St Paul (1 Cor. vii. 1) [brought by Fortunatus, Stephanas, and Achaicus (1 Cor. xvi. 17)].

8. St Paul writes 1 Corinthians at or near Easter [and sends it by Titus and a brother; the collection for the poor is now organized (1 Cor. xvi. 1; 2 Cor. viii. 6, xii. 18), and Titus then returns to the Apostle at Ephesus].

9. [Timothy arrives at Corinth.] Fresh difficulties arise in the Corinthian Church; the Apostle's authority is questioned, and by some is defied (2 Cor. x. 7, 10, xi. 23, xii. 16, 17). [Timothy leaves, unable to deal with the crisis.]

10. St Paul hears of this [from Timothy] and pays a short visit to Corinth (2 Cor. ii. 1, xii. 14, xiii. 1), during which he is grossly insulted by some Corinthian Christian (2 Cor. ii. 5–8, vii. 12).*

11. St Paul sends Titus to Corinth with a severe letter (ii. 3, 9, vii. 8–12), [the greater part of which is preserved in 2 Cor. x.–xiii.]. Titus is instructed [to press for the collection for the Palestinian Relief Fund and] to return to St Paul through Macedonia and Troas (ii. 12, 13, vii. 5, 6).

12. [Longer stay in Ephesus having become perilous,] St Paul leaves Ephesus for Troas, and being intensely anxious about the effect of the severe letter, he leaves Troas for Macedonia, in order to meet Titus the sooner and get his report (ii. 12, 13).

13. He meets Titus in Macedonia and receives from him a most encouraging report as to the end of the grave crisis in Corinth (vii. 6–16).

---

* This visit ought possibly to be placed earlier, either between 3 and 4 or between 4 and 5. If the former, then it would be mentioned in the lost letter of 1 Cor. v. 9, and this would account for its not being mentioned in 1 Corinthians.

14. He writes **2** Corinthians [i.–ix.] **and sends it** from Macedonia by Titus and two brethren (viii. 16–24).*

15. St Paul reaches Corinth, and during a stay of three months there (Acts xix. 21, xx. 3) writes the Epistle to the Romans (see Sanday and Headlam, *Romans*, pp. xxxvi f.).

The most speculative portions of this scheme are those which are placed in square brackets in the sections numbered 4 and 9. That Titus was the bearer of the first letter written by the Apostle to Corinth, and that he then began to urge the Corinthians to raise money for the poor Christians in Judaea, is not improbable, but there is little evidence for either conjecture. That Timothy reached Corinth and was a failure there is possible, but the silence about his doing anything there is equally well explained by the hypothesis that he never got so far. If he reached Corinth and was contemptuously treated, he probably returned as quickly as possible to St Paul at Ephesus, and his report of the grave condition of things at Corinth would account for the Apostle's decision to hurry across to Corinth himself. But the bad news from Corinth may easily have reached St Paul in some other way.

§ III. Place, Date, and Contents.

Both place and date can be fixed within narrow limits. **The** country was Macedonia (ii. 13, vii. 5, viii. 1, ix. 2–4); and it is possible that the subscription of the Epistle, which is certainly early (B², Syr-Pesh. Syr-Hark. Copt.), is correct in saying that the city was Philippi. It has already been shown (*1 Corinthians*, p. xxxiii) that the First Epistle was probably written in the spring of A.D. 55, and it is probable that the Second Epistle was written in the autumn of the same year. In neither case, however, is the year quite certain. For the First Epistle nearly all modern writers allow some margin ; Harnack, A.D. 50–53 ; C. H. Turner, 52–55 ; Ramsay, 53–56 ; Lightfoot, Lewin, and Wieseler, 54–57. For the Second Epistle, Harnack says 53, Turner 55, Ramsay 56, Lightfoot, Lewin, and Wieseler 57. There is no serious objection to assigning both Epistles to the same year, even for those who believe that between the two letters St Paul paid a brief visit to Corinth. In favourable weather that might be accomplished in less than three weeks. All the events enumerated above, 8–14, might take place in seven or eight months. But Jülicher and others think that we must place about a year and a half between the two Epistles.

* This is at least the *third* mission of Titus to Corinth (8, 11), and may be the *fourth*, if Titus was the bearer of the first letter, now lost (4).

With regard to the letter itself it is better to talk of "contents" rather than "plan." Beyond the three clearly marked
divisions (i.–vii.; viii., ix.; x.–xiii.) there is not much evidence
of plan. In these main divisions the Apostle seems to have
dictated what he had to say just as his thoughts and feelings
moved him, without much consideration of arrangement or
logical sequence. We may conjecture that the last four chapters
were dictated at one sitting, without much pause until the last
chapter was reached. But between vii. and viii., and between
ix. and x. there were doubtless breaks of some duration, if not
between viii. and ix.; and it is not likely that the first seven
chapters were dictated all at one time. Hence the rapid
changes (as they seem to us) of topics and temper; but something more than a break in the time of dictating is required to
account for the immense change from ix. to x. The following
analysis of the three main divisions is offered as a help to a
study of the Epistle in detail. It is not meant to imply or
suggest that the Apostle had any such scheme in his mind as he
dictated the various paragraphs. As in the first Epistle, there is
a mixture of precept and instruction with personal matter; but
the proportion of the two elements is reversed. In 1 Corinthians
the personal element is comparatively slight and appears incidentally. In 2 Corinthians the personal element is the main thing,
especially in the first and last divisions; what is didactic, however important, is not the leading topic or series of topics. It is
the Apostle's conduct and authority that comes to the front
throughout.

Epistolary Introduction, i. 1-11.

    A. *The Apostolic Salutation*, i. 1, 2.

    B. *Preamble of Thanksgiving and Hope*, i. 3-11.

I. Review of his recent Relations with the Corinthians,
    i. 12–vii. 16.

    A. *Defence of his Conduct with regard to his promised
        Visit and the great Offender*, i. 12–ii. 17.
        The postponement of the intended Visit, i. 12–
        ii. 4.
        The Treatment of the great Offender and the
        Result of the severe Letter, ii. 5–17.

    B. *The Glory of the Apostolic Office*, iii. 1–vi. 10.
        The Superiority of the New Ministration to the
        Old, iii. 1–11.

These contents, however we may interpret them in detail, reveal a situation very different from that which is exhibited by the First Epistle. Even with regard to the features which are the same in both letters there is difference. The old relations between Apostle and converts may remain, but they have been, and perhaps still are, severely strained. Some of the old features have vanished and new features have appeared. The Apostle is no longer so serenely sure of the Corinthians' affection and loyalty. They had sometimes criticized him before, and had raised questions as to his being an Apostle (1 Cor. iv. 3, ix. 1, 2); but now he has been openly insulted, defied, and laughed at, and his Apostleship has been denied. He says that self-praise is no recommendation, but they say that he is always singing his own praises and asserting his own importance. Although we hear no more of the four factions of which St Paul speaks with disapproval in 1 Cor. i. 12, 13, yet faction of a far more virulent kind is manifest, and it threatens the Church of Corinth with ruin. Corinth has been invaded by a band of fanatical Jewish Christians, who have a narrow and bigoted view of the spirit of the Gospel and an intense hatred of St Paul's free interpretation of it. They did not attempt to enforce circumcision, as similar fanatics were endeavouring to do among the Galatians, for they probably saw that such attempts would have no success in Greece; but they did their utmost, by accusation and insinuation, to undermine and overthrow the influence of St Paul. We can measure the malignity of their attack by the vehemence of the Apostle's language in repelling it, and indeed we have to attribute atrocious conduct to them in order to understand how he could regard as justifiable all the strong expressions which he uses. This applies specially to xi. 13–15. See Menzies, *ad loc.*, and McFadyen, pp. 247, 248.

§ IV. INTEGRITY.

Among the many features in which 2 Corinthians differs from 1 Corinthians is that of structure. The First Epistle exhibits an evenness of style so complete that its unity, although disputed by a few eccentric critics, as Hagge and Völter, is not open to serious question. A few words in the traditional text are wanting in authority, as 'and in your spirit, which are God's' (vi. 20); and a few are open to suspicion, but not well-grounded suspicion, as possible glosses, as xiv. 34, 35, xv. 56. But proposals to treat the Epistle which has come down to us in the familiar form as a conglomeration of several letters, or of portions of several letters, are not worthy of consideration. The same cannot be said of the Second Epistle. There is considerable probability that it is composite, and that chapters i.–ix. are the greater part of a conciliatory letter, while chapters x.–xiii. are the greater part of a sharp and severe letter which was written before the conciliatory letter was sent; and there is a possibility that part ot a third letter, written before either of the Epistles which have come down to us, is embedded in it (vi. 14–vii. 1). Moreover, doubts have been raised as to whether both viii. and ix. belong to the same letter, some critics regarding ix. as an intruder while a few regard viii. as the intruder. Nor is this all. The verses which tell of the Apostle's escape from Damascus (xi. 32, 33) come so abruptly and prosaically in a passage of lofty feeling and language, that they also are suspected of being out of their original position. They may be a fragment from some other letter, or they may have been accidentally omitted from this letter and then reinserted in the wrong place. A less violent conjecture is that St Paul inserted them after the letter was finished, without caring whether they were quite in harmony with the context.

But the large majority of the critics who are inclined to adopt one or more of these hypotheses are agreed that all the passages in question, vi. 14–vii. 1, viii., ix., xi. 32, 33, and x.–xiii., were written by St Paul. This consensus is specially strong with regard to the last four chapters. There are a few wild critics who contend that not one of the Pauline Epistles is genuine, and their criticisms carry no weight. To accept Galatians, Romans, 1 Corinthians, and 2 Cor. i.–ix. as by St Paul, and reject 2 Cor. x.–xiii. as spurious, would be an amazing result to reach by any kind of argument.

It must always be remembered that in every one of these four cases the doubts as to their being part of the Second Epistle, as St Paul dictated it, *are based entirely on internal evidence.* No MS., no version, and no patristic quotation supplies any evidence that the Epistle was ever in circulation anywhere with any one of these four portions omitted.

It will be convenient to take the four shorter passages first, in the order of their occurrence, reserving the more important question respecting the last four chapters for more detailed treatment after the other passages have been discussed.

1. The strength of the case against vi. 14–vii. 1 lies in the facts that (1) the six verses violently interrupt the sequence of thought, and that (2), when they are removed, vii. 2 fits admirably to vi. 11–13. 'My lips are unlocked to tell you everything; my heart stands wide open. There is no restraint in my feeling towards you; the restraint is in your own affections. But love should awaken love in return; let your heart be opened

wide to receive me. Make room for me; I have never wronged any of you in any way.' The connexion is excellent between πλατύνθητε καὶ ὑμεῖς and χωρήσατε ἡμᾶς, whereas it is difficult to see what the connexion is between vi. 13 and 14, and between vii. 1 and 2. These facts justify the statement that, in its present position, the passage "looks like an erratic boulder." And, when it is pointed out that the letter mentioned in 1 Cor. v. 9 dealt with the same subject as that which is treated in this passage, viz. careful abstention from the pollutions of heathendom, and that the strict charge given in 2 Cor. vi. 14–vii. 1 might be easily misunderstood in the way mentioned in 1 Cor. v. 10, the suggestion that we have here a fragment of that lost letter becomes attractive. This view is accordingly adopted by Dobschütz, Franke, Hilgenfeld, Lisco, Moffatt, Sabatier, Von Soden, and Whitelaw. Others, with less probability, think that the original position of the passage was in 1 Cor. vi. or 1 Cor. x., an hypothesis which has the additional difficulty of there being no external evidence that it ever occupied that position. Consequently we have two great difficulties,—to account for its being universally omitted there and universally admitted here. Others again regard it as a fragment from another letter without attempting to define the original place. If the passage is an erratic boulder, the conjecture that it comes from the letter of 1 Cor. v. 9 is the best that can be made as to its origin; Bacon (*Intr. to N.T.* p. 95) somewhat doubtfully inclines to it.

The least probable hypothesis is that these six verses are not by St Paul, but are an interpolation by another hand. The arguments used in support of this theory are not of great weight.* (*a*) We have in these six verses six words which St Paul uses nowhere else, and which are found nowhere else in N.T.; ἑτεροζυγοῦντες, μετοχή, συμφώνησις, Βελίαρ, συνκατάθεσις, μολυσμοῦ. That fact counts for very little. The subject of intimacy with the heathen is rarely discussed by St Paul, and this topic accounts for some of these six words: and when a writer, in order to vary his language, requires five different words to express 'intimacy,' he is likely to employ some that are less usual. Σύμφωνος occurs in 1 Corinthians, and μετέχω is frequent there, as also in Hebrews. (*b*) It is said that this stringent prohibition is inconsistent with 1 Cor. v. 9 f. and x. 27 f. But that is not correct. There, the Apostle tolerates the idea of a Christian caring to accept a heathen's invitation to dinner; here, he strictly forbids intimate combinations with heathen—a very different thing from an exceptional sharing of a meal. (*c*) It is

---

* "Neither the language nor the ideas justify a suspicion of the genuineness of the passage" (Moffatt).

urged that 'defilement of flesh and spirit' is not Pauline. St Paul treats 'the flesh' as the seat of sin and defilement, and 'the spirit' as the opponent of 'the flesh.' The latter statement is true of the Apostle's common practice, when he is writing theologically. Here he is not doing so. In popular language 'flesh and spirit' is an expression which covers the whole of man's nature. The Apostle says in conclusion that Christians must keep themselves free from what would defile them (as we might say) 'body and soul.' St Paul often uses 'flesh' in the sense of the weak physical part of man, without any idea of its being the seat of sin and opposed to the spirit (v. 5, xii. 7 ; Gal. ii. 20, iv. 13). 'That life which I now live in the flesh I live in faith, the faith which is in the Son of God' (Gal. ii. 20), shows clearly that with St Paul 'flesh' is not always essentially sinful. See Gifford, *Romans*, in the *Speaker's Commentary*, p. 50.

But all these hypotheses as to this passage being no part of our Epistle in its original form, labour under the grave difficulty that there is no MS. evidence to support them. How is it that *all* our witnesses have the passage, and have it in this place ? A fragment of the letter mentioned 1 Cor. v. 9 might easily survive ; but how did it come to be inserted here ? Why place it where it does not seem to fit ? If it be supposed that a stray leaf from one letter has accidentally got among the leaves of another letter, then we have to suppose that the stray leaf chanced to begin and end with a complete sentence, and that, of the leaves between which it was erroneously inserted, one chanced to end with a complete sentence and the other to begin with one. Such a combination of chances is improbable.

It seems, therefore, safer to abide by the external evidence and regard the passage as being not only Paul's, but as having been placed by him in this apparently unsuitable place. Abrupt digressions are more possible in dictating than in writing. While he was imploring the Corinthians to be as frank and affectionate towards him as he was towards them, he may have remembered that their refusal to comply with his demand that they should make no compromises with heathendom was one of the chief causes of the constraint which kept them apart from him. In that case he might there and then repeat his demand and the reasons for it, before going on with his tender appeal. Zahn (*Intr. to N.T.* i. p. 350) goes so far as to suggest that the connexions between vi. 13 and 14 and between vii. 1 and 2 are better than the connexion between vi. 13 and vii. 2. While Baljon, Clemen, Pfleiderer, and others favour the excision of the passage, Bachmann, Bousset, and Lietzmann regard the reasons for treating it as an interpolation as inadequate. Adeney (*Biblical Intr. to N.T.* p. 371) seems to think that the hypothesis does not need to be mentioned. Allen and Grensted (*Intr. to the Books of N.T.* p. 129) mention it without expressing any opinion of its merits. K. Lake (*Earlier Epistles of St Paul,* pp. 123, 162) says that, although "to some extent the very strongly supported theory which divides 2 Cor. x.–xiii. from 2 Cor. i.–ix. lends strength to the much more doubtful hypothesis that 2 Cor. vi. 14–vii. 1 is an interpolation," yet this hypothesis "from its nature can never be regarded as more than a probable guess."

2. The proposal to separate ch. viii. from i.–vii. has met with very little approval, and it may be safely rejected. The sequence is quite natural, and any change in tone is adequately accounted for by the change of subject. One does not ask favours in the same tone as that in which one claims rights.

3. Still less has the proposal of Semler to separate ch. ix. from ch. viii., and make the former a letter to the Christians of Achaia, found favour. The audacious theory of A. Halmel (*Der zweite Korintherbrief des Apostles Paulus,* Halle, 1904) needs little more than mention. He divides our Epistle into nine portions, of which the largest is x. 1–xiii. 10, and this is supposed to be the second of three letters. The first letter contains viii., the last contains ix.* As will be shown in the notes, so far from there being a manifest break between viii. and ix., the division of the chapters is clumsily made. The first verses of ix. are linked to the end of viii. The one thing that is probable in this extreme theory is that x. 1–xiii. 10 ought to be separated from i.–ix. "The attempts to isolate viii. as a separate note (Hagge), written later than ix. (Baljon), or as part of the Intermediate Letter (Michelsen), break down for much the same reason as the cognate hypothesis that ix. itself was a subsequent letter sent to the Achaian churches (Semler). The unity of the situation pre-supposed in viii. and ix. is too well-marked to justify any separation of the chapters either from one another or from the letter i.–ix., whose natural conclusion they furnish" (Moffatt).

4. The case of xi. 32, 33 is somewhat similar to that of vi. 14–vii. 1. We have a violent transition in the vein of thought; and if we omit the verses which produce this abrupt change, we have a good sequence of thought. But the two cases are very different. Here the transition is not nearly so violent as there; and, when the verses which seem to interrupt the flow of idea are omitted, we do not obtain so good a junction of thought and language as in the former case. Indeed, those who propose to excise the sentences which seem to cause a difficulty are not agreed as to how much ought to be cut out in order to make a good junction. Some would omit only xi. 32, 33. Some would

---

* We may say with C. R. Gregory (*Einl. in das N.T.* p. 666); *Das ist alles völlig aus der Luft gegriffen.*

omit these two verses and the first half of xii. 1 ; others, these two and the whole of xii. 1. But it is by no means incredible that St Paul dictated just what has come down to us. No one always writes letters that are perfectly consecutive in thought. Certainly St Paul does not; and those who habitually dictate their letters are apt to make sudden digressions from which they return with equal suddenness. How often, when we read a letter over, we note that the omission of a sentence or two would have made it read more smoothly. It is possible that the story of the Apostle's escape from Damascus had been embroidered, in order to make his descent in a basket laughable. Therefore, when he is recounting τὰ τῆς ἀσθενείας μου, he mentions it and solemnly declares that his account of what took place is the truth. It is, however, possible that in dictating he omitted the incident, and that, when he decided that it ought to be inserted, his amanuensis put it in the margin not quite in the best place. It would come better immediately after xi. 23. Even if this passage stood alone, there would be no need to doubt that the event took place ; and it is confirmed by Acts ix. 23–25.

The Last Four Chapters.

5. We come now to the much larger, more important, and more interesting question, whether the four concluding chapters, x.–xiii., or at any rate x. 1–xiii. 10, ought not to be separated from the first nine chapters and regarded as the main portion of a very different letter, which probably preceded the first nine chapters.

We may at once set aside the second alternative. If the theory is true in any shape, it must include the whole of the last chapter. To say that no one could write xiii. 10, and then immediately afterwards write v. 11, is dogmatic assumption. The sudden change of tone, so far from being incredible, is natural, especially in one who was so full of shifting emotions as St Paul. The most unwelcome task of denouncing malignant enemies and threatening impenitent offenders is accomplished. He will not utter another word in that strain. He ends with a few words of exhortation, a few words of affection, and his fullest benediction.

Moreover, if we assume that the whole of the last four chapters form one piece, viz. the middle and conclusion of a different letter, which had lost its beginning, we can more easily understand how this came to be joined to the main portion of another letter, which had lost its end. It is much less easy to understand how a large portion of a letter, without either beginning or end, came to be inserted between the main portion of another letter and its conclusion. As a conclusion, xiii. 11–13 (14) belong to the last four chapters and not to the first nine. In the discussion which follows, that point is assumed. We are dealing with the supposed conjunction of a letter that has lost its conclusion with a letter that has lost its beginning, not with the insertion of a large fragment of one letter into a break near to the conclusion of another letter. See p. 385.

The hypothesis that x.–xiii. ought to be separated from i.–ix. is almost always combined with the hypothesis that x.–xiii. is part of the severe letter to the Corinthians (2 Cor. ii. 3, 9, vii. 8), as to the effect of which the Apostle was so anxious when he left Ephesus for Troas, and still more so when he left Troas for Macedonia in order to meet Titus as soon as possible and receive his report of the state of Corinth (ii. 12, 13, vii. 6). This is a convenient place, therefore, for considering the problem of this severe "intermediate" letter. Although scholars of great eminence have declared that it is not impossible that 1 Corinthians is the letter which was written 'out of much affliction and anguish of heart . . . with many tears' (2 Cor. ii. 3), the sending of which he at one time regretted (vii. 8), that hypothesis may once for all be abandoned as untenable. On the other hand, we may well believe that much of 2 Cor. x.–xiii. was written in anguish, and that there are things in these scathing criticisms, especially in x. and xi., which he sometimes regretted having written. As in the case of the intermediate visit, there is great difference of opinion respecting this intermediate letter.

Its existence is *doubted or denied* by Alford, Beet, J. H. Bernard, Conybeare and Howson, Denney, Lias, McFadyen, Meyer, B. Weiss, Zahn; in fact by all who would identify the letter of 2 Cor. ii. 3, 9 and vii. 8 with 1 Corinthians.

It is regarded as *wholly lost* by Bachmann, Barth, Bleek, Bousset, Credner, Drummond, Ewald, Farrar, Findlay, Godet, Heinrici, Klöpper, Jacquier, Jülicher, Lietzmann, Menzies, Neander, Olshausen, Sabatier, Sanday, Weizsäcker, Ziegler.

It is regarded as *probably preserved in part* in 2 Cor. x.–xiii. by Adeney, Bacon, Clemen, Cone, Cramer, Hausrath, Kennedy, König, K. Lake, Lipsius, Lisco, McGiffert, Massie, Michelsen, Moffatt, Paulus, Peake, Pfleiderer, Rendall, Schmiedel, R. Scott, Seufert, Völter, Von Soden, Wagenmann, Weisse. G. Milligan inclines to this view.

There is yet another theory respecting these four chapters. Drescher, Krenkel, and Weber regard them as constituting a separate letter, which, however, they place *after* 2 Cor. i.–ix. So also in the main does Schnedermann.* The supposition is that, after 2 Cor. i.–ix. had been despatched to Corinth, bad reports

---

* Such a theory requires us to believe that Titus had been utterly mistaken in the excellent report which he had just brought from Corinth.

of the state of the Corinthian Church reached the Apostle, and that he then wrote and sent x.–xiii. Drescher places the intermediate visit between the sending of i.–ix. and the sending of x.–xiii.

It is plain from these facts that there is a very large consensus of opinion in favour of there having been a severe letter of the Apostle to Corinth which cannot be identified with 1 Corinthians, and that among those who hold this opinion, which is doubtless correct, not a few favour the hypothesis that a great deal of this severe letter survives in 2 Cor. x.–xiii. Thus far, however, the case for the latter hypothesis is not a strong one. St Paul tells us that before writing 2 Cor. i.–ix. he had in affliction and anguish written a letter to Corinth which was so severe that at times he wished that he had not sent it, and that for weeks he was intensely anxious about the result; and in 2 Cor. x.–xiii. there is a good deal that harmonizes with those statements. But there are stronger reasons for the identification than this general harmony. We have to take into account (1) the extraordinary change of tone which is manifest when we pass from ix. to x.; (2) the apparent inconsistency between passages in i.–ix. and passages in x.–xiii., which make it difficult to believe that statements so inconsistent can have been penned in one and the same letter ; (3) the fact that there are passages in i.–ix. which seem to refer to passages in x.–xiii., and therefore indicate that x.–xiii. was written and sent to Corinth before i.–ix. was written ; (4) the fact that x. 16 is expressed naturally, if the writer was in Ephesus, where the severe letter was written, but not naturally, if the writer was in Macedonia, where i.–ix. was written. All these points added to the general harmony between x.–xiii. and the Apostle's statements about his severe letter make a really strong case.

(1) The extraordinary change of tone which begins at x. 1 and continues to xiii. 10 is generally admitted, and is sometimes described in adequate language by those who nevertheless maintain the integrity of the whole Epistle. K. Lake, who surrenders the integrity, says tersely and truly enough ; " There is not only no connexion between 2 Cor. i.–ix. and 2 Cor. x.–xiii., but there is an absolute break between them. . . . There never has been, and indeed there never can be, any dispute as to the fact that the whole tone of the Epistle changes suddenly at ch. x. 1, and that, if 2 Cor. x.–xiii. had existed in a separate form, no one would ever have dreamt of suggesting that it was the continuation of 2 Cor. i.–ix." (pp. 155, 157). There is not only logical inconsistency, as will be seen in the next section, there is psychological maladroitness. The change is not only surprising in its intensity, it is in the wrong direction. When one wishes to re-establish friendly relations with persons, one may begin by stating one's own grievances frankly and finding fault freely, and

then pass on to say all that is conciliatory, showing a willingness to forgive and a desire for renewed affection. But here the Apostle does the opposite. Having written in tender language of his intense longing for reconciliation and his intense joy at having been able to establish it, he suddenly bursts out into a torrent of reproaches, sarcastic self-vindication, and stern warnings, which must almost have effaced the pacific effect of the first seven chapters. Nor is this all. In between these strangely inharmonious portions there is placed a delicate and somewhat hesitating, yet eager, petition for increased interest in the collection for the poor Christians at Jerusalem. This follows naturally enough after affectionate relations have been re-established by the first seven chapters. But it is strange policy, immediately after imploring freshly regained friends to do their duty, to begin heaping upon them reproaches and threats.

(2) The logical inconsistency is not so conspicuous as the psychological, and it might escape observation ; but in certain particulars it is striking enough. A writer might say first one and then the other of two inconsistent statements, if each was in a different letter, especially if the less pleasing statement was sent first ; but he would hardly put them in the same letter, writing first what was pleasing and then what was the reverse. At any rate he would not act thus towards people with whom he wished to be on good terms. The contrasts will be best seen if the inconsistent passages are placed side by side.

2 COR. i.–ix.	2 COR. x.–xiii.
i. 24. By your faith ye stand ; *i.e.* as regards belief, ye are sound. vii. 16. I rejoice that in everything I am of good courage concerning you. viii. 7. As ye abound in everything, in faith, and utterance, and knowledge, and in all earnestness, and in your love to us.	xiii. 5. Try your own selves, whether ye be in the faith. xii. 20, 21. I fear lest by any means there should be strife, jealousy, wraths, factions, backbitings, whisperings, swellings, tumults ; lest I should mourn for many of them that have sinned heretofore, and repented not of the uncleanness and fornication and lasciviousness which they committed.
ii. 3. My joy is the joy of you all. vii. 4. Great is my glorying in your behalf ; I am filled with comfort.	x. 2. I beseech you, that I may not when present show courage with the confidence wherewith I count to be bold against some, which count of us as if we walked according to the flesh.
vii. 11. In everything ye approved yourselves to be pure in the matter.	xi. 3. I fear lest by any means your minds should be corrupted from the simplicity and purity that is toward Christ.
iii. 2. Ye are our epistle, written in our heart.	xiii. 10. I write these things while absent, that I may not when present deal sharply.

The hypothesis that x.–xiii. is part of a stern letter, which was sent to Corinth before the conciliatory first chapters were written, puts these divergent statements in their logical order. Fears and warnings are expressed while a very rebellious spirit is prevalent in the Corinthian Church. Joyous commendation is expressed after the rebels have submitted and shown regret.

(3) Let it be admitted that divergent statements such as the above would be not impossible in a letter written, as 2 Corinthians must have been, at intervals, in some cases of hours, and possibly of days; for the thirteen chapters cannot have been dictated at one sitting. There are, however, passages in i.–ix. which appear to make a reference to things in x.–xiii. As in the case of the previous argument, the effect of these passages is cumulative. One or two might be accidental; but if all of them are mere coincidences, we have here a literary phenomenon which is very remarkable. As before, we will place the passages in question side by side, but in the reverse order, in order that the probability of the second being an allusion to the first may be judged.

2 COR. x.–xiii.	2 COR. i.–ix.
x. 1. I have confidence *against* you (θαρρῶ εἰς ὑμᾶς).	**vii. 16.** I have confidence *in* you (θαρρῶ ἐν ὑμῖν).
x. 2. With the confidence (πεποιθήσει) wherewith I count to be bold.	**viii. 22.** By reason of much confidence (πεποιθήσει) to youward.

In both of these cases St Paul seems to be purposely repeating in a friendly sense an expression which in the former letter he had used in a stern and unpleasing sense.

x. 6. Being in readiness to avenge all disobedience, when your obedience (ὑπακοή) shall be fulfilled.	**ii. 9.** To this end also did I write, that I might know the proof, whether you are obedient (ὑπήκοοι) in all things.
xii. 16. But being crafty (πανοῦργος) I caught you with guile.	**iv. 2.** Not walking in craftiness (πανουργίᾳ).
xii. 17. Did I take advantage (ἐπλεονέκτησα) of you?	**vii. 2.** We took advantage (ἐπλεονεκτήσαμεν) of no one.
xiii. 2. If I come again I will not spare (οὐ φείσομαι).	**i. 23.** To spare you (φειδόμενος) I forbore to come to Corinth.
xiii. 10. I write these things while absent, that I may not when present deal sharply.	**ii. 3.** I wrote this very thing that I might not by coming have sorrow.

The last two examples are very remarkable, and they come very near to one another, especially in what seems to be the later letter. It is also to be noted that, when the severe letter was written there was some doubt about St Paul's returning to Corinth (*If* I come again). When i.–ix. was written there was no such doubt. It is quite true that even when i.–ix. was written,

c

the Apostle might say ἐὰν ἔλθω εἰς τὸ πάλιν : but such an expression would be more suitable in the earlier letter.

It is possible that in v. 13, 'Whether we were beside ourselves' (ἐξέστημεν), we have a reference to the earlier letter, especially to the account of his being 'caught up even to the third heaven' (xii. 2). He may have anticipated that this and other things would lead the Corinthians to say, "The man must be mad." In connexion with this it may be noticed that only in the chapters which we are assuming to be part of the severe letter does he use the strong words ἄφρων (xi. 16, 19, xii. 6, 11) and ἀφροσύνη (xi. 1, 17, 21) of the 'folly' with which he was sometimes charged; and elsewhere in N.T. the words are rare. In 1 Corinthians he always uses μωρός (i. 25, 27, iv. 10) and μωρία (i. 18, 21, 23, ii. 14, iii. 19) in relation to the apparent 'foolishness' of his preaching. In 2 Cor. i.–ix. none of these words occur. Here, therefore, there is another marked difference between i.–ix. and x.–xiii.

Kennedy (*Hermathena*, XII. xxix., 1903, p. 343) points out a difference in the use of the words καυχᾶσθαι, καύχησις, and καύχημα, which is similar to the difference pointed out in the first two examples quoted above; viz. in the later letter repeating in a pleasing sense expressions which in the earlier letter had been used in an unpleasing sense. Of these three words Kennedy says; "We find that, while these expressions occur ten times in the first nine chapters, there is not one of the paragraphs in which any of them is to be found which does not contain a marked compliment to the Corinthians—a compliment which is paid in every instance by the use of one or more of these very words. We find, further that, in these nine chapters the writer (after i. 12) never speaks of himself as boasting of anything, except of the Corinthians; or of them as boasting of anything, except of him. When, however, we pass beyond the break at the end of ix., a new and opposite (an apparently contrasted) use of these words begins. We meet them nineteen times in these four chapters; but never once do we find the least approach to the complimentary use of them which characterized the former section. On the contrary, they are here employed again and again to describe the writer's indignant vindication of his claims against the disloyalty of the Corinthians." There is, therefore, some reason for believing that the changed application of these words in i.–ix. is intended to take the sting out of their application in x.–xiii. K. Lake, *Earlier Epistles of St Paul*, p. 161.

To these cases in which i.–ix. seems to contain references to what is said in x.–xiii. the passages in the latter in which he commends himself, and those in the former in which he declares that he has no intention of doing so any more, should be added.

2 COR. x.–xiii.	2 COR i.–ix.
x. 7. Even as he is Christ's, so also are we.	iii. 1. Are we beginning again to commend ourselves?
xi. 5. I am not a whit behind those pre-eminent apostles.	
xi. 18. I will glory also.	
xi. 23. Are they ministers of Christ? I more.	v. 12. We are not again commending ourselves to you.
xii. 12. Truly the signs of an apostle were wrought among you.	viii. 8. I speak not by way of commandment.

(4) In x. 16, St Paul looks forward to an extension of his missionary labours beyond Corinth; 'so as to preach the gospel even unto the parts beyond you' (εἰς τὰ ὑπερέκεινα ὑμῶν). We know that soon after writing 2 Corinthians, St Paul had thoughts of visiting Rome and Spain (Rom. xv. 24, 28), and we may suppose that 'the parts beyond you' mean Italy and Spain. 2 Cor. i.–ix. was written from *Macedonia* (ii. 13, vii. 5, viii. 1, ix. 2–4), and a person in Macedonia would hardly use such an expression as 'the parts beyond you' in reference to Corinth, if he was thinking of Italy and Spain. But the severe letter was written from *Ephesus*, and a person in Ephesus might well say 'the parts beyond Corinth,' and by this mean Italy and Spain. Here again, therefore, we seem to have another indication that x.–xii. is part of the severe letter which had preceded the letter written from Macedonia after Titus had brought the good news of the Corinthians' return to loyalty and obedience.

These arguments, when taken together, do constitute a strong case for the theory that 2 Cor. i.–ix. and x.–xiii. are the main portions of two different letters, and that x.–xiii. is part of the severe letter which St Paul sent to Corinth before he wrote 2 Cor. i.–ix. The theory cannot be set aside as gratuitous and superfluous. It solves in a reasonable and complete manner a grave difficulty by supplying a satisfactory explanation of the extraordinary change of tone which begins suddenly at x. 1. Nevertheless, this useful theory, supported though it be by a remarkable amount of corroborative evidence drawn from the documents themselves, is doubted or rejected by a considerable number of critics of the first rank, and it is necessary to weigh what is urged on the other side.

1. It is said that the taunt which the Apostle quotes in x. 10, 'His letters, they say, are weighty and strong,' includes the severe letter, and indeed is a direct reference to it. Therefore it is impossible that ch. x. can be part of the severe letter; and no one has proposed to separate x. from xi.–xiii.

That, of course, is conclusive, if it is correct. But there is little reason for believing that it is correct. The letter mentioned in 1 Cor. v. 9 would be weighty and strong, and 1 Corinthians is certainly of that character. There is no need to bring in the severe letter of ii. 3 and vii. 8. The painful visit, from which the Apostle returned insulted and defeated, explains the second part of the taunt.

2. It is urged that this theory cannot be brought into harmony with the plan of the promised double visit to Corinth (2 Cor. i. 15).

We have no reason, however, to suppose that the double visit was promised. The Apostle says that he 'was wishing' to make it. How soon the Corinthians were aware of this wish, we do not know; still less do we know of his sending them a promise about it. See notes on i. 15.

3. Nor has the argument that the severe letter must have included some notice of the case of the incestuous person of 1 Cor. v., whereas it is not alluded to in x.–xiii., any force; and that for two reasons. Perhaps no one now maintains that x.–xiii. is the whole of the severe letter; and the case of incest may have been mentioned in the part that is lost. Secondly, there is no difficulty in supposing that the severe letter contained no allusion to this case. St Paul had recently been in Corinth (the short and unsuccessful visit), and during that he would have said all that need be said about that painful matter.

4. Still less force has the argument that there are more than 20 words, some of which are not common in the Pauline Epistles, which occur both in i.–ix. and x.–xiii., the inference being that both are parts of the same letter; e.g. ἀγνότης, ἀγρυπνία, ἀκαταστασία, ἀπλότης, δοκιμάζω, δοκιμή, δυνατέω, ἕτοιμος, θαρρέω, κατὰ σάρκα (always in reference to the Apostle himself), κατεργάζομαι, κόπος, νόημα, ὅπλα, πέποιθα, πεποίθησις, περισσεία, περισσότερος, περισσοτέρως, πλεονεκτέω, ταπεινός (of himself), ὑπακοή. An argument the other way, and at least as strong, may be drawn from similar facts. There are more than 30 words, not found elsewhere in the Pauline Epistles, which occur in x.–xiii. but not in i.–ix.; and more than 50 words, not found elsewhere in the Pauline Epistles, which occur in i.–ix. and not in x.–xiii. Moreover we have δόξα 19 times, παρακλῆσις 11 times, θλίψις 9 times, and χαρά 4 or 5 times, in i.–ix., and none of them in x.–xiii.; also ἀσθένεια and ἀσθενέω each of them 6 times in x.–xiii., and neither of them in i.–ix.

Such statistics can prove very little as to whether the two parts formed one letter or not. For according to both theories the two parts were written by the same person, to the same persons, about the same subject, viz. the condition of the

Corinthian Church, with a brief interval between the writing of
the two parts, in the one case an interval of perhaps a few days,
in the other an interval of a few weeks. In either case there
would be similarities as well as differences of expression.

5. It is urged that the surprising change of tone which begins
abruptly at x. 1 can be explained without the violent hypothesis
of two separate letters, and the following explanations are offered.

(*a*) The first part is addressed to the submissive majority who
have become reconciled to the Apostle, while the last part is
addressed to the still rebellious and impenitent minority. This
is simply untrue. It is quite clear that both i.–ix. and x.–xiii.
are addressed to the Corinthian Church as a whole. In neither
case is there any hint at a limitation ; and in x.–xiii. there is no
appeal to the example of the supposed submissive majority.
This is repeatedly pointed out in the notes.

(*b*) It is asserted that St Paul's appeal for a collection on
behalf of the Jerusalem poor skilfully "prepares for the polemic
against his Judaistic opponents in the third" part. This is assertion without evidence, and also assumes that only the Judaistic
opponents are addressed in x.–xiii. Few people would think
that it was politic to make an urgent, yet somewhat diffident
request for a generous subscription to a charity fund, and then
at once begin to hurl sarcastic reproaches and threats at the
people who were asked to give.

(*c*) It is suggested that "the change of tone is sufficiently
accounted for by a change of mood such as every busy and
overburdened man is subject to, especially if his health is not very
robust (cf. 2 Cor. i. 8, 9 and xii. 7)." Lietzmann thinks that a
sleepless night might account for it. Such explanations are
strangely inadequate.

(*d*) It is suggested that grave news had come from Corinth
after i.–ix. had been written, news so serious that it made a
radical change in the attitude of the Apostle to the Corinthian
Christians. This might be an adequate explanation, but in
x.–xiii. there is no mention of such news having arrived. The
excellent news brought by Titus is spoken of with affectionate
enthusiasm (vii. 6–16), but there is no hint of a more recent
report totally different in character.

(*e*) Perhaps the best argument is that we are so very much in
the dark as to the details of the situation at Corinth, that we are
hardly competent to say what St Paul might or might not write
in the circumstances ; the change of tone would seem more
intelligible, if we knew what St Paul knew. Yet in any case we
have to explain how he came to write so vehemently severe an
attack as x.–xiii. 10 after being so intensely anxious about the
effect of his former severe words.

6. By far the strongest argument in favour of the integrity of the Epistle as it has come down to us is that the proposal to make i.–ix. and x.–xiii. parts of two different letters *rests entirely upon internal evidence* and receives no support whatever from MSS., versions, or quotations. That is solid ground; and so long as no documentary evidence can be found in favour of the proposal, those who reject it can do so with reason. But the internal evidence in favour of this hypothesis is so cogent in detail, and so coherent as a whole, and the difficulty from which it frees us is so great, that there will probably always be some who prefer it to the traditional view. The case is not parallel to that of the more recent hypothesis that in Mk. xiii. 5–37 we have a Christian Apocalypse, in which a few genuine Sayings of Christ are embedded, but which was "composed to meet a definite crisis"; its main purpose being "to encourage the despondent by showing that the delay of the Parousia and the intervening events had been foretold by the Master, and especially to warn believers against the false Christs who were expected to precede the Parousia" (*Studies in the Synoptic Problem*, p. 165). This hypothesis is gratuitous. It solves no difficulty, unless it be a difficulty that in this one place Mark gives us a discourse of Christ as distinct from short Sayings. There is nothing in the discourse which is unworthy of Christ, and nothing which is unlike Mark; on the contrary, the characteristics of his style are rather abundant. The one thing in which the two cases resemble one another is that neither is supported by any documentary evidence. But in the one we have an hypothesis which is based on weak internal evidence, and which is not of any service to us; while in the other we have an hypothesis based on evidence which not a few regard as convincing, and one which frees us from a perplexing difficulty of great magnitude.

§ V. The Opponents.

In the Second Epistle we find no traces of the four factions which were disturbing the Church when the First was written (1 Cor. i. 12). That evil appears to have been not very grave; it did not amount to rebellion: but in principle it was quite wrong, as tending to schism. Enthusiasm for one's teacher may be a good thing; but championship for one leader as against another is not, for it is contrary to the spirit of the Gospel and may end in disaster. To cry up Paul or Apollos or Kephas as rivals, if not opponents of one another, was wrongheaded enthusiasm; and to bring the name of Christ into such a connexion was to degrade Him who bore it. St Paul thinks that it is enough to point out and condemn this error. He does not use severe language, and he does not come back to the subject. In the interval between the two Epistles the evil appears to have passed out of sight, driven under perhaps by other causes of excitement.

In the Second Epistle, however, we do find traces, if not of the earlier 'Christ' party, yet of one which was akin to it, and which had perhaps absorbed the 'Christ' party together with some of the more fanatical members of the party of Kephas. It seems to have continued the exclusive claim to the name of the Master. People who say ' *We* are Christ's,' when the whole Church is included (cf. 1 Cor. iii. 23), use language which is right enough. But the Corinthian cry, ' *I* am of Christ,' had implied ' I am His, and you are not,' or 'He is mine and not yours.' There seems to have been something of the same spirit, but a good deal intensified, in the new party with which St Paul is in actual conflict some months later. ' If any man trusteth in himself that he is Christ's, let him consider this again with himself, that even as he is Christ's, so also are we' (2 Cor. x. 7 ; cf. xi. 3, 4).

Among the obscurities of 2 Corinthians there are various stray hints which enable us to conjecture with considerable probability the genesis of this new 'Christ' party, if such it may be called. The Corinthian Church had been invaded by a band of teachers who perhaps were making a missionary tour through various Churches. St Paul sarcastically calls them, or their leaders, 'the super-eminent apostles' (xi. 5, xii. 11), apparently because they falsely claimed the honourable title of 'apostle' (xi. 13), while they denied it to him (xii. 12). They said that they were true Jews, and he was not (xi. 22). They were 'ministers of righteousness' (xi. 15), who insisted on the Law, while he ignored it and even declared it to be obsolete. They were 'ministers of Christ' (xi. 23), and he was not. It is possible that some of them said, and not untruly, that they had been actual hearers of Christ, which he had not been ; but it is perhaps more probable that in saying that they were 'ministers of Christ' they claimed that their teaching was much nearer to that of Christ, who had kept the Law, than was St Paul's. Quite certainly their teaching about Jesus was very different from his (xi. 4).

It would appear that these invaders had come with 'letters of commendation' (iii. 1), and this is sometimes thought to point to their having come from Jerusalem ; but we cannot assume this with any certainty. They must have been Greek-speaking Jews, or they could not have preached to Corinthian Christians, nearly all of whom were Gentiles ; and they may have been Hellenists, like St Paul himself. Their 'letters of commendation' may have been from the Churches which they had recently visited in their tour. But if they had letters of commendation from some members of the Church at Jerusalem, we may be sure that they had none from any of the Twelve, although they would no doubt wish it to be believed that the Twelve sanctioned their mission to Corinth. In the Apostle's prolonged and vehement attack on these invaders, there is not a hint that he supposes them to have the support of the Twelve or of the Church at Jerusalem. His friendly relations with the Twelve remain as they were; he and they teach the same thing (1 Cor. xv. 11). The letters of commendation would come from Jewish Christians who wished the Law to be made as binding as the Gospel (Acts xv. 5, 24).

We know that when these new missionaries arrived in Corinth they found Gentile converts who continued the practice of heathen vices (xii. 21). If they came to Corinth for the purpose of attacking St Paul, this feature in the lives of many of his converts would intensify them in their desire to oppose a preacher whose teaching had had such results; and if they came without any such definite purpose, this feature would be likely to turn them into opponents, for it would seem to show that there must be something radically wrong in his teaching. It is probable that they were prejudiced against him before they arrived; and it is evident that they soon became malignant assailants, who seem to have regarded any weapon as admissible in the effort to defeat so dangerous a teacher. They were not content with trying to prove that he was no true Apostle, and that as a preacher he was miserably ineffective, but they bitterly assailed his private character. He was altogether, as in public, so also in his private life, a despicable person. He never knew his own mind, or at any rate he would never declare it clearly; he was always trying to say 'Yes' and 'No' in the same breath (i. 17, 18). He was a tyrant, lording it over his converts (x. 8); and, like many tyrants, he was a coward, who said that he would come to Corinth, and yet did not dare to show himself there (i. 23, xiii. 2). He could be very brave on paper, but he was utterly ineffective face to face (x. 10). At the beginning of his career he had run away from Damascus in quite a ludicrous fashion (xi. 32, 33); and now quite recently he had run away from Corinth, unable to stand up against determined opposition (ii. 1, xiii. 2). During his stay he would not accept the maintenance of an Apostle, because he knew that he was not a true Apostle; this was his real reason, but he made a great parade of this refusal, as if it was a proof of great generosity (xi. 7–9, xii. 14). And all the while, although he accepted nothing openly or directly, yet he was getting support in an underhand way through his agents (vii. 2, xii. 17, 18). Indeed it was by no means certain that he did not appropriate some of the money collected for the poor Christians at Jerusalem

(viii. 20, 21). And yet the man who was capable of this despicable behaviour was never tired of asserting himself as a person
of exceptional authority (iii. 5, iv. 5), and praising himself as a
person of exceptional merit and success (iii. 1, x. 8, xi. 16–18,
xii. 1, 11). The only reasonable explanation of his conduct was
that he was mad (v. 13). There is, however, no reason for believing that even these wild and unscrupulous assailants ever insinuated
that, in spite of all his strong words against impurity, Paul was
himself a man of impure life. That is not the meaning of x. 2.

Some of these supposed accusations or insinuations are
inferences from what St Paul says about himself, and in one or
two cases the inference may be erroneous ; but about the majority
of charges made against the Apostle by these opponents there
is no doubt, and they form a consistent whole. They are just
the kind of things which exasperated controversialists have in all
ages been apt to say about those whose teaching they regarded
as heretical and poisonous. In a similar way we can gather the
other side of the picture. The invaders evidently had a very bad
opinion of St Paul ; we may now look at the estimate which he
had formed of them. Like the fraudulent seller who adulterates
his wares, these men corrupted the Gospel which they preached
(ii. 17, iv. 2, xi. 3, 13). Their Gospel was utterly different from
St Paul's (iii. 5–10, xi. 4) ; indeed it was little better than a diabolical caricature of it (xi. 14). They lowered the spiritual
standard down to their own moral level, and then they lauded
themselves and one another for having reached that low standard
(x. 12). They professed to have a great zeal for religion, but
they did not go among the heathen and labour to win converts ;
they followed in the footsteps of genuine workers and tried to take
the credit for what had been done before they came (x. 15, 16).
And wherever they obtained influence they used it in a tyrannical
and grasping manner, not only accepting maintenance (xi. 12),
but exacting it by brutal and violent means (xi. 20). In a word,
they were 'Satan's ministers' (xi. 15).

One sees what monstrous distortion there is in the description which these invaders gave of the Apostle's character and
teaching. Is there no exaggeration in the picture which he draws
of them ? A teacher who was so absolutely absorbed in his work
as was St Paul, who had seen his work so marred, and for a time
almost wrecked, by the intrusion of these bigoted propagandists,
and whose personal character had been so venomously assailed
by them, would have been almost superhuman, if he had been
able to form and state a perfectly just estimate of such opponents.
We are not competent to decide whether the estimate which he
gives us is just or not. We must leave the matter in the obscurity
which blurs so many of the details of this tantalizing Epistle.

Reitzenstein and K. Lake think that the opponents of St Paul at Corinth were not Judaizers, but 'spirituals.' They accounted themselves as πνευματικοί, and were "inspired by a desire to go still further than St Paul in the direction of freedom from the Law, and to lay even greater stress on the spiritual nature of Christianity" (*Earlier Epp. of St Paul*, p. 219). In favour of this view appeal is made to 2 Cor. x. 2, xii. 11–15; and it is suggested that x. 3–18 is not a reply to a vulgar attack on St Paul's personal appearance (*v.* 10), but to an argument that he "had not got the impressive powers which resulted from the gift of the Spirit" (p. 224). It is also contended that the right interpretation of the difficult passage v. 16 (see notes there) confirms the view that St Paul's opponents were πνευματικοί. Saul of Tarsus had once known Christ as a teacher of lawlessness and falsehood, who was rightly put to death and had never been raised: but that was long ago, and now he had a lofty and spiritual conception of Him. In this matter he had long been as 'spiritual' as his opponents claimed to be.

It may be doubted whether the passages in question will bear the interpretation thus put upon them. At the outset it is almost startling to be told of Jewish Christians who assailed St Paul as a dangerous teacher because he did not go far enough in throwing off the yoke of the Law. In that case would it have been necessary for him to declare so passionately that he was just as much a Hebrew, an Israelite, the seed of Abraham, as any of them? Would he have spoken of them as false *apostles*? In all his vehement language about them he nowhere accuses them of being libertines who by their antinomian doctrines were undermining the moral law and opening the door to licentiousness. When he expresses a fear that many of the Corinthian Christians have not repented of their former uncleanness and lasciviousness (xii. 21), he gives no hint that they have been led astray by the false teachers. On the other hand it is easy enough to believe that Judaizing Christians, coming to Corinth and finding much licentiousness among the converts there, would assail St Paul as a cause of the evil, owing to his abrogation of the Jewish Law. On the whole there does not seem to be sufficient reason for abandoning the usual view that these Jewish teachers were Judaizers who insisted on the Law to an extent which was fatal to Christian freedom. The contrast drawn in ch. iii. between the transient character of the old dispensation and the permanence of the new, looks like an indirect condemnation of the teaching which Judaizers had, with much success, been giving to the Corinthians. If it be asked why St Paul does not make the Judaizing character of his opponents more clear, we may reply that the Corinthians did not need to have it made clear to them; they knew what these men taught. That is the puzzle all through the Epistle; allusions which were perfectly obvious to the Corinthians then are obscure and perplexing to us now, because we do not know the details of the situation.

§ VI. DOCTRINE.

As already stated, in 2 Corinthians the didactic element is secondary; doctrine and instruction are found in it, but they are incidental : the primary element is a personal one, viz. the vindication of the Apostle's authority and character. The First Epistle is not a doctrinal treatise; only one great doctrine is discussed in it, that of the Resurrection, because it had been denied at Corinth. But there is far less instruction as to either doctrine or rules of life in the Second Epistle. Nevertheless there are some topics which need consideration.

With regard to *the writer's own relation to the Master* there is the same position as before. He is 'an Apostle of Christ Jesus by God's will' (i. 1), and this position is strenuously asserted as one which can be demonstrated in the face of all who question or deny it. Its proof lies in the Corinthians themselves (iii. 2, 3), *i.e.* in the existence of the Church at Corinth, and in the 'signs and wonders and mighty works' which he had wrought among them (xiii. 12). It is by God that he was made sufficient as a minister (iii. 5, 6, iv. 7), and not by any commission received from man.

The *Christology* is the same. Jesus Christ is the 'Son of God' (i. 19), and it is 'in Him' that all Christians live (i. 21, ii. 14, 17, etc.). His pre-existence is implied in the statement that 'for your sakes he became poor' (viii. 9), which refers to the Word becoming flesh. In His human life Jesus did not make any sacrifice of wealth; He was poor from His birth. But by taking on Himself human life He sacrificed more than man can understand. He died for all (v. 15), and through Him God has reconciled us to Himself (v. 18–21), a statement of deep import.* He has been raised from the dead, and with Him we also shall be raised (iv. 14). Statements made in O.T. of Jehovah are often transferred to Christ.

In neither Epistle is there any clearly defined *Trinitarian doctrine*, but in the Benediction at the end of 2 Corinthians we are nearer to such definite doctrine than in 'the same Spirit

---

* "This memorable passage is the culminating point of the Apostle's teaching in this Epistle, and is perhaps the profoundest and most important utterance in the whole of his writings" respecting the mystery of the Atonement (C. R. Ball, *Preliminary Studies on N.T.* p. 143).

. . . the same Lord . . . the same God' (1 Cor. xii. 4–6). See
notes on i. 2, 22 and iii. 17 for other evidence.

In one particular it has been thought by some that we have
a development in St Paul's thought amounting to a change of
view, viz. with regard to the *manner of our resurrection.* Certainly
he expresses himself very differently in each Epistle. See
Additional Note on v. 1–10. It may be said of his theology
generally, that there is no system in it, and that to suppose that
out of his various statements we can construct the theological
system which was in his mind when he delivered his various
statements about God, Christ, the Spirit, redemption, etc., is
utterly to misunderstand him. This is specially true of what is
commonly spoken of as his "Eschatology." What distinguishes
it and his theology generally is its want of system. In each
utterance his object is to make his meaning clear to those to
whom he is writing; and he does not stop to think whether
what he says is logically coherent with what he may have said
elsewhere. Hence the frequent occurrence of what have been
called "the Antinomies of St Paul." Like Ruskin and Westcott, he is not afraid of a verbal contradiction. Deissmann goes
so far as to contend that "what is called the 'Eschatology' of
Paul has little that is 'Eschatological' about it. . . . Paul did
not write *de novissimis.* . . . One must be prepared for a surging
hither and thither of great thoughts, feelings, expectations"
(*Theol. Lit. Zeit.*, 1898, Sp. 14; cited by Milligan, *Thessalonians*,
p. lxix, and by Kennedy, *St Paul's Conceptions of the Last
Things*, p. 21 n.). Sometimes there is a Judgment (v. 10), sometimes there seems to be no room for one (1 Thess. iv. 16, 17).
Sometimes God is the Judge (Rom. xiv. 10), sometimes Christ
(1 Cor. iv. 4; 2 Cor. v. 10). "We must keep the two categories
of passages together, without attempting any artificial reconciliation of apparent discrepancies in order to attribute to the Apostle
a complete system of Eschatology" (Weinel, *St Paul, the Man
and His Work*, p. 49). The Jewish Apocalypses are full of
contradictory notions on a variety of points. St Paul in this
matter was a man of his age, and it is not improbable that at
different times he was under the influence of different Jewish ideas,
which, however, were always tested by his own penetrating thought.

In the somewhat crude picture which is put before us in
1 and 2 Thessalonians nothing is said about the nature of the
resurrection-body. In 1 Cor. xv. he deals with this question,
not perhaps because he himself regarded it as of very great
moment, but because there were Christians at Corinth who
thought it incredible that a body which had been dissolved in
the grave should be restored, and who therefore denied that the
dead could be raised. The Apostle had to answer this objec-

tion, and in doing so he would naturally think of answers which were prevalent among Jews with regard to a resurrection. We can distinguish four views.

1. The Book Ecclesiasticus says that the soul of man is not immortal (xvii. 30), but that the wise man's name will never die, τὸ ὄνομα αὐτοῦ ζήσεται εἰς τὸν αἰῶνα (xxxvii. 26). This is not very different from the old idea that Sheol is the end of man, for existence in Sheol is hardly to be called life. St Paul would be familiar with this idea, whether he knew Ecclesiasticus or not.

2. Almost certainly he knew the Book of Wisdom (Sanday and Headlam, *Romans*, pp. 51, 52, 267; Gregg, *Wisdom*, pp. lvi–lix), and in that we have not only the immortality (i. 15, ii. 23, iii. 1, iv. 7) but the pre-existence of souls (viii. 20). This, however, is immortality for the soul alone; it is the spirit that is raised from sleep, and there is no resurrection of the body (*Enoch* xci. 10, xcii. 3, ciii. 3, 4; *Jubilees* xxiii. 31). We cannot with any certainty get the idea of a return to a golden age on earth from the picturesque language in Wisd. iii. 7–9 and v. 16–23 (Gregg, p. xlviii).

3. In 2 Macc. 9–11, xiv. 46 we have the resurrection of the body in the most literal sense. The very limbs in which men die are to be restored, according to the popular idea that bodies will come out of their graves at the resurrection, as out of their beds every morning during life,—an idea which is certain to prevail wherever the resurrection is represented in sculpture or painting (2 Esdr. vii. 32). Even Rabbis taught that the righteous after resurrection would beget children and feast on the flesh of Leviathan, the latter being a gross misunderstanding of Ps. lxxiv. 14 (see Briggs, *ad loc.*). In the *Apocalypse of Baruch* we have both this view (l. 1) and the next (see below). It was this idea which seemed to the sceptics at Corinth to be quite incredible, and St Paul does not ask them to believe it.

4. In *Enoch* li. 4, civ. 6, as in the *Apocalypse of Baruch* li. 5, 10, there seems to be some idea that the resurrection-body will be the material body transfigured into a spiritual body, such as Angels have. This is not a creation of a new body, in which case there would be no resurrection; it is a marvellous transformation of the earthly body. This is the idea which the Apostle adopts (see on 1 Cor. xv. 35). When is the spiritual body received by the person who dies? It is on this point that St Paul's view appears to have undergone a change. When 1 Cor. xv. was written he seems to have thought that the spiritual body was received at the resurrection. When 2 Cor. v. was written he seems to have thought that it was received at death. Some such change as the following *may* have taken place. Formerly

he expected that he and nearly all Christians would live to see the Coming of Christ, and the brief interval between death and the Coming in the case of the few who died before the Coming did not impress him. But since writing 1 Corinthians he himself had been in great and prolonged peril of death,* other Christians had died, and it was still uncertain when Christ would come. Were the dead to wait till the day of resurrection for the spiritual body which fits them for eternal life with the Lord? Surely not. At death we are immediately clothed upon with this glorified body, in which we at once enter into full communion with the glorified Christ. Comp. the words of the dying Stephen (Acts vii. 59), words which St Paul had heard.

Commentators differ as to whether the way in which St Paul expresses himself in 2 Cor. v. amounts to a change of view from 1 Cor. xv. Lightfoot (on Phil. i. 23) simply says; "The one mode of representation must be qualified by the other." Vincent (on Phil. i. 23) holds that "the assumption that Paul's views had undergone a change" is "beside the mark." Kennedy (*St Paul's Conceptions of the Last Things*, p. 163) is convinced of "the futility of postulating schemes of gradual development in St Paul's Eschatology." On the other side see Cohu, *St Paul and Modern Research*, pp. 320–324. Alford (on 2 Cor. v. 1) thinks that the question need not be raised at all, but quotes a variety of opinions.

§ VII. MYSTERY RELIGIONS.

The theories that St Paul is the real founder of Christianity by bringing into prominence doctrines which went far beyond, and at last almost eclipsed, the simple teaching of Christ, and that in so doing he borrowed a great deal from the Mystery Religions which were in vogue in his own day, would seem to be finding their proper level. Criticism has shown that only in a very limited and qualified sense is there truth in either of them. No doubt there are differences between the teaching of St Paul as we have it in his letters, and the teaching of Christ as we have it in the Synoptic Gospels. That was inevitable, seeing that the personal experiences of each were so different, and the requirements of their hearers were so different also. But with this controversy we need not concern ourselves here, for it has no special connexion with 2 Corinthians. The reader who desires to

---

* This fact might influence him in opposite ways. It might make him think that another such crisis would probably kill him. Or it might lead him to hope that, as he had been preserved through this, he would be preserved till the Coming.

consider it may turn to *Cambridge Biblical Essays,* to Knowling's *The Testimony of St Paul to Christ,* and to Maurice Jones' *The N.T. in the Twentieth Century.* The other controversy lies somewhat more in our path, not only because some of the words which are thought to be technical terms in Mystery Religions are used in this Epistle, but also because of the 'revelation' in xii. 1–7, which is supposed to mark some affinity with Mystery Religions. Among these technical expressions are ranked ἀπο-κάλυψις (xii. 1, 7), ἄρρητα ῥήματα (xii. 4), γνῶσις (iii. 18), δόξα (*passim*), εἰκών (iv. 4), ἐνδύομαι (v. 3), σοφία (i. 12), σφραγίζομαι (i. 22), σωτηρία (i. 6, vi. 2, vii. 10); and it may be remarked that most of them might easily be employed by a writer who had never heard of a Mystery Religion, and that not one of them is conclusive evidence of acquaintance with the language of such cults; although, when St Paul's Epistles are considered as a whole, acquaintance with the language of some of these cults need not be doubted. But knowledge and use of certain technical terms which were current in connexion with Mysteries is one thing; borrowing from the Mysteries themselves in order to construct a new Gospel is quite another. Before the latter is allowed to be probable there is much to be considered.

1. The amount that we really know about the Mysteries has been exaggerated; a great deal of what modern writers tell us about them is conjectural, for evidence is insufficient. This is specially the case with regard to Mithraism, the most important of all the Mystery Religions of which we have any knowledge. This is fully admitted by F. Cumont in the Preface to *Die Mysterien des Mithra.* Inscriptions are our only sure guides, and they are scanty enough. A great deal of what is told us about Mithra-worship is inference from the interpretations which have been put upon pieces of sculpture in which the figure of Mithra appears. But are the interpretations right? There are sculptures which are undoubtedly Christian, but which our intimate knowledge of the Christian religion does not enable us to interpret with certainty. Where should we be if our knowledge of Christianity depended upon the interpretation of the sculptures? As Cumont says, about the conflict between Mithraism and Christianity we know only the result. Mithraism was vanquished, and its defeat was inevitable, not merely because of its intrinsic inferiority, but also because, although both were of Eastern origin, Christianity could, while Mithraism could not, adapt itself permanently to the thought and life of the West. This is the more remarkable, because Christianity was exclusive and Mithraism was not. Mithraism could co-exist with almost any other religion. It was specially popular in the legions, and with them reached the Roman Wall along the Tyne; and it is

perhaps true to say that in the second century Mithra had more worshippers than Christ. The two religions started about the same time, and at first they did not often come into collision. The battle was fought out later in Africa, Gaul, and Rome. It may be doubted whether much was known about Mithra in Corinth at the time when St Paul was at work there.

With regard to the extent to which meagre evidence is supplemented by conjecture, Schweitzer has some useful remarks. "Those who are engaged in making these comparisons are rather apt to give the Mystery Religions a greater definiteness of thought than they really possess, and do not always give sufficient prominence to the distinction between their own hypothetical reconstruction and the medley of statements on which it is based. Almost all popular writings fall into this inaccuracy. They manufacture out of the various fragments of information a kind of universal Mystery Religion which never actually existed, least of all in Paul's day" (*Paul and his Interpreters*, p. 192). Dieterich in his work on the *Mithrasliturgie* admits that we have very little exact knowledge regarding the sacred meals of the Mystery Religions, about which so much is sometimes urged in connexion with the institution of the Eucharist; that they were believed to have supernatural effects is perhaps all that can be said with certainty.

2. Chronology is often fatal to the supposition that St Paul borrowed a great deal from this or that Mystery Religion, for few of them had made much way in the Roman Empire until about A.D. 100. Our knowledge of them often comes from sources which belong to the second century or later, and then the question at once arises whether, in the details which are really analogous, —and these are not so numerous as is sometimes supposed,— the Mystery Religion has not borrowed from Christianity. At Tarsus, Antioch, Ephesus, and elsewhere St Paul would learn something about Oriental Mysteries; and in Greece he would learn something about the Eleusinian Mysteries and perhaps some other Greek cults, enough probably to enable him to make skilful but cautious use of some of the language which was used by the initiated. But we must always bear in mind the possibility that the Apostle sometimes uses in its ordinary sense language which afterwards became technical in connexion with the Mysteries; also that, where he consciously uses the language of the Mysteries, he uses it in a new sense.* Records of prayer for 'Salvation,' says Ramsay, are found in many villages of Asia Minor. "St Paul may have caught the Greek word from the

---

* See F. B. Westcott, *A Letter to Asia*, pp. 122, 123 n. ; Ramsay, *The Teaching of Paul in Terms of the Present Day*, pp. 283–305 ; Maurice Jones, *The N.T. in the Twentieth Century*, pp. 144–149.

lips of thousands of pagans. It is the same word that became
specially characteristic of Christian teaching. Yet it would be a
serious error to argue that, because pagans and Christians alike
longed and prayed for 'Salvation,' therefore the thing that they
sought for was the same. . . . Paul in the last resort was an
uncompromising enemy of the religious ideas embodied in the
Mysteries" (pp. 285, 303).

There is this amount of truth in the theory that the Mystery
Religions have influenced St Paul. In a very real sense Christianity is a Mystery Religion, the best that the world has ever
seen. Many of the Apostle's converts had some knowledge of
what the Mystery Religions of the East, or of Egypt, or of
Greece, professed to offer to those who accepted them. We may
regard it as certain that some of his converts had been initiated in
one or other of these cults ; and their experiences of initiation and
membership might easily lead them to inquire about, and finally
to be admitted to, the Christian Church. To such converts the
Gospel would seem to be the best Mystery Religion of which
they had ever heard ; and the Apostle in instructing them would
naturally at times use language with which they were already
familiar, and which could now be employed of Christian
Mysteries in a far deeper and more spiritual sense. It is perhaps
going too far to say with H. A. A. Kennedy (*Expositor*, July
1912, p. 67) that " he must have gained a first-hand acquaintance
with those religious conceptions by which they (the initiated) had
attempted to reach spiritual peace." But Kennedy is certainly
right in his criticism of Heinrici, that " we know too little about
the organization either of Pagan or early Christian societies to
accept his conclusion that the Christian community at Corinth
was nothing else than a heathen religious guild transformed."
" We know far less about the actual ritual and doctrines of the
Mystery Religions in the Graeco-Roman world than we do of
their wide diffusion and potent influence. This is not surprising,
for, on the one hand, their votaries were strictly enjoined to
keep silence on their most sacred experiences, and, on the other,
stern critics of Paganism like the early Christian Fathers must
inevitably have been biassed in their casual representation of the
facts. The literary remains of these communities are very scanty "
(p. 60). " Extreme divergence of opinion prevails as to the full
significance and effect of the ritual and its accompaniments. . . .
Considerable caution must be employed in attempting to define
with any certainty the beliefs or ritual of these cults at special
moments in their history. For that history remains exceedingly
dim, especially for the period when Oriental faiths were confronted
with Greek culture in Asia " (pp. 70, 72). In particular, it is
difficult to determine the period at which such savage and

d

barbaric ritual as the gashing themselves with knives, and the
taurobolium or bath of blood, became associated with deeper and
saner religious ideas, such as self-sacrifice, purification from sin,
and the securing of immortality by union with the deity.   In any
given case this momentous change may have taken place at a
period long after the lifetime of St Paul; and it is precisely in
these deeper and saner ideas that resemblances between Christianity and Mystery Religions can be found.   One idea would
in any case be new to converts who had previously been initiated
in some heathen cult, new both in language and in thought,—the
doctrine of Christ crucified.   "The Cross is the peculiar property
of the Gospel" (Bigg, *The Church's Task under the Roman
Empire*, p. xi).

Clemen, *Primitive Christianity and its Non-Jewish Sources*,
supplies much valuable criticism on the theory that St Paul and
other N.T. writers borrowed largely from Mystery Religions.

§ VIII. Characteristics, Style, and Language.

As literature the Second Epistle does not rank so high as the
First.   Powerful as is the language of the Great Invective
in the last four chapters, which sometimes has a rhythmical and
rhetorical swing that sweeps one along in admiration of its im-
passioned intensity,* there is nothing in the whole letter which
rises to the sustained beauty and dignity of 1 Cor. xiii. and xv.
The ease and smoothness and orderly arrangement of the earlier
letter are wanting, and the rapid changes in the series of con-
flicting emotions are not conducive to literary excellence.   The
mixture of human weakness with spiritual strength, of tenderness with severity, of humility with vehement self-vindication, of
delicate tact with uncompromising firmness, produces an impression of intense reality, but at the same time bewilders us as to
the exact aim of this or that turn of expression.   The Greek is
harder to construe than that of the First Epistle, owing to the
ruggedness which results from dictating when the feelings are
deeply stirred.

Sanday and Headlam (*Romans*, lvii f.) have shown that there
is much resemblance, both in style and vocabulary, between the
four great Epistles of this period of the Apostle's life.   The
resemblance is stronger when Romans is omitted from the comparison, and it is strongest of all when only Galatians and
2 Corinthians are compared.   One reason for this resemblance is
that all four letters were written during the time when the brief
but bitter conflict between Gentile and Judaistic Christianity

---

* See especially the paraphrase of xi. 16–33.

was at its height. Traces of this conflict come to the surface in 1 Corinthians and Romans, but other topics keep it in abeyance : in Galatians and 2 Corinthians one is in the thick of the battle. The personal element is least prominent in Romans, the latest of the four great Epistles, rather more so in 1 Corinthians, much more so in Galatians, and most of all in our Epistle. The feature which is specially characteristic of all four letters is intense sincerity, to which we may perhaps add sureness of touch. In common with other Pauline Epistles they have a marked argumentative form. See Introduction to *1 Corinthians*, pp. xlviii, xlix, for other features.

The use of such words as αὐτάρκεια (ix. 8), ἐπιείκεια (x. 1), τὸ καλόν (xiii. 7), πραότης (x. 1), προαιρέομαι (ix. 7), συνείδησις (i. 12, iv. 2, v. 11), and φαῦλος (v. 10) may be taken as indicating some knowledge of Greek philosophical language.

Words peculiar to 2 Corinthians in N.T.

In this list it will be of some interest to separate the words which are found only in the first nine chapters from those which are found only in the last four ; but, as has been pointed out already, no sure inference can be drawn from such statistics. An asterisk indicates that the word is not found in the LXX.

The following words occur in i.–ix. :

* ἀγανάκτησις (vii. 11), * ἀδρότης (viii. 20), ἀνακαλύπτω (iii. 14, 18), * ἀνεκδιήγητος (ix. 15), * ἀπαρασκεύαστος (ix. 4), ἀπεῖπον (iv. 2), * ἀπόκριμα (i. 9), αὐγάζω (iv. 4), * αὐθαίρετος (viii. 3, 17), * Βελίαρ (vi. 15), δολόω (iv. 2), δότης (ix. 7), δυσφημία (vi. 8), εἰσέχομαι (vi. 17), * ἐκδημέω (v. 6, 8, 9), ἐλαττονέω (viii. 15), * ἐλαφρία (i. 17), * ἐνδημέω (v. 6, 8, 9), ἐνπεριπατέω (vi. 16), * ἐντυπόω (iii. 7), ἐξαπορέομαι (i. 8, iv. 8), ἐπακούω (vi. 2), * ἐπενδύω (v. 2, 4), * ἐπιπόθησις (vii. 7, 11), ἐπιτιμία (ii. 6), * ἑτεροζυγέω (vi. 14), * εὐφημία (vi. 8), ἡνίκα (iii. 15, 16), * ἱκανότης (iii. 5), ἱλαρός (ix. 7), κάλυμμα (iii. 13, 14, 15, 16), * καπηλεύω (ii. 17), * κατάκρισις (iii. 9, vii. 3), * κατοπτρίζομαι (iii. 18), μολυσμός (vii. 1), μωμάομαι (vi. 3, viii. 20), παραυτίκα (iv. 17), πένης (ix. 9), * πέρυσι (viii. 10, ix. 2), προαιρέω (ix. 7), * προενάρχομαι (viii. 6, 10), * προκαταρτίζω (ix. 5), * προσκοπή (vi. 3), πτωχεύω (viii. 9), σκῆνος (v. 1, 4), σπουδαῖος (viii. 17, 22), στενοχωρέομαι (iv. 8, vi. 12), * συμφώνησις (vi. 15), * συνκατάθεσις (vi. 16), * συνπέμπω (viii. 18, 22), * συννπουργέω (i. 11), * συστατικός (iii. 1), * φειδομένως (ix. 6), φωτισμός (iv. 4, 6).

The following words occur in x.–xiii. :

* ἀβαρής (xi. 9), * ἄμετρος (x. 13, 15), * Ἀρέτας (xi. 32), ἁρμόζω (xi. 2), * ἄρρητος (xii. 4), βυθός (xi. 25), Δαμασκηνός

xi. 32), ἐθνάρχης (xi. 32), * ἐκδαπανάω (xii. 15), ἐκφοβέω (**x.** 9),
* ἐνκρίνω (x. 12), * ἐπισκηνόω (xii. 9), * ἐφικνέομαι (x. 13, 14),
* ἥδιστα (xii. 9, 15), καθαίρεσις (x. 4, 8, xiii. 10), * καταβαρέω
(xii. 16), * καταναρκάω (xi. 9, xii. 13, 14), * κατάρτισις (xiii. 9),
* νυχθήμερον (xi. 25), ὀχύρωμα (x. 4), παραφρονέω (xi. 23),
πεντάκις (xi. 24), * προαμαρτάνω (xii. 21, xiii. 2), σαργάνη (xi. 33),
σκόλοψ (xii. 7), συλάω (xi. 8), συναποστέλλω (xii. 18), ὑπερβαλλόντως (xi. 23), * ὑπερέκεινα (x. 16), * ὑπερεκτείνω (x. 14),
* ὑπερλίαν (xi. 5, xii. 11), * φυσίωσις (xii. 20), * ψευδαπόστολος
(xi. 13), ψιθυρισμός (xii. 20).

The following occur in both divisions of the letter :
ἀγρυπνία (vi. 5, xi. 27), προσαναπληρόω (ix. 12, xi. 9), and perhaps * ἀγνότης (vi. 6, xi. 3), but the reading in xi. 3 is doubtful.

Phrases peculiar to 2 Corinthians in N.T.

παλαιὰ διαθήκη (iii. 14).
ὁ θεὸς τοῦ αἰῶνος τούτου (iv. 4).
ὁ ἔξω ἡμῶν ἄνθρωπος (iv. 16).
κατα βάθους (viii. 2).
ἄγγελος φωτός (xi. 14).
τρίτος οὐρανός (xii. 2).
ἄγγελος σατανᾶ (xii. 7).

Quotations from the O.T.

For this subject Swete, *Introduction to the O.T. in Greek*,
pp. 381–405, should be consulted; also Sanday and Headlam,
Romans, pp. 302–307. Even when the difference in length
between the two Epistles is taken into consideration, the number
of quotations in the Second is less than in the First. In
1 Corinthians (pp. lii f.) we found about thirty quotations
from eleven different books. In 2 Corinthians there are about
twenty quotations from nine or more different books. Not many
of these are given as direct quotations, and all such are in the
first nine chapters : καθάπερ (iii. 12), κατὰ τὸ γεγραμμένον (iv. 13),
λέγει (vi. 2), καθὼς εἶπεν ὁ Θεός (vi. 16), καθὼς γέγραπται (viii. 15,
ix. 9). In the last four chapters quotations of any kind are few.
In the first nine chapters we have quotations from Exodus
(iii. 3, 7, 10, 13, 16, 18, viii. 15), Leviticus (vi. 16), 2 Samuel
(vi. 18), Psalms (iv. 13, vi. 9, 11, ix. 9), Proverbs (iii. 3, viii. 21,
ix. 7), Isaiah (v. 17, vi. 2, 17, vii. 6, ix. 10). There are possible
citations from Ezekiel (iii. 3, vi. 16, 17), Hosea (vi. 18, ix. 10),
and Amos (vi. 18), but where the wording of the original passages
are similar, the source of the quotation becomes doubtful, and

in some cases we may have a mosaic of several passages. In the last four chapters we have quotations from Genesis (xi. 3), Deuteronomy (xiii. 1), and Jeremiah (x. 17). In some instances it is possible that St Paul is not consciously reproducing the language of the LXX, but his mind is full of that language, and it comes spontaneously as the natural wording in which to express his thoughts. Like other N.T. writers, he was very familiar with the LXX, and, although he was also familiar with the Hebrew, his quotations are commonly either in exact agreement with the Greek Version or very close to it. As Swete remarks, "it is impossible to do justice" to the N.T. writings "unless the reader is on the watch for unsuspected references to the Greek O.T., and able to appreciate its influence upon the author's mind" (*Intr. to the O.T. in Greek*, p. 452).

In this Epistle we have five cases of exact agreement with the LXX.

iv. 13 = Ps. cxvi. 10 [cxv. 1].	ix. 9 = Ps. cxii. [cxi.] 9.
vi. 2 = Is. xlix. 8.	ix. 10 = Is. lv. 10.
viii. 15 = Exod. xvi. 18 (slight change of order).	

In five cases the agreement is close.

viii. 21 = Prov. iii. 4.	x. 17 = Jer. ix. 24.
ix. 7 = Prov. xxii. 8.	xi. 3 = Gen. iii. 13.
	xiii. 1 = Deut. xix. 15.

In one place, vi. 16–18, it is possible that recollection of the Hebrew may have influenced the composite quotation of Lev. xxvi. 11, 12 and other passages: cf. Is. lii. 11; Ezek. xi. 17, xx. 33, 34, xxxvii. 21, 27; 2 Sam. vii. 8, 14; Zeph. iii. 20; Zech. x. 8. But the remarkable expression ἐνοικήσω ἐν αὐτοῖς, which is stronger than 'walk among them' or 'tabernacle among them,' is not found in any of the passages; and this seems to be a case in which the Apostle has changed the wording in order to make the quotation more suitable to his purpose. Cf. the substitution of σοφῶν for ἀνθρώπων in 1 Cor. iii. 20 = Ps. xciii. [xciv.] 11, and the substitution of ἀθετήσω for κρύψω in 1 Cor. i. 19 = Is. xxix. 14.

§ IX. THE TEXT.

There is no special problem in determining the text of 2 Corinthians. In the Pauline Epistles, as elsewhere, B is the most constant single representative of the 'Neutral' text, but it occasionally admits readings of the 'Western' type. The term 'Western' is misleading, for this type of text seems to have originated in the East and thence to have spread in the West.

But the term holds its place against the proposed substitutes, 'Syro-Latin,' which better describes it, and 'δ-text,' which suggests connexion with codex D and yet commits one to no theory as regards origin. ℵ admits Western elements more often than B does, but in the Pauline Epistles ℵ does this less often than elsewhere. Western readings are found chiefly in D E F G, in the Old Latin and the Vulgate, and in 'Ambrosiaster,' among which E, as a copy of D, and F, as the constant companion of G, are comparatively unimportant. An examination of the texts of d and g side by side with that of Ambrosiaster shows what divergence there was in the Old Latin texts, and how much need there was of revision. Perhaps it may also to some extent explain the surprising inadequacy of Jerome's revision, especially in the Epistles. Jerome may have thought that, if he made all the changes that were required, his revision would never be accepted. In the notes in this volume the imperfections of the Vulgates are often pointed out. It is clear that Jerome not only left many times uncorrected, but also sometimes corrected unsystematically. See Index IV.

In his valuable *Atlas of Textual Criticism*, p. 43, Mr. E. A. Hutton remarks that the combinations B D and B F in the Pauline Epistles are by no means always to be condemned off hand.† Yet even B D F G may be rejected when ℵ A C are ranged on the other side, for the latter group may represent the Neutral text, while the former may be Western. But in 2 Corinthians, A is defective from iv. 13 to xii. 6, and C is defective from x. 8 to the end, so that only from i. 1 to iv. 13 is the combination ℵ A C possible. This fragment of the Epistle, however, yields at least two examples of the weight of this combination. In iii. 1 συνιστάνειν (ℵ A C K L P) is to be preferred to συνιστᾶν (B D), and in iii. 7 ἐν γράμμασιν (ℵ A C K L P) is to be preferred to ἐν γράμματι (B D F G). Perhaps we may add iii. 5, where ἐξ ἑαυτῶν (ℵ A C D E K L P) may be preferable to ἐξ αὐτῶν or ἐξ αὑτῶν (B F G). Even when A or C is absent, ℵ C or ℵ A (especially when supported by other witnesses) may be preferable to B D F G. In v. 3 εἴ γε (ℵ C K L P) is perhaps to be preferred to εἴπερ (B D F G), in ix. 5 εἰς ὑμᾶς (ℵ C K L) is to be preferred to πρὸς ὑμᾶς (B D F G), and in ix. 10 σπέρμα (ℵ C K L P) is to be preferred to σπόρον (B D F G). The transfer of K L P to the other side does not turn the scale. In iii. 16 ἡνίκα δὲ ἐάν (ℵ* A 17) may be preferable to ἡνίκα δ'ἄν (B D F G K L P), where C has neither

---

† In xi. 4 ἀνέχεσθε (B D* 17) is probably to be preferred to ἀνείχεσθε (ℵ D³ E G K L M P); in xi. 32 we should probably omit θέλων with B D*, d e f Vulg. against ℵ D³ K L M P and F G, g Copt.; in xii. 3 χωρίς (B D*) is certainly to be preferred to ἐκτός (ℵ D² and ³ F G K L M P); in xii. 5 the omission of μου (B D* 17, 67) is doubtless to be followed.

ἐάν nor ἄν. In v. 10 we may adopt φαῦλον (ℵ C 17, 37 and other cursives) rather than κακόν (B D F G K L P); in xii. 15 we may adopt ἀγαπῶ (ℵ A) rather than ἀγαπῶν (B D F G K L P); and in xii. 20 ἔρις (ℵ A) is certainly to be preferred to ἔρεις (B D F G K L P). The ninth century uncials K L P represent the late 'Syrian' or 'Antiochian' or 'a-text,' and a reading which is purely Syrian cannot be right; *e.g.* ὑπὲρ δύναμιν in viii. 3, and the omission of τοῦτο after τρίτον in xii. 14. The untrustworthy character of the combination B D F G K L P shows that a reading may be both Western and Syrian and yet be wrong, for "width of attestation is no proof of excellence"; and hence the perplexing διό (ℵ A B F G) in xii. 7 must be retained, although D E K L P, Latt. Syrr. omit. The two great Alexandrine witnesses, B and ℵ, when united are seldom wrong. Relying on them we may omit the ἡ after ἐπὶ Τίτου in vii. 14, although almost all other witnesses repeat the article; in xi. 21 we may adopt ἠσθενήκαμεν (ℵ B) against ἠσθενήσαμεν (D E F G K L M P); and in xii. 10 we may adopt καὶ στενοχωρίαις (ℵ* B) against ἐν στενοχωρίαις (ℵ³ D E F G K L P). Hutton has collected a number of passages in 2 Corinthians in which triple readings, Alexandrine, Western, and Syrian, are found, and in all the cases the Alexandrine reading supported by ℵ B is to be preferred. See critical notes on ii. 3, iii. 9, iv. 10, vi. 16, x. 8, xi. 21.

AUTHORITIES FOR THIS EPISTLE.

Greek Uncial MSS.

ℵ (Fourth century). Codex Sinaiticus; now at Petrograd, the only uncial MS. containing the whole N.T.

A (Fifth century). Codex Alexandrinus, now in the British Museum. All of 2 Corinthians from ἐπίστευσα iv. 13 to ἐξ ἐμοῦ xii. 6 is wanting.

B (Fourth century). Codex Vaticanus.

C (Fifth century). Codex Ephraemi, a Palimpsest; now at Paris, very defective. Of 2 Corinthians all from x. 8 onwards is wanting.

D (Sixth century). Codex Claromontanus; now at Paris. A Graeco-Latin MS. The Latin (d) is akin to the Old Latin. Many subsequent hands (sixth to ninth centuries) have corrected the MS.

E (Ninth century). At Petrograd. A copy of D, and unimportant.

F (Late ninth century). Codex Augiensis (from Reichenau); now at Trinity College, Cambridge.

G (Late ninth century). Codex Boernerianus; at Dresden.
   Interlined with the Latin (in minuscules). The Greek
   text is almost the same as that of F, but the Latin (g)
   shows Old Latin elements.

H (Sixth century). Codex Coislinianus, very valuable, but
   very incomplete. The MS. has been used in bindings
   and is in seven different libraries; 2 Cor. iv. 2–7 is at
   Petrograd, and x. 18–xi. 6 at Athos.

I² (Fifth century). Codex Muralti vi. Fragments at Petrograd.
   Two leaves contain 2 Cor. i. 20–ii. 12.

K (Ninth century). Codex Mosquensis; now at Moscow.

L (Ninth century). Codex Angelicus; now in the Angelica
   Library at Rome.

M (Ninth century). Codex Ruber, in bright red letters; two
   leaves in the British Museum contain 2 Cor. x. 13–
   xii. 5.

O (Ninth century). Two leaves at Petrograd contain
   2 Cor. i. 20–ii. 12.

P (Ninth century). Codex Porfirianus Chiovensis, formerly
   possessed by Bishop Porfiri of Kiev, and now at
   Petrograd.

R (Eighth century). Codex Cryptoferratensis. One leaf at
   Grotta Ferrata contains 2 Cor. xi. 9–19.

Minuscules or Cursive MSS.

About 480 cursives of the Pauline Epistles are known. Very
few of them are of much weight in determining readings, but
others have some interest for special reasons. Excepting No. 17,
very few are mentioned in the critical notes in this volume.

7. At Basle. Used by Erasmus for his first edition (1517), but
   not of special weight.

17. (Evan. 33, Acts 13. Ninth century). Now at Paris. "The
   queen of the cursives" and the best for the Pauline
   Epistles; more than any other it preserves Pre-Syrian
   readings and agrees with B D L.

37. (Evan. 69, Acts 69, Apoc. 14. Fifteenth century). The
   well-known Leicester codex; belongs to the Ferrar group.

47. (Eleventh century). Now in the Bodleian. Akin to A and
   B, which are nearer to one another in the Epistles than
   in the Gospels.

67. (Eleventh century). At Vienna. Has valuable marginal
   readings (67**) akin to B and M; these readings must
   have been copied from an ancient MS., but not from the
   Codex Ruber itself.

73. (Acts 68). At Upsala. Resembles 17.

80. (Acts 73. Eleventh century). In the Vatican. Akin to the Leicester codex; used by John M. Caryophilus (d. 1635) in preparing his edition of the Greek Testament.

Versions.

The Old Latin text is transmitted in d e f g, the Latin companions of the bilingual uncials D E F G. But in no MS. is the Latin text always an exact translation of the Greek text with which it is paired; in some passages the Latin presents a better text than the Greek. This is specially the case with d, which often agrees with the quotations in Lucifer of Cagliari (d. A.D. 370), while e f g approximate more to the Vulgate. Besides these four witnesses we have also

x (Ninth century). Codex Bodleianus; at Oxford. The text often agrees with d. The whole Epistle.

m (Ninth century). Speculum pseudo-Augustinianum; at Rome. Fragments.

r (Sixth century). Codex Frisingensis; at Munich. Fragments.

Respecting the Vulgate, Egyptian, Syriac, Armenian, and Gothic, the reader is referred to Sanday and Headlam, *Romans,* pp. lxvi f. No MS. of the Old Syriac is extant. The Harkleian revision (seventh century) preserves some ancient readings.

§ X. COMMENTARIES.

These are not so numerous as in the case of the First Epistle, but they abound, as the formidable list in Meyer shows; and that list has continued to increase. See also the Bibliography in the 2nd ed. of Smith, *Dictionary of the Bible,* i. pp. 658, 659; Hastings, *DB.* i. pp. 491, 498, iii. p. 731. In the selection given below, an asterisk indicates that information respecting the commentator is to be found in the volume on the First Epistle, pp. lxvi f., a dagger that such is to be found in Sanday and Headlam on *Romans,* pp. xcviii f.

Patristic and Scholastic: Greek.

*† Chrysostom (d. 407). Tr. Oxford, 1848.
*† Theodoret (d. 457). Migne, *P.G.* lxxxii.
*† Theophylact (d. after 1118). Migne, *P.G.* cxxv.

Patristic and Scholastic: Latin.

*† Ambrosiaster or Pseudo-Ambrosius (fl. 366–384).
Pseudo-Primasius. Migne, *P.L.* lxviii. An anti-Pelagian edition of Pelagius. This has been established by the investiga-

tions of Zimmer (*Pelagius in Irland*), C. H. Turner (*JTS.* Oct. 1902, pp. 132–141), and above all of A. Souter (*The Commentary of Pelagius on the Epistles of Paul: The Problem of its Restoration*). Turner suggested that Pseudo-Primasius is the commentary on the Pauline Epistles evolved out of Pelagius and Chrysostom by Cassiodorus and his monks of Vivarium, and Souter has proved that this surmise is correct. The original commentary of Pelagius was anonymous. Apparently the symbol P was wrongly interpreted by Gagney (1537) to mean ' Primasius,' and hence the error, which has continued to the present time, of quoting this commentary as 'Primasius.' It is an authority of great importance for determining the Vulgate text of the Pauline Epistles.

Bede (d. 735). Mainly a *catena* from Augustine.
* Atto Vercellensis (Tenth century). Migne, *P.I.* cxxxiv.
* Herveius Burgidolensis (Twelfth century). Migne, *P.L.* clxxxi.
Peter Lombard (d. 1160).
† Thomas Aquinas (d. 1274).

Modern Latin.

Faber Stapulensis, Paris, 1512.
Cajetan, Venice, 1531.
† Erasmus (d. 1536).
*† Calvin, Geneva, 1539–1551.
* Estius, Douay, 1614.
† Grotius, Amsterdam, 1644–1646.
*† Bengel, Tübingen, 1742 ; 3rd ed. London, 1862.
*† Wetstein, Amsterdam, 1751, 1752.
R. Cornely, S.J. Roman.

English.

*† H. Hammond, London, 1653.
† John Locke, London, 1705–1707.
Edward Burton, Oxford, 1831.
T. W. Peile, Rivingtons, 1853.
† C. Wordsworth, Rivingtons, 4th ed. 1866.
F. W. Robertson, Smith and Elder, 5th ed. 1867.
† H. Alford, Rivingtons, 6th ed. 1871.
* A. P. Stanley, Murray, 4th ed. 1876.
E. H. Plumptre in *Ellicott's Commentary*, n.d.
J. Waite in the *Speaker's Commentary*, 1881.
* W. Kay (posthumous), 1887.
J. Denney in the *Expositor's Bible*, 1894.
J. A. Beet, Hodder, 6th ed. 1895.
J. Massie in the *Century Bible*, n.d.

J. H. Bernard in the *Expositor's Greek Testament*, Hodder, 1903.
G. H. Rendall, Macmillan, 1909.
J. E. McFadyen, Hodder, 1911.
A. Menzies, Macmillan, 1912.
The more recent commentaries are, in general, the more helpful; but Alford and Waite retain much of their original value.

New Translations into English.

The Twentieth Century New Testament, Part II., Marshall. 1900.
R. F. Weymouth, *The New Testament in Modern Speech*, Clarke, 2nd ed. 1905.
A. S. Way, *The Letters of St Paul*, Macmillan, 2nd ed. 1906.
W. G. Rutherford (posthumous), *Thessalonians and Corinthians*, Macmillan, 1908. Ends at 2 Cor. ix. 15.
J. Moffatt, *The New Testament, a New Translation*, Hodder, 1913.
E. E. Cunnington, *The New Covenant, a Revision of the Version of A.D. 1611*, Routledge, 1914.

German.

Billroth, 1833; Eng. tr., Edinburgh, 1837.
Olshausen, 1840; Eng. tr., Edinburgh, 1855.
† De Wette, Leipzig, 3rd ed. 1855.
Kling, 1861; Eng. tr., Edinburgh, 1369.
Maier, Freiburg, 1857. Roman.
† Meyer, 5th ed. 1870; Eng. tr., Edinburgh, 1877. Re-edited by B. Weiss, and again by Heinrici, 1896 and 1900; again by J. Weiss, 1910.
Schnedermann, in Strack and Zöckler, Nördlingen, 1887.
* Schmiedel, Freiburg, i. B., 1892.
* B. Weiss, Leipzig, 2nd ed. 1902; Eng. tr., New York and London, 1906. Also his *Textkritik d. paul. Briefe* (xiv. 3 of *Texte und Untersuchungen*), 1896.
Lietzmann, Tübingen, 1907.
Bousset, in J. Weiss's *Die Schriften des N.T.*, Göttingen, 1908.
Bachmann, in Zahn's *Kommentar*, Leipzig, 1909.
The last five are of great value.

General.

The literature on the life and writings of St Paul is enormous and is rapidly increasing. In the volume on the First Epistle, p. lxx, a selection of modern works is given, to which the following may be added:—

O. Pfleiderer, *Hibbert Lecture,* 1885.
Das Urchristentum, 3nd ed. 1902 ; Eng. tr., 1907.
G. Matheson, *The Spiritual Development of St Paul,* 1890.
G. B. Stevens, *Pauline Theology,* 1892.
A. Hausrath, *History of N.T. Times ; Time of the Apostles,* 1895.
E. L. Hicks, *St Paul and Hellenism,* 1896.
A. B. Bruce, *St Paul's Conception of Christianity,* 1896.
A. Sabatier, *L'Apôtre Paul,* 3rd ed. 1896.
O. Cone, *Paul, the Man, the Missionary, and the Teacher,* 1898.
P. Faine, *Das gesetzfreie Evang. des Paulus,* 1899.
H. A. A. Kennedy, *St Paul's Conception of the Last Things,* 2nd ed. 1904.
C. Clemen, *Paulus, sein Leben und Wirken,* 1904 ; much information in the foot-notes.
B. Lucas, *The Fifth Gospel, being the Pauline Interpretation of The Christ,* 1907.
W. Sanday, *Paul,* Hastings' *DCG.* ii., 1908.
B. W. Bacon, *The Story of St Paul.*
A. B. D. Alexander, *The Ethics of St Paul,* 1910.
P. Gardner, *The Religious Experiences of St Paul,* 1911.
K. Lake, *The Earlier Epistles of St Paul,* 1911.
A. Deissmann, *St Paul, a Study in Social and Religious History,* 1912.
A. Schweitzer, *Paul and his Interpreters,* 1912.
S. N. Rostron, *The Christology of St Paul,* 1912.
W. Ramsay, *The Teaching of St Paul in Terms of the Present Day,* 1913.
A. C. Headlam, *St Paul and Christianity,* 1913.
E. B. Redlich, *St Paul and his Companions,* 1913.

The Apocryphal Correspondence.

The apocryphal letters between St Paul and the Corinthians are of some interest as illustrating the clumsiness with which forgers sometimes execute their work, and the uncritical spirit which allows such work to pass muster as genuine. Stanley gives a translation of the letters in an appendix to his commentary on 1 and 2 Corinthians, and he exposes various blunders. Harnack has edited them in his *Geschichte d. altchrist. Literatur,* 1897 ; and there is a convenient edition of them in Lietzmann's excellent *Materials for the use of Theological Lecturers and Students,* 1905. Other literature on the subject is mentioned in Moffatt, *Intr. to the Literature of the N.T.* pp. 129 f.

THE SECOND
EPISTLE TO THE CORINTHIANS

---◆---

I. 1, 2. THE APOSTOLIC SALUTATION.

Paul, a divinely chosen Apostle, and Timothy our brother, give Christian greeting to the Corinthian Church and to the Christians near it.

¹ Paul, an Apostle by divine appointment, and Timothy whom ye all know, give greeting to the body of Corinthian Christians and to all Christians in the Province. ² May the free and unmerited favour of God be yours, and the peace which this favour brings! May our Heavenly Father and the Lord Jesus Christ grant them to you!

The Salutation has the usual three parts; the writer, those addressed, and the greeting.

1. Παῦλος ἀπόστολος Χριστοῦ Ἰησοῦ. St Paul states his own claim to be heard before mentioning Timothy, who is ἀδελφός and not ἀπόστολος. *Vos Corinthii mihi debetis obedire, et falsos apostolos respuere, quia sum Paulus apostolus Jesu Christi, id est mirabilis legatus Salvatoris Regis. Apostolus sum, non usurpative, sed per voluntatem Dei Patris. Pseudo autem apostoli, nec a Christo sunt missi, nec per Dei voluntatem venerunt. Ideoque respuendi sunt* (Herveius Burgidolensis).

In nearly all his letters, including the Pastorals, St Paul introduces himself as an Apostle, with or without further description; and here, as in Phil. i. 1 and Col. i. 1, he is careful not to give to Timothy the title of ἀπόστολος. Cf. the opening words of 1 and 2 Thess., Phil., and Philemon. We find the same feature in 1 and 2 Pet. The amplification, Ἰησοῦ Χριστοῦ διὰ θελήματος Θεοῦ, is specially in point in Epistles in which he has to contend with the opposition of false teachers, some of whom claimed to have a better right to the title of Apostle than he had (Batiffol, *Primitive Catholicism*, p. 42). We find it in 1 Cor., Eph., Col., 2 Tim.; and in Gal. i. 1 the fact that his Apostleship is of God and not of man is still more clearly stated. It did not come to him in the ordinary course of events, but by a definite Divine decree.

Τιμόθεος ὁ ἀδελφός. He is mentioned, like Sosthenes in 1 Cor., to show that what St Paul sends by Apostolic authority has the approval of one who can regard these matters from the Corinthians' own point of view, as a fellow-Christian, without authority over them (i. 19; Acts xviii. 5). The Apostle might be prejudiced by his high position; Timothy is influenced simply by his brotherly affection. 'He agrees with me in what I have to say to you.' Timothy is joined with Paul in the addresses of five other Epistles (1 and 2 Thess., Phil., Col., Philemon) and is mentioned at the close of two others (1 Cor. xvi. 10; Rom. xvi. 21; cf. Heb. xiii. 23).* He was converted by St Paul at Lystra during the First Missionary Journey, and afterwards seems to have been more often with the Apostle than not. Very possibly he was the Apostle's amanuensis for some of the Epistles; but this does not follow from his being included in the Salutations: Tertius (Rom. xvi. 2) is not mentioned in the address of that Epistle. But, whether or no he acted as scribe, it is not likely that Timothy here, or Sosthenes in 1 Cor., or Silvanus and Timothy in 1 and 2 Thess., had much to do with the composition. Whoever acted as amanuensis may have made an occasional suggestion; but in every case we may be sure that the letter is St Paul's and not a joint production. St Paul had been anxious about the reception which Timothy would have at Corinth (1 Cor. xvi. 10), and here he shows how highly he thinks of Timothy. But nowhere in 2 Cor. does he say anything about Timothy's reception at Corinth. Either Timothy never reached Corinth (Lightfoot, *Bibl. Essays*, p. 220), or (more probably) he was so badly received that St Paul does not think it wise, after the submission of the Corinthians, to recall Timothy's ill-success in trying to induce them to submit (K. Lake, *Earlier Epistles of St Paul*, p. 134; Paley, *Horae Paulinae*, IV.). What is certain is that the mission of Timothy to Corinth, whether carried out or not, is done with when 2 Cor. was written. There is no need to mention it. (Redlich, *S. Paul and his Companions*, p. 279.)

ὁ ἀδελφός. This does not mean 'my spiritual brother'; Timothy was St Paul's spiritual son (1 Tim. i. 2; 2 Tim. i. 2);

---

* In Origen's phrase, "the concurrence of Paul and Timothy flashed out the lightning of these Epistles."

nor does it mean ὁ συνεργός μου (Rom. xvi. 21). It means 'one of the brethren,' a member of the Christian Society. Deissmann (*Bible Studies*, pp. 87, 88, *Light from the Anc. East*, pp. 96, 107, 227) has shown from papyri that ἀδελφός was used of members of pagan brotherhoods. While the Master was with them, Christ's adherents were described in their relation to Him; they were His 'disciples': in the Gospels, μαθητής occurs more than 230 times. After His presence had ceased to be visible they were described in their relation to one another as 'brethren,' and in relation to their calling as 'saints': in the Epistles, μαθηταί nowhere occurs; its place is taken by ἀδελφοί and ἅγιοι. In Acts all three terms are found.

τῇ ἐκκλησίᾳ τ. Θεοῦ. Having reminded them of his high authority as 'an Apostle *of Christ Jesus*,' he at the same time reminds them of their own high position as 'the Church *of God*.' In both cases the genitive is possessive. The Society of which they are members has as its Founder and Ruler the Creator of the world and the Father of all mankind. St Paul is not hinting that in Corinth there is an ecclesia which is not 'of God.' Rather, as Theodoret suggests, by reminding them of their Lord and Benefactor, he is once more warning them against divisions —εἰς ὁμόνοιαν πάλιν συνάπτων: what God has founded as one body they must not divide. It is probable that, wherever he uses this phrase, τοῦ Θεοῦ is not a mere otiose amplification, but always has point (1 Thess. ii. 14; 2 Thess. i. 4; 1 Cor. i. 2, x. 32, xi. 16, 22, xv. 9; Gal. i. 13; 1 Tim. iii. 5 without articles). Everywhere else in this Epistle we have ἐκκλησίαι in the plur., showing that local Churches are meant (viii. 1, 18, 19, 23, 24, xi. 8, 28, xii. 13); and here ἡ ἐκκλησία is expressly limited to Corinth; so that nowhere in the letter is the Church as a whole mentioned. In Rom. xvi. 16 we have αἱ ἐκκλ. τοῦ Χριστοῦ, an expression which occurs nowhere else in N.T. In Acts xx. 28 both reading and interpretation are doubtful. In LXX we have ἐκκλησία Κυρίου and other expressions which show that the ἐκκλ. is a religious one. There is no instance of ἐκκλ. being used of religious assemblies among the heathen. The οὔσῃ implies that the Church was now established in Corinth (Acts xiii. 1; cf. v. 17, xiv. 13, xxviii. 17); it had ceased to be a congregation of hearers.

We can draw no reasonable inference as to change in the Apostle's feelings from the brevity of the description of the Church in Corinth here when compared with that in 1 Cor. i. 2.

σὺν τ. ἁγίοις πᾶσιν τ. οὖσιν ἐν ὅλῃ τ. Ἀχαίᾳ. 'With all the saints which are in the whole of Achaia.' All Christians are 'holy' in virtue, not of their lives, but of their calling; they are set apart in a holy Society as servants and sons of the Holy God.

Chrysostom thinks that St Paul addresses 'all,' because all alike need correction. In Thess. he does not include all in Macedonia, nor in Rom. all in Italy. Achaia may be used loosely for the district of which Corinth was the chief city. St Paul does not mention other *Churches* in Achaia (contrast Gal. i. 2), and therefore we can hardly regard this as a circular letter. But there were Christians in Athens and Cenchreae, and probably in other places near Corinth, and the Apostle includes all of them in the address. We may perhaps, with Lietzmann, regard this as the germ of the later Metropolitan constitution. See on 1 Cor. i. 2. The Corinthians were apt to be exclusive and to plume themselves upon a supposed superiority. St Paul may be reminding them that they are not the whole Church (1 Cor. xiv. 36), even in Achaia; at any rate he lets Christians outside Corinth know that they are not forgotten. The whole of Greece may possibly be included.

Χριστοῦ Ἰησοῦ (אּ B M P 17) rather than Ἰησοῦ Χρ. (A D E G K L, Latt. Copt. Arm. Aeth. Goth.). F, f omit. In the best texts of the earlier Epp. (1 and 2 Thess. Gal.) always Ἰ. Χρ. ; in the later Epp. (Phil. Eph. Col. Philem. 1 and 2 Tim.) almost always Χρ. Ἰ. In the intermediate Epp. (1 and 2 Cor. Rom.) the readings vary, and St Paul's usage may have varied. While Χριστός was a title, it was naturally placed after Ἰησοῦς, which was always a name. But Χρ. became a name, and then the two words in either order, became a name. See on Rom. i. 1, and Sanday, *Bampton Lectures*, p. 289.

2. χάρις ὑμῖν κ. εἰρήνη. So in all the Pauline Epp. (except 1 and 2 Tim.) and in 1 and 2 Pet. In N.T., 'peace' probably has much the same meaning as in Jewish salutations,—freedom from external enmity and internal distraction. The two Apostles "naturally retain the impressive term traditional with their countrymen, but they subordinate it to the term 'grace,' which looked back from the gift to the Giver, and which the Gospel had clothed with special significance. This subordination is marked not only by the order, but by the collocation of ὑμῖν, which invariably precedes καὶ εἰρήνη" (Hort on 1 Pet. i. 2 ; see on 1 Cor. i. 3). It is the grace which produces the peace. In 2 Macc. i. 1 we have χαίρειν . . . εἰρήνην ἀγαθήν, and in 2 Macc. i. 10, ix. 19, we have the frequent combination χαίρειν κ. ὑγιαίνειν, which is found in the oldest Greek letter known to us, 4th cent. B.C. (Deissmann, *Light from Anc. East*, p. 149). See J. A. Robinson (*Eph.* pp. 221 f.) on χάρις in Bibl. Grk., and G. Milligan (*Thess.* p. 127 f.) on St Paul's use of current epistolary forms and phrases.

ἀπὸ Θεοῦ πατρὸς ἡμῶν καὶ κυρίου Ἰ. Χρ. As at the beginning of the earliest book in N.T. (1 Thess. i. 1) we find the notable phrase 'God the Father,' so here we find Christ called 'Lord,'

the usual title of God, and we find Christ linked with God the
Father under one preposition, which shows that the Apostle
regards the two as on an equality. "In the appellation
'Father' we have already the first beginning—may we not say
the first decisive step, which potentially contains the rest?—of
the doctrine of the Trinity. . . . The striking thing about it is
that the Son already holds a place beside the Father" (Sanday,
Outlines of the Life of Christ, p. 218). "It is well known that
the phrase 'God the Father' is especially common in these
opening salutations. We cannot think that it is a new coinage
of St Paul. It comes to his pen quite naturally, and not as
though it needed any explanation. We may safely set it down
as part of the general vocabulary of Christians. Its occurrence
in Q is proof that it was familiar in circles far removed from
Pauline influence" (*Christ in Recent Research,* p. 131). It is
not probable that the Spirit is omitted because *eo tempore
nullus errabat de Spiritu.* St Paul is not consciously teaching
Trinitarian doctrine; he uses language which indicates, without
his intending it, how much he held of that doctrine. Cf. xiii. 13.

This Salutation exhibits undoubted resemblances in form to
secular letters that have come down to us from the same period.
But the differences are greater, and that in three respects.
There is the firm assertion of Apostolic authority, the clear
indication that those whom he addresses are not ordinary
people but a consecrated society, and the spiritual character of
the good wishes which he sends them. Comparison with a
letter from some religious official, addressed to those who had
been initiated into one of the Mysteries, if we did but possess
such, would be of great interest.

The Thanksgiving which follows the Salutation, in accordance with St Paul's almost invariable practice, is also a common
feature in secular letters; cf. 2 Macc. ix. 20. Deissmann
(*Light from Anc. East,* p. 168) gives a close parallel to this one
in a letter from Apion, an Egyptian soldier, to his father, 2nd
cent. A.D. After the usual greeting and good wishes he says:
"I thank the Lord Serapis, that, when I was near being
drowned in the sea, he saved me straightway"—εὐχαριστῶ τῷ
κυρίῳ Σεράπιδι, ὅτι μου κινδυνεύσαντος εἰς θάλασσαν ἔσωσε εὐθέως.
See also *Bibelstudien,* p. 210, an example not given in *Bible
Studies.* St Paul usually thanks God for some grace bestowed
on those whom he addresses, and hence his omission of the
Thanksgiving in the stern letter to the Galatians; here and in
1 Tim. i. 12 he gives thanks for benefits bestowed on himself.
But his readers are not forgotten (*vv.* 6, 7); it is largely on their
account that he is so thankful. The Thanksgiving is in two
parts; for Divine Comfort (3–7) and for Divine Deliverance (8–11).

I. 3–11. PREAMBLE OF THANKSGIVING AND HOPE.

I bless God for the recovery and comfort which enables us to recover and comfort the fallen and distressed.

[3] Blessed be the God and Father of our Lord Jesus Christ,—the Father who is full of compassion and the God who is the Source of all comfort. [4] Blessed be He, for He ever comforts us all through our affliction, and He does this as a lesson to us how to comfort other people in any kind of affliction whether of body or soul, viz. by using the same way of comforting that God uses with us. [5] For if, through our intimate union with the Christ, we have an abundant share of His sufferings, to just the same extent, through His merciful mediation, we can draw upon an abundant fund of comfort. [6] So then, whatever happens to us, you reap an advantage : for, if we receive afflictions, it is to bring comfort and spiritual well-being to you ; and if we receive comforting in our afflictions, our comforting is for your benefit, for God makes it effective to you when you courageously accept the same kind of sufferings as He lays upon us. And our confidence in your future is too well founded to be shaken, [7] because we know well that, as surely as you share our sufferings, so surely do you share our comfort.

[8] When I speak of our sufferings, I mean something very real. I do not wish you, my Brothers, to be in any uncertainty about that. Affliction so intense came upon us in Asia that it prostrated us beyond all power of endurance ; so much so that we despaired of preserving even life. [9] Indeed, when we asked within ourselves, whether it was to be life or death for us, our own presentiment said ' Death,'—a presentiment which God sent to teach us not to rely any more on our powers, but on Him who not only can rescue from death but restores the dead to life. [10] Of course He can do both ; for it was He who delivered us out of such imminent peril of death and will do so again ; and it is on Him that we have set our hope that He will continue to deliver us, [11] while you also join in helping on our behalf by your intercessions for us. And the blessed result of this will be that from many uplifted faces thanksgivings on our behalf will be offered by many for the mercy which has been shown to us.

As in Eph. i. 3–14 (see Westcott), the rhythmical flow of the passage will be felt, if it is read according to the balance of the clauses, which is very marked in the first half.

Εὐλογητὸς ὁ Θεὸς καὶ πατὴρ τοῦ κυρίου ἡμῶν Ἰησοῦ Χριστοῦ,
  ὁ πατὴρ τῶν οἰκτιρμῶν καὶ Θεὸς πάσης παρακλήσεως,
  ὁ παρακαλῶν ἡμᾶς ἐπὶ πάσῃ τῇ θλίψει ἡμῶν,
εἰς τὸ δύνασθαι ἡμᾶς παρακαλεῖν τοὺς ἐν πάσῃ θλίψει
διὰ τῆς παρακλήσεως ἧς παρακαλούμεθα αὐτοὶ ὑπὸ τοῦ Θεοῦ.
ὅτι καθὼς περισσεύει τὰ παθήματα τοῦ Χριστοῦ εἰς ἡμᾶς,
  οὕτως διὰ τοῦ Χριστοῦ περισσεύει καὶ ἡ παράκλησις ἡμῶν.
εἴτε δὲ θλιβόμεθα, ὑπὲρ τῆς ὑμῶν παρακλήσεως,
  εἴτε δὲ παρακαλούμεθα, ὑπὲρ τῆς ὑμῶν παρακλήσεως.

3. Εὐλογητὸς ὁ Θεὸς κ. πατὴρ τοῦ κυρίου ἡμῶν Ἰ. Χρ. The AV. is inconsistent here in separating ὁ Θεός from τ. κυρίου κ.τ.λ., while in xi. 31, as in Eph. i. 3 and 1 Pet. i. 3, it takes both nominatives with the following genitive; 'Blessed be the God and Father of our Lord Jesus Christ.' The latter is probably right, in accordance with 1 Cor. xv. 24; Eph. i. 17; Rev. i. 6, iii. 12; Mk. xv. 34; Jn. xx. 17. If St Paul had meant ὁ Θεός to be separated from πατήρ, he would probably have written ὁ Θεός μου, as in Rom. i. 8; Phil. i. 3; Philem. 4. It is remarkable that the Apostles Paul, Peter, and John, while thinking of Christ as God and giving Him Divine attributes, do not shrink from saying that God is not only Christ's Father but also His God. *Benedictus Deus, qui Christum secundum humanitatem creavit et secundum divinitatem genuit, atque ita est Deus et Pater ejus* (Herveius). 'God who is also Father of our Lord Jesus Christ' is a possible translation, in accordance with Col. i. 3; 'God the Father of our Lord Jesus Christ'; but it is not the most natural rendering. See on Rom. xv. 6, and Hort on 1 Pet. i. 3.

Εὐλογητός occurs eight times in N.T., chiefly in Paul (xi. 31; Rom. i. 25, ix. 5; Eph. i. 3), and always of God. When human beings are called 'blessed,' εὐλογημένος is used, but this occurs only in the Gospels. In a few passages in LXX (Deut. vii. 14; Ruth ii. 20; 1 Sam. xv. 13, xxv. 33), εὐλογητός is used of men. The adjective implies that blessing ought to be given, the participle that it has been received. This difference is pointed out by Philo (*De Migr. Abrah.* 19); but it cannot be rigidly insisted upon in exegesis. In Dan. iii. 52–56, εὐλογητός and -ημένος are used indifferently of God, εὐλογητός being more frequent (4 to 2) in LXX, and εὐλογημένος (4 to 2) in Theod. Grammatically, we may understand either ἔστω (εἴη) or ἐστίν. In Rom. i. 25, ἐστίν is expressed, as also in 1 Pet. iv. 11, which is not quite parallel; here, as in Eph. i. 3 and 1 Pet. i. 3, we almost certainly have a wish: but in Eph. i. 3 the Old Latin has *benedictus est.* Eusebius (*Praep. Evang.* ix. 34) quotes from Eupolemus of Alexandria a letter from Surom (Hiram)* to Solomon which begins thus; Σούρων Σολομῶνι Βασιλεῖ Μεγάλῳ χαίρειν. Εὐλογητὸς ὁ Θεός, ὃς τὸν οὐρανὸν καὶ τὴν γῆν ἔκτισεν, ὃς εἵλετο ἄνθρωπον χρηστὸν ἐκ χρηστοῦ ἀνδρός. ἅμα τῷ ἀναγνῶναι τὴν παρὰ σοῦ ἐπιστολὴν σφόδρα ἐχάρην καὶ εὐλόγησα τὸν Θεὸν ἐπὶ τῷ παρειλη-φέναι σὲ τὴν βασιλείαν.

τοῦ κυρίου ἡμῶν. A translation of the Aramaic *Maran* (1 Cor. xvi. 22) or *Marana*, and a continuation of the title by which the disciples commonly addressed the Master. Christ refers to Himself as ὁ κύριος ὑμῶν (Mt. xxiv. 42; cf. xxi. 3). The general use of *Maran* after the Ascension is strong evidence for at least occasional use during our Lord's ministry. See Bigg on 1 Pet. i. 3; Plummer, *Luke*, p. xxxi; Dalman, *Words of Jesus*, p. 328. "It may be said with certainty that, at the time when Christianity originated, 'Lord' was a divine predicate intelligible to the whole Eastern world. St Paul's confession of 'our Lord Jesus Christ' was, like the complemental thought that the worshippers are the 'slaves' of the Lord, understood in its full meaning by everyone in the Hellenistic East, and the adoption of the Christian term of worship was vastly facilitated in consequence" (Deissmann, *Light from Anc. East*, p. 354). 'Lord' or 'the Lord' is very frequent as a name for Christ in 1 and 2 Thess., eight times without, and fourteen times with, the article. But this lofty title, so full of meaning in the Apostolic age, "has become one of the most lifeless words in the Christian vocabulary" (Kennedy on Phil. ii. 11: with Klöpper, Lipsius, and B. Weiss, he holds that Κύριος is the 'Name above every name' which God has given to Christ).

ὁ πατὴρ τ. οἰκτιρμῶν κ. Θεὸς π. τ. παρακλήσεως. The two genitives are probably not quite parallel, although Theodoret makes them so by rendering the first ὁ τοὺς οἰκτιρμοὺς πηγάζων. The first is probably qualifying or descriptive; 'the Father who shows mercy,' 'the merciful Father,' as in ὁ π. τ. δόξης (Eph. i. 17), τὸν Κύριον τ. δόξης (1 Cor. ii. 8), ὁ Θεὸς τ. δόξης (Acts vii. 2), and perhaps the difficult expressions, ὁ πατὴρ τ. φώτων ͺnd τ. Κυρίου ἡμῶν Ἰ. Χριστοῦ τῆς δόξης (Jas. i. 17, ii. 1). But there is not much difference between 'the merciful Father' and 'the Father from whom mercy flows.' The plur. τῶν οἰκτιρμῶν does not refer to separate merciful acts, "Father of *repeated* compassions"; it is a Hebraism, very frequent in LXX, even

* Other forms of the name are Hirom (1 K. v. 10, 18) and Sirom (Hdt. vii. 98).

when combined with ἔλεος in the sing. (Ps. cii. [ciii.] 4; Is. liii. 15; 1 Macc. iii. 44). In N.T., excepting Col. iii. 12, the plur. is invariable. *Recte igitur non Pater judiciorum vel ultionum dicitur, sed* Pater misericordiarum, *quod miserendi causam et originem sumat ex proprio, judicandi vel ulciscendi magis ex nostro* (S. Bernard, *In Nativ. Dom.* v. 3).

Theodoret's explanation is right of the second genitive ; 'the Supplier' or 'Source of all comfort.'* Vulg. has *Deus totius consolationis*, instead of *omnis*; and this has misled some commentators who interpret *totius* as meaning *integrae* or *perfectae*. In *v.* 4, *in tota tribulatione* (ἐπὶ πάσῃ τῇ θλ.) might have been better than *in omni tribulatione*. The threefold πάσης, πάσῃ, πάσῃ, intensifies the idea of abundance; and the whole passage illustrates St Paul's fondness for alliteration, especially with the letter π.

παρακλήσεως. The word occurs six times in these five verses, with παρακαλεῖν four times.† AV. spoils the effect by wavering between 'consolation' and 'comfort.' 'Comfort' for both substantive and verb preserves the effect. Vulg. also varies between *consolatio* and *exhortatio*, and between *consolari* and *exhortare*. The change to *exhortatio* and *exhortare* in *vv.* 4 and 6 confuses the Apostle's meaning, and the double change in *v.* 4 causes great confusion.

4. Vulg. *Qui consolatur nos in omni tribulatione nostra, ut possimus et ipsi consolari eos qui in omni pressura sunt, per exhortationem qua exhortamur et ipsi a Deo.*

ὁ παρακαλῶν. 'Who continually comforts us'; not once or twice, but always; the παράκλησις is without break (Chrys.); and it is supplied in various ways—*vel per Scripturas, vel per alios sanctos, vel per occultam inspirationem, vel per tribulationis allevationem* (Herveius).

The ἡμᾶς need not be confined to Paul and Timothy, still less to Paul alone. It probably includes all missionaries, and perhaps indirectly all sufferers; Is. xl. 1. It is unreasonable to suppose that St Paul always uses the 1st pers. plur. of himself in his Apostolic character, and the 1st pers. sing. when he speaks as a private individual; and it would be rash to assert that he

---

* Cf. ὁ Θεὸς τῆς ὑπομονῆς καὶ παρακλήσεως (Rom. xv. 5), τῆς ἐλπίδος (xv. 13), τῆς εἰρήνης (xv. 33): also αἱ παρακλήσεις σου ἠγάπησαν τὴν ψυχήν μου (Ps. xciii. [xciv.] 19).

† In the first eight chapters παράκλησις occurs eleven times, in the four last chapters not at all, and in the rest of the Pauline Epistles only eight times; in the rest of N.T. (Lk., Acts, Heb.) only nine times. The verb is specially frequent in Acts and Paul, who uses it in all three senses ; 'beseech' 18 times, 'exhort' 17 times, 'comfort' 13 times, of which 7 are in this Epistle, where the verb occurs 17 times. Bernard, *ad loc.*

never uses the plur. without including others; but the latter statement is nearer the truth than the former.   He seems to use the 1st pers. plur. with varying degrees of plurality, from himself with one colleague to himself with all Christians or even all mankind; and he probably uses it sometimes of himself alone. Some elasticity may be allowed in this passage.   Each case must be judged by its context.   But we cannot be sure that, when he employs the plur. of himself, he is emphasizing his official authority, for Milligan (*Thess.* p. 131) has shown that this use of the plur. is found in the ordinary correspondence of the time, and also in inscriptions.   In Epistles written without any associate (Gal. Rom. Eph. Past.), the sing. is dominant.   In 2 Cor., the plur. is frequent, and sometimes changes rapidly with the sing. (i. 13, v. 11, vii. 2, 3, 4, 5, 6, 7, 12, 14, ix. 4, x. 2, 8, xi. 6, 21, xii. 19, 20, xiii. 6–10).   It is very unlikely that all the plurals are virtually singular and also official; but in vii. 5 ἡ σὰρξ ἡμῶν must mean St Paul only.   See Lightfoot on 1 Thess. ii. 4.

ἐπὶ πάσῃ τῇ θλίψει ἡμῶν.   As in vii. 4 and 1 Thess. iii. 7, the ἐπί expresses the occasion *on* which the comfort is given; and the article indicates that the θλίψις is regarded as a whole, 'in all our affliction,' whereas ἐν πάσῃ θλ. means 'in every kind of affliction' that can occur, whether of mind or body (Blass, *Gram. d. N.T. Gr.* § 47. 9, p. 158).   There is no exception on God's side (Ps. xciv. 19), and there must be none on ours.   Both AV. and RV. mark the difference by change from 'all' to any.' The change from ἐπί to ἐν can hardly be marked in English without awkwardness: Latin versions make no change, and some Greek texts read ἐν for ἐπί.   Θλίψις (or θλῖψις) is found in all Pauline groups, except the Pastorals.   It is rare in class. Grk.,— perhaps never before Aristotle, and then always in the literal sense of 'crushing.'   In LXX it is very frequent, especially in Psalms and Isaiah.   AV. obliterates its frequency here by varying between 'tribulation' and 'trouble' (*vv.* 4, 7, 8) and 'affliction' (ii. 4, iv. 17, etc.).   RV. has 'affliction' always in 2 Cor., but in other Epistles has 'tribulation' also : it retains 'tribulation' always in Rev. and in the Gospels, except Jn. xvi. 21, where 'anguish' is retained.   Vulg. usually has *tribulatio,* which is not classical, but sometimes has *pressura*: in *v.* 4 it has both, as if St Paul used two different words.   In Col. i. 24 it has *passio.*

εἰς τὸ δύνασθαι κ.τ.λ.   With the construction comp. 1 Cor. ix. 18.   The teleological standpoint is Pauline : *non sibi vivebat Apostolus, sed Ecclesiae* (Calv.).   Evangelists are comforted, not for any merit of their own, but in order that they may be able to comfort others.   In missionary work sympathy is the great condition of success (1 Cor. ix. 22), and it was part of the training of the Apostles that they should need and receive comfort in order to know how to impart it; and the comfort is deliverance, not necessarily from the suffering, but from the anxiety which suffering brings. There is the assurance that sufferers are in the hands of a loving Father, and this assurance they can pass on to others in all their afflictions. But we need not confine ἡμᾶς to Apostles and missionaries; the words apply to all Christians. It is, however, exaggeration to say that only those who have received consolation know how to impart it.

It is not impossible that St Paul is here thinking of the affliction which the Corinthians had recently been experiencing in their agony of self-reproach and remorse when the severe letter of the Apostle and the remonstrances of Titus, who had brought the letter to them, had convinced them that they had treated their spiritual father abominably in listening to the misrepresentations and slanders of the Judaizing teachers and in rebelling against him. These emotional Greeks, as Titus had reported to St Paul, had been crushed by the thought of their own waywardness and ingratitude. The Apostle, hardly less emotional than themselves, longs to comfort them, and he knows how to do it. They, by their rebellion and maltreatment of him had taught his tender and affectionate heart what affliction, in one of its most intense forms, could be; and God had comforted him and sustained him in it all. Now he knows how to comfort them. "The affliction had intensified Paul's capacity as a son of consolation" (Massie, *The Century Bible*, p. 71).

ἧς παρακαλούμεθα. This kind of attraction is not common in N.T.; comp. τῆς χάριτος αὐτοῦ, ἧς ἐχαρίτωσεν ἡμᾶς and τῆς κλήσεως, ἧς ἐκλήθητε (Eph. i. 6, iv. 1). In these cases it may be "simplest" to take ἧς as ᾗ; but in all of them the acc. is possible, as in Mk. x. 38 and Jn. xvii. 26; and in all five cases a substantive is followed by its cognate verb. Eph. i. 19, τὴν ἐνέργειαν . . . ἣν ἐνέργηκεν, and ii. 4, τὴν πολλὴν ἀγάπην αὐτοῦ, ἣν ἠγάπησεν ἡμᾶς, suggest the acc. rather than the dat. The attraction of the dat. is very rare, but we find it Ps. xc. 15; Hag. ii. 18.

For ἐπί, C, Eus. Chrys. have ἐν. M, Hil. Ambr. omit ἡμῶν. For εἰς, F has ἵνα. Vulg. ins. καί before ἡμᾶς. D E F G, Latt. (not r) ins. καί before αὐτοί. For ὑπό, F has ἀπό.

5. ὅτι καθὼς κ.τ.λ. 'Because just as the sufferings of the Messiah abound unto us, so through the Messiah our comfort also aboundeth.' For καθὼς . . . οὕτως . . . see 1 Thess. ii. 4. The sufferings are those *quas Christus prior pertulit et nobis perferendas reliquit* (Herveius). The preachers of the Kingdom have to suffer persecution as He had (1 Pet. iv. 13); but

Chrys. gives too much meaning to περισσεύει, when he interprets it as meaning that Christ's ministers suffer more than He did. 'The sufferings of the Messiah' are those which He was destined to suffer, which ἔδει παθεῖν τ. Χριστόν (see on Lk. xxiv. 26 and cf. Acts xvii. 3; 2 Cor. iv. 10; Rom. vi. 5; Phil. iii. 10, with Lightfoot's note).* 'Sufferings endured for Christ's sake' is wrong as translation (cf. iv. 11), and inadequate as exegesis. 'Sufferings which the glorified Christ suffers when His members suffer' is questionable exegesis, which is not justified by the Apostle's use of τοῦ Χριστοῦ instead of τοῦ Ἰησοῦ as in Gal. vi. 17. It is the sufferings of the Messiah that he is pointing to, for his recent opponents were Jews. Moreover, τ. Χριστοῦ is necessary in the second clause, for not the historical Jesus who suffered is the Consoler, but the glorified Christ; and it would have marred the antithesis to have 'Jesus' in the first clause and 'Christ' in the second. In iv. 10, he has 'Jesus' in both clauses. In the background is the thought of the absolute unity between Christ and His members; and although we can hardly think of Him as still liable to suffering when His members suffer, yet their sufferings are a continuation of His, and they supplement His (Col. i. 24) in the work of building up the Church. One purpose of His sufferings was to make men feel more certain of the love of God (Rom. viii. 32). Cf. iv. 10; Rom. vi. 5, viii. 17; Phil. iii. 10; Mt. xx. 22, xxv. 40, 45). It is less likely that he is hinting at opponents who had said that his sufferings were richly deserved. So far as possible, he wishes to suppress all allusion to the unhappy past, and hence the obscure wording of this paragraph. What he desires to emphasize is the comfort which he and those who had opposed him now enjoy, owing to their submission. In N.T., πάθημα is confined to the Pauline Epp., Heb. and 1 Pet. The change from plur. to sing. is effective; *illa multa sunt, haec una, et tamen potior* (Beng.). D E have τὸ πάθημα to match ἡ παράκλησις.

περισσεύει εἰς ἡμᾶς. Cf. ix. 8; Rom. v. 15; Eph. i. 8.

διὰ τοῦ Χριστοῦ. 'Through the Messiah': it is through His instrumentality that the reconciliation between the Jew of Tarsus and his Jewish antagonists in Corinth, which has been such a comfort to both sides, has come about. This use of διά is freq. of the Son (1 Cor. viii. 6; Col. i. 16; Heb. i. 2), but it is also used of the Father (1 Cor. i. 9; Rom. xi. 36; Heb. ii. 10), and therefore, as Chrys. remarks, is not derogatory to the Divinity of the Son. It is He who sends His Spirit to bring comfort. He has become πνεῦμα ζωοποιοῦν (1 Cor. xv. 45).

καὶ ἡ παράκλησις ἡμῶν. This does not mean the comfort

* See Briggs, *The Messiah of the Apostles*, p. 122.

which we give, but the comfort which we receive. After περισσεύει we may understand εἰς ὑμᾶς. St Paul and Timothy have received abundant comfort and have abundant comfort to impart.

DEFG 17, 37, Latt. Copt. ins. καὶ after οὕτως. Vulg. omits καὶ before ἡ παράκλησις.

6. εἴτε δὲ θλιβόμεθα. 'But whether we be afflicted, it is for your comfort [and salvation].' How this is the case, has been shown in v. 4. The teachers' sufferings and subsequent consolations have taught them how to comfort others; so that all their experiences, whether painful or pleasing, prove profitable to the Corinthians.

τῆς ὑμῶν παρακλήσεως. We have ὑμῶν between article and substantive twice in this verse. The arrangement is peculiar to Paul (vii. 7, 15, viii. 13, 14, xii. 19, xiii. 9, etc.). The alternatives, εἴτε . . . εἴτε, are almost peculiar to Paul, and are very frequent in 1 and 2 Cor. Elsewhere in N.T., 1 Pet. ii. 3 only.

εἴτε παρακαλούμεθα. 'Or whether we be comforted, it is for your comfort, which is made effective in the endurance of the same sufferings which we also suffer'; *i.e.* the comfort which their teachers receive overflows to them, when the sufferings of both are similar.

Are we to suppose that there had been persecution of the Christians at Corinth? The πειρασμός in 1 Cor. x. 13 might mean that some who had refused to take part in idolatrous practices had been denounced as disloyal. But, if there is a reference to persecution at all, it is more probable that St Paul is thinking of the possibility of future trouble, as ἡ ἐλπίς indicates. The fact that ἐνεργουμένης and ἐστε are presents must not be pressed; they are timeless and refer to what is normal. St Paul expected further persecution for himself (v. 10): he would neither cease to preach, nor preach a rigid Gospel pleasing to Judaizers, nor preach an elastic Gospel pleasing to freethinking Hellenists and Gentiles.

ἐνεργουμένης. Lightfoot has sanctioned the view that the passive of ἐνεργεῖν does not occur in N.T. J. A. Robinson (*Eph.* p. 245) has given reasons for doubting this. The instances, with the exception of Jas. v. 16, are all in Paul (iv. 12; 1 Thess. ii. 13; 2 Thess. ii. 7; Gal. v. 6; Rom. vii. 5; Eph. iii. 20; Col. i. 29). In all of them it is difficult to decide between the middle and the passive, and even in Jas. v. 16 the passive is not impossible. Here Chrys. seems to regard the participle as passive, for he points out that St Paul says ἐνεργουμένης and not ἐνεργούσης. The comfort does not work of itself, but 'is made to work' by him who bestows it. If we regard it as middle, the meaning will be 'which makes itself felt.' See Blass, § 55. 1.

ἐν ὑπομονῇ. Manly endurance without cowardly shrinking (vi. 4, xii. 12) is meant. The word is found in all groups of the Pauline Epp. Cf. ἡ θλίψις ὑπομονὴν κατεργάζεται (Rom. v. 3). In LXX it generally means patient expectation and hope, a meaning which prevails even in Ecclus. (ii. 14, xvi. 13, xvii. 24, xli. 2); but in 4 Macc., which was written not long before this Epistle, the N.T. meaning is found: τῇ ἀνδρείᾳ καὶ τῇ ὑπομονῇ (i. 11), τῆσδε τῆς κακοπαθείας καὶ ὑπομονῆς (ix. 8), ἀρετὴ δι' ὑπομονῆς δοκιμάζουσα (xvii. 12; also 17, 23). See on Luke viii. 15; Trench, Syn. § liii.

τῶν αὐτῶν παθημάτων. Note the attraction of ὧν. Not the identical sufferings, as if the Corinthians were pained whenever the Apostle was pained, in which case the καί would be meaningless; but the same in kind, arising out of devotion to Christ. Communio sanctorum egregie representatur in hac epistola (Beng.).

The text is confused as to the order of the clauses. The received Text, which is followed in AV., was made by Erasmus without MS. authority. The two arrangements, between which the choice lies, are given by WH., one in the text and one in a foot-note. The former, which is preferable, runs thus ; εἴτε δὲ θλιβόμεθα, ὑπὲρ τῆς ὑμῶν παρακλήσεως καὶ σωτηρίας· εἴτε παρακαλούμεθα, ὑπὲρ τῆς ὑμῶν παρακλήσεως τῆς ἐνεργουμένης ἐν ὑπομονῇ τῶν αὐτῶν παθημάτων ὧν καὶ ἡμεῖς πάσχομεν, καὶ ἡ ἐλπὶς ἡμῶν βεβαία ὑπὲρ ὑμῶν (א A C M P). The other runs thus ; εἴτε δὲ θλιβόμεθα, ὑπὲρ τῆς ὑμῶν παρακλήσεως [καὶ σωτηρίας] τῆς ἐνεργουμένης ἐν ὑπομονῇ τῶν αὐτῶν παθημάτων ὧν καὶ ἡμεῖς πάσχομεν καὶ ἡ ἐλπὶς ἡμῶν βεβαία ὑπὲρ ὑμῶν· εἴτε παρακαλούμεθα, ὑπὲρ τῆς ἡμῶν παρακλήσεως καὶ σωτηρίας (B D E F G K L). B 17, 176 omit the first καὶ σωτηρίας. Assuming that the text of א A C M P is original, we may explain the origin of the other arrangement by supposing that, owing to homoeoteleuton (παρακλήσεως to παρακλήσεως), the words καὶ σωτηρίας εἴτε παρακαλούμεθα ὑπὲρ τῆς ὑμῶν παρακλήσεως were accidentally omitted and afterwards written in the margin, and that the next copyist inserted them in the wrong place.

Editors differ as to the punctuation and the division of the verses, according as they regard ἡ ἐλπὶς ἡμῶν as connected with what precedes or with what follows. Some place only a comma at πάσχομεν and a colon or full stop at ὑπὲρ ὑμῶν. Others place a colon or full stop at πάσχομεν and only a comma at ὑπὲρ ὑμῶν. The latter is better, and καὶ ἡ ἐλπὶς κ.τ.λ. is rightly assigned to v. 7.

7. καὶ ἡ ἐλπὶς ἡμῶν βεβαία ὑπὲρ ὑμῶν. 'And our hope is sure concerning you.' See Deissmann on βεβαίωσις, Bible Studies, pp. 104–109. Wetstein gives examples of the expression ἐλπὶς βεβαία. There may be trouble in store for both sides, but those who have shared distress and consolation on a large scale may face the future without dismay. This is much higher praise than he bestows on the Thessalonians (1 Thess. iii. 2, 3, 5).

εἰδότες. 'Because we know'; cf. 1 Cor. xv. 58; Col. iii. 24;

Eph. vi. 8. Strict grammar would require εἰδότων, but this use of the nom. participle, not in agreement with the noun, is common in Paul and in papyri; *e.g.* θλιβόμενοι (vii. 5), στελλόμενοι (viii. 20), πλουτιζόμενοι (ix. 11), ἐροιζωμένει (Eph. iii. 17), ἀνεχόμενοι (iv. 2), διδάσκοντες (Col. iii. 16), ἔχοντες (Phil. i. 30), etc. Some refer εἰδότες here to the Corinthians; 'because *ye* know,' which is improbable. It is expressly said that the knowledge is the security for '*our* hope.'

κοινωνοί ἐστε . . . τῆς παρακλήσεως. He does not claim the credit of comforting them: they receive comfort from the same source that he does—from God through Christ. For the construction, cf. 1 Pet. v. 1; 2 Pet. i. 4; for ὡς . . . οὕτως, Rom. v. 15, 18.

For ὡς (א A B C D* M P 17), D² and 3 K L have ὥσπερ.

8–11. The Thanksgiving still continues, these verses explaining (γάρ) why he blesses God for mercies to himself rather than for graces bestowed on them, and the wording continues to be obscure. The obscurity may be due to reference to a delicate matter which is understood rather than expressed. This would be very intelligible, if the 'affliction' is the Corinthian rebellion against the Apostle, and the 'comfort' is their submission and reconciliation to him. But a reference to persecution is not impossible.

8. Οὐ γὰρ θέλομεν ὑμᾶς ἀγνοεῖν, ἀδελφοί. The formula is used six times by St Paul (1 Cor. x. 1, xii. 1; Rom. i. 13, xi. 25; 1 Thess. iv. 13), always with ἀδελφοί, as if the information given was an appeal to their affection and sympathy. Excepting 1 Cor. xii. 3, where ἀδελφοί has preceded, the similar expression, γνωρίζω (-ομεν) ὑμῖν, is also followed by ἀδελφοί (viii. 8; 1 Cor. xv. 1; Gal. i. 11). The less frequent θέλω ὑμᾶς εἰδέναι (1 Cor. xi. 3; Col. ii. 1) is not so followed. Similar expressions are found in papyri; γινώσκειν σε θέλω is often placed at the beginning of letters. It is not quite exact to say that logically the οὐ belongs to ἀγνοεῖν: there is something which he does not wish. The expression is not parallel with οὐκ ἔφη χρήσειν, which does not mean that she did not say that she would, but that she said that she would not. St Paul does not wish the Corinthians to remain in ignorance of the intensity of his recent affliction, for when they know how greatly he has suffered, they will regard their own sufferings more patiently, and will also appreciate his present comfort and derive comfort from it.

τῆς θλίψεως ἡμῶν τῆς γενομένης ἐν τῇ Ἀσίᾳ. Evidently the θλίψις is something which the Corinthians already know, for the vague statement that it 'took place in Asia' is enough to tell them what he means. He gives no particulars, but merely enlarges upon the terrible effect which the affliction had upon himself. This leaves plenty of room for conjecture, and there are many guesses. We must find something very severe and capable of being regarded as 'sufferings of the Christ.' Neither illness nor shipwreck seem to be very suitable, and a shipwreck would hardly have been described as taking place 'in Asia.' News that his beloved Corinthians had rebelled against him, and thereby had set an example of revolt to other Churches in Europe, is more probable. Such tidings might go far towards making so sensitive and affectionate a worker think that he could not live any longer. On the other hand, it is perhaps a little improbable that, after the joyous reconciliation, he should revive the past by telling them that they had almost killed him by their misbehaviour. Yet he might do this in order to show them how intensely everything that they do affects him.* If this conjecture is set aside as improbable—and the language of *vv.* 8–10 does seem to be rather strong for the effect of painful news—we may fall back upon the hypothesis of persecution, not by officials, but by furious mobs, consisting of, or hounded on by, exasperated Jews, so that he was nearly torn in pieces by them (1 Cor. xv. 31, 32). Such θλίψις would fitly be compared with 'the sufferings of the Messiah.' This is Tertullian's view (*De Resur. Carnis*, 48) ; the *pressura apud Asiam* refers to *illas bestias Asiaticae pressurae*. Those who, with Paley, think that the reference is to the uproar raised by Demetrius at Ephesus (Acts xix. 23–41) must admit that, in that case, St Luke has given an inadequate account of St Paul's peril, for he gives no hint that he was near being killed. Paley's argument suffices to show that *vv.* 8, 9 cannot have been written by a forger who wished to make an allusion to Acts xix. ; a forger would have made the allusion more distinct ; but it does not prove that the allusion is to Acts xix. There may easily have been a much worse outbreak at Ephesus somewhat later, and even a plot to kill St Paul, as in Acts xxiii. 12, and this peril may have hastened his departure from Ephesus. It is probably right to assume that 'in Asia' means in Ephesus. Ephesus was the metropolis of the Roman province of Asia, which contained the Seven Churches of Rev. i. 11. See on 1 Cor. xvi. 19. In Ephesus he had

---

* G. H. Rendall, on i. 4, argues strongly for the view that the anguish was caused by the revolt and estrangement of the Corinthian converts. See also the *Camb. Grk. Test.*, 1903, p. 28. It is perhaps best to leave the question open. "This trial, which the Apostle does not explain more definitely, surpassed all bounds, and exceeded his powers of endurance. He despaired of life. He carried within his soul a sentence of death. And now his unhoped for deliverance seems like an actual resurrection" (A. Sabatier, *The Apostle Paul*, p. 181).

'many adversaries' (1 Cor. xvi. 9). If Timothy shared this great affliction, either it took place before he started for Corinth, or he had returned to the Apostle before the latter left Ephesus. καθ' ὑπερβολὴν ὑπὲρ δύναμιν ἐβαρήθημεν. Some teachers and leaders insist upon their glories and successes; St Paul insists rather on his sufferings (xii. 5, 9, 10). Whatever this θλίψις may have been, he hints that it was far worse than what the Corinthians had to endure. He says that he (and Timothy?) 'were weighed down exceedingly beyond our power.' Does καθ' ὑπερβολήν qualify ὑπὲρ δύναμιν or ἐβαρήθημεν? Our English is as amphibolous as the Greek. The placing of ὑπὲρ δυν. after ἐβαρήθημεν (E K L) is an attempt to decide the point. Only once in LXX does καθ' ὑπερβολήν occur, in one of the latest books (4 Macc. iii. 18), and there of acute physical suffering, τὰς τῶν σωμάτων ἀλγηδόνας καθ' ὑπερβολὴν οὔσας. St Paul has it five times (iv. 17; 1 Cor. xii. 31; Gal. i 13; Rom. vii. 13), all in this group of Epistles.

ὥστε ἐξαπορηθῆναι ἡμᾶς καὶ τοῦ ζῆν. 'So that we were utterly without way of escape, were utterly at a loss, were quite in despair, even of life' (iv. 8 only; in LXX, Ps. lxxxvii. 16 only). This is the right meaning, which is preserved in the Old Latin, *ut de vita haesitaremus* (Tert. *De Res. Carn.* 48), and by Jerome (on Eph. iii. 13), *ita ut desperaremus nos etiam vivere.* But Vulg. supports the less probable meaning, that he did not wish to live any longer, *ut taederet nos etiam vivere.* We have a braver strain in iv. 8 and in Phil. iv. 3. St Paul has many moods, and he has no wish to conceal from the Corinthians how profoundly great trouble had depressed him. On τοῦ, see J. H. Moulton, pp. 217, 200.

ὑπὲρ τῆς (B K L M) is more likely to be original than περὶ τῆς (א A C D E F G P 17); περὶ is the usual constr. after ἀγνοεῖν (1 Cor. xii. 1; 1 Thess. iv. 13), and hence the change here. Cf. viii. 23, xii. 8; 2 Thess. ii. 1; Rom. ix. 27. א³ D² and ³ E K L, Syrr. Copt. ins. ἡμῖν after γενομένης, א* A B C D* F G M P 17, Latt. Arm. omit. ὑπὲρ δύναμιν before ἐβαρήθημεν (א A B C M P 17) rather than παρὰ δύν. after ἐβαρ. (D F G).

9. ἀλλὰ αὐτοὶ ἐν ἑαυτοῖς. Cf. Rom. viii. 23. 'Nay, we ourselves had the sentence of death within ourselves.'* We may render ἀλλά either 'Nay,' *i.e.* 'It may seem incredible, but,' or 'Yea,' *i.e.* 'One may put the matter still more strongly.' The ἀλλά confirms what has just been said (vii. 11, viii. 7, x. 4), and is equivalent to our colloquial, 'Why.' In his own mind the Apostle was convinced that in all human probability his hours were numbered.

* Rutherford would render ἐν ἑαυτοῖς 'in a tribunal composed of ourselves.' But the Apostle felt the sentence of death rather than pronounced it on himself. Rutherford explains the ἀλλά as due to the negative implied in ἐξαπορηθῆναι.

2

With ἐσχήκαμεν comp. ἔσχηκα (ii. 13), πεποίηκα (xi. 25), πεποίηκεν (Heb. xi. 28). Here we might explain the perf. as expressing the permanent effects of the ἀπόκριμα as vividly recalling the moment when the ἀπόκριμα was recognized. But there seems to be a "purely aoristic use of the perfect" (Winer, p. 340), especially in late Greek. In Rev. v. 7 we have aor. and perf. combined, and the same in reverse order in Rev. iii. 3, viii. 5, xi. 17. See J. H. Moulton, pp. 143–146; Blass, § 59. 4.

Both AV. and RV. express doubt whether 'sentence' or 'answer' is the better translation of ἀπόκριμα. Vulg. has *responsum*. The word occurs nowhere else in Biblical Greek, but Josephus and Polybius use it for a decision of the Roman Senate; and Deissmann (*Bible Studies*, p. 257) quotes an inscription dated A.D. 51 in which ἀπόκριμα is used of a decision of the Emperor Claudius. Both Chrys. and Thdrt. use τὴν ψῆφον as an equivalent, to which Chrys. adds τ. προσδοκίαν and τ. ἀπόφασιν. Cf. ὦ θάνατε, καλόν σου τὸ κρίμα ἐστίν, and μὴ εὐλαβοῦ κρίμα θανάτου (Ecclus. xli. 2, 3).

ἵνα μὴ πεποιθότες ὦμεν ἐφ᾽ ἑαυτοῖς. A thoroughly Pauline touch. He has told us of one Divine purpose in sending afflictions and comfort, viz. to train him for administering comfort to others who are in affliction (*v.* 4). Here he tells us of another. Suffering of great intensity has been sent to prove to him his own helplessness, and to teach him to trust in God, who has the power of life and death (2 Kings v. 7), and can not only recover the dying but restore the dead (iv. 14; Rom. iv. 17). We need not water down ἵνα into a mere equivalent to ὥστε: the telic force is quite in place here. This dreadful trial was sent to him in order to give him a precious spiritual lesson (xii. 7–10).

τῷ ἐγείροντι. Timeless present participle expressing a permanent attribute, like ὁ παρακαλῶν in *v.* 4. Cf. Heb. xi. 19, where δυνατός (not δύναται) gives a Divine attribute. In such extreme danger and dread, human aid was worthless; real relief could come only from Him who had power to raise the dead: and to be rescued from so desperate a condition was almost a resurrection. Bousset refers to the "Eighteen-petition-prayer" of the Jews, the *Schmone-Esre* or chief prayer which each Jew ought to say thrice daily. It really contains nineteen petitions, as Schürer (*Gesch. d. Jüd. Volk.* ii. pp. 460–462, 3rd ed. 1898) has shown. In the second petition we have, "Thou art almighty for ever, O Lord, for Thou makest the dead to live. Thou art mighty to help, Thou who sustainest the living through Thy mercy, and makest the dead to live through Thy compassion. . . . Who is like unto Thee, O King,

who killest and makest alive and causest help to spring up.
And true art Thou in making the dead to live." This is the
great mark of Divine power—restoring the dead to life.
Chrys. thinks that it is mentioned here because the possibility of resurrection was questioned at Corinth (1 Cor. xv. 12).
But the mention is quite natural, without any polemical purpose.
A reflexion on Corinthian scepticism is more probable in iv. 14
and v. 15. Thdrt. and some others weaken the meaning greatly
by substituting ἐγείραντι for ἐγείροντι, as if it referred to the single
act of raising Christ from the dead. Even *in Deo qui suscitat
mortuos* (Vulg.) is not quite adequate: *in Deo mortuorum
resuscitatore* is the full meaning. Of the whole clause, ἵνα μὴ
κ.τ.λ., we may admit that *facit locus iste contra eos qui suis aliquid
meritis tribuere praesumunt* (Pseudo-Primasius).

10. ὃς ἐκ τηλικούτου θανάτου ἐρύσατο ἡμᾶς. 'Who out of so
great a death delivered us.' He says 'death' rather than 'peril
of death,' because he had regarded himself as a dead man; the
ἐκ (not ἀπό) seems to imply peril rather than death personified,
but Wetstein shows that ἐρύσατο ἐκ θανάτου is a common expression. This may be one of the rare N.T. reminiscences of
the Book of Job; * ἐρύσατο τὴν ψυχήν μου ἐκ θανάτου (xxxiii. 30).
A comparison with ἐρύσθην ἐκ στόματος λέοντος. ῥύσεταί με ὁ
κύριος (2 Tim. iv. 17, 18) and ἵνα ῥυσθῶ ἀπὸ τῶν ἀπειθούντων
ἐν τῇ Ἰουδαίᾳ (Rom. xv. 31) rather favours the hypothesis that
the great θλίψις in Asia was violent persecution. As in Heb. ii.
3, τηλικοῦτος here means 'so *great*' as to require such a Saviour:
cf. Rev. xvi. 18; Jas. iii. 4. In LXX the word is found in Macc.
only; in class. Grk. it is used more often of age than of size, 'so
old,' and sometimes 'so young.'

καὶ ῥύσεται. This is superfluous, anticipating and somewhat
spoiling the next clause. Hence some witnesses read ῥύεται or
omit, and some editors either omit the word or adopt awkward
punctuation: see critical note. But St Paul, in dictating, might
easily repeat himself, toning down the confident 'He will
deliver' into a confident hope that He will do so. Thus affliction is set before us as a school of sympathy (*v.* 4), a school of
encouragement (*v.* 5), and a school of hope (*v.* 10). He proclaims that the rescue in all cases is God's work, not their own:
it must come from Him, if at all.

εἰς ὃν ἠλπίκαμεν [ὅτι] καὶ ἔτι ῥύσεται. 'Unto whom we have
directed our hope *that* He will *also* still deliver us'; or, omitting
ὅτι, '*and* He will still deliver us'; or καί may be intensive, '*that*
He will *indeed* deliver us.' *Praescit se adhuc passurum qui sperat*

* Cf. 1 Cor. iii. 19; Rom. xi. 35; Phil. i. 19; 1 Thess. v. 22; 2 Thess.
ii. 8.

se liberandum (Pseudo-Primasius). He had enough experience of perils of death (xi. 23; 1 Cor. xv. 31) to feel that he must be prepared for others in the future. Cf. προαποθνήσκω πόλλους, θανάτους ὑπομένων (Philo, *In Flaccum*, 990 A); μενέτω ἐν ταῖς ψυχαῖς ἀκαθαίρετος ἡ ἐπὶ τὸν σωτῆρα Θεὸν ἐλπίς, ὃς πολλάκις ἐξ ἀμηχάνων καὶ ἀπόρων περιέσωσε τὸ ἔθνος (*Leg. ad Caium*, 574). For ἐλπίζειν εἰς, see Jn. v. 45; 1 Pet. iii. 5; ἐλπίζειν ἐπί is more common (Rom. xv. 12; 1 Tim. iv. 10, v. 5, vi. 17); *in quo spem repositam habemus* is nearer to ἐπί.

Origen (on Lev. xi. 2), with too rigid logic, argues that, as it is not to be supposed that St Paul expected to be immortal, he cannot mean physical death when he says that he hopes that God will *continue* to deliver him from deaths; he must mean sins. Origen evidently read ἐκ τηλικούτων θανάτων, with Vulg. (*de tantis periculis*) Syrr., Jerome (on Eph. i. 13), Rufinus (*ad loc.*), Ambrst. He also read καὶ ῥύεται with D³ E F G K L M, Latt. Goth., Chrys. But ἐκ τηλικούτου θανάτου and καὶ ῥύσεται is to be preferred with ℵ B C P 17, Copt. Arm. A D* omit καὶ ῥύσεται. B D* M omit ὅτι, and F G place it after καί. Goth. Aeth. omit both καί and ἔτι. B. Weiss proposes to read εἰς ὃν ἠλπίκαμεν. καὶ ἔτι ῥύσεται.

11. συνυπουργούντων καὶ ὑμῶν κ.τ.λ. 'Ye also helping together on our behalf by your supplication,' which may mean either 'provided you help' or 'while you help.'* The latter is more probably right; the Apostle is as secure of the intercession of the Corinthians as he is of God's protection, and the one will contribute to the other. *With whom* do the Corinthians cooperate? Various answers have been given to this question. 'With the Apostle, in his hope or in his prayers' (Rom. xv. 30); or, 'with one another'; or, 'with the particular purpose.' He has just said that God will rescue, and he adds that the Corinthians will help. Their intercessions are part of the machinery which God has provided for preserving His Apostle from deadly peril. "Even if God doeth anything in mercy, yet prayer doth mightily contribute thereto" (Chrys., who, however, takes συνυπουργ. of the Corinthians uniting with one another in intercession). We need not take ὑπὲρ ἡμῶν after τῇ δεήσει: it goes well with συνυπουργ.

As a word for 'prayer,' δέησις is almost as general as προσευχή, with which it is often joined. It is commonly an expression of personal need (see on Lk. i. 13), but is often used of intercession; ix. 14; Rom. x. 1; Phil. i. 4 (see Lightfoot); 2 Tim. i. 3; Heb. v. 7. Cf. the letter of Agrippa in Philo, *Leg. ad Caium*, § 36 *sub init.* (ii. p. 586); γραφὴ δὲ

* St Paul was a strong believer in the value of intercession, whether of others for him (Rom. xv. 30; 1 Thess. v. 25; 2 Thess. iii. 1), or of himself for others (Rom. i. 9; Eph. i. 16: Phil. i. 4; 1 Thess. i. 2; 2 Tim. i. 3; Philem. 4). Ἔργον *est Dei*, ὑπουργεῖν *est apostolorum*, συνυπουργεῖν *Corinthiorum* (Beng.).

μηνύσει μου τὴν δέησιν, ἣν ἀνθ᾽ ἱκετηρίας προτείνω . . . δέομαι ὑπὲρ ἁπάντων.

ἵνα ἐκ πολλῶν προσώπων . . . ὑπὲρ ἡμῶν. A perplexing sentence. Among the doubtful points are (1) whether πολλῶν qualifies προσώπων or is the gen. after προσώπων (*ex multorum personis*, Vulg.); (2) whether τὸ εἰς ἡμᾶς χάρισμα refers to God's rescue of the Apostle from death or to the Corinthians' intercessions for him; (3) whether διὰ πολλῶν is masc. or neut.; (4) the meaning of προσώπων. (1) The meaning is much the same whether we say 'many πρόσωπα' or 'the πρόσωπα of many,' but the former is almost certainly right. (2) The context strongly suggests that τὸ εἰς ἡμᾶς χάρισμα means the Divine favour in delivering St Paul from death. That deliverance had already taken place, and was a more conspicuous subject for thanksgiving than the intercessions of the Corinthians on his behalf. Here, as in 1 Pet. iv. 10, χάρισμα means an external blessing. All the other passages in N.T. in which χάρισμα occurs are in Paul (1 Cor., Rom., 1 and 2 Tim.), and it is commonly used of a spiritual gift, especially of some extraordinary power. (3) It is true that, if διὰ πολλῶν is masc., it is superfluous after ἐκ πολλῶν προσώπων. But St Paul is dictating, and such repetitions as ῥύσεται . . . ῥύσεται (*v.* 10) and ἐκ π. πρ. . . . διὰ π. are quite natural. Similarly, ὑπὲρ ἡμῶν is superfluous after τὸ εἰς ἡμ. χαρ., and yet is quite natural. Moreover, it is not easy to find a satisfactory meaning for διὰ πολλῶν, if πολλῶν is neut. 'With many thanks' (*ingentes gratias*), or 'with many words' (*prolixe*), makes poor sense, even if such a translation is possible. We may safely regard διὰ πολλῶν as meaning 'through many people' (*per multos*, Vulg.). (4) The meaning of πρόσωπον is less easily determined. The word occurs twelve times in this letter; in eight places it certainly means 'face,' iii. 7 (*bis*), 13, 18, viii. 24, x. 1, 7, xi. 20; in one it means 'face' in the sense of outward appearance (v. 12); in three it may mean either 'face' or 'person' (here, ii. 10, iv. 6). Herveius renders *ex personis multarum facierum* and interprets *homines multarum aetatum et qualitatum diversarum*. Ambrosiaster has *multorum faciebus*. Bengel is much less happy than usual in giving the impossible *ex multis respectibus*. The conjectural emendation, προσευχῶν for προσώπων, has not found much support. 'From many persons' makes excellent sense, and this late use of πρόσωπον is abundantly illustrated in the Greek of the period. But the literal sense is more probable and more attractive. It is difficult to explain ἐκ, if persons are meant; and we can well believe that the Apostle, as he dictates, sees in thought the many upturned faces, lighted up with thankfulness, as praises for this preservation rise up from their lips. Some, however, while giving this meaning to ἐκ π. προσώπων, understand it of the intercessions for the Apostle's protection; others (AV., RV.) give this meaning to διὰ πολλῶν.

Certainty is unattainable; but the following renderings are intelligible; (1) 'that from many mouths, for the favour shown to us, thanks may be offered by means of many on our behalf'; or (2) 'that the benefit accruing to us from the intercessions of many persons may through many be a matter of thanksgiving on our account'; or (3) 'that for the gift bestowed upon us by means of many, thanks may be given by many persons on our behalf' (RV.). The last is questionable; it involves taking τὸ εἰς ἡμ. χαρ. διὰ πολ. as if it were τὸ διὰ πολ. εἰς ἡμ. χαρ. The second is still more questionable; it involves taking ἐκ π. προσ. τὸ εἰς ἡμ. χαρ. as if it were τὸ ἐκ π. προσ. εἰς ἡμ. χαρ. The first is more accurate and makes equally good sense. But in any case the words show what an impression this great affliction had made on St Paul, as if "even in a life of peril this peril in Asia had marked an era" (J. Agar Beet, p. 322).

διὰ πολλῶν εὐχαριστηθῇ. Lit. 'may be thanked for by many,' *i.e.* may be made a subject of thanksgiving through the instrumentality of many thankful persons. The passive occurs nowhere else in either N.T. or LXX. By Justin it is used of the eucharistic bread which has been dedicated with thanks (*Apol.* i. 65).

For ὑμῶν ὑπὲρ ἡμῶν, A has ἡμῶν ὑπὲρ ὑμῶν, while D* F have ὑμῶν περὶ ἡμῶν and G has ὑμῶν περὶ ὑμῶν. For ἐκ πολλῶν προσώπων, F G M have ἐν πολλῷ προσώπῳ, g *in multa facie.* For εὐχαρ. ὑπὲρ ἡμῶν (ℵ A C D* G M 17, Vulg. Syrr. Copt. Arm. Goth.), B D³ E F K L P, Chrys. have εὐχαρ. ὑπὲρ ὑμῶν. Baljon would omit both διὰ πολλῶν and the second ὑπὲρ ἡμῶν as glosses. Neither of them has the look of a gloss, but both might be omitted without injury to the meaning.

I. 12–VII. 16. REVIEW OF RECENT RELATIONS WITH THE CORINTHIANS.

This is the first of the main divisions of the Epistle, and it may be divided into three sections; i. 12–ii. 17, iii. 1–vi. 10, vi. 11–vii. 16. But the Second Epistle does not present such clearly marked divisions as the First. There the Apostle takes up the matters which had been reported to him and the questions which had been asked, disposes of them one by one, and passes on. Here it is his strong feeling rather than any deliberate arrangement that suggests the order of his utterances. Nevertheless, although exact analysis is seldom possible owing to digressions and repetitions, yet some divisions are fairly clear, and the letter becomes more intelligible when they are noted.

The headings given to the different sections are tentative: they are offered, not as adequate summaries of the contents of each section, but as stating what seems to be its dominant thought, or one of its dominant thoughts. In each section we have often to be content with highly conjectural explanations of the language used, seeing that we are in complete ignorance of the circumstances to which the Apostle alludes, and about which he perhaps sometimes writes, from feelings of delicacy, with studied vagueness. In some cases the meaning of individual words is uncertain.

I. 12–II. 17. DEFENCE OF HIS CONDUCT WITH RE- GARD TO HIS INTENDED VISIT AND THE GREAT OFFENDER.

The first verses (12–14) are transitional, being closely connected (γάρ) with the preceding expression of thanksgiving and hope, and at the same time preparing the way for the vindication of his character and recent actions. He can conscientiously say that in all his dealings he has endeavoured to be straightforward. Some editors attach these verses to what precedes, and treat them as the concluding part of the Thanksgiving. But a new note is struck by the words ἐν ἁγιότητι κ. εἰλικρινία, which anticipate ταύτῃ τῇ πεποιθήσει in v. 15, and on the whole it seems better to regard the verses as introductory to what follows.

My motives have been disinterested, and I believe that you are willing to admit this.

12 For if we have any right to glory, it is because our conscience bears testimony that whatever we did was done in purity of motive and in a sincerity which had its source in God, in reliance, not on worldly cleverness, but on the gracious help of God. This is true of all our conduct in the world, and it is more abundantly so of our relations to you. 13 Do not believe for a moment that I write one thing at one time and another at another. I write nothing different from what I have written before. My meaning lies on the surface; you read it and you recognize it as true; and I hope that the time will never come when you will refuse to recognize it as such: 14 just as, in fact, you have recognized about us—some of you, at any rate—that you have good reason to glory in us, even as we also look forward to glorying in you in the Day of the Lord Jesus.

12. Ἡ γὰρ καύχησις ἡμῶν αὔτη ἐστίν. 'For our glorying is this,'—viz. the testimony that, etc. To make ὅτι depend upon αὔτη, and take what lies between in opposition, is forced and unnecessary. The γάρ is perhaps an indefinite conjunction without special reference. But we can give it special reference by connecting it with v. 11. 'I may count upon your prayers and thanksgivings for me, for I have done nothing to estrange you. Some of you think that I am too fond of glorifying myself and my office. What I do pride myself upon is my sincerity, especially towards you.' The cognate words, καύχημα (thrice), καύχησις (six times), καυχᾶσθαι (twenty times) are more frequent in this letter than in all the rest of the N.T. ; and the frequency ought to be reproduced in translation. AV. has 'rejoicing' here, which is never the meaning, and elsewhere 'glorying' and 'boasting'; Vulg. has *gloria* and *gloriatio*, and the Old Latin sometimes has *exsultatio*. The distinction between words in -μα and words in -σις has lost its sharpness in N.T., but in some cases it still holds good, as here in vv. 12 and 14 (see on 1 Cor. v. 6 ; Lightfoot on Gal. vi. 4); and καύχησις more often preserves its special meanings as the 'act of glorifying' than καύχημα as the 'ground for glorying' or the 'completed boast.'

τὸ μαρτύριον τῆς συνειδήσεως ἡμῶν. "Virtue is better than praise ; for virtue is content with no human judgment, save that of one's own conscience" (Aug. *De Civ. Dei*, v. 12). While μαρτυρία is the act of testifying or bearing witness, μαρτύριον is the testimony or evidence ; but μαρτυρία is sometimes used in the latter sense. Except in 1 Tim. iii. 7 and Tit. i. 13, St Paul always uses μαρτύριον. For συνείδησις, 'reflexion on the value of the actions which we are conscious of doing,' see on Rom. ii. 15 and 1 Pet. ii. 19; also Westcott on Heb. ix. 9, p. 293 ; Cremer, *Lex.* p. 233 ; Hastings, *DB.* i. p. 468. The word is rare in LXX, but the picture of a guilty person with an accusing conscience is given Wisd. xvii. 11 (cf. Tennyson's *Sea Dreams*); it is frequent in the Pauline Epistles and in Hebrews ; cf. Rom. ix. 1, and, for the construction, 1 Thess. iv. 3.

ἐν ἁγιότητι καὶ εἰλικρινίᾳ τ. Θεοῦ. The expression is strange, especially τ. Θεοῦ : see critical note. Rückert's conjecture of ἀγνότητι is attractive. The apparent inappropriateness of ἁγιότητι, and its rarity in LXX and N.T., may have caused the change to ἁπλότητι, which is more in point and a better com- panion to εἰλικρινίᾳ. The etymology of the latter word is a puzzle, but it appears to mean 'transparency' and hence 'ingenuous- ness' or 'sincerity' (1 Cor. v. 8 ; see Lightfoot on Phil. i. 10). B. Weiss paraphrases, "in the holiness of God, which is separ- ated from all uncleanness of the world, and in an uprightness which, even if examined by the most brilliant light of the sun,

will show no defects." See WH. ii. p. 154 on the change of
termination, -εια to -ια.   The exact force of τοῦ Θεοῦ is uncertain;
'superlative,' 'approved by God,' 'divine,' 'godlike,' 'godly'
have been suggested and are possible; but 'derived from God'
or 'God-given' is more likely to be right, and the gen. probably belongs to both nouns; 'God-given holiness (simplicity)
and sincerity.'   St Paul is free from all πανουργία and δόλος (iv. 2)
and the sin of καπηλεύειν τὸν λόγον τ. Θεοῦ (ii. 17).   He passed
on the truth to them without adulteration, and he passed it on
gratis.

οὐκ ἐν σοφίᾳ σαρκικῇ ἀλλ' ἐν χ. Θ.   The ἐν in all three places
indicates the element in which his life moved; but the antithesis
in these two qualities is somewhat strange.   It is the opposition
between the man who relies simply on his own natural cleverness, which suggests unprincipled dealing, and the man who
relies upon the grace of God.   By professing to be all things to
all men, St Paul had laid himself open to the charge that he was
an unscrupulous schemer.   It is possible that in σοφίᾳ σαρκικῇ
he just glances (ἠρέμα καθαπτόμενος, Chrys.) at teachers who *per
hypocrisim faciunt quidquid boni facere videntur* (Herveius), and
also at heathen culture—τὴν ἔξω παίδευσιν (Chrys.).   In these
Epistles St Paul repeatedly points out that he does not rely upon
worldly wisdom or human ability (x. 4; 1 Cor. i. 17, ii. 4, 13)
The word σαρκικός is Pauline, five times against twice elsewhere:
in LXX it does not occur.   Cf. μὴ περιπατοῦντες ἐν πανουργίᾳ
(iv. 2).

ἀνεστράφημεν.   Life is movement, and this is abundantly
suggested by various expressions for conduct and manner of life;
περιπατεῖν (iv. 2, v. 7, x. 2, etc.), πορεύεσθαι (1 and 2 Pet. and
Jude, but in Paul always of actual travelling) ἀναστρέφεσθαι
(Eph ii. 3; 1 Tim. iii. 15; Heb. x. 33, xiii. 18).   Of these three,
περιπατεῖν and πορεύεσθαι belong to Hebrew thought; both are
found fairly often in LXX in the sense of pursuing a particular
mode of life, a use foreign to class. Grk.   But ἀναστρέφεσθαι and ἀναστροφή (Gal. i. 13; Eph. iv. 22; 1 Tim. iv. 12)
belong to Greek thought.   Deissmann (*Bible Studies*, pp. 88, 194)
shows from inscriptions that the ethical use of these words is
common in current Greek from B.C. 150 onwards.   Polybius
(iv. 82. 1) uses it of Philip's general conduct.   Vulg. has *conversari*
and *conversatio*; but RV. rejects the old rendering 'conversation,' which has now become misleading.

περισσοτέρως δὲ πρὸς ὑμᾶς.   'More abundantly in our relations to you.'   He does not mean that he had been less scrupulous in his dealings with others than in his dealings with the
Corinthians, but that they had had more opportunity than others
(Acts xviii. 11) of knowing how scrupulous he was.   He had

been on the most intimate terms with them for many months. It is possible that there is something of a compliment to the Corinthians in the comparison. In the wicked heathen world (ἐν τῷ κόσμῳ, cf. 1 Cor. v. 10) he might have been tempted to use the world's underhand and slippery methods, but among the brethren at Corinth there was no such temptation. There may, however, be no comparison: 'our conduct has been straightforward everywhere, and certainly it has been so among you.'

The evidence for ἁγιότητι (א *A B C K M P 17, 37, 67**, Copt. Arm., Clem.-Alex. Orig.) is certainly superior to that for ἁπλότητι (א³ D F G L, Vulg. Syrr. Goth., Chrys. Ambst.), and no one would change ἁπλότητι, which is so suitable, to ἁγιότητι, which is much less so. But, by transcriptional error, απλοτητι might become αποτητι, and then αγιοτητι. ἁγνότητι (vi. 6 and perhaps xi. 3) is a good conjecture. A ins. ἐν before εἰλικρινίᾳ. F G K L P omit τοῦ before θεοῦ.

13. οὐ γὰρ ἄλλα γράφομεν. He justifies the περισσοτέρως πρὸς ὑμᾶς by answering a charge which has been made against him, that he writes shuffling letters, in which one has to read between the lines in order to see that what he seems to say is not what he really means. 'The testimony of my conscience, that I am sincere in my dealings with you is true, *for* I never write anything but what you see the meaning of, or even accept the meaning of, from what you know of me.' His letters are always consistent in themselves, and with one another, and with his conduct, of which the Corinthians have large experience. There are no reserves and no cunningly contrived phrases. Some commentators, however, confine γράφομεν to the present letter; 'I am not writing now anything different from the things which you read in my previous letters.' That is an unnecessary restriction. At this time St Paul had sent the Corinthians at least three letters,—the one mentioned in 1 Cor. v. 9, 1 Corinthians, and a severe letter, of which the greater part probably survives in 2 Cor. x.–xiii. This correspondence, added to their personal experience of him, gave them sufficient means of judging whether the claim made in *v.* 12 was just, especially the 'more abundantly to you-ward.'

It is impossible to reproduce in English the play upon words in ἃ ἀναγινώσκετε ἢ καὶ ἐπιγινώσκετε, 'that which you read, or even recognize as true.' 'Assent to, or even consent to,' is perhaps the nearest approach that can be made, but it is not satisfactory. *Quae legitis aut etiam intelligitis* is better, but it is not found in any Latin version.* We have *legitis et cognoscitis* (some MSS.), *legistis et cognoscitis* (Am. Ambrst.), *legistis et cognovistis* (Vulg.-Clem.). St Paul is fond of playing upon words in various ways, by alliteration, by bringing together words com-

* Wetstein quotes the saying, *legere et non intelligere negligere est.*

pounded with different prepositions, by interchanging simple and compound words, and so forth; iii. 2, iv. 8, vi. 10, vii. 4, 10, viii. 22, ix. 8, x. 6, 12; 1 Cor. iv. 3, vi. 1–6, vii. 31, xi. 29–32, etc. See on 1 Cor. ii. 15.

There can be little doubt that both here and in iii. 2 ἀναγινώσκειν means 'read,' although in both places 'recognize,' which is its frequent meaning in class. Grk., makes sense. The verb is very common both in LXX and N.T., and its dominant meaning is 'read,' often in the sense of 'read *aloud*' (iii. 15), which is its almost universal sense in class. Grk., when the verb is used of reading. In iii. 15 it certainly means 'read,' and hardly less certainly it has this meaning here and in iii. 2 : its position between γράφομεν and ἐπιγινώσκετε is almost conclusive here. And it may mean 'read aloud,' 'read publicly,' so that all knew what he said. In papyri it is found in both senses 'read' and 'read aloud.'

This is the only passage in which St Paul uses the 1st pers. plur. of his letters: elsewhere he has either γράφω (xiii. 10; 1 Cor. iv. 14, xiv. 37; Gal. i. 20; 2 Thess. iii. 17; 1 Tim. iii. 14) or ἔγραψα (ii. 3, 4, 9, vii. 12; 1 Cor. v. 9; Gal. vi. 11; Philem. 19, 21). The γράφομεν probably covers all his correspondence with the Corinthians, and perhaps the plur. indicates that in all his letters to them some one else was associated with him in writing. This would be some guarantee for his sincerity.

ἕως τέλους. Cf. 1 Cor. i. 8. In the Gospels we have εἰς τέλος, as in 1 Thess. ii. 16; in Heb. μέχρι or ἄχρι τέλους. In such expressions there is some vagueness. 'To the end of the world' and 'to the end of your lives' would for the Apostle and the Corinthians mean much the same. Cf. ἀπ᾽ ἀρχῆς, ἐξ ἀρχῆς.

ἀλλ᾽ ἢ ἅ may be safely adopted as the right reading. B F G omit ἀλλ᾽. A 17 omit ἢ ἅ. Goth. Arm. omit ἤ. D* omits ἅ. The somewhat mixed construction (see on Lk. xii. 51) has caused confusion, but the meaning is clear, and the construction is classical. Winer, p. 552 ; Blass, § 77. 13 ; ἕως τέλους (א A B C D* E F G, Latt. Copt. Goth. Arm.) rather than ἕως καὶ τέλους (D³ K L M P). AV. follows the latter, '*even* to the end.' The punctuation is doubtful, and editors differ considerably : place a comma after ἐπιγινώσκετε and a colon after ἐπιγνώσεσθε. It is a drastic remedy for the uncertainty as to the connexion of the clauses to cut out all that any text omits and even more, so as to read οὐ γὰρ ἀλλὰ γράφομεν ὑμῖν ἢ ἅ γινώσκετε· ἐλπίζω δὲ κ.τ.λ. So Baljon and others.

14. καθὼς καὶ ἐπέγνωτε ἡμᾶς ἀπὸ μέρους. 'As also you did acknowledge us in part.' His reason for hoping that they will now always form a right estimate of his letters is that they have already formed a right estimate of himself—at any rate to some extent. The ἀπὸ μέρους is an afterthought, to qualify the statement. The qualification may be understood in two ways,— 'part of you,' or 'part of me.' Either, 'There are some of you

who still misjudge me,' or, 'There is something in me which none of you quite understands.' Thdrt. adopts the former; οὐχ ἁπλῶς προστέθεικεν, ἀλλὰ νύττων αὐτούς, ὡς μὴ παντελῶς ἀποσαμένους τὰς κατ᾽ αὐτοῦ γεγεννημένας διαβολάς. Chrys. with more probability adopts the latter, and thinks that St Paul is contrasting the imperfect estimate of his sincerity which the Corinthians now have with that which will be theirs when the secrets of all hearts are revealed at the Last Day. So also Pseudo-Primasius; *quia nondum est finis; cum autem venerit finis, tunc ex integro cognoscetis.* In Rom. xi. 25 and xv. 24 there is a similar ambiguity as to what is the exact force of ἀπὸ μέρους. But the two interpretations might both be true. Some Corinthians had been more prejudiced against the Apostle than others, and none fully appreciated him. His irony might easily puzzle them. As Lietzmann remarks, *Beschränkte Leute halten oft Ironie für Zweideutigkeit.*

The change from ἐπιγινώσκετε to ἐπιγνώσεσθε is intelligible enough: the change to ἐπέγνωτε is not so clear. To what period does the aorist refer? Probably to the time before their rebellion against him. But it may refer to the time of their estrangement: he is willing to believe that even then they did not wholly distrust him.

ὅτι καύχημα ὑμῶν ἐσμέν. There are three ways of taking ὅτι. 1. It = 'because,' and gives the reason for their past recognition of him. 2. It = 'that,' and depends upon ἐπιγινώσκετε, the intervening words being parenthetical. 3. It = 'that,' and depends upon ἐπέγνωτε: 'ye acknowledged us in part, that we are your glorying—something that you are proud of.' The last is the best, and the first is the worst, of the three possible constructions. In these chapters (i.–ix.) καύχησις and καύχημα "have an apologetic note and refer to the self-glorying forced upon him when composing x.–xiii. (x. 8, 13, 15, 16, 17, xi. 10, 12, 16, 17, 18, 30, xii. 1, 4, 5, 6, 9). In this Epistle (i.–ix.) all glorying in personal claims or services is set aside; the letter is a reaction from the unwelcome temper of rights, of claims, of authority, of reproof, to the satisfactions of reconciliation, the fruitions of friendship, the understandings of confidence and love. For himself his one boast is sincerity; above all, sincerity of relation to themselves (*v.* 12); apart from that the one thought of glorying is that they could find some cause of glorying in him, as he abundantly in them (i. 14, v. 12, vii. 4, 14, viii. 24, ix. 2, 3). The whole of this is sacrificed and unsaid if x.–xiii. is read as a continuation and part of i.–ix.; and the end miserably stultifies the beginning" (G. H. Rendall, *The Epistles of St Paul to the Corinthians,* pp. 49, 51). The change from καύχησις (*v.* 12) to καύχημα is probably intentional: the difference between the act of

glorying and the material for it is here quite in point. The
ἐσμέν is a timeless present expressing a permanent relationship,
a relationship so real that it will stand the scrutiny of the Day
of the Lord. καθάπερ καὶ ὑμεῖς ἡμῶν. He has been suspected of glorifying
himself and looking down on them. That is a double mistake.
He does glory, but not about himself; and, so far from looking
down on them, it is about them that he glories. He is just as
proud of them as his spiritual children (1 Cor. iv. 15) as (he
feels sure) they are of him as their spiritual father. The καθάπερ
brushes away all idea of his claiming superiority; ὡς μαθηταῖς
ὁμοτίμοις διαλεγόμενος οὕτως ἐξισάζει τὸν λόγον (Chrys.). He
thus cuts at the root (ὑποτέμνεται) of all jealousy (ibid.) by
making the glorying mutual and equal. St Paul rather frequently brings in the thought of the Day of the Lord as a
sort of test of the value of his missionary work and its results
(1 Cor. iii. 12, 13, iv. 5 ; Phil. ii. 16 ; 1 Thess. ii. 19, 20, which is a
close parallel to this). The Attic καθάπερ is frequent in N.T., and,
excepting Heb. iv. 10, is wholly Pauline (iii. 13, 18, viii. 11 ; etc.).

τῇ ἡμέρᾳ κ.τ.λ. Non in nocte praesentis saeculi, sed in die et
clarificatione Domini nostri Jesu Christi (Herveius) ; ubi et veri
magistri et boni discipuli probabuntur (Pseudo-Primasius). St
Paul still believed that the Day of the Lord would come soon
(1 Cor. vii. 29, x. 11, xv. 51), and had imparted this belief to his
converts (see on Rom. xiii. 11–14, p. 379) ; it is therefore no
remote date to which he appeals. Cf. 1 Thess. ii. 19.

A C D E K L omit ἡμῶν before Ἰησοῦ. ℵ* A B C D² and 3 K L omit
Χριστοῦ after Ἰησοῦ, and it is probably not original. Even if the evidence
were less strong, its insertion would be more probable than its omission.
Nearly all Versions have the addition.
In LXX, ἡμέρα Κυρίου (MSS. differ as to ἡ ἡμ. and τοῦ K.) is frequent
in the Prophets. St Paul uses ἡ ἡμέρα of the Parousia, with τ. Κυρίου
(1 Cor. v. 5 ; 2 Thess. ii. 2), or τ. Κυρ. Ἰησοῦ (here) ; also ἡμέρα, with
Ἰησοῦ Χριστοῦ (Phil. i. 6) or Χριστοῦ only (Phil. i. 10. ii. 16). The fullest
form is ἡ ἡμ. τ. Κυρ. ἡμῶν Ἰ. Χριστοῦ (1 Cor. i. 8). The Day in which the
thoughts of all hearts shall be revealed is mentioned here in confirmation of
the Apostle's claim to perfect sincerity. He is not afraid of what will then
be revealed about his heart. The mention of it forms a solemn conclusion
to this introduction (vv. 12–14) to his defence of his conduct. We have
similar solemn conclusions ii. 17, iv. 6, v. 10, ix. 15, xi. 15.

I. 15–II. 4. The Postponement of the Intended Visit.

*It was out of consideration to you that I abandoned my
original plan of coming to see you.*

15 In the confidence that we stood on these terms of mutual
trust and esteem, and that you would not take it amiss if I was

obliged after all to change my plans, I entertained the desire to come first to you, so that I might give you the pleasure of two visits from me on the same tour, 16 one on my way to Macedonia and one on my way back from it, and then be helped forward by you to Judæa. 17 Well, that was my desire. Do you suppose that I did not care whether I fulfilled it or not? that I make plans and unmake them, like a man of the world, just as the fancy of the moment takes me, and that, when I give a promise, I always hold myself free to break it, if I please. 18 But, whatever you think of me, God is faithful, and of this you have evidence, in that the Gospel which we preach to you is no uncertain message wavering between 'Yes' and 'No.' 19 For the Son of this same faithful God, Christ Jesus, who was proclaimed among you by us—by me and Silvanus and Timothy—was not found by you to be a waverer between 'Yes' and 'No'; a steadfast 'Yes' has ever been found in Him. 20 For however many promises God may have made to us, they are all of them assured to us in Christ with His affirming 'Yes': He is their fulfilment. And so it is through Him that the 'Amen' goes up to God in thankful assent, and He is glorified through the faith of us who are His ministers. 21 And it is God who causes us, yes, and you also, to be securely established in the life of His Anointed, and it is God who anointed us, 22 and sealed us as His own, and gave us the presence of His Spirit in our hearts as an earnest and foretaste of future blessings.

23 Now it is this same faithful and never-failing God that I who have been distrusted by you call as a witness ; and, as my life shall answer for it, I assert that it was from a wish to spare you pain that I abandoned my original plan of coming to Corinth. 24 Do not misunderstand me again. We have no wish to domineer over you as regards your faith ; not at all. But we do wish to have a share in making you happy in your faith. You need no one now to tell you what to believe; as regards that your condition is sound. II. 1 For I made up my mind for my own sake not to come again to see you in pain and grief; it would be better to stay away. 2 For if I of all men make you grieve, who then is to cheer me when I need cheering but the very people who receive pain and grief from me ? 3 This is just what I said in the letter which I wrote instead of coming ; that it was better not to come at all, if, instead of the happiness

which I might expect to have from you, I was to have only
pain and grief by coming; because I was and am confident,
with regard to every one of you, that what gives me happiness
is a happiness to all of you. ⁴ For that letter was the outcome of intense affliction and anguish of heart. I shed many
tears as I wrote it. Yet it was not written to make you grieve,
but to make you see how abundantly my love overflows towards
you.

15. Καὶ ταύτῃ τῇ πεποιθήσει. Placed first with great emphasis. It looks back to *vv.* 13, 14, and repeats the ἐλπίζω
in a more confident form. With the dative comp. those in
1 Cor. viii. 7; Gal. vi. 12; Rom. xi. 31. The noun is late
Greek (Hatch, *Biblical Greek*, p. 13), and occurs in LXX only
once, in Rabshakeh's taunt, 2 Kings xviii. 19. In N.T., no one
uses it but St Paul; four times in 2 Cor. (here, iii. 4, viii. 22,
x. 2), and Eph. iii. 12; Phil. iii. 4. He is also fond of πέποιθα
and πεποιθώς, which are rare elsewhere in N.T. He has glanced
at the Last Day when all secrets shall be revealed, and his confidence in the Corinthians and in his own sincerity is unshaken.
He is not conscious of any reason why he should have felt
shy of paying them a visit. Their salvation is the only thing
which he has tried to gain: *nihil aliud vestrum quaesivimus, quam
salutem* (Pseudo-Primasius).

The changes from 1 pers. plur. to 1 pers. sing. and *vice versa*
are here very rapid : γράφομεν . . . ἐλπίζω (13), ἐσμέν (14),
ἐβουλόμην (15). Such things are found in secular correspondence. Bachmann quotes a letter from Dinon, an official
personage, to Harimuthes (*Hibeh Pap.* 44); ἐγράψαμέν σοι
πρότερον . . . ὁρῶντες δέ σε καταρυθμοῦντα ᾤμην δεῖν καὶ νῦν
ἐπιστεῖλαί σοι . . . ἀπόστειλον πρὸς ἡμᾶς.

ἐβουλόμην πρότερον πρὸς ὑμᾶς ἐλθεῖν. 'I was wishing to come
first to you,' *i.e.* before going to Macedonia. He is speaking of
the time before his relations with the Corinthians became so
strained ; when he was on as good terms with them as he is now,
he had this desire. Authorities vary as to the position of
πρότερον, but the above order is almost certainly right, and
almost certainly it is to be taken with ἐλθεῖν rather than
ἐβουλόμην : it deprives it of force to translate 'I was formerly
desiring.'* And πρότερον does not mean 'sooner than I was

* K. Lake thinks that, in the 'Koine' Greek πρότερον is more commonly
used in the sense of 'originally,' with no comparative sense beyond that
involved in a contrast between past and present, than in the more classical
significance ; and he holds that this is "almost indisputably its meaning in
all the ten passages in which it is found in the N.T." (*The Earlier Epp. of
St Paul*, p. 226).

able to come,' but 'before going to Macedonia.' It is uncertain whether he communicated to the Corinthians this desire to visit them twice; he does not say 'I promised,' or 'I said,' or 'I wrote to you,' but simply that at one time he was wishing to pay them a double visit, and no doubt intended to do this. He may be merely giving evidence of his devotion to them. He had promised one visit (see on 1 Cor. xvi. 6), but we do not know that he had promised two. He had been hindered more than once in paying an intended visit to the Thessalonians (1 Thess. ii. 18), and often in paying one to the Romans (Rom. xv. 22, where τὰ πολλά means 'these many times'). Bachmann contends for the view that in *vv.* 15–17 St Paul is telling the Corinthians of a plan for visiting them of which they had hitherto known nothing (p. 66). For ἐβουλόμην, see Lightfoot on Philem. 13.

ἵνα δευτέραν χαρὰν σχῆτε. We are again in uncertainty. To what does this 'second joy' refer? Various suggestions are made. The first long visit in which he converted the Corinthians was the first joy; the projected visit would be a second joy. Those who do not believe in a second visit, short and painful, can adopt this suggestion easily. Those who do believe in the painful visit must suppose that it does not count when χαρά is under consideration. To make 1 Cor. the first joy or grace (Chrys., Atto) is very unsatisfactory. The best interpretation is that St Paul is referring to the two visits which he had wished to pay instead of only the one promised in 1 Cor. xvi. 5, the second of which would be a second joy to them. The objection that he has not yet mentioned two visits is not a serious one. He is dictating, he has the two visits in his mind, and he mentions them in the same breath. There is no difficulty, either, if χάριν be adopted as the right reading: the visit of an Apostle might confer some χάρισμα πνευματικόν and be ἐν πληρώματι εὐλογίας Χριστοῦ (Rom. i. 11, xv. 29).

πρότερον after ἐβουλόμην (A B C D E F G M P 17, Latt. Syrr. Arm. Goth.) rather than after ἐλθεῖν (K, Copt., Thdrt.); א* omits. πρὸς ὑμᾶς ἐλθεῖν (א A B C M P, Arm., Chrys.) rather than ἐλθεῖν πρὸς ὑμ. (D E F G K L, Latt. Copt. Goth., Thdrt.). χαράν (א³ B L P, Thdrt.) is perhaps better than χάριν (א* A C D E F G K, Latt.). As in 3 Jn. 4, a copyist may have substituted a more spiritual word: in N.T., χάρις is far more frequent than χαρά. Chrys. adopts χάρις, but explains it as χαρά: Thdrt. adopts χαρά, but explains it as human χάρις, which in N.T. is not probable, although in the Κοινή examples of χάρις = 'courtesy' are found. σχῆτε (א B C P, Thdrt.) rather than ἔχητε (A D E F G K L): confusion between Σ and E would be easy.

16. καὶ δι' ὑμῶν . . . εἰς τ. Ἰουδαίαν. Both AV. and RV. are somewhat misleading, and neither marks the sequence of prepositions (εἰς . . . πρὸς . . . εἰς) correctly. 'Pass by you'

may mean 'go past without visiting you'; and 'by you to pass' may mean 'to be sent on by you'; both of which are wrong. Translate, 'Through you to pass on unto M., and again from M. to come to you, and by you to be set forward on my way unto Judaea.'

διελθεῖν (אBCD³EKL, Latt.) rather than ἀπελθεῖν (AD*FGP, Copt. Arm.).

17. τοῦτο οὖν βουλόμενος κ.τ.λ. 'With this, then, as my wish, did I at all show levity?' The art. τῇ ἐλαφρίᾳ may be generic, but it possibly means 'the levity with which you have charged me.' Vulg. has *cum ergo hoc voluissem*; but *vellem* would be right; and 'levity' is perhaps nearer to ἐλαφρία than 'fickleness.' The word is found nowhere else in N.T. or LXX, and, like πεποίθησις, belongs to late Greek. Polybius uses ἐλαφρός in an ethical sense of the unthinking multitude which needs to be kept in order by a religion of some kind (VI. lvi. 11). "'Ελαφρία does not mean change of mind; but rather the lightness of character of a man who has no mind, who makes a promise without any real intention of fulfilling it, or, if he does at the time intend to do so, forgets it almost as soon as it is made. St Paul's answer to this charge seems to be, that, while the Corinthians supposed him to be careless about them, he was all the time wishing and planning to visit them, if only he could do so without having to exercise severity" (Kennedy, *The Second and Third Epistles to the Corinthians*, p. 36; cf. p. xxv). Bachmann takes a similar view (pp. 64–66). Cf. *v.* 23. Other charges are answered iii. 5, iv. 2.

The μήτι here, as elsewhere (xii. 18), anticipates a negative answer. 'Of course he was not exhibiting levity when he acted in this manner.' The AV. spoils Jn. iv. 29 by not observing this. The ἄρα after an interrogative particle points to some antecedent statement. 'Did I in that case?' *num igitur?* It is frequent in the Synoptists (Mt. xviii. 1, xix. 25, 27, xxiv. 45, etc.), but is not found elsewhere in Paul, fond as he is of argumentative questions. 'Was then my intention so flimsy and fleeting, that I did not care whether I acted upon it or not?'

ἢ ἃ βουλεύομαι. The change from the aorist (ἐχρησάμην), of what took place on a particular occasion, to the pres. (βουλεύομαι), of what is habitual, must not be overlooked. 'Or the things which I (at any time) purpose, do I (always) purpose them in accordance with (the fitful fancies of) my lower nature (*v.* 12), without reference to reason or spirit?' The second question is far more comprehensive than the first; it covers his life as a whole.

ἵνα ᾖ παρ᾽ ἐμοί. In late Greek the distinction between ἵνα

3

and ὥστε becomes somewhat blurred, and the idea of purpose can scarcely be included here (Blass, § 69. 3); see on 1 Jn. i. 9. But J. H. Moulton (p. 210) takes ἵνα here as final; "Paul is disclaiming the mundane virtue of unsettled convictions, which *aims* at saying yes and no in one breath." So also Beet. The exact meaning of what follows is uncertain. The art. τὸ Ναὶ ναί and τὸ Οὒ οὔ, like the art. in τῇ ἐλαφρίᾳ, may be either generic or 'that with which you charge me.' The repetition gives emphasis. The charge which he is rebutting is probably that of blowing hot and cold with the same breath, and always having retraction of what he says in reserve. Others make the charge to be one of inflexibility, of never modifying when he has once said 'Yes' or 'No'; but it is difficult to get this out of the Greek, and it does not fit the facts. It was his change of plans that had brought him into disrepute. The Greek has to be altered in order to get the meaning 'that with me No should be Yes, and Yes No'; for there is no such reading. It is, of course, impossible that St Paul is alluding to Mt. v. 37, for that Gospel was not yet written; but he may be alluding to some tradition, or even written record, of our Lord's words which was known to him. Yet the difference between the way in which Ναὶ ναί, Οὒ οὔ is used in the Saying and in this passage is so considerable that allusion is not very probable. See J. B. Mayor on Jas. v. 12, p. 155, and Plummer on Mt. v. 37, p. 84. For κατὰ σάρκα, see v. 16, x. 2, xi. 18; Rom. viii. 4, 12, 13; Jn. viii. 15: it means 'on external grounds,' such as expediency, likes and dislikes, without internal principle. St Paul contends that, though his plans changed, yet his principles did not; he was always loyal to the Gospel and to his converts.

βουλόμενος (אABCFGP, Vulg. Copt.) rather than βουλευόμενος (DEK, g Syrr. Arm. Aeth. Goth.) or βουλευσόμενος (L). Note that G supports βουλ. and g βουλευ.

18. πιστὸς δὲ ὁ Θεὸς ὅτι κ.τ.λ. There is doubt whether this is an adjuration or not. In favour of its being an adjuration (Genevan, AV., RV.) is the fact that 'as God is faithful' makes excellent sense, and that it seems to be analogous to such expressions as ζῶ ἐγώ, ὅτι (Rom. xiv. 11 from Is. xlv. 23, where LXX has κατ' ἐμαυτοῦ ὀμνύω), ζῇ Κύριος ὅτι (1 Sam. xx. 3; 2 Sam. ii. 27, xii. 5; etc.). Bousset and Lietzmann adopt the rendering, *Bei Gottes Treue.* But there is much to be said against this interpretation. The formula, πιστὸς ὁ Θεός, is used elsewhere by St Paul in places where it is not an adjuration (1 Cor. i. 9, x. 13; cf. 1 Thess. v. 24; 2 Thess. iii. 3). In adjurations and solemn asseverations he uses forms which are quite different; *e.g.* μάρτυρα τ. Θεὸν ἐπικαλοῦμαι (*v.* 3), Θεὸς μάρτυς (1 Thess. ii. 5, 10), μάρτυς

γάρ μού ἐστιν ὁ Θεός (Rom. i. 9), μάρτυς γάρ μου ὁ Θεός (Phil. i. 8), ὁ Θεὸς οἶδεν (xi. 11), ὁ Θ. καὶ πατὴρ τ. Κυρίου Ἰησοῦ οἶδεν ὅτι οὐ ψεύδομαι (xi. 31), ἰδοὺ ἐνώπιον τ. Θεοῦ ὅτι οὐ ψεύδομαι (Gal. i. 20), διαμαρτύρομαι ἐνώπιον τ. Θεοῦ (1 Tim. v. 21; cf. 2 Tim. ii. 14, iv. 1), παραγγέλλω σοι ἐνώπιον τ. Θεοῦ (1 Tim. vi. 13). Wiclif, Tyndale and Cranmer follow the Vulgate (*Fidelis autem Deus*) in not making this an adjuration. Schmiedel has, *Treuer Bürge ist Gott.*

This use of πιστός as a special attribute of God is frequent in N.T. and LXX (*e.g.* 2 Tim. ii. 13; Heb. x. 23, xi. 11; Deut. vii. 9; Is. xlix. 7); cf. πιστὸς Κύριος τοῖς ἀγαπῶσιν αὐτόν, and πιστὸς ὁ Κύριος ἐν πᾶσι τοῖς κρίμασιν αὐτοῦ (Ps. Sol. xiv. 1, xvii. 12). As in Jn. ii. 18, ix. 17, ὅτι = 'in that'; 'God is faithful in that our word toward you is (not 'was,' AV.) not a wavering between Yes and No.' They have his letters, they have in their minds what he and others taught them, and there is no inconsistency or insincerity in the Gospel which they possess; it is a reflexion of the faithfulness of God. Chrys. paraphrases, 'Mistrust not what is from God, for what is from God cannot be untrue.' The argument is one from "ethical congruity." God is faithful *in the fact that* the Gospel which is proclaimed by His messengers is not a Gospel of duplicity, full of misleading statements and of promises which are not fulfilled.

οὐκ ἔστιν (א* A B C D* F G P 17, Latt. Copt. Goth. Arm.) rather than οὐκ ἐγένετο (א³ D² and ³ E K L, Syrr. Aeth.), which is assimilation to *v.* 19.

19. ὁ τοῦ Θεοῦ γὰρ υἱός. The usual order would be ὁ γὰρ υἱὸς τ. Θ. The transfer of γάρ from the second to the fourth place throws great emphasis on τ. Θεοῦ and marks the connexion with what precedes. 'For it is this faithful God's Son.' Comp. the position of μέν in x. 1, and of οὖν in 1 Cor. viii. 4, where, as here, some MSS. put the particle back to the usual place. Winer, p. 699; Blass, § 80. 4. 'That ὁ πιστὸς Θεός should have a Son who was Yes and No would be a monstrous contradiction, and it is His Son who is the subject of ὁ λόγος ἡμῶν.' Ἀντὶ τοῦ κηρύγματος αὐτὸν κηρυττόμενον τέθεικε (Thdrt.) His title is given with solemn fulness. The full expression, ὁ υἱὸς τοῦ Θεοῦ, is used by St Paul in only two other places, Gal. ii. 20, Eph. iv. 13 (in Rom. i. 4, υἱὸς Θεοῦ), in both of which there is an emphatic change of titles from 'Christ' to 'the Son of God.' See J. A. Robinson, *Ephesians*, pp. 100, 183. The rareness of use may be accidental, for St Paul often refers to Christ as the 'Son' (1 Cor. i. 9, xv. 28; 1 Thess. i. 10; Gal. i. 16, iv. 4, 6; Rom. i. 3, 9, v. 10, viii. 3, 29, 32; Col. i. 13), *i.e.* in all groups, excepting the Pastorals. St Paul's usage has to be compared with the evidence of papyri and inscriptions, in which

Θεοῦ υἱός, or in Latin inscriptions *divi filius*, is frequently used of Augustus. In a votive inscription from Magnesia on the Menander, now at Pergamum, for Nero between his adoption by Claudius and his accession (A.D. 50–54), Nero is called "the son of the greatest of the gods, Tib. Claudius," τὸν υἱὸν τοῦ μεγίστου θεῶν Τιβερίου Κλαυδίου. Deissmann gives an illustration of it, *Light from Anc. East*, p. 351 ; see also *Bible Studies*, p. 166. Hence two opposite suggestions. St Paul used υἱὸς Θεοῦ rarely, because its evil associations would cause it to be misunderstood by converts from heathenism. He uses it, and the still stronger ὁ υἱὸς τοῦ Θεοῦ, and frequently uses υἱός of Christ's relationship to God, because he wished to point out that there was only one Son to whom the title rightly belonged. See Milligan, *Thessalonians*, p. lxvi ; F. H. Stead, *Expositor*, 3rd series, 1888, vii. pp. 386–395. The full title is found Heb. iv. 14, vi. 6, vii. 3, x. 29, and very often in 1 Jn. See on 1 Jn. i. 3 ; also Swete, *Apost. Creed*, pp. 24 f. ; Menzies, *2 Corinthians*, p. lii.

ὁ ἐν ὑμῖν δι' ἡμῶν κηρυχθείς. The verb is very frequent in Paul (all four groups) of preaching Christ and the Gospel (iv. 5, xi. 4 ; 1 Cor. i. 23, xv. 12 ; Phil. i. 15 ; 1 Tim. iii. 16 ; etc.). The Apostle places the two related pronouns in close proximity, bound together in one expression between the article and the participle ; the Christ 'who was preached among you by our instrumentality' (διά not ὑπό). He is not claiming what belongs to ὁ αὐξάνων Θεός. He and his colleagues are only διάκονοι δι' ὧν ἐπιστεύσατε : see on 1 Cor. i. 5, 6. This διά is also used of Christ (*vv.* 5, 20, iii. 4, etc.), and therefore is no evidence that St Paul regarded himself as a mere machine ; but he is not the supreme worker. Here he is appealing to the probability that there is moral resemblance between master and servant. The Son of the God who cannot lie is one who may be trusted and has proved to be trustworthy. Therefore the message which His ministers bring—ὁ λόγος ἡμῶν ὁ πρὸς ὑμᾶς—is likely to be trustworthy. On St Paul's use of ὁ λόγος, often with a genitive following,—τοῦ Θεοῦ, τοῦ Κυρίου, τῆς ἀληθείας, and (*v.* 19) τῆς καταλλαγῆς,—see Harnack, *The Constitution and Law of the Church*, pp. 339–343. It is clear from *v.* 20 that 'the Son of God, Jesus Christ,' does not mean '*the doctrine about* Jesus Christ.' The meaning of *v.* 19 is not doubtful. The Apostle reminds the Corinthians of the way in which he and his colleagues proclaimed Christ among them at first. To make it quite clear what is meant by 'proclaimed by us,' he names the missionaries. Paul and Silvanus were working together in Corinth for a time before Timothy, who had been left behind at Beroea and had afterwards been sent to Thessalonica, joined them. All three are associated in writing 1 and 2 Thess.* Chrys. may be right in suggesting that the appeal to the preaching by three different agents is given as a guarantee for consistency. Calvin suggests that these three had been specially maligned by the Apostle's opponents. More probably St Paul is simply recalling the time when all three were working happily together.† He does not mention Apollos, who came later, after St Paul had left.

We may safely assume that the Silvanus of the Pauline Epistles and of 1 Pet. v. 12 and the Silas of Acts may be identified, and that the proposal to identify him with St Luke is to be rejected. See Bigg, *St Peter and St Jude*, pp. 85, 86, art. 'Silas' in Hastings' *DB*. iv., art. 'Acts' in Smith, *DB*., 2nd ed. We know very little about him after his work in Corinth.

οὐκ ἐγένετο Ναί καὶ Οὔ, ἀλλὰ Ναί ἐν αὐτῷ γέγονεν. 'The Son of God, who was proclaimed by us among you, did not prove to be Yes and No, but in Him Yes has proved true.' The Corinthians' experience of Him had shown that He was a Son who faithfully fulfilled the promises of His faithful Father.‡ The change to the perfect (γέγονεν) marks the permanent result: comp. the change from ἐκτίσθη to ἔκτισται (Col. i. 16). For this use of γίνεσθαι, comp. γινέσθω ὁ Θεὸς ἀληθής (Rom. iii. 4), 'prove to be,' 'be seen to be.' Ἐν αὐτῷ means 'in Christ.'

ὁ τοῦ Θεοῦ γάρ (ℵ A B C P) rather than ὁ γὰρ τοῦ Θεοῦ (D E F G K L; F G omit τοῦ); correction to more usual order. Χριστὸς Ἰησοῦς (ℵ* A C) may be right, but Ἰησ. Χρ. is powerfully supported (ℵ³ B D E F G K L P, Vulg.). 17 omits Χριστός. See critical note on v. 1. D E F G have Σιλβανοῦ for Σιλουανοῦ, but f g have *Silvanum*.

20. ὅσαι γὰρ ἐπαγγελίαι Θεοῦ. This is an independent clause, 'For how many soever are the promises of God'; it is not (as AV.) the subject, of which the next clause is the predicate, which obscures the meaning. With ἐν αὐτῷ τὸ Ναί we may understand γίνεται from v. 19: 'For of all the promises of God, however many they may be, in Him is found the fulfilment': ἐν αὐτῷ again means 'in Christ,' who sums up the historical development of Divine revelation. By 'the promises' are meant those which were made to the Jews, and through them to man-

* On the supposed influence of Silas on St Paul's movements, see Redlich, *S. Paul and his Companions*, pp. 66, 82–84, 272.

† On the striking coincidence between this passage and Acts, see Knowling on Acts xviii. 5, and Paley, *Horae Paulinae*, iv. and viii.

‡ That St Paul is here opposing Judaizing teachers, who preached a different Jesus, and that he names Silvanus and Timothy in order to exclude the Judaizers, is an unnecessary hypothesis.

kind, with reference to the coming of the Messiah (Rom. ix. 4, xv. 8 ; Gal. iii. 14). The word is frequent in N.T., but is hardly ever used of anything else but Divine promises, for which it is the constant expression. It implies that what is promised by God is freely offered, it is not an engagement extracted by negotiation. See Lightfoot on Gal. iii. 14. The word is rare in LXX, and there it has no such special meaning. In Eph. i. 13, iii. 6, the Gentiles are said to share in the promise through Christ. What is said here is that to all God's promises Christ is the never-failing Yes, the Yes that assures, confirms, and fulfils.

διὸ καὶ δι' αὐτοῦ τὸ 'Αμήν. 'Wherefore also through Him is the Amen.' This doubtless refers to the Amen in public worship (Deut. xxvii. 15 f. ; Neh. v. 13, viii. 6 ; Ps. xli. 14) which the Church had taken over from the Synagogue : see on 1 Cor. xiv. 16. This does not imply that 'Amen through our Lord Jesus Christ' was already the usual formula for closing each prayer in public worship. About the response of 'Amen' by the congregation there is ample evidence, and in this way the Corinthian converts had again and again given their adhesion to the teaching of St Paul and his colleagues. Their saying, 'Jesus is Lord' (1 Cor. xii. 3), was of a similar character. The article, τὸ 'Αμήν, means 'the customary Amen,' and ἐστίν, or possibly γίνεται, is to be understood. Calvin erroneously makes the clause a wish ; quare et per ipsum sit Amen Deo ad gloriam per nos. The reading, καὶ ἐν αὐτῷ, followed in AV., makes the 'Αμήν a repetition of the Ναί, like 'Abba, Father,' which is weak. The clause is not a mere amplification of the first part of the verse, but a deduction from it. The fact that in Rev. iii. 14 Christ is called ὁ 'Αμήν, ὁ Μάρτυς ὁ πιστός, probably helped to cause the corruption of the text.

τῷ Θεῷ πρὸς δόξαν δι' ἡμῶν. These words belong to τὸ 'Αμήν exclusively, to the saying of Amen by the Corinthians in public worship, not to the first half of the verse ; and τῷ Θεῷ is placed first with emphasis. It is to God, for His glory, that this assent by the congregation is given. In 1 Cor. x. 31 we have εἰς δόξαν Θεοῦ. For the history of the word δόξα, see Milligan on 1 Thess. ii. 12 ; Parry, St James, pp. 36 f. ; Hastings, DCG. i. pp. 648 f. The δι' ἡμῶν repeats the δι' ἡμῶν of v. 19 : 'all this comes to pass nostro ministerio, through our preaching of Christ to you.' It is the Corinthians who are inconsistent if, in the face of their own public asseveration, they tax their teachers with inconsistency. Others understand δι' ἡμῶν as meaning that the 'Amen' is said by the Apostle and his colleagues as the spokesmen of the congregation ; which weakens the argument. Still farther from the Apostle's meaning is the corrupt reading which omits δι' and makes ἡμῶν the genitive after πρὸς δόξαν, 'to *our* glory.' There is no καύχησις ἡμῶν (*v.* 12) here : he is answering the charge of levity. People who cause glory to be given to God for His faithfulness are not likely to be unfaithful.

δὶὸ καὶ δι' αὐτοῦ (ℵ A B C F G O P 17, 37, Latt. Copt. Goth. Arm.) rather than καὶ δι' αὐτοῦ (D* d e Ambrst.) or καὶ ἐν αὐτῷ (D² and ³ E K L, Chrys. Thdrt.). πρὸς δόξαν δι' ἡμῶν (ℵ A B D E F G K P) rather than πρὸς δόξαν ἡμῶν (C L O, *ad gloriam nostram* f Vulg.). The addition of *dicimus* after *ad gloriam nostram* in some Latin writers is a gloss without authority in any Greek text.

21. ὁ δὲ βεβαιῶν ἡμᾶς σὺν ὑμῖν εἰς Χριστὸν καὶ χρίσας ἡμᾶς Θεός. It is better to take this as a complete sentence of which Θεός is the predicate than to make it the subject of a long sentence of which *v.* 22 is the predicate. It is doubtful whether σὺν ἡμῖν is to be carried on to the second ἡμᾶς and to the ἡμᾶς and ἡμῶν in *v.* 22 : the fact that ἡμᾶς is repeated while σὺν ἡμῖν is not, is rather against the carrying on, but is by no means decisive. The change of tense from present to aorist does not affect this question. Both teachers and taught are included in ἡμᾶς σὺν ἡμῖν : the following ἡμᾶς and ἡμῶν *may* mean the officials only, and the anointing and sealing may refer to their being 'separated' (Acts xiii. 2) for ministerial work. The "χρίσας is evidently suggested by Χριστόν, and it is implied that the Apostle and his colleagues shared the unction with which Christ was anointed, *i.e.* the power of the Spirit. In 1 Jn. ii. 20, 27 this is extended to all believers" (Swete, *The Holy Spirit in the N.T.*, p. 385). Elsewhere in the same work Swete takes *this* passage as applying to all believers (pp. 193, 220, 232); see especially p. 298, "The Epistles of the N.T., which are silent about the fact of the Lord's Baptism (except the allusions in 1 Tim. iii. 16 ; 1 Jn. v. 6), as they are about most of the other facts of the Gospel history, speak freely of the anointing received *by all Christians* from the Holy One, *i.e.* the ascended Christ (2 Cor. i. 21 ; 1 Jn. ii. 20, 27)." This agrees with Neander's view ; *Es ist dies die Weihe des allgemeinen Priesterthums.* If we confine χρίσας and σφραγισάμενος to the teachers, then the aorists refer to the time when they were set apart for missionary work. If we regard all Christians as included in the ἡμᾶς, then the aorists refer to their conversion and baptism. In either case, the change of tense indicates that God continually establishes those whom He once for all consecrated to Himself. The χρίσας does not imply any actual ceremony of unction : the anointing is with the Spirit ; and in order to bring out the connexion between Χριστόν and χρίσας, the former might be translated 'the Anointed.' 'But He who confirmeth us and you also unto the Anointed and who anointed us is God.' We must

keep in mind that St Paul is dictating and not always adhering
to the form of sentence which he originally had in his mind.
'Who confirmeth us' is another blow at the charge of levity; it
indicates that the relationship established between us and Christ
cannot be impugned; there is no flaw in it, and it is legally
indestructible.   See Deissmann, *Bible Studies*, p. 109; in
papyri βεβαιωτήρ is often used of a 'surety.'

ἡμᾶς σὺν ὑμῖν. The σὺν ὑμῖν is a conciliatory addition, like
καὶ ὑμεῖς ἡμῶν in *v.* 14. In this permanent βεβαίωσις the
Corinthians share equally with their teachers, and this is a strong
guarantee for the sincerity of the latter. 'It is absurd to suppose
that we who remain united with you in such a relationship treat
you with levity.' The addition of ἐσμὲν ἀλλήλων μέλη in Eph.
iv. 25 is similar; joint membership in the same body conduces
to truthfulness.

εἰς Χριστόν. 'In relation to Christ,' ὁ μὴ ἐῶν ἡμᾶς παρασαλεύ-
εσθαι (Chrys.). This is another security against levity and
caprice. One is tempted to translate, '*into* the Anointed so as
to abide *in* Him'; but the present participle is against this.
'They entered into Christ as members of His Body when they
became Christians, and God is continually confirming them
in that relationship. The '*in* Christ' of AV. and RV. is right,
cf. Col. ii. 7.

καὶ χρίσας ἡμᾶς. If σὺν ὑμῖν is not carried on, this refers to
the consecration of the Apostle and others for missionary work.
But all Christians receive unction from God (see on 1 Jn. ii.
20, 27), and we cannot with any certainty restrict the χρίσας to
the officials. The mention of Χριστόν has suggested χρίσας, but
there is probably no direct reference to the anointing of Christ
at His Mission to bring the good tidings (Lk. iv. 18; Acts iv. 27,
x. 38; cf. Jn. x. 36). Heb. i. 9 should not be quoted in this
connexion, for there the glorified Son is anointed with the oil of
gladness at the completion of His work, not with power at the
beginning of it (Lk. iv. 14).*

For ἡμᾶς σὺν ὑμῖν, which is overwhelmingly attested, C and the Harlean
Syriac with a few cursives have ὑμᾶς σὺν ἡμῖν. The scribe of B perhaps
had the same reading; he has written ὑμᾶς σὺν ὑμῖν, with ὑμᾶς after χρίσας.

For χρίσας Vulg. has *qui unxit.* Cornely points out that *ungere* in
N.T. is used to translate four different Greek words; ἀλείφειν (Mt. vi. 17;
Mk. vi. 13, xvi. 1; Lk. vii. 38, 46; Jn. xi. 2, xii. 3; Jas. v. 14), μυρίζειν
(Mk. xiv. 8), ἐπιχρίειν (Jn. ix. 11), and χρίειν (Lk. iv. 18; Acts iv. 27,
x. 38; 2 Cor. i. 21; Heb. i. 9). The first three words are always
used in the literal sense, while the last is nowhere so used; χρίειν is
always symbolical, as also is χρίσμα (1 Jn. ii. 20, 27). In LXX,
χρίειν is very frequent, and almost always in the literal sense.

---

* An allusion to the rubbing of athletes with oil before gymnastic contests
is not probable.

22. ὁ καὶ σφραγισάμενος ἡμᾶς. The ὁ is omitted in important authorities, but is probably genuine. Deissmann (*Bible Studies*, pp. 108 f.) has thrown much light on both σφραγισάμενος and ἀρραβῶνα. Sealing is mentioned in O.T. in the literal sense as a security against secret opening (Dan. vi. 17) and as a substitute for signature (1 Kings xxi. 8); and in a figurative sense (Deut. xxxii. 34 ; Job xiv. 17, xxxiii. 16, xxxvii. 7 ; Is. viii. 16). But the papyri show that sealing had a very extended and important use in the East, especially for legal purposes, to give validity to documents, to guarantee the genuineness of articles, and that sacks and chests convey the specified amount, etc. The meaning here may be that, in confirmation of a covenant, God sealed us as His own (mid.) and attested our value (see J. A. Robinson on Eph. i. 13, 14, and Swete on Rev. vii. 2). 'He not only anointed us, but *also* (καί) sealed us and gave us'; this is a further security. The first καί does not anticipate the second, '*both* sealed us *and* gave'; it introduces a fresh argument. We need not suppose that St Paul is referring to supernatural spiritual gifts as signs of an Apostle. An allusion to rites for initiation into certain mysteries is perhaps possible; but it is more probable that an allusion to Christian baptism is meant, a rite for which at a later period the metaphor of 'sealing' was often used. The aorists point to some definite occasion. See on Rom. iv. 11, xv. 28.

τὸν ἀρραβῶνα τοῦ πνεύματος. Lightfoot has a full note on the strange word ἀρραβών, *Notes on the Epistles of St Paul*, pp. 323 f. ; see also Ellicott on Eph. i. 14. It may be Phoenician. Cf. the Scotch 'arles' and the German *Angeld* or *Handgeld*. It is more than a pledge (*pignus*, ἐνέχυρον); it is μικρόν τι μέρος τοῦ πάντος (Thdrt.), an instalment, *i.e.* delivery of a small portion, whether of money or goods, as an earnest that the remainder would be delivered later. Comp. the use of ἀπαρχή in Rom. viii. 23. In v. 5 the expression occurs again. Papyri show that the ἀρραβών was sometimes a considerable portion of the total, and that, if the buyer failed to deliver the remainder, he lost his ἀρραβών; on the other hand, if the seller failed to fulfil his side of the bargain, he had to pay twice the amount of the ἀρραβών *plus* interest on it. The genitive is one of apposition ; the Spirit is the earnest, the earnest of eternal life ; *quantum ergo praemium est, cujus tanta est arrha ! id est gratia Spiritus* (Pseudo-Primasius). The Spirit is the anointing, the sealing, and the first instalment of eternal life ; and the three metaphors are perhaps meant to form a climax. The incidental, and probably unintentional, suggestion of Trinitarian doctrine is noteworthy. *God* confirms both teachers and taught to *Christ* ; as a security He gave His *Spirit*. See on xiii. 14, on 1 Cor. xii. 4–6, and comp. Eph. iv. 4–6; also Clem. Rom. *Cor.* xlvi. 3, lviii. 2. In the last two passages, as here, we have the order, God, Christ, Spirit; in the other passages the order varies, and sometimes Christ or the Spirit is mentioned first. In the Apostolic age there was evidently a pervading thought that in some sense the Divine Essence is threefold.

ἐν ταῖς καρδίαις ἡμῶν. ' Our hearts are the sphere *in* which the gift of the Spirit is displayed '; cf. ἐν ταῖς ἐκκλησίαις, ἐν τῷ εὐαγγελίῳ (viii. 1, 16), and especially ἐκκέχυται ἐν ταῖς καρδίαις ἡμῶν (Rom. v. 5).

ὁ καὶ σφραγ. (א³ B C³ D E L O) rather than καὶ ὁ σφραγ. (F G, Latt.), or καὶ σφραγ. (א* A C* K P).

Jerome notes that the Latin version has *pignus* here and v. 5, instead of *arrabo* (or *arrha*). *Pignus* = ἐνέχυρον (Deut. xxiv. 10–13), a word not found in N.T. Nevertheless, in the Vulgate, Jerome has left *pignus* in both passages. This is one of many pieces of evidence that Jerome's revision of the Epistles was very perfunctory. Augustine also points out the inaccuracy of *pignus* as a translation ; *Melius dicitur* arrha *quam* pignus ; *haec enim duo similia videntur inter se, sed tamen habent aliquam differentiam non negligendam* (*Serm.* 378). In LXX ἀρραβών occurs Gen. xxxviii. 18–20, and there it means *pignus*, a pledge, and not an instalment.

McFadyen takes this paragraph (15–22) as evidence of "the heights upon which Paul was habitually living." He repels a charge of insincerity by showing how impossible it must be for a minister of *Christ*, the eternal affirmation of all God's promises, to be insincere. "For a moment he loses sight of himself and his pain in the contemplation of Christ as the Everlasting Yea . . . the finished realization of the divine purpose."

Here the chapter ought to have ended ; or still better at *v.* 14. The next two verses (23, 24) are closely connected with ii. 1–4. See on 1 Cor. xi. 1.

23. Ἐγὼ δέ. With great emphasis. He returns to his own individual case, in which Silvanus and Timothy are not included. Having shown how antecedently improbable it is that a minister of Christ should be guilty of levity and faithlessness, he now tells the Corinthians the actual reason why he changed his plans. It was not out of caprice, nor out of cowardice (xiii. 10; 1 Cor. iv. 18, 19), nor simply for his own convenience ; it was out of consideration to them. The δέ marks the relation between the Apostle's attitude and what has just been stated respecting God. ' He who continually confirms us is the faithful God ; but *I* call *Him* as a witness, etc.' These strong appeals (*v.* 18, iii. 1, iv. 2, v. 11) are evoked by his opponents' charges of untrustworthiness and timidity.

μάρτυρα τὸν Θεὸν ἐπικαλοῦμαι ἐπὶ τ. ἐμὴν ψυχήν. ' *I* call God for a witness upon my soul '; we might render ' I call *this* God, 'the God whom I have just described.' 'He knows every corner of the soul and all its secrets; the most subtle deceit would not escape Him ; and I should at once be convicted if I were lying.' The rendering '*against* my soul' is possible (see on Lk. ix. 5, and cf. Acts xiii. 51); in which case the idea is that, if he is lying, his soul, the seat of his physical life (Rom. ii. 9), will pay the penalty. Vulg. has *in animam meam*, Aug. *super animam meam.* In one of his letters (*Ep.* 157), Augustine says that many people do not know what constitutes swearing. They think that if they do not say '*Per Deum,*' but use expressions which are found in St Paul, they are quite safe. They say *Testis est Deus* (Rom. i. 9; Phil. i. 8), *Scit Deus* (2 Cor. xii. 2), *Testem invoco Deum super animam meam* (i. 23), without thinking. There is no sin in swearing to what is true ; but swearing falsely is a very grievous sin, and those who swear frequently are likely to fall into it. *Non ideo, quia in suis epistolis juravit Apostolus, vir in veritate firmissimus, ludus nobis debet esse juratio.*

Calling Heaven to witness is freq. in literature from Homer onwards. Hector proposes to Achilles that each shall offer to the other the witness of his own gods as a guarantee of good faith (*Il.* xxii. 254);

ἀλλ' ἄγε δεῦρο θεοὺς ἐπιδώμεθα· τοὶ γὰρ ἄριστοι
μάρτυροι ἔσσονται καὶ ἐπίσκοποι ἁρμονιάων.

Still closer to the present passage we have τόν τε Παιᾶνα, ἐπικαλούμενος μάρτυρα τῶν λεγομένων ἀληθείας πέρι (Plato, *Laws,* ii. 644 C) ; ἐπικαλεῖσθαι θεοὺς καθορᾶν τὰ γιγνόμενα (Xen. *Hell.* II. iii. 55) ; in all which cases the mid. indicates that Heaven is invoked as a witness on one's own side.* Harveius combines the ideas of '*upon* my soul to search it' and '*against* my soul to condemn it'; *Deum invoco in animam meam, ut ipse inspiciat, si verum dico, et testis mihi sit,—si autem mentiar, puniat.*

ψειδόμενος ὑμῶν.   Emphatic; 'it was in order to spare you.' Levity was not the cause, but consideration for them ; he did not wish to come ἐν ῥάβδῳ to punish offenders (see on 1 Cor. iv. 21, vii. 28), so he gave them time to come to a better mind.   In this he was not shirking a painful duty.   If they had not yielded to his severe letter and to Titus, he would have come in all sharpness (xiii. 10).   Delay was a gain to both sides, but it was not prompted by timidity or σοφία σαρκική (*v.* 12).

οὐκέτι ἦλθον εἰς Κόρινθον.   'I came no: any more to Corinth.' The Greek cannot mean 'I came not as yet' (AV.), and can hardly mean 'I forbare to come' (RV.).   Comp. οὐκέτι γιγνώσκομεν (*v.* 16), οὐκέτι ὑπὸ παιδαγωγόν ἐσμεν (Gal. iii. 25), and with past

---

* The expression is Greek rather than Hebrew.   In LXX we have μάρτυς κύριος (1 Sam. xii. 5, 6, xx. 23, 42), but not this phrase.

tenses, οὐκ εἶδεν αὐτὸν οὐκέτι (Acts viii. 39), οὐκέτι αὐτὸ ἑλκύσαι ἴσχυον (Jn. xxi. 6). 'I came not any more,' or 'I came not again,' harmonizes so well with the theory of a second and painful visit to Corinth, even if it does not actually imply it, that those who reject the theory prefer some other manner of translation, as that in RV. See on *1 Corinthians*, pp. xxi–xxiv, for arguments in support of the theory, and pp. xxxi–xxxiii for arguments against it.

The theory that 2 Cor. x.–xiii. is part of the severe letter written between 1 Cor. and 2 Cor. i.–ix. is strongly confirmed by this verse. In xiii. 2 he writes, 'If I come again I will not spare'; here he writes, 'To spare you I came not any more to Corinth.' This parallel combined with those between xiii. 10 and ii. 3, and between x. 6 and ii. 9, make a strong case. "It seems difficult to deny that St Paul, in each case, is referring to the same thing,—in the passage from x.–xiii. in the present tense, and in that from i.–ix. in the past" (K. Lake, *The Earlier Epp. of St Paul*, p. 160). See also Kennedy, *Second and Third Corinthians*, pp. 79 f.; G. H. Rendall, p. 55.

24. Epanorthosis. At once the thought strikes the Apostle that what he has just said may be misunderstood, especially by the emotional Corinthians, who are so jealous of their own independence. The power to spare implies the power to punish, and this seems to imply a claim to control everything. He hastens to assure them that he makes no such claim. This nervous anxiety about seeming to presume is so unlike the tone of x.–xiii. that it is difficult to think that both belong to one and the same letter.

οὐχ ὅτι. Elliptical for οὐ λέγω τοῦτο ὅτι. The ellipse is very intelligible, and seems to have been in common use; iii. 5, vii. 9; Phil. iii. 12, iv. 17; 2 Thess. iii. 9; etc. Winer, p. 746. 'Not that' is in common enough use in English.

κυριεύομεν. He includes his colleagues once more; *v.* 23 is purely personal. And he is perhaps once more glancing at the rival teachers who did try to domineer and dictate as to what the Corinthians must accept (xi. 20). 'Do not think that we are attempting anything of the kind. Our work is to awaken, to instruct, to entreat.' *Non quia dominatur fidei vestrae* (Vulg.); 'have dominion over' (AV.), 'have lordship over' (RV.). *Fides non necessitatis sed voluntatis est, dominatus necessitatis causa est. Fides per dilectionem operatur* (Gal. v. 6) *non per dominium cogitur* (Herveius). Faith must be free. What power, asks Chrysostom, can make an unconvinced man believe? All you can do is to make him say that he believes. With regard to faith, Apostles are not tyrants but ministers and stewards (see on 1 Cor.

iv. 1); they labour to help their flocks, not to oppress them,* The construction is not quite certain. 'Lord it over your faith is simple enough, but everywhere else in N.T. κυριεύειν has a gen. of the person (Rom. vi. 9, 14, vii. 1, xiv. 9; 1 Tim. vi. 15; Lk. xxii. 25), not of the thing, and here the meaning may be 'lord it over you,' τῆς πίστεως being added as an afterthought, either because he had been accused of undue pressure (see on 1 Cor. vii. 35, and comp. 2 Cor. x. 8, xiii. 10) in matters of faith, or because other teachers had used such pressure. In LXX such expressions as κυριεύειν τῆς θαλάσσης, τῆς γῆς, τῆς οἰκουμένης, are common enough (1 Es. iv. 15; Dan. ii. 39, iii. 2; etc.). Nevertheless, the position of ὑμῶν is in favour of its dependence on κυριεύομεν rather than on τῆς πίστεως, especially in contrast with τῆς χαρᾶς ὑμῶν. See critical note. Erasmus would supply ἕνεκα to govern τῆς πίστεως.

συνεργοί ἐσμεν. 'So far from being tyrants we are fellow-workers'—of course with the Corinthians. There is nothing in the context to suggest 'with God' or 'with Christ'; in 1 Cor. iii. 9, Θεοῦ is expressed; in LXX the word is very rare; in N.T. usually of St Paul's colleagues.†

τῆς χαρᾶς ὑμῶν. This comes rather as a surprise, for it forms no contrast with τῆς πίστεως, which might have been repeated. 'We do not force a creed upon you, but we help you in your quest of one.' But, as he goes on to state, they no longer need such help, for they have found the truth. Yet they have not reached the full happiness which the Gospel can give them (Gal. v. 22); their teachers can and do help them to greater *joy* in believing. It is the χαρὰ τῆς πίστεως (Phil. i. 25), the χαρὰ καὶ εἰρήνη ἐν τῷ πιστεύειν (Rom. xv. 13) that they labour with their converts to produce.‡ He mentions the χαρά of the Gospel in contrast to the λύπη which has to be mentioned (ii. 1) in connexion with his change of plans. See Chadwick, *The Pastoral Teaching of St Paul*, p. 175.

τῇ γὰρ πίστει ἑστήκατε. Not 'by faith' (AV., RV.), nor 'by your faith' (RV. marg.), but '*in* your faith.' In that sphere the position of the Corinthians was correct and firm, and κυριεύειν would have been altogether superfluous. It was not in their faith that they needed guidance and control, but it ought to

---

* *Fides enim prorsus ab hominum jugo soluta liberrimæque esse debet*, says Calvin. He goes on to remark that, if any man had a right to have dominion in matters of faith, it would be St Paul; yet he disclaims it. Whence Calvin infers that the only rule of faith is Scripture.

† St Paul uses συνεργός eleven or twelve times, 1 Thess. iii. 2 being doubtful; elsewhere only 3 Jn 8.

‡ "It is implied in this, that joy is the very end and element of the Christian life, and that it is the minister's duty to be at war with all that restrains it, and to co-operate in all that leads to it" (Denney).

have more influence on their lives. If the Gospel had its right effect among them, there would be no fear of λύπη either for them or for him. Some take the words as meaning that it is by faith that Christians have a secure foothold; but such a statement has no point here. St Paul is explaining why he has no wish to lord it over them as regards faith; it is because he is confident that they need nothing of the kind; their faith is sure. Could he afterwards, in the same letter, have written, 'Try your own selves whether ye be in the faith' (xiii. 5)? If that was written when they were disgracing the faith by rebellion, and 'in your faith you stand firm' was written after they had submitted, all becomes intelligible.

With the dat. here comp. τῷ σώματι καὶ τῷ πνεύματι (1 Cor. v. 34) and ταῖς φρεσίν (xiv. 20). Papyri yield examples; e.g. οὐκ ἔμενεν τῇ γενομένῃ μεσιτείᾳ. Bachmann would make it a *dativus ethicus*. For ἑστήκατε, see 1 Cor. xv. 1.

ὑμῶν τῆς πίστεως (‫א‬ A B C K L O P) rather than τ. πίστεως ὑμ. (D E F G), which is an unintelligent assimilation to τῆς χαρᾶς ὑμῶν. The difference of order has point.

II. 1. *Quisquis fuerit capitum divisor, fecit hic ineptam sectionem*, says Calvin with justice. The connexion with what goes before is very close. The Apostle is continuing his answer to the charge of levity. He had changed his plans in order to spare them. Having stated what he did not mean when he spoke of sparing them (i. 24), he now explains what that expression does mean.

ἔκρινα δὲ ἐμαυτῷ τοῦτο. It is not easy to decide whether δέ or γάρ is the right reading. External evidence seems to be somewhat in favour of δέ, but γάρ is more likely to have been changed to δέ than *vice versa*, and γάρ makes a good connexion; 'It was to spare you that I gave up the idea of another visit to Corinth, *for* I determined this for myself.' But another γάρ immediately after τῇ γὰρ πίστει ἑστήκατε is unpleasing and somewhat unlikely, and δέ makes quite a natural connexion, whether one renders it by 'and' or 'but.' 'It was to spare you, and⎫ but⎭ as regards myself, etc.' For ἔκρινα, see on 1 Cor. ii. 2 and vii. 37; in the latter passage we have, as here, τοῦτο pointing forward to what is coming. The verb at once excludes the idea of levity or caprice; he thought the matter over and came to a definite conclusion; cf. v. 14; also Rom. xiv. 13, where we have exactly the same construction as here, κρίνειν with an anticipatory τοῦτο, followed by τὸ μή with the infinite; ἀλλὰ τοῦτο κρίνατε μᾶλλον, τὸ μὴ τιθέναι πρόσκομμα τῷ ἀδελφῷ. In 1 Jn. τοῦτο commonly refers to what follows (iii. 1, 8, iv. 3); so also in

1 Cor. (i. 12, vii. 29, xv. 50). Ἐμαυτῷ is *dat. commodi* rather than *dat. ethicus*, which would have been μοι rather than ἐμαυτῷ. It was chiefly for their sakes that he postponed his visit; but he came to the conclusion that *for his own sake* he had better not have the pain. AV., following the Vulg., *statui autem hoc ipsum apud me*, has 'But I determined this *with* myself,' which would require παρ' ἐμαυτῷ or ἐν ἐμαυτῷ, a reading found in no text. And *ipsum* is in the wrong place; we should have *statui autem* (or *enim*) *mihi ipsi hoc.**

τὸ μὴ πάλιν ἐν λύπῃ πρὸς ὑμᾶς ἐλθεῖν. There is little doubt that this is the right order of the words; see below. The translation of them is disputed. Those who hold that xii. 14 and xiii. 1 compel us to believe that St Paul had already paid two visits to Corinth, translate, 'Not again in sorrow to come to you.' 'Again in sorrow' is to be taken together and is emphatic by position. He has had to come once in sorrow ; and if he visited them on his way to Macedonia, he would have again to come in sorrow. This he decided not to do. The distressing visit cannot refer to the long stay during which he converted them; therefore there must have been a second visit, which was probably short. See Introduction; also G. H. Rendall, p. 57. Among recent writers, "Is it not plain," says K. Lake, "that this passage (ii. 1–11) implies a recent visit which had ended so unpleasantly that St Paul had determined not to come back if he was likely to undergo similar experiences?" (*Earlier Epp.* p. 150).

On the other hand, those who think that the silence of Acts and the difficulty of fixing a time for this second visit are fatal to the supposition that it took place, translate thus, 'Not to come to you again (and this time) in sorrow,' or, 'Not at my second coming to come to you in sorrow.' He had paid them one very happy visit, and he would not revisit them in circumstances which must make the second visit a sad one. There is no need to determine whether λύπη means the sorrow which the Apostle must cause or that which he must feel : the context shows that he is thinking of both.

The AV. has 'heaviness' for λύπη here, with 'sorrow' in *v*. 3, ii. 7, vii. 10; Phil. ii. 27, etc. ; and 'sorrow' is used to translate other Greek words. Even the R.V. uses 'sorrow' for both λύπη (often) and ὀδύνη, which in Rom. ix. 2 it renders 'pain.'

B 17, 37, Syr-Hark. Copt. support γάρ : D*, Aeth. support τε : almost all others support δέ. T.R. with a few cursives reads πάλιν ἐλθεῖν ἐν λύπῃ. Nearly all authorities have πάλιν ἐν λύπῃ πρὸς ὑμᾶς ἐλθεῖν, but D E G, Syr. Pesh. have π. ἐν λ. ἐμθεῖν πρὸς ὑμᾶς. Copt. omits πάλιν and has ἐλθεῖν πρὸς ὑμᾶς ἐν λύπῃ.

* The Vulg. varies much in the translation of κρίνω : *statuo, aestimo, judicio subjicio*, and (most often) *judicio*.

2. εἰ γὰρ ἐγὼ λυπῶ ὑμᾶς κ.τ.λ. 'For if *I* (with emphasis) make you sorrowful, who then is he that maketh me glad, but he that is made sorrowful by me.' 'Sorry' and 'sorrowful' (vi. 10) are not synonymous, and the latter is what is meant here: see on *v.* 5. The καί makes the τίς emphatic and thus adds force to the question, 'Why, who is there to make me glad?' *Ja wo ist denn dann noch einer, der mich erfreute?* So Bachmann. The answer to this question is 'No one, for the only people who can cheer me have been made sad by me.' The καί accepts the previous statement, and the question shows what a paradox it involves; cf. *v.* 16; Mk. x. 26; Jn. ix. 36. See Winer, p. 545; Blass, § 77. 6. The singular ὁ εὐφραίνων, ὁ λυπούμενος, does not allude to any individual. The rhetorical τίς is necessarily singular, and thus the community is spoken of as an individual. The point is delicately put. 'You Corinthians are my fount of joy; how could I be the one to wish to trouble with sorrow the source whence I draw my own gladness?' But ὁ λυπούμενος does not refer to the penitent rebel who has been pained by the process of conversion; and *ad hoc vos contristo ut gaudeam de vobis* (Pseudo-Primasius) is certainly not the meaning of the verse. Ambrosiaster is far better; *ideo noluit ire, ne forte corripiens paucos multos contristaret, ipse etiam contristatus; compatiuntur enim omnia membra unius moerori.*

καὶ τίς without ἐστιν (‭א‬ A B C, Copt.): other authorities insert. It is probably not original.

3. ἔγραψα τοῦτο αὐτό. This may be accepted as the right reading (see below), but its meaning is not certain, for both ἔγραψα and τοῦτο αὐτό may be understood in more ways than one.

Is ἔγραψα a simple aorist referring to a previous letter? Or is it an epistolary aorist referring to the present letter? In other words, ought it to be translated 'I wrote' or 'I am writing'? It is not quite certain that there is anywhere in N.T. an instance of ἔγραψα as an epistolary aorist meaning 'I am writing,' although there are several cases which may be such. It is not such in vii. 12, or 1 Cor. v. 9, or 3 Jn. 9: in all three cases ἔγραψα refers to a previous letter. It may be an epistolary aorist in 1 Cor. ix. 15 (see note there), but more probably it refers to an earlier part of the letter (see on 1 Jn. ii. 21, 26); and this is clearly the meaning of προέγραψα in Eph. iii. 3. See Lightfoot on Gal. vi. 11, where ἔγραψα may mark the place where St Paul ceased to dictate and began to write himself; also on Philem. 19, where ἔγραψα seems to show that he wrote the whole letter with his own hand. Ἐγράψαμεν near the opening of the Martyrdom of Polycarp is a clear instance, and there are instances in papyri.

There is no doubt that ἔπεμψα is used in the sense of 'I am sending' in viii. 18, ix. 3; Phil. ii. 28; Philem. 12; and there is an interesting example in the papyrus letter quoted above (introd. to i. 3) from Apion to his father; ἔπεμψά σοι τὸ εἰκόνιν μου διὰ Εὐκτήμονος, "I am sending you by Euctemon the little portrait of me." *   Other examples might be quoted.

What is stated here and what is stated in vii. 8–12 show that ἔγραψα does not mean 'I am writing,' in reference to this part of 2 Cor.; it means 'I wrote,' in reference to some earlier letter. Like ἔκρινα in v. 1, ἔγραψα refers to what took place in the past; and it is possible that both aorists refer to the same period in the past.   In that case the meaning would be that, when he decided not to come to Corinth, he sent a letter instead of com ng.   That is thoroughly intelligible and natural, and we may regard as certain that ἔγραψα does not refer to 2 Cor. i.–ix. It is equally certain that it does not refer to 1 Cor.   The language of vi. 3, 4 and of vii. 8–12 has to be explained in an unnatural manner, or indeed has to be explained away (see below), in order to make it fit 1 Cor.

The meaning of τοῦτο αὐτό may be 'for this very reason.' That rendering is linguistically possible; see on 2 Pet. i. 5; Winer, p. 178; Blass, § 49.   But elsewhere (v. 5; Rom. ix. 17, xiii. 6.; Col. iv. 8) St Paul writes εἰς αὐτὸ τοῦτο to express this; and in v. 9; 1 Thess. iii. 3; 1 Tim iv. 10 we have εἰς τοῦτο with a similar meaning.   Nowhere else does St Paul use τοῦτο αὐτό or αὐτὸ τοῦτο, without εἰς, in the sense of 'for this reason,' and the probability is that it is not used in that sense here. 'This very thing' is the simpler and more probable rendering; and what precedes shows what 'this very thing' was,—viz. that to spare them he had given up the idea of coming, because he did not wish to pay a (second) painful visit, and was dealing with them by letter instead of coming.   It is quite possible that in these verses he is quoting his earlier letter, just as in 1 Cor. he sometimes quotes the Corinthians' letter; but we cannot detect the quotations with any certainty.   We may, however, feel sure that there was not only a letter from St Paul to Corinth before 1 Cor. (see on 1 Cor. v. 9), but also a letter between 1 Cor. and 2 Cor.†

That 2 Cor. x.–xiii. is part of the latter letter is a theory which here finds further confirmation (see on i. 23).   In xiii. 10

---

* In the frayed original only νιν is legible; and εἰκόνιν = εἰκόνιον is a better restoration than ὀθόνιν, which was an earlier conjecture.

† Wieseler thinks that these verses may refer to the letter of 1 Cor. v. 9, but they evidently refer to something more recent, and to the last letter which he had sent them.   As this cannot be 1 Cor., it must be a letter written later than 1 Cor

4

he says, 'For this cause when absent I write these things, that when present I may not deal sharply.' Here, with apparent reference to those very words, he says, 'I wrote this very thing that I might not by coming have sorrow.' It is natural that what he called 'dealing sharply' when they were in revolt, he should call 'having sorrow' now that they have submitted.

ἵνα μὴ ἐλθὼν λύπην σχῶ. 'In order that I might not by coming have sorrow.' He does not say ἵνα ἐλθὼν μὴ λ. σχῶ, 'that when I came I might not have sorrow.' AV. and RV. rather imply the latter reading.

ἀφ' ὧν ἔδει με χαίρειν. 'From the hands of those from whom I ought to have been rejoicing,' if he had come. They were his spiritual children who ought to be making him happy by following his wishes and example (see on 1 Cor. iv. 16).

πεποιθὼς ἐπὶ πάντας ὑμᾶς. 'Because I had reposed trust on you all.' Even when they were rebels he was confident that there was real sympathy with him, and that they would wish to please him. Confidens vos omnes intelligere, quia tunc verum gaudium habitis, si ego gaudeo (Pseudo-Primasius). In the fulness of his heart he expresses what he hopes rather than what he knows; μέγα τι οἰκονομῶν (Chrys.). For the construction cf. οἱ πεποιθότες ἐπὶ Κύριον (Ps. cxxv. 1); also 2 Thess. iii. 4. Contrast i. 9, x. 7; Philem. 21, where we have the more classical dative.

ἔγραψα without ὑμῖν (א A B C O P 17, Am. Copt., Ambst.): other authorities insert. C O, Chrys. have αὐτὸ τοῦτο: A, Copt. Arm. omit αὐτό: other authorities have τοῦτο αὐτό, which D E F G, Latt. Goth., Aeth. place before ἔγραψα. D F, Latt. insert ἐπὶ λύπην after λύπην. σχῶ (א* A B O P, Chrys.) rather than ἔχω (א³ C D E F G K L); cf. i. 15; Rom. i. 13; Phil. ii. 27.

4. ἐκ γὰρ πολλῆς θλίψεως . . . διὰ πολλῶν δακρύων. These strong words, expressive of deep emotion and intense distress, are quite in place, if they refer to a letter of which x.–xiii. formed a chief part. That passionate outburst of feeling might well have been written in 'deep affliction and anguish of heart amid a flood of tears.' But, as a description of the state of his mind when he wrote 1 Cor., the language is extravagant.* It might apply to the short section about the incestuous person, but that is only a fragment of the Epistle; and nowhere in the range of his extant letters can we find any considerable portion to which this statement would so fitly apply as to x.–xiii.

It is interesting and instructive to compare the Apostle's description of his own condition during the writing of this vindication of his own authority with J. H. Newman's statements

* " These words cannot be referred to our first canonical Epistle, and no more characterise its general tone than what he says about his second visit describes his first mission " (Orello Cone, *Paul*, p. 121).

respecting himself, while he was writing the marvellous *Apologia
pro Vita sua* in the spring of 1864. He wrote to Sir F.
Rogers on April 22 ; " During the writing and reading of my Part 3 I
could not get from beginning to end for crying." He wrote to
Mr. Hope-Scott on May 2 ; " I have been writing without inter-
ruption of Sundays five weeks. I have been constantly in tears,
and constantly crying out with distress."

The Apostle's statement explains (γάρ) how it came about
that one whose function it was to be a 'helper of their joy'
(i. 24) should write a letter which was sure to cause great sorrow.
That incongruity was only too keenly felt by the writer, and it
caused *him* intense distress. Yet the object of the letter was
not to spare himself and inflict pain on them, but to prove the
reality of his affection. He had had more than enough of λύπη.

The change from ἐκ to διά has significance. It was out of a
condition of affliction that the letter was written, and it passed
through a flood of tears. We should more naturally say 'amid
many tears.' There is a similar change from ἐκ to διά in Rom.
ii. 27 : for διά of "attendant circumstances," cf. Rom. iv. 11,
viii. 25, xiv. 20. Both πολλῆς and καρδίας may be taken with
both substantives ; ' out of much affliction of heart and much
anguish of heart.' In class. Grk. συνοχή is nearly always literal,
of actual contraction, junction or check. It occurs Lk. xxi. 25
and nowhere else in N.T. In LXX it occurs Judg. ii. 3 ; Job
xxx. 3 ; Jer. lii. 5 ; Mic. v. 1 (iv. 14), with a variety of meanings.
Jerome's carelessness in revision is seen again in his rendering of
the word. In Lk. 23, 25 he has *pressura* for both ἀνάγκη and
συνοχή, although Lat. Vet. distinguishes with *compressio* and
necessitas, and here he has *angustia* for συνοχή.

In his speech to the Ephesian elders at Miletus, St Paul
twice mentions his frequent tears (Acts xx. 19, 31). One may
call it softness, as Calvin remarks, but it is more worthy of a
hero than *illa ferrea durities Stoicorum* would have been. The
Apostle was no Stoic, and for him the suppression of all emotion
was no road to perfection. The sympathy which he felt he
showed, with utter disregard for Stoical ἀπάθεια and ἠρεμία, and
Epicurean ἀταραξία : ἄλογος καὶ παρὰ φύσιν ψυχῆς κίνησις is a
doctrine to which he could never subscribe.

ἀλλὰ τὴν ἀγάπην ἵνα γνῶτε. Placing τ. ἀγάπην in front of ἵνα
throws great emphasis on the word ; cf. τῶν πτωχῶν ἵνα
μνημονεύωμεν (Gal. ii. 10). He could have spared himself the
pain of writing such a letter ; he could have come at once and
used severity, without giving them time to return to their obedience : but his love for them would not allow him to do either.
As Chrys. points out, the run of the sentence requires 'not that
you should be made sorrowful, but that *you should be induced to*

repent.' Instead of this he substitutes 'that you should know the exceptional love which I have for you.' It was affection, not cold or cruel severity which made him write. He bears 'Corinth' written on his heart; i. 12, iii. 2, xii. 15; 1 Cor. iv. 15, ix. 2: καταγλυκαίνει τὸν λόγον βουλόμενος ἐπισπάσασθαι αὐτούς (Theophyl.). That ἀγάπη is not a word of Biblical origin has been shown by Deissmann (*Bible Studies*, p. 199). It has been found in Egypt in papyri of the Ptolemaic period.

II. 5-17. The Treatment of the Great Offender and the Result of the Severe Letter.

The offender ought now to be freely forgiven. And for the intense relief caused by the report of you brought by Titus I thank God who does not allow ministers that work in sincerity to fail.

⁵ As regards him who has been the cause of the sorrow, it is not so much to me that he has caused it (I do not wish to be considered at all) as to all of you; and perhaps not to all of you, for there may be exceptions, and I do not wish to be hard upon any one. ⁶ I think, therefore, that the punishment which was inflicted by the majority is sufficient in the circumstances, and those who thought it inadequate need not insist upon anything more; ⁷ on the contrary, you may now turn round and forgive and encourage him. ⁸ If you fail to do this, a person in his circumstances may sink down in despair in the excess of his grief. I therefore implore you to leave him no longer in suspense, but at once, by some formal act, put into execution, not any sentence of further punishment, but the renewal of your love for him. ⁹ This request that you should forgive him is not at all inconsistent with the letter which I sent instead of coming, for I wrote that letter, not so much in order to be severe on him, as to have a sure test whether in all respects you are prepared to obey me. ¹⁰ You have proved your loyalty by punishing where punishment was due; but now, if you decide to forgive, you may rest assured that I agree with that decision; for—and this is one more point—if there has been anything for me to forgive, it is for your sakes that I have forgiven it, not thoughtlessly, but as in the presence of Christ. ¹¹ Satan is always on the watch to get an advantage over us. He did get an advantage when he

caused this member of our body to sin so grievously.   Are we to
let him have another advantage—over a sinner that has repented ?

¹² My disturbing anxiety about you is now removed ; but it
was so intense that, although, when I came to Troas to preach
the Gospel, God gave me openings there which were very
favourable, ¹³ yet I could not settle to any fruitful work, because
Titus, who was to bring me news of you, was not to be found
there.   In my eagerness to learn what success he had had among
you I said good-bye to Troas and went on to Macedonia to
meet him the sooner.   ¹⁴ But, God be thanked, all has turned
out for the best.   God, as always, led us along in His triumphal
train with Christ, using us as His instruments to diffuse the
sweet odour of His Gospel in every place.   ¹⁵ For it is of the
fragrance of Christ that we ourselves are a sweet savour to God
among both those who are in the way to deliverance and those
who are in the way to destruction, ¹⁶ to the one being a savour
exhaled from death and breathing death, to the other a savour
exhaled from life and breathing life.   It is an awful charge, and
what ministers are competent to undertake it ?   ¹⁷ Some are not,
but by God's grace we are.   For, unlike most teachers, we are
not men who for their own ends corrupt God's message.   No ;
with sincerity in our hearts, nay with God in our hearts, and
with His eye upon us, as befits those who are members of Christ,
we deliver our message.

5-11.   This paragraph about the great offender is not really
a digression (Meyer), and the fact that we should have a good
sequence of thought if it were omitted does not prove it to be a
digression.   It is part, and not on unimportant part, of St Paul's
vindication of himself.   The Corinthians' chief grievance was
his sending them a severe letter instead of coming to them for
the long and happy visit indicated in I Cor. xvi. 5–7.   But there
was also the treatment of the ringleader against Apostolic
authority.   The majority censured him in a way which some
thought inadequate.   The Apostle assures them that the action
of the Church in condemning the offender satisfies the requirements, all the more so as the person condemned is very penitent.
He assures them that he is more than ready to join in their
formal restoration of the man to favour ; and there is now no
bar to his coming.

We are ignorant as to the exact nature of the penalty which was inflicted by the majority, but apparently it was not that which St Paul was believed to require. Possibly it was that suggested in 1 Cor. v. 11, τῷ τοιούτῳ μηδὲ συνεσθίειν, as also in 2 Thess. iii. 14, μὴ συναναμίγνυσθαι αὐτῷ, ἵνα ἐντραπῇ, where we have the important addition, καὶ μὴ ὡς ἐχθρὸν ἡγεῖσθε, ἀλλὰ νουθετεῖτε ὡς ἀδελφόν. In accordance with this addition, the Apostle now pleads earnestly for a generous forgiveness. Punishment had been inflicted in order to rescue him from perdition by inducing him to repent; and he had repented. If punishment were continued, it might drive him to perdition by making him desperate.

We are ignorant also as to who this offender was and as to what was the exact nature of his offence. But "it should no longer require to be proved that this offender is not the incestuous person of 1 Cor. v. 1, but some one who had wronged Paul himself" (Moffatt, *Int. to the Literature of the N.T.*, p. 122). This theory is still advocated by Zahn (1909), McFadyen (1911), and others, and therefore it is necessary to point out once more how untenable it is. Tertullian's vigorous argument almost suffices without any others (*De Pudic.* 13). After quoting this passage (5–11) he asks whether the Apostle could possibly have written in this effusively indulgent way about a man who had been guilty of fornication aggravated by incest, and this without one word of severity about the past or warning about the future.* We must remember that, if the offender here is the incestuous person of 1 Cor. v. 1, then the incest was of a specially monstrous character, for the sinful union was contracted in the lifetime of the man's father. This passage and vii. 12 refer to the same case, and there, if ὁ ἀδικήσας is the incestuous son, ὁ ἀδικηθείς must be the woman's injured husband, who was still alive when St Paul wrote.† This adds immense force to Tertullian's question. Moreover, it is unlikely that St Paul would view such a sin simply as an injury inflicted by one man on another.

---

* The omission is all the more astonishing when we remember that St Paul had ordered that the offender should be handed over to Satan, and that (on this hypothesis) the sentence had not been executed.

† McFadyen is inconsistent. On 1 Cor. v. 1 he says that it is uncertain whether the father was dead when the son took his father's wife; on 2 Cor. vii. 12 he assumes that the father was alive when the son formed this revolting union.

When he treats of incest in 1 Cor., it is the *infection of the whole Church* upon which he enlarges (v. 6, 7, 11, 13). Lastly, it is incredible that St Paul would say (*v.* 9) that he had insisted upon the punishment of so grievous a sin, merely to test the Corinthians, whether they were ready to obey him in all things.

If ὁ ἀδικηθείς is the Apostle himself, the language used here and in vii. 12 is quite natural. This man had grossly wronged St Paul, but the particulars are unknown to us.* Of such an offender St Paul might reasonably say that he had demanded his punishment to test the loyalty of his converts. This man had insulted and defied him. The personal affront St Paul could treat as nothing, but he could not allow his authority to be defied. The man must be punished, and punished by the community; that would test their loyalty. If this was done, the amount of punishment was of comparatively small importance; and when the man had expressed contrition, prolongation of his punishment would do more harm than good. On this interpretation, everything falls into its place. From a feeling of delicacy, St Paul uses indefinite language; it sufficed to tell the Corinthians what he meant, but it does not suffice to tell us.†

5. Εἰ δέ τις. The indefiniteness begins at once. 'But if any one has caused sorrow, it is not to me that he has caused it.' The personal element is brushed on one side at once; the injury to the Church, whose members are members of Christ, is what matters. The argument that we have here a τις and a τοιοῦτος (*v.* 6) and Σατανᾶς (*v.* 11), and that in 1 Cor. v. we have also a τις (*v.* 1) and a τοιοῦτος (*v.* 5) and Σατανᾶς (*v.* 5), and that therefore this passage refers to the same case as that, is very shallow. In every sinful πρᾶγμα (vii. 11) there is a τις and a τοιοῦτος, with Satan at work also. The use of τοιοῦτος in

---

* *Es muss sich hier um eine schwere persönliche Kränkung des Paulus und um einen persönlichen Beleidiger handeln* (Bousset, p. 175). See also Hastings, *DB.* i. p. 493; *Enc. Bibl.* i. 902; G. H. Rendall, p. 61; Schmiedel, p. 221. Bleek, Hilgenfeld, Ewald, Godet, Bachmann, Lietzmann and others take a similar view: the offence was a personal attack on St Paul.

† Krenkel's suggestion that the offender had wronged a fellow-Christian in a matter of property has found little support. It is more probable than the supposed reference to 1 Cor. v. 1; but the only reasonable hypothesis is that the ἀδικία was against St Paul himself. Against Timothy is not impossible, but it is improbable.

the two places is different. In the other case St Paul refuses
to stain his letter with the name of such a transgressor, and
perhaps intimates that any one who transgresses in a like manner
will receive the like punishment. In this case, he refrains from
naming him out of consideration for the offender's feelings, whose
case he states hypothetically; '*if* there is such a person': in
v. 10, vii. 14, x. 7 we have a similar use of εἰ. So also there is
difference in the way in which Satan is introduced in each
case. There he was made the instrument of chastisement;
here he is to be guarded against as a crafty enemy.

ἀλλὰ ἀπὸ μέρους (ἵνα μὴ ἐπιβαρῶ) πάντας ὑμᾶς. This is the
best arrangement of a sentence which has suffered by being
dictated; 'He hath caused sorrow, not to me, but in part (that
I press not too heavily) to you all.' So RV. and others. He
does not wish to be severe, but it is really the whole Corinthian
Church that has been troubled by this man's ἀδικία. A qualifying
ἀπὸ μέρους is inserted, because there were a few who were not
distressed by the scandalous treatment of the Apostle.

It is possible, with Mosheim, Olshausen, and others, to
include πάντας in the parenthesis and make it the acc. after
ἐπιβαρῶ, 'that I press not too heavily upon all.' But this gives
a weak position to πάντας, and leaves ὑμᾶς awkwardly alone
after the parenthesis. If πάντας is taken with ὑμᾶς, we have a
pointed and almost necessary antithesis to ἐμέ, 'not me but all
of you.'

The AV. rendering, 'He hath not grieved me but in part:
that I may not overcharge you all,' follows Tertullian, Vulgate,
Luther and others, but it cannot stand, for ἀλλά does not mean
'except' (Mk. x. 40), and St Paul is not urging that he has
been distressed even 'in part'; he is dismissing the personal
affront altogether. It is not quite certain whether ἀπὸ μέρους
means that not quite all the Corinthians had been distressed, or
that all of them had been distressed to some extent; but the
former is much more probable as being more true, and this is
an additional objection to the rendering in AV. B. Weiss
understands ἀπὸ μέρους as limiting the action of the λελυπηκώς:
the offender was only partly the cause of the Corinthians' grief;
the other part was caused by the Apostle's severe letter. Hofmann gives ἀπὸ μέρους the highly improbable meaning of 'for
a time,' and with perverted ingenuity makes the first part of the
verse interrogative; 'If any one has caused sorrow, is it not to
me that he has caused it?' The answer to this question is,
'Yes; nevertheless, *for a time* (that I may not press too heavily
on you all) sufficient to such a one, etc.' This is a very clumsy
construction, and—what is far more serious—it destroys the
tact and delicacy of the Apostle's appeal by laying the whole

emphasis on the personal injury to himself—the thing about which he desires to say as little as possible.*

In Biblical Greek, ἐπιβαρεῖν is peculiar to Paul, who always uses it in a metaphorical sense (1 Thess. ii. 9; 2 Thess. iii. 8) and with the acc. Appian has it several times, always with the dat. (examples in Wetstein); and it is found in inscriptions. Cf. καταβαρεῖν, xii. 16. On the whole verse see Stanley and Alford.

6. ἱκανὸν τῷ τοιούτῳ ἡ ἐπιτιμία αὕτη. 'A sufficient thing for such a person is this punishment.' We may understand ἔστω, but ἐστιν is more probable. This substantival use of the neuter adjective accompanied by a feminine substantive is found elsewhere; ἀρκετὸν τῇ ἡμέρᾳ ἡ κακία αὐτῆς (Mt. vi. 34); ἀρεστόν ἐστιν τοῖς Ἰουδαίοις ἡ ἐπιχείρησις αὐτοῦ (the reading of D and other authorities, Acts xii. 3); ἡ ψυχὴ πλεῖόν ἐστιν τῆς τροφῆς (Lk. xii. 23). Blass, § 31. 2, quotes also ἱκανόν ἐστιν (Lk. xxii. 38), but the meaning there is, 'Enough of this subject,' not, 'two swords are a sufficient thing.' There is perhaps a slight difference of meaning between ἱκανόν and ἱκανή. The latter would mean that the existing ἐπιτιμία need not be prolonged. The former means that no additional penalty need be imposed. But this cannot be insisted on.† The meaning here is that 'the punishment is a sufficient thing.' It is not said that it is adequate to the offence, but that it satisfies the requirements of the case.‡ Apostolic authority has been defied, and the Church, acting through the majority, has censured the offender. Nothing further is necessary.

In Wisd. iii. 10 we have οἱ δὲ ἀσεβεῖς καθ᾽ ἃ ἐλογίσαντο ἔξουσιν ἐπιτιμίαν, but nowhere else in Bibl. Grk. does ἐπιτιμία occur. In Attic Grk. it means 'possession of political rights,' 'citizenship.' The transition to 'punishment' is curious, the intermediate step being 'getting one's due': the citizen gets his due, and the criminal gets his. Cf. the Biblical use of ἐπιτιμᾶν = 'rebuke, censure severely,' and the classical use of τὸ ἐπιτίμιον = 'legal penalty.' The Latin renderings of ἐπιτιμία vary; increpatio (Tert.), correptio (Aug.), objurgatio (Vulg.); in Wisd. iii. 10, Vulg. has correptio. It is possible that both ἱκανόν and ἐπιτιμία are forensic terms. In 2 Thess. i. 9 St Paul has δίκη = 'punishment,' a word of somewhat similar history, passing from

---

* If the offender were the incestuous man, could St Paul have said, 'He has not pained me at all'? For the moral of these words see Chadwick, *The Pastoral Teaching of St. Paul,* p. 239.

† Bachmann quotes what Zeus says about the parasites (Lucian, *Timon,* 10), ἱκανὴ καὶ αὕτη τιμωρία ἔσται αὐτοῖς, viz. that of seeing Timon rolling in money, which tells against the supposed distinction.

‡ *Sufficiens non quantum ad Dei judicium, sed quantum expediebat tempori.*

'customary rights,' through 'legal action' to 'penalty.' 'Punish'
and 'punishment' are freq. in O.T., but not so in N.T.
ἡ ὑπὸ τῶν πλειόνων. 'Which was inflicted by the many' (RV.)
or 'by the majority,' rather than 'by many' (AV.). A similar
correction should be made iv. 15, ix. 2 ; 1 Cor. x. 5 ; Phil. i. 14 ;
cf. 1 Cor. xv. 6. It may be lawful to translate οἱ πλείονες 'many'
or even 'several' (Blass, § 44. 4), but in this and other places in
N.T. 'the many' or 'the majority' is probably right. They
are contrasted with a minority who did not concur in what was
done by οἱ πλείονες, and it is often assumed that this minority
opposed the infliction of the ἐπιτιμία as being excessive, or as
being altogether undeserved. Those who hold this view remind
us that there was an anti-Pauline party at Corinth which would
be sure to refuse to punish a man whose only offence was that
of having defied St Paul. But there is no hint that this
minority had been patronizing a rebel. St Paul tells them that
'*contrariwise* they should rather forgive' the rebel, which implies
that hitherto they had refused to forgive him. It is more likely
that the minority were the Paul party (1 Cor. i. 12, 13), who
thought that one who defied the Apostle ought to be much more
severely punished ; and it is this minority whom he is specially
addressing. Kennedy, *Second and Third Corinthians*, pp. 100 f. ;
Lake, *Earlier Epistles*, p. 171.

7. ὥστε τοὐναντίον μᾶλλον κ.τ.λ. 'So that on the contrary
you may rather forgive him fully and comfort him.' The ὥστε
gives the natural consequence of the view that the penalty
which has been imposed satisfies the requirements. So far
from imposing anything more, they may put an end to what
has been imposed. He is not telling them what they *must* do ;
there is no δεῖν. He tactfully points out the logical consequence
of admitting the ἱκανόν, and leaves them to act upon it. The
μᾶλλον is probably genuine (see below), and it indicates that
there were still some who felt that the punishment was insufficient.
For χαρίσασθαι, which implies making the man a present of the
remainder of the penalty,* and forgiving him absolutely, cf. xii.
13 ; Lk. vii. 42, 43 ; Col. ii. 13, iii. 13 ; Eph. iv. 32.

μή πως τῇ περισσοτέρᾳ λύπῃ καταποθῇ ὁ τ. 'Lest by any
means such a one should be swallowed up by his overmuch
sorrow.' Neither here nor ix. 4 nor xii. 20 does the AV. give
the right force to μή πως : it does so 1 Cor. ix. 27 ; Gal. ii. 2.
Various conjectures are made as to what the Apostle feared

---

* Vulg. here and elsewhere uses *donare* to translate χαρίζεσθαι, and
donare may mean 'to forgive' ; *culpa gravis precibus donatur saepe suorum*
(Ov. *Pont.* II. vii. 51). The idea that an offence involves a debt to be wiped
out by punishment lies at the back of such language.

might be the result; apostasy, reckless indulgence in sin, suicide. It is more important to notice that this implies that the man had already repented; he was no longer rebellious; and *vera poenitentia est jam cessare a peccato* (Herveius). Evidently, his grief was already great, and there was danger of his despairing of being restored to favour in Christian society. For καταπίνειν in the metaphorical sense cf. v. 4; 1 Cor. xv. 54; 1 Pet. v. 8. It is freq. in LXX. The 'swallowing,' as Chrys. says, may be ὡς ἐπὶ θηρίου, ὡς ἐπὶ χειμῶνος, ὡς ἐπὶ κλύδωνος. In the Ep. of the Churches of Lugdunum and Vienna those who had apostatized are said to have been swallowed by the Beast, ἵνα ἀποπνιχθεὶς ὁ θήρ, οὓς πρότερον ᾤετο καταπεπωκέναι, ζῶντας ἐξεμέσῃ (Eus. *H.E.* v. ii. 6). The rather superfluous repetition of ὁ τοιοῦτος at the end of the sentence gives a touch of compassion, enforcing the plea. *Locus diligenter observandus*, says Calvin; *docet enim qua aequitate et clementia temperanda sit disciplina Ecclesiae, ne rigor modum excedat. Severitate opus est ne impunitate (quae peccandi illecebra merito vocatur) mali reddantur audaciores. Sed rursus, quia periculum est, ne is qui castigatur animum despondeat, hic adhibenda est moderatio; nempe ut Ecclesia simulatque resipiscentiam illius certo cognoverit, ad dandam veniam sit parata.* He goes on to contrast the cruel sentences of the penitential system. The comment is remarkable as coming from so rigorous a disciplinarian.

H. C. Lea points out that in the Roman Catholic version of the N.T. there is a note appended to this text explaining that "the Apostle here granted an indulgence or pardon in the person and by the authority of Christ to the incestuous Corinthian whom he had put under penance, which pardon consisted in a releasing of part of the temporal punishment due to sin." This, says Lea, is "a typical instance of the facility with which men read into Scripture whatever they desire to find there" (*Hist. of Auricular Confession and Indulgences*, iii. p. 5).*

A B, Syr-Pesh., Aug. omit μᾶλλον, which is found before ὑμᾶς in אC K L O P, Syr-Hark. Vulg. Copt. Arm., Chrys. Ambrst. and after ὑμᾶς in D E F G 17, Goth., Thdrt. Tert.

8. διὸ παρακαλῶ ὑμᾶς. He does not invoke his Apostolic authority and command the forgiveness; as an equal he entreats them to grant it. The community had selected and enforced the penalty, whatever it may have been, and he leaves to them the removal of it. He respects the democratic feeling of the

---

* Until the Reformation it was not seriously disputed that indulgences were comparatively modern. But the Council of Trent (Sess. xxv.) declared them to have been used *antiquissimis temporibus*, and this view is authoritatively upheld.

Corinthian Church, and he respects the spirit of the Lord's
commission to the whole Church. " It is a fact of the highest
importance and clearly established by the documents, that the
commission given on the evening of the first Easter Day—the
'Great Commission '—was given to the Church and not to any
class in the Church—to the whole Church and not to any part of
it, primarily. ' Receive ye the Holy Ghost; whosoever sins ye
forgive, they are forgiven unto them ; whosoever sins ye retain,
they are retained' (Jn. xx. 22 f.). The words are the Charter of
the Christian Church, and not simply the Charter of the Christian
Ministry " (Westcott, *Ephesians*, pp. 169 f.). On that first Easter
evening, not all the Apostles were present, and others were
present who were not Apostles. The commission, in the first
instance, was to the community as a whole. The Apostle here
makes his appeal to the whole community, and not to any class
of officials, and he leaves the community free to act. The
change of meaning from παρακάλεσαι, 'to comfort' (*v.* 7), to
παρακαλῶ, ' I beseech ' (*v.* 8), should be noted : see on i. 4.

παρακαλῶ ὑμᾶς κυρῶσαι εἰς αὐτὸν ἀγάπην. *Oro vos, constitu-
atis in eum dilectionem* (Tert.). *Obsecro vos, ut confirmetis in
illum caritatem* (Vulg.). The differences are characteristic, and
constituo is perhaps better than *confirmo*, in the sense of ' make
effective ' ; we have *constituere libertatem, victoriam, pacem, con-
cordiam fidem*, etc. We need not suppose that κυρῶσαι implies
that a formal resolution, rescinding the previous sentence, is to
be passed, any more than ' ratify' would imply that in English.
What the Apostle cares about is the change from censure to
affection ; the way in which the affection is to be made effective
he leaves to them. What it is that they are to ratify is kept with
effect to the last. Comp. Lk. xiv. 18, where παραιτεῖσθαι comes
as a surprise at the end ; one would have expected just the
opposite. At Corinth there were some who wished for a more
severe punishment on the offender than censure and separation.
The Apostle says, Ἐνώσατε τὸ μέλος τῷ σώματι, συνάψατε τῇ ποίμνῃ
τὸ πρόβατον, θερμὴν αὐτῷ διάθεσιν δείξατε· προσήκει γὰρ ὑμᾶς μὴ
μόνον τέμνοντι συνεργεῖν ἀλλὰ καὶ συνάπτοντι (Thdrt.). With
κυρῶσαι εἰς αὐτὸν ἀγάπην comp. ἐκυρώθη ὁ ἀγρὸς τῷ Ἀβραάμ
(Gen. xxiii. 20). In papyri (Oxyrh. 513, 4) ἐκυρώθην οἰκίαν.
Thuc. VIII. lxix. 1, ἡ ἐκκλησία κυρώσασα ταῦτα διελύθη.

9. εἰς τοῦτο γὰρ καὶ ἔγραψα. 'For it was just for this that I
also wrote ' ; the 'just' marks the emphasis on εἰς τοῦτο, which
looks forward to ἵνα γνῶ. As in *v.* 3, ἔγραψα refers to the letter
between 1 Cor. and 2 Cor., of which 2 Cor. x.–xiii. is probably a
part. The καί marks the agreement of this letter with that, not
of this letter with what he had said, or of this passage with the

earlier part of this letter.   And we must not translate as if we had καὶ γὰρ εἰς τοῦτο.   The proof of you, *i.e.* he wished to have them tested ; *ut cognoscam probationem vestram* (Tert.), which is better than *ut cognoscam experimentum vestrum* (Vulg.).   In ii. 9, viii. 2, xiii. 3, Vulg. has *experimentum* for δοκιμή, as also in Phil. ii. 22 ; but in ix. 13 and Rom. v. 4 it has *probatio*.   AV. has 'experience,' 'experiment,' 'trial,' and 'proof,' but without following Vulg. in its changes.

εἰ εἰς πάντα ὑπήκοοί ἐστε.   'Whether in all respects ye are obedient,' 'whether to every call of duty you lend your ear.' They were not to be obedient just so far as the claims made on them pleased them.   The ἐστέ implies that the proof was satisfactory ; they are obedient in all points ; cf. ἐστε ἄζυμοι (1 Cor. v. 7).   Here, as in vii. 12, St Paul seems to be interpreting his original intention in writing the letter by the light of the actual results of the letter.

The reading ᾗ for εἰ may possibly be right;* it refers to δοκιμήν, 'the proof *whereby* ye are, etc.'   This would strengthen the ἐστέ in indicating that they are found to be perfectly obedient. St Paul does not say, and perhaps does not mean, that they are obedient to *himself* : rather, they are obedient to the principles of the Gospel.

Once more we have considerable confirmation of the theory that x.–xiii. is part of the severe letter to which allusion is made by ἔγραψα here and in *v.* 3.   In x. 6 he says, 'Being in readiness to avenge all disobedience when your obedience shall be fulfilled ' ; here he says, 'For it was just for this that I also wrote, that I might know the proof of you, whether you are obedient in all things.'   As in *v.* 3 and i. 23, he here writes in the past tense of the same thing as that of which in x.–xiii. he writes in the present tense.   It is quite natural that in the previous letter written in severity, he should speak of 'avenging disobedience,' and that in this letter of reconciliation he should omit all allusion to such a possibility.   That within the compass of a dozen verses we should have three close parallels between i.–ix. and x.–xiii., and all of the same character, make a case of considerable strength.   And we shall find other facts pointing in the same direction.

A B 17 have ᾗ, other authorities εἰ.   Cf. Heb. vi. 14, where εἰ μήν has been corrupted to ἢ μήν.

10.   ᾧ δέ τι χαρίζεσθε, κἀγώ.   They had joined with him in condemning ; he joins with them in forgiving.   They had shown

* The corruption of η to ει occurs elsewhere ; ἀρέσῃ to ἀρέσει (1 Cor. vii. 32).

obedience in consenting to censure ; let them now be sure of
his consent if they desire to give love instead of blame. The
Apostle is not promising always to follow their lead in exercising
leniency : although the statement is general, it is manifestly
limited to the particular case ; and with regard to that he is not
acting in the dark. He has the report of his official representative Titus to guide him, and that made it clear to him that
generous treatment of the offender would do a great deal of good
and little or no harm.

και γὰρ ἐγὼ ὃ κεχάρισμαι. *Here* we have και γάρ (contrast
v. 9), introducing an additional reason, and ἐγώ is emphatic ;
' For also what *I* have forgiven,' I on my side as distinct from
you. AV. is faulty in turning the perfects into aorists.

εἴ τι κεχάρισμαι. A gracious parenthesis ; ' if I have forgiven
anything,' *i.e.* ' if I have had anything to forgive.' He is not suggesting a doubt as to whether he has granted forgiveness, but he
puts the fact of there being something for him to forgive as a
mere hypothesis. The hypothetical statement is exactly parallel to
εἴ τις λελύπηκεν : ' if there is such person, he has received forgiveness so far as I am concerned.' Some would translate, ' what I
have been forgiven, if I have been forgiven anything,' which is
grammatically possible, but it spoils the appeal, and is out of
harmony with δι' ὑμᾶς ἐν προσώπῳ Χρ. St Paul is not thinking of
the Corinthians' change of attitude towards himself, but of his
own towards the offender and them. It is ' for their sakes '
that he has so entirely blotted out the thought of the man's
offence. Their relation towards the offender has been a painful
one, but it need not continue ; let it be changed for a happy
one.

ἐν προσώπῳ Χριστοῦ. 'In the presence of Christ' ; *in facie
Christi,* or *in conspectu Christi* (Calv.) ; ὡς τοῦ Χριστοῦ ἐφορῶντος
και ἀρεσκομένου τοῖς γενομένοις (Thdrt.). Cf. εὐφραινόμην ἐν
προσώπῳ αὐτοῦ ἐν παντὶ καιρῷ (Prov. viii. 30). This is more
probable than ' in the person of Christ ' (AV., RV.) ; *in persona
Christi* (Vulg.), *an Christi Statt* (Luth.), or ' unto the glory of
Christ' (Chrys.). See on i. 11. But, however we may translate
the expression, the purpose of it is to correct a possible misunderstanding of δι' ὑμᾶς. Although it was for their sakes that
he acted as he did, yet he remembered whose eye was upon him
to approve or condemn his action.

κἀγώ (אᵃ*A B C² D E O P) rather than και ἐγώ (א³ C* F G K L), as
in most places where such crasis is possible. ὃ κεχ. εἴ τι κεχ. (א A B C F G O)
rather than εἴ τι κεχ. ᾧ κεχ. (D² K L 17). Baljon suggests that εἴ τι κεχ.
is a gloss. It would be a very clever gloss,—subtly Pauline. As in the
case of i. 6, 7, there is difference of opinion about the division of the verses.
Some editors assign ἵνα μὴ . . . Σατανᾶ to *v.* 10.

11. ἵνα μὴ πλεονεκτηθῶμεν ὑπὸ τ. Σατ.   'To prevent our being overreached by Satan.' The man is penitent and is freeing himself from Satan ; what a grievous error to aid Satan in getting control over him again ! Chrys. remarks that the Apostle is quite right in speaking of the πλεονεξία of Satan, of his getting more than his due. That Satan should take man by sin is proper to him, but that he should do so through man's repentance is too much, for repentance is our weapon, not his. Vulg. has *ut non circumveniamur a Satana*,* which is not so good as *ne fraudemur* (Tert.), but better than *ne possideamur* (Aug. Ambrst.). The verse explains the δι' ὑμᾶς. It was to the Corinthians' advantage and the Apostle's as well (his including himself in this gain is a delicate touch) that Satan should not be allowed to gain through a Christian's penitence : *debemus cavere ne remedium nostrum fiat ejus triumphus* (Ambrose). Nowhere else in Bibl. Grk. is the passive of πλεονεκτεῖν found. In LXX the verb is rare ; in N.T. both πλεονεκτεῖν and πλεονέκτης are peculiar to Paul. The 'us' or 'we' means the Church as a whole, not the Apostle.

οὐ γὰρ αὐτοῦ τὰ νοήματα ἀγνοοῦμεν. This is probably an intentional play upon words, but it can hardly be imitated in English ; 'for we are not unwitting of his wiles' : *non ignoramus astutias ejus*. This is the rendering of Pseudo-Cypr. (*De sing. cler.* 19) and of Ambrst. Sedulius has *versutias* ; Tert. *injectiones*. Vulg. is very capricious in its translation of νοήματα, a word which in N.T. is almost peculiar to 2 Cor., in which it always has a bad sense. Here it has *cogitationes*, in iii. 14 (with Cypr. *Test.* i. 4) and in xi. 3 it has *sensus*, in iv. 4 *mentes*, in x. 5 *intellectum* (sing.), and in Phil. iv. 7 *intelligentias*. Chrys. gives a variety of expressions to represent τὰ νοήματα, all of them pointing to the wiliness of the evil one ; τὸ δολερόν, τὸ κακομήχανον, τὸ ποικίλον, τὸ ἐπὶ προσχήματι εὐλαβείας ἐπηρεαστικόν : and this thought is freq. in Paul (iv. 4, xi. 14 ; 1 Cor. vii. 5 ; 2 Thess. ii. 9). See on iii. 14.

Of the Scriptural designations of the evil one, four are found in this Epistle ; 'Satan' (here, xi. 14, xii. 7), 'the serpent' (xi. 3), 'Beliar' (vi. 15), 'the god of this age' (iv. 4). Elsewhere St Paul calls Satan 'the tempter' (1 Thess. iii. 5), 'the devil' (Eph. iv. 6, etc.), 'the evil one' (Eph. vi. 16), 'the prince of the power of the air' (Eph. ii. 2). It is not necessary to dwell on the obvious fact that here and elsewhere he regards the evil power which opposes God and the well-being of man as a personal agent. Excepting xii. 7, Σατανᾶς always has the article in the Pauline Epp. So also most frequently in the rest of the

---

* Vulg. always has *circumvenire* for πλεονεκτεῖν (vii. 2, xii. 17, 18 ; 1 Thess. iv. 6) : so also has Cyprian (*Test.* iii. 88).

N.T. But, whether with or without the article, Σατανᾶς in N.T. is always a proper name which designates the great Adversary of God and man.

12, 13. From the λύπη caused by the great offender the Apostle returns to the θλίψις which was nearly fatal to him in Asia, from which the news brought by Titus enabled him to recover. But the joyous recollection of the recovery makes him omit to mention the news. This dropping a subject and taking it up again is very natural, especially in a man of strong feeling, who dictates his letters.

12. Ἐλθὼν δὲ εἰς τὴν Τρῳάδα. 'Now' (not 'furthermore,' AV.) 'when I came to Troas.' The words might mean 'to the Troad,' the region between the Hellespont and Mount Ida, but a town must be meant.* St Paul would not tell Titus to meet him in a large district, and the city of Troas was a convenient landing-place from Macedonia. Its full name was Alexandria Troas, Ἀλεξάνδρεια ἡ Τρῳάς, Τρῳάς being an adjective to distinguish it from other places called Ἀλεξάνδρεια; and while in N.T. and Pliny it is called simply Troas, in Strabo it is called simply Alexandria. Its modern name is *Eski Stambui* or *Eski Stamboul*, Old Constantinople. It was one of the few Roman colonies in Asia Minor, and Suetonius says that there was a widely spread rumour that Julius Caesar meant to transfer the capital of the Empire to this colony.† A coast-road ran northwards from Ephesus through Adramyttium to Troas, and when St Paul left Ephesus (Acts xx. 1) for Troas he probably followed it; but he may have gone by sea. Troas is a few miles south of Novum Ilium, which was on the site of the Homeric Troy. See *Enc. Bib.* iv. 5215.

εἰς τὸ εὐαγγέλιον τοῦ Χριστοῦ. 'For,' that is, 'to preach the Gospel (that tells) of the Christ.' This was his primary object. Such missionary work would take time, and during this time he expected that Titus would arrive with news as to the state of affairs at Corinth. If the report of Titus was encouraging, St Paul was conveniently placed for going on to Corinth through Macedonia.

θύρας μοι ἀνεῳγμένης ἐν Κυρίῳ. 'Although a door stood open to me in the Lord.' See on 1 Cor. xvi. 9 and Lightfoot on Col. iv. 3 and 1 Thess. i. 9, where ὁποίαν εἴσοδον ἔσχομεν is used of an excellent opening for missionary work. It was hardly necessary to add ἐν Κυρίῳ after τοῦ Χριστοῦ, but he wishes to

---

* Cf. Acts xx 5, 6, where the art. is omitted and inserted of the same place in consecutive verses.

† *Valida fama percrebuit migraturum Alexandriam vel Ilium, translatis simul opibus imperii* (Julius, 79).

make it quite clear that he had come for the work of a Christian
missionary, and that it was precisely *in that sphere* that he found
a promising opportunity. This intensifies the significance of
what follows. In spite of all this he found it impossible to
remain and work.

εἰς τὸ εὐαγγέλιον with almost all authorities, except F G, Latt., which
have διὰ τὸ εὐαγγέλιον, *propter evangelium.* D E here do not agree with
d e, but have διὰ τοῦ εὐαγγελίου : see critical note on *v.* 17. For θύρας μοι
ἀνεῳγμένης, F G, Latt. have θύρα μοι ἦν ἀνεῳγμένη, *ostium mihi apertum
esset.* Some editors assign οὐκ ἔσχηκα ἄνεσιν . . . ἀδελφόν μου to *v.* 12,
not without reason. There is similar difference between *vv.* 10 and 11 ;
see above.

13. οὐκ ἔσχηκα ἄνεσιν τῷ πνεύματί μου. 'I had no relief for
my spirit.' He uses the same expression in vii. 5, οὐδεμίαν
ἔσχηκεν ἄνεσιν ἡ σὰρξ ἡμῶν, where the change from πνεῦμα to
σάρξ has no special significance : it is the seat of human emotion
and sensation that is meant in each case. We talk of 'weariness
of the spirit' and 'weariness of the flesh,' without much change
of meaning. We may explain the perf. as vividly recalling the
moment when the Apostle had this experience and could say 'I
have not got relief'; but more probably this is another instance
of the aoristic use of the perf. See on i. 9.

Like νόημα, ἄνεσις is specially freq. in this letter (vii. 5,
viii. 13) and occurs elsewhere in N.T. only in 2 Thess. 1. 7 ;
Acts xxiv. 23. Vulg. usually renders it *requies,* but 'relaxation'
in the sense of loosening some kind of tension or restriction is
its meaning rather than 'rest.' Being set free from θλίψις is the
main idea in this letter, as in 2 Thess. In Ecclus. xv. 20, xxvi.
10, it means freeing from wholesome restraint, licence. So also
in the Epistle of Barnabas iv. 2 ; μὴ δῶμεν τῇ ἑαυτῶν ψυχῇ ἄνεσιν
ὥστε ἔχειν αὐτὴν ἐξουσίαν μετὰ ἁμαρτωλῶν καὶ πονηρῶν συντρέχειν.
With the dat. '*for* my spirit,' comp. οὐχ εὑροῦσα ἡ περιστερὰ
ἀνάπαυσιν τοῖς ποσὶν αὐτῆς (Gen. viii. 9).

τῷ μὴ εὑρεῖν με Τίτον τὸν ἀδελφόν μου. 'Because I found
not Titus my brother.' For some reason, he fully expected to
find Titus there, and his failing to do so seems to have robbed
him of the power of work ; his anxiety about Corinth was so
great. Chrys. thinks that St Paul may have wished to remain at
Troas, but that God required him to go on. St Paul tells us
that he could not endure remaining at Troas ; he was so miserable there. There is no hint of any other reason. Thdrt. thinks
that the Apostle felt that he must have a colleague ; that a
missionary working alone was wasted. What is intimated here is
quite an intelligible reason. The Apostle was very human ; he
was so anxious about the effect of his severe letter, that he
decided to shorten the time of torturing suspense by going where

5

he could meet Titus the sooner. Moreover, he may have reasonably thought that the rescue of the Corinthian converts from disaster was more important than making new converts at Troas. We know little of Titus, except what can be gathered from 2 Cor. and Gal. St Paul evidently had the highest opinion of him. Here he calls him 'my brother,' and in viii. 23, 'my comrade and fellow-worker in your interest'; in xii. 18 he mentions him as one who was utterly incapable of being mean or grasping. Ἕλλην ὤν, Titus is the first missionary of purely 'Greek' and pagan origin that is known to us (Gal. ii. 3). But in N.T. Ἕλλην means no more than 'Gentile,' and we cannot be sure of the nationality of Titus. Nevertheless, his acceptability among the Corinthians, and his success in the delicate mission which St Paul entrusted to him, are evidence of his being, by race a Greek. K. Lake, *Earlier Epp.* pp. 146 f., 275 f. Titus is mentioned nine times in 2 Cor. and is highly praised. In 1 Cor. he is not mentioned at all. The reason may be that he was the bearer of 1 Cor. Ramsay, *Paul the Traveller*, p. 284.

There is no parallel in N.T. to the causal dat. τῷ μὴ εὑρεῖν, 'by reason of my not finding'; in 1 Thess. iii. 3 the true reading is τὸ μηδένα σαίνεσθαι, not τῷ. But examples are found elsewhere; τῷ μὴ καὶ ταῦτα πανταχοῦ μηδ' ἐν τοῖς δημοσίοις ἀποκεῖσθαι τόποις (Jos. *Ant.* XIV. x. 1). Moulton quotes from papyri, ἄλλως δὲ τῷ μηθέν' ἔχειν πλὴν τοῦ Πτολεμαίου. See Winer, p. 413 for other references.

ἀποταξάμενος αὐτοῖς. The same words occur Mk. vi. 46, the only place in N.T. in which the verb occurs outside the writings of Paul and Luke, and where αὐτοῖς is as indefinite as here. In N.T. the mid. only is found, and its meaning is 'to bid farewell to friends,' in Mk. probably to the disciples, here obviously to the converts at Troas; cf. Lk. ix. 61, xiv. 33; Acts xviii. 18, 21. The word suggests that he left them with reluctance. In Josephus it is used of Esther's fasting, τροφῇ καὶ ποτῷ καὶ ἡδέσιν ἀποταξαμένη (*Ant.* XI. vi. 8). Hence it comes to mean 'to renounce,' as in the baptismal formula, ἀποτάσσομαι τῷ Σατανᾷ καὶ συντάσσομαι Χριστῷ· ἀποτάσσομαί σοι, Σατανᾶ, καὶ τοῖς ἔργοις σου. Suicer gives many references. Vulg. has *vale facere* here and in Acts, but in Lk. *renunciare*. See Index IV.

ἐξῆλθον εἰς Μακεδονίαν. In Acts xvi. 10, xx. 1 we have ἐξελθεῖν εἰς τὴν Μακ., and in each case it is needless to ask whether ἐξελθεῖν refers to leaving the town or leaving the province. Both Asia and Macedonia were Roman provinces. See Index IV.

In these two graphic verses (12, 13), St Paul once more shows the Corinthians how erroneous it was to suppose that his not visiting them at the time proposed was due to levity or any want of care for them. For their sakes he abandoned a very promising field of missionary enterprise. He is so overwhelmed with thankfulness at the thought of the ultimate result, that, without going on with his narrative, he bursts out into a hymn of praise. We can imagine the surprise of his amanuensis, as the Apostle suddenly changed his line of thought and began to dictate the next four verses. See vii. 5 f. for the narrative.

It is difficult to believe that the man who had just been freed from an agony of anxiety as to the effect of a severe letter to the Corinthians should forthwith write the severe reproaches and sarcasms contained in x.–xiii. 10, and should send them to the Corinthians in the same letter in which he tells them of this agony of anxiety.

For τῷ μή (א³ A B C* G K) L P have τὸ μή and א* C² have τοῦ μή, both of which may safely be disregarded, while D E 17 have ἐν τῷ μή, which Blass is inclined to adopt. Schmiedel rightly rejects the conjectures that *vv.* 12, 13 originally came after i. 22, or were written by Paul as a marginal note to i. 16. The conjectures are quite unnecessary.

14. Τῷ δὲ Θεῷ χάρις. St Paul generally writes χάρις τῷ Θεῷ (viii. 16, ix. 15 ; Rom. vi. 17, vii. 25), but here, as in the similarly sudden transition to thanksgiving in 1 Cor. xv. 7, he puts τῷ Θεῷ first with great emphasis. The two thanksgivings should be compared. In each case we have a noble digression of irrepressible gratitude. And the gratitude here is evoked by the thought of the intense revulsion of feeling from anxiety to joy when he met Titus and heard that all was well in Corinth. To seek for any other explanation is unintelligent waste of time. The remembrance of the victory of God's cause at Corinth leads him on to think of the triumph of the Gospel generally, and of the very subordinate but glorious share which Apostolic missionaries have in that triumph. He thinks of its progress as a magnificent procession moving onwards through the world. The victorious commander is God, and the Apostles are—not His subordinate generals, but His captives, whom He takes with Him and displays to all the world. St Paul thanks God, not for ‘ always *causing* him to triumph ’ (AV.), but for ‘ at all times *leading* him in triumph.’ The Apostles were among the first to be captured and made instruments of God's glory. When a Roman *imperator* triumphed, clouds of incense arose all along the route ; and in the triumph-train of the Gospel the incense of increased knowledge of God is ever ascending. The Apostles cause this increase of knowledge, and therefore they themselves are a fragrance to the glory of God, a fragrance that is life-giving to those that are on the road to salvation, but will prove deadly to those who are on the other road. The atmosphere of the Gospel is one which only those who are prepared to welcome it can breathe with safety and delight ; to others it is a peril and a pain.

Some editors make *vv.* 14–17 a separate paragraph ; but the connexion with *vv.* 12, 13 should not be broken.

τῷ πάντοτε θριαμβεύοντι ἡμᾶς. 'Who at all times leadeth us in triumph' is almost certainly right. It is true that some verbs in -ευω acquire a causative sense : μαθητεύω may mean 'I make a disciple of' (Mt. xxviii. 19 ; Acts xiv. 21) as well as 'I am a disciple' (Mt. xxvii. 57), and βασιλεύω may be 'I make to be king' (Is. vii. 6) as well as 'I am a king' (Lk. xix. 14, 27). But we do not know that θριαμβεύω ever means 'I cause to triumph,' although that meaning would make good sense here and is adopted by various interpreters ; *qui facit ut semper triumphemus* (Beza), *qui triumphare nos facit* (Calvin). But in Col. ii. 15 θριαμβεύω has its usual meaning of 'I lead in triumph,' and that is likely to be its meaning here. Earlier writers have *nos in triumpho circumduco.* This is Thdrt.'s explanation ; τῇδε κἀκεῖσε περιάγει δήλους ἡμᾶς πᾶσιν ἀποφαίνων. And Chrys. is similar ; τῷ πᾶσι ποιοῦντι περιφανεῖς. Oecumenius also ; τῷ φανεροῦντι ἡμᾶς καὶ καταδήλους ποιοῦντι.* See on 1 Cor. iv. 9, where we have a similar metaphor, and the leading idea in both places is that of exhibiting, displaying to the world. As to the usual signification of θριαμβεύω one example may suffice ; Cleopatra, captured by Caesar, says to the Manes of Mark Antony, whom she had recently buried, μηδ' ἐν ἐμοὶ περιίδῃς θριαμβευόμενον σεαυτόν (Plut. *Ant.* 84). Wetstein gives other examples. See also Field, *Notes on Translation of the N.T.* p. 181, who, however, questions the allusion to a Roman triumph. The derivation of θρίαμβος, like that of εἰλικρινία (i. 12), is a problem, but its meanings are well established. Originally a hymn sung in processions in honour of Bacchus, it was used as equivalent to the Roman *triumphus,* probably through similarity of sound and of association. Thus Polybius says that the Senate can add glory even to the successes of generals by bringing their achievements in tangible form before the eyes of the citizens in what are called 'triumphs' (VI. xv. 8).† Wetstein well sums up the meaning of the passage ; "God leads us round as it were in triumph, so that we do not stay in one place or move on to another according to our own will, but as seems good to our all-wise Director. The man whom He vanquished at Damascus He leads in triumph, not at Rome, and just once, but through the whole world, as

---

* Suidas gives δημοσιεύσας as the equivalent of θριαμβεύσας.

† St Paul uses a number of words to express his relation to God as a minister of the Gospel. It is λειτουργία and διακονία (ix. 12), πρεσβεία (v. 20), στρατεία (x. 4), ὑπηρεσία and οἰκονομία (1 Cor. iv. 1) ; but this metaphor of being led in triumph by Him is the most striking of all.

long as he lives." See also McFadyen, *ad loc.*, and also on the
Pauline phrase 'in Christ' in *Truth in Religion*, pp. 242–259,
from which much of the next note is taken.

ἐν τῷ Χριστῷ. Cf. ἐν Κυρίῳ in *v.* 12. The expressions, ἐν
Χριστῷ, ἐν τῷ Χριστῷ, ἐν Χριστῷ Ἰησοῦ, ἐν Ἰησοῦ Χριστῳ, ἐν τῷ
Χριστῷ Ἰησοῦ, ἐν Κυρίῳ Ἰησοῦ Χριστῷ, occur upwards of fifty
times in N.T., and nearly all of them are found in the Pauline
Epp. The exceptions are 1 Pet. v. 10, 14, of which v. 10 is
doubtful, and both may be due to Pauline influence. Of the
six forms of expression (which cover all four groups of the
Pauline Epp.), the first three are very common, while the last
three are rare, occurring only once or twice each. The differences in the forms of expression may not mean much, but the
total amount may show channels of thought in which the Apostle's
mind habitually ran. 'In Christ' or 'in Christ Jesus' was a
sphere in which his inner life ever moved. To us the phrase
has a conventional sound; it is like a coin much defaced by
frequent use, and it needs to be taken back to the mint in
which it was fashioned, the mint of experience. St Paul had
been persecuting the followers of Jesus as being the worshippers
of a false and dead Messiah. Experience had confronted him
with the same Jesus and had compelled him to recognize Him
as the true Messiah, victorious over death, and able to make
Himself known to living men. Further experience had proved
that Jesus the Messiah was one in whom was revealed all that
men could know about God, and that the way to learn the truth
about God was to be united with His Christ. Henceforth
St Paul thought of himself as '*in* Christ,' and these words tell
us of a man with a changed consciousness of life.* The chief
element of change was a sense of freedom, freedom from the
bondage of the Law and from the bondage of sin: but it was not
the only element. 'In Christ' we have indeed a sphere of
liberty, but we have also a sphere of work; for freedom is
freedom to *do* something, and to be 'in Christ' is to be working
in His service, as fellow-workers not only of Apostles (viii. 23),
but of God Himself (1 Cor. iii. 9). To be working in this
atmosphere of liberty is an experience which makes men 'new
creatures in Christ Jesus' (v. 17), with new estimates of things,
new aims and hopes, and new powers wherewith to attain and
fulfil them.

---

* "Ask different persons what is the leading doctrine of the Apostle of
the Gentiles, and you will get different answers. Some will reply, justification
by faith, others, the liberty of the Gospel. You will find that for once when
either of these doctrines is referred to, union with Christ will be mentioned
ten times. They are indeed prominent. But it underlies the whole "
(Lightfoot, *Sermons in St Paul's*, p. 227).

Whether intended to do so or not, ἐν τῷ Χριστῷ at the end
of this clause balances τῷ Θεῷ at the beginning of it.   It is for
being perpetually led in triumph '*in* Christ' that the Apostle
gives rapturous thanks to *God.*   And the central word is πάντοτε,
which is repeated in another form in ἐν παντὶ τόπῳ.   Neither in
time nor in space is there any point at which this being led in
triumph ceases.

τὴν ὀσμὴν τῆς γνώσεως αὐτοῦ.   Sweet odours often reveal the
presence of what cannot be seen ; *odor ideo, quia sentitur potius
quam videtur* (Pseudo-Primasius).   God makes manifest through
the labours of His ministers the fragrance which a knowledge
of the Christ who reveals Him always brings.   The genitive is
probably one of apposition ; the knowledge is the fragrance ; cf.
τὸν ἀρραβῶνα τοῦ Πνεύματος (i. 22).   This metaphor of fragrance
suggests the penetrating strength of the revelation and the delight
which it brings to those who receive it.   We have here one of
many passages in N.T.—more common in St John than in St
Paul—in which we are in doubt whether a pronoun refers to God
or to Christ.   Here αὐτοῦ may mean either ; but the preceding
ἐν τῷ Χριστῷ and the Χριστοῦ εὐωδία which follows make the
reference to Christ more probable.   In any case it is in Christ
that the knowledge of God is acquired ; iv. 6.

φανεροῦντι δι' ἡμῶν ἐν παντὶ τόπῳ.   The choice of the verb is
determined by τῆς γνώσεως rather than by τὴν ὀσμήν.*   As in
i. 19 and 1 Cor. iii. 5, the Apostles are not independent agents,
but instruments.   Cf. the frequent διὰ τοῦ προφήτου.   It is a
mistake to refer δι' ἡμῶν to St Paul alone.   He is not claiming
an exclusive revelation.   Ἐν παντὶ τόπῳ and πάντοτε show that
there is no special reference to the crisis at Corinth.   It is
fanciful to find in ὀσμή any allusion to the anointing of priests,
or in φανεροῦντι any suggestion of the opening of a box of
unguents.   The verb is very freq. in the Johannine and Pauline
writings, and occurs nine times in this Epistle.

15. ὅτι Χριστοῦ εὐωδία ἐσμὲν τῷ Θεῷ.   By way of explanation
(ὅτι) the metaphor of the sweet savour is used in a different way
to express the work of those who preach the Gospel.   In spreading the fragrance of it they are themselves a fragrance to God.
Here Χριστοῦ is emphatic, as τῷ Θεῷ is in *v.* 14, 'For it is of
Christ that we are a sweet odour to God.'   'Of Christ' means
that the fragrance comes from Him, for it is He whom the
missionaries preach, and such preaching is pleasing to God.
It is possible that τῷ Θεῷ is added because of the frequency of
ὀσμὴ εὐωδίας Κυρίῳ or τῷ Κυρίῳ in LXX.   Codex Mosquensis (K)
omits τῷ Θεῷ, and J. Weiss regards it as an editorial insertion ;

* In LXX, the most common verbs with ὀσμήν are ποιεῖν and διδόναι.

but it has point. The preaching is always εὐωδία to God, but not always to men, to some of whom it breathes death.* It is worth noting that the sacrificial phrase ὀσμὴ εὐωδίας, so frequent in LXX, is not used here, and this makes any allusion to sacrifice doubtful. Contrast Eph. v. 2, where see J. A. Robinson. In Phil. iv. 18, ὀσμὴν εὐωδίας, θυσίαν δεκτήν is used of the gifts of the Philippians to the Apostle. Cf. Ezek. xx. 41; Mal. iii. 4. In N.T. εὐωδία is found only in Paul. See Index IV.

ἐν τοῖς σωζομένοις καὶ ἐν τοῖς ἀπολλυμένοις. The repetition of the ἐν shows how different the two classes are; 'among those that are being saved (pres. part.; Lk. xiii. 23; Acts ii. 47; see on 1 Cor. i. 18) and among those who are perishing' (iv. 3; 1 Cor. i. 18; 2 Thess. ii. 10). The 'perfective' verb ἀπόλλυμαι (Lk. xv. 17; Mt. viii. 25) gives the idea of something which is regarded as certain at the moment of utterance. The ἀπολλύμενοι are not merely on the road to ἀπώλεια: ἀπώλεια is regarded as their end, unless some complete change takes place. J. H. Moulton, *Gr.* p. 114. The two expressions are far more pregnant and significant than 'believers' † and 'unbelievers.' Cf. 1 Cor. x. 9, xv. 18; Rom. ii. 12; Phil. i. 28, iii. 18.

16. ἐκ θανάτου εἰς θάνατον . . . ἐκ ζωῆς εἰς ζωήν. The classes just mentioned are taken in reverse order: chiasmus is freq. in these Epistles (iv. 3, vi. 8, ix. 6, x. 11, xiii. 3; 1 Cor. iii. 17, iv. 10, viii. 13, xiii. 2). 'A savour from death to death . . . a savour from life to life.' It may be doubted whether the double ἐκ . . . εἰς ought to be pressed and rigidly interpreted. Perhaps nothing more is meant than continuous succession, as when we say 'from day to day,' 'from strength to strength.' In such cases it would be misleading to insist upon 'out of' and 'into' as the meaning of 'from' and 'to,' and then ask, 'out of what?' and 'into what?' It is easy to see that to some persons the Gospel message may be εἰς θάνατον. 'What should have been to their wealth' becomes, through their own fault, 'an occasion of falling' lower and lower. But it is not easy to see how the Gospel can be ἐκ θανάτου, in the sense that it proceeds 'out of

* "Wherever Christ's servants are, there should be fragrance. A Christian without this redolence is as impossible as incense whose presence is unfelt by those who come near it. It penetrates the atmosphere and compels attention;—so plainly that their presence is, as it were, a perpetual challenge to their environment, repelling some, attracting others. They constitute a living standard, which compels men involuntarily to expose the inner quality of their life" (McFadyen, pp. 274 f.).

† Other terms used by St Paul in reference to the fate of unbelievers are θάνατος (Rom. vi. 23, viii. 6), φθορά (Gal. vi. 8), ὀργή Rom. ii. 5, 8, v. 9; 1 Thess. i. 10, v. 9). But he is much more concerned to remind his readers that believers can be sure of salvation in Christ than to discuss the future of those who refuse to believe on Him.

death.' Progress from one evil condition to another is what is meant, movement from bad to worse. They were in a condition that was virtually fatal when the Gospel came to them, and its effect was to confirm that fatal tendency. The idea of pestilential air coming from a corpse is not required. Nor need we, with Bousset, bring in the oriental idea that the perfumes of heaven, or other strong smells (Tobit viii. 2, 3), will drive demons back to hell. Chrys. does not help us with the remark that ointment is said to suffocate swine, nor Thdrt. with the popular belief that sweet odours drive away vultures. Evidence of this curious belief is given by Wetstein. It is better to abide by the comment of Gregor. Nyss.; κατὰ τὴν προσοῦσαν ἑκάστῳ διάθεσιν ἢ ζωοποιὸς ἐγένετο ἢ θανατηφόρος ἡ εὔπνοια. So also Jerome (*Ep.* cxx. 11); *Nominis Christi in omni loco bonus odor sumus Deo et praedicationis nostrae longe lateque spirat fragrantia. Sed odor noster qui per se bonus est, virtute eorum qui suscipiunt sive non suscipiunt in vitam transit aut mortem, ut qui crediderint salvi fiant, qui vero non crediderint pereant.* Schoettgen and Wetstein quote Jewish sayings to the effect that the words of the Law are medicine to the wise and poison to fools. As regards the Χριστοῦ εὐωδία, Saul of Tarsus and Paulus the Proconsul illustrate the one side, Simon Magus and Elymas Magus the other side.

καὶ πρὸς ταῦτα τίς ἱκανός; 'Well, if that is true (see on *v.* 2), who is sufficient for these responsibilities?' What kind of a minister ought he to be who preaches a Gospel which may prove fatal to those who come in contact with it? Vulg. has *et ad haec quis* tam *idoneus?* The *tam* has no authority in any Greek text, and it makes the question still more surprising in form; 'Who is so competent as we are?' *Quis tam* may be a mistake for *quisnam.*

We do not know enough about the situation to see why St Paul prepares the way for his elaborate vindication of the Apostolic office and of the Gospel (iii. 1–vi. 10) by flashing out this question in a way which, even without the *tam*, is almost offensive, and is certainly very abrupt. Augustine and Herveius interpret the question as meaning, 'Who is competent to *understand* these things?' which does not fit the context. 'Who is equal to such responsibilities?' is the meaning. The answer is not stated, but is clearly implied in the next verse; ' *We are*, for, etc.'

ἐκ is omitted in both places by D E F G K L, Latt. Arm.; probably because of the difficulty of seeing how Χριστοῦ εὐωδία could be ἐκ θανάτου, Goth. has the second ἐκ, which is easy, and omits the first, which is difficult. We must read ἐκ in both places with ℵ A B C, Copt. Aeth., Clem-Alex. Orig.

17. οὐ γάρ ἐσμεν ὡς οἱ πολλοί. The γάρ indicates the reply to the question just asked. ' *We* are sufficient for these things, *for* we are not as the many teachers.' Here we have for the first time in the Epistle a passage that is manifestly polemical. The Apostle's opponents may have been in his thoughts in earlier places, but here it is quite certain that he is censuring other teachers for doing what the Apostle and his colleagues never do ; they garble the word of God, in order to make the preaching of it more profitable to themselves. There are similar polemical hits in iii. 1, iv. 2, v. 12, while x.–xiii. teems with them, *e.g.* x. 12, 18, xi. 12, 13, 20, xii. 14. With ὡς οἱ πολλοί comp. ὥς τινες (iii. 1). Here, as in Rom. v. 15, 19, AV. ignores the article before πολλοί and translates 'many' instead of 'the many.' But we need not give the article its strongest force and make οἱ πολλοί mean 'the majority,' although it is likely that at Corinth the majority of the teachers were misleading the converts, and that the Judaizers on the one hand, and the advocates of Gentile licence on the other, far outnumbered the Apostle, Silvanus, and Timothy with whatever helpers they may have had. The meaning here seems to be 'the mob of teachers,' without comparing them in number with the Apostle and his colleagues. On the opposition to St Paul see K. Lake, *Earlier Epp.* pp. 219 f. In what sense he claims ἱκανότης for himself and his fellow-workers he tells us at once in iii. 5, 6 ; none are sufficient, excepting those whom God has made so, and it is evident whom He has made sufficient, viz., those who preach His word as He would have it preached.

καπηλεύοντες τὸν λόγον τοῦ Θεοῦ. 'Adulterating the word of God.' The participle belongs to ἐσμέν. not to οἱ πολλοί : 'We are not people who adulterate the word.' Vulg. has *adulterantes* for καπηλεύοντες here and for δολοῦντες iv. 2. 'Adulterate' suggests more clearly than 'corrupt' (AV., RV.) that the corruption is done for the sake of some miserable personal gain. The word occurs nowhere else in Biblical Greek, but κάπηλος, 'a retail dealer,' occurs twice in LXX. In Is. i. 22 we have οἱ κάπηλοί σου μίσγουσι τὸν οἶνον ὕδατι, 'Thy hucksters mix their wine with water,' in order to cheat the buyers ; and Ecclus. xxvi. 29, οὐ δικαιωθήσεται κάπηλος ἀπὸ ἁμαρτίας, 'An huckster shall not be judged free from sin.' St Paul may have had Is. i. 22 in his mind in using καπηλεύοντες. The Talmud counts the huckster as one whose business involves robbery, and Deut. xxx. 13 is interpreted to mean that the Law cannot be found among hucksters or merchants. Plato says, "Knowledge is the food of the soul ; and we must take care that the sophist does not deceive us when he praises what he sells, like those who sell the food of the body, the merchant and the hawker (κάπηλος):

for they praise all their wares, without knowing what is good or bad for the body. In like manner those who carry about items of knowledge, to sell and hawk (καπηλεύοντες) them to any one who is in want of them, praise them, all alike, though neither they nor their customers know their effect upon the soul" (*Protag.* 313 D). Lucian says that philosophers dispose of their wares just as hucksters (κάπηλοι) do, most of them giving bad measure after adulterating and falsifying what they sell (*Hermotimus*, 59): κάπηλος is frequently used of a retailer of *wine.* Other illustrations in Wetstein.

The expression, 'the word of God,' ὁ λόγος τοῦ Θεοῦ, is very freq. in N.T., nearly forty times in all, without counting the expression, which is also freq., 'the word of the Lord,' ὁ λόγος τοῦ Κυρίου. It is specially common in Acts (twelve times) and in the Pauline Epp. (iv. 2 ; 1 Cor. xiv. 36 ; Rom. ix. 6 ; Col. i. 25 ; 1 Thess. ii. 13 ; 2 Tim. ii. 9 ; Tit. ii. 5). Its usual meaning, as here, is the Gospel as preached, the contents of the new religion, as set forth in the O.T. and in the life and teaching of Christ. Often ὁ λόγος, without τοῦ Θεοῦ, is used in much the same sense, and in interpreting it in the Pauline Epp. we must bear in mind 1 Cor. ii. 2, 'I determined not to know anything among you, save Jesus Christ, and Him crucified,' so that the preaching of the word means the preaching of Jesus Christ, crucified and raised again. It was this λόγος that was being adulterated at Corinth. See J. H. Bernard, *Past Epp.* pp 74 f. ; Harnack, *Constitution and Law of the Church*, pp. 332 f.

As to the manner of the adulteration, *omnis doctor qui auctoritatem Scripturarum, per quam potest audientes corripere, vertit ad gratiam et ita loquitur ut non corrigat sed delectet audientes, vinum Scripturarum violat et corrumpit sensu suo* (Jerome on Is. i. 22). As Chrys. puts it, such teachers τὰ αὐτῶν ἀναμιγνύουσι τοῖς θείοις.

ἀλλ' ὡς ἐξ εἰλικρινίας, ἀλλ' ὡς ἐκ Θεοῦ. 'But as from sincerity, nay, as from God.' Sincerity (see on i. 12) is the internal source, and God is the external source, of what the missionaries preach. Their message rings true, for it comes from an honest and good heart (Lk. viii. 15), and is inspired by the faithful God (i. 18) who cannot lie (Tit. i. 2). Cf. οὐ γὰρ ὑμεῖς ἐστε οἱ λαλοῦντες, ἀλλὰ τὸ πνεῦμα τοῦ πατρὸς ὑμῶν τὸ λαλοῦν ἐν ὑμῖν (Mt. x. 20). The ὡς means 'as any one acts who acts ἐξ εἰλ., ἐκ Θ.' The repetition of ἀλλά gives emphasis in an ascending scale; vii. 11 ; 1 Cor. vi. 11 ; ὡς as in Mt. vii. 49; Jn. i. 14.

κατέναντι Θεοῦ. Cf. xii. 19; Rom. iv. 17, etc. Neither κατέναντι nor κατενώπιον is classical ; both are found several times in N.T. and LXX. There is no ἀλλ' ὡς before κατ. Θ., and there should be no comma either before or after these words ; 'but as from God in the sight of God speak we in Christ.' God is the source of what they preach and the witness of it ; what greater guarantee of truthfulness cou:d there be? ἐν Χριστῷ. See on v. 14. Neither *Christi nomine* (Grot.), nor *secundum Christum* (Calv.), nor *de Christo* (Beza), but, quite literally, *in Christo* (Vulg.) ; it is ' in Christ,' as members of His Body, that ministers of the Gospel do their work, in the power that flows from union with Him. The branches bear fruit by being *in* the vine, and in no other way (Jn. xv. 4).

In this last verse (17), St Paul states both negatively and positively some leading characteristics of the minister who is equal to the responsibility of delivering a message which is so crucial that it may determine, not only the salvation of those who are already seekers after truth, but also the ruin of those who have set their faces against it. Such a minister is not one who, in order to win converts on easy terms, waters down the claims which the Gospel makes upon those who accept it. He is one who teaches with the openness and fulness which come from the God who inspires him ; and in God's presence he works as befits a member of Christ. He has, as the motive of all that he does or says, not his own gain or glory or satisfaction, but the desire to serve God by causing others to perceive the sweetness and the saving power of knowing something of Him. St Paul's own experiences lie at the root of all this. He never forgets how Saul the persecutor was changed into Paul the Apostle.

οἱ πολλοί (אA B C K, d e f Vulg. Copt. Aeth.) rather than οἱ λοιποί (D E F G L, g Syrr. Arm.). F G, d e f g Vulg. Copt. Goth. omit the second ὡς. F G, d e f g omit the second ἀλλ'. In all three cases, as in that of εἰς τὸ εὐαγγέλιον in v. 12, D E do not agree with d e. κατέναντι (א* A B C P 17) rather than κατενώπιον (א³ D E F G K L). The second Θεοῦ without τοῦ (א* A B C D* 17) rather than with τοῦ (א³ D² and ³ E F G K L P). On the difference between Θεός and ὁ Θεός see Westcott, additional note on I Jn. iv. 2.

III. 1–VI. 10. THE GLORY OF THE APOSTOLIC OFFICE.

The first three verses, like i. 12–14, are transitional. They are closely connected with the preceding expression of thankfulness and confidence, for ἑαυτοὺς συνιστάνειν clearly looks back to ἐξ εἰλικρινίας . . . λαλοῦμεν. But μὴ χρήσομεν κ.τ.λ. equally clearly anticipates πεποίθησιν τοιαύτην, and there is more pause between the chapters than between vv. 3 and 4. These three verses, therefore, are best regarded as introductory to the Apostle's vindication, not only of himself, but of the high office which he holds, and of the message which he is commissioned to deliver.

The first verse gives us further insight into the opposition

which confronted St Paul at Corinth.   Evidently one of the
charges brought against him was that he was always asserting
himself and singing his own praises,—of course because nobody
else praised him.   A man who has often to speak with authority
is open to this kind of criticism, and there are passages in 1 Cor.
which would lend themselves to such a charge; ii. 6–16, iii. 10,
iv. 3, 14-21, ix. 1–6, xi. 1, xiv. 18.   But more probably it was
the severe letter, of which x.–xiii. may be a part, which provoked
this criticism.   There is plenty of material for such criticism in
those four chapters.   Titus, no doubt, had reported the existence
of these cavillings, and perhaps he knew that they had not been
completely silenced.   The Apostle does not assert that they
still exist, but he meets the possibility of their existence with a
tactful question.   Then he still more tactfully asks a question
which can be turned against his opponents.   Finally, he makes a
statement which is likely to go home to the hearts of the
Corinthians and win those who are still wavering back to their
devotion to him.   The readiness with which the passionate outburst of ii. 14–17 is turned to account for the vindication of the
Apostolic office is very remarkable.

III. 1–3.   *I have no desire to commend myself.   The only
testimonial which I need I have in you, and all the world
can read it.*

¹ In claiming to be competent to deliver a message which
involves the momentous alternative of ultimate life and death, do
I seem to be commending myself once more?   I was obliged to
assert myself in my last letter, but I have no need to do so now.
There are people who bring letters of recommendation to you,
and ask you to give them such; and no doubt they require
them.   ² But what need have I of such things, when you yourselves are my letter of recommendation written on my very heart,
a letter which the whole world can get to know and construe,
wherever I go and tell of you?   ³ It is made plain to all that
you are a letter composed by Christ and published by me;
written not with the blackness of perishable ink, but with the
illuminating Spirit of the living God ; written not, like the Law,
on dead tables of stone, but on the living tables of sensitive
human hearts.

1. Ἀρχόμεθα πάλιν ἑαυτοὺς συνιστάνειν;   'Are we beginning
again to commend ourselves?'   It makes no difference whether
we take πάλιν with ἀρχόμεθα or with συνιστάνειν.   The sentence
is certainly a question.   Taking it as a statement involves a

clumsy insertion in order to get a connexion with ἢ μὴ κ.τ.λ., such as, 'Or *if you object to our commending ourselves, I reply with this question,* Do we need, etc.' Ἀρχόμεθα is a sort of echo of the supposed criticism; 'He is beginning to belaud himself again.' The πάλιν plainly shows that St Paul is aware that this charge of self-praise had been made. He alludes to it again iv. 5, v. 12, vi. 4. It may have been an insult offered to him by ὁ ἀδικήσας, the great offender; but, whoever started it, it was accepted as true by some of the Corinthians. There are passages 1 Cor. which would give a handle to such a charge; ix. 15, xiv. 18, xv. 10; cf. iv. 16, vii. 40, xi. 1; 2 Cor. i. 12.

The question may be a direct reference to τῶν ἑαυτοὺς συνιστανόντων (x. 12) and to ὑφ' ὑμῶν cυνίστασθαι (xii. 11). If they are, we have further evidence that x.–xiii. is part of the severe letter written between 1 Cor. and 2 Cor. i.–ix. These three verses are strangely out of harmony with the last four chapters, *if* those chapters are part of the same letter : they are natural enough, if those chapters had been previously sent to Corinth and had occasioned, or intensified, the charge that St Paul was too fond of praising himself. See Rendall, p. 65.

We find συνιστάνειν or συνιστάναι, 'to bring together,' used in two senses in N.T. (1) 'To bring persons together,' to introduce or commend them to one another; iv. 2, v. 12, vi. 4, x. 12, 18; Rom. xvi. 1. (2) 'To put two and two together,' to prove by argument and evidence ; viι. 11 ; Gal. ii. 18 ; Rom. v. 8. This difference of meaning is not clearly marked in LXX, but in Susann. 61, Theod. has συνέστησεν of Daniel's proving that the elders have borne false witness. See on Rom. iii. 5. In these two senses the verb is peculiar to Paul in N.T. and is found chiefly in this Epistle. It occurs elsewhere only Lk. ix. 32 and 2 Pet. iii. 5, in quite other senses. The position of the reflexive pronoun is to be noted. In this Epistle we have ἑαυτοὺς συν., in a bad sense, iii. 1, v. 12, x. ι2, 18; and συν. ἑαυτούς, in a good sense, iv. 2, vi. 4, vii. 11.

ἢ μὴ χρῄζομεν ὥς τινες; 'Or is it the fact that we need, as some people do?' This side-stroke at the false teachers is very effective; he alludes to the οἱ πολλοί of ii. 17 and others like them. St Paul often speaks of his opponents as 'certain persons,' τινες (x. 2; 1 Cor. iv. 18, xv. 12; Gal. i. 7; 1 Tim. i. 3, 19). The μή, implying a negative answer, throws back its force on the previous question, and shows that the suggested criticism is unjust. Harnack thinks that the Apostles required a fresh commission for each missionary expedition. That was clearly not the case with St Paul.

συστατικῶν ἐπιστολῶν πρὸς ὑμᾶς ἢ ἐξ ὑμῶν. These words tell us three things : that the Judaizers had brought letters of recommendation from some one; that they had already left Corinth; and that before leaving they had obtained, or had tried to obtain, letters of recommendation from the Corinthian Church. We know nothing, however, as to who gave recommendations to the Judaizers; perhaps leading persons in Palestine did so. It is not likely that they had obtained credentials from any of the Twelve or from the Church at Jerusalem.* Letters of this kind were commonly brought by travelling brethren as evidence that they were Christians and honest persons. The Epistle to Philemon is a συστατικὴ ἐπιστολή for Onesimus; and ἐλάβετε ἐντολάς, ᾿Εὰν ἔλθῃ πρὸς ὑμᾶς, δέξασθε αὐτόν (Col. iv. 10) probably refers to a previous letter of recommendation. St Paul sometimes commends individuals to the Church whom he addresses; *e.g.* Titus and his companion (viii. 22 f.), Timothy (1 Cor. xvi. 10 f.), Phoebe (Rom. xvi. 1). Cf. Acts xv. 25 f., xviii. 27; 2 Jn. 12. Papyri yield examples; Deissmann (*Light from the Ancient East*, p. 226) says that the letters in *Epistolographi Graeci*, Hercher, pp. 259, 699, begin, like Rom. xvi., with συνίστημι. Suicer (ii. 1194) gives instances of such letters in the early Church. The Latins called them *epistolae commendaticiae* or *literae formatae*. How necessary they were is shown by Lucian, who says that an adroit unscrupulous fellow, who has seen the world, has only to get among these simple-hearted Christians, and he can soon make a fortune out of them (*Perigr. Prot.* 13). Diogenes condemned γράμματα συστατικά as useless; nothing but personal experience of men, he said, was of any real value (Arrian, *Epict.* ii. iii. 1). This, however, was what existed between St Paul and the Corinthians; and it was πάσης συστατικώτερον ἐπιστολῆς. Cf. Acts xxviii. 21, and see Harnack, *Mission and Expansion*, i. p. 328.

If we are right in inferring from this verse that the Judaizers had left Corinth, we have a strong argument for the view that x.–xiii. was written before i.–ix., for in x.–xiii. the Judaizers are denounced as a present plague in Corinth.

If the reading εἰ μή be adopted, we must translate, 'unless it possibly be the case that we are needing, etc.'; and we must interpret this as a sarcasm; 'unless it be the case that we are so unable to get recommendations that we are compelled to praise ourselves.' This sarcasm shows that the

* The relation of the Judaizers to the Twelve is unknown to us, as also are the details of their teaching. "It was the life, not the teaching of the original Apostles which appeared to support the Judaizers. They continued in attendance upon the Temple services. To a superficial observer, they were simply pious Jews. They were not simply pious Jews. But the Judaizers failed to penetrate beneath the outward appearance. Because the original Apostles continued to observe the Jewish Law, the Judaizers supposed that legalism was of the essence of their religion" (J. G. Machen, *Princeton Biblical Studies*, p. 555).

charge of St Paul's praising himself is ridiculous. So clumsy an interpretation need not be accepted, for the balance of evidence is decisive against εἰ μή. ℵ B C D E F G, Latt. and other versions have ἢ μή, A K L P, Arm. have εἰ μή. B D 17 have συνιστᾶν, F G συνιστάναι, all other witnesses συνιστάνειν. A D have ὥσπερ τινες, other authorities ὥς τινες. D E F K L P, d e Syrr. add συστατικῶν after ἐξ ὑμῶν, and F G add συστ. ἐπιστολῶν. Omit both words with ℵ A B C 17, 67**, Vulg. Copt. Arm. Aeth., Chrys. Ambrst.

2. ἡ ἐπιστολὴ ἡμῶν ὑμεῖς ἐστέ. The asyndeton is effective, and the two pronouns are in telling juxtaposition. The convincing statement is flashed out with emphatic suddenness and brevity ; 'The letter of recommendation which we have to show are ye.' * No other testimonial is needed, either *to* the Corinthians or *from* them. They know what Apostolic teaching has done for them ; and all the world can see this also. Their changed life is an object lesson to themselves and to all outside ; and both they and the outsiders know how this change has been produced ; it is writ large in the history of the foundation of a Church in such a city as Corinth. The Apostle appeals, not to written testimony, which may be false, but to the experience of all who know the facts. There seems to be an allusion to this passage in the Ep. of Polycarp (xi. 3), where he says "among whom the blessed Paul laboured, who were his letters in the beginning." See on iv. 14 and viii. 21.

The details which follow are neither quite clear nor quite harmonious. St Paul dictates bold metaphors, in order to set forth the convincing character of his credentials, and he does not stop to consider whether they can all be combined in one consistent picture. 'Written in our hearts' does not agree well with 'read by all men,' and yet both were true. The Christian life of the Corinthians was impressed in thankful remembrance on the hearts of those who had converted them, and it was recognized by all who knew them. It was also impressed on the hearts of the Corinthians themselves. See on 1 Cor. ix. 2. Experience showed to the teachers that their ministry had been blessed by God ; the existence of the Corinthian Church convinced them of this, and they could appeal to that conviction with a good conscience. Experience also taught the world at large that the men who had produced this change at Corinth were no charlatans ; and it had taught the Corinthians themselves the same truth.

* "Observe the remarkable expression of the Apostle ; his *letter* ! He was writing on men's hearts ; and each man here is writing something ; and his writing lasts for ever. Pilate uttered a deeper truth than he thought when he said, 'What I have written, I have written.' For deeds are permanent and irrevocable : that which you have written on life is for ever. You cannot blot it out : there it is for ever ; your Epistle to the world, to be known and read of all men " (F. W. Robertson).

ἐγγεγραμμένη ἐν ταῖς καρδίαις ἡμῶν. There is probably no
allusion to Aaron 'bearing the names of the children of Israel
in the breastplate (pouch) of judgment upon his heart, when
he goeth in unto the holy place, for a memorial before the
Lord continually' (Ex. xxviii. 36). The idea of intercession is
foreign to this passage. 'Written on our hearts' suggests to
us the idea of deep affection, and Chrys. interprets the words of
the love to the Corinthians which causes Paul to sing their
praises in other Churches. But it may be doubted whether this
is the exact meaning of the words. The context seems to require
some such meaning as this; 'Our own hearts tell us that you
are our recommendation, and everybody else can see this also.'
The compound ἐνγεγρ. implies that this fact cannot slip from
our hearts, cannot be forgotten; cf. ἦν ἐγγράφου σὺ μνήμοσιν
δέλτοις φρενῶν (Aesch. *Pr. V.* 789); and ἐπίγραψον ἐπὶ τὸ πλάτος
τῆς καρδίας σου (Prov. vii. 3). The plur. 'hearts' probably
implies that other teachers are included with the Apostle;
contrast 'our heart' in vi. 11. The 'heart' in Scripture is the
inner man, the centre of personality, known only to God; Rom.
v. 5, viii. 27; Eph. i. 18, iii. 17; 1 Pet. iii. 4; Rev. ii. 23. See
art. 'Heart' in Hastings, *DB.* and *DCG.*; *Milligan* on 1 Thess.
ii. 4.

Lietzmann and Bousset would read ὑμῶν for ἡμῶν with ℵ 17 after
καρδίαις. Confusion between the two pronouns is often found in MSS.,
and might easily be made at the outset in dictating, the pronunciation being
similar.
'My testimonial is written in *your* hearts and can be read by all, for all
can see that you are Christians.' Schmiedel and J. Weiss would omit the
whole clause as a gloss.

γινωσκομένη καὶ ἀναγινωσκομένη. Note the change from perf.
to pres. participles. It was written long ago and the writing
still remains, and this is continually becoming known and being
read. See on i. 13 respecting the word-play* and the meaning
of ἀναγινωσκομένη. Some suggest that these participles are in
the wrong order, for one reads a letter before one knows its
purport. Has St Paul been careless, or has he sacrificed sense
to sound? Probably neither: one recognizes the hand-writing
before one reads the letter; at any rate, one perceives that it is
a letter before one reads it.

ὑπὸ πάντων ἀνθρώπων. Another blow, whether intended or
not, to his opponents, whose testimonials were not published.

3. φανερούμενοι. The construction is continued from ὑμεῖς
ἐστέ, and the meaning is continued from ἀναγινωσκομένη. 'Ye

* Cf. μηδὲν ἐργαζομένους ἀλλὰ περιεργαζομένους (2 Thess. iii. 11); μὴ
ὑπερφρονεῖν παρ' ὃ δεῖ φρονεῖν (Rom. xii. 3); γινώσκεις ἃ ἀναγινώσκεις (Acts
viii. 30).

are our epistle, read by all, for you are being made manifest.'
The idea of ' making manifest ' is freq. in this part of the letter ;
iv. 10, 11, v. 10, 11, vii. 12.

ἐπιστολὴ Χριστοῦ.   Is the genitive subjective, objective, or
possessive?   Probably the first, and in that case it may be
another hit at the false teachers ; 'their testimonials have little
authority, but ours were written by Christ.'*   Or he may be
merely disclaiming all credit ; ' Christ is the agent to whom the
composition of the letter is due ; I am only the instrument.'
Chrys. takes the genitive as objective ; ' a letter which tells of
Christ.'   Some moderns make it possessive ; 'ye are a letter
belonging to Christ,' i.e. ' ye are Christians.'

διακονηθεῖσα ὑφ' ἡμῶν.   We need not seek an exact interpretation and ask whether, if Christ is the author of the letter, διακ.
ὑφ' ἡμῶν means that St Paul was His amanuensis, or that he
carried the letter to its destination.†   The metaphor is not
thought out in detail.   The words mean that St Paul and his
colleagues were Christ's ministers in bringing the letter of
recommendation into existence by converting the Corinthians.
See on 1 Cor. iii. 5, iv. 1.   We have ὑπό here, not, as in i. 19,
iii. 4, the more usual διά.   Chrys. understands διακονηθεῖσα of St
Paul's preparation of their hearts ; 'for as Moses hewed the
stones and tables, so we your souls.'   Per ministerium nostrum
scripsit Christus in vobis fidem spem caritatem ac reliqua bona
(Herveius).   We have the passive διακονεῖσθαι, as here, in viii. 19,
of the service rendered ; in Mk. x. 45 it is used of the person
who receives the service.

οὐ μέλανι.   Cf. 2 Jn. 12 ; 3 Jn. 13 ; Jer. xxxvi. 18.   See artt.
' Ink ' and ' Writing ' in Hastings, DB., atramentum and tabulae
in Dict. of Ant.   Ink could be blotted out (Ex. xxxii. 33) or
washed off (Num. v. 23, where see Gray's note).   Non atramento
scriptum est, id est non ita ut possit deleri, sicut ea quae atramento
scribuntur ; sed Spiritu Dei vivi, id est ut aeternaliter et vivaciter
in cordbus nostris aut vestris permaneat, sicut ille qui scripsit vivit
et aeternus est (Herveius).   See the beautiful passage in Plato,
Phaedrus, 276 C, in which it is said of the good teacher, that he
does not much care to write his words in perishable ink, tracing
dumb letters which cannot adequately express the truth, but
finds a congenial soul, and then with knowledge sows words
which can help themselves and him who planted them, and can
bear fruit in other natures, making the seed everlasting and the
possessor of it happy.

* Christum facit auctorem, se vero organum, ut calumniatores intelligant
sibi cum Christo esse negotium, si maligne contra obtrectare pergant (Calvin).
† See Swete, The Holy Spirit in the N.T., pp. 193 f. ; Deissmann, Light
from the Anc. East, p. 379.

6

πνεύματι Θεοῦ ζῶντος. See on 1 Cor. xii. 3 and Rom. viii. 9, 14. The epithet ζῶντος is not otiose; the Spirit is an efficient force, and the letter which it produces consists of living persons. Moreover, the epithet accentuates the contrast between the abiding illumination of the Spirit and the perishable blackness of inanimate ink. In the Pauline Epp. and Hebrews, Θεὸς ζῶν is frequent; in Mt. xvi. 16, xxvi. 63; Rev. xv. 7, we have the less common ὁ Θεὸς ὁ ζῶν. For the difference see Westcott on Heb. iii. 12.

οὐκ ἐν πλαξὶν λιθίναις. This again is not quite in harmony. It would have agreed better with the metaphor of a letter to have said 'not on parchment' (ἐν μεμβράναις, 2 Tim. iv. 13), or 'not on papyrus' (ἐν χάρτῃ, 2 Jn. 12). But the Apostle has already in his mind the contrast between the Mosaic and the Christian ministry (vv. 4–11), and he therefore introduces here 'tables of stone' (Ex. xxxi. 18, xxxiv. 1) rather than ordinary writing materials. He suggests that the living 'letter of Christ,' which is his testimonial, is superior, not only to the formal letters brought by the Judaizing teachers, but even to the tables at Sinai. Those tables were indeed written with the finger of God; yet they remained an external testimony, and they had no power of themselves to touch men's hearts; whereas the credentials of the Christian teachers are internal, written on the yielding hearts both of themselves and of their converts. The Corinthians cannot disregard a commendation written on their own hearts. The law written externally is a terror to evil-doers; the internal law is an inspiration to those who do well. As soon as the Apostle's thought had reached the 'tables of stone,' the current contrast between 'the heart of stone' and a 'heart of flesh,' τὴν καρδίαν τὴν λιθίνην and καρ. σαρκίνην (Ezek. xi. 19, xxxvi. 26; cf. Jer. xxxi. 33, xxxii. 38), would easily come in to strengthen the comparison.

Omitting details, which give fulness but somewhat disturb the metaphor, we have as the main thought this; 'That which *Christ* by the *Spirit* of *God* has written on your hearts is recorded in our hearts as commending us to all mankind.' Once more (see on i. 22) we can perceive how the elements of Trinitarian doctrine lie at the base of the Apostle's mind and influence his thought and language; cf. Rom. xv. 16.

ἐν πλαξὶν καρδίαις σαρκίναις. This difficult expression is the better attested reading: καρδίας is a manifest correction, for no one would alter καρδίας to καρδίαις. Unless with WH. and Wendland we suspect a primitive error, such as the accidental insertion of the second πλαξίν, we must accept the harder reading and take καρδίαις in apposition with πλαξίν. Two ways are possible, according as σαρκίναις is taken with πλαξίν or with καρδίαις. The former is very awkward : 'on tables (viz. hearts) of flesh.' It does not follow, because σαρκίναις balances λιθίναις, and λιθίναις agrees with πλαξίν, that therefore σαρκίναις agrees with πλαξίν. But Syr-Hark. takes it so ; 'on tables of flesh—on hearts.' 'On tables (which are) hearts of flesh' is less awkward, but not pleasing. In dictating, St Paul might easily utter the words slowly in the order in which we have them, ἐν πλαξίν— καρδίαις — σαρκίναις. But the proposal to omit πλαξίν is attractive. Both λιθίναις and σαρκίναις indicate the *material* of the πλαξίν, which in each case has ἐν, while the instruments (μέλανι, πνεύματι) have no preposition ; σαρκικαῖς (i. 12, x. 4 ; see on 1 Cor. iii. 1) would indicate *quality*, especially ethical quality.

B, f Vulg. insert καί before ἐνγεγραμμένη. K has γεγραμμένη. καρδίαις (א A B C D E G L P, Syr-Hark., Eus.) rather than καρδίας (F K, Latt. Syr-Pesh. Copt. Aeth. Arm. Goth., Iren. and perhaps Orig. Did. Cyr-Alex.).

III. 4–11. The Superiority of the New Ministration to the Old.

God alone made us competent to be ministers of the new covenant, which in splendour immeasurably surpasses the old.

⁴ This confidence, that you are a letter composed by Christ testifying to the effectiveness and validity of our commission, is no fiction of my own invention : it comes through Christ, and it looks reverently to God as its source. ⁵ It is not a confidence that of ourselves we are competent to form any estimate of results, as though we made ourselves sufficient. All our competence to form such an estimate has its source in God. ⁶ For of course He did not leave us incompetent of serving Him when He called us to be ministers of His new covenant with men,—a covenant which consists, not of a lifeless written code, but of an active penetrating Spirit. For the written code imposes a sentence of death, but the Spirit breathes new life.

⁷ Now if the Law's dispensation of death, which was a thing of letters graven on stones, was inaugurated with such dazzling manifestations of glory that the Children of Israel could not look steadily at the brightness on the face of Moses, a brightness which was already beginning to fade away, ⁸ how much greater must be the glory of the dispensation of the Spirit ! ⁹ For, surely, if the dispensation which sentences men to death can be a manifestation of God's glory, then the dispensation which offers righteousness as a gift to men must be a far greater manifesta-

tion. ¹⁰ For the former may be said to have had no real glory, because its glory pales and vanishes before the overwhelming glory of the latter. ¹¹ For if that which comes and soon passes away has somewhat of glory, much more must that which for ever abides be arrayed in glory.

4. Πεποίθησιν δὲ τοιαύτην ἔχομεν. 'And confidence of this kind we possess through Christ to God-ward.' He refers to the πεποίθησις just expressed, viz. that he has no need of any credentials other than the testimony which the existence of the Corinthian Church bears : that fact by itself suffices to prove his Apostleship. But he at once hastens to show that in this confidence there is no self-praise and no claim to credit; for it is conditioned in two ways which entirely exclude vain-glorious thoughts; it is through Christ, and it is towards God. In LXX πεποίθησις occurs only in the taunt of Rabshakeh, Τί ἡ πεπ. αὕτη ἦν πέποιθας; but it is fairly freq. in other versions. It is found six times in Paul and nowhere else in N.T. See Index IV.

διὰ τοῦ Χριστοῦ. 'Therefore not through any innate power of our own. Apart from Him we could do nothing (Jn. xv. 5). He gave us the power that we have'—τοῦτο ἡμῖν δεδωκότος τὸ θάρσος (Thdrt.).

πρὸς τὸν Θεόν. *Erga Deum,* which is the second security against boastfulness. 'The quiet confidence which gives us strength (Is. xxx. 15) is not directed towards anything earthly as the ultimate source of strength, but towards God' (Rom. xv. 16). The idea is that of looking towards the person on whom one relies. This use of πρός is rare; the usual prepositions after πεποίθησις are εἰς (viii. 22) and ἐν (Phil. iii. 4), and after πεποιθέναι, which is very freq. in N.T. and LXX, εἰς, ἐν, and ἐπί with dat. (i. 9) or acc. (ii. 3). In 2 Thess. iii. 4 we have πεποίθαμεν δὲ ἐν Κυρίῳ ἐφ' ὑμᾶς, a construction which would have stood very well here.

5. οὐχ ὅτι . . . ἀλλ'. The πεποίθησις is further explained, both negatively and positively, in order to exclude still more emphatically the suspicion of self-commendation. 'I do not mean that (i. 24) of ourselves we are sufficient (ii. 16) to account anything as originating with ourselves.' He does not claim the right or power to judge that he and his fellows are the real authors of any part of the work ; they claim no credit whatever. Experience has proved that as ministers they are competent, for the Corinthian Church exists; but all their competency comes from above.

The statement is particular, not general ; and it has reference simply to the successful work at Corinth. The Apostle is not denying free will, nor is he declaring that the natural man can do nothing but evil. Calvin's remark, *Paulus non poterat igitur magis hominem nudare omni bono*, is altogether beside the mark. By a fanciful derivation, El Shaddai, as a name for God, was sometimes interpreted as meaning 'The Sufficient One.' In Ruth i. 20, 21, ὁ Ἱκανός, and in Job xxi. 15, xxxi. 2, xxxix. 32 [xl. 2], Ἱκανός is used as a Divine name. It is just possible that St Paul had this in his mind here; 'Our sufficiency comes from the Sufficient One.' Nowhere else in LXX or N.T. is ἱκανότης found.

ἀφ' ἑαυτῶν should be placed before ἱκανοί ἐσμεν (אBC, Copt. Arm.) rather than after λογ. τι (ADEFGP, Latt.) or after ἱκ. ἐσμεν (KL, Syr-Hark.) or be omitted (17, Syr-Pesh.). λογίσασθαι (אABKLP) rather than λογίζεσθαι (CDEFG). For ἐξ ἑαυτῶν, BFG have ἐξ αὐτῶν (WH. ii. p. 144).

6. ὃς καὶ ἱκάνωσεν ἡμᾶς. 'Who also made us sufficient as ministers,' where 'who' = 'for He.' No English version before the RV. marks the repetition, ἱκανοί, ἱκανότης, ἱκάνωσεν: nor does the Vulgate, which has *sufficientes, sufficientia, idoneos fecit*. There is a similar repetition in διακονηθεῖσα, διακόνους, διακονία, and this is followed by δόξα (eight times in five verses), δεδόξασται, τὸ δεδοξασμένον. As in 1 Cor. iii. 5, διάκονος is used in quite a general sense. There is no evidence that at this time διάκονος had an exclusively official sense, or designated any particular class of Christian minister: see Westcott on Eph. iv. 12. The aorist ἱκάνωσεν points to the time when St Paul was called to be an Apostle; at that crisis he was made competent (Col. i. 12) to respond to the call. See Index IV.

καινῆς διαθήκης. 'Of a new covenant' (RV.): 'of the New Testament' (AV.) is misleading. The covenant is fresh and effective, with plenty of time to run, in contrast to the old covenant, which is worn out and obsolete. This is the constant meaning of καινός as distinct from νέος, so that καινός always implies superiority to that which is not καινός, whereas what is νέος may be either better or worse than what is not νέος. See Trench, *Syn.* § lx. and Lightfoot on Col. iii. 10.

The usual word for 'covenant' is συνθήκη, which occurs thirteen times in LXX, but not at all in N.T. It is not suitable for a covenant between God and man, for it suggests that the parties meet on equal terms. See on 1 Cor. xi. 25. Here the emphasis is on καινῆς. Contrast διαθήκης καινῆς μεσίτης (Heb. ix. 15), where the emphasis is on διαθήκης. To be ministers of the old covenant was no great distinction; there were large numbers of them, and their duties were largely matters of routine. But to be made competent ministers of a new covenant with God was an extraordinary grace. In Heb. xii. 24 we have διαθήκης νέας μεσίτης, the only passage in which διαθήκη νέα occurs. Christianity was both νέα and καινή, it was of recent origin and it was effective, whereas Judaism was old and effete. It was also αἰωνία. 'I will make a new covenant (διαθήκην καινήν) with the house of Israel' (Jer. xxxi. 31). 'And I will make an everlasting covenant (δ. αἰωνίαν) with them, 'that I will not cease to do them good' (Jer. xxxii. 40).

We are not yet in a position to say the final word respecting the rendering of διαθήκη in N.T., where the word occurs thirty-three times, mostly in Paul (nine) and in Hebrews (seventeen). Probably the extremists on both sides are in error. It seems to be reasonable to hold that διαθήκη cannot always be rendered 'covenant' in accordance with LXX use, and that it cannot always be rendered 'testament' in accordance with the usage of classical writers and that of Greek-speaking populations in the East in the first century. Among the crucial passages are Gal. iii. 15–18 (see Lightfoot) and Heb. ix. 16, 17 (see Westcott). It does not follow that, because 'covenant' is the meaning elsewhere in N.T., therefore 'covenant' is the meaning in both these passages; or that, because 'testament' is the meaning in one or both of these, therefore 'testament' is the meaning everywhere. Deissmann (*Light from Anc. East*, p. 341; *Licht von Osten*, p. 243) says; "There is ample material to back me in the statement that no one in the first century A.D. would have thought of finding in the word διαθήκη the idea of 'covenant.' St Paul would not, and in fact did not. To St Paul the word meant what it meant in his Greek O.T., 'a unilateral enactment,' in particular 'a will or testament.' This one point concerns more than the superficial question whether we write 'New Testament' or 'New Covenant' on the title-page of the sacred volume; it becomes ultimately the great question of all religious history; a religion of grace, or a religion of works? It involves the alternative, was Pauline Christianity Augustinian or Pelagian?" On this Lietzmann rightly remarks that, however true it may be that διαθήκη almost always means 'testament' in profane literature, yet in the very numerous passages in LXX in which a διαθήκη between God and man is mentioned it cannot have this meaning; and this is true also of the passages in N.T. which have been influenced by the LXX. "I know of no instances of 'a unilateral enactment' (*einseitige Verfügung*). We must abide by the Hebrew and translate 'covenant.' One instance of this usage we at any rate have in Aristoph. *Birds*, 440. Peisthetairos refuses to have any dealings with the birds, ἢν μὴ διάθωνταί γ' οἴδε διαθήκην ἐμοί—not to peck him." See Ramsay's valuable dissertation, *Galatians*, §§ 33, 34, pp. 349–370; A. Lukyn

Williams, *Galatians*, pp. 68–70; Wickham, *Hebrews*, pp. 71–73; *Expositor*, Dec. 1908, pp. 563–565; E. Riggenbach, *Der Begriff der Diatheke im Hebraerbrief*, 1908; Muntz, *Rome, St Paul, and the Early Church*, pp. 146 f., 165 f.

οὐ γράμματος ἀλλὰ πνεύματος. 'Not of letter, but of spirit, for the letter puts to death but the spirit gives life.' This saying holds good of many other things besides the Law and the Gospel; everywhere letter prescribes, spirit inspires. But we must not be misled by the common contrast in English between 'letter' and 'spirit,' which means the contrast between the literal sense and the spiritual or inward sense of one and the same document or authority. By γράμμα and πνεῦμα St Paul means two different authorities; γράμμα is the written code of the Law, πνεῦμα is the operation of the Spirit in producing and promulgating the Gospel. See on Rom. ii. 29, vii. 6.* This passage is almost a summary of the Ep. to the Romans. St Paul mentioned the tables of stone (*v.* 3) in preparation for this comparison between the old ministration and the new. The old put forth a written code of duty, so onerous as to kill hope and love; the new is inspired by the spirit, which is able to revive what is ready to die. See Swete, *The Holy Spirit in N.T.*, p. 319.

We see here once more (see on 1 Cor. ix. 20; Dobschütz, *Probleme*, p. 82) how completely St Paul had broken with the Jewish Law.† He has now reached the main topic in this portion of the Epistle (iii. 1–vi. 10), viz. the glory of Apostleship under the new covenant. The Judaizing teachers had not been able to extricate themselves from the trammels of the old covenant. But experience has taught St Paul that the embrace of the Law has now become deadly. It is effete and cannot adapt itself to the new conditions. It is purely external; 'Thou shalt not do this overt act,' 'Thou shalt do this overt act.' It has no power to set free and strengthen the moral elements in man. It makes heavy demands, but it gives nothing. It commands and imposes a punishment for disobedience; but it gives no power or encouragement to obey. The spirit of Christianity is the opposite of this. It is a living force. Instead of pressing the man down from without, it lays hold of him from within; it supplies, not slavish rules, but emancipating principles. It enriches and quickens those who welcome it, and it makes them

---

* "No idea is more familiar to us than the distinction between the spirit and the letter. . . . Yet, so far as I am aware, it occurs in S. Paul for the first time. No doubt the idea was floating in the air before. But he fixed it; he made it current coin" (Lightfoot, *Sermons in St Paul's*, p. 206).

† "The third chapter is a polemic against the doctrine that believers in Christ ought to pay respect to the Law of Moses" (Menzies, p. xxv).

both desirous and able to follow its inspirations. " The Law,"
says Chrys., "when it takes a murderer, puts him to death;
grace, when it takes a murderer, gives him light and life."

It is evident from the language used that the Apostle is
contrasting the spirit of the Gospel, not merely with ceremonial
regulations, but with the whole code, whether ceremonial or
moral, of the Mosaic Law. That Law said to the Jew, " Obey,
or it will be worse for you." The Christian says to the Gospel,
" Obedience is the thing that I long for."

The genitives, γράμματος and πνεύματος, probably depend on
διακόνους (see *v.* 8); but the meaning is much the same if we
take them after διαθήκης. They are qualifying or characterizing
genitives and are equivalent to adjectives: we might translate,
'not letter-ministers, but spirit-ministers.' Winer, p. 297 ; Blass,
§ 35. 5.

τὸ γὰρ γράμμα ἀποκτ. This does not refer to capital punishment, which the Law inflicted for a variety of crimes, such as
adultery, blasphemy, dishonour to parents, idolatry, murder,
prophesying falsely, sabbath-breaking, witchcraft, etc., although
there may be some indirect allusion. In a much more serious
sense the Law kills, in that it sends men along the road which
leads to eternal death. It does this by its prohibitions, which
at once suggest the doing of what is prohibited, and also make
men conscious of having sinned and merited punishment. " By
giving edge to the conscience, it intensifies the sense of remorse.
A child will go on doing a wrong act ignorantly, till it has
become a habit, without any inward dissatisfaction ; till at
length some authoritative voice says, ' That is a wicked act.'
Then everything is changed. Each recurrence of the evil habit
brings misery to the child. It has the sentence of condemnation in itself. The commandment has slain the child " (Lightfoot). Again, the letter kills by setting up lofty standards, which
it does not help men to reach, and which without help they
cannot reach. This takes the heart out of them, for they feel
from the first that disastrous failure is certain. Moreover, the
Law held out no hope of a resurrection, by means of which the
failures of this life might be rectified. *Lex non est adjutrix
legentium, sed testis peccantium quae mortificat peccatores* (Pseudo-
Primasius). *Spiritus vivivicat qui intus docet animam qualiter
ea quae audit intelligere debeat* (Herveius). With St Paul the
principle that ' the letter puts to death ' is an axiom ; and it was
confirmed by his own experience. See on Rom. vii. 7–25,
pp. 184–189. But this verse would have been very obscure if
we had not possessed Romans, which was written in Corinth
and shows what St Paul had been teaching there. In all this
disparagement of τό γράμμα there was no danger of seeming to

disparage Christian writings, for as yet there were no Christian
Scriptures. The Apostle, without being aware of it, was beginning to make such writings.

The excellent cursive 17 has οὐ γράμματι ἀλλὰ πνεύματι, which is
supported by Lat-Vet. *non litera sed spiritu*; but Vulg. has *non litterae
sed spiritus*. B has ἀποκτείνει, א G K P 17 have ἀπ϶κτέννει, a form said
to be Aeolic, A C D E L ἀποκτενει, which D³ L accentuate ἀποκτένει.

7. ἡ διακονία τοῦ θανάτου. See on 1 Cor. xv. 56 and comp.
Gal. iii. 10, which quotes Deut. xxvii. 26 : διακονία is not abstract
for concrete, 'ministry' for 'ministers'; it means the whole
dispensation of the Mosaic Law. The Apostle's main object is
to show the superiority of the Christian ministration. This
involves disparaging the Jewish ministration, which he does in
strong language, because of the mischief done by the Judaizers.
"See," says Chrys., "how he again cuts the ground from under
the Judaistic point of view." He adds that the Apostle does not
say that the Law produced death, but that its ministry tended to
death, when it declared 'the soul that sinneth, it shall die'
(Ezek. xviii. 4).* The inferiority of the Law to the Gospel is
shown in three different aspects, the second of which is an
explanation or justification of the first : it is a ministration of
death, a ministration of condemnation, and a ministration which
was designed to be only temporary.

ἐν γράμμασιν, ἐντετυπωμένη λίθοις. 'In letters, and engraven
on stones.' It is necessary to insert 'and,' in order to make
clear that we have here two attributes of the διακονία, which was
in writing that might never be read or understood, and written
on dead and heavy material. 'Graven in letters on stones'
would give only one of these ideas. Κεκολαμμένη ἐν ταῖς
πλαξίν is said of the writing made by God on the *first* tables
(Ex. xxxii. 16). It is not said who wrote on the second tables
(the nom. may be God or Moses), nor whether the writing was
engraved or not (Ex. xxxiv. 28). The Commandments, as
the centre and basis of the Mosaic code, are here put for the
whole of it, as the Sermon on the Mount is sometimes put for
the whole of the Christian code. 'In writing' would be better
than 'in letters'; but the connexion between γράμμα and ἐν
γράμμασιν must be preserved.

ἐγενήθη ἐν δόξῃ. 'Came into existence in glory,' *i.e.* had a
glorious inauguration; or 'came to be in glory,' *i.e.* was trans-
ported into a glorious condition. Bachmann defends the latter
rendering by a number of instances from papyri in which γίγνεσθαι

---

* *Ministratio mortis lex est, quae ostenso revelatoque peccato confundit,
conterret et occidit conscientiam* (Melanchthon, *Loci Theologici*, p. 65, ed.
Volbeding).

ἐν seems to mean 'pass into a certain state'; ἐν νόσῳ γενόμενος, ἐν ἀσφαλεῖ γενέσθαι, κ.τ.λ. This use is not rare in N.T. Cf. [Lk. xxii. 44]; Acts xxii. 17; Phil. ii. 7; 1 Tim. ii. 14; Rev. i. 10, iv. 2; but it does not fit the context here. The Law was not given in an inglorious condition and afterwards promoted to a glorious one; it was ἐν δόξῃ from the first. Driver notices that St Paul's key-words in this passage (δόξα, δεδόξασται) are suggested by the LXX rendering of 'shone' in Ex. xxxiv. 29, 35, viz. δεδόξασται. We may contrast the aor. here with the fut. ἔσται in v. 8; the latter implies permanence, the former not.

ὥστε μὴ δύνασθαι ἀτενίσαι. Ex. xxxiv. 30 says no more than that 'they were afraid to come nigh him'; but Philo (Vita Moys. i. 2, p. 665) gives the current belief; κατέβαινε πολὺ καλλίων τὴν ὄψιν ἢ ὅτε ἀνῄει, ὡς τοὺς ὁρῶντας τεθηπέναι καὶ καταπεπλῆχθαι, καὶ μηδὲν ἐπιπλέον ἀντέχειν τοῖς ὀφθαλμοῖς δύνασθαι κατὰ τὴν προσβολὴν ἡλιοειδοῦς φέγγους ἀπαστράπτοντος. There was a Jewish tradition that the light which shone in Moses' face was the light which inaugurated the Creation. Vulg. here varies the translation of πρόσωπον in a capricious way; *ut non possent intendere filii Israhel in faciem Mosi propter gloriam vultus ejus, quae evacuatur.* See Index IV. On the difference between ὥστε with the infinitive and ὥστε with the indicative, see T. S. Evans in *Expositor*, 3rd series, iii. p. 3. Excepting here and v. 13, ἀτενίζειν is peculiar to Luke in N.T.; it is freq. in Acts. In LXX it is rare and late.

τὴν καταργουμένην. 'Which was being done away'; imperfect participle. It was very splendid, but it was very transient. This is not stated in Exodus, but it seems to be implied, and it is brought in here with much effect at the end of the sentence, to be enlarged upon as a separate point of inferiority in v. 11. 'Was to be done away' (AV.) is certainly wrong,* and 'was passing away' (RV.) is doubtful. In v. 14, as generally in Paul, the verb is passive, and it may be passive here and in vv. 11, 13; see on 1 Cor. i. 28, xv. 26 and on Luke xiii. 7 for the meaning of the verb.

γράμμασιν (א A C D² and ³ E K L P, d e f g Vulg. Copt. Syr-Pesh. Goth.) rather than γράμματι (B D* F G). f Vulg. omit the ἐν before γραμμ. א^c D² and ³ E K L, d e f Vulg. Arm. insert ἐν before λίθοις. In all three cases note the divergence between Greek and Latin in bilingual MSS.

8. πῶς οὐχὶ μᾶλλον. 'How shall not to a greater extent the ministration of the spirit be in glory?' The ἔσται does not point to the future coming of the Messianic Kingdom; it indicates that διακονία τ. πνεύματος will continue to be in an

---

* The same error is made by Beza, *quae gloria erat aboelenda*, and is repeated in v. 13, *in finem ejus quod abolendum est*, where AV. inconsistently has 'is abolished.'

atmosphere of glory. Or ἔσται may be the logical future, of the natural consequence of what has been stated. Cf. εἰ δὲ ἀπεθάνομεν σὺν Χριστῷ, πιστεύομεν ὅτι καὶ συζήσομεν αὐτῷ (Rom. vi. 8).

9. εἰ γὰρ ἡ διακονία τῆς κατακρίσεως. The second point of contrast is explanatory (γάρ) of the first; the Law is a διακ. τ. θανάτου because it is διακ. τ. κατακρ., for condemnation results in death. 'If such a ministration is glory, to a much greater extent the ministration of righteousness is superabundant in glory.'* The use of the pres. here is against ἔσται being the logical future. By 'righteousness' is meant that which is attributed to man when he is justified. Through faith in Christ man is more than forgiven; his debt is cancelled and he has something placed to his credit.

The ἐν which is usual after περισσεύειν (viii. 7; Eph. i. 8; etc.) is omitted here, probably to balance δόξα in the first clause. In the first contrast we have ἐν δόξῃ . . . ἐν δόξῃ: in the second, δόξα . . . δόξῃ. Cf. 1 Thess. iii. 12; Acts xvi. 5; here many texts insert ἐν.

ἡ διακονία τ. κατ. (B D² E K L P, f g Vulg. Copt. Goth.) is probably to be preferred to τῇ διακονίᾳ τ. κατ. (א A C D* F G 17 d e Syrr.); but the latter may be original; 'For if the ministration of condemnation *has* glory.' D E G have ἐστιν after δόξα. א³ D E F G K L F, Latt. Arm. have ἐν before δόξῃ.

10. καὶ γὰρ οὐ δεδόξασται τὸ δεδοξασμένον. 'For indeed that which has been made glorious in this respect has been deprived of glory by reason of the glory which exceeds it?' It is outshone by something which is much more dazzling and beautiful. When the sun is risen, lamps cease to be of use; *orto sole lumen lucernae caecatur.* In this way the paradox becomes true that 'what had been made glorious was not made glorious.' In comparison with the glory which superseded it, it seemed to have had no glory at all. Cf. ὅμοιοι τοῖς τυφλοῖς ἂν ἦμεν ἕνεκά γε τῶν ἡμετέρων ὀφθαλμῶν (Xen. *Mem.* iv. iii. 3). Stallbaum on Plato, *Rep.* 329 B gives other examples of this use of ἕνεκα.

If ἐν τούτῳ τῷ μέρει be taken with τὸ δεδοξασμένον, the meaning will be 'in respect of the illumination of Moses' countenance.' But it is better to take the words with οὐ δεδόξασται and under-

* "Paul, then, must be not less distinguished than Moses; this is the extraordinary claim made by the Apostle in this passage. To have set up a genuine and lasting spiritual movement in a society like the Church at Corinth is proof that it is so; for Moses produced no such result; the opposite is the result of what he did. And what is being done at Corinth is being done in other places also; mankind is passing into the final stage of its history" (Menzies).

stand them as anticipating what follows; 'in this respect,' viz.
because of the overwhelming glory of the Gospel. The phrase
is repeated ix. 3, and nowhere else in N.T. Ὑπερβάλλειν is
found only ix. 14; Eph. i. 19, ii. 7, iii. 19; and its derivative
ὑπερβολή is also purely Pauline in N.T., peculiar to this group,
and most freq. in 2 Cor. (i. 8, iv. 7, 17, xii. 7); in LXX only
4 Mac. iii. 18.

For οὐ δεδόξ. a few cursives and a few Latin texts have οὐδὲ δεδόξ. Vulg.
has *nec* and also spoils the oxymoron by rendering *nam nec glorificatum est
quod claruit in hac parte.* εἵνεκεν (א A B D E G P) rather than ἕνεκεν
(C K L).

11. Third contrast; again explanatory (γάρ) and in support
of what precedes. 'For if that which was being done away was
through glory, to a much greater extent that which abideth is in
glory.' What is given to last only for a time is as nothing in
comparison with what is given to last for ever. Christianity is
εὐαγγέλιον αἰώνιον (Rev. xiv. 6), a Gospel reaching forward into
eternity and bringing with it σωτηρίαν αἰώνιον (Is. xlv. 17; Heb.
v. 9), and its ministers are ministers διαθήκης αἰωνίου (Heb. xiii.
20). They have not the transitory glory of Moses in their faces,
but in their souls they have the everlasting glory of the message
which they deliver. Supply ἐστίν rather than ἔσται with ἐν
δόξῃ.

The change from διὰ δόξης to ἐν δόξῃ may indicate the
difference between what passes and what abides. We have a
similar change Rom. v. 10, in a sentence very similar in construction to this; εἰ γὰρ ἐχθροὶ ὄντες κατηλλάγημεν τῷ Θεῷ διὰ τοῦ
θανάτου τοῦ υἱοῦ αὐτοῦ, πολλῷ μᾶλλον καταλλαγέντες σωθησόμεθα ἐν
τῇ ζωῇ αὐτοῦ. In Eph. i. 7 we have the converse change from
ἐν to διά, from what is permanent to what was transitory; ἐν ᾧ
ἔχομεν τὴν ἀπολύτρωσιν διὰ τοῦ αἵματος αὐτοῦ. St Paul is fond
of changes in prepositions; 1 Cor. xii. 8; Gal. ii. 16; Rom.
iii. 30.

These verses (7–11) show what a revolution had taken place
in the mind of St Paul since he had exchanged the Law for the
Gospel. Christianity is so superior to Judaism that it has
extinguished it. Even in its best days, when it also was a
Divine revelation to the human race, Judaism had a glory which
was infinitesimal compared with that which was inaugurated by
Christ. A rich variety of expressions is used to bring this out.
The Gospel is μᾶλλον ἐν δόξῃ, is πολλῷ μᾶλλον ἐν δόξῃ, πολλῷ
μᾶλλον περισσεύει δόξῃ, and the δόξα is ὑπερβάλλουσα. It secures
from death, it secures from condemnation, and it abides. In
this argument the Apostle has chiefly in view the Judaizers who
made the Law indispensable and superior to the Gospel. Beet,
p. 349.

III. 12–IV. 6. The Great Boldness of the New Ministers.

Conscious of the vast superiority of the New Covenant, we need no veil to cover deficiencies, but deliver our message with boldness and openness.

¹² Seeing, therefore, that we servants of the Gospel have a sure expectation that the glory of the new covenant will prove as superior in duration as it is in splendour, and will never disappear before a far greater glory, we venture to preach with great confidence, frankness, and courage, at the risk of being accused of self-commendation. ¹³ Unlike our opponents, we have nothing to conceal. We have no need to act as Moses did. He used to put a veil over his face, to prevent the children of Israel from gazing at the gradual dying away of the glory which the presence of the Lord had imparted to his countenance. The passing away of that glory symbolized the transitory character of the Mosaic dispensation ; and by concealing the former from the people Moses might seem to be concealing the other also. ¹⁴ But, so far from seeing what the fading of the glory signified, or profiting by our plain speaking, their spiritual perceptions were deadened. For down to this very day, when the records of the old covenant (which might teach them so much) are read, the same veil of ignorance as to the transitory character of the Law lies still upon their minds, still unlifted, because by becoming members of Christ, and in that way alone, is it done away. ¹⁵ And unto this very day, whenever the Law of Moses is read in their synagogues, a veil of miscomprehension lies upon their hearts. ¹⁶ But just as Moses, when he returned to the presence of the Lord, removed the veil from his face, so, when any one of them turns to the Lord, the veil is removed from his heart, and he sees that the dispensation of the Law has come to an end. ¹⁷ Now the Lord to whom such an one turns is the Spirit of Christ, and where the Spirit of Christ is, there is emanicipation from the bondage of the Law and of sin. ¹⁸ And all we Christian men, freed from the Law and freely obeying a higher commandment, have a glory which resembles that of the unveiled Moses. As we gaze with unveiled face upon the glory of the Lord Christ, before which the glory of Moses vanished away, we are daily being transformed into spiritual likeness to Him, from one degree of brightness to another,—an

amazing transformation, but not beyond belief, when we remember that the power which transforms us is a Spirit which is Lord.

IV. [1] Seeing then that the Gospel is so glorious and is so unreservedly made known, and that we by God's mercy have been made competent for the ministration of it, we have a courage which corresponds with that mercy. [2] We are not cowardly schemers,—far from it. We have from the first refused to adopt underhand methods of unworthy trickery; we follow no courses of unscrupulous cunning; we do not tone down or in any way tamper with God's message. On the contrary, we set forth the truth so clearly and purely that this at once commends us to the conscience of our hearers, however much it may differ in different men. If, however, the verdict of all human consciences may err, we are not afraid to appeal to the judgment of God. [3] I do not deny that the Gospel which we proclaim so openly and honestly does not penetrate to the hearts of all who hear it; a veil intervenes. That is true, but only of those who are lost, [4] in whose case the god of this evil dispensation has blinded their understandings, unbelievers, as they are, so that for them there is no morning-glow from the light which is shed by the Gospel,—the Gospel which is charged with all the glory of Christ, who is the image of God. [5] Yes, the glory of Christ; for it is not our own claims that we press, but those of Christ Jesus, as the risen and glorified Lord. Our relation to you is that of bondservants, in the service of Him who Himself took the form of a bondservant. [6] I say that we do not press our own merits, because we have none; all that is of value in us is derived. To the God who in the beginning said, Out of darkness light shall shine, we owe the light that has shined in our hearts, the light which springs from the knowledge of the glory of God, which we must pass on to others. I have knowledge of that glory, for I have seen it myself on the face of Christ.

The closing words of this section are a complete explanation of the statement made at the beginning of it and elaborated in iv. 2. The man who has always in his heart the Divine light which shone into it from the face of the glorified Lord cannot be guilty of tricky artifices and double-dealing with a view to commending himself and winning applause. The light trans-

figures him, and he is ever transparent and open. He works to
impart the light to others, not as coming from himself, but from
God through Christ.

We may notice the close correspondence between the last
seven verses of this chapter and the first six verses of the next
chapter. In both we have three subjects in the same order;
the excellence of the Gospel ministry, the sad condition of those
who are so blind as to be unable to see the excellence of the
Gospel, and the Divine source of the excellence. Both passages
begin with similar words expressing the rich possession of those
to whom the ministry of the Gospel has been entrusted, and in
both the metaphor of the veil is used. In the first passage this
metaphor is applied to the unbelieving Jews, in the second to
unbelievers generally, especially, but not exclusively, Gentiles.
The repetition of ἔχομεν and ἔχοντες of the treasure possessed by
Christian misssionaries should be noted (iii. 4, 12, iv. 1, 7, 13).
See below on iv. 1.

12. Ἔχοντες οὖν τοιαύτην ἐλπίδα. That he says 'hope' rather
than 'confidence' (v. 4) does not prove that ἔσται is to be
supplied with ἐν δόξῃ in v. 11. The glory of the Gospel has
already begun, and therefore ἐστίν rather than ἔσται is required.
But that the Gospel will prove permanent (τὸ μένον) is a matter of
hope, and therefore ἐλπίδα is here quite in place. 'Because, therefore, we have a sure hope that our glory will continue, we use
great boldness.' For οὖν following a participle see i. 17, v. 6, 11,
vii. 1; 1 Cor. xi. 20; Rom. v. 1; Heb. iv. 14, x. 19; 1 Pet. ii. 1.

πολλῇ παρρησίᾳ χρώμεθα. He had been accused of having in
one matter used such levity that his word could not be relied on
(i. 17). He says here that he habitually uses great boldness and
openness of speech, because he is in possession of a great hope.
The word παρρησία implies that the boldness is exhibited either
in speech or in action. It is opposed, not only to timidity, but
to reserve, and it is sometimes misunderstood, for it may seem
to imply self-confidence and self-commendation.* But it has
quite other sources. Ministers who feel that God has made
them competent (ii. 16, 17), and that their work will endure,
have ground for παρρησία. Chrys. expands, οὐδὲν ἀποκρυπτόμενοι,
οὐδὲν ὑποστελλόμενοι, οὐδὲν ὑφορώμενοι. Calv., *aperta et plena*

---

* Arrian in his letter to Lucius Gellius, introductory to his report of the
Discourses of Epictetus, says that they are memoirs of the philosopher's
thought and freedom of speech (παρρησία), the aim of which was simply to
move the minds of his hearers to the best things; but it may not have this
effect on those who read the report of these utterances.

Christi manifestatio. It is possible that in explaining the nature of this παρρησία the Apostle is not only following up his answer to the charge of ἑαυτοὺς συνιστάνειν (*v.* 1), but also again glancing at the hole-and-corner methods of his Judaizing opponents; but what follows is on a higher level than mere controversy.

In Vulg. παρρησία is generally *fiducia*, but also *constantia* (Acts iv. 13), and *confidentia* (Heb. x. 35), while μετὰ παρρησίας is *audenter* (Acts ii. 29), and παρρησίᾳ (adv.) is *palam* or *manifeste.* Beza's *in loquendo evidentia* is no improvement on *fiducia*, and Erasmus goes wrong in changing *utimur* (Vulg.) to *utamur.* See Index IV.

13. καὶ οὐ καθάπερ Μωυσῆς. The structure is defective, but the sentence is quite intelligible; 'And we do not put a veil over our faces, as Moses used to put a veil over his face.' Comp. Mk. xv. 8, where there is nothing to correspond to καθὼς ἐποίει αὐτοῖς and 'to do' has to be supplied. From the lofty position in which God has placed him the Apostle looks down even on Moses. Moses and the Prophets often spoke obscurely, for they did not always understand their own message, and much had not been even dimly revealed to them that was clearly known to the Apostles. 'Many prophets and righteous men desired to see the things which ye see and saw them not' (Mt. xiii. 17). 'Concerning which salvation the prophets sought and searched diligently.' And 'not unto themselves but unto you did they minister these things' (1 Pet. i. 10, 12). For καθάπερ see on i. 14.

πρὸς τὸ μὴ ἀτενίσαι. 'That the children of Israel should not look steadfastly upon the end of that which was passing away.' There is no δύνασθαι in this verse, and we have πρὸς τὸ μή, and not ὥστε μή. In *v.* 7 'could not look steadfastly' is right; but here 'could not' (AV.) is incorrect and misleading. The difference is considerable. In *v.* 7 it is said that the glory was so dazzling that the people could not look steadily at it. This is not stated in Ex. xxxiv. 29 f., but it is not inconsistent with what is stated there. Here it is said that Moses used to veil his face so that the people should not see the fading away of the glory on it. This is inconsistent with the AV. of *v.* 33; '*Till* Moses had done speaking with them he put a veil on his face'; which means that the people were terrified by the brightness and would not come near him, and so he wore a veil all the time that he was addressing them. This is erroneous. The correct translation is, '*When* Moses had done speaking with them he put a veil on his face.' He knew that the brightness was caused by converse with Jehovah, and would fade away when he was absent from the Divine presence. He did not wish the people to see the disappearance of the brightness, and therefore, when he had delivered his message, he covered his face, until he returned to the presence of the Lord. This is plain in LXX and Vulg.,* as also in RV., but it is quite obscured in AV. Apparently we are to understand that this practice was continued by Moses throughout the wanderings in the wilderness.

The Apostle's main point is this fading of the glory, which he treats as symbolizing the temporary nature of the Mosaic Law. He does not say that it was intended to convey this lesson ; but, as in 1 Cor. x. 2–4 and Gal. iv. 21–26, he takes the O.T. record and gives it a spiritual meaning. The meaning of πρὸς τό with the infinitive is in N.T. generally final, expressing the subjective purpose, 'with a view to,' 'in order that.' Mt. v. 28, xxvi. 12, and Lk. xviii. 1 seem to be exceptions. St Paul has it four times (here ; 1 Thess. ii. 9 ; 2 Thess. iii. 8 ; Eph. vi. 11), and in each case it expresses the purpose of the agent or agents. In this case it was the purpose of Moses that the Israelites should not witness the vanishing of the glory from his face. This does not imply that Moses understood the vanishing to be a sign of the transitory character of the Law ; still less that he wished to conceal its transitory character from the Israelites. He wished to conceal from them the *end* of the fading illumination. He did not wish them to go on watching him till there was no more glory to watch.

It is the Apostle who makes the passing away of the glory a symbol of the transitoriness of the Law, and the veil a symbol of obscurity and concealment. In these two respects the Gospel ministration is greatly superior to that of the Law. It is permanent, and it conceals nothing that its adherents can understand. Its ministers deliver a message which reaches out into eternity, and they deliver it fearlessly, with entire frankness and freedom.

τὸ τέλος τοῦ καταργουμένου. The whole phrase and the context make the meaning of τέλος certain : 'the end of that which was passing away,' or (passive) 'was being done away,' means the cessation of the glory. We may set aside 'the end of that which is abolished' (AV.), which seems to mean Christ as the end of the abolished Law (Rom. x. 4). This meaning of τὸ τέλος is adopted by Aug. and Thdrt., but it does not stand investigation. St Paul could not mean that Moses veiled his face to prevent the Israelites from seeing Christ. Nor does τὸ τέλος mean the final cause, the aim and object of the Law. Why should that be concealed from the people, and how would the use of a veil conceal it ? And Luther is certainly wrong in

* ἐπειδὴ κατέπαυσεν λαλῶν πρὸς αὐτούς, ἐπέθηκεν ἐπὶ τὸ πρόσωπον αὐτοῦ κάλυμμα : *impletisque sermonibus, posuit velamen super faciem suam.*

making τοῦ καταργουμένου masc., 'of him who is passing away,' viz. Moses, which is quite alien from the context. The Vulg. is puzzling, *in faciem ejus, quod evacuatur*, but the *quod* shows that this reading gives no support to the view that τοῦ καταργ. is masc.

αὐτοῦ (A B C G L P 17) rather than ἑαυτοῦ (א D E K). For τέλος, A has πρόσωπον, which some copyist may have taken from the previous line or from *v.* 7.   f Vulg., Ambrst. have *faciem* for *finem*.

14. ἀλλὰ ἐπωρώθη τὰ νοήματα αὐτῶν. 'But their minds were dulled.' The ἀλλά looks back to the preceding μή. 'Dulled' is perhaps better than either 'blinded' (AV.) or 'hardened' (RV.). The Rhemish version has 'their senses were dulled,' following the Vulg., which has *obtunsi sunt sensus eorum*. Vulg. generally has *excaecare*, but Jn. xii. 4, *indurare*. 'Harden' is the original meaning of the verb, but this does not agree well with 'minds'; minds are blinded, blunted, dulled. As 'blinded' is wanted for ἐτύφλωσεν (iv. 4), 'blunted' or 'dulled' will be better here. J. A. Robinson (*Ephesians*, pp. 264–274) gives a full history of πωρόω and πώρωσις, and comes to the conclusion that from the original idea of petrifaction the words come to indicate insensibility, especially of the eyes. The meaning generally required by the context in the N.T. is obtuseness or intellectual blindness rather than hardness. Lightfoot on 2 Thess. ii. 8 remarks that St Paul sometimes uses καταργεῖν in opposition to 'light' (1 Cor. ii. 7; 2 Tim. i. 10) as here in *vv.* 7, 13, and this is somewhat in favour of 'blinded' or 'dulled' rather than 'hardened.' Strictly speaking, νοήματα are the products of νοῦς, and therefore 'thoughts' rather than 'minds': but here, as in iv. 4 and xi. 3, νόημα seems to mean the thinking faculty. The same difference of meaning is found in class. Grk.* See on ii. 11.

It is not necessary to decide whether St Paul is speaking of the Jews of his own day, as what follows seems to intimate, or of the contemporaries of Moses, as what precedes rather implies. He is thinking of the nation as a whole without distinction of time. The aor. may be timeless, and in that case may be rendered 'have been dulled' or 'are dulled.' Nor need we ask whether their minds were dulled by God, or by the evil one, or by themselves: in different ways all three contributed to the result. The indefinite passive has the advantage of raising no side issue; the one important fact is the intellectual πώρωσις of the Jews, which is a warning to the Corinthians not to exchange Christian clearness and freedom for the obscure entanglements of Judaism.

* In Agathon's speech in praise of Eros, he ends with mention of the beautiful song which Eros sings, θέλγων πάντων θεῶν τε καὶ ἀνθρώπων νόημα (Plat. *Symp.* 197 E).

To what does · But' (ἀλλά) refer? To the main topic of
these verses, the παρρησία of the Apostle and his colleagues.
'We do not use concealments, as Moses did; we speak openly
to the people ; but (*aber*) in spite of that, they do not understand. Even the free preaching of the Gospel is powerless
against the deep-seated insensibility of Jewish prejudice. This
is one of the strongest of St Paul's strong statements against
Judaism. Others explain, 'But (Moses had no need to hide
anything, for) their minds were dulled.' This is a less obvious
connexion.

ἄχρι γὰρ τ. σήμερον ἡμέρας. It must have been insensibility,
for it remains unyielding still. "Why are ye perplexed that the
Jews believe not Christ? They do not even believe the Law.
They are ignorant of grace also, because they did not know even
the Old Covenant, nor the glory which was in it. For the glory
of the Law is to turn men to Christ" (Chrys.). *Nisi enim
credideritis, non intelligetis* (Pseudo-Primasius).

τὸ αὐτὸ κάλυμμα. Not of course the same veil that Moses
used, but one which had the same effect, viz. preventing them
from recognizing that the Mosaic dispensation was transient.
Aug. evidently thought that Moses wore the veil while he was
speaking to the Israelites, for he says on this passage, *sonabat
enim vox Moysi per velum, et facies Moysi non apparebat ; sic et
modo Judaeis sonat vox Christi per vocem Scripturarum veterum :
vocem earum audiunt, faciem sonantis non vident* (*Serm.* lxxiv. 5).
The *tallith*, which Jews now wear as a scarf on the shoulder
when worshipping in the synagogue, was formerly worn on the
head. It is just possible that there may be some reference to
this. A reference to the wrappers in which the rolls of the
sacred books were kept is not probable.

ἐπὶ τῇ ἀναγνώσει. 'At the reading.' This use of ἐπί of the
occasion on which or circumstances in which something takes
place is common enough (i. 4, vii. 4; 1 Cor. xiv. 6; etc.). It
makes rather strange sense to take ἐπὶ τ. ἀν. after μένει, for a veil
abiding on reading is a picture difficult to realize. We know
from Acts and other sources that the synagogues, where the O.T.
was publicly read (Acts xiii. 15), were often the headquarters of
hostility to the Gospel (Acts xiii. 45, 50, xiv. 2, 19, etc.). Aug.
De Civ. Dei, xvii. 7, says; "The O.T. from Mount Sinai which
gendereth to bondage, profiteth nothing, except so far as it bears
witness to the N.T."

τῆς παλαιᾶς διαθήκης. 'The Old Covenant' and 'the
New Covenant' are such familiar expressions to us that we are
apt to forget their enormous significance to those who first used
their equivalents. This is plainly stated in Heb. viii. 13; 'In
that he saith, A new covenant, he hath made the first old. But

that which is becoming old and waxeth aged is nigh unto vanishing away.' Nowhere else in N.T. is the expression παλαιὰ διαθήκη found, and it is possible that St Paul was the first person to declare the abrogation of the covenant made with Israel by speaking of the Pentateuch as ἡ παλαιὰ διαθήκη. Παλαιός implies far more than ἀρχαῖος does, that what is 'old' is the worse for wear. Trench, *Syn.* § lxvii.

μὴ ἀνακαλυπτόμενον. This probably agrees with τὸ κάλυμμα just mentioned; 'the same veil abideth, *without being lifted, because* it is in Christ (and in Him alone) that it is done away.' But μὴ ἀνακ. may be a nom. or acc. absolute; 'the same veil abideth, *the revelation not having been made that* it is done away in Christ.' Field suggests a third method; 'the same *mystery* remains unrevealed, *viz.* that it is done away in Christ.' The second method labours under two disadvantages; (1) the clumsy absolute case, which, however, is not without examples; see Winer, p. 669, who rejects it as inapplicable to this passage; (2) the meaning given to ἀνακαλυπτόμενον, which in this context seems almost necessarily to refer to the moving of the veil; see *v.* 18. The third method avoids these drawbacks, but involves one which is more serious, *viz.* taking κάλυμμα in a different sense from that which it bears both before and after this verse. Everywhere else it means the veil and not the thing veiled, *i.e.* a mystery. The second method may be right; it is strongly supported by Meyer, Stanley, Alford, Bachmann, and others, and is admitted to RV. marg. But with AV., RV., most ancient writers, Waite, Way, Weymouth, J. H. Bernard, Massie, De Wette, Neander, B. Weiss, Schmiedel, Bousset, and others, it seems better to take μὴ ἀνακαλυπτόμενον with τὸ κάλυμμα.

ὅτι ἐν Χριστῷ καταργεῖται. AV. and RV. read ὅ τι, and translate, 'which veil is done away in Christ.' But this use of ὅ τι for ὅ is open to question. Reading ὅτι, our rendering will depend on the rendering of μὴ ἀνακ. Either, 'abideth without being lifted, *for* it is in Christ that it is done away'; or 'abideth, the revelation not having been made *that* it is done away in Christ.' Adopting the former, we make the sentence a parenthetical explanation of μένει μὴ ἀνακαλυπτόμενον, for it is union with Christ which does away with the veil, and this union the unconverted Jews reject. Note the emphatic position of ἐν Χρ. It is in union with Him, and in that alone, that the removal of this ignorance takes place. The difference between ἐν (i. 14, 17) and διά (*v.* 4, i. 5) should be observed. The number of passages in which ὅτι may be either 'because' = 'for,' or 'that,' is considerable (i. 14, vii. 9, 13, 16; 1 Cor. i. 5, 14; etc.). They are specially common in Lk. (i. 45, vii. 16, 39, ix. 22, x. 21, xi. 38, xxii. 70).

τῆς σήμερον ἡμέρας is the reading of nearly all authorities, but K L Syr·
Pesh. Aeth., under the influence of *v.* 15, omit ἡμέρας.

15. The metaphor of the veil is changed in a way somewhat
similar to that in which the metaphor of the epistle is changed in
vv. 1–3. Previously, the veil was something external to themselves which hid from them the truth that the dispensation of
the Law was temporary and vanishing. Now it is something
within them which keeps them from recognizing and welcoming
the truth, viz. their prejudice in favour of the old dispensation;
see on Lk. v. 39. It is probably because of this change of
meaning that κάλυμμα has no article; '*the* veil' would mean
'veil' in the same sense as before, and AV. obscures the sense
by inserting the definite article. In *v.* 16, τὸ κάλυμμα means
the veil mentioned in *v.* 15.

ἀλλ' ἕως σήμερον ἡνίκα ἂν ἀναγινώσκηται. 'But unto this day,
whenever Moses is read, a veil lies upon their heart.' The
ἀλλά refers to μὴ ἀνακαλυπτόμενον, 'not lifted up, but (so far
from that) a veil lies on their heart.' 'Heart,' as often in
Scripture, and especially in Paul, is the seat of the intelligence
(iv. 6; 1 Cor. ii. 9; Rom. x. 6, 8, 10; Phil. iv. 7) as well as of
the affections. Therefore it is beside the mark to say that the
veil is said to be on the heart and not on the head, because "it
was moral and not intellectual blindness which caused their
unbelief." If any contrast is implied in ἐπὶ τ. καρδίαν αὐτῶν, it is
to the effect that the existing veil does not lie on the head of
Moses, hiding the vanishing of the glory of the Law, but on the
hearts of his people, hiding the dawn of the glory of the Gospel.
We might have expected τῇ καρδίᾳ, but ἐπί with acc. usurps the
place of ἐπί with dat., not only where motion previous to rest
may be implied (Mk. ii. 14, iv. 38, etc.), but where there has
been no previous motion (Mk. viii. 2; Lk. i. 33; etc.). Blass,
§ 43. 1. With ἕως σήμερον (Ecclus. xlvii. 7) comp. ἕως ἄρτι
(1 Cor. iv. 13, viii. 7, xv. 6).

ἡνίκα ἂν with ℵ A B C (17 has ἐάν): D F E G K L P omit ἂν. ἀναγινώσκηται (ℵ A B C D E P) rather than ἀναγινώσκεται (F G K L).
There is no sufficient reason for suspecting with Heinrici that the verse
is a gloss. The ἡνίκα in *v.* 16 looks like a reference to ἡνίκα here.

16. ἡνίκα δὲ ἐὰν ἐπιστρέψῃ πρὸς Κύριον. 'But, whensoever a
man shall turn to the Lord, at once the veil is taken away.' The
emphasis on περιαιρεῖται justifies 'at once'; 'away the veil is
taken.' The nom. to ἐπιστρέψῃ is probably τις (so Origen); anyone in the synagogue, any who hears the Law read. Others make
ἡ καρδία αὐτῶν the nom., or Israel, or Moses as the representative, either of the old Israel, or of the new. The last is Calvin's
idea. No doubt St Paul has Ex. xxxiv. 34 in his mind; ἡνίκα

δ' ἂν εἰσεπορεύετο Μωσῆς ἔναντι Κυρίου λαλεῖν αὐτῷ, περιῃρεῖτο τὸ κάλυμμα ἕως τοῦ ἐκπορεύεσθαι. But that does not prove that here he is thinking of Moses as a type, or that here περιαιρεῖται is midd., as περιῃρεῖτο is in Exodus. Whenever Moses turned to the Lord (in the tabernacle), he took off the veil from his head ; whenever a Jew turns to the Lord (Christ), the veil is taken off from his heart. The compound verb expresses the removing of something which envelops.

In ἐπιστρέψῃ πρὸς Κύριον we have another echo of Ex. xxxiv., and possibly more than one. When the people were afraid to come near him, Moses called them, καὶ ἐπεστράφησαν πρὸς αὐτόν. And St Paul probably says Κύριον rather than Χριστόν, because of ἔναντι Κυρίου in Exodus. Frequently the Apostle transfers to Christ expressions which in O.T. are used of Jehovah ; and Κύριον here clearly means Christ, for it balances ἐν Χριστῷ, and Jews had no need to turn to Jehovah. He is speaking of devout Jews worshipping in the synagogue, and perhaps he is thinking of his own conversion.

It is difficult to decide between ἡνίκα δὲ ἐάν (א*A 17) and ἡνίκα δ' ἂν (א³ B D E F G K L P) : the latter may be assimilation to v. 15, where, however, D E F G K L P omit ἄν. There is good reason for suspecting that, independently of v. 15, ἄν may be a correction to literary form. Cf. ὃ ἐὰν ποιήσῃ (1 Cor. vi. 18) ; οὓς ἐὰν δοκιμάσητε (1 Cor. xvi. 3) ; ὃ γὰρ ἐὰν σπείρῃ (Gal. vi. 7). In many places WH. have restored ἐάν, in accordance with the best MSS., where inferior texts have ἄν. The evidence of papyri is overwhelming as to this use of ἐάν for ἄν after ὅς, ὅστις, ὅπου, etc., being very common in the vernacular Greek of the first three centuries. "It seems that in this small point the uncials faithfully reproduce originals written under conditions long obsolete" (J. H. Moulton, p. 43). See Deissmann, Bible Studies, pp. 202 f. ; he gives numerous examples.

17. These two abrupt sentences supply premises in support of the emphatic statement, 'away is taken the veil.' They might be omitted without loss to the argument, for no proof is required for the assertion that whenever men turn to the Lord, the veil which hides Him from them is taken away, and v. 18 would follow well immediately after v. 16. Using these two sentences as premises, we get an argument in this form ; 'The Lord is the spirit,' 'Where the spirit is, is freedom.' Therefore, 'Where the Lord is, the bondage of the letter is taken away.' Or, as Pseudo-Primasius puts it, *Dominus spiritus est. Liber est spiritus. Idcirco non potest velamen accipere, sed magis ipse revelat.* Injected statements and appeals are found elsewhere in Paul ; 1 Cor. xv. 56, xvi. 13, 14 ; Gal. iii. 20.

In these two verses (17, 18) the fluctuation between τὸ πνεῦμα as that which is opposed to τὸ γράμμα, and to τὸ πνεῦμα as the spiritual nature or the inspiring power of Christ, must be allowed for. The contrast between Moses and Christ is one between letter and spirit, between compulsion and inspiration; that is the main fact.   How far St Paul thinks of the Spirit as a power distinct from Christ is not clear ; at any rate Christ and the Spirit work in the same way and produce the same effects.   See on 1 Cor. ii. 12.

The two verses have a rhythm and swing, the balance of which is easily felt in reading aloud.

ὁ δὲ Κύριος τὸ πνεῦμά ἐστιν.
οὗ δὲ τὸ πνεῦμα Κυρίου, ἐλευθερία.
ἡμεῖς δὲ πάντες ἀνακεκαλυμμένῳ προσώπῳ
τὴν δόξαν Κυρίου, κατοπτριζόμενοι
τὴν αὐτὴν εἰκόνα μεταμορφούμεθα
ἀπὸ δόξης εἰς δόξαν,
καθάπερ ἀπὸ Κυρίου πνεύματος.

These rhythmical passages, of which there are several in the Epistle, are evidence of exalted emotion, and perhaps of rhetorical skill that has been acquired by study.   In the next chapter note the correspondence in structure between *v.* 4 and *v.* 6 and the evenly balanced clauses in *vv.* 8–10.

ὁ δὲ Κύριος τὸ πνεῦμά ἐστιν.   This statement has been mis-used controversially; on the one side to prove the Divinity of the Holy Spirit, on the other to show that St Paul identifies the Holy Spirit with the Lord Christ.   The Apostle is not con-structing metaphysical propositions respecting the Divine Nature.   He has still in his mind the distinction between ἡ διακονία γράμματος and ἡ διακονία πνεύματος, the former of which is transient and is obscured by ignorance and exclusiveness, while the latter is permanent, informing, and open.   Moses placed restrictions on external conduct; Christ transforms the inner life.   Therefore to turn from Judaism to Christianity is to turn from the letter which enslaves to the spirit which gives free-dom, and to welcome Christ is to receive in oneself the Spirit of the Lord.   "It is impossible in the Pauline Epistles to make a rigid distinction between the Holy Spirit and the Spiritual Christ.   Life in Christ and life in the Spirit are the same.   It is by partaking of the Holy Spirit that believers grow into Christ. In 1 Cor. xv. 45 Paul says that the last Adam, that is Christ, was made a life-giving Spirit.   In 2 Cor. iii. 17 he says, 'The Lord is the Spirit.'   Paul sometimes falls into the way of speak-ing of the Christian community as a manifestation of the Divine Spirit, and sometimes he speaks of the indwelling Christ.   In Rom. viii. 9, 10 the words 'Spirit of God,' 'Spirit of Christ,' 'Spirit' and 'Christ' are all used interchangeably" (P. Gardner, *The Religious Experience of St Paul*, pp. 176 f.).

It is in the interests of the Trinitarian doctrine that the

possible, but most improbable translation, 'The Spirit is the Lord,' is sometimes adopted. Grammar allows it, for both terms have the article; but the preceding πρὸς Κύριον, which shows that ὁ Κύριος means Christ, and the order of the words forbid it. Lias, in Appendix I., has collected patristic interpretations; Meyer-Heinrici gives several modern suggestions. It is a passage, about the exact meaning of which we must be content to remain in doubt. It is well treated by Headlam, *St Paul and Christianity*, pp. 106 f.

οὗ δὲ τὸ πνεῦμα Κυρίου, ἐλευθερία. ' He who possesses the Spirit of Christ has liberty.' Spiritual freedom of all kinds is meant, with special reference to the bondage of the Law and of sin; cf. 1 Cor. ix. 1, 19, x. 29; Rom. viii. 15; Gal. iv. 6, 7. In Rom. vi. 15-23, vii. 1-6, St Paul expounds the freedom which comes by leaving the strictness of the Law for union with Christ. He compares it to release from slavery and to marriage with a second husband after the death of the first. In each case there is the substitution of new ties for old ones, not the abolition of all ties. Christian freedom is not licence; it is the free acceptance of the ties of affection instead of the enforced acceptance of bonds of fear. Service voluntarily rendered to Him who is the Truth is the most perfect freedom of which a creature is capable; ἡ ἀλήθεια ἐλευθερώσει ὑμᾶς. ἐὰν οὖν ὁ υἱὸς ὑμᾶς ἐλευθερώσῃ ὄντως ἐλεύθεροι ἔσεσθε (Jn. viii. 32, 36).* *Ubicunque est Spiritus Filii, ibi est mentis libertas, ut remoto servili velamine possit libere mens veritatem inspicere* (Herveius). Cf. 1 Cor. vii. 22, and Seneca, *De vita beata*, xv. 6, *In regno nati sumus ; Deo parere libertas est.*

Several conjectural emendations of the text have been suggested. In the first sentence for ὁ δὲ κύριος Baljon and others would read οὗ δὲ κύριος or οὗ δ' ὁ κύριος, ' Now where the Lord is, there is the Spirit.' In the second sentence, for Κύριου Hort would read κύριον, ' Where the Spirit (or, ' the spirit,' in opposition to the letter) is Sovereign, is freedom.' But Hort admits that there is no obvious difficulty in the universally attested reading; and St Paul would be familiar with the expression πνεῦμα Κυρίου in LXX (1 Kings xviii. 12 ; 2 Kings ii. 16 ; Is. lxi. 1).

L has τὸ ἅγιον instead of Κυρίου. The ἐκεῖ before ἐλευθερία should be omitted with ℵ* A B C D* 17, 67**, Syr-Pesh. Copt. Elsewhere St Paul does not write ἐκεῖ answering to οὗ (Rom. iv. 15, v. 20).

18. ἡμεῖς δὲ πάντες. ' And *we* Christians, *all* of us.' ' And ' rather than ' But ' (AV., RV.), for there is probably no contrast in δέ, but mere transition from 'liberty' to those who have been set free. The main contrast is marked by the very emphatic

* " There can be no liberty of thought without the love of truth " (Paget, *The Spirit of Discipline*, p. 106). The chapter is a good comment on this text. " By the use of one of the splendid paradoxes of the higher life, the acceptance of the service of God is equated with a supreme and glorious liberty " (P. Gardner, *The Religious Experience of St Paul*, p. 34).

ἡμεῖς : 'we freed believers, unlike the servile Jews, *qui fidei carent oculis*' (Erasmus). A second contrast is marked by πάντες, which is in antithesis to the one Moses. But this contrast is greatly weakened if, with Bengel and others, we confine ἡμεῖς, as in *vv.* 1–12, to 'we ministers of the Gospel.' There is a tone of triumph in πάντες, which would be out of place if the meaning were confined to a handful of teachers. The contrast is between the one Hebrew leader and the whole body of Christians. Then only one was illuminated, and his illumination was hidden from all the rest; now all are illuminated and there is no concealment. Point after point in the comparison is brought out, and in most of them superiority is brought out also. The rhythm throughout the two verses (17, 18) is jubilant.

ἀνακεκαλυμμένῳ προσώπῳ. This is a third contrast. 'In our case there is no need of concealment ; there is no fear and there is nothing to hide. We Christians know that the glory which is seen in us is permanent, and no one will see it vanishing away. Neither 'with open face' nor 'with unveiled face' gives quite distinctly the full meaning of ἀνακεκαλυμμένῳ. More clearly than ἀκατακάλυπτος (1 Cor. xi. 5, 13) or ἀκάλυπτος (not in N.T. and rare in LXX), ἀνακεκαλυμμένος shows that there has been a veil and that it has been removed. We might have expected καρδία rather than προσώπῳ, for the veil was on their heart before conversion (*v.* 15); but the comparison here is chiefly with Moses, whose face was veiled.

τὴν δόξαν Κυρίου. 'The glory of the risen and glorified Christ,' which is given here as equivalent to the glory of Jehovah in the Holy of Holies or on the Mount. It is inadequate to interpret this of Christ's moral grandeur and beneficence during the life of His humiliation. It is rather the glory of Him 'in whom dwelleth all the fulness of the Godhead bodily' (Col. ii. 9), and who was revealed to Stephen as 'standing at the right hand of God' (Acts vii. 55, 57 ; cf. vi. 15). See Briggs, *The Messiah of the Apostles,* pp. 127, 128 ; *The Messiah of the Gospels,* pp. 292, 293.

κατοπτριζόμενοι. Pres. part. of what continually goes on ; either 'beholding as in a glass' (AV.), or 'reflecting as a mirror' (RV.). The former is clearly the meaning in Philo, *Legis Alleg.* iii. 33, where he expands the prayer of Moses in Ex. xxxiii. 13 thus ; Ἐμφάνισόν μοι σαυτόν, γνωστῶς ἴδω σε, μὴ γὰρ ἐμφανισθείης μοι δι' οὐρανοῦ ἢ γῆς ἢ ὕδατος ἢ ἀέρος ἢ τινος ἁπλῶς τῶν ἐν γενέσει, μηδὲ κατοπτρισαίμην ἐν ἄλλῳ τινι τὴν σὴν ἰδέαν, ἢ ἐν σοὶ τῷ Θεῷ. The latter meaning is adopted by Chrys., and it makes excellent sense. When Moses spoke to the people, he covered with a veil the reflexion of the Divine glory which shone in his face ; but it is with unveiled face that Christians reflect the glory of Christ and make known their changed condition with openness and boldness.   The force of the participle is 'by continually reflecting'; it is by this process that the metamorphosis takes place.

The Latins adopt the other meaning and translate κατοπτριζό-μενοι *speculantes* or *contemplantes*, neither of which preserves the allusion to κάτοπτρον, 'a mirror.' *Speculantes* seems to preserve it, but does not, for *speculari* is 'to see from a watch-tower' (*specula*), not 'see in a mirror' (*speculum*).   In any case, τὴν δόξαν Κυρίου is in an emphatic position in reference to κατοπτριζό-μενοι, as τὴν αὐτὴν εἰκόνα in reference to μεταμορφούμεθα.

τὴν αὐτὴν εἰκόνα μεταμορφούμεθα.   'Are transformed' (RV.) is better than 'are changed' (AV.), for 'to be changed' is the rendering of ἀλλάσσεσθαι (1 Cor. xv. 51, 52 ; etc.).   But 'are *being transfigured*' brings out both the force of the pres. and also the fact that we have here the same word that is used of the Transfiguration (Mk. ix. 2 ; Mt. xvii. 2), and nowhere else, excepting Rom. xii. 2.*   Vulg. has three different words in the four passages ; *transfigurari* in the Gospels, *transformari* here, and *reformari* Rom. xii. 2.   Comp. μετασχηματιζόμενοι in xi. 13, where a less complete change is implied than that which is indicated here.   See on Rom. xii. 2, Lightfoot's detached note on Phil. ii. 7, and Trench, *Syn.* § lxx.   Seneca (*Ep.* vi. 1) has *Intelligo, Lucili, non emendari me tantum, sed transfigurari.* Again (*Ep.* xciv. 48), *Philosophiam qui didicit nondum sapiens est nisi in ea quae didicit animus ejus transfiguratus est.*

'The same image' means the image of Christ reflected in the mirror.   St Paul may have in his mind the εἰκόνα Θεοῦ (Gen. i. 27), the image of God, marred in Adam and restored in Christ. The construction of τὴν αὐτὴν εἰκόνα is regular.   Beza and others say that κατά rather than εἰς is to be understood : but nothing is to be understood.   Like other compounds of μετά which mean change, μεταμορφοῦσθαι means 'to be transformed *into*.'   Thus, μεταβάλλειν is often 'to change to.'   When Menelaus taxes Agamemnon with acting very differently before and after gaining power, he says, κᾀτ' ἐπεὶ κατέσχες ἀ̣ ̣ ̣άς, μεταβαλὼν ἄλλους τρόπους, and with being shifty about the surrender of Iphigeneia, κᾀθ' ὑποστρέψας λέληψαι μεταβαλὼν ἄλλας γραφάς (Eur. *Iph. in Aul.* 343, 363).   Similarly Plato has μεταβάλλειν καινὸν εἶδος, μεταβ. τὴν φιλοπονίαν (*Rep.* iv. 424 C, vii. 535 D), and μεταλλάσσειν χώραν ἑτέραν ἐξ ἑτέρας (*Parm.* 138 C).   In all these cases the verb means 'to make a change *and adopt.*'   The omission of εἰς in the last example is conclusive.   Again, while μετατίθεσθαι τῆς γνώμης is 'to change from one's opinion,' μετατίθεσθαι τὴν γνώμην is 'to change to one's new opinion' (Hdt. vii. 18).   This usage is regular and not rare, whereas we lack evidence that τὴν

* Cf. ἐν δόξῃ in iii. 7 with ἐν δόξῃ in Lk. ix. 31, and ἔλαμψεν in iv. 6 with ἔλαμψεν in Mt. xvii. 2.

αὐτὴν εἰκόνα can be used absolutely like τὸν αὐτὸν τρόπον, τοῦτον τὸν τρόπον, τόνδε τὸν τρόπον, and τρόπον τινά. See Stallbaum's note on Plat. *Rep.* iv. 424 C, where he renders μεταβάλλειν *mutando assumere.*

Driver says of the narrative in Ex. xxxiv. 29–35, that it is "a beautiful symbolical expression of the truth that close converse with God illumines the soul with Divine radiance, and that those who ' with unveiled face ' behold spiritually as in a mirror the glory of the Lord, are gradually through its influence transformed more and more completely into His likeness " (*Exodus*, p. 376). We find similar ideas in the *Book of Enoch*, where it is said that the righteous "will become angels in heaven," and "their faces will be lighted up with joy because the Elect One has appeared " (li. 45), "the glory will not pass away " (lxii. 16), " and they will be resplendent for times without number, for righteousness is the judgment of God " (cviii. 13). Again, in the *Apocalypse of Baruch*; "Their splendour will be glorified in changes, and the form of their face will be turned into the light of their beauty, that they may be able to acquire and to receive the world which does not die, which is then promised to them." " They shall be changed into every form they desire, from beauty into loveliness, and from light into the splendour of glory " (li. 3, 10). This *Apocalypse* is contemporaneous with the chief writings of the N.T. Its authors were orthodox Jews, and it is a good representative of the Judaism against which the Pauline dialectic was directed " (R. H. Charles, Preface).

ἀπὸ δόξης εἰς δόξαν. There is no fading away, as in the case of Moses, for it is no superficial glory. It penetrates to the spiritual nature of the inner man and makes that, like the Lord from whom it comes, a source of light. Yet it is no sudden change, completed, as if by magic, in an instant ; that might end in stagnation. It is a continual and gradual progress, ' from strength to strength' (Ps. lxxxiv. 7), ' shining more and more unto the perfect day ' (Prov. iv. 18). It passes on from this world to the next, from what is temporal to what is eternal. Less probably, ἀπὸ δόξης is interpreted of the Divine glory imparted, and εἰς δόξαν of that which is received. Thus Bengel ; *a gloria Domini ad gloriam in nobis*: and Neander ; 'from the glory which we contemplate to the glory which we receive in ourselves.' Thdrt. perhaps means the same. Aug. *De Trinitate*, xv. 8 ; *de gloria creationis in gloriam justificationis, vel etiam ; de gloria fidei in gloriam speciei, de gloria, qua filii Dei sumus, in gloriam, qua similes ei erimus, quoniam videbimus eum sicuti est.* 'From the glory of Moses to that of the Spirit' (Ambrose), and 'from the glory lost in Paradise to the glory to be received in Heaven' (Ephraem) are curiosities of exegesis.

καθάπερ ἀπὸ Κυρίου πνεύματος. Like the first half of *v.* 17, this is a passage about the exact meaning of which we are obliged to remain in doubt. It is impossible to decide with certainty what the words mean. Every possible translation has been advocated. Are the genitives in apposition? or is one dependent on the other? If the latter, which of the two is dependent? Is the definite or the indefinite article to be supplied in each case? If the definite with one and the indefinite with the other, which is to have which? May the article, whether definite or indefinite, be in either case omitted in English? May κυρίου be an adjective? AV. and RV. give us four renderings, which may be reduced to three, for AV. marg. is almost the same as RV. text. These three are; 'by the spirit of the Lord' (AV.), 'from the Lord the Spirit' (RV.), 'from the Spirit which is the Lord' (RV. marg.). Add to these renderings three more; 'from the Lord of the Spirit,' 'from the Lord who is spirit,' and 'from a sovereign Spirit,' *i.e.* a Spirit which exercises lordship, making κυρίου an adjective. These six do not exhaust the possibilities in English, but they probably include the right rendering.

It will help us to select one or more of these as more probable than the others, if we consider why these words are added. The καθάπερ (see on i. 14), 'even as,' means 'as one would expect,' 'as is natural,' and the words which follow καθάπερ explain how it is that the marvellous transfiguration into the very image of Christ is possible. It is because the Lord is spirit that He effects this change. A spiritual effect must have a spiritual cause, and from a cause of the highest order we may expect very high effects. On the other hand, a spiritual effect of the greatest magnitude requires an adequate cause. The Lord of glory as the giver of glory satisfies these conditions, and the Apostle shows *talem gloriam dari, quae sublimitati congruat dantis* (Ambrst.). These considerations are in favour of 'Even as from the Lord who is spirit' (Jn. iv. 24), 'the Lord' being Christ, as is shown by ἐν Χριστῷ and πρὸς Κύριον. It is the glory of Christ that is reflected in Christians; for which reason 'Even as from a Spirit who is Lord,' or 'Even as from the Spirit which is the Lord,' is less probable. 'Even as from the Lord of the Spirit,' *i.e.* from Christ who sends the Spirit (Jn. xvi. 7), is the simplest translation grammatically, unless κυρίου is an adjective; but it has against it (1) the absence of the articles, which would have made this meaning clearer, and (2) the fact that St Paul generally represents God as the giver of the Spirit (i. 22, v. 5; 1 Cor. ii. 12, vi. 19; 1 Thess. iv. 8), through the instrumentality of Christ (Tit. iii. 6). Hort's proposal to make κυρίου an adjective is attractive, but it has against it the fact that nowhere else in Scripture is κύριος thus used, and this is a strong objection, for the fact can hardly be accidental.* Writers would avoid using as a mere epithet a word which was so constantly employed as one of the Divine names. 'Even as from the Lord who is spirit,' or 'from the Lord, the Spirit,' is on the whole to be preferred. AV. text is not likely to be right.

There is no transforming power so effectual as spirit, and in this case it is the Lord Christ Himself who is the transforming power. Spiritual agency is here at its highest. The most wonderful changes are not only possible but natural, when such a cause is operating. But the conditions must be observed, and they are mainly three. There is the turning to the Lord; every veil that might hide Him must be removed; and it is His glory and no other that is reflected. When these three things are secured, by continual reflexion of the Lord's glory Christians are transfigured into the very image of Him whose glory they have caught and retained, and step by step the likeness becomes more and more complete—εἰς μέτρον ἡλικίας τοῦ πληρώματος τοῦ Χριστοῦ, 'unto the full measure of the maturity of the fulness of Christ' (Eph. iv. 13).

IV. 1. Here again, as between i. and ii., the division of chapters is unintelligently made. The first six verses of this chapter belong to the preceding one, and the close connexion between the two paragraphs is obvious: the opening verses of this chapter show how close it is, for the Apostle is still urging the claims of his office, especially against those who charge him with insincerity and self-commendation.

The six verses run in couplets; the glory of the new ministry (1, 2); the condition of those who are too blind to see the glory of the Gospel (3, 4); the source of the glory (5, 6). A fresh departure is made at *v.* 7. With 1–6 comp. 1 Thess. ii. 1–12, which is a similar vindication of Apostolic authority on behalf of St Paul and his colleagues, and contains several similar expressions.

Διὰ τοῦτο. In 1 Cor. iv. 17 both AV. and RV. have 'For this cause,' which might well be retained here, vii. 13, and xiii. 10, in order to mark a difference between διὰ τοῦτο, διό (iv. 16), which might be 'wherefore,' and οὖν (v. 20), which is usually 'therefore.' Vulg. has *ideo* for διὰ τοῦτο, *propter quod* for διό, and *ergo* for οὖν, not invariably, but in this Epistle. See Index IV.

---

* The familiar language of the Creed, "the Lord, and Giver of Life," is based on these verses (iii. 6, 17, 18). The Greek, τὸ Κύριον τὸ ζωοποιόν, shows that it is wrong to rehearse the words as if they meant "the Lord of life and the Giver of life."

καθὼς ἠλεήθημεν. 'Even as we received mercy.' The words belong to what precedes; 'seeing that, in full accordance with God's mercy, we have this ministry.' It is of God's goodness, and not of any merit of his own, that he has a calling of so high an order. *Habentes eam, non ex meritis, sed ex Dei misericordia, quae nos ministros suos fecit* (Herveius). Cf. the similar use of καθάπερ in iii. 18 to show how Divine action is the explanation of wonderful results. Hort, on 1 Pet. ii. 10, points out that this verb is used "in reference to the signal mercy of the gift of the Gospel." St Paul uses it several times of his own conversion and call (here; 1 Cor. vii. 25; 1 Tim. i. 13, 16). The use of so humble an expression respecting his appointment to the Apostle-ship had special point in writing to Corinth, because there he had been accused of being self-asserting and aggressive. Cf. 1 Cor. xv. 9, 10. For διακονία see on v. 18.

In these six verses, as in the preceding chapter, St Paul is sometimes answering charges which had been brought against himself, and sometimes indirectly bringing charges against his Judaizing opponents by hinting that they do what he declares that he himself does not do; and we cannot always decide which of the two he is doing. In some cases he may be doing both. It is also difficult to decide whether the 1st pers. plur. includes Timothy or anyone else. Apparently the Apostle is thinking mainly of himself.

οὐκ ἐγκακοῦμεν. 'We do not lose heart.' The verb indicates the timidity which shrinks from coming forward and speaking out. Such faintheartedness takes refuge in silence and inactivity, in order to escape criticism, and therefore is the opposite of παρρησία. In Eph. iii. 13, μὴ ἐνκακεῖν follows a mention of παρρησία. The consciousness that he owed his ministry to the graciousness of God inspired the Apostle with courage and frankness. *Misericordia Dei, per quam ministerium accipitur, facit strenuos et sinceros. Etiam Moses misericordiam adeptus est, et inde tantam invenit admissionem* (Beng.). Chrys. paraphrases, οὐ καταπίπτομεν, ἀλλὰ καὶ χαίρομεν καὶ παρρησιαζόμεθα. In short, the Apostle acts up to his own exhortation, ἀνδρίζεσθε, κραταιοῦσθε (see on 1 Cor. xvi. 13). Cf. οὐ γὰρ ἔδωκεν ἡμῖν πνεῦμα δειλίας (2 Tim. i. 7).

Excepting Lk. viii. 1 (where see note), the verb is found only in Paul (*v.* 16; 2 Thess. iii. 13; Gal. vi. 9; Eph. iii. 13), and everywhere there is a *v.l.* ἐκκακ. Here we should read ἐγκακ. (א A B D* F G 17, 67**) rather than ἐκκακ. (C D³ E K L P). In all five passages D³ K L P have ἐκκακ., in four they are joined by C and E, and in three by F and G. The other uncials vary between ἐνκακ., which is right in Lk. xviii. 1, and may be right in Gal. vi. 9 and Eph. iii. 13. The evidence is tabulated by Gregory in *Prolegomena* to Tisch. ed. 8, p. 78. The verb is not found in LXX, but ἐγκακ. is used by Symmachus four times, and ἐκκακ. once. Polyb. IV.

xix. 10 has τὸ πέμπειν τὰς βοηθείας ἐνεκάκησαν of the Lacedemonians dis-
honourably neglecting to send the promised reinforcements; and Philo, *De
confus. ling.* § 13, has οὔτε ἐκκακούμενος ἐκνάμφθην, ἀλλὰ ἐρρωμένως ὠνείδισα
τοῖς ἐξ αὐτῶν μοι καταρωμένοις. Vulg. here has *non deficimus*, d and e *non
deficimus*, g *non fiamus segnes*, Ambrst. *non infirmemur.*

2. ἀπειπάμεθα. The verb both in act. and mid. has a variety
of meanings, but there is no doubt as to its meaning here; 'we
have renounced' or 'we renounce,' *abdicamus occulta dedecoris*
(Vulg.). The aor. is timeless, or "ingressive," J. H. Moulton,
pp. 109, 134. This is more probable than that the aor. refers
to the same period as ἠλεήθημεν. It is not likely that St Paul
means that at his call he definitely renounced certain things.
And of course ἀπειπάμεθα does not mean that he had previously
practised what he here says that he has renounced, as was the
case with St Matthew and Zacchaeus as toll-collectors. He
means that these practices are quite alien to the work of an
Apostle. On this 1st aor. in -a see WH. App. p. 164; Winer,
p. 103; Blass, § 21. 1. The mid. of ἀπεῖπον is not found in
classical Attic, and the dictum of Thomas Magister (57) that
ἀπειπάμην is better Greek than ἀπεῖπον may be doubted. In
Joseph. *Ant.* XVII. iii. 1 we have ἀπείπεσθαι τήνδε τὴν γαμετήν,—a
very rare instance of the 2nd aor. mid.

τὰ κρυπτὰ τῆς αἰσχύνης. The exact meaning of 'the hidden
things of shame' is not clear; but they are the opposite of παρρησία. 'The hidden things which bring disgrace when they are
known,' or 'which make a man ashamed of himself,' or 'which
shame makes a man conceal.' The general sense is much the
same however we analyse the expression. He is not thinking of
heathen vices (Eph. v. 12), but of the underhand methods of the
false teachers. An allusion to circumcision (Thdrt.) is certainly
not intended. See on τὰ κρυπτὰ τοῦ σκότους (1 Cor. iv. 5).
'The hidden things of dishonesty' (AV.) was not far wrong in
1611, when 'dishonesty' might mean 'disgrace,' and 'honesty'
(1 Tim. ii. 2) might mean 'decorous behaviour,' and 'honest'
(Rom. xii. 17) 'honourable,' or 'of good report.' This usage
still survives in the expression "to make her an honest woman,"
but 'dishonesty' here is now misleading.

μὴ περιπατοῦντες ἐν πανουργίᾳ. 'So that we do not walk in
craftiness'; *non ambulantes in astutia* (Vulg.). This is a result
of renouncing τὰ κρυπτὰ τ. αἰσχύνης. By πανουργίᾳ is meant
unscrupulous readiness to adopt any means in order to gain one's
ends. Excepting Lk. xx. 23, only in Paul (xi. 3; 1 Cor. iii. 19;
Eph. iv. 14). The Apostle had been accused of being a πανοῦργος (xii. 16), and if x.–xiii. is part of the intermediate severe
letter, this passage may be a reference to that, or to xi. 3. If
πανουργία refers to the manoeuvres of the Judaizers, it may point

to their efforts to undermine the influence of the Apostle. In our ignorance of the circumstances, there is abundant room for conjectures. See on 1 Cor. iii. 3 for περιπατεῖν of daily conduct, a very freq. use in Paul, = *versari*; also Hort on 1 Pet. i. 15; Milligan on 1 Thess. ii. 12; Lukyn Williams on Gal. i. 13. μηδὲ δολοῦντες τ. λόγον τ. Θεοῦ. See on iii. 17. The verb occurs nowhere else in N.T. and only twice in LXX (Ps. xv. 3, xxxvi. 2). Here, as in ii. 17 and 1 Cor. xiv. 36, ὁ λόγος τ. Θεοῦ means the Gospel message, which is its usual, though not invariable, meaning in Paul (1 Thess. ii. 13; Phil. i. 14; Col. i. 25; 1 Tim. iv. 5; 2 Tim. ii. 9; Tit. ii. 5). See Harnack, *The Constitution and Law of the Church*, p. 340. By δολοῦντες he means using fallacious arguments and misinterpretations, and falsifying the relation of the old revelation to the new. The Judaizers of course resented his use of the O.T. and his disregard of the letter of the Law.

ἀλλὰ τῇ φανερώσει. 'But, on the contrary, by manifestation.' The word occurs in Biblical Greek only here and 1 Cor. xii. 7: it is selected in opposition to τὰ κρυπτὰ τῆς αἰσχύνης. Cf. i. 12, iii. 12, xi. 3.

τῆς ἀληθείας. In opposition to δολοῦντες. 'By the manifesta-tion of the truth' stands first with emphasis; by that, and by nothing else, do they commend themselves; no letters of recommendation, no wily arts, no crying of 'peace' when there is no peace (Jer. vi. 14, viii. 11). In Gal. ii. 5, 14, where St Paul is dealing with similar opponents, we have the more definite expression ἡ ἀλήθεια τ. εὐαγγελίου, and in Col. i. 5, ὁ λόγος τῆς ἀληθείας τ. εὐαγγελίου. In all these places the expression is a protest against misrepresentations of the Gospel and spurious substitutes for it, especially such as destroyed Christian liberty. *Veritas quam manifestamus nos ipsos efficit commendabiles* (Herveius).

συνιστάνοντες ἑαυτούς. This looks back to iii. 1–6. Re-membering who sent him and made him competent for the work, he is not afraid to magnify his office, although he knows that his doing so may be maliciously misinterpreted. Reflexive pronouns of the 3rd pers. with verbs of the 1st pers. plur. are freq. (*v.* 5, v. 12, 15, vi. 4; 1 Cor. xi. 31; Rom. viii. 23, xv. 1; etc.). The simplification is convenient where it causes no ambiguity.

πρὸς πᾶσαν συνείδησιν ἀνθρώπων. 'Unto the human con-science *in all its forms*'; see Westcott on Eph. i. 3, iv. 8, and cf. Rom. ii. 9; Eph. i. 8, iv. 19, 31, v. 3, 9, vi. 18; etc. Passion and prejudice are no safe judges; reason cannot always be trusted; even conscience is not infallible, for the conscience of this or that individual, or class, or profession may give a faulty decision. St Paul takes a wider range. He appeals to *every kind* of conscience among men, confident that they will *all* admit the justice of his claim ; and *securus judicat orbis terrarum.* For this use of πρός comp. πρὸς τὸν Θεόν in iii. 4 ; for συνείδησις see on i. 12.

ἐνώπιον τοῦ Θεοῦ. The accumulation of solemn language in this verse here reaches a climax. He has felt the seriousness of the charges which had been openly formulated, or secretly insinuated, against him by his wily opponents, and he meets them seriously and without compromise. He appeals, not only to every form of human conscience, but to Him to whose mercy (*v.* 1) he owes the high calling which has subjected him to so much criticism, and under whose eye every conscience works : τοὺς εὖ φρονοῦντας ἔχομεν μάρτυρας καὶ τὸν τοῦ συνειδότος Ἐπόπτην (Thdrt.). The appeal can go no higher. *Magnum esset, si hoc solummodo de hominibus diceret ; sed, quia homines falli possunt, ideo subjunxit quod majus est incomparabiliter* (Atto Vercellensis). Cf. vii. 13 ; Rom. xiv. 22.

The reading συνιστάνοντες (A ? B P 47, 67**, 80) is not quite certain ; συνιστάντες (א C D* F G 17, 39) is preferred by some editors : either is to be preferred to συνιστῶντες (D³ E K L). Winer, p. 94, note.

3. εἰ δὲ καὶ ἔστιν κεκαλυμμένον τὸ εὐαγγέλιον ἡμῶν. 'But even though the Gospel which we preach really *is* veiled.' The use of εἰ καί (*v.* 16, v. 16, xii. 11) rather than καὶ εἰ, and the emphatic position of ἔστιν, which here cannot be enclitic, show that St Paul concedes what is stated hypothetically to be actually a fact. Winer, p. 554. In spite of the φανέρωσις τῆς ἀληθείας, the good tidings were not recognized as such by all. Some denied that there had been any φανέρωσις : his preaching was obscure and shifty. He had said that a veil hid the meaning of the Law from them ; it was more true to say that a veil hid his Gospel from them. The Apostle here admits this ; a veil has hid and does hide (perf. part.) the Gospel from them, but the veil is on their own hearts (iii. 15). It is not the fault of the Gospel or of those who preach it that it is rejected by some ; it is the hearers' own fault, because they listen in an attitude that is fatal. They desire, not the truth, but the confirmation of their own views.

The sublimity of St Paul's teaching and his paradoxical expressions laid him open to the charge of saying 'things hard to be understood' (2 Pet. iii. 16). But that was not the cause of the vehement opposition to his teaching. His chief offence was his declaring the Law to be obsolete, and thereby (his enemies said) opening the door to boundless licence. So they declared that his Gospel was imperfect. He had never known the Christ, nor had been intimate with those who had known Him. They, on the contrary, had authentic information.

8

ἐν τοῖς ἀπολλυμένοις. 'In the case of those who are perishing' (see on ii. 15). The ἐν is not superfluous (Blass, § 41. 2); nor does it mean 'in the hearts of,' for the Gospel had not reached their hearts; nor 'in their judgment,' like ἐν ἐμοί, 1 Cor. xiv. 11, for the question is one of fact, not of opinion; but 'in their case.' The uses of ἐν in late Greek are very various; J. H. Moulton, p. 103. Calvin comments on the confidence of the Apostle in this declaration; *magnae fiduciae argumentum est, quod pro reprobis ducere audet omnes qui doctrinam respuunt.* And then, perhaps remembering his own attitude towards those who dissented from him, he adds, *Verum simili fiducia instructos esse convenit, quicunque pro Dei ministris haberi volunt; ut intrepida conscientia non dubitent omnes doctrinae suae adversarios ad Dei tribunal citare, ut illiuc damnationem certam referant.* See on 1 Jn. iv. 16, where the writer says that he and his fellow-teachers receive their inspiration from God, and their message is rejected only by those who are not of God and are not striving to know Him.

4. ὁ θεὸς τοῦ αἰῶνος τούτου. The expression occurs nowhere else; but St Paul speaks of τὸν ἄρχοντα τῆς ἐξουσίας τοῦ ἀέρος (see on Eph. ii. 2), while St John, in three utterances attributed to Christ, has ὁ ἄρχων τοῦ κόσμου τούτου. In Mk. iii. 22 = Mt. xii. 24 and Lk. xi. 15 (Mt. ix. 34), Christ's opponents say that He casts out demons ἐν τῷ ἄρχοντι τῶν δαιμονίων. In all these cases Satan is meant, and in harmony with these passages St John says that the whole κόσμος, *i.e.* the whole of the moral and intellectual universe, so far as it is estranged from God, lies in the power of the evil one (see on 1 Jn. v. 19). This does not mean that God abdicates or surrenders any portion of His dominion to Satan, but that those to whom He has granted free will place themselves under the power of darkness.* Here it is not this κόσμος, *mundus*, but ὁ αἰὼν οὗτος, 'this age,' *seculum*, that is said to have Satan for its god. During the time—believed by St Paul to be short—which would elapse before the Coming of the Lord, Satan reigned wherever there was opposition to the will of God, and this was an enormous sphere.

St Paul speaks frequently of ὁ αἰὼν οὗτος (1 Cor. i. 20, ii. 6, 8, iii. 18; Rom. xii. 2; Eph. i. 21), or ὁ νῦν αἰών (1 Tim. vi. 17; 2 Tim. iv. 10; Tit. ii. 12), or ὁ νῦν καιρός (Rom. iii. 26, viii. 18,

---

* See the *Ascension of Isaiah* x. 11, 12. "The point of this bold comparison seems to lie in this, that as the true God by His Spirit illumines the minds of believers, enabling them to behold the glory of Christ in the Gospel, so the false god of the present age has a counter-spirit at work (or is a counter-spirit) which blinds the minds of the unbelieving that the light of the glory of Christ should not dawn upon them" (G. Vos, *Princetown Biblical Studies,* p. 251).

xi. 5), or ὁ αἰὼν ὁ ἐνεστώς (Gal. i. 4), where it is especially stigmatized as πονηρός, or, in a remarkable expression which combines both terms, ὁ αἰὼν τοῦ κόσμου τούτου (Eph. ii. 2). The
opposite of this evil age or world is ὁ αἰὼν μέλλων (Eph. i. 21 ;
cf. Heb. vi. 5 ; Lk. xviii. 30, xx. 35), which is more commonly
designated ἡ βασιλεία τοῦ Θεοῦ, the period or realm in which God
reigns supreme.   If Satan is the ruler of this limited age, God
is the King of the countless ages which are to follow it ; He is
ὁ βασιλεὺς τῶν αἰώνων (1 Tim. i. 17 ; Tob. xiii. 6, 10; cf. Ps.
cxlv. 13, and see J. H. Bernard on 1 Tim. i. 17).   In [Clem.
Rom.] ii. 6 it is said ἔστιν δὲ οὗτος ὁ αἰὼν καὶ ὁ μέλλων δύο ἐχθροί,
and as we cannot be friends of both, we must detach ourselves
from this one and cling firmly to the other.

It is startling to find one who had all his life held idolatry
in abomination, and been zealous for the glory of the one true
God, using this *grandis et horribilis descriptio Satanae* (Beng.)
and electing to apply the term θεός to the arch-enemy of God
and of mankind (P. Gardner, *The Religious Experience of St
Paul*, p. 203); but what he says about the worship of demons
(see on 1 Cor. x. 20) is some explanation of his view.   There was
a Rabbinical saying, "The first God is the true God, but the
second God is Samael," and Irenaeus (I. v. 4) says that the
Valentinians called the devil Κοσμοκράτωρ.   See J. A. Robinson
on Eph. vi. 12 ; Dalman, *Words*, p. 165.

This verse contains the strongest item of evidence for what
is called "the dualistic element in the thinking of St Paul," *i.e.*
the recognition of a power or powers other than God, external
to man, exerting influence over human affairs, and in some sense
independent of God; and it has been maintained that on this
point the dualism of the N.T. is sharper than that of contemporary Judaism.   It may be so.   Increased recognition of the
mystery of 'the unsearchable riches of Christ' would lead to
a deeper appreciation of 'the mystery of lawlessness.'

Fear of giving Apostolic support to the Manichaean doctrine
of a good God and an evil one caused various Fathers, both
Greek and Latin, to interpret this passage of God.   Irenaeus
(III. vii. 1) and others (Orig. Chrys. Thdrt. Tert. Hil. Aug.)
adopt the device of taking τοῦ αἰῶνος τούτου as the gen. after
τῶν ἀπίστων—'in whom God has blinded the minds of the
unbelievers of this world'; and 'the unbelievers of this world'
is interpreted to mean those who have no part in the other
world, the world of light and bliss.   Aug. (*c. Faust.* xxi. 2) says
that *plerique nostrum* take the sentence in this way.   He and
others seem to be aware that this is questionable exegesis; but
they are of opinion that, as Atto of Vercelli expresses it, because
to interpret the words as meaning Satan brings us near to error,

we must understand them as meaning God Himself. Calvin's comment on this is to the point; *Videmus quid faciat contentionis fervor in disputationibus: si composito animo legissent illi omnes Pauli verba, nemini eorum in mentem venisset ita in coactum sensum torquere: sed quia urgebant adversarii, magis de illis propulsandis quam de inquirenda Pauli mente solliciti fuerunt.* See Chase, *The Lord's Prayer in the Early Church,* pp. 88 f.

ἐτύφλωσεν τὰ νοήματα τῶν ἀπίστων. 'Blinded the minds of the unbelieving.' Nothing is gained by making τ. ἀπίστων proleptic, 'so that they did not believe'; on the contrary, it spoils what is the probable meaning. It was because they refused to believe that Satan had power to blind them. They resisted the influence of light until they lost the power of appreciating it. If the adjective had been proleptic, we should have had ἄπιστα rather than τῶν ἀπίστων, which is a kind of after-thought added to explain how the disastrous blinding became possible. Neither ἀνεγκλήτους in 1 Cor. i. 8 (see note there), nor σύμμορφον in Phil. iii. 21 (see note) is parallel to τῶν ἀπίστων here. As in iii. 14, νοήματα here must mean 'minds' rather than 'thoughts': to speak of blinding men's thoughts is somewhat incongruous. In LXX ἄπιστος is very rare; in N.T. it is specially freq. in 1 and 2 Cor., and is almost always used of unconverted Gentiles But here there is such constant allusion to the Judaizers that we can hardly limit τῶν ἀπίστων to heathen. Cf. Tit. i. 15.

In dictating, St Paul has packed his sentence too full, and the construction is so nearly broken that the meaning is in some respects obscure. It is not clear whether οἱ ἀπολλύμενοι and οἱ ἄπιστοι are coextensive. If not, which of the two includes the other? The latter question can be answered with some certainty, if it arises. It is not likely that οἱ ἀπολλύμενοι is the larger class, of which only some are ἄπιστοι. But it is possible that οἱ ἄπιστοι is a large class, some of whom, by being blinded, become ἀπολλύμενοι. We must translate ἐν οἷς 'in whose case,' not 'among whom': either 'in whose case Satan has blinded the understandings of some who believed not'; or, 'in whose case Satan blinded their understandings because they believed not.' The latter is more probably correct, as being the simpler construction. If we adopt it, then all the ἄπιστοι are blinded and become ἀπολλύμενοι, and the two classes are coextensive. The interest of the discussion lies in the question whether St Paul contemplated the possibility of 'unbelievers' who were not 'perishing.'

εἰς τὸ μὴ αὐγάσαι. The verb may be either transitive, 'to see,' or intransitive, 'to dawn'; therefore either, 'that they should not see the illumination of the Gospel of the glory of the Christ,' or, 'that the illumination of the Gospel, etc., should not

dawn' upon them.   Both AV. and RV. take the latter meaning ;
RV. marg. takes the former, which has in its favour the order of
the words and the absence of αὐτοῖς, which is not genuine, but
has been inserted in some texts in order to make the latter
meaning more possible.   *Qui oculos ad lucem claudunt justum est
ut eis lux occultetur* (Herveius) ; or, as Thdrt. puts it, ἀσθενοῦσι
γὰρ ὀφθαλμοῖς πολέμιος ἥλιος.   The rapid sequence, 'see' or
'dawn,' 'illumination,' 'good-tidings,' 'glory,' 'the Christ,'
'image of God,' shows how anxious St Paul is to give some idea
of the amazing brightness and beauty which was lost when
unbelievers came into the power of Satan.   There is something
stately both here and in *v.* 6 in the series of four genitives in
succession.   In N.T. αὐγάζειν occurs nowhere else, and in LXX
it is very rare ; φωτισμός occurs here and *v.* 6 and six times in
LXX.   It is possible that here we have a trace of the influence
of the Book of Wisdom on St Paul ; cf. ἀπαύγασμα γάρ ἐστιν
φωτὸς ἀϊδίου, καὶ ἔσοπτρον ἀκηλέδωτον τῆς τοῦ θεοῦ ἐνεργείας
(Wisd. vii. 26).   See on v. 1, 4.   In the Testaments (*Levi* xiv.
4), τὸ φῶς τοῦ νόμου τὸ δοθὲν εἰς φωτισμὸν παντὸς ἀνθρώπου.   As
we might expect, neither αὐγάζειν nor φωτισμός has been found
in papyri ; they deal with subjects that do not require the use of
such words.

τῆς δόξης τοῦ Χριστοῦ.   The Gospel 'which contains and
proclaims the glory of the Messiah.'   This was precisely what
the Gospel preached by the Judaizers did not do.*   The addition
of these words was perhaps suggested by the glory of Moses.
In 1 Tim. i. 11 we have 'the Gospel of the glory of the blessed
God.'   Neither expression is inconsistent with ὁ λόγος τοῦ σταυροῦ,
which is foolishness τοῖς ἀπολλυμένοις (see on 1 Cor. i. 18).   It
was the cross which led direct to the glory : ' He became obedient
to the death of the cross ; *wherefore* also (διὸ καί) God highly
exalted Him' (Phil. ii. 9 ; cf. Jn. x. 17 ; Heb. ii. 9).†

ὅς ἐστιν εἰκὼν τοῦ Θεοῦ.   Here again, as in ἐνώπιον τοῦ Θεοῦ
(*v.* 2), we reach the supreme climax.   This addition to the
sentence, which is complete without it, is made in order to show
what 'the glory of the Christ' means ; *hinc satis intelligi potest,
quanta sit gloria Christi* (Beng.).   It means the glory which is
shed abroad by the one visible Representative of the invisible
God, a glory which cannot be seen by those whom Satan has
blinded.   See on Phil. ii. 6 and Col. i. 15, and comp. χαρακτὴρ
τῆς ὑποστάσεως αὐτοῦ (Heb. i. 3).   This is one of the passages

---

* It weakens the force of τῆς δόξης to treat it as a characterizing genitive,
'the glorious Gospel of Christ' (AV.).

† It is here that 'the Gospel of the glory of God' (1 Tim. i. 11) and 'the
Gospel of the grace of God' (Acts xx. 24) are coincident.   God's grace in
sending His Son is His special glory.

in which St Paul comes near to the Johannine doctrine of the
Λόγος. See Bernard, *ad loc.* The Alexandrian school interprets
the εἰκὼν Θεοῦ of the Λόγος : see Lightfoot on Col. iii. 10, and
Foundations, pp. 192 f. Cf. Jn. viii. 19 ; Wisd. vii. 26.

Baljon and others suggest that τῶν ἀπίστων is a gloss ; Bachmann, that
the original reading may have been αὐτῶν τῶν ἀπίστων or simply αὐτῶν.
αὐγάσαι (א B F G K L P) rather than καταυγάσαι (C D E H) or διαυγάσαι
(A 17). After αὐγάσαι D² and ³ E K L P, Syrr. Vulg. Aeth. Goth. add
αὐτοῖς, which some editors accept ; but א A B C D* F G H 17, Lat-Vet.
omit, and insertion to smooth the construction is more probable than
accidental omission. For Χριστοῦ, C has Κυρίου. After τοῦ Θεοῦ, א³ L P,
Syr-Hark. add τοῦ ἀοράτου from Col. i. 15.

5. οὐ γὰρ ἑαυτοὺς κηρύσσομεν. In spite of such strong dis-
claimers as 1 Cor. i. 13, St Paul was accused of preaching
himself. His giving himself as a pattern to be imitated (1 Cor.
iv. 16, vii. 7, xi. 1 ; etc.) would serve as a handle for this charge ;
see on iii. 1. It is less probable that by this accusation his
enemies meant that his revelations were delusions or deliberate
fictions ; he had never seen Jesus and knew nothing about Him ;
what he called "preaching Christ" was preaching his own fancies.
This does not suit the context very well. The γάρ refers to the
preceding verses. 'I call it "our Gospel" (*v.* 3), because we
preach it, but its contents are "the glory of Christ" (*v.* 4) ; *for* it
is not *ourselves* that we preach, but (what is very different) Christ
Jesus as Lord.' Ἑαυτούς is emphatic by position, but κυρίους
is not to be understood with it. 'It is not ourselves that we
preach as lords, but Christ Jesus that we preach as Lord' is an
antithesis which St Paul would not be likely to make. To
'preach Christ as Lord' is to preach Him as crucified, risen, and
glorified, the Lord to whom 'all authority in heaven and earth
has been given.' To confess Him as Lord is to declare oneself a Christian (Rom. x. 9 ; 1 Cor. xii. 3). Κύριον suggests the
δούλους which follows as an antithesis.

ἑαυτοὺς δὲ δούλους ὑμῶν. 'While (we account) ourselves as
your bondservants.' Grammatically, κηρύσσομεν governs the
second ἑαυτούς as well as the first, but that is not what the
Apostle means. He has just stated that he does not preach
himself, which is to be understood absolutely. From no point of
view and in no capacity does he do that ; but the position which
he assumes in relation to his converts is not that of Saviour, but
of a slave. In 1 Cor. iii. 5 he said διάκονοι, 'servants': in
1 Cor. iv. 1, ὑπηρέται, 'underlings'; here he says δοῦλοι,
'slaves.' Elsewhere he calls himself the δοῦλος of Jesus Christ
(Rom. i. 1 ; Phil. i. 1) ; and the qualifying words which he adds
here show that this is his meaning here. It is because Christian
ministers are the bondservants of Christ that they are the bond-

servants of those to whom they minister; and only so far as service to them does not interfere with service to Him, is it allowable to be bondservants to men. This is the only passage in which St Paul speaks of being the δοῦλος of his converts. See Chadwick, *Pastoral Teaching of St Paul*, p. 128. Cf. 1 Cor. vii. 23, ix. 19.

διὰ 'Ιησοῦν. *Propter Jesum*, 'for Jesus' sake.' The use of this name without Χριστόν commonly denotes our Lord in the time of His humiliation (*vv.* 10–14; 1 Thess. i. 10, iv. 14); see on 1 Cor. ix. 1; J. A. Robinson, *Ephesians*, pp. 23, 107. It is rare in the Pauline Epistles, but it has special point here. It is not in order to curry favour with the Corinthians, or to flatter their conceit, that he counts himself as their δοῦλος, but he does so for the sake of Him who ἑαυτὸν ἐκένωσεν μορφὴν δούλου λαβών (Phil. ii. 7); for the sake of Him who commanded His Apostles to be ready for the meanest service (Jn. xiii. 14–16). *Non ad gloriam nostram praedicamus Evangelium, sed ad claritatem Christi, cui obedimus, dum vobis in ministerio verbi servimus non propter vestrum meritum, sed propter Domini praeceptum* (Herveius). For His sake they made themselves the servants of all, in order to bring the more adherents to Him; see on 1 Cor. ix. 19.

Some editors make *vv.* 3 and 4 parenthetical and treat this verse as a continuation and explanation of *v.* 2. Others, with more reason, make this verse a parenthesis. Clearness is not gained by either arrangement. The connexion (γάρ) of *v.* 5 with *vv.* 3 and 4 has been pointed out. There is perhaps yet another thought. 'We do not preach ourselves but Jesus as Lord; therefore those unbelievers who reject our preaching reject, not us, but the Lord Jesus.' On the other hand, the connexion between *v.* 4 and *v.* 6 is close.

This is one of the places in which it is hard to decide between Χριστὸν Ιησοῦν (B H K L, Syr-Pesh. Copt. Arm.) and 'Ιησ. Χρ. (א A C D E, Latt. Syr-Hark. Goth.). F G have Κύριον before 'Ιησ. Χρ. P omits Κύριον. Vulg-Clem. and some inferior Latin authorities insert *nostrum* after *Dominum*; 'we preach Jesus Christ our Lord.' For διὰ 'Ιησοῦν, א* A** C 17, Latt. (*per*, not *propter*) Copt. have διὰ 'Ιησοῦ, 'through Jesus.'

6. ὅτι. This explains why they must preach Christ and not themselves; 'Because the God who said, Out of darkness light shall shine, is He who shone in our hearts.' This is another reason for not treating *v.* 5 as a parenthesis. 'Out of darkness' should come before 'light shall shine' in English, as in the Greek. To omit ὅς is a needless simplification; ἐστιν is to be supplied with ὅς. The statement is in antithesis to *v.* 4, which has influenced the structure of this verse. The unbelieving opponents have been blinded by Satan; the Apostle has been illumined by God Himself, the Creator of Light. Satan reduced them from unbelief to total blindness; God has brought him from darkness to light. In this verse the 1st pers. plur. must mean primarily the Apostle, for the reference to his own experiences on the road to Damascus and in Damascus are almost as clear as his reference to 'Let there be light.' With regard to that, it is possible that some recollection of ἐξανέτει-λεν ἐν σκότει φῶς (Ps. cxi. 4), or of φῶς ποιήσας ἐκ σκότους (Job xxxvii. 15), has influenced his wording. He wants for his purpose ἐκ σκότους as well as φῶς: it was out of darkness, both physical and spiritual, that God rescued him. God blinded his bodily eyes for three days as a means towards healing his spiritual blindness. How could a man who had had these experiences preach himself?

ὁ εἰπών, Ἐκ σκότους φῶς λάμψει. The Apostle reminds his converts of the first creative word that is recorded. The God who is Light (see on 1 Jn. i. 5), the nature of which is to communicate itself and expel darkness, and who is 'the Father of lights' (Jas. i. 17), and therefore the Source of all intellectual and spiritual illumination, is the God who illuminated the Apostles, and in a special manner St Paul. God did not allow darkness to reign over the material universe. With the first utterance attributed to Him He dispersed it. *Magnum opus*, as Bengel remarks. It is not likely that He would allow darkness to prevail throughout the spiritual world. From the first He provided means for dispersing that also. The old lamps, however, were going out; but better ones have taken their place, and some of them have been sent to Corinth.

ὃς ἔλαμψεν ἐν ταῖς καρδίαις ἡμῶν. 'Is He who shone in our hearts,' illuminating our whole moral and spiritual being. He who over the primeval chaos said, 'Let there be light,' and provided sun, moon, and stars to preserve and spread it, has shed light into the chaos of our souls, and has thus provided instruments for the perpetual φανέρωσις τῆς ἀληθείας (v. 2). The details of this process in the case of St Paul himself are told us to some extent in Gal. i. 15, 16. As λάμψει must be intransitive in the previous clause, it is probable that ἔλαμψεν also is intransitive. Some, however, understand φῶς, which is the nom. to λάμψει, as the acc. after ἔλαμψεν, 'made light to shine.' But in class. Grk. the transitive use of λάμπειν is poetical and somewhat rare.

πρὸς φωτισμὸν τῆς γνώσεως τῆς δόξης τοῦ Θεοῦ. The stately series of genitives is parallel to that in v. 4. In both cases the first genitive is subjective; 'the illumining which the knowledge of the glory (or, the Gospel of the glory) produces.'* In v. 4, φωτισμὸς τ. εὐαγγελίου cannot mean 'the enlightenment which produces the Gospel,' and it is unlikely that φωτ. τ. γνώσεως means 'the enlightenment which issues in knowledge.' The knowledge which has this illumining power is in the Apostles, imparted to them by God with a view to (πρός) their employing it to illuminate others. In the account of his conversion given by St Paul to King Agrippa he states that Christ told him of this purpose at the outset; 'To this end (εἰς τοῦτο) have I appeared to thee, to appoint thee a minister and a witness, delivering thee from the People and from the Gentiles, to whom I send thee, to open their eyes that they may turn from darkness to light, and from the power of Satan unto God' (Acts xxvi. 16–18). 'With a view to illumining men with the knowledge of the glory of God' gives the sense. Some would limit the action of φωτισμός to ἐν ταῖς καρδίαις ἡμῶν, 'God shone in our hearts to illumine *them*,' so that the scope of the statement does not extend beyond the Apostles and preachers; but vv. 3 and 4 clearly cover those to whom they preached, and the hearers are probably included here.

ἐν προσώπῳ Χριστοῦ. Like ὅς ἐστιν εἰκὼν τ. Θεοῦ in v. 4, this is an addition to a sentence which would be complete without it, yet an addition which is full of meaning. Christ is the image of God, and in His face is revealed so much of the Divine glory as can be communicated to men, and it is this which Apostles know and have to make known. It may be that St Paul is still thinking of the reflexion of the Divine glory on the face of Moses, and hence says ἐν προσώπῳ Χριστοῦ rather than ἐν Χριστῷ.† But it is more probable that he is thinking of the Divine glory in the face of Christ, which he himself saw on the road to Damascus. Elsewhere he merely affirms that he has seen the Lord (1 Cor. ix. 1, xv. 8), or that God revealed His Son to him (Gal. i. 15). Here he seems to be desiring to tell, as in the narratives in Acts, the splendour of the vision. Christ was revealed to him by God in a glory which was Divine. When he speaks of having knowledge 'of the glory of God in the face of Christ,' he is speaking of what he himself has *seen*. See Bousset, *ad loc*. For προσώπῳ see on ii. 10.

On this lofty level St Paul leaves for a while (till v. 11) the glorification of Apostleship, which is a different thing from

---

* In the Apostles, not in St Paul alone. He is not claiming to be the one original transmitter of the light, any more than he claimed to be the one original diffuser of the perfume (ii. 14).

† Cf. *Book of Enoch* xxxviii. 4; "They will not be able to behold the face of the holy, for the light of the Lord of Spirits is seen on the face of the holy and righteous and elect."

glorification of himself. God does wonderful work with very humble instruments, and takes His instruments sometimes from very unexpected quarters. St Paul often remarks how true this is of himself. But whatever his demerits may be, they only enhance the glory of the Apostleship. What he has accomplished is due to the grace given to an Apostle, not to the abilities of Saul of Tarsus.

It is often debated whether the experiences which produced his conversion were objective or subjective, whether there was any light that was seen by others and any voice that was heard by others. The accounts agree about the sight, but not about the sound. May there not be an error about both? May not the whole of the experiences have been mental, and confined to the future Apostle? * These questions will continue to be asked, and no answer to them can be proved to be true. What is certain is that these experiences produced in St Paul a conviction, which lasted the whole of his life and influenced his whole life, that he had seen and held a conversation with the risen Lord Jesus. In this passage he himself seems to give us both a subjective and an objective element. In ὃς ἔλαμψεν ἐν καρδίαις ἡμῶν we have an internal experience; in ἡ δόξα τοῦ Θεοῦ ἐν προσώπῳ Χριστοῦ we have an external one. Comp. ἐν ἐμοί (Gal. i. 16) with the one and ἑώρακα (1 Cor. ix. 1) with the other (Klöpper, ad loc.). The reasonableness of believing in both these elements is well put by A. T. Robertson, *Epochs in the Life of St Paul*, ch. iii.; and by J. H. Ropes, *The Apostolic Age*, pp. 107–110. See also Ramsay, *The Teaching of Paul in Terms of the Present Day*, p. 15.

λάμψει (א* A D* 67**, Syrr. Aeth.) rather than λάμψαι (א³ C D³ E F G H K L P, Latt. Goth. Arm.), which was perhaps substituted because the wording is so different from Gen. i. 3; 'who commanded the light to shine out of darkness' avoids divergence as to the form of the command. D* F G, Chrys. Tert. Ambrst. omit ὅς before ἔλαμψεν, which simplifies the construction. C*D*F G, d e g r Aeth. substitute αὐτοῦ for τοῦ Θεοῦ. ἐν προσώπῳ Χριστοῦ (A B 17, Arm. (codd.), Orig. Chrys. Tert.) rather than ἐν πρ. Ἰησοῦ Χρ. (א C H K L P, Syrr. Copt. Goth.) or ἐν πρ. Χρ. Ἰησοῦ (D E F G, Latt.).

IV. 7–V. 10. The Sufferings and Supports of an Apostle.

It may seem strange that so glorious a dispensation should be proclaimed by such frail and suffering ministers; but that proves that the power of it is from God and not

* See Cohu, *S. Paul and Modern Research*, pp. 78–80; he gives a useful table of the three narratives in parallel columns. See also Weinel, *St Paul*, pp. 79–84. It is strange that the hypothesis that Wisd. vii. 25, 26 is the basis of the story of St Paul's conversion should be called "attractive."

from them.   They are sustained by God's power and by the
prospect of future blessedness.   The sure hope that present
suffering leads on to eternal glory enables them to bear all
things in the service of Christ.

⁷ But this glory has another side.   This illuminating power is
entrusted to unattractive and worthless persons, as treasure is
stored in earthen jars, in order that it may be patent to all that
the excellence of power which we exhibit is God's gift, and does
not emanate from us.   ⁸ In our conflicts we suffer heavily, but
are never utterly defeated.   Often hard pressed, yet not driven
to surrender; in desperate plight, yet not in despair; ⁹ chased
from the field, yet not left to the mercy of the foe; beaten to
the earth, yet not killed outright; ¹⁰ always carrying about in
the body the imminent danger of dying as Jesus died, in order
that by the continual escapes and deliverances of our bodies it
might be manifest to the world that Jesus is still alive.   ¹¹ Yes,
every day that we live we are continually being handed over to
death for the sake of Jesus, in order that in just that part of us
which is liable to death it might be made manifest to all that the
living Jesus is at work.   ¹² So then it is His death that takes effect
in us while it is His life which, through its power in us, takes
effect in you.   ¹³ There is a Psalmist who has written, ' I believed,
therefore I spoke.'   That is just our case.   We have exactly the
same spirit of faith and trust that he had, and therefore we do
not keep silence.   ¹⁴ We also speak with confidence, because we
know that He who raised the Lord Jesus from the grave will, in
virtue of His Resurrection, raise us up also, and will bring us
into His presence, side by side with you.   ¹⁵ For all that we do
and all that we suffer is done and suffered for your benefit, in
order that the grace which is bestowed on us, being augmented
by the increasing number of those who believe with us and pray
for us, may cause a greater volume of thanksgiving to rise both
from us and from them to the glory of God.

¹⁶ No wonder, therefore, that, with your salvation to work for
and this faith to sustain us, we do not lose heart and act as
cowards.   On the contrary, although our physical powers are
wasting away, yet what is spiritual in us is being ceaselessly
made fresh and strong.   ¹⁷ By this I mean that our present
afflictions, which may seem heavy and protracted, are really

light and momentary compared with the enduring substantiality of glory which they are working out for us in an ever increasingly preponderating degree. [18] And we are sure of this, because we direct our gaze, not towards the fleeting things which we now see around us, but towards the lasting realities which to us are at present unseen.

V. [1] I affirm this because we know well that, if the tentlike body which is our earthly dwelling should be taken down, God supplies us with a better building, a dwelling that is supernatural, lasting, with its site not on earth but in heaven. [2] For truly in this tent-dwelling we sigh and groan, desiring greatly to have our heavenly home put over us, [3] sure that this putting of it on will secure us from being found at Christ's coming without any house at all. [4] For verily we that are still in our tent, awaiting His return, have reason to sigh and groan, feeling oppressed because, while we shrink from the idea of losing it by death, we desire to have the better dwelling placed over it, in order that all that is perishable in the one may be swallowed up by the imperishable nature of the other. [5] Our feelings may seem to be a poor security for this, but we have a far stronger one. He who has schooled us for this very change is none other than God Himself; and He has given us, as a guarantee that we shall have it, no less than His Holy Spirit.

[6] Having, therefore, at all times such a sure ground for confidence, and knowing that so long as we are still at home in the body we are in a sort of exile from our home in the Lord— [7] for here we have to guide our steps by means of faith, because the realities which shape our lives cannot be seen—[8] we have, I say, a sure ground for confidence, and in that confidence we are well content rather to go into exile from our home in the body, and take up our abode in our home with the Lord. [9] Having such a preference, we are not only well content to leave the body, but we earnestly desire that, whether we are still in it or already out of it, we may find acceptance with Him. [10] This desire, in all conditions of existence to be acceptable to Him, is inevitable, when we remember that, by God's decree, from which we cannot escape, there is not one of us but will have the whole of his life and character laid bare before Christ at His judgment-seat, in order that he may receive recompense for the things of which his body was the instru-

ment, in exact requital for his conduct, whether it was meritorious or worthless.

Edmund Waller's lines on Old Age may serve as a prelude to this part of the Epistle.

> The soul's dark cottage, battered and decayed,
> Lets in new light through chinks that Time hath made :
> Stronger by weakness, wiser men become
> As they draw near to their eternal home.
> Leaving the old, both worlds at once they view
> That stand upon the threshold of the new.

The subject remains the same,—the value of the Apostolic office ; but it is regarded from a new point of view. He has shown the exceeding glory of the new dispensation and its superiority to the old, especially with regard to the courage and frankness exhibited by its ministers (iii. 4–iv. 6). That does not mean that the ministers are magnificent persons. In the Apostle's case, so far from external magnificence, there is constant weakness with frequent suffering and depression. But in the weakness of the preachers the Divine power of the Gospel becomes all the more conspicuous, and they know that they may count upon the necessary support here and an eternal reward hereafter.

These sufferings and compensating supports are discussed in three aspects ; in reference to the difficulties of ministerial work (7–15), in reference to the hope of resurrection (16–v. 5), and in reference to life, death, and judgment (v. 5–10). In the first of these he is possibly referring once more to his opponents' reproaches. They may have said that his frequent sufferings were a judgment on him for his false teaching about the Law. We know that they had laughed at his mean appearance and want of eloquence (x. 10). But, he now urges, the contents of a vessel cannot always be inferred from the character of the vessel.

7. Ἔχομεν. The Apostle again and again dwells upon the goodly *possessions* of the Christian, and especially of the Christian minister ; πεποίθησιν τοιαύτην (iii. 4), τοιαύτην ἐλπίδα (iii. 12), τ. διακονίαν ταύτην (iv. 1), θησαυρὸν τοῦτον (iv. 7), τὸ αὐτὸ πνεῦμα τῆς πίστεως (iv. 13), οἰκοδομὴν ἐκ Θεοῦ (v. 1), πάντα (vi. 10), ταύτας τὰς ἐπαγγελίας (vii. 1) ; and he often builds an argument upon these goodly possessions.

Ἔχομεν δὲ τὸν θησαυρὸν τοῦτον. The δέ marks the contrast between the glory on which he has been enlarging and the humiliations about to be described ; ' *But* there is a great deal to be said on the other side.' The contrast is skilfully drawn :

1. it confirms the declaration that the preachers do not preach themselves, for in themselves they are despised and persecuted; 2. it works round to a conclusion which is much in favour of the Corinthians (*vv.* 12–15). 'This treasure' is the illumining power of the knowledge of Divine glory. The power is limitless, but it is stored in very unlikely receptacles.

ἐν ὀστρακίνοις σκεύεσιν. The expression σκεῦος ὀστράκινον occurs four times in Leviticus, and ἄγγος or ἀγγεῖον ὀστρ. is common elsewhere in LXX. Here we have to determine the literal meaning of σκεύη and from this to reach the metaphorical use. The word in its literal sense has a wide range. Articles of furniture in a house (Lk. xvii. 31), differing greatly in value and use (Rom. ix. 21–23; 2 Tim. i. 20), are σκεύη. Not only a vessel for holding things (Jn. xix. 29), but a sheet (Acts x. 11), is a σκεῦος. A σκεῦος is inanimate; it is an instrument or implement, as distinct from a ζῶον (Plat. *Rep.* x. 601 D, *Gorg.* 506 D). It is doubtful whether σκεῦος in its literal sense ever means a body. Its metaphorical sense in N.T. is commonly assumed to be taken from the meaning 'vessel,' but this is not always correct. In Acts ix. 15, σκεῦος ἐκλογῆς, 'a vessel of election,' 'a chosen vessel,' should rather be 'an elect instrument.' In 1 Pet. iii. 7, ὡς ἀσθενεστέρῳ σκεύει, 'as to the weaker vessel,' should rather be 'as to the weaker chattel': both husband and wife are articles of furniture in God's house, and one of them is stronger than the other. In 1 Thess. iv. 4 the meaning of τὸ ἑαυτοῦ σκεῦος remains doubtful and does not help us here. In this passage 'vessel' is certainly right; treasure was frequently stored in earthen jars, a fact of which Wetstein gives numerous illustrations.*

If the treasure is the illumining power of the knowledge τῆς δόξης τοῦ Θεοῦ, what are the vessels in which it does its work? We perhaps give too limited an answer when we say, 'the *bodies* of the chosen ministers.' It is quite true that the human body is often spoken of as a mean vessel or vase which holds the much more precious mind or soul. It is one of those metaphors which are so obvious as to be inevitable. Cicero (*Tusc. Disp.* i. 22), *vas animi.* Seneca (*Ad Marciam Consolatio,* 11), Quid est homo? *Quodlibet quassum vas, et quodlibet fragile . . . imbecillum corpus, ad omnem fortunae contumeliam projectum.* Philo (*Quod deterius potiori insid. sol.* § 46), τὸ τῆς ψυχῆς ἀγγεῖον, τὸ σῶμα. And again (*De Migr. Abr.* § 35) ὁ μὲν γὰρ ἡμέτερος νοῦς

---

* The words are repeatedly quoted by Jerome, who tells Eustochium that her mother Paula often repeated them; *In languoribus et crebra infirmitate dicebat, Quando infirmor, tunc fortior sum. Et, Hobemus thesaurum istum in vasis fictilibus* (*Ep.* cviii. 19). He often quotes St Paul as the *vas electionis.*

περιέχεται ὡς ἐν ἀγγείῳ τῷ σώματι. See also the parallel Wisd. ix. 15. Marcus Aurelius (x. 38) bids us remember that what is within the vessel, τὸ ἔνδον ἐγκεκρυμμένον is the real ἄνθρωπος, and τὸ περικείμενον ἀγγειῶδες ought not to be included. Chrys., Thdrt., and others think that the ὀστρ. σκεῦος here means the human body, and that the epithet 'earthen' refers to man being made of the dust of the earth. The reference to the creation of light in v. 6 makes such an allusion not impossible; but in that case we should have expected χοῦν ἀπὸ τῆς γῆς (Gen. ii. 7) to have suggested either χοϊκός (1 Cor. xv. 47), or γηγενής (Wisd. viii. 1), or γήϊνος, rather than ὀστράκινος. Gideon's ὑδρείαι (Judg. vii. 16, 19) have no epithet, and they were used to hide light. Tertullian understands the vessels here as meaning bodies; he translates (*De Res. Carn.* 7, 44) *in testaceis vasculis* or *vasis,* and adds *scilicet in carne.* Vulg. has *in vasis fictilibus.*

But it is not impossible that here the σκεῦος is the whole personality. It was in the man as a whole, and not in his body in particular, that the Divine treasure which was to enrich the world was placed to be dispensed to others. In this work the body was indispensable, but it was not the only factor. The participles in *vv.* 8–10 apply partly to the body and partly to the mind, and they apply more to the former than to the latter, because the metaphors are taken from bodily contests; and the epithet ὀστρακίνοις indicates the general unattractiveness and insignificance of the men who preached the Gospel, and not merely the fragile character of their bodies. The metaphor of earthenware as representing human beings is common in O.T. (Is. xxix. 16, xxx. 14, xlv. 9, lxiv. 8; Jer. xviii. 6; Lam. iv. 2; Job x. 9), and in such passages it is the whole man, and not merely his body, that is contemplated. Cf. 4 Esdr. iv. 11; *quomodo poterit vas tuum capere Altissimi viam?* The epithet here is chosen because of the treasure, inestimable worth in a worthless vessel; and ὀστράκινος is sometimes used in the sense of worthless. Epictetus applies ὀστράκινος to discourse, opinions, pursuits, desires; "Your utensils," he says, "are of gold, and your discourse of earthenware," χρυσᾶ σκεύη, ὀστράκινον δὲ λόγον κ.τ.λ. (*Dis.* iii. 9).

ἵνα ἡ ὑπερβολὴ τῆς δυνάμεως ᾖ τοῦ Θεοῦ. '(In order) that the exceeding greatness (xii. 7) of the power may be God's and not from us.' Here 'may be' means 'may be seen to be,' φανῇ or εὑρεθῇ: in Rom. iii. 4, γινέσθω is used in the same sense, and in Rom. vii. 13, γένηται. Cf. οὐκ ἀφ᾽ ἑαυτῶν . . . ὡς ἐξ ἑαυτῶν (iii. 5). 'Of God and not of us' (AV.) obliterates the difference between τοῦ Θεοῦ and ἐξ ἡμῶν. 'May be perceived to belong to God and not to originate with ourselves' is the meaning. Dei, *non modo* ex Deo; *Deus non modo largitur* virtutem, *sed semper*

praestat (Beng.).   The reading ἐκ τ. Θεοῦ (Baljon and others) is
pure conjecture.   By ὑπερβολή (see on i. 8) is meant that the
power is a great deal more than is sufficient for its purpose;
it triumphs over all opposition.   The δύναμις is the power of his
preaching (1 Cor. ii. 4), with which we may perhaps couple the
power of his miracles, and certainly that of his endurance,—all
the power which produced the conversion of so many in spite of
such great obstacles.   *Ut sublimitas sit virtutis Dei, et non ex
nobis* (Vulg.) is misleading, the *sit* being misplaced.   It is
possible to translate 'that the exceeding greatness may be of the
power of God and not from ourselves,' but the position of ᾖ is
against it, and ὑπερβολή without further definition is awkward;
superabundance of what?   Those who take the sentence in this
way give very different answers to this question.   Elsewhere
Jerome takes the more probable construction; *ut abundantia
fortitudinis nostrae sit ex Deo et non ex nobis (Con. Pelag.* iii. 9).
So also Augustine; *ut eminentia virtutis sit Dei et non ex nobis*
(*Serm.* 169, 12).   God designed that the power in speading the
Gospel should be recognized as His; He therefore chose
humble instruments who could not be supposed to have produced such effects by their own powers.

8–10.   The rhythm in these three verses is clearly marked by
the balance of the clauses.   We have four illustrations of the
way in which the frailty of the instruments might have been fatal
to any other cause, but in this case were not allowed to be so.
The fifth instance is different.   They are all taken from the
Apostle's own experience.

8.   ἐν παντὶ θλιβόμενοι.   We have the same words in vii. 5;
'in everything pressed.'   In i. 6 it was necessary to translate
θλιβόμεθα 'are afflicted,' because of the frequent 'affliction' in
that passage.   But here the radical signification of 'pressure'
(Mk. iii. 9) must be retained, because of στενοχωρούμενοι.   The
pressure is that of persecution (1 Thess. iii. 4; 2 Thess. i. 6, 7;
Heb. xi. 37).   The indefinite ἐν παντί is to be understood with
all the pairs of participles.   Chrys. paraphrases, 'in respect of
foes and friends, of those who are hostile and those who are
of one's own household.'   Ἐν παντί occurs ten times in 2 Cor.
Elsewhere in Paul, 1 Cor. i. 5 only.

οὐ στενοχωρούμενοι.   'Not in hopeless straits,' not in a plight
from which extrication is impossible: *nunquam deest exitus*
1 Cor. x. 13); *in inviis vias salutis invenimus*; ἐν ἀπόροις πράγ-
μασιν πόρους εὑρίσκομεν σωτηρίας (Thdrt.)   He is speaking of
external difficulties, not of mental anxiety: that comes next.

Here we have οὐ with a participle (which is rare in N.T.)
four times in two verses; but there are eight other examples in the

Pauline Epistles; see on 1 Cor. ix. 26; J. H. Moulton, p. 231;
Blass, § 75. 5. We have στενοχωρία, Rom. ii. 9, viii. 35.
ἀπορούμενοι, ἀλλ' οὐκ ἐξαπορούμενοι. Once more a play upon
words (see on i. 13); 'in despondency, yet not in despair';
indigemus, sed non perinde indigemus (Tert. Scorp. 13).* There
may be the greater anxiety and perplexity, so that one does not
know what to do, and yet confidence that all will end well.
Such a state of mind is quite compatible with expectation of
death (see on i. 8).

9. διωκόμενοι, ἀλλ' οὐκ ἐγκαταλειπόμενοι. 'Pursued by men
(1 Cor. iv. 12), yet not forsaken by God.' 'Pursued by foes,
yet not left in the lurch by friends' (Plat. Symp. 179 A), might be
the meaning, but it has less point. The ruling idea throughout
is that God manifests His power in His servants' weakness.
Whatever hostile agents, whether human or diabolical, may do,
the earthen vessels are able to bear the shock and continue to
render service. In LXX, the verb is used of the Divine
promise; οὐ μή σε ἐγκαταλείπω (Gen. xxviii. 15; Josh. i. 5; cf.
Deut. xxxi. 6, 8).

καταβαλλόμενοι, ἀλλ' οὐκ ἀπολλύμενοι. 'Struck down, yet not
destroyed'; struck down, either ἐν ρομφαίᾳ (2 Kings xix. 7), or
ἐν μαχαίρᾳ (Jer. xix. 7), or any other weapon (Hdt. iv. 64).

It is probable that the last two illustrations, and possible that
all four, are taken from combatants in battle or in the arena;
'hard pressed, yet not hemmed in; in difficulties, yet not in
despair; pursued, yet not abandoned; smitten down, yet not
killed.' But ἐγκαταλειπόμενοι must not be understood of being
left behind in a race, nor καταβαλλόμενοι of being thrown in
wrestling. The four form a climax.

10. The fifth illustration sums up the preceding four, and
carries the climax to the supreme point, 'always dying, yet
always alive.' The four kinds of suffering are condensed as
ἡ νέκρωσις τοῦ Ἰησοῦ, and the four kinds of deliverance as ἡ ζωὴ
τ. Ἰ. The emphatic πάντοτε repeats the emphatic παντί (v. 8)
and anticipates the emphatic ἀεί (v. 11), from which it should
be distinguished in translation; 'at all times' (ii. 14, v. 6,
ix. 8).

τὴν νέκρωσιν τ. Ἰ. The meaning of this 'putting to death of
Jesus' is explained (γάρ) in the next verse. The missionaries
were perpetually being delivered unto death for Christ's sake.
They were never free from peril. Enemies were always seeking
their lives, as they sought His life, and to a large extent the

* Herveius, though he knows better, suggests for ἀπορούμενοι, laborando
sudamus nam poros etc.

9

enemies in both cases were Jews. All this He and they endured, because it was so decreed in accordance with the will of
God. They shared His sufferings, including the process which
in His case ended in death, and which at any time might so end
in their case (see on Phil. iii. 10 and 1 Cor. xv. 31). This
shows that St Paul taught his converts details in the history of
Jesus, especially His sufferings ending in death. Here he
assumes that they know. In this late Greek the different shades
of meaning attached to terminations become somewhat in-
distinct. See on i. 12, 14 and on ix. 10. Here νέκρωσις has
the old force of indicating a process, whereas in Rom. iv. 19
νέκρωσις means 'deadness' rather than 'putting to death' or
'deadening.' Epictetus says that most people take all means
to prevent the mortification (ἀπονέκρωσις) of the body, while
few care much about the mortification of the soul (*Dis.* i. 5).
The Apostle's life, like the Lord's, was a perpetual martyrdom, ending at last in actual putting to death; with this
difference, that Christ knew, up to the arrest in Gethsemane,
that His hour was not yet come, whereas St Paul had no such
knowledge.

Here again the Apostle expresses in mystic and paradoxical
language his union with Christ. In his frail, weary, battered
person he ever bears the *dying* of Jesus, in order that the *life*
also of Jesus may be exhibited to the world. This may mean
that the frequent deliverances from difficulty, danger, and death
are evidence that the Crucified is still alive and has Divine power;
cf. i. 5; Col. i. 24; 2 Tim. ii. 12; 1 Pet. iv. 13, v. 1.* See on
1 Pet. iii. 18, p. 161. Thdrt. and others explain the ἵνα . . .
φανερωθῇ of the hope of a future resurrection and immortality.
But ἐν τῇ θνητῇ σαρκὶ ἡμῶν in v. 11, which paraphrases v. 10,
compels us to confine the explanation to this life. From the
repetition of τοῦ 'Ιησοῦ (see on v. 5) we see that St Paul does not
separate the historic Jesus from the glorified Christ. To him it
is the same Jesus.† Bengel thinks that St Paul repeats the
name Jesus, because *singularitur sensit dulcedinem ejus.* That
thought inspired St Bernard's "Joyful Rhythm," *Jesu dulcis
memoria,* well known through Caswall's translation, "Jesu, the
very thought of Thee," and the *Jesu dulcedo cordium* of the Paris
Breviary; to which we may add Newton's "How sweet the

---

* F. A. Clarke (*Sermons,* p. 158) puts it thus; "As Christ's weakness
and dying on the Cross opened the gate to a new and glorious life, so in the
living death of His servant, the cross-bearing in the mortal flesh, there would
be made manifest the vigour of an immortal life, the undying energy of faith
and love."

† Only here and in Eph. iv. 21 does St Paul put the article before
'Ιησοῦς.

name of Jesus sounds " (*Olney Hymns*, No. 57, ed. 1779): but
it may be doubted whether it is the cause of the repetition
here.   The point here is that the dying and living of one
and the same Jesus are found in one and the same servant
of Jesus.   In περιφέροντες we have an allusion to missionary
journeys.

For the first τοῦ Ἰησοῦ, D* F G, d e f g have τοῦ Χριστοῦ, and between
τοῦ and Ἰησοῦ, K L, Syr-Hark. insert Κυρίου.   See Blass, § 46. 10, who
points out that the art. with Ἰησοῦς is usual in the Gospels, but rare in the
Epistles and Rev.   After the first τῷ σώματι, D E F G, Latt. Syr-Pesh.
Copt. add ἡμῶν.   For the second τῷ σώματι, ℵ, Vulg. have τοῖς σώμασιν.

11. ἀεὶ γὰρ ἡμεῖς οἱ ζῶντες.   'For always we who are alive are
being handed over unto death.'   Death is a monster that
devours victims who are alive.   All their life long, the missionaries are being thrown, like Daniel, into peril of almost certain
death, and are as wonderfully delivered (2 Tim. iv. 17; see on
1 Cor. xv. 31, 32).   Hence the pointed insertion of οἱ ζῶντες:
'we are ever a living prey.'   It was natural to use παραδιδόμεθα
in such a context; but the verb may have been chosen because
tradition habitually used it of Christ being 'handed over' to His
blood-thirsty enemies (Mk. ix. 31, x. 33, xiv. 10, 18, 21, etc.):
we have παραδοῦναι εἰς θάνατον 2 Chron. xxxii. 11.

διὰ Ἰησοῦν.   Here Vulg. rightly has *propter Jesum*, not, as in
v. 5, *per Jesum*.   The constant risking of life is well worth facing
for His sake, and the risking is thus amply justified.   For lower
reasons it might be wrong.

ἐν τῇ θνητῇ σαρκὶ ἡμῶν.   This comes at the end in a tone of
triumph and repeats the paradox of *v*. 10 in a stronger form; so
that, while the first half of *v*. 11 elucidates the first half of *v*. 10,
the second half intensifies the second.   In just that element of
our nature which is liable to death, the life of Jesus is to be
manifested.   Hence the change from σῶμα to σάρξ and the
addition of θνητή, a word found only in this group of Epistles in
N.T.   This manifestation of the life of Jesus probably does not
refer to the transformation of the physical body into a spiritual
body which envelops and absorbs it (*v*. 1–5; see on 1 Cor. xv.
40–44).   Such an explanation destroys the parallel between ἐν τῷ
σώματι and ἐν τῇ θνητῇ σαρκί.   Rather it refers to the case which
Dryden (*Abs. and Achit.* i. 156) describes;

A fiery soul, which, working out its way,
Fretted the pygmy-body to decay.

To whom is the life of Jesus thus made manifest?   Not so
much ἡμῖν as ὑμῖν, to the converts rather than to the missionaries.
This is plain from *v*. 12.   The many deliverances of the Apostle
and others from physical death are evidence of the power of the

risen Jesus.* So also is the activity, and very successful activity, of which these frail bodies are made capable. The first half of *v.* 12 refers to the former, the second half to the latter. Ignatius probably had this passage in his mind when he wrote of Christ, δι᾽ οὗ ἐὰν μὴ αὐθαιρέτως ἔχωμεν τὸ ἀποθανεῖν εἰς τὸ αὐτοῦ πάθος, τὸ ζῆν αὐτοῦ οὐκ ἔστιν ἐν ἡμῖν.

For Ἰησοῦ, C has Χριστοῦ, D* F G, d e g have Ἰησοῦ Χριστοῦ.

12. ὥστε. Another paradox ; 'So then, it is the death that takes effect in us, while it is the life that takes effect in you.' The antithesis is mainly verbal, for ὁ θάνατος is wholly physical and ἡ ζωή is chiefly spiritual ; 'we have the physical suffering and loss ; you have the spiritual comfort and gain.' Moreover, ἡ ζωή was active in the Apostle no less than in the Corinthians.

Calvin and others are so surprised at this conclusion (ὥστε), that they think that it must be ironical. But the literal meaning is quite intelligible, and it is a mark of the Apostle's characteristic tact, for the conclusion which he draws is a compliment to the Corinthians. 'You are now in the way that leads to life. It is marvellous that you should owe this enormous blessing to so insignificant and depressed a person as myself : but that strange fact manifests the power of God.' Schmiedel thinks that St Paul is here indirectly showing that his sufferings are not judgments on him for exceptional sinfulness. But would any one see this? Others make ἡ ζωή physical. 'I am always ill, while your illnesses and deaths (1 Cor. xi. 30) are diminishing.' This interpretation gives a very low meaning to the statement. Herveius is also misleading, when he makes the sentence a rebuke ; *mors, qua quotidie pro Salvatore morimur, operatur in nobis vitam aeternae felicitatis ; sed e contrario vita, qua delectamini in terrenis, operatur in vobis mortem aeternam.*

The articles probably indicate the θάνατος and the ζωή mentioned in the previous verse, and in that case should be translated. In the true text there is no μέν to anticipate the δέ, so that the second clause comes as a surprise. K L and Syr-Hark. insert μέν. Almost certainly ἐνεργεῖται is middle, not passive, a use not found in N.T. Even if admissible, 'is wrought' makes poorer sense than 'takes effect.'

13. 'But the fact that we have the death while you have the life is no reason why we should be silent.' *Nullo metu suppli-*

---

* "As the death of Jesus, which seemed to disprove His Messiahship, gave occasion for the great proof of it, viz. His Resurrection, so the Apostles' perils, which seemed to be inconsistent with their claim to be ambassadors of God, really supported this claim by giving occasion for display of the preserving powers of God" (Beet).

ciorum omittimus loqui ea quae credimus (Herv.). 'Trust in God inspires us as it did the Psalmist.' As in most of the quotations in the Pauline Epistles, the quotation is from the LXX, without material change (cf. vi. 2, viii. 15, ix. 9; see on 1 Cor. vi. 16, x. 7): also Swete, *Introd. to O.T. in Greek*, p. 400. This practice of the Apostle is remarkable here, because, although the exact meaning of the Hebrew is uncertain, yet the LXX, ἐπίστευσα, διὸ ἐλάλησα, is certainly wrong. The Hebrew may mean 'I believed (or believe), for I will speak,' *i.e.* must speak, must confess it: or, 'I believe, though I speak it,' *i.e.* although I utter the desponding words which follow, 'I was greatly afflicted; I said in my alarm, All men are liars.' And there are other possibilities. In the Hebrew the passage is central, cxvi. 10, 11. But the LXX, Syriac, Arabic, and Ethiopic, against clear internal evidence, unite Ps. cxv. with Ps. cxiv. and cut xvi. in two, making xvi. 10 the beginning of cxvi. (cxv.).

ἔχοντες. See on *v.* 7; 'because we have,' as in iii. 12.

τὸ αὐτὸ πνεῦμα τῆς πίστεως. 'The same spirit of faith as the Psalmist'; *quem habuerunt et illi qui scripserunt, Credidi, propter quod locutus sum* (Aug.); not 'the same spirit as you Corinthians'; nor 'the same spirit among ourselves,' *i.e.* that all the preachers have the same inspiration. Chrys. appeals to this as evidence that the O.T. and N.T. are inspired by the same Spirit; and many Fathers understand πνεῦμα here to mean the Holy Spirit as the bestower of faith, which is probably incorrect.

κατὰ τὸ γεγραμμένον. This formula of quotation appears in papyri in reference to legal documents, and is found in one of about the same date as this Epistle (Deissmann, *Bible Studies*, p. 250). Here it explains τὸ αὐτὸ πνεῦμα. It does not look forward to καὶ ἡμεῖς πιστεύομεν (Meyer), as if the Apostle's belief was regulated by the Psalmist. As often in his quotations, St Paul seems to have the whole passage in his mind, although he quotes only a few words.

καὶ ἡμεῖς. 'We also, as well as the Psalmist, believe; and therefore we also speak.' This is how it comes to pass that 'life takes effect in you.' Faith cannot be silent.

ℵ F G, Syrr. Arm. Goth. insert καί before ἐλάλησα, B C D E K L P, Latt. omit. There is no καί in LXX, and some editors treat the omission of καί here as assimilation to LXX.

14. From faith he passes on to hope, hope of the Resurrection. His faith is based on knowledge which produces hope. Polycarp (ii. 2) has a loose quotation of this; see on iii. 2.

εἰδότες. 'Because we *know* that He who raised up the Lord Jesus (Rom. viii. 11) will raise up us also *with* Jesus.' This does not mean that Jesus will be raised again when we are raised, but that our resurrection is absolutely dependent on His, as effect on cause, and that in being raised we share His glory. There may be also the thought of the union between Christ and His members. The difficulty of σύν caused the change in some texts to the simpler διά.

In 1 Cor. vii. 29, x. 11, xv. 51, St Paul regards the Second Advent as near, and he expects to be alive when it comes. Here he contemplates the possibility of not being alive. Nowhere does he state what will certainly be the case. It is exaggeration to say that we have here "the language of a man who does not expect to live to witness the coming of the Lord," or who has "the growing conviction that he would not live to witness the Parousia." He *fears* that he *may* not do so; that is all.

παραστήσει σὺν ὑμῖν. 'Will present us with you; as a bride is presented to the bridegroom' (xi. 2; Col. i. 22; Eph. v. 6). Thdrt. and others prefer 'will present us before the judgment-seat (a meaning found in papyri), where we shall be approved and told to enter into the joy of the Lord.' Some understand ζῶντας with παραστήσει, 'will present us alive' (Acts i. 3, ix. 41). It is probable that τῷ βήματι (v. 10; Rom. xiv. 10) would have been expressed in the one case, and ζῶντας (Rom. vi. 13) in the other, if this had been the Apostle's meaning. The verb is freq. in Paul. Comp. the absolute use of παριστάναι in Num. i. 5, τὰ ὀνόματα τῶν ἀνδρῶν οἵτινες παραστήσονται μεθ᾽ ὑμῶν : with Κυρίῳ added, Zech. iv. 14, vi. 5.

B 17, r Vulg. Arm. omit κύριον. For σὺν Ἰησοῦ (א* B C D E F G P, Latt. Copt. Arm. Aeth.), which is doubtless original, א³ D³ K L, Syrr. Goth. have διὰ Ἰησοῦ.

15. τὰ γὰρ πάντα δι᾽ ὑμᾶς. 'I say, he will present us with you, for all things are for your sakes.' All things that the Apostles and others do and suffer, as recounted in *vv.* 7–13, are done and suffered, not for their own benefit, but for that of their converts, and, through their converts, not to their own glory, but to the glory of God. Chrys. explains τὰ πάντα of the Death and Resurrection of Christ, which is alien to the context, however true in itself.

ἵνα ἡ χάρις πλεονάσασα κ.τ.λ. An obscure clause, which, like i. 11, may be construed in several ways, and the meaning of which, when construed, is not clear. Does διὰ τῶν πλειόνων belong to πλεονάσασα or to περισσεύσῃ, and is περισσεύσῃ transitive (ix. 8; Eph. i. 8; 1 Thess. iii. 12) or intransitive (i. 5, viii. 2, ix. 12)? We note the play on words between χάρις and εὐχαριστία, and the alliteration, πλεονάσασα . . . πλειόνων, which is slightly in favour of taking διὰ τῶν πλειόνων with πλεονάσασα, and the climax from πλεονάσασα to περισσεύσῃ, which is slightly in favour of the intransitive use of the latter. With this guidance we may translate with Chrys., 'In order that the grace, being made more by means of the more, may cause the thanksgiving to abound to the glory of God.' So RV., Alford, Bachmann, J. H. Bernard, Bousset, Heinrici, Lias, Meyer, etc. The grace given to him by God and augmented by the increasing number of converts, makes both him and them thankful, and their thanksgiving glorifies God. The increase of converts encourages him, and their prayers help him, and thus χάρις and εὐχαριστία are increased. This makes good sense, but other translations are possible. (1) 'In order that the grace, having abounded, may, through the greater number of converts, make thanksgiving to abound.' So Emmerling, De Wette, Waite. (2) 'In order that grace, having abounded, may, through the thanksgiving of the greater number, superabound.' So Luther, Beza, Bengel, Grotius. (3) 'That grace, having increased the thanksgiving by means of the greater number, may abound, etc.' This last makes πλεονάζειν transitive, a use found once or twice in LXX and once in N.T., 1 Thess. iii. 12. It is not likely to be right here. The order of the Greek is against it, and it does not yield as good sense as the other methods.

IV. 16–V. 5. The sufferings and supports of an Apostle are now considered in reference to the hope, or rather the certainty (εἰδότες, v. 14) of resurrection and reward. This life of daily deliverance from death may end at any moment in death. But what of that? Death has been conquered once for all. The passage has been called "The Hymn of the Home Eternal" (Way).

16. Διὸ οὐκ ἐγκακοῦμεν. 'No wonder that we do not lose heart.' See on v. 1 and v. 6. Elevation of thought again affects the Apostle's style. The rhythmic swing, which can be noticed at the end of ch. iii. and in iv. 8 f., is easily felt here, and it continues till v. 5.

ἀλλ᾽ εἰ καί. 'But (so far from our losing heart), although our outward man is being destroyed.' As in v. 3, εἰ καί states hypothetically what is conceded as being actually the case.

ὁ ἔξω ἡμῶν ἄνθρωπος. The expression is unique, but its meaning can be determined with some certainty from the correlative term ὁ ἔσω ἄνθρωπος, which occurs here, Rom. vii. 22, and Eph. iii. 16. Cf. ὁ παλαιὸς ἡμῶν ἄνθρωπος, 'our old self' (Rom. vi. 6 ; Col. iii. 9 ; Eph. iv. 22). This use of ἄνθρωπος, very much as we use 'self,' is common in Paul and goes back to Plato, but ὁ ἐντὸς ἄνθρωπος (*Rep.* 589 A) is not parallel to ὁ ἔσω ἄνθρωπος : see A. J. Robinson on Eph. iii. 16, and cf. 1 Pet. iii. 4.

The two expressions here, ὁ ἔξω and ὁ ἔσω ἄνθρ., correspond

only roughly to what we call "the lower and the higher self,"
and not quite exactly to the material and immaterial parts of our
nature. Our bodies, with all physical powers, emotions, and
appetites, belong to the ἔξω ἄνθρ., but not all immaterial elements
belong to the ἔσω ἄνθρ. The latter expression is always used in
a good sense, of that part of us which is opposed to worldliness
and is rooted in God. It is the highest part of our immaterial
being; that which is capable of being the home of the Holy
Spirit and of being ruled by Him. But in all these expressions,
'flesh' and 'spirit,' 'body' and 'soul,' 'lower' and 'higher'
self, it is impossible to define the differences with logical exact-
ness; our ignorance is too great. See on Rom. vii. 14.

Aug. (c. Faust. xxiv. 2) points out that there is here no room
for Manichaean dualism. "The Apostle uses *the inward man*
for the spirit of the mind, and *the outward man* for the body and
this mortal life, but we nowhere find him making these two
different men, made by two different powers. The two constitute
one personality, the whole of whom was created by one and the
same God. Nevertheless, this one person is made in the image
of God, only as regards the inward man, which is not only
immaterial but rational; and it is this which distinguishes him
from the brutes. . . . The whole of this man, both in his inward
and outward parts, has become old because of sin, and is liable
to death. Yet there is a renovation now for the inward man,
when it is reformed according to the image of its Creator, by the
putting off of unrighteousness, that is, the old man, and the
putting on of righteousness, that is, the new man. But hereafter, when what is sown a natural body shall rise a spiritual
body, the outer man also shall acquire the dignity of a celestial
condition (*habitudinis*) ; so that all that has been created may be
recreated, and all that has been made be remade, by Him who
created and made it."

Still less is there here any room for Tertullian's strange idea
that the soul is corporeal.

ἀλλ᾽ ὁ ἔσω ἡμῶν ἀνακαινοῦται. 'Yet our inward man is being
renewed' (Col. iii. 10; ἀνακαίνωσις, Rom. xii. 2 ; Tit. iii. 5). In
class. Grk. as in LXX, ἀνακαινίζειν (Heb. vi. 6) is more usual.
This form of the verb, like the idioms, ὁ ἔξω, ἔσω, παλαιός, καινός
(νέος), ἄνθρωπος, connects Epistles, such as Ephesians and
Colossians, whose genuineness is still, though less frequently,
disputed, with Romans and 1 and 2 Corinthians, whose genuineness is not questioned by critics whose judgment counts. The
verb does not necessarily mean that something which had
perished is restored, but that in some particular that which
ἀνακαινοῦται is being made as good as new. By comparing it
with διαφθείρεται we obtain the meaning of both verbs. In the

case of the physical powers there is a ceaseless wearing away, under the pressure of hard work, ill health, anxiety, and persecution; in the spiritual powers there is a ceaseless increase of strength. The one process, in spite of frequent Divine deliverances, must end in death; the other, by Divine decree, ends in eternal life. The force of the pres. must be preserved, 'is being destroyed,' 'is being renewed'; cf. τὸν ἀνακαινούμενον in Col. iii. 10, and the significant changes of tenses in Eph. iv. 22–24. "How is it being renewed?" asks Chrys., and replies, "By faith, by hope, by zeal." The ἀλλά marks strong contrast, 'nevertheless.' ἡμέρᾳ καὶ ἡμέρᾳ. 'Day by day'; there is no cessation in the progress; each day shows some advance. The form of expression is not found in LXX, nor elsewhere in N.T. It is commonly said to be a Hebraism (Esth. iii. 4), but papyri may show that it was colloquial; Blass, § 38. 4; Winer, p. 581. Tert. (*Scorp.* 13) has the literal *die et die* and (*De Res. Carn.* 40) *de die et die*; Vulg. has the more usual *de die in diem.*

There is much the same division of evidence here between ἐγκακοῦμεν (ἐνκ.) and ἐκκακοῦμεν as in iv. 1; see note there. A few cursives, Latt. Copt. Goth., Tert. omit ἡμῶν after ὁ ἔσω. D² and ³ E K L have ὁ ἔσωθεν for ὁ ἔσω ἡμῶν, and this may be the reading represented by Latt. Copt. Goth., Tert.

17. τὸ γὰρ παραυτίκα ἐλαφρὸν τ. θλ. 'I mean that our present light amount of affliction'; a thoroughly classical form of diction. The γάρ introduces the explanation of the apparent paradox that a process of destruction and a process of renewal is going on in the same persons, not alternately, but simultaneously and ceaselessly, day by day; and thus γάρ becomes equivalent to 'I mean that.' He is stating the same fact in a different way. In this verse, as in 4 and 6, there is an accumulation of words of deep meaning, in order to express, so far as language can do it, the overwhelming superiority of the glory; cf. iii. 8–11 and see on Rom. viii. 18.

The adjectival use of παραυτίκα is freq. in class. Grk., *e.g.* ἡ παραυτίκα λαμπρότης in the peroration of the famous speech of Pericles; "the immediate splendour of great actions and their subsequent glory abides in a way that no one can forget"; and τὴν παραυτίκα ἐλπίδα, "no man among them would have given up for all the world the immediate hope of deliverance" (Thuc. ii. 62, viii. 82). The adverb occurs only here in N.T. and only twice in LXX (Ps. lxix. 3; Tob. iv. 14). It indicates a short amount of *present* time, viz. till life ends or the Lord comes, and here it balances antithetically αἰώνιον in the next clause, as ἐλαφρόν balances βάρος and θλίψεως balances δόξης. We are accustomed to think of glory as transient and affliction as lasting. But the Apostle reverses that. In comparison with the glory, affliction **is** shortlived, and permanence is on the other side.* Still more are we accustomed to attribute weight to affliction rather than to glory. The Apostle reverses that also. The simple and common idea of scales is in his mind; weighed against one another, the glory goes down and the affliction kicks the beam. All the daily wear and tear of life, with its losses, sicknesses, and sufferings, are as nothing, and the result of the comparison would be much the same if that scale were empty. However great may be our estimate of the θλίψις, it has no weight or solidity against αἰώνιον βάρος δόξης.

It is possible that both here and in 1 Thess. ii. 6 the Apostle has in his mind the other sense of βάρος, viz. 'dignity,' *gravitas*; *e.g.* of Pericles, οὐδεὶς βάρος ἐχὼν ἰσόρροπον οὐδ᾽ ἀξίωμα πρὸς τοσαύτην ἡγεμονίαν ἐφαίνετο (Plut. *Per.* 37). The Latins render βάρος in N.T. variously; *pondus, onus, gravitas*. While βάρος refers to weight and ὄγκος (Heb. xii. 1 only) to bulk, both may be burdensome; but here it is solid and lasting value that is meant. For the constr. τὸ ἐλαφρὸν τῆς θλίψεως see on viii. 8.

καθ᾽ ὑπερβολὴν . . . κατεργάζεται ἡμῖν. 'Worketh out for us more and more beyond measure'; *supra modum in sublimitate operatur nobis* (Vulg.); *per supergressum in supergressum* (Tert. *bis*). The verb is almost exclusively Pauline in N.T., Jas. i. 3 and 1 Pet. iv. 3 being the only exceptions; and in the Pauline Epistles it occurs almost exclusively in Romans and Corinthians, Eph. vi. 13 and Phil. ii. 12 being the only exceptions. Its meaning is 'to produce' or 'to accomplish,' and it implies a prolonged process, a working *out*; *e.g.* πλειόνων περὶ ταῦτα πραγματευομένων, ἐλάττους οἱ κατεργαζόμενοι γίγνονται (Xen. *Mem.* IV. ii. 7). AV. here goes wrong in taking καθ᾽ ὑπερβολὴν εἰς ὑπερβολήν with βάρος instead of with κατεργάζεται. See Index IV.

The Council of Trent (Sess. VI. *De justific.* xvi.) uses this passage in support of the doctrine of *meritum ex condigno*, taking κατεργάζεται in the sense of 'earns,' as if suffering constituted a claim to heavy compensation; but it adds, *absit tamen ut Christianus homo in se ipso vel confidat vel glorietur, et non in Domino, cujus tamen est erga omnes homines bonitas, ut eorum velit esse merita, quae sunt ipsius dona.*

D* E G, Latt. Goth. Arm. insert πρόσκαιρον καὶ before ἐλαφρόν. B C², Syr-Pesh. omit ἡμῶν. אֵ* C* K, Syr-Hark. Copt. Arm. Aeth. Goth. omit εἰς ὑπερβολήν, which Naber and Baljon suspect as accidental dittography.

---

* Cf. *The Apocalypse of Baruch* xv. 7, 8; "As regards what thou didst say touching the righteous, that on account of them has this world come, nay more, even that which is to come is on their account. For this world is to them a trouble and weariness with much labour, and that accordingly which is to come, a crown with great glory." See also xxi. 24, xlviii. 50, li. 14.

18. μὴ σκοπούντων ἡμῶν. 'Since we do not direct our gaze,' or 'Provided we do not'; *nobis non intuentibus* (Tert. *Scorp.* 13); *non contemplantibus nobis* (Vulg.). If ἡμῶν means 'us Christians,' then Chrys. may be right in preferring 'provided we do not,' ἂν τῶν ὁρωμένων ἀπάγωμεν ἑαυτούς. The Latins vary between *dum si* and *quia*. We have seen that St Paul uses the 1st pers. plur. sometimes of himself alone and sometimes of himself with other teachers ; and he also sometimes changes quickly from the wider meaning to the widest of all ; Col. i. 12–14. All true Christians direct their thoughts and desires towards τὰ αἰώνια, and therefore, even with this interpretation of ἡμῶν, 'since we do not' may be right. That we have μή and not οὐ proves nothing, for οὐ with participles is rare in N.T., even when the participle states a matter of fact. See on 1 Cor. i. 28 and ix. 26. Grammar might have suggested μὴ σκοποῦσι, but the change to the gen. abs. is natural, and is common in N.T. Examples in Blass, § 74. 5. Cf. 1 Macc. i. 6. The construction is freq. in papyri ; but in class. Grk. the superfluous pronoun (ἡμῶν) is commonly omitted. Yet we find it in Thuc. iii. 22 ; λαθόντες τοὺς φύλακας, ἀνὰ τὸ σκοτεινὸν μὲν οὐ προιδόντων αὐτῶν.

τὰ μὴ βλεπόμενα. The μή is quite in place, and in class. Grk. we should have μή here rather than οὐ, 'things which to us are at present unseen'; *nam multa quae non cernuntur erunt visibilia confecto itinere fidei* (Beng.). Contrast *vv.* 8, 9, and see on 1 Cor. xiii. 12. Heb. xi. 1 we have πράγματα οὐ βλεπόμενα, and Heb. ix. 11, οὐ ταύτης τῆς κτίσεως.

The contrast is between our experiences of the world of sense and our hopes of the glories of the kingdom of God. Jewish ideas about future glory were for the most part sensuous and frequently political ; lofty and spiritual elements often came in, but they did not become supreme. Hence Christ in His teaching about the Kingdom admits sensuous pictures, such as eating and drinking, as symbolical of future bliss. Such language was before long seen to be symbolical, and St Paul here wholly dispenses with it. There is much force in the apparent contradiction, 'fixing our gaze on the things which we cannot see.' The kingdom is an invisible, spiritual world, without limitations of time or space.* But it is possible that the much discussed term αἰώνιος has here the idea of time. The opposition may be between very short duration and very long duration, rather than between time and timelessness. Seneca (*Ep.* lviii. 24) says of things of sense ; *Ista imaginaria sunt, et ad tempus aliquem faciem ferunt: nihil horum stabile, nec solidum est: et nos tamen cupimus tanquam aut semper futura, aut semper habituri. Imbecilli fluidique*

---

* See a sermon by R. W. Church on this text in the *Expositor*, 3rd series, vi. pp. 28–38, 1887.

per invalla consistimus : mittamus animum ad illa quae aeterna sunt.   Again (*Ep.* lxi. 2) he finely says : *Paratus exire sum, et ideo fruor vita : quia quam diu futurum hoc sit non nimis pendeo. Ante senectutem curavi, ut bene viverem : in senectute, ut bene moriar.*   Herveius makes the contrast one between *figura* and *veritas ; Figura deperit, veritas permanet,* which agrees with the words which J. H. Newman chose for inscription on his tomb ; *Ex umbris et imaginibus in veritatem.*

V. 1-5.   Here again, as between i. and ii., and between iii. and iv., the division of chapters is not well made.   There is no clear break at this point, and *vv.* 1–5, or indeed *vv.* 1–10, have a closer connexion with what precedes than with what follows them. In *vv.* 1–5 the subject of the sufferings and compensations of Christ's servants in reference to the hope of the Resurrection is continued.

The opening words show that once more we have an explanation of what has just been stated, especially of οὐκ ἐγκακοῦμεν. Οἴδαμεν γάρ here is equivalent to εἰδότες in iv. 14, 'because we *know,*' *fide magna* (Beng.).   In both cases St Paul goes far beyond human experience, and yet he says, 'we know.'   He could say that experience had taught him that the Lord Jesus had been raised from the dead, and that he himself had been often rescued from imminent death.   But experience had not taught him that God will raise us from the dead, if we die before the Lord comes ; or that He will supply us with spiritual bodies, in exchange for our material bodies, if we are still alive when He comes.   Yet he has a sureness of conviction which we may perhaps call a Divine intuition.   He is confident that in these matters he possesses knowledge which transcends experience, and with the inspiration of a Prophet he declares what has been revealed to him.   See on 1 Cor. xv. 20 and 51.   For some there will be a resurrection ; for others there will be a transformation; for all there will be a spiritual body suitable to the new state of existence.   The contrast between material bodies which are daily being wasted and spirits which are daily being renewed, will not continue much longer.   Cf. 1 Thess. iv. 15.

Men of science have contended that in this last point St Paul is confirmed by science ; "The same principles which guide us from the continuous existence of the outer world to acknowledge an Unseen, lead us, on the assumption of our own existence after death, to acknowledge a spiritual body. . . . We certainly hold that, if we are to accept scientific principles, one of the necessary conditions of immortality is a spiritual body, but we as resolutely maintain that of the nature of this spiritual body we are and must probably remain profoundly ignorant " (*The Unseen*

Universe, by Balfour Stewart and P. G. Tait, 4th ed. pp. 7, 8 ; see also p. 203).

1. Οἴδαμεν γάρ. St Paul frequently uses this verb of things which are known by experience and which any Christian may come to know (1 Cor. viii. 1, 4; Rom. ii. 2, iii. 19, viii. 28 ; etc.), although for such knowledge γινώσκειν would be the more suitable word. But here οἴδαμεν is used of intuitive knowledge. *Haec scientia non est humani ingenii, sed ex Spiritus sancti revelatione manat* (Calvin). Comp. the οἶδα γάρ of Job xix. 25, 27, where there is much which resembles this passage, and see on 1 Cor. xv. 51. Bousset thinks that St Paul is appealing to apocalyptic traditions known to him and the Corinthians, but no longer known to us.*

ὅτι ἐάν. ' That if our earthly tent-dwelling were taken down.' There is no καί, and we must not translate ' that *even* if, etc.' He is merely taking the case of those who do not live to see the Lord's return, which he still thinks will be exceptional; most people will live to see it.

ἡ ἐπίγειος ἡμῶν οἰκία τοῦ σκήνους. ' The earthly house of our tabernacle.' Vulg. is interesting, but not accurate ; *Scimus enim quoniam si terrestris domus nostra hujus habitationis dissolvatur, quod aedificationem ex Deo habeamus.* Here ὅτι is translated twice, by *quoniam*, and then superfluously by *quod*. *Hujus* is also superfluous, but it is meant to represent τοῦ. In 1 Cor. i. 20, ὁ κόσμος is rendered *hoc seculum*, and in iii. 19, iv. 13, v. 10, xiv. 10, *hic mundus*.† *Habitatio* is trebly unsatisfactory. (1) It makes no sufficient contrast to *aedificatio*, the one being temporary and fragile, the other permanent and solid. (2) In *v. 2*, *habitatio* is used to translate the permanent οἰκητήριον. (3) In *v. 4*, σκῆνος is rendered *tabernaculum*. The metaphor of a tent to indicate the human body would readily occur to a σκηνοποιός (Acts xviii. 3), but St Paul employs it only this once, and it is common enough in literature, although not in N.T. (cf. Jn. i. 14; 2 Pet. i. 13, 14) or in O.T. (cf. Is. xxxviii. 12). Modern writers may have had this passage in their minds, as in J. Montgomery's well-known verse ;

> Here in the body pent
> Absent from Him I roam,
> Yet nightly pitch my moving tent
> A day's march nearer home.

---

* It is hardly necessary to point out that there is no warrant for limiting the ' we ' in this section (1–10) to the Apostle, as if he expected to be made an exception to believers in general.

† See also Rom. v. 12. In the early versions, *hic* often represents the Greek article, and Jerome has allowed this to stand in various places in the Epistles which he seems to have revised much less carefully than the Gospels. In the Gospels he has not allowed *hic mundus* to stand for ὁ κόσμος.

Ἐπίγειος certainly means 'earthly' and not 'earthy' or
'earthen'; it is opposed to ἐπουράνιος (1 Cor. xv. 40; Phil. ii.
10; Jn. iii. 12), and denotes what exists on earth and is connected with this world. Vulg. commonly renders it *terrestris*,
which likewise cannot mean 'earthen,' but in Phil. ii. 10 and
Jas. iii. 15 has *terrenus*, which might mean that. Clem. Alex.
(*Strom.* v. 14, p. 703, ed. Potter) says that Plato called man's
body γήϊνον σκῆνος, and in Wisd. ix. 15 we have τὸ γεῶδες σκῆνος,
but in neither case does the epithet seem to be quite congruous.
It is probable that St Paul knew Wisdom, and that here and
elsewhere that book has influenced his language, if not his
thought; the verse runs φθαρτὸν γὰρ σῶμα βαρύνει ψυχὴν καὶ
βρίθει τὸ γεῶδες σκῆνος νοῦν πολυφρόντιδα. With this passage
comp. Wisd. iii. 1–4, and see Sanday and Headlam, *Romans*,
pp. 51, 52, 267. In Job iv. 19, οἰκίας πηλίνας, '*houses* of clay,'
there is no incongruity, and there the reference to the material of
which man was made is expressed; ἐξ ὧν καὶ αὐτοὶ ἐκ τοῦ αὐτοῦ
πηλοῦ ἐσμεν. There is no doubt that ἡ ἐπίγειος οἰκία τοῦ σκήνους
means the body, but some understand ἐπίγειος of the earth on
which we dwell. The genitive is one of apposition, a house that
is a tent, a 'tabernacle-house' or 'tent-dwelling.'

Field thinks that the use of σκῆνος for the human body comes
from Pythagorean philosophy. In this he follows Wetstein, who
says that the Pythagoreans compared man's skin to the skins of
which tents were made. Wetstein gives abundant quotations in
which the body is called σκῆνος. Hippocrates, "the Father of
Medicine," has ἀπολείπουσα ἡ ψυχὴ τοῦ σώματος σκῆνος (*Aph.*
viii. 18), and he may have been a disciple of Hippocrates the
Pythagorean. Philo (*De Somn.* i. 20) uses the less depreciatory
term οἶκος—τὸν συμφυᾶ τῆς ψυχῆς οἶκον, τὸ σῶμα, and it is οἰκία
which is the leading term here; τοῦ σκήνους is adjectival. An
allusion to the camp-life of the Israelites is possible, but the passage
is quite intelligible without it; see Lightfoot on Phil. i. 23. The
general meaning is that life here is only a pilgrimage. Christians
are citizens of a realm that is in heaven, and on earth they are only
sojourners; see Hort on πάροικος and παρεπίδημος in 1 Pet. ii. 11.

The idea that life in this world is only a pilgrimage towards
a better and permanent abode is not peculiar to Christianity.
Cicero has it often. He says that *animos, cum e corporibus
excesserint, in caelum, quasi in domicilium serum, pervenire* (*Tusc.*
I. xi. 24); and again, that the soul is in the body as in a house
that does not belong to it, *aliena domus*; heaven is its home
(*Tusc.* I. xxii. 51).* Again, *Ex vita ita discedo tanquam ex*

---

* Cicero suggests that it is because corpses are buried in the ground, that
people believe that the life of the dead is spent under the earth; *quam opinionem
magni errores consecuti sunt* (*Tusc.* I. xvi. 36; see also *De Rep.* vi. 15, 26, 29).

hospitio, non tanquam e domo; commorandi enim natura diversorium nobis, non habitandi, dedit (*De Sen.* xxiii. 84). And Pope (*Essay on Man,* i. 97) follows him.

> The soul, uneasy and confined from home,
> Rests and expatiates in a life to come.

So also in the well-known lines of the Emperor Hadrian, who, however, is doubtful about the future home; *Animula, vagula, blandula, hospis comesque corporis, quae nunc abibis in loca, pallidula, rigida, nudula?* See the account which Josephus (*B.J.* II. viii. 11) gives of the creed of the Essenes; the freed souls are borne aloft, μετεώρους φέρεσθαι.

Two genitives, depending in different relations on the same substantive, ἡμῶν οἰκία τοῦ σκήνους, are not rare either in Greek or Latin, the most common instances being, as here, where one is of a person, the other of a thing; Phil. ii. 30; 2 Pet. iii. 2; Heb. xiii. 7. Cicero (*Tusc.* I. xv. 35) defines *labor* as *functio quaedam vel animi vel corporis gravioris operis.*

καταλύθῃ. 'Dissolved' (AV., RV.), 'destroyed' (Tyn. Cran. Genevan). Neither houses nor tents are 'dissolved,' although the human body may be. 'Pulled down' would apply to both houses and tents, and would not be inappropriate to our bodily frames. Bengel calls καταλύθῃ *mite verbum,* but in the case of buildings it commonly implies destruction (Mt. xxiv. 2; Mk. xiv. 58; Lk. xxi. 26; Acts vi. 14), being the opposite of οἰκοδομεῖν (Gal. ii. 18).

οἰκοδομὴν ἐκ Θεοῦ ἔχομεν. If ἐκ Θεοῦ belonged to ἔχομεν, it would have been placed first or last. It belongs to οἰκοδομήν, 'a building proceeding from God as Builder.' In 1 Cor. iii. 9 (see note there), οἰκοδομή is the building *process,* which results in an edifice. Here we seem to be half-way between the process and the result, 'a building in course of erection,' the result being οἰκίαν, a word in which there is no intimation of a process. The inner man is being renewed day by day, and the production of the spiritual body is connected with that. The shade of difference between the words is well preserved in AV. and RV. by 'building' for οἰκοδομήν and 'house' for οἰκίαν, as in Vulg. by *aedificatio* and *domus.* In N.T., οἰκοδομή is almost peculiar to Paul (15/3), and chiefly in 1 and 2 Cor. (9/6). See Lightfoot on 1 Cor. iii. 9 and J. A. Robinson on Eph. ii. 21. By ἔχομεν is meant 'we come into possession of.'

ἐκ Θεοῦ. Cf. 1 Cor. i. 30, viii. 6, xi. 12. It is true that the σκῆνος, the material body, proceeds from God (see on 1 Cor. xii. 18, 24), but man takes part in the production of it. The spiritual body is wholly His creation (see on 1 Cor. xv. 38).

Lietzmann, A. Sabatier, and Bousset would press ἔχομεν to

mean that the spiritual bodies of those who are still in the flesh on earth are awaiting them in heaven, "created perhaps from all eternity." It is not necessary to believe that this is the Apostle's meaning. The present tense is often used of a future which is absolutely certain. The spiritual body is so certain to take the place of the material frame when the latter is pulled down, that we may be said to have it already. See on 1 Jn. v. 15. The idea of a disembodied spirit was abhorrent to both Jew and Gentile. A spirit which survives death must have a body of some kind, and it is this spiritual body which is raised. Its relation to the material body is real, but it cannot be defined.*

οἰκίαν ἀχειροποίητον. 'A house not made with hands,' *i.e.*, supernatural, immaterial, spiritual; Heb. ix. 11, 24. The human body is not made with hands, but it is natural and material. The difference is that between πνευματικός and ψυχικός (see on 1 Cor. xv. 44). In LXX χειροποίητα is used of idols.

αἰώνιον. Here, as in iv. 18, the idea may be that of indefinite durability rather than of timelessness; cf. Lk. xvi. 9.

ἐν τοῖς οὐρανοῖς. It is in heaven that this supernatural habitation has its proper environment, but heaven is not the habitation. We often think of heaven as the home of departed spirits; but St Paul thinks of each departed spirit as having an οἰκία of its own, the site of which is in heaven. The three attributes, ἀχειροποίητον, αἰώνιον, and ἐν τοῖς οὐρανοῖς, are in antithesis to ἐπίγειος τοῦ σκήνους: ἐν τοῖς οὐρανοῖς does not belong to ἔχομεν, 'we already possess in heaven.'

D E F G, Latt. Goth. insert a second ὅτι before οἰκοδομήν. In English there is a tendency to insert a superfluous 'that' in such sentences; 'We know that, if the makeshift dwelling which we have in this world be pulled down, [that] there is a much better one to replace it.'

2. καὶ γὰρ ἐν τούτῳ. AV. ignores the καί—'For in this.' The καί is either intensive, 'For verily' (RV.), 'For in fact,' 'For indeed,' introducing some important reason; or argumentative, ·For also,' 'For moreover,' introducing an additional reason. Either of these makes good sense. Again, ἐν τούτῳ may be either 'in this tent-dwelling' (*v.* 1), or 'hereby,' or 'herein,' lit. 'in this fact'; Jn. xv. 8; 1 Jn. ii. 3, 5; see on 1 Cor. iv. 4. The last meaning is specially freq. in the Johannine writings, where it commonly points forward to what is about to be stated. The first meaning is simplest here; 'For

* Spenser seems to have thought that the form of the natural body is derived from the soul. In his *Hymne in Honour of Beutie* he says; "For of the soule the bodie forme doth take; For soule is forme, and doth the bodie make." Philo thought otherwise; ὁ ἡμέτερος νοῦς οὐ δεδημιούργηκε τὸ σῶμα, ἀλλά ἔστιν ἔργον ἑτέρου (*De Migr. Abr.* § 35).

truly in this tabernacle-house we groan.¹* The words which
immediately follow (τὸ οἰκητήριον κ.τ.λ.) seem to show that St
Paul is still thinking of the σκῆνος when he says ἐν τούτῳ. Comp.
Rom. viii. 12, 13 and 18–23. But 'herein' makes good sense,
looking forward to ἐπιποθοῦντες.

τὸ οἰκητήριον . . . ἐπιποθοῦντες. The participle explains and
gives the reason for στενάζομεν : 'we groan, because we yearn.'
St Paul has ἐπιποθεῖν in all four groups (1 Thess. iii. 6 ; Rom.
i. 11 ; Phil. i. 8, ii. 26 ; 2 Tim. i. 4). Elsewhere in N.T., Jas.
iv. 5 and 1 Pet. ii. 2, where see Hort. Everywhere else in Paul
it expresses the longing for absent friends, to which the longing
for a permanent and glorious home is analogous. He regards
this yearning as evidence of the reality of the thing yearned for :
*si desiderium naturae non est frustra, multo minus desiderium
gratiae frustra est* (Aquinas). In late Greek, compounds take
the place of simple verbs without much increase of meaning, and
in N.T. ποθεῖν does not occur. The ἐπι- may indicate direction ;
cf. ἐπιπόθησις (vii. 7, 11). In LXX ποθεῖν is rare, except in
Wisdom. See Index IV.

τὸ οἰκητήριον. Not a diminutive ; it denotes a permanent
abode or home (Jude 6) ; cf. λογιζόμενος τὴν πόλιν Ἕλλησιν
οἰκητήριον ποιήσειν (2 Macc. xi. 2). The difference between
οἰκία and οἰκητήριον is that the latter implies an οἰκητήρ, an
inhabitant, while the former does not.

ἐπενδύσασθαι. A double compound which is not found elsewhere in N.T. or LXX. Cf. ἐπενδύτης (Jn. xxi. 7 ; Lev. viii. 7 ;
the A text of 1 Sam. xviii. 4). The body may be regarded either
as a dwelling or as a garment, and here we have the two ideas
combined ; 'longing to be clothed upon with our habitation
which is from heaven.' The more permanent dwelling is to be
drawn over the less permanent one, as one garment is drawn over
another, and is to take its place. In some way not described,
the now useless σκῆνος is destroyed, without being dissolved in
the grave, as in the case of those who die before the Lord comes.
The change from the carnal to the spiritual body is regarded as
instantaneous (1 Cor. xv. 52), and the change is longed for.

We may therefore be content to adopt as the more probable
rendering ; 'For indeed, in this tent-dwelling we groan, because
we long to put on over it our true habitation, which comes to
us from heaven.' This last point is a repetition of ἐκ Θεοῦ in *v.* 1.
In all cases it is God who furnishes the spiritual body, through
Christ (Phil. iii. 21), but the method differs : the dead receive
their spiritual body through resurrection, the living through
transfiguration (1 Cor. xv. 38, 51), and it is the living who

* See the beautiful passage in Plat. *Phaedo*, 66, 67. But *non agnoscit
fides philosophicum corporis a Creatore dati fastidium* (Beng.).

10

are described here. Comp. μετασχηματιζόμενος εἰς ἀφθαρσίαν (4 Macc. ix. 22). See Briggs, *The Messiah of the Apostles*, p. 130. We may set aside as improbable, if not impossible, the suggestion that στενάζομεν ἐπιποθοῦντες is to be treated as equivalent to ἐπιποθοῦμεν στενάζοντες, the main idea being in the participle, and not in the finite verb. It is doubtful whether any such usage is found in N.T. Nor is it likely that the ἐπί in ἐπενδύσασθαι indicates mere succession; that the clothing with the οἰκητήριον comes *after* the clothing with the σκῆνος. The context, especially *v.* 4, shows that the former comes *over* the latter and extinguishes or absorbs it. It is probable that fondness for alliteration has led to the juxtaposition of the two compounds, ἐπενδύσασθαι ἐπιποθοῦντες.

It is not easy to decide how far this idea of clothing living Christians with spiritual bodies is to be identified with that of the bright robes which adorn the saints in glory. In some passages the two seem to be identical, while in others the identification is doubtful. In Rev. iii. 5, 18, iv. 4, the saints have ἱμάτια λευκά, in Rev. vi. 11, vii. 9, 13, στολαὶ λευκαί: in 2 (4) Esdr. ii. 39, *splendidae tunicae*: in Herm. *Sim.* viii. 2, ἱματισμὸς λευκός. These "garments of glory," and "garments of life," which will not grow old (*Enoch* lxii. 15, 16) are a frequent feature in Jewish apocalypses, and in some of them we have an approach to what is stated here. In 2 (4) Esdr. ii. 45, *Hi sunt qui mortalem tunicam deposuerunt, et immortalem sumpserunt, et confessi sunt nomen Dei; modo coronantur, et accipiunt palmas*. In the *Book of the Secrets of Enoch* xxii. 8, "And the Lord said to Michael, Go and take from Enoch his earthly robe, and anoint him with My holy oil, and clothe him with the raiment of My glory." In the *Ascension of Isaiah* ix. 16 this raiment is said to be stored in heaven; "But the saints shall come with the Lord, with their garments which are laid up on high (*supra repositae sunt*) in the seventh heaven; with the Lord they shall come, those whose spirits are reclothed, they shall descend and shall be in the world (1 Thess. iv. 15–17); and He will confirm (?) those who shall be found in the flesh with the saints, in the garments of the saints, and the Lord will serve those who shall have watched in this world (Lk. xii. 37; cf. Jn. xiii. 4). And after that, they shall be changed in their garments [from] on high, and their flesh shall be left in the world." Again, ix. 9, "I saw those who had put off their garments of flesh and were now in garments from on high (*exutos stolis carnalibus et existentes in stolis excelsis*), and they were as angels"; and ix. 17, "Then shall there ascend with Him many of the just, whose souls have not received their garments until the Lord Christ is ascended and they have ascended with Him"; and xi. 40 we have the final charge; "And do you watch in the Holy Spirit, to receive your garments, thrones, and crowns of glory, which are laid up in the seventh heaven." AV. places a full stop at the end of *v.* 2, RV. a colon: a comma is all that is needed.

3. εἴ γε καὶ ἐνδυσάμενοι. Here the metaphor of the garment becomes more distinct; '*if* so be that being clothed we shall not be found naked,' *i.e.* without either a material or a spiritual body.* This possibility is excluded by the fact that the heavenly οἰκητήριον envelops the earthly σκῆνος, which is not destroyed until it is replaced by something very much better. The force of the καί is to strengthen the doubt expressed by εἴ γε, and this may be done by emphasizing the 'if.' Comp. Xen. *Mem.* III. vi. 13, Λέγεις παμμέγαθες πρᾶγμα, εἴ γε καὶ τῶν τοιούτων ἐπιμελεῖσθαι δεήσει. 'Of course, on the supposition that,' is the meaning. The ἐνδυσάμενοι refers to the same fact as ἐπενδύσασθαι, for here the simple verb suffices, and its relation to εὑρησόμεθα shows that it refers to some future clothing, which, when it takes place, will prevent the calamity of being found γυμνοί, like the souls in Sheol, without form, and void of all power of activity.† Some would place a comma after ἐνδυσάμενοι, and treat ἐνδυσάμενοι, οὐ γυμνοί as a case of asyndeton, like γάλα, οὐ βρῶμα (1 Cor. iii. 2), προσώπῳ, οὐ καρδίᾳ (1 Thess. ii. 17); 'on the supposition that we shall be found clothed, not naked.' The construction is not admissible, and the instances quoted in support of it are not parallel to it, being both of them pairs of substantives, not an aorist participle with an adjective. Others would understand some such word as 'wondering' or 'doubting' before εἴ γε, which might be implied in στεν. ἐπιποθοῦντες, 'we groan, wondering whether we really shall be found clothed, not naked.'

The sentence is a kind of afterthought, added to *v.* 2, as if to anticipate a misgiving, or objection. Some might suggest that our στενάζομεν ἐπιποθοῦντες proves no more than that we have a strong desire to be freed from the suffering body; it gives no security for the acquisition of a better body. Such an objection might easily be felt by those Corinthians who doubted about a resurrection. The Apostle rejects it with decision. No one yearns for the γυμνότης of being a bodiless spirit, and God has better things in store for us.

---

* This use of γυμνός is found in Plato, *e.g. Cratylus* 403, *Gorgias* 523, 524.

† Rom. xv. 4, προεγράφη is repeated as ἐγράφη, Eph. vi. 13, ἀντιστῆναι as στῆναι, 1 Pet. i. 10, ἐξηραύνησαν as ἐρευνῶντες (J. H. Moulton, p. 115).

εἴ γε (א C K L P) is perhaps to be preferred to εἴπερ (B D F G 17). ἐνδυσάμενοι (א B C D³ E K L P, Vulg. Syrr. Copt. Arm. Aeth. Goth.) is certainly to be preferred to ἐκδυσάμενοι (D* F G, d e g, Tert.), which is an early alteration to avoid apparent tautology. Pseudo-Primasius adopts the Vulg. *vestiti* and yet explains *expoliati corpore*.

4. καὶ γὰρ οἱ ὄντες ἐν τῷ σκήνει. 'For verily we that are still in the tent'—the tent-dwelling mentioned in *v.* 1; 'we who are in no immediate danger of being separated from our mortal body by death.' After the supplementary remark in *v.* 3, he returns to the contents of *v.* 2, viz. our present deplorable condition; and here the plur. seems to mean all Christians.

στενάζομεν βαρούμενοι. Not a mere repetition of στενάζομεν ἐπιποθοῦντες. In the one case groaning is caused by a feeling of intense longing, in the other by a feeling of intense depression. At first sight this seems to mean, 'we groan because we are oppressed by the sufferings of the body.' But these sufferings would lead to a desire to be rid of the body,* and what follows shows that there is no such desire. The groaning is caused by the oppressive thought that death may come before the Lord returns, and may leave us γυμνοί, without any bodies at all. The use of βαρούμενοι here looks like another reminiscence of Wisd. ix. 15; see on *v.* 1 and ii. 6 (ἐπιτιμία). Aug., after quoting these verses, remarks that "the cause of the burdensomeness is not the nature and substance of the body, but its corruptible character. We do not desire to be deprived of the body, but to be clothed with its immortality. For then also there will be a body, but it will no longer be a burden, being no longer corruptible" (*De Civ. Dei,* xiv. 3). For καὶ γάρ, Vulg. has *Nam et* in both *v.* 2 and *v.* 4; Aug. is more accurate with *etenim,* which serves to subjoin a corroborative clause, 'For verily'; a freq. use in Cicero.

ἐφ' ᾧ. This may mean either 'wherefore' (Lightfoot on Phil. iii. 12) or 'because,' ἐπὶ τούτῳ ὅτι, *propterea quod* (Rom. v. 12). The latter is better here. 'We feel oppressed, because we do not wish to be unclothed, *i.e.* to be divested of our body by death'; in other words, 'because we shrink from the idea of being left without a body.'† AV. and RV. transpose the negative, in order to smooth the construction, 'not for that we would be unclothed'; but the smoothness weakens the sense. The οὐ belongs to θέλω, and, as in the case of οὐ θέλω ὑμᾶς ἀγνοεῖν (see on i. 8), there is something which is very far from being wished; the total loss of the body is a thought of horror.

---

* This desire is frequently expressed by philosophers, especially of the Platonic and Neo-Platonic School, but it is not expressed here. The Jewish belief was that the soul, *furnished with a body,* constitutes a man.

† "The common ἐφ' ᾧ c. *fut. indic.*, ' on condition that,' does not appear in the N.T." (J. H. Moulton, p. 107).

Tantam vim habet corporis et animae dulce consortium. . . . Sub terrena tunica gemimus, ad coelestem festinamus, illam volumus accipere, istam nolumus ponere (Herveius). St Paul regards this instinctive horror of being without a body as strong evidence that a heavenly body will be given to us. To him, as to many Greeks, a disembodied spirit seemed to be utterly against nature. But there is no intimation here or elsewhere of a *third* body, an *interim* body, to be occupied between the earthly body and the resurrection body.

ἀλλ' ἐπενδύσασθαι. 'But (we wish) to be clothed upon,' to be invested with the heavenly body before the earthly one is taken away, so that there may be no interval of separation between soul and body.

ἵνα καταποθῇ. 'In order that the mortality of the one may be swallowed up by the immortal life of the other.' In Irenaeus (IV. xxxvi. 6) we have *Nolumus exspoliari, sed superindui, uti absorbeatur mortale ab immortalitate*; and (V. xiii. 3) *ut absorbeatur mortale a vita.* Only what is mortal perishes; the personality, consisting of soul and body, survives. The Apostle again seems to have Is. xxv. 8 in his mind; see on 1 Cor. xv. 54. Theodoret says that the imperishable life makes corruption to vanish in much the same way as the entrance of light counteracts darkness. Conversely, Chrys. says that corruption can no more conquer incorruption than wax can conquer fire.

After σκήνει, D E F G, Syrr. Copt. Aeth. Goth. add τούτῳ. ℵ B C K L P, Vulg. Arm. omit. For ἐφ' ᾧ (all uncials) a few cursives have ἐπειδή.

5. ὁ δὲ κατεργασάμενος ἡμᾶς. Both AV. and RV. have 'Now' for δέ, yet it seems to imply a certain amount of contrast; 'You may think that this is fanciful, and that our feelings of longing or of horror prove nothing as to the reality of what is desired or dreaded; *but* He who wrought us out for this very thing, viz. to expect that our mortal garb will be absorbed by a heavenly one, is God.' As in i. 21, Θεός comes at the close with great emphasis; cf. Heb. iii. 4 and see Westcott's additional note on 1 Jn. iv. 12. Chrys. refers κατεργασάμενος to the creation; it refers rather to the καινὴ κτίσις, to our regeneration, as what follows shows. The Latins vary between *operari, facere, perficere, efficere,* and *consummare* for κατεργάζεσθαι, and Vulg. has all five in different places, *e.g.* iv. 17, xii. 12; Rom. vii. 18; 2 Cor. v. 5; 1 Pet. iv. 3, *operari* being the usual translation, *e.g.* iv. 17, vii. 10, 11, ix. 11; etc. But nowhere does *instruere, praeparare, disponere, concinnare* or *elaborare* seem to be used. The fact that no less than five different translations have been allowed to remain is further evidence that Jerome's revision of

the Epistles was somewhat perfunctory. In the Gospels κατεργάζεσθαι does not occur. See Index IV. and footnote on *v.* 1.

ὁ δοὺς ἡμῖν. This explains *how* God prepared us for this
sure hope of receiving a spiritual body ; ' He gave us the earnest
of the Spirit.' That implies that He has placed Himself in the
position of a debtor who has paid an instalment ; and He is a
debtor who is sure to pay the remainder in full. The Spirit
inspires the longing and is the security that our longing for the
spiritual body, the σῶμα τῆς δόξης (cf. iii. 18, iv. 17), will be
satisfied. See on i. 22 for the doctrine that the Spirit is given
to us as an instalment. On this difficult verse see Salmond,
Christian Doctrine of Immortality, pp. 565–575 : also Briggs,
The Messiah of the Apostles, p. 130, who takes a different view.

ὁ δοὺς (א* B C D* G P 67**, Vulg. Syr-Pesh. Copt. Arm. Aeth.) rather
than ὁ καὶ δοὺς (אᶜ D² and ³ E K L, Syr-Hark. Goth.).

6–8. ' Confident, therefore, at all times, and knowing that
while we are at home in the body we are in exile from
the Lord,—for we walk by means of faith and not by means of
what we can see,—we are confident, I say, and are well pleased
to go into exile from the body and to go home unto the Lord.'
The construction of *v.* 6 is broken by the parenthetical *v.* 7, and
then a new construction is started in *v.* 8.

St Paul does not mean that while we are in the body we are
absent from the Lord ; our union with Him both in life and in
death is one of his leading doctrines (iv. 10, 11 ; 1 Thess. v. 10).
He is speaking relatively. The life of faith is less close and
intimate than the life of sight and converse. The passage
assumes that the dead are conscious, conscious of the Lord
(Phil. i. 20–23 ; Lk. xxiii. 43 ; Acts vii. 59) ; otherwise departure
from the body would be a worse condition, with regard to Him,
than being in the body. In agreement with this, Polycarp (*Phil.*
9), following Clement of Rome (*Cor.* 5), says that St Paul and
other Apostles εἰς τὸν ὀφειλόμενον αὐτοῖς τόπον εἰσὶν παρὰ τῷ
Κυρίῳ. See on iii. 2.

6. θαρροῦντες οὖν πάντοτε. Both in LXX (Prov. i. 21) and
in N.T. (vii. 16, x. 1, 2 ; Heb. xiii. 6) θαρρεῖν is rare, θαρσεῖν
being the common form. Vulg. varies between *audere* (here and
x. 2) and *confidere* (vii. 16 and x. 1). *Confidere* would be better
here, for the notion of ' daring ' is foreign to the passage. Θαρρεῖν
is a favourite word with the Stoics. See Epictetus, *Dis.* ii. 1,
where he shows in what sense we can be both confident and
cautious. The οὖν means, ' because we have God as our
security ' (*v.* 5), and πάντοτε (ii. 14, iv. 10, ix. 8) means that ' in
every event,' whether we die soon or live till the Lord returns,
we have this confidence. It is worth while to distinguish

between πάντοτε and ἀεί: Vulg. has *semper*, and AV. and RV. have 'always' for both.   See on iv. 10.

καὶ εἰδότες. Co-ordinately with θαρροῦντες, εἰδότες looks onwards to εὐδοκοῦμεν.

ἐνδημοῦντες . . . ἐκδημοῦμεν. Neither verb is found in LXX, and neither occurs in N.T. except in these verses.* Tertullian has *immorari* and *peregrinari* throughout. Vulg. varies the translation of both verbs capriciously ; *dum sumus in corpore peregrinamur a Domino* (6) ; peregrinari *a corpore et* praesentes esse *ad Deum* (8) ; *sive* absentes *sive* praesentes (9). *Domi esse* and *exsulare* would express the respective meanings better. *Quamdiu domi sumus in hoc corporis habitaculo* is the paraphrase of Erasmus ; and it is evident that St Paul is thinking of the house in which we dwell rather than of the city or country in which we dwell.   But ἐκδημ. is a great deal more than 'out of the house'; it means 'away from home.'   The true home is with the Lord ; *nam peregrinator patriam habet, sive cito sive tardius eo perventurus* (Beng.).   In papyri we have both ἐκδημεῖν and ἀποδημεῖν, 'to go abroad' and 'to be abroad,' in opposition to ἐνδημεῖν, 'to stay at home' or to 'be at home.'   See critical note below.

ἀπὸ τοῦ Κυρίου.   'Separate from the Lord'; cf. Rom. ix. 3. This is true, in spite of His constant presence (Mt. xxviii. 20) and of our union with Him (1 Cor. vi. 15, xii. 27); *quia non exhibet se coram videndum, quia adhuc exulamus ab ejus regno, et beata immortalitate, qua fruuntur angeli qui cum eo sunt, adhuc caremus* (Calvin).

For ἐνδημοῦντες, D G have ἐπιδημοῦντες, and for ἐκδημοῦμεν, D E G have ἀποδημοῦμεν.   For Κυρίου, D G, Copt. have Θεοῦ.

7. διὰ πίστεως γὰρ κ.τ.λ.   The Apostle seems to feel that ἐκδημ. ἀπὸ τοῦ Κυρίου may cause perplexity, and he hastens to explain in what sense such an expression is true.   'It is through a world of faith that we walk here, not through a world of visible form'; and *non videre prope tantundem est atque disjunctum esse* (Beng.).   In this life we have to walk under conditions of faith, not under conditions of what is seen.   Belief, however strong, cannot be the same as sight ; and from a Christ whom we cannot see we are to that extent separated, just as a blind man is cut off from the world to which he nevertheless belongs ; νῦν αὐτὸν τοῖς τοῦ σώματος ὀφθαλμοῖς οὐχ ὁρῶμεν, τότε δὲ καὶ ὀψόμεθα καὶ συνεσόμεθα (Thdrt.).   AV. and RV. give the general sense of the verse correctly, but εἶδος cannot mean 'sight.'   It means 'that which is seen,' *species*. Cf. ἐν εἴδει καὶ οὐ δι' αἰνιγμάτων (Num.

* In the *Testament of Abraham* 15 (p. 95, ed. James), ὁ ἀσώματος Michael says to Abraham, ποίησον διάταξιν περὶ πάντων ὧν ἔχεις· ὅτι ἤγγικεν ἡ ἡμέρα ἐν ᾗ μέλλεις ἐκ τοῦ σώματος ἐκδημεῖν καὶ ἔτι ἅπαξ πρὸς τὸν Κύριον ἔρχεσθαι.

xii. 8); τὸ δὲ εἶδος τῆς δόξης Κυρίου (Ex. xxiv. 17), *species gloriae Domini*. *Haec erit species*, Augustine says, *quando faciet quod dixit*, *Ostendam me ipsum illi*. And again, *Neque enim jam fides erit qua credantur quae non videantur, sed species, qua videantur quae credebantur* (*De Trin*. xiv. 2). There is a slight change from διὰ πίστεως to διὰ εἴδους, the former being subjective and the latter objective, but it causes no difficulty. In this world the Christian is under the condition of belief in Christ, not under the condition of His visible form. Here we have faith only; hereafter both faith and sight.* Faith is a virtue which 'abideth'; see on 1 Cor. xiii. 13.

8. θαρροῦμεν δὲ καὶ εὐδοκοῦμεν. After the parenthetical explanation in *v.* 7 the θαρροῦντες of *v.* 6 is taken up again by the δέ, for which 'I say' (AV., RV.) is a good equivalent. Without the injected explanation the sentence would have run θαρροῦντες . . . εὐδοκοῦμεν, but in his emotion at the thought the Apostle forgets the original construction and resumes with θαρροῦμεν καὶ εὐδοκοῦμεν, 'we are confident and are well pleased.' The emphatic word, as is shown in both places by its position and here by its repetition, is θαρρεῖν. It takes the place of στενάζειν in *vv.* 4 and 6. The thought which there suggested sighing and groaning, now that it is further considered, suggests confidence. Even the possibility of being left γυμνός for a time loses its terrors, when it is remembered that getting away from the temporary shelter furnished by the body means getting home to closer converse with the Lord.† The change from presents (ἐνδημοῦντες, ἐκδημοῦμεν) to aorists (ἐκδημῆσαι, ἐνδημῆσαι) must be observed, and the force of the aorists may be expressed by 'getting.' With ἐκδημῆσαι comp. 'He has got away,' which in the North of England is a common expression for 'He is dead'; and with ἐνδημῆσαι comp. the German *heimgegangen*.

εὐδοκοῦμεν. 'We are *well pleased*,' as both AV. and RV. in Mt. iii. 17, xii. 18, xvii. 5; Mk. i. 11; Lk. iii. 22; 1 Cor. x. 5; 2 Pet. i. 17; and as RV. in 1 Thess. ii. 8. The verb is used both of God and of men. When used of men (xii. 10; Rom. xv. 26, 27; 1 Thess. ii. 8, iii. 1; 2 Thess. ii. 12), it expresses hearty goodwill and perfect contentment, and it is often used of giving consent, especially in legal transactions. This goodwill

---

* Comp. *Venit ad nos ex his, quos amamus, etiam absentibus, gaudium: sed id leve et evanidum. Conspectus et praesentia et conversatio aliquid habet vivae voluptatis: utique si non tantum quem velis, sed qualem velis, videas* (Seneca, *Ep*. xxxv. 2, 3).

† The approximation to this in Wisd. iii. 1–5 is worth considering. 'The souls of the righteous are in the hand of God, and no torment shall touch them. . . . Because God made trial of them, and found them worthy of Himself.' See on *vv.* 1 and 4.

and contentment is not quite the same as θέλομεν (*v.* 4) or ἐπιποθοῦντες (*v.* 2). It is possible to long for one thing, and yet be content with, or even prefer, another, because one knows that the latter is well worth having, and perhaps better for one. St Paul longed to have a spiritual body, in exchange for his material body, without dying : but rather than remain in his material body he was quite ready to die. It was better to see the Lord than to be deprived of this bliss through being in the body ; and to be sure of seeing Him robbed death of its terrors. Comp. *Proinde intrepidus horam illam decretoriam prospice: non est animo suprema, sed corpori. Quidquid circa te jacet rerum, tanquam hospitalis loci sarcinas specta : transeundum est. Detrahetur tibi haec circumjecta, novissimum velamentum tui cutis : detrahetur caro et suffusus sanguis. Dies iste, quem tanquam extremum reformidas aeterni natalis est* (Seneca, *Ep.* ciii. 24, 25).

Perhaps in no other case is the caprice of the Vulg. so conspicuous as in the translation of εὐδοκεῖν. The verb occurs fifteen times in the Epistles, and it is translated in ten different ways ;—*bonam voluntatem habemus* (here), *placeo mihi* (xii. 10), *placuit* with a dat. (1 Cor. i. 21 ; Rom. xv. 27 ; Gal. i. 15 ; 1 Thess. iii. 1 ; Heb. x. 6, 38), *beneplacitum est Deo* (1 Cor. x. 5), *probaverunt* (Rom. xv. 26), *complacuit* (Col. i. 19), *cupide volebamus* (1 Thess. ii. 8), *consensuerunt* (2 Thess. ii. 12), *placita sunt tibi* (Heb. x. 8), *mihi complacui* (2 Pet. i. 17). And in this case the Gospels are not more uniform than the Epistles. The verb occurs six times in them, and it is translated in five different ways, three of which differ from all the renderings in the Epistles ; *mihi complacui* (Mt. iii. 17), *bene placuit animae meae* (Mt. xii. 18), *mihi bene complacui* (Mt. xvii. 5), *complacui* (Mk. i. 11), *complacuit* with a dat. (Lk. iii. 22, xii. 32).

πρὸς τὸν Κύριον. Here, as in Phil. i. 23–25, his reason for wishing to depart from the body is the same, viz. to be with the Lord, σὺν Χριστῷ εἶναι· πολλῷ μᾶλλον κρεῖσσον. But his reasons for wishing to remain in the body differ. There it is for the sake of others, because his beloved Philippians still need him. Here it is for his own sake, because he desires to be alive when the Lord comes, and thus to escape dying. In both passages he implies that at death there is immediate entrance into closer fellowship with Christ. Comp. Seneca, *Ep.* cii. 22 ; *Cum venerit dies ille qui mixtum hoc divini humanique secernat, corpus hoc, ubi inveni, relinquam : ipse me diis reddam. Nec nunc sine illis sum, sed terreno detineor carcere.*

Once more Plato (*Apol.* 40, 41), followed by Cicero (*Tusc.* 1. xli. 98), to some extent anticipates Christian thought. "If indeed when the pilgrim arrives in the world below, he finds sons of God who were righteous in their own life, that pilgrim-

age will be worth making.   What would not a man give if he
might converse with Orpheus and Musaeus and Hesiod and
Homer?   What infinite delight would there be in conversing
with them and asking them questions!"   Still more closely
Philo (*Leg. Alleg.* iii. 14), "It is not possible for one who is
dwelling in the body, in a race that is mortal, to hold communion
with God, but God floods one who is free from the prison."
And again (*De Migr. Abr.* § 34, 466 Mang.) ; " Rouse yourselves
and seek for that migration hence which proclaims to us, not
death, but deathlessness."   *Non est vivere, sed valere, vita* (Mart.
vi. lxx. 15).

For θαρροῦμεν, א 17, Orig. Tert. have θαρροῦντες.   For Κύριον, D* 17,
Vulg. have Θεόν.

9. διὸ καὶ φιλοτιμούμεθα.   'Wherefore also we make it our
aim.'   Both διό, which looks back to εὐδοκοῦμεν, and καί, which
adds something to it, show that a new section does not begin
here, as Calvin and Bachmann suppose.   The verb may in this
place retain its classical meaning (*Haec una ambitio legitima,* as
Beng. says) ; but in late Greek (1 Thess. iv. 11 ; Rom. xv. 20)
it need not mean more than 'desire earnestly,' or ' make it one's
aim ' (RV.), which is probably right here.   Xenophon and Plato
seem sometimes to use it in this sense, followed, as here, by an
infinitive.   In meaning and construction it is thus equivalent to
σπουδάζειν (1 Thess. ii. 17 ; Gal. ii. 10 ; Eph. iv. 3 ; 2 Tim. ii.
15).   'We make it a point of honour,' *wir setzen unsre Ehre
darein* (Bousset, Bachmann), is a translation which looks neat,
but is not preferable to ' desire earnestly' or ' make it our aim.'

εἴτε ἐνδημοῦντες εἴτε ἐκδημοῦντες.   Two questions have been
much discussed with regard to these two participles.   (1) How
are they to be understood?   (2) Do they belong to φιλοτιμούμεθα or to εὐάρεστοι αὐτῷ εἶναι ?   The answer to the second
question depends upon the answer to the first.

(1) As to the meaning of the participles there are three
suggestions.   (a) They refer to one's *place of abode* in this world ;
' whether we are at home or away from home.'   This interpretation may be safely rejected as having no point and as unworthy of the dignity of the passage.   (β) They refer to the
communion with Christ just mentioned, πρὸς τὸν Κύριον being
understood with ἐνδημοῦντες and ἀπὸ τοῦ Κυρίου with ἐκδημοῦντε .
This is better, but the order is against it, for the Apostle would
hardly have mentioned the future condition before the present
one ; he would have written εἴτε ἐκδ. εἴτε ἐνδ., and a few
authorities have this order ; see critical note below.   (γ) The
participles refer to the *body* just mentioned, ἐν τῷ σώματι being
understood with ἐνδημοῦντες and ἐκ τοῦ σώματος with ἐκδημοῦντες.

This is almost certainly right. It makes good sense in itself and it fits the context. 'Whether we are at home in the body, or away from home out of it,' is the meaning. But ἐκδημοῦντες is not to be rendered '*going* from home,' ' *migrating* from the body,' *i.e.* dying. The alternative is not between *staying* and *leaving*, but between *being in* the body and *being out of* the body, between ἐνδυσάμενοι and ἐκδυσάμενοι (*v.* 2).

(2) With this explanation of the participles there can be little doubt that they belong to εὐάρεστοι αὐτῷ εἶναι. It would hardly be congruous to say that, when we are absent from the body and at home with the Lord, we 'desire earnestly' or 'make it our aim' to be acceptable to Him; in that blissful condition we *are* εὐάρεστοι αὐτῷ. It is in this life that we desire and strive to please Him.

The meaning of the verse is, therefore, 'We aim at winning the Lord's approval, whether at His Coming He finds us in the body or already out of it.' Again we have a parallel in Seneca (*Ep.* cii. 29); *Haec cogitatio nihil sordidum animo subsidere sinit, nihil humile, nihil crudele. Deos omnium rerum esse testes ait, illis nos approbari, illis in futurum parari jubet, et aeternitatem proponere.* The whole letter should be compared with this passage.

εὐάρεστοι. 'Acceptable.' RV. has 'well-pleasing,' which is right in meaning, but cannot well be used by those who translate εὐδοκοῦμεν 'we are well pleased.' The word is late Greek; only twice in LXX (Wisd. iv. 10, ix. 10), although εὐαρεστεῖν is common. See Deissmann, *Bible Studies*, p. 214. Excepting Heb. x. 6, the word in N.T. is exclusively Pauline, eight times in all, and in all groups, except Thessalonians. Cf. Eph. v. 10; Col. iii. 20; Phil. iv. 18. In nearly all places it is used of what is acceptable to God or to Christ. So also in Wisd. iv. 10, ix. 10, from which book St Paul may have got the word; see on ἐπίγειος in *v.* 1. Vulg. varies between *placens* (Rom. xii. 1, 2), *beneplacitum* (Eph. v. 10), *placitum* (Col. iii. 26), and *placere* (here).

f g and Syr-Pesh. have the order εἴτε ἐκδημοῦντες εἴτε ἐνδημοῦντες: see above, p. 154 *sub fin.*

10. τοὺς γὰρ πάντας ἡμᾶς. 'We have good reason for making this our aim, *for* every one of us, whether in the body or out of it, must be made manifest (1 Cor. iv. 5) before the judgment-seat of Christ.' A desire to be persons who are acceptable to Him must abide in us, when we remember that our whole life will be laid open before Him and judged according to its exact deserts. All Christians, without exception, are summed up under τοὺς πάντας ἡμᾶς. And they have not only to 'appear' (φαίνεσθαι), but to have their whole character 'made manifest' (φανερωθῆναι). It is probable that, as in the Parables of the Talents and of the Sheep and the Goats, being made manifest to one's own conscience and to other persons is included; * but it is manifestation to the Judge whose approval is desired that is specially meant. See on 1 Cor. iv. 4, 5. He reminds the Corinthians, who are so prone to criticize, that a time is coming when they themselves will be laid bare to the most searching criticism. 'Appear' (AV.) is inadequate.

δεῖ. By Divine decree which cannot be evaded.

ἔμπροσθεν τοῦ βήματος τοῦ Χριστοῦ. Cf. 2 Tim. iv. 1. In Rom. xiv. 10 it is 'the judgment-seat of God,' God being said to do Himself what He does through His Son (Jn. v. 22). In the Gospels, as here, Christ is the Judge. In the Apocalypse it is 'He that sitteth upon the throne,' i.e. the Almighty Father, who judges (Swete on Rev. xx. 11). Polycarp (Phil. 6) combines our verse with Rom. xiv. 10; πάντας δεῖ παραστῆναι τῷ βήματι τοῦ Χριστοῦ, καὶ ἕκαστον ὑπὲρ ἑαυτοῦ λόγον δοῦναι. See on iii. 2.

The βῆμα is the tribunal, whether in a basilica for the praetor in a court of justice,† or in a camp for the commander to administer discipline and address the troops. In either case the tribunal was a platform on which the seat (sella) of the presiding officer was placed. In LXX, βῆμα commonly means a platform or scaffold rather than a seat (Neh. viii. 4; 1 Esdr. ix. 42; 2 Macc. xiii. 26). In N.T. it seems generally to mean the seat (Mt. xxvii. 19; Jn. xix. 13; Acts xviii. 12, xxv. 6, etc. Seven times in Acts in this sense). But in some of these passages it may mean the platform on which the seat was placed. On Areopagus the βῆμα was a stone platform; ὅστις κρατεῖ νῦν τοῦ λίθου τοῦ 'ν τῇ Πυκνί (Aristoph. Pax, 680): cf. Xen. Mem. III. vi. 1. Fond as St Paul is of military metaphors, and of comparing the Christian life to warfare, he is not likely to be thinking of a military tribunal here. Other N.T. writers speak of the Divine judgment-seat as a θρόνος (Mt. xix. 28, xxv. 31; Rev. xx. 11; cf. Dan. vii. 9, 10). The idea of a judgment-seat is frequent in the Book of Enoch, and it is the 'Elect One' or the 'Son of Man' who sits on the throne of His glory to judge (xlv. 3, lv. 4,

---

* Augustine speaks of a certain divine power, qua fiet ut cuique opera sua vel bona vel mala cuncta in memoriam revocentur et mentis intuitu mira celeritate cernantur, ut accuset vel excuset scientia conscientiam, atque ita simul et omnes et singuli judicentur (De Civ. Dei, xx. 14).

† Stanley is in error in stating that "when the Basilica became the model of the Christian place of worship, the name of βῆμα (or tribunal) was transferred to the chair of the bishop." The βῆμα was the space inside, and sometimes in front of, the apse, containing the altar, the seats of the presbyters, and the cathedra of the bishop, the last being in the centre of the wall of the apse.

lxii. 3, 5). He has been placed thereon by the Lord of Spirits and all judgment has been committed to Him (lxi. 3, lxii. 2, lxix. 27, 29). See Charles on xlv. 3. In the *Assumption of Moses* the Eternal God rises from His royal throne and goes forth to judge and punish (x. 3, 7). Though nearer in date to St Paul (perhaps A.D. 20), this is further from him in thought.

ἵνα κομίσηται ἕκαστος τὰ διὰ τοῦ σώματος. 'In order that each one may *receive as his due* the things done by means of his body.' This corrects the false inference which might be drawn from τοὺς πάντας ἡμᾶς. We shall not be judged *en masse*, or in classes, but one by one, in accordance with individual merit. "St Paul does not say merely that he shall receive according to what he has done in the body, but that he shall receive the things done—the very selfsame things he did; they are to be his punishment" (F. W. Robertson, *Lectures on the Epp. to the Corinthians*, p. 377). Chrys. points out that men are not much influenced by the prospect of losing possible blessings; the dread of possible pains is more influential. But *present* gains and losses are the most influential of all. Cf. εἰδότες ὅτι ἕκαστος, ἐάν τι ποιήσῃ ἀγαθόν, τοῦτο κομίσεται παρὰ Κυρίου (Eph. vi. 8), and ὁ γὰρ ἀδικῶν κομίσεται ὃ ἠδίκησεν (Col. iii. 25). In all three passages, κομίζεσθαι, 'to get what is one's own,' comes to mean 'to get as an equivalent,' 'to be requited.' Hort (on 1 Pet. i. 9) says that κομίζεσθαι "always in N.T. means not simply to receive but to receive back, to get what has belonged to oneself but has been lost, or promised but kept back, or what has come to be one's own by earning." This use is freq. in LXX also; Gen. xxxviii. 20, κομίσασθαι τὸν ἀρραβῶνα: Lev. xx. 17, ἁμαρτίαν κομιοῦνται: Ps. xl. 15; Ecclus. xxix. 6; 2 Macc. viii. 33, xiii. 8; etc. De Wette points out that the metonymy by which we are said to receive *back* what we have done is not a mere idiom, but "lies deeper in the identity of the deed and its requital." In papyri we find the same usage. This is not always brought out in Vulg., which again varies greatly in its renderings. In the eleven passages in which κομίζεσθαι occurs it uses five different words, some of which do not bear this meaning; *referre* (here), *percipere* (Eph. vi. 8; 1 Pet. v. 4; 2 Pet. ii. 13), *recipere* (Col. iii. 25; Mt. xxv. 27), *reportare* (Heb. x. 36; 1 Pet. i. 9), and *accipere* (Heb. xi. 13, 19, 39). The words from which this shade of meaning is absent are those which are most frequently employed. The renderings of this clause in Tertullian, Cyprian, and the Vulgate are worth comparing. Tert. (*Adv. Marc.* v. 12) *ut recipiat unusquisque quae per corpus admisit, sive bonum sive malum*; (*De Res. Carn.* 43) *uti unusquisque reportet quae per corpus secundum quae gessit, bonum sive malum*; (*ibid.* 60) *ut quis referat per corpus prout gessit,* where *quis* is probably a slip for *quisque.* Cypr. (*Test.* ii. 28 and iii. 56) *ut reportet unusquisque sui corporis propria secundum quae egit sive bona sive mala.* Vulg. *ut referat unusquisque propria corporis prout gessit, sive bonum sive malum,* where *referat, prout gessit, bonum, malum* agree with Tertullian, *propria corporis* with Cyprian. The latter expression points to a reading ἴδια for διά, a reading which is attested also by d e f g Goth. Arm., Ambrst., and several of the Fathers. In the Pelagian controversy it came to the front, because infants have no ἴδια sins, and could not be supposed to be justly liable to punishment.

τὰ διὰ τοῦ σώματος. 'Done by means of the body,' and therefore, as Herveius points out, *dum in corpore fuit*; and these include words and thoughts as well as deeds, for the tongue and the brain are instruments in producing them. In Plato we have ὁ μηδὲν φροντίζων τῶν ἡδονῶν αἳ διὰ τοῦ σώματός εἰσιν (*Phaedo,* 65); and again, ὄψις ἡμῖν ὀξυτάτη τῶν διὰ τοῦ σώματος ἔρχεται αἰσθήσεων, ᾗ φρόνησις οὐχ ὁρᾶται (*Phaedr.* 250): cf. αἱ κατὰ τὸ σῶμα ἡδοναὶ ἀπομαραίνονται (*Rep.* 328 D). In Xenophon (*Mem.* I. v. 6) οὐ μόνον τῶν διὰ τοῦ σώματος ἡδονῶν ἐκράτει, ἀλλὰ καὶ τῆς διὰ τῶν χρημάτων. The διά is probably instrumental, but it may be temporal, 'during his bodily lifetime,' *bei Leibesleben.* So Aug. *De Civ. Dei,* xvii. 4.

πρὸς ἃ ἔπραξεν. Works are needed as well as faith, and it is habitual moral action (πράσσειν), rather than mere performance and production (ποιεῖν), that has weight. Cf. xii. 21; 1 Cor. v. 2; Rom. ii. 1, 2, vii. 15, 19, xiii. 4, where πράσσειν is used of doing what is morally evil; 1 Cor. ix. 17; Phil. iv. 9, of what is morally good; and Rom. ix. 11, as here, of both : see on Rom. i. 32, vii. 15, 19, xiii. 4; Jn. iii. 20, 21, v. 29, where both verbs occur. Vulg. distinguishes with *ago* for πράσσω and *facio* for ποιέω. Although this cannot be pressed, for the difference between the two verbs is often very slight, yet πράσσειν is more appropriate here. With regard to both verb and preposition comp. ὁ μὴ ποιήσας πρὸς τὸ θέλημα αὐτοῦ (Lk. xii. 29). Noble ancestors, even righteous ancestors, says Chrys., will not count. Only a man's own deeds will be of any value; and, as Thdrt. adds, there will be exact correspondence between action and requital (καταλλήλους τὰς ἀντιδόσεις). Cf. κατὰ τὰ ἔργα (Rom. ii. 6; Rev. ii. 23, xx. 12). See on xi. 15.

εἴτε ἀγαθὸν εἴτε φαῦλον. The change to the neuter singular is significant. It seems to imply that, although persons will be judged one by one and not in groups, yet conduct in each case will be judged as a whole. In other words, it is character rather than separate acts that will be rewarded or punished. It is a mistake to suppose that any act, however heroic, can secure eternal

life. We must ask, not τί ποιήσας κληρονομήσω; (Lk. x. 25), but
τί με δεῖ ποιεῖν; (Acts xvi. 30). It is habitual action that will be
judged. And this explains the aorist; it is what he did during
his lifetime that is summed up and estimated as a total. Human
tribunals deal with crime; they have punishments, but no rewards. The Divine tribunal has both. See on 1 Cor. iii. 13
and iv. 5.

There are two things about which the Apostle is silent. He
does not say when the φανερωθῆναι will take place, whether at
death or at the Second Advent, but he seems to imply that the
requital will follow immediately upon the manifestation. Moreover, while he states that the period spent in the body is a time
of probation, and that there will be a scale of requitals pro-
portionate to our conduct here (cf. ix. 6), he says nothing about
the possibility of further probation hereafter, and he seems to
imply that there will be no further opportunity. But it is
going beyond what is written to say that the idea of a 'second
chance' is contrary to what St Paul asserts here. Here, as
elsewhere in Scripture, that possibility is veiled. See on 1 Cor.
x. 22.

Here again we have Pauline doctrine partly anticipated on
philosophical grounds by Plato (*Gorgias*, 523, 524). After
telling the story how Zeus was led to decree that men must not
be judged till after death, "because there are many who have
evil souls clad in comely bodies," and that they must be stripped
of these misleading coverings in order to be fairly judged,
Socrates continues; "This story, Callicles, I have heard and
believe to be true, and from it I think that some such inference
as this may be drawn. Death, it seems to me, is nothing else
than the separation of two things from one another, the soul and
the body. And when they are separated from one another, each
of them has pretty much the same character which it had when
the man was alive. If he was tall, fat, long-haired, scarred,
misshapen, the same characteristics are found on the dead
body, either all of them, or most of them, for some time. The
very same thing, it seems to me, Callicles, holds good of the
soul. When the soul is stripped of the body, all its natural
qualities and all those which the man acquired through his
devotion to this or that pursuit, are laid bare to view. And
when the souls come to the judge, he takes that of some
potentate, whose soul is full of the prints and scars of perjuries
and crimes with which his conduct has marked it, and has many
crooked places, because of lying and vanity, and has no straight-
ness, because he lived without truth. This soul the judge looks
at and sends away to a place where it must undergo the treatment which it requires."

There is no doubt that ἔπραξεν, not κομίσηται, is to be understood with εἴτε ἀγαθὸν εἴτε φαῦλον: it is the conduct, not the recompense, that is thus characterized. The recompense would not be called φαῦλον, 'worthless,' whether it were reward or punishment, and κομίσηται has τὰ διὰ τοῦ σώματος as its object. What a man does may be worthless, ξύλα, χόρτον, καλάμην (1 Cor. iii. 12), without being so evil as to exclude from the Kingdom. It may be doubted whether the Apostle is here taking account of those who are excluded; if so, they are quite in the background. Excepting Jn. v. 29 there is perhaps no passage in N.T. in which a resurrection of the wicked is clearly indicated. St Paul seems to regard it as a blessing reserved for members of Christ. Here it is genuine Christians, τοὺς πάντας ἡμᾶς, of whom he is speaking. All their shortcomings and failures will one day be exposed, and therefore they 'make it their aim' to avoid such defects.

Both Orig. and Thdrt. seem to have known the reading τά ἴδια τοῦ σώματος, but it is found in no Greek MS. L omits τὰ διὰ τ. σωμ., and Baljon would bracket the words as a gloss. D G have ἃ διὰ τοῦ σώματος ἔπραξεν. It is difficult to decide between φαῦλον (ℵ C 17 and other cursives) and κακόν (B D F G K L P); but it is more probable that κακόν, as the usual antithesis to ἀγαθόν, should be substituted for the less usual φαῦλον, than vice versa. But φαῦλον might come from Rom. ix. 11. The word occurs in four other passages in N.T., always of what is morally bad (Jn. iii. 20, v. 29; Tit. ii. 8; Jas. iii. 16); Aristotle has it often in this sense. Only in Jas. iii. 16 does Vulg. distinguish φαῦλον from κακόν: there it has pravum, elsewhere malum. In Eccles. xii. 14 we have σύμπαν τὸ ποίημα ὁ Θεὸς ἄξει ἐν κρίσει ἐὰν ἀγαθὸν καὶ ἐὰν πονηρόν.

ADDITIONAL NOTE ON V. 1–10.

Two questions have been discussed, with a minuteness and fulness out of proportion to their importance; and conclusions respecting them have been asserted, with a positiveness which is not warranted by the evidence which is at our disposal. Can what is stated here be reconciled with what is stated in 1 Cor. xv. 20–55? If not, are we to suppose that the painful experiences which troubled the Apostle in the brief interval between the writing of the two Epistles caused him to modify his beliefs respecting the Resurrection, the Parousia, and the Judgment? Or it is possible that further acquaintance with Alexandrian ideas, which he may have obtained through Apollos, led him to change his views? Again, can what is said in v. 6–10 be reconciled with what is said in v. 1–5? If not, how can we account for the Apostle's uttering two discordant views almost in the same breath?

It is to be remembered that in dealing with death, the condition of the departed, resurrection, and judgment, the language, not only of St Paul, but of Scripture generally, is highly symbolical, and that it is impossible to find symbols that are in all respects harmonious. Moreover, it is not justifiable to draw inferences from metaphors and treat the inferences as original statements. Thirdly, we are not to suppose that St Paul had a clearly defined theory respecting these mysterious topics, and that he kept this theory in mind and was careful to make all his statements respecting these topics in a form which would harmonize with the preconceived theory. He was fully convinced of the truth and importance of certain things, *e.g.* that Christ died and has been raised, that Christians who die will be raised, that they will be requited in accordance with their conduct in this life, and that neither in life nor in death are they separated from Christ; and each time that he has to handle any of these subjects he states his conviction in words which at the time seem to be forcible and fitting. The Epistles to the Corinthians are written in the glow of intense feeling, which varies according to the subject; and it is unreasonable to interpret them as if they were parts of a carefully elaborated system of theology.

"The man who wrote the great Resurrection-chapter in 1 Corinthians," says Wernle, "did not possess the capacity for altering his opinions which belongs to the modern theologian. For him, his hope, which he there expresses, is a truth for which he is willing to live and die. . . . The yearning to die and to be with Christ is for him the same thing as the hope of resurrection. His yearning overleaps all between death and resurrection, and hurries to its goal for reunion with Jesus" (H. A. A. Kennedy, *St Paul's Conception of the Last Things*, p. 272). That is the reasonable explanation of the apparent difference between this passage and 1 Cor. xv. There he is dealing with those who rejected the Resurrection because it was incredible that the material body will be resuscitated. He assures these sceptics that the resurrection-body will be something quite different from the material body. The material body will be destroyed. Here he is dealing with the contrast between the Christian's sufferings in this life and his hope of future glory. The latter is so strong that it far outweighs the sufferings, and even drives away the natural horror of leaving the material body. In 1 Cor. xv. the argument is directed against an error which assumed an interval between death and resurrection. Here no such interval comes into view; it is neither assumed nor denied. Those who live to see the Parousia will have their material bodies changed to spiritual bodies. Those who die before the Parousia will be better off than they were in this life, for they will be nearer to Christ. Whether there will be an interval between death and

11

the reception of a body suitable to the new conditions of life is lost sight of.* To one who believed that the Lord was near at hand, and that at His Coming all would receive spiritual bodies, the condition of those who died before His Coming was not a matter of much interest, and he tells us only one thing respecting their condition. They are happier, because they are in closer communion with Christ, than they were when they were in the body. This implies that they are conscious; they are not, in any literal sense, asleep: see on 1 Cor. xi. 30.

Jewish thought on the subject seems to have gone through several stages, which were not always logically consecutive. They may be stated roughly in some such way as this.

In Jer. li. 57 the sleep is not only said to be perpetual (αἰώνιος), but one from which the sleepers shall not wake (μὴ ἐξεγερθῶσιν). All rewards and penalties are given in this life; good and bad alike go to Sheol, which is almost equivalent to annihilation.

In Is. xxvi. and *Enoch* lxxxiii.–xc. there is to be a resurrection of the righteous Israelites.

In Dan. xii. there is to be a resurrection of the exceptionally righteous and the exceptionally wicked among the Israelites; but resurrection is of the spirit only, not of the body. This implies that Sheol is only a temporary abode for those who are to be raised, which leads to a division of Sheol.

In 2 Macc. and *Enoch* xxxvii.–lxx. there is to be a bodily resurrection of the righteous, and perhaps of all Israelites. Part of Sheol is Paradise, and part is Gehenna.

In 2 (4) Esdras and the *Apocalypse of Baruch* there is to be a bodily resurrection of both righteous and wicked; but retribution begins immediately after death.

With regard to bodily resurrection there are two views; (1) that the material body would be resuscitated; (2) that there would be a transfigured body. It is with this latter view that St Paul has sympathy.

But throughout his Epistles, wherever he touches upon this subject, he seems to be thinking almost (if not quite) exclusively of the resurrection of believers, of genuine Christians. It is not easy to decide whether he expected a general resurrection. If retribution begins immediately after death, there is no *necessity*

---

* G. B. Redman, in his essay on the Theology of St Paul in *The Parting of the Roads*, pp. 213–238, after working through the evidence in the Epistles, comes to this conclusion; "Hence the theory of a gradual development of St Paul's thought, involving the abandonment of the old idea of the coming of the Lord to inaugurate a new order of things, in favour of a conception of the gradual improvement of earthly conditions by the work of the Spirit, seems insufficiently supported by the evidence. The Advent Hope retains a permanent place in his scheme of Christianity."

for a resurrection of the wicked; and if resurrection depends
upon union with Christ, there is no *possibility* of it.   St Paul says
little about it.   Cf. 2 (4) Esdras viii. 38, 39; 'For indeed I will
not think on the fashioning of them which have sinned, or their
death, their judgment, or their destruction : but I will rejoice
over the framing of the righteous, their pilgrimage also, and the
salvation, and the reward, that they shall have'; where AV. is
seriously misleading.   St Paul held that all men, whether
believers or not, would be judged; but it does not follow from
this that he looked forward to a general resurrection.

The apparent want of harmony between the first five verses
of this chapter and the next five verses lies in this, that in *vv.*
1–5 he seems to contemplate an immediate passage from life in
the mortal body to life in an immortal body, and to have a
horror of physical death, which might leave him without a body
of any kind; whereas in *vv.* 6–10 he says that all believers must
be judged before entering upon immortal life, and that it is well
worth while to migrate from the mortal body.   On neither point
is there any real contradiction.   He does not speak of a great
assize in which all souls will come up simultaneously for judgment.   What he is concerned to insist upon is that every
individual soul will be judged; none can escape.   Whether
multitudes are before the judgment-seat together, and whether
there is an interval between death and judgment, are questions
which are not raised.   They do not affect the main issue.   On
the other point he encourages himself and others to conquer the
natural fear of death by remembering that parting from the
mortal body means entering upon closer union with the Lord.
On the passage generally the following remarks are worthy of
consideration.

"Questions about the *How* of the future life, about the
conditions of existence between death and the resurrection,
about the process of the resurrection itself, or about the nature
of the resurrection body, have little place in Paul's doctrine.
His concern is much more with the fact than with the mode of
the resurrection.   He suggests that there may be preservation of
identity along with far-reaching change of form.   Theologians
have asked, What is it that makes identity?   How is the new
body to be provided?   Out of what material shall it grow?
What shall be its relation to the present body?   How shall it
preserve its sameness together with a difference which seems
essential?

St Paul gives us to understand that the new body will be *our*
body, related to the former body, but superior to it in incorrupti-
bility, in power, in ability to discharge its function.   He states
the broad principle that 'God gives to each its own body.'   And

for his last answer he refers us to his great word 'in Christ.' Our union with Christ is his final solution of all difficulties, his final reason for the certain hope of a resurrection.

The doctrine of the resurrection is in essential harmony with Hebrew faith and Hebrew hope, and in essential distinction from Greek thought and Greek surmise. It is in the Pauline writings that the Biblical doctrine of a future life is seen in its sharpest contrasts with the Hellenic, which regarded the life of mind as the only real life and made man himself ultimately only a soul. It stands absolutely apart from the speculations of the great Greek sages and from the teaching of thinkers like Philo, in whom Hebrew thought was sunk in the wisdom of the Greek schools.

Paul never bases the hope of a hereafter for man on psychological considerations. He never contemplates a simple immortality of the soul. He proceeds on the O.T. view of man as a being made in God's image, a free personality destined for life. The Pauline hope is not the Platonist hope of a release from the shackle and sepulchre of the body, not the hope of the survival of an immortal principle in man, but the hope of the endurance of the man himself. Its kinship is with the O.T. doctrine of the unity of man's nature, the royalty of his being, his affinity with God. It reveals a consummation which is to be realized in his elevation to a condition of existence in which he shall live in the full integrity of his being, and his body, transformed and glorified, shall be the perfect instrument of a perfect life" (Abbreviated from S. D. F. Salmond, *The Christian Doctrine of Immortality*, pp. 570-577. See also 'Eschatology' in Hastings, *DB.*, and in *Enc. Bibl.*, and the literature there mentioned; J. A. Beet, *The Last Things*, 1897 and 1905; H. A. A. Kennedy, *St Paul's Conceptions of the Last Things*, 1904; J. R. Cohu, *S. Paul in the Light of Modern Research*, 1911).

V. 11-VI. 10. The Life of an Apostle.

I re-assert my sincerity, and I do so to enable you to answer those who question it. You can show them that for one's work as an Apostle one has a high motive, a sure basis, and full credentials.

11 With the thought of the Judgment in our minds, and knowing from experience what the fear of Christ as Judge means, we endeavour to convince men that they have good security against any insincerity on our part. To God, who has no prejudices against us, we have all along been laid as open as we

shall be at the Judgment ; and I trust that to the conscience of each one of you also our characters have been equally transparent.   [12] Do not misunderstand me ; I am not beginning again to praise myself, as some persons say that I am so fond of doing. What I am doing is giving you an opportunity of saying a word on our behalf by glorying in your own experience of us.   I want you to have an opportunity of answering our opponents, who constantly boast of their superficial advantages, because they have no reality of character to boast of.   [13] That I am not a selfish impostor is clear from this, that when I was beside myself, as these men say, it was with zeal for God, and now when I am sane and sober, I am working for you.   There is no room for selfishness in either case.   [14] I must be devoted to God and to you, for Christ's love keeps me from all selfish motives.   [15] Long ago I came to the following conclusion.   The Representative of the human race died for the sake of us all, and so His death was ours.   Why did He die for all?   In order that the living, now that they know that they died in Christ, should never again live for themselves, but should henceforth live for Him who for their sakes died and was raised again.   There you have our motive.

[16] This being understood, whatever our opponents or other people may do, we ministers of Christ, from the time that we came to this conclusion, value no one because of his external qualities.   Even if there was a time when we appreciated Christ in this way, yet, since we have been united with Christ, this has quite ceased to be true, and it is futile to recall it.   [17] This also follows ;—if any man is in Christ, he is a new creature ; the old condition of things passed away when he entered into that relation, and a new condition took its place.   [18] But all these new conditions come from God ; they are His creation.   Because of the Death and Resurrection of Christ He regarded us as reconciled to Himself (we ministers needed that as much as other men) and commissioned us to make this offer of reconciliation to others.   [19] We are to tell them that, from the first, God was in Christ reconciling the world to Himself, namely, by forbearing to count against men their transgressions, and by depositing with us His message of reconciliation.

[20] It is on behalf of Christ, therefore, that we are acting as ambassadors, seeing that it is God who entreats through us.   We beseech on Christ's behalf, Become reconciled to God.   [21] Do

you ask how this is possible? Him who never became acquainted
with sin, God for our sakes made to be sin, in order that we
might become God's righteousness by being merged in Him.

VI. ¹ But I have more to say than this. We are fellow-
workers with God in the work of converting the world. God has
given His grace; our part is to entreat *you* not to fail in profiting
by it. ² (For He says, 'In a season of acceptance, I gave ear to
thee; on a day of deliverance I succoured thee.' I tell you, the
season of acceptance is come; we are now at the day of deliverance.) ³ In all that we do in conjunction with Him, we strive to
put no cause of stumbling in anybody's way, so that no one may
have a handle for ridiculing or reviling the ministry. ⁴ On the
contrary, in everything we endeavour so to frame our conduct
that it may commend itself in a way that is worthy of God's
ministers.

The evidence that we are God's ministers may be seen
    In our abundant and varied endurance,
  Amid afflictions, necessities, and straits,
    scourgings, imprisonments, and riots,
    toilsome days, sleepless nights, foodless times;
  In innocence of life, and in knowledge of the truth,
    in patient long-suffering, and in kindliness of heart,
    in a spirit that is holy, and in love that is unfeigned,
    in a teaching that is true, and in a power that is Divine;
  Through weapons of righteousness for the right hand and the
    left,
        through repute and disesteem,
        through ill and good report;
    As impostors, and yet truthful,
  as nobodies to these, and celebrities to those,
  as ever at death's door, and yet behold! we live on,
  as chastened for our sins, yet never killed by chastisement,
  as sorrowing much, but always full of joy,
  as paupers ourselves, but able to enrich thousands,
  as having nothing, yet holding the whole world in possession.

It is difficult to summarize this section (v. 11-vi. 10) as a
whole, and the connexion between portions of it is sometimes
obscure. On the whole, as distinct from the sufferings and
supports of one who has the responsibilities of an Apostle, this
section re-asserts St Paul's sincerity, and gives further explana-

tions of his conduct. This is done, not so much in order to convince the Corinthians that they do well in admitting his Apostolic authority, as to supply them with sound answers to give to those who question it and accuse him of being a self-advertising impostor. He points to three things which character-ize his work as a preacher. The *motive* of it is the fear of Christ as our Judge and Christ's love for us as our Redeemer (11–15). The *basis* of it is the creation of new conditions and the recon-ciliation won for us by Christ (16–19). The *credentials* which attest its authority are his having been made an ambassador of Christ and a minister of God (v. 20–vi. 10). With these facts his personal sincerity and his Apostolic position can be made as evident to men as they are to God.

It is strange that anyone should suppose that in vi. 3–10 St Paul is maintaining that, not only he himself, but all Christians, are free from sin. With regard to Christians in general, it is enough to point to the stern reproofs and warnings which he at times administers to his converts (xii. 20, 21 ; 1 Cor. i. 11, iii. 3, v. 1, 11, viii. 11, x. 14, xi. 30; Gal. iii. 1 ; etc.) : he knows well that Christians do sometimes sin grievously. With regard to himself, he says that acquittal by his own conscience proves nothing as to his innocence (1 Cor. iv. 4); therefore for him to claim to be sinless, because his conscience did not reprove him, would be vain ; and the vivid picture which he draws of the inward struggle between right and wrong (Rom. vii. 17–25) is evidently drawn from tortures which he had himself experienced. And how unreal would be the appeal to a future judgment (v. 10 ; Rom. iv. 10), if he felt sure that he had no sins to answer for !

In vi. 3–10 he is sketching the Apostolic ideal which he has set before himself, and which their knowledge of him can tell that he is trying to realize. There is enough of these features in his life for them to be able to assure others that he is really an ambassador and minister of God. Teachers who have none of these features cannot be recognized as such. *Tria ergo hic agit Paulus : docet quae sint virtutes, quibus censeri debent Evangelici doctores : deinde his virtutibus se praeditum esse demonstrat : tertio admonet Corinthios, ne pro Christi servis agnoscant, qui se aliter gerunt* (Calv.). In his own day the error about him was some-what different.

It is strange that one who was so conspicuously self-sacrific-ing as St Paul should be charged with self-seeking and self-praise. But his opponents' fanatical hatred of his teaching distorted their judgment and depraved their consciences. They misinterpreted all that he said and did, and they thought that in such a con-flict all weapons were lawful, including insinuation, slander, and abuse.

11. Εἰδότες οὖν. 'Therefore, because we are conscious of,' 'because we feel the influence of'; an appeal to actual experience. 'We know what the fear of the Lord means.' The οὖν refers to the contents of *v.* 10. Bachmann gives illustrations from papyri of this use of εἰδώς.

τὸν φόβον τοῦ Κυρίου. The fear excited by the thought of standing before the judgment-seat of Christ and having one's whole life exposed and estimated. In O.T., 'the fear of the Lord' or 'the fear of God' is the whole of piety. It is 'wisdom' (Job xxviii. 28) and 'the whole duty of man' (Eccles. xii. 13); cf. Deut. x. 12; Prov. i. 7, ix. 10, xvi. 6. St Paul makes 'the fear of Christ' a principle of conduct (Eph. v. 21), and here he states that he knows that his own actions are guided by it. It is the fear which he feels (vii. 1; Rom. iii. 18), not 'the terror' (AV.) which Christ inspires, *terrorem illum Domini* (Beza), τὸ φοβερόν (Heb. x. 27, 31, xii. 21) τοῦ Κυρίου (Chrys.), that is meant. Vulg. is right with *timorem Domini*. To translate, 'We persuade men as to the fear of the Lord,' *i.e.* teach them to fear Him, is perverse misconstruction.

ἀνθρώπους πείθομεν, Θεῷ δὲ πεφανερώμεθα. 'We persuade men, but we are made manifest to God.' The AV. loses the antithesis by separating the second clause from the first and attaching it to what follows; 'We persuade men; but we are made manifest to God, and I trust also, etc.' The antithesis is effective and ought to be preserved; 'God knows all about us through and through, but we have to persuade men to believe in our sincerity'; τοὺς περὶ ἡμῶν ψευδεῖς ἔχοντας δόξας ἐπανορθοῦν πειρώμεθα (Thdrt.). The omission of μέν after ἀνθρώπους is not owing to inadvertence in dictation. The contrast between men's mistrust and God's full knowledge is all the more forcible because no μέν prepares the reader for what is coming. That τὸν φόβον does not mean τὸ φοβερόν is confirmed by πείθομεν. He does not say 'we frighten,' but 'we persuade.' The thought that he will have to answer for all that he does in his ministry makes him anxious to convince men that they need not hesitate to accept his ministry. He appeals to God's knowledge of him; *Deo notum esse qua animi sinceritate agat* (Calv.); in Him there are no prejudices to be removed. And the perfect has its full force; 'have been made manifest and remain so,' 'all along we have been open to God's view'; at any given moment the manifesting is complete.

Gal. i. 10 should be compared; ἄρτι γὰρ ἀνθρώπους πείθω ἢ τὸν Θεόν; 'For am I now trying to win men over or to win God over?' This may be a reply to a charge that he was always trying to get people over to his side. 'Yes,' he says; 'yet it is not men, but God, that I wish to have on my side.' Strictly speaking, to talk of persuading God is inadmissible, but by a kind of zeugma he uses the expression in answer to an accusation. Here also he may be replying to criticism, such as, 'You know how to talk men over, but you will not be able to talk God over.' 'Certainly,' he says, 'I try to induce men to believe in me; the fear of a judgment to come makes me do so; but to God I am perfectly transparent. The conviction that He sees me and that I must one day give account compels me to be sincere.' Here he avoids using πείθειν of God and takes the verb used in *v.* 10 : πείθειν may be the word used by his critics.

Others interpret, 'We persuade men that we strive to please Christ who is to be our Judge.' This is not very different from 'we persuade men that we are sincere.' Chrys. points out that it is a duty to remove unjust suspicions from ourselves. A minister is hindered in his work by being credited with misdeeds of which he is innocent.

It is not likely that ἀνθρώπους πείθομεν means ' we persuade men to become Christians,' *homines ad fidem adducimus* (Beza). Such an interpretation is foreign to the context, and it makes the contrast between persuading men and being fully known to God pointless.

ἐλπίζω δὲ καὶ ἐν ταῖς συνειδήσεσιν ὑμῶν πεφανερῶσθαι. 'And I hope that in your consciences also we have been made manifest.' Against the mistrust of men he has appealed to God, who sees him through and through. He trusts that he may appeal also to what his converts know about him. After all that he has explained about his motives and actions, is he not as transparent to them as he is to God? The rapidity with which he alternates between 1st pers. plur. and 1st pers. sing. is here conspicuous,— πείθομεν, ἐλπίζω, συνιστάνομεν. We cannot safely infer that all three have exactly the same meaning. The plur. may mean the Apostle as the representative of other ministers, while the sing. is strictly personal; his hopes are his own.

After ἐλπίζω we commonly have the aor. infin. (1 Cor. xvi. 7 ; Phil. ii. 19, 23 ; 1 Tim. iii. 14), but here the previous perf. determines the case, the meaning in both cases being the same, —that his character has been, and still is, laid bare. Blass (§ 61 note) says that ' hope ' here means ' think ' (as often in English) and hence the perf.

ταῖς συνειδήσεσιν ὑμῶν. Their consciences, rather than their intellects, on which they prided themselves : *conscientia enim longius penetrat quam carnis judicium* ; conscience goes deeper than criticism (Calv.). St Paul says ' consciences ' and not ' conscience,' because he appeals to the individual conscience of each of them : *pluralis habet gravitatem* (Beng.). Nowhere else in Biblical Greek does the plural occur ; contrast **i.** 12 ; 1 Tim iii. 9, iv. 2 ; etc.

12. οὐ πάλιν ἑαυτοὺς συνιστάνομεν ὑμῖν. 'Do not think that we are again commending ourselves to you.' The remark has the same relation to v. 11 as iii. 1 to ii. 17. He sees that what he has just stated gives a handle to those who said that he was always praising himself, and he hastens to show that he has no such aim. He is not commending himself to them; if the hope just expressed is correct, there is no need for him to do that; he is helping them to answer the cavils of his opponents. The accusations against him, sometimes very plausible, were a great hindrance to his work, and he constantly takes opportunity to answer them. Often, although we feel that he is referring to some objection, our ignorance of the nature of the objection renders his words obscure. Here we can see our way fairly clearly. See on iii. 1.

ἀλλὰ ἀφορμὴν διδόντες ὑμῖν καυχήματος ὑπὲρ ἡμῶν. 'On the contrary (we say this) by way of giving you some grounds for glorying on our behalf.' With this free use of the participle comp. θλιβόμενοι (vii. 5), χειροτονηθείς and στελλόμενοι (viii. 19, 20). Winer, p. 442; Blass, § 79. 10. Vulg. smooths the construction by making the participle a finite verb; *sed occasionem damus vobis gloriandi pro nobis.* If the consciences of the Corinthians do recognize his sincerity, they can use their estimate of him in replying to his Jewish detractors. This is a hint that they might have done this without his having to suggest it. They might have said, "Each one of us has had personal experience of Paul and his work, and we are unanimously convinced of his authority and integrity." With the very doubtful exception of Lk. xi. 54, ἀφορμή is peculiar to Paul in N.T. (xi. 12; Rom. vii. 8, 11; Gal. v. 13; 1 Tim. v. 14, as here, with διδόναι). It means 'a basis of operations,' 'a place to start from,' and hence 'good grounds': *argumenta vobis praebemus gloriandi de nostra integritate; tantum abest ut demum opus esse commendatione nostri putem* (Beng.). In 3 Macc. iii. 2, ἀφορμή means 'motive,' a meaning found also in papyri, where it seems sometimes to mean 'excuse'; see Bachmann. Here, as in 1 Cor. v. 6, καύχημα does not mean *materies gloriandi* (Meyer), but *gloriatio* (Beng.), *i.e.* glorying uttered. Cf. ix. 3, and see T. S. Evans on 1 Cor. v. 6.

ἵνα ἔχητε πρὸς τοὺς κ.τ.λ. 'That ye may have (it ready) against those who, etc.' Something is to be understood after ἔχητε, either τι or τι λέγειν, or better, either καύχημα or ἀφορμήν. In deciding between the last two it is little to the point that in Rom. iv. 2 and Gal. vi. 4 we have καύχημα ἔχειν, and nothing to the point that in Rom. vii. 8, 11 we have ἀφορμὴν λαβεῖν, for λαβεῖν and not ἔχειν is required for the sense. Understand ἀφορμήν here; 'that you may have this resource ready to your hand.'

τοὺς ἐν προσώπῳ καυχωμένους καὶ μὴ ἐν καρδίᾳ.   The resemblance to 1 Thess. ii. 17 is verbal only.   There the antithesis means that out of sight is not out of mind.   Here it means that what men see is not what God sees ; ἄνθρωπος ὄψεται εἰς πρόσωπον, ὁ δὲ Θεὸς ὄψεται εἰς καρδίαν (1 Sam. xvi. 7).   The Judaizers gloried in what was patent to the world, the superficial advantages which made an outward show, such as their descent from Abraham, their exclusiveness, their scrupulous keeping of the Law, perhaps also their intimacy with James, the Lord's brother.   What were all these external characteristics compared with a good conscience and the fear of God?   Paul had the latter, as the Corinthians knew, for it was out of the goodness of his heart that light and truth had come to their consciences ; whereas the Judaizers had given them no evidence of their possessing these spiritual characteristics.   As usual in N.T., we have ἐν after καυχᾶσθαι, and μή with the participle.   In LXX, ἐν is usual, but ἐπί sometimes occurs.   Here many texts have οὐ instead of μή.

Three other ways of interpreting the opposition between πρόσωπον and καρδία are suggested.   (1) 'Who glorify me to my face, but not in their hearts.'   This is inadmissible, for τ. καυχωμένους cannot mean ' those who glorify me ' ; it means ' those who glory,' ' those who glorify themselves.'   (2) 'Who boast in the presence of other people, but not in their own hearts.'   This also is inadmissible, for the πρόσωπον and the καρδία belong to the same persons, viz. those who boast, an objection which holds good against (1) also.   (3) 'Whose boasting is seen in their faces, but is not felt in their hearts.'   This is possible, but it is not probable. In N.T., as in LXX, ἐν after καυχᾶσθαι introduces that in which people glory (x. 15–17, xi. 12, xii. 9 ; 1 Cor. i. 31 ; etc.).*   The more probable meaning is, ' Who glory in external privileges, not in internal worth ' ; welche sich äusserer Dinge und nicht der rechten Herzensverfassung rühmen (Bousset).   But (3), with emendation, may be right ; ' Who glory in what is seen in their faces, but not in what exists in their hearts ' ; i e. they hypocritically profess a satisfaction which they do not feel, or they wear a look of apostolic virtue which they do not possess.

οὐ πάλιν (א B C D* G 67**, e Vulg. Syrr. Goth. Copt. Arm.) rather than οὐ γὰρ πάλιν (D³ E K L).   For ὑπὲρ ἡμῶν, א B 17, Aeth. have ὑπὲρ ὑμῶν, a common confusion.   καὶ μή (א B 17 and other cursives, Thdrt.) is probably to be preferred to καὶ οὐ (C D³ E K L P) or καὶ οὐκ (D* F G).   ἐν καρδίᾳ (א B D* F G 17, 37, Latt.) rather than καρδίᾳ (C D³ E K L P).

13.   εἴτε γὰρ ἐξέστημεν, Θεῷ· εἴτε σωφρονοῦμεν, ὑμῖν.   ' I do not commend myself ; indeed I do nothing on my own account ; for

* We find gloriari in in the same sense ; non pudet philosophum in eo gloriari quod haec non timeat (Cic. Tusc. I. xxi. 48) ; in virtute recte gloriamur (Nat. Deor. III. xxxvi. 87).   More often gloriari has no preposition or de.

when I was beside myself, it was on God's account, and when
I am sane, it is on yours.' The selection of this surprising
alternative of ἐκστῆναι and σωφρονεῖν was probably caused by the
declaration of some of his opponents that he was not only paradoxical and obscure (iv. 3), but quite crazy. Jews thought that
Paul went mad when he was converted on the road to Damascus,
and ἐξέστημεν might refer to that. Festus had impulsively said
that he was mad (Acts xxvi. 24), and his Judaizing critics had
brought the same charge (xi. 1, 16), as the Jewish critics of his Master
had done in His case (Mk. iii. 21; Jn. vii. 48). The Judaizers'
charge against the Apostle was not pure invention. He claimed
to have been 'caught up even to the third heaven' (xii. 2), to
'speak with Tongues more than all' of them (1 Cor. xiv. 18),
in which condition he spoke 'not to men but to God' (xiv. 2),
and his 'understanding was unfruitful' (xiv. 14). Speaking with
Tongues easily led to the charge of being mad (xiv. 23), and it
may have done so in the case of one who was so frequently
ecstatic as St Paul. If, as is probable, the 'stake for the flesh'
from which he suffered was epilepsy, this again would cause his
sanity to be questioned. The reply here is pointed and tactful.
'My ecstasies concerned only God and myself; my normal
condition is always at your service. The two together sum up
my life, which accordingly is devoted either to God or to you.'
*De nobis potestis gloriari, quia quidquid agimus, vel honor Dei est,
vel utilitas proximi* (Herveius).

Augustine several times refers to this passage, and he always
takes ἐξέστημεν (*mente excessimus*) as meaning ecstasy; but it may
refer to other features in the Apostle's life, as suggested above.
In Is. xxviii. 7, ἐξέστησαν is used of prophets beside themselves
with strong drink. It is not certain that ἐξέστησεν refers to past
time; it may be a timeless aorist; RV. has 'are' in the text and
'were' in the margin. Cf. ἐξέστη, 'He *is* beside Himself' (Mk.
iii. 21). Winer, p. 346; Blass, § 59. 3; J. H. Moulton, p. 134;
and see Hort on 1 Pet. i. 24. For the datives comp. Rom.
xiv. 4, and see Blass, § 37. 2.

Some think that both alternatives refer to a definite accusation, one that he was mad, the other that he was worldly wise;
but σωφρονεῖν never means the latter. A more reasonable suggestion is that ἐξέστημεν refers to his self-commendation, which
his critics said amounted to a mania. Cf. τὸ καυχᾶσθαι παρὰ
καιρὸν μανίαισιν ὑποκρέκει, "To glory out of season is to sound
the same note as madness" (Pind. *Ol.* ix. 39). Thdrt. adopts
this interpretation. Other suggestions are: (1) Ἐξέστημεν refers
to the vigour with which the Apostle followed his own advice of
being 'instant εὐκαίρως, ἀκαίρως' (2 Tim. iv. 2) in proclaiming
the word. But his preaching was ὑμῖν as well as Θεῷ. (2) He

is referring to the comments made on the letter which he sent between 1 Corinthians and this Epistle,—the severe letter, about the effects of which he was so anxious. If x.–xii. formed part of that letter, some Corinthians might easily say, "The man must be mad"; and he himself foresaw the possibility (xi. 1, 16, xii. 6). Herveius seems to agree with Augustine in restricting the reference to ecstasy; *sive enim mente omnia temporalia excedimus, ut contemplemur aeterna, Deo id facimus, sive ab illa mentis ebrietate ad communem sensum redimus, hoc fit in vestram utilitatem, ut vos nimirum docere possimus.* All that is certain is that ἐξέστημεν refers to exceptional, and σωφρονοῦμεν to ordinary conditions, and that these two cover the whole of his behaviour, which, therefore, is never self-seeking.

14. ἡ γὰρ ἀγάπη τοῦ Χριστοῦ συνέχει ἡμᾶς. 'We are influenced, not only by *future* rewards and punishments, whether in this world or the next; there is something in the present which affects us, for Christ's love controls us : The love which Christ has for us (Gal. ii. 20) keeps us back from all self-seeking, and confines our aims to the service of God and of our fellow-men.' In the Pauline Epp., the genitive of the person after ἀγάπη seems always to mean that the person exhibits, not receives, the love (xiii. 13 ; 2 Thess. iii. 5 ; Eph. ii. 4; etc.), and in them ἀγάπη seems never to be used of man's love to Christ or to God. In any case it is love and not fear (*v.* 12) which operates. As regards the meaning of συνέχει, comp. συνέχομαι ἐκ τῶν δύο, 'I am hemmed in on both sides, restrained from inclining either way' (Phil. i. 23; see Lightfoot). 'The love of Christ constraineth us' (AV., RV.) is doubly ambiguous; it may mean 'our love for Christ urges us on.' 'Our love for Christ' is certainly wrong, as *v.* 15 shows; and 'urges us on' is probably wrong, although Chrys. takes it so, as does Vulg., *urget nos.* The verb implies the pressure which confines and restricts (Lk. viii. 45, xii. 50, xix. 43 ; Acts xviii. 5). It is true that restriction may lead to concentration, which may produce an increase of activity. Nevertheless, restricting men is opposed to pushing them on, and here 'restrains us from self-seeking' rather than 'urges us on to service' seems to be the meaning. 'Urges us on to avoid self-seeking' is a curious way of adopting one translation and keeping the meaning of the other. Bousset makes συνέχει refer to ἐξέστημεν, 'restrains us from madness and extravagance,' 'keeps us sane and sober'; *hält uns bei Sinnen.* It is more probable that it refers to ἑαυτοὺς συνιστάνομεν, 'restrains us from self-praise.' Papyri give no help; they merely repeat the usages found in N.T.

15. κρίναντας τοῦτο. 'Having reached this decision'; *judicio verissimo. Amor et judicium non obstant inter se apud spirituales* (Beng.). He probably refers to the period of reflexion between his conversion and his missionary activity (Gal. i. 17, 18). Both AV. and RV. ('because we thus judge'), as also Aug. (*judicantes*) and Vulg. (*aestimantes*) treat the aor. part. as a present. Some editors assign this clause to *v.* 14.

ὅτι εἷς ὑπὲρ πάντων ἀπέθανεν. 'That one died on behalf of all,' as their representative ; not ἀντὶ πάντων, 'instead of all,' as their substitute. He died in their interest; cf. ὑπὲρ ἡμῶν in *v.* 12. Only in connexion with the metaphor of a ransom is ἀντί used of Christ's death ; λύτρον ἀντὶ πόλλων (Mk. x. 45 = Mt. xx. 28) : cf. ἀντίλυτρον ὑπὲρ πάντων (1 Tim. ii. 6). For ὑπέρ see Rom. viii. 32 ; Gal. i. 4, ii. 20, iii. 13 ; Eph. v. 2 ; Tit. ii. 14. But the ideas of representation and of substitution easily run into one another, as in ἵνα ὑπὲρ σοῦ μοι διακονῇ (Philem. 13), and in the formula, which is freq. in papyri, ἔγραψα (or ἔγραψεν) ὑπὲρ αὐτοῦ, the nominative to the verb being the name of the scribe who wrote the letter for some person who was unable to write. For examples see Deissmann, *Light from the Ancient East*, pp. 153, 335.

ἄρα οἱ πάντες ἀπέθανον. 'Therefore all died'; lit. 'the all' (the 'all' for which He died) died in the dying of Him who, as Origen says, is the ἀνακεφάλωσις καὶ συγκεφάλωσις πάντων. 'Then were all dead' (AV.) is inaccurate and obscures the meaning; and there are similar mistranslations Rom. vi. 2 and Col. iii. 3. 'Therefore all must die' is equally erroneous and misleading. Seeing that the Representative of the whole race died, His death was their death ; and they all died in Him in the sense that His supreme act of love extinguished in them the old life of worldly interests in which the centre of gravity was self.* Although there is a vast difference between their death and His, yet there is this similarity. In each case there is the dying to the old self in order to rise again to something far higher ; in His case a dying to the life of suffering to rise to the life of glory ; in their case a dying to the life of sin to rise to the life of righteousness (Rom. vi. 6–11 ; Col. iii. 3). The life of love, inherent in Him, was kindled in them. This was the Apostle's own experience. Saul the persecutor was filled with consuming indignation, when he saw that one who had died the most shameful of all deaths was being proclaimed as the Messiah   When the risen Jesus appeared to him and convinced him that He was the Messiah, he was filled with consuming love and gratitude towards a Messiah who, for the sake of mankind, had submitted to such a death. "The mixture of love and gratitude forms one of the

* See J. A. Beet in the *Expositor*, 3rd se ies, vi pp. 140–150 (1887).

strongest passions which can dominate the heart of man," and the Apostle never wearies of declaring how Christ's immense love for us calls for a generous return (Rom. v. 15–21, viii. 35; Gal. ii. 20, v. 24, vi. 14; Eph. iii. 19, v. 2, 25; Tit. ii. 14). See P. Gardner, *The Religious Experience of St Paul*, p. 188. In N.T. ἄρα is sometimes placed first in a sentence (vii. 12; Rom. x. 17; Gal. v. 11; etc.); rarely in LXX (Ps. cxxiii. 2, 3, 4, cxxxviii. 11; Wisd. v. 6); never in class. Grk. See on vii. 12.

ἵνα οἱ ζῶντες μηκέτι ἑαυτοῖς ζῶσιν. 'In order that those who live should no longer (now that they know that they died in Christ) live to themselves.' How can those for whom Christ died go on living for themselves and not for Him? Rom. xiv. 7–9. Does οἱ ζῶντες mean those who are alive in the body and are still in this world, or those who have died to their old selves and are spiritually alive in Christ? The context favours the former meaning, and this is confirmed by iv. 11. It is not true that 'those who are still alive in the world' is superfluous and pointless here. The ζῶσιν which follows gives point; 'that the *living* should never again *live* to themselves.'

τῷ ὑπὲρ πάντων. These words probably belong to both participles; and, as it cannot be said that Christ was raised *instead* of us, therefore ὑπὲρ πάντων does not mean 'instead of all' but 'on behalf of all,' as ὑπὲρ ἡμῶν in v. 12 means 'on our behalf.' Nevertheless, it is possible to translate 'for Him who died for the sake of all, and was raised,' or 'who died instead of all, and was raised.'

AV. has '*if* one died for all,' following the reading of אᵃC*, f Vulg. Copt. Arm.; ὅτι εἰ εἷς. The εἰ might accidentally be either lost in the εἷς or produced by reduplication from it. Probably it was inserted for smoothness to anticipate ἄρα, as in 1 Cor. xv. 14, 17; cf. 2 Cor. vii. 12. Rom. v. 10, 15, 17 might be in the copyist's mind. Here the insertion of εἰ weakens the terseness of what is overwhelmingly attested as the original reading (א* B C² D E F G K L P, d e g Syrr. Aeth. Goth. RV.). AV. and RV. assign κρίναντας τοῦτο . . . ἀπέθανον to v. 14. See above on the divisions between i. 6, 7, ii. 10, 11, ii. 12, 13.

16–19. Having stated the motive of his work as a preacher, the Apostle now goes on to show the *basis* of it in the new conditions produced by being in Christ and in the reconciliation brought about for us by Him.

16. The verse is one of those parenthetical remarks which are so characteristic of St Paul, and so natural in one who dictated his letters; cf. *v.* 7; 1 Cor. xv. 56; Rom. v. 25. There is no need to conjecture that he inserted it afterwards; still less that a copyist inserted it. A copyist would have inserted something much more simple, and no copy exists without it. Verse

15 would easily suggest it,* and *v.* 17 is parallel to it. The parenthesis is quite in place. Christ died for all in order that all should cease to live for themselves, and should live for Him and for others in Him. That implies that our estimate of others must be based, not on the πρόσωπον, but on the καρδία, not on the external circumstances which the world values, but on the character and the inner life.

The details of this difficult verse are very variously explained, and it would be tedious, and not very profitable, to quote all the variations. What follows is offered as a tenable interpretation, and a few that seem to be less tenable are added.

ὥστε ἡμεῖς ἀπὸ τοῦ νῦν. The pronoun is emphatic, and so also, in a lower degree, is the adverbial phrase. 'Wherefore whatever others may do, we ministers of Christ, from the time when we arrived at this decision (κρίναντες).' The others are the many who care chiefly for earthly considerations, in their estimate of men; and it is implied that 'we' once did so, but have been effectually cured. The meaning of ἀπὸ τ. νῦν is uncertain, but it cannot mean 'from the present moment, the time of writing,' and there is nothing in the context that is obvious, except the conclusion drawn from the death of Christ. Recognition of the true meaning of the death of Christ has put an end to κατὰ σάρκα : now all is κατὰ πνεῦμα.

οἴδαμεν. The verb is used in the same sense as in 1 Thess. v. 12, 'we appreciate, we value.' '*Agnoscere' hic significat Habere rationem aut respectum* is Calvin's remark. In 1 Cor. xvi. 18, ἐπιγινώσκετε is used in much the same sense; see note there and comp. καλῶς ἔχει Θεὸν καὶ ἐπίσκοπον εἰδέναι (Ign. *Smyr.* 9). 'We value no one because of his external attributes.' The differences between king and clown, rich and poor, master and slave, genius and dunce, do not come into the estimate; what counts is the person's character as a Christian.

κατὰ σάρκα. *Secundum statum veterem, ex nobilitate, divitiis, opibus, sapientia* (Beng.). 'In the world's way,' 'by human standards,' 'as men know one another' are not accurate renderings. They make κατὰ σάρκα subjective, qualifying the view of the person who estimates; whereas κατὰ σάρκα is objective, qualifying the aspect of the person who is estimated, 'according to external distinctions,' 'by what he is in the flesh.'

εἰ καὶ ἐγνώκαμεν κατὰ σάρκα Χριστόν. 'Even though we have appreciated Christ after the flesh.' The change from εἰδέναι to γινώσκειν is of little moment here: it is the change of tense that

* The connexion is of this kind. To live for oneself means that one estimates others by purely external distinctions (κατὰ σάρκα); ever since we recognized the meaning of Christ's death we have ceased to assign any value to such distinctions: it is the internal qualities that count.

matters.   A perfect is wanted, and, as εἰδέναι has no perfect, a change of verb becomes necessary.   As usual, εἰ καί concedes the point which is stated hypothetically.   St Paul seems to be referring to some charge which had been made against him, that he had known Christ according to the flesh, and he admits that at one time this was true.   Then what does St Paul mean when he admits that he once knew Christ κατὰ σάρκα?   The phrase κατὰ σάρκα occurs often, in very different contexts, and no explanation of it will suit them all.   In each case the context must decide (i. 17, x. 2, 3; 1 Cor. i. 26, x. 18; Gal. iv. 23; Rom. iv. 1, viii. 4, 5, 12, ix. 3, 5; etc.).   Our answer to the question will depend upon the period in St Paul's career at which this erroneous appreciation of Christ is placed.

Almost certainly he is alluding to some time *previous* to his conversion.   On that hypothesis various explanations have been suggested.   (1) At that time he knew Christ as an heretical and turbulent teacher, who was justly condemned by the Sanhedrin and crucified by the Romans.   Consequently, he persecuted His adherents and caused them to be imprisoned and slain.   This explanation seems to be the best.*   (2) At that time he had the very carnal idea that the Messiah must be an earthly potentate who would conquer the Romans and set Israel free. But the passage implies, and the next verse shows, that it is the actual Christ, and not the Jewish idea of the Messiah, that the Apostle admits that he knew, and knew superficially and wrongly.   (3) At that time he had seen Christ at Jerusalem or elsewhere.   But would St Paul lay any weight on the fact (if it was a fact) that he had once known Christ by sight?   And what meaning, in that case, could ἀλλὰ νῦν οὐκέτι γινώσκω have? Moreover, if he had seen Christ before the Crucifixion, would he not have mentioned it xi. 22, 23?   (4) He is admitting this merely for the sake of argument.   'Supposing that I have seen Christ in the flesh, as some of my opponents claim to have done, I put no value upon that accidental circumstance.   On that hypothesis, I am in no better position as a teacher than if I had never seen Him.'   But we do not know that any of the Apostle's opponents did claim to have seen Christ during His ministry, or that on this account they professed to be superior to St Paul.   Nevertheless, this explanation of the passage is worth considering.

* P. Gardner may perhaps be claimed as a supporter of it when he says; "This reference is not to the human life of Jesus, which Paul had probably not witnessed, but to the kind of knowledge which is only of the senses, and has not become a process of the spirit" (*The Religious Experience of St Paul*, p. 200). See also Headlam, *St Paul and Christianity*, pp. 51 f., and *Foundations*, p. 188.

12

There are some, however, who think it more probable that St Paul is referring to a time *subsequent* to his conversion. (5) He is confessing that at an immature stage of his ministry he still retained some of the low ideas about Christ which he had inherited from Judaism. Jowett (*Introduction to Thessalonians*, pp. 8–12) strongly advocates this view. He says that St Paul "acknowledged a time when he had more nearly approximated to their (his opponents') Judaizing tenets, or in other words, had known Christ after the flesh. Whatever softening the skill of interpreters may introduce into these latter words, they must have a meaning; that meaning is that there was something which the Apostle had left behind him, which he had once thought, and no longer thought, to be a part of the faith of Christ" (p. 9). This view has also been held by Baur, Holsten, and others. The objection to it is that no trace of it is to be found in any of the Epistles. St Paul admits more than once that he had been a persecuting Jew (1 Cor. xv. 19; 1 Tim. i. 13), and seems to allude to it elsewhere. But he nowhere confesses that he had once preached a Judaizing Gospel: in Gal. ii. 15–19 he declares that he had done the opposite. For Beyschlag's criticism of this interpretation, and for other interpretations, see Knowling, *The Witness of the Epistles*, pp. 2, 3. Kirsopp Lake, who places the time in which St Paul knew Christ after the flesh in the period before his conversion, remarks that the Apostle "had once been an anti-Christian Jew; but when had he ever been a Judaizing Christian?" (*Earlier Epistles of St Paul*, p. 224).* It is possible to take this last view also on the same lines as (4) in reference to (3). We may say, (6) St Paul is admitting this merely for the sake of argument. 'Let us grant, if you like, that at one time I preached much the same unspiritual Gospel that my Judaizing opponents do. I certainly do nothing of the kind now, and therefore it is idle to reproach me with it. Am I right, or are they right, now? That is the only question.' But it is difficult to believe that his opponents had asserted that at one time he had agreed with them about the Gospel. And, unless they had done so, why should he, even hypothetically, concede that he might have agreed with them? Their view of him was that he had gone mad from the first.

We must be content to leave the exact meaning of the words in uncertainty; but this much is fairly clear. The Apostle is alluding to some charge which had been made against him, and he admits that at one time it was true; but he declares that there is no truth in it now. This excludes the (on other grounds)

* See also J. G. Machen in the *Princeton Biblical Studies*, p. 559, and H. R. Mackintosh, *The Doctrine of the Person of Jesus Christ*, p. 52.

improbable view that (7) seeing Christ on the road to Damascus
was knowing Him after the flesh.

See the fine comment of Aug. (*De Doc. Chris.* i. 38), to the
effect that this passage teaches us not to cling to the details of
Christ's earthly life, although they were done for our salvation,
but pass over them quickly, in order to reach Christ Himself,
who has freed our nature from earthly things and placed it at the
right hand of God.

ἀλλὰ νῦν οὐκέτι γινώσκομεν. He might have said οἴδαμεν, and
it is perhaps excess of accuracy to make in this place any difference between οἴδαμεν, 'we know,' and γινώσκομεν, 'we come to
know.' St Paul wants the present once more, and he naturally
takes the present of ἐγνώκαμεν. The important thing in translation is to distinguish the perfect from the present on each side
of it. This the Vulg. does with *novimus, cognovimus, novimus.*
The νῦν means from the moment of his conversion.

εἰ καὶ (א* B D* 17, Arm.) rather than καὶ εἰ (F G, Latt. Syr-Pesh.),
or εἰ δὲ καὶ (א³ C² D² and ³ L P), or εἰ δέ (K, Copt.) D E G add κατὰ σάρκα
after γινώσκομεν.

17. ὥστε εἴ τις ἐν Χριστῷ, καινὴ κτίσις· τὰ ἀρχαῖα παρῆλθεν.
The ὥστε may imply a second consequence from *v.* 15, parallel to
the ὥστε in *v.* 16 ; or it may imply a consequence from *v.* 16 ; or
a consequence from *vv.* 15 and 16 combined. It is difficult to
decide ; but the first has this advantage, that here, as in *v.* 15, the
Apostle is speaking of all Christians, whereas ἡμεῖς in *v.* 16 means
St Paul and his fellow-ministers. We can deduce the case of
the ministers from that of all believers ; but it is less logical to
argue from the ministers to all believers. We may, however,
argue legitimately from both combined. The sequence of
thought seems to be this. 'If we have died with Christ to our old
selves and have risen with Him to a new life, we share His
spiritual life and are in Him ; and if any man is in Christ, he is a
new creature ; the old things passed away when he became such.'
Or we may translate, 'there is a new creation' (Gal. vi. 15), with
much the same meaning. By 'is in Christ' is meant 'has become
a Christian, has become a member of Christ.' St Paul is not
thinking of the Christ-party and hinting at the difference between
being Χριστοῦ (x. 7 ; 1 Cor. i. 12) and ἐν Χριστῷ. It is gratuitous
to introduce that difference here.

Vulg. and some Latin authorities greatly weaken the force of
the passage by making καινὴ κτίσις the subject of a protasis, of
which τὰ ἀρχαῖα παρῆλθεν is made the apodosis ; 'If therefore
there be any new creation in Christ, the old things have passed
away,' *si qua ergo in Christo nova creatura, vetera transierunt.*
So also Tert. *Adv. Marc.* v. 12 ; *si qua ergo conditio nova in
Christo, vetera transierunt.* Cornelius a Lapide, although he

rightly makes τις masculine, has the same feeble arrangement ; *si quis ergo mecum est in Christo regeneratus, vetera transierunt.* This is almost tautology ; of course, if one is created anew, old things have passed away. Tert. adds, *impleta est Esaiae prophetia.* He means Is. xliii. 18, 19, lxv. 17, lxvi. 22. But it may be doubted whether the Apostle has any of these passages in his mind. In LXX there is resemblance in the words used, but there is not much affinity in the meaning. Wetstein, *ad loc.*, and Schöttgen, i. p. 704, show that καινὴ κτίσις was a common Rabbinical term for a Gentile brought to the knowledge of the true God (Lightfoot on Gal. vi. 15). It is a stronger expression than μεταμορφούμεθα (iii. 18 ; Rom. xii. 2) or παλιγγενεσία (Tit. iii. 5), though it means much the same as the latter ; and Tit. iii. 5 should be compared.

τὰ ἀρχαῖα παρῆλθεν· ἰδού, γέγονεν καινά. These words explain καινὴ κτίσις. What took place was no less than this ; 'the old things passed away ; behold they are become new.' It no longer matters whether a man is by birth a Jew or Gentile, bond or free ; the one thing that is of weight is whether he has the right spiritual relation to Christ. Even the Commandments are made new when they are informed with the spirit of the Gospel.* The Hebraic ἰδού gives a tone of triumph to the passage. Evidently the thought of the change from old to new makes the Apostle enthusiastically jubilant. The Crucifixion and Resurrection of Christ constitute for him the dividing line in the world's history, and if he did not foresee all the blessings which the Gospel would bring to mankind, he saw something of its immense potentialities. Out of his own experience of God's dealing with himself and others he declares that one who is in Christ is a new creature. Christ is the source of a new and higher life (see on 1 Cor. xv. 45 and on Rom. v. 12–19). The Apostle calls to mind that the narrowness and exclusiveness of Judaism, the intolerable burden of the Law, and the still more intolerable burden of sin, have passed away from those who believe in Christ, and that a dispensation of comprehension, freedom, and peace has taken their place. This is no longer the hope of a prophet, or the guess of an apocalyptic dreamer, but an abiding fact.

It is a needless narrowing of the Apostle's meaning to confine it, as Thdrt., to getting free from the old Nessus-garment of sin, τὸ τῆς ἁμαρτίας ἀπεκδύσασθαι γῆρας. The old feelings, desires, and determinations of the will are re-created and directed into a new channel ; cf. Phil. iii. 7. Chrys. narrows the meaning in

---

* It is possible that here, as sometimes in classical Greek, ἀρχαῖος has the meaning of ἀρχαϊκός, ' antiquated,' ' old-fashioned ' ; *haec appellatio fastidium aliquod ostendit* (Beng.).

another direction when he analyses it thus; instead of the Law,
the Gospel; instead of circumcision, baptism; instead of
Jerusalem, heaven; and so forth. The very essence of the new
creation is that it is moral and spiritual, not, as is often pictured
in prophetic and apocalyptic literature, an actual new heaven
and new earth. It is a merit of the *Book of Jubilees* that it
recognizes this. "And after this they will turn to Me in all
uprightness and with all heart and soul, and I will create in them
a holy spirit, and I will cleanse them, so that they shall not turn
away from Me from that day unto eternity" (i. 23). "Mount
Zion will be sanctified in the *new creation* for a sanctification of
the earth; through it will the earth be sanctified from all guilt
and uncleanness throughout the generations of the world"
(iv. 26). "And He made for all His works a new and righteous
nature, so that they should not sin in their whole nature for ever,
but should be all righteous each in his kind alway" (v. 12). See
also xxiii. 26–31.

D² and ³ E K L P, Syr-Hark. Goth. AV. Tert. have καινὰ τὰ πάντα :
א B C D* F G 67**, Vulg. Copt. RV. omit τὰ πάντα.

18. τὰ δὲ πάντα ἐκ τοῦ Θεοῦ. 'But all these new things come
from God.'* They are His creation. The καινὴ κτίσις is no
spontaneous development, and it is not man's own work on himself; Apostles do not claim to be the cause of it. It is wholly
ἐκ τοῦ Θεοῦ (*v.* 5, i. 21, ii. 14, iv. 6; 1 Cor. viii. 6, xi. 12; Rom.
xi. 36). In the same breath in which he declares this, St Paul
goes on to explain *how* it is that God brings this about.

τοῦ καταλλάξαντος ἡμᾶς ἑαυτῷ διὰ Χριστοῦ. 'Who reconciled
us to Himself through Christ.' This is the usual language of
N.T., in which the change which brings about the reconciliation
between God and men is regarded as taking place in them rather
than in Him. Greeks thought of God as estranged from men,
and it was He who needed to be won over. Jews thought
rather that it was men who by their sins were estranged from
God, and the sins had to be 'cleansed,' or 'purged,' or 'covered,'
in order to bring about reconciliation (see on 1 Jn. ii. 2).† St
Paul follows Jewish rather than Hellenic thought. It is man
who is reconciled to God, rather than God to man ; οὐ γὰρ αὐτὸς

* In ii. 16, iii. 5, v. 1, xii. 6, RV. corrects 'of' to 'from,' but here it
leaves 'of' unchanged.
† Ephraim Levine, in his essay on the Breach between Judaism and
Christianity in *The Parting of the Roads*, p. 288, points out that Jews insisted
on sincere penitence and complete reparation as necessary preliminaries to a
reconciliation with God. He quotes *Mishna Yoma* ; "Sins between man
and man cannot be atoned for till the sinner has acknowledged his guilt and
made reparation " ; and he refers to C. G. Montefiore's article on the Jewish
conception of repentance in the *Jewish Quarterly Review* (1903).

ἡμῖν κατηλλάγη, ἀλλ' ἡμᾶς ἑαυτῷ κατήλλαξεν· ἐνεχείρισε δὲ ἡμῖν τὰ τῶν καταλλαγῶν εὐαγγέλια (Thdrt.). This is insisted on by Lightfoot on Col. i. 21, and by Westcott in his additional note on 1 Jn. ii. 10, p. 85, also on Heb. x. 10, p. 347. It is well to be reminded that God is not a man that He should repent or change His mind, and that His unchanging love is always waiting for the penitent sinner. But in order to get another side of this vast truth we are obliged to use language which involves us in a seeming contradiction. Scripture speaks of God being angry with impenitent sinners and ceasing to be angry with those who are penitent. Scripture also speaks of 'propitiation' as a means to reconciliation (1 Jn. ii. 2, iv. 10; cf. Rom. iii. 25; Lk. xviii. 13), and in this relation it is God and not man who is propitiated. In both cases we have to affirm or imply change in One who was before said to be incapable of change. As so often, in trying to express deep spiritual truths, we have got down to "the bed-rock of a contradiction." See additional note on Rom. v. 10, the only other passage in N.T. in which καταλλάσσειν occurs of this relation between God and man. It can be used either of one of the two estranged parties reconciling the other, or of a third reconciling them both ; cf. συναλλάσσειν (Acts vii. 26). St Paul also uses ἀποκαταλλάσσειν (Eph. ii. 16 ; Col. i. 20, 21) and καταλλαγή (Rom. v. 11, xi. 15), but not ἱλάσκεσθαι (Heb. ii. 17 ; Lk. xviii. 13) or ἱλασμός (1 Jn. ii. 2, iv. 10).

καὶ δόντος ἡμῖν τὴν διακονίαν τῆς καταλλαγῆς. This is the climax. One who persecuted His Son and the Church, God has not only reconciled to Himself through His Son, but has committed to him the ministry of reconciliation for the benefit of the Church.

The rapidity with which St Paul makes changes between the 1st pers. plur. and 1st pers. sing. has been pointed out (vv. 11, 12), and some see rapid changes in the meaning of ἡμεῖς here. In v. 16, ἡμεῖς is 'we ministers'; in v. 18, ἡμᾶς seems to be 'us Christians' and to be equivalent to κόσμον in v. 19, while ἡμῖν is certainly 'to us ministers,' as διακονίαν in v. 18 and ἐν ἡμῖν (not ἐν αὐτοῖς) in v. 19 show. But it is not certain that ἡμᾶς in v. 18 = κόσμον in v. 19 = 'us Christians.' St Paul may be continuing to think only of himself and his colleagues, and in that case all runs smoothly. He is deeply conscious, and is anxious to avow, that an Apostle has as much need as anyone of the reconciliation which was effected through Christ. Not till v. 19 does his thought go beyond the circle of preachers, and then he shows how they share in making the reconciliation of the human race, which has been won by Christ, effectual to individual souls.

The use of διακονία of Apostles (here, iv. 1, vi. 3 ; Rom

xi. 13; 1 Tim. i. 12; and often in Acts) shows that they are not regarded as αὐθένται. They do not act on their own independent authority, but are commissioned by God to continue Christ's διακονία of reconciliation. The word is found in all groups of the Pauline Epistles, except Thessalonians, and it evidently has no fixed application to any particular kind of ministry. The renderings in AV. and RV. vary greatly; 'ministry,' 'ministering,' 'ministration,' 'administration,' 'serving,' 'service,' and 'relief.'

D³ E K L, AV. have Ἰησοῦ before Χριστοῦ: א B C D* F G P, Latt. Syrr. Copt. RV. omit.

19. ὡς ὅτι Θεὸς ἦν ἐν Χριστῷ κόσμον καταλλάσσων ἑαυτῷ. The exact force of ὡς ὅτι is not clear. Greek commentators substitute καὶ γάρ and the Latins render it *quoniam quidem*. We may analyse it, 'as was the case, because,' or 'how that,' or 'namely, that,' which is much the same as 'to wit, that' (AV. RV.).* Of the four possible constructions, (1) that of AV., which agrees with Luther, Calvin, Beza, and Bengel, is to be rejected; 'God was in Christ, reconciling the world to Himself.' Almost certainly, ἐν Χριστῷ belongs to καταλλάσσων, being parallel to διὰ Χριστοῦ in v. 18. The same objection holds good against (2) 'was reconciling to Himself the world that is in Christ,' *i.e.* those that are His members. This would require τὸν ἐν Χριστῷ κόσμον. And do those who are already in Christ need reconciliation? (3) 'There was God, in Christ reconciling the world to Himself.' This is Theodoret's rendering, reading ὁ Θεός. It is awkward, but it puts ἐν Χριστῷ in the right place. (4) Almost certainly, ἦν καταλλάσσων is the analytical imperfect of which Lk. is so fond (i. 21, ii. 51, iv. 20, v. 1, 16, 18, etc.). This periphrastic tense expresses, more decidedly than the simple imperfect, the duration of the action. There was a lasting process of reconciliation; 'God in Christ was reconciling the world to Himself.' The 'world' means all mankind. God did all that on His side is necessary for their being reconciled to Him; but not all men do what is necessary on their side. Aug. (*In Joann. Tract.* lxxxvii. 2, 3, cx. 4) characteristically explains *mundus* as meaning only those who are predestined to salvation, the Church of the elect gathered out of the world.

For κόσμος without the art. comp. Rom. iv. 13; Gal. vi. 14: ἐν κόσμῳ (1 Cor. viii. 4, xiv. 10) is not quite parallel, because there was a tendency, which appears in papyri, to omit the art. after a preposition; J. H. Moulton, p. 82.

* In Xen. *Hellen.* III. ii. 14, the MSS. have εἰπὼν ὡς ὅτι ὀκνοίη, but editors reject the ὅτι. In late Greek ὡς ὅτι seems to be used as equivalent to ὅτι. See Milligan on 2 Thess. ii. 2.

μὴ λογιζόμενος . . . καὶ θέμενος. Just as τοῦ καταλλάξαντος ἡμᾶς explains how God brought about the new conditions, so these two participles explain how He brings about the reconciliation ; 'viz. by not reckoning to men their trespasses, and by having deposited with His ministers the message of reconciliation.' Note the change from pres. part., of a process that is going on, to aor., of one that is complete. Although the μὴ λογιζόμενος (Rom. iv. 7, 8 ; Col. i. 14) is free and universal, yet it has to be made known to individuals, in order that they may appropriate it ; hence the θέμενος ἐν ἡμῖν. By μὴ λογιζόμενος He does His part, and by θέμενος κ.τ.λ. He aids men to do their part, in the work of reconciliation.

Both λογίζεσθαι and παράπτωμα are favourite words with Paul, especially the former. Παράπτωμα is a *lapse* from righteousness, and it sometimes indicates an offence that is less serious than ἁμαρτία, as perhaps in Gal. vi. 1, and more clearly in Ps. xviii. 13, 14 ; but this occasional distinction cannot be pressed. Comp. Eph. i. 7, ii. 1, 5 and Col. ii. 13, which are parallel in sense to this passage ; and see Westcott, *Ephesians*, p. 166 ; Trench, *Syn.* § lxvi. For παράπτωμα in the Gospels, Vulg. always has *peccatum*; in the Epistles, always *delictum*, except Eph. i. 7, ii. 5, where it has *peccatum*.

τὸν λόγον τῆς καταλλαγῆς. Cf. τ. λόγον τῆς ἀληθείας (Eph. i. 13 ; Col. i. 5), λόγον ζωῆς (Phil. ii. 16), ὁ λόγος τῆς σωτηρίας (Acts xiii. 26). "In determining the meaning of λόγος in Paul one must always keep in mind 1 Cor. ii. 12 ; 'I determined not to know anything among you, save Jesus Christ, and Him crucified'" (Harnack, *The Constitution and Law of the Church*, p. 341).

Before τ. λόγον τ. καταλλαγῆς, D* E G, g insert (τοῦ) εὐαγγελίου.

V. 20–VI. 10. From the declaration that he is one of those to whom God has committed the word of reconciliation the Apostle goes on to show his *credentials* as a preacher of the Gospel. He is God's ambassador, fellow-worker, and minister, and as such has had to suffer a great deal. This again is some evidence of his sincerity.

20. Ὑπὲρ Χριστοῦ οὖν πρεσβεύομεν. 'On behalf of Christ, therefore, we are acting as ambassadors.' * Cf. ὑπὲρ οὗ πρεσβεύω ἐν ἁλύσει (Eph. vi. 20), and see on Philem. 9. Deissmann (*Light from the Ancient East*, p. 379) points out that these "proud words of St Paul stand in quite different relief when we know that πρεσβεύω and πρεσβευτής were the proper words in

---

* Klöpper points out that ὑπὲρ Χρ. cannot mean 'in Christ's stead,' which is **not** given in *vv.* 18, 19 ; it means 'in Christ's interest,' *Christi causam agens.* The Apostle is God's ambassador to further the cause of Christ.

the Greek East for the Emperor's Legate." Both verb and substantive are found in this sense in inscriptions, the latter very
frequently. The dignity of an Apostle comes once more to the
front. He is the representative of Christ the Reconciler, and
behind Christ is God. As in i. 1; 1 Cor. i. 1; Gal. i. 16, he
holds his office, not from any human being however distinguished, but from the Father. It is a high position, and it
involves a great responsibility. "The ambassador, before acting,
receives a commission from the power for whom he acts.
The ambassador, while acting, acts not only as an agent, but as a
representative of his sovereign. Lastly, the ambassador's duty is
not merely to deliver a definite message, to carry out a definite
policy; but he is obliged to watch opportunities, to study
characters, to cast about for expedients, so that he may place it
before his hearers in its most attractive form. He is a diplo-
matist" (Lightfoot, *Ordination Addresses*, p. 48). This is what
St Paul means when he says that he becomes all things to all
men, that he may by all means save some (1 Cor. ix. 32).

ὡς τοῦ Θεοῦ παρακαλοῦντος. Neither 'as though God did
beseech' (AV.), nor 'as though God were entreating' (RV.),
is quite exact; better, 'seeing that God is entreating.' The
force of ὡς with a genitive absolute is not always the same. The
ὡς always gives a subjective view of what is stated by the gen.
abs., but that subjective view may be shown by the context to be
either right or wrong. When it is given as right, as in 2 Pet. i. 3,
ὡς may be rendered 'seeing that,' which RV. has in that place.
Where the subjective view is given as wrong, ὡς = 'as though,'
which RV. correctly has in 1 Cor. iv. 18; 1 Pet. iv. 12; Acts
xxvii. 30, following the Vulg. *tamquam*. Here it is manifest that
God's entreating is given as a fact, yet AV. and RV. have 'as
though,' and Vulg. has *tamquam*. Here Schmiedel rightly condemns *als ob*, and with Lietzmann adopts *indem*. Bachmann
agrees, with *indem ja*. The fact that 'God is entreating by us'
is a momentous one, and the declaration of it is analogous to
the formula of the Hebrew Prophet, 'Thus saith the Lord.'

δι' ἡμῶν. Cf. i. 23. The acc. after παρακαλοῦντος is omitted,
as also after δεόμεθα, because he is thinking of a wider field than
Corinth. He is an Apostle to the Corinthians (1 Cor. ix. 2),
but to many others besides, and so both verbs are left as general
as possible in their scope. The second half of the verse is
addressed *urbi et orbi*.

δεόμεθα ὑπὲρ Χριστοῦ, καταλλάγητε τῷ Θεῷ. 'We beseech on
Christ's behalf, Become reconciled to God.' "He said not,
Reconcile God to yourselves, for it is not He that bears enmity
but you; for God never bears enmity" (Chyrs.). In RV. the
reader naturally puts an emphasis on 'ye'; 'Be *ye* reconciled to

God'; and there should be no emphasis, for ὑμεῖς is not expressed. It is better, therefore, to omit it in translation. 'Become reconciled,' *efficite ut Deo reconciliemini*, effects this and does justice to the tense. 'In Christ's stead' (AV.) is probably wrong; see on ὑπὲρ πάντων and ὑπὲρ αὐτῶν in *vv.* 14, 15. Chrys. expands ὑπὲρ Χριστοῦ thus; 'Do not think that it is we who are asking you; it is Christ Himself who asks you, it is the Father Himself who entreats you, through us. What can be compared with such love? God's innumerable benefits have been treated with contumely, and He not only exacted no penalty, but even gave His Son, that we might be reconciled. And when those to whom He was first sent were not reconciled to Him, but put Him to death, He has again sent other messengers, and it is by sending them that He is asking you.' By the repeated ὑπὲρ Χριστοῦ St Paul is characterizing the authority of an Apostle; it is of the highest, but it is official, not personal. An Apostle does not exhort in his own name or on his own behalf; he acts for Christ. On the other hand, those whom they exhort do not work out their reconciliation by themselves; they *receive* it (Rom. v. 11). Their part in the process lies in their appreciating and appropriating it.

For δεόμεθα, D* F G, d e g, Hil. Ambrst. have δεόμενοι, and for καταλ-λάγητε, D* F G, d e g Goth. have καταλλαγῆναι. Both changes weaken the forcible independent clauses of the original text.

21. τὸν μὴ γνόντα ἁμαρτίαν. 'Him who came to no acquaintance with sin.' Aug. (*Con. duas epp. Pelag.* i. 23) compares our Lord's words to the wicked, 'I know you not' (Mt. vii. 23), "although, beyond a doubt, nothing is hidden from Him." The asyndeton makes the announcement of this amazing paradox all the more impressive, a fact which was not felt by the copyists who inserted γάρ. The Apostle anticipates the question which his urgent καταλλάγητε is sure to provoke; How is it possible for sinners such as we are to become reconciled to God? His reply is as epigrammatic as it is startling.

We cannot press the classical force of μή as necessarily indicating a subjective view, because in N.T. μή with participles is the usual construction, although οὐ still survives; see on 1 Cor. ix. 26. But here μή is probably subjective, and if so, it is God's view that is meant; 'Him who in God's sight came to no knowledge of sin.' These opening words of the paradox have parallels enough in Scripture (1 Pet. ii. 22; 1 Jn. iii. 5; Heb. iv. 15, vii. 26); and in the front of them we may place Christ's own challenge to His opponents, that none had ever convicted Him of sin (Jn. viii. 46). So far from knowing sin, He was, as Chrys. says, Αὐτοδικαιοσύνη, Righteousness itself. He had known sin in others, had Himself been tempted to it, but His conscience had never accused Him of having yielded. The commandments never roused in Him, as they did in His Apostle (Rom. vii. 7–11), the consciousness that He had transgressed in act or will.

With the **very** doubtful exception of 2 Thess. ii. 3, ἁμαρτία in the sing. is not found in any other group of the Pauline Epistles. In this group it is found in all four Epistles (xi. 7 ; 1 Cor. xv. 56 ; Gal. ii. 17, iii. 22 ; Rom. iii.–viii. often, xiv. 23). The plur. is found in all four groups. St Paul rarely uses ἁμάρτημα (1 Cor. vi. 18 ; Rom. iii. 25 ; elsewhere only Mk. and 2 Pet.). Westcott, *Ephesians*, p. 165.

Note the chiasmus between τὸν μὴ γνόντα ἁμαρτίαν and ἁμαρτίαν ἐποίησεν, and comp. iv. 3, vi. 8, ix. 6, x. 11, xiii. 3.

ὑπὲρ ἡμῶν ἁμαρτίαν ἐποίησεν. 'On our behalf He made to be sin.' *Quis auderet sic loqui, nisi Paulus praeiret* (Beng.). The nearest approach to this startling utterance comes also from St Paul, when he speaks of Christ as γενόμενος ὑπὲρ ἡμῶν κατάρα (Gal. iii. 13). Both passages are probably influenced by the language of LXX respecting the sin-offering and the guilt-offering in Lev. iv., and respecting the scape-goat in Lev. xvi. The authority of Augustine, who states the view repeatedly, especially in his anti-Pelagian treatises, has caused many to solve the difficulty of 'made him to be ἁμαρτία' by supposing that ἁμαρτία, *peccatum*, here means 'sin-offering.' Lev. iv. 25, 29 *perhaps* may be quoted in support of this ; but no support for it can be found in N.T., and it cannot stand here, because of ἁμαρτίαν in the previous clause, where it must mean 'sin.' Nor can the other suggestion of Aug. be accepted, that ἁμαρτία may mean human nature, as being liable to suffering and death, which are the penalties of sin ; so that ἁμαρτίαν ἐποίησεν means that God made Christ assume human nature. This is improbable enough in itself ; and, as before, the previous ἁμαρτίαν forbids it.* We must face the plain meaning of the Apostle's strong words. In some sense which we cannot fathom, God is said to have identified Christ with man's sin, in order that man might be identified with God's own righteousness. The relationship expressed by 'Christ in us and we in Him' is part of the solution. It is by union of Christ with man that Christ is identified with human sin, and it is by union of man with Christ that man is identified with Divine righteousness. No explanation of these mysterious words satisfies us. They are a bold attempt to express what cannot even be grasped in human thought, still less be expressed in human language ; and it is rash to put our own interpretation

---

* Gregory of Nyssa, who quotes the statement several times, would make 'sin' mean 'flesh,' the seat of sin.

on the verse, build a theory of the Atonement upon that interpretation, and then claim for the theory the authority of St Paul.
St Paul is giving a courageous answer to a difficult question; he
is not starting or summarizing a systematized doctrine of reconciliation. In his answer he has given a striking illustration of
the truth of J. H. Newman's words, made so famous by Charles
Kingsley; "It is not more than an hyperbole to say, that, in
certain cases, a lie is the nearest approach to the truth." St
Paul's words here cannot be true, and yet it is possible that they
are the best way of stating what is true. We have once more
got down to "the bed-rock of a contradiction." "But it raises
one's opinion of the extraordinary sanity of Paul's judgment, and
his insight, that he could be so near to the substitutionary view
of the Atonement without accepting it. He was in fact kept
from accepting it by his view of the nature of faith, which was of
an extremely practical kind. He regarded salvation as consisting
in the continuing of the life of Christ and sharing His obedience,
but not in being merely justified, as in a law-court, by a fictitious
claim to merit which one did not possess" (P. Gardner, *The
Religious Experience of St Paul*, p. 195).

ἵνα ἡμεῖς γενώμεθα. 'In order that *we* might become.' It is
for our gain, not His; the whole process is ὑπὲρ ἡμῶν. For ἡμεῖς
he might have said oἱ μὴ γνόντες δικαιοσύνην.

δικαιοσύνη Θεοῦ. It is God's, not ours (Rom. x. 3); it is the
righteousness which characterizes Him and which He imparts as
a grace to man (Rom. v. 17). See on Rom. i. 17; also Briggs,
The Messiah of the Apostles, pp. 123–126; Bruce, *St Paul's
Conception of Christianity*, p. 176.

ἐν αὐτῷ. It is in Christ, *i.e.* through our union with Him
and our sharing in the outcome of His Death and Resurrection,
and not in our own right, that we become righteous in God's
sight. Ἐν αὐτῷ in this clause corresponds to ὑπὲρ ἡμῶν in the
previous clause; but the same preposition could not be used in
both places. St Paul could not have said that Christ was made
to be sin 'in us'; still less that we become righteous ' on Christ's
behalf.' See on Rom. iii. 26.

For numerous theories of the Atonement see Ritschl, *Justification and Reconciliation*, 2nd ed. 1902; H. N. Oxenham, *The
Catholic Doctrine of the Atonement*, 1881; Dale, *The Doctrine of
the Atonement*, 1875; A. Lyttelton in *Lux Mundi*, 1889; Westcott, *The Victory of the Cross*, 1889; J. M. Wilson, *Hulsean
Lectures*, 1899; G. B. Stevens, *Christian Doctrine of Salvation*,
1905; R. C. Moberly, *Atonement and Personality*, 1907.

ℵ³ D³ E K L P, Syrr. Arm. Aeth. Goth. AV. insert γάρ after τόν:
ℵ* B C D* F G 17, 67**, Latt. Copt. RV. omit. Aug. (*Enchir.* 41) knew
of a text *in quibusdam mendosis codicibus* which had ὁ μὴ γνοὺς ἁμαρτίαν,

is qui non noverat peccatum, pro nobis peccatum fecit, "as if," says Augustine, "for our sakes Christ committed sin!"

VI. 1–10. There is once more an unintelligent division of the chapters: vi. 1 is closely connected with v. 20, 21, and the first ten verses of this chapter are a continuation of the Apostle's self-vindication from another point of view; they set forth his conduct and his experiences as God's ambassador, and as a minister to whom has been entrusted the message of reconciliation. After an earnest appeal to the Corinthians not to lose through neglect the grace offered to them, the spiritual exaltation of the Apostle once more gives a rhythmic swing to his language, as if he were singing a song of triumph. *Magna res est, et granditer agitur, nec desunt ornamenta dicendi* (Aug. *De Doc. Chris.* iv. 20). Way calls it a "Hymn of the Herald of Salvation." There is no good reason for supposing that St Paul here turns to "the better-disposed heathen believers." He is addressing weak believers, who were in danger of a lapse into heathen laxity, through making so poor an attempt to reach a Christian standard of holiness. He points to the way in which an Apostle does his work, and to what he has to endure: these are things which the Corinthians can appreciate.*

1. Συνεργοῦντες δὲ καὶ παρακαλοῦμεν. 'But there is more to be said than this (δὲ καί): as working together with God we entreat that *you* do not accept the grace of God in vain.' God had committed the message of reconciliation to His ambassadors; St Paul had brought it to the Corinthians; they must do their part and make a right use of it. Where συνεργεῖν (1 Cor. xvi. 16; Rom. viii. 28) or συνεργός (i. 24, viii. 23; 1 Cor. iii. 9) or other compounds of σύν occur, it is plain that the force of the συν- depends on the context. But that principle is not decisive here, because there are several possibilities in the context. Five connexions have been suggested. (1) 'Co-operating with *God*'; which is the natural inference from v. 18, 21, and it is confirmed by 1 Cor. iii. 9. (2) 'With *Christ*'; which might be inferred from v. 20, *if* ὑπὲρ Χριστοῦ means 'in Christ's stead.' (3) 'With *you*' (so Chrys.); the Corinthians have co-operated with the missionaries in listening to their message, and so the Apostle is a fellow-worker with them. The objection to this is that the whole context is concerned with the preachers' part rather than with that of the hearers. (4) 'With *other teachers*.' This explanation assumes that the 1st pers. plur. refers to St Paul alone. If it included other teachers, the συν- would be meaningless;

---

* This chapter was the Second Lesson at Evensong on 8 June 1688, after the Seven Bishops had been imprisoned in the Tower. See also Job xi. 14–20, which was part of the First Lesson.

'co-operating with ourselves.' (5) 'With *our exhortations,*' *i.e.* adding our example to our precept. If this had been meant, it would have been expressed in a plainer manner.

εἰς κενόν. 'To no profit'; *in vacuum* (Vulg.), *frustra* (Beza). The expression is freq. in LXX (Lev. xxvi. 20; Job xxxix. 16; Is. xxix. 8; Jer. vi. 29, xxviii. 58), but in N.T. it is peculiar to Paul (1 Thess. iii. 5; Gal. ii. 2; Phil. ii. 16). It is probable that δέξασθαι is a timeless aorist after παρακαλεῖν, like κυρῶσαι (ii. 8), παραστῆσαι (Rom. xii. 1), συναγωνίσασθαι (Rom. xv. 30), περιπατῆσαι (Eph. iv. 1), and may be rendered *ne recipiatis* (Vulg.). The reference is to the present time; acceptance of grace is continually going on, and there ought to be good results. But the aorist may have the force of a past tense and be rendered *ne reciperetis* (Beza). In this case the reference is to the time of their conversion; he exhorts them not to have accepted the grace of God in vain, *i.e.* not to show by their behaviour now that they accepted it then to no profit. Chrys. seems to take it in the latter way, for he interprets ἐς κένον as losing through unfruitfulness the great blessings which they have received. In any case, ὑμᾶς comes last with much emphasis; 'you, whatever the rest of the κόσμος may do.' 'We are commissioned to preach to all mankind; I beseech you not to let the preaching prove vain in *your* case.'

2. As in v. 7, 16, we have a Pauline parenthesis. He remembers an O.T. saying which will drive home the exhortation that he has just given, Is. xlix. 8, and he injects it. In a modern work the verse would be a foot-note. As usual, he quotes the LXX with little or no change; cf. iv. 13, viii. 15, ix. 9. Here there is no change. In LXX the words are introduced with οὕτως λέγει Κύριος, and we readily understand ὁ Θεός here (Blass, § 30. 4) from the context. But λέγει (Rom. xv. 10; Eph. iv. 8) and φησίν (see on 1 Cor. vi. 16), without subject, are common forms of quotation, equivalent to inverted commas. The conjecture is often repeated that δέξασθαι suggested the passage about καιρὸς δεκτός. It may be so; but a deeper reason is possible. The passage may have occurred to St Paul because of the resemblance of his own case to that of the Prophet. In Is. xlix. the Prophet points out that the Lord has formed him from the womb to be His servant, and to reconcile Israel again to Him; but also to give him as a light to the Gentiles, that His salvation may be to the end of the earth. The servant has delivered his message, and a period of labour and disappointment follows (LXX of *v.* 4). Then come the encouraging words which St Paul quotes, and comforting thoughts arise. Although men despise him, God will honour him by confirming his message; and the God who has had compassion on Israel in spite of their sins, will have compassion on all the nations (see Driver, *Isaiah*, p. 149; W. E. Barnes, *ad loc.*). Word for word, this is true of the Apostle; and he also has his καιρὸς δεκτός, δεκτός to all the parties concerned. In Phil. iv. 18, δεκτήν means acceptable to God, and τῷ Θεῷ is expressed. In Lk. iv. 19, δεκτόν means acceptable to man, and here the meaning is probably the same; the time in which such benefits are offered is welcome to the human race. On God's side it is 'a season of favour,' on man's it is 'a season to be welcomed.' Εἰσακούειν, freq. in LXX, occurs here only in N.T.

ἰδοὺ νῦν. The Apostle at once applies the words of the Prophet to his readers; they are to take the saying to heart. By νῦν is meant all the time between the moment of writing and the Advent. The common application of the 'now,' viz. 'act at once, for delay is dangerous,' is not quite the meaning of the νῦν here. The point is rather that the wonderful time which the Prophet foresaw is now going on; the Apostle and his readers are enjoying it. His comment is equivalent to that of Christ, Lk. iv. 21, but this carries with it the warning already given, not to neglect golden opportunities. To some persons the νῦν may be very short. *Ex quo in carne Salvator apparuit semper est acceptabile tempus. Unicuique tamen finitur hoc tempus in hora obitus sui* (Herveius).*

εὐπρόσδεκτος. In LXX δεκτός is freq., especially in the Psalms, and εὐπρόσδεκτος is not found, but St Paul prefers the compound, probably as being stronger; he uses it again viii. 12 and Rom. xv. 16, 31; and his use of it here indicates his jubilant feeling; 'Behold now is the welcome acceptable time.' The word is found of heathen sacrifices; κατανοεῖν εἰ εὐπρόσδεκτος ἡ θυσία (Aristoph. *Pax*, 1054).

D* F G, d e g have καιρῷ γὰρ λέγει for λέγει γάρ· καιρῷ.

3. μηδεμίαν ἐν μηδενὶ διδόντες προσκοπήν. The construction shows that *v.* 2 is a parenthesis, the participles in *vv.* 3 and 4 being co-ordinate with συνεργοῦντες in *v.* 1. Aug. (*De Doc. Chris.* xx. 42) has *nullam in quoquam dantes offensionem*, which is more accurate than Vulg. *nemini dantes ullam offensionem*. Luther follows in making ἐν μηδενί masc., and he makes διδόντες an exhortation; *lasset uns aber niemand irgend ein Aergerniss geben*. Both context and construction show that this is wrong. It is the exhorters themselves who aim at 'giving no cause of stumbling in anything whatever.' Ἐν μηδενί embraces πρεσ-

* Calvin finds meaning in the order of the clauses ; *Prius tempus bene-volentiae ponitur, deinde dies salutis ; quo innuitur ex sola Dei misericordia tanquam ex fonte manare nobis salutem.*

βεύομεν, δεόμεθα, παρακαλοῦμεν, and all the details of the διακονία τῆς καταλλαγῆς. Here again, as in v. 21, the μή probably has its subjective force; 'not giving what could be regarded as a προσκοπή.' Note the Pauline alliteration; cf. viii. 22, ix. 5, 8, x. 6. Nowhere else in Bibl. Grk. does προσκοπή occur; πρόσκομμα and σκάνδαλον are the usual words. All three denote what causes others to stumble, in behaviour or belief, such as vainglory, self-seeking, insincerity, inconsistency of life. *Necesse est ejus praedicationem negligi, cujus vita despicitur* (Greg. M.).

ἵνα μὴ μωμηθῇ ἡ διακονία. 'That the ministry may not be vilified,' *vituperetur* (Vulg.), *verspottet*. The verb is rare (Prov. ix. 7); St Paul, who has it again viii. 20, may have got it from Wisd. x. 14, ψευδεῖς τε ἔδειξεν τοὺς μωμησαμένους αὐτόν (Joseph), which AV. vaguely renders 'those that accused him.' Heinrici quotes Lucian, *Quom. hist.* 33, ὃ οὐδεὶς ἄν, ἀλλ' οὐδ' ὁ Μῶμος μωμήσασθαι δύναιτο, where Μῶμος is mocking criticism personified. Wetstein quotes Apollonius, *Lex.* μωμήσονται, οἱονεὶ καταπαίξονται· μῶμος γὰρ ὁ μετὰ ψόγου καταπαιγμός. In class. Grk. the verb is mostly poetical (Hom. Aesch. Aristoph.), and in late prose it often implies ridicule as well as blame, with disgrace as a result. Here the thought of being made a laughingstock may be included.* In any case, it is man's criticism and abuse that is meant, not Divine condemnation. The Apostle is not thinking of the Judgment-seat of Christ (v. 10); neither προσκοπή nor μωμηθῇ would be used in reference to that. He may be thinking of the insults offered to him by ὁ ἀδικήσας (vii. 12).

After διακονία, D E F G, Latt. Syrr. Sah. Goth. add ἡμῶν : א B C K L P, Copt. omit. The insertion spoils the sense. He is thinking of the Apostolic office in general ; his conduct must not cause it to be reviled. In what was done at Corinth, the credit of the cause for which all ministers laboured was at stake. RV. wrongly substitutes 'our ministration' for 'the ministry.'

4.   ἀλλ' ἐν παντὶ συνιστ. ἑαυτούς. 'On the contrary, in every·thing commending ourselves, as God's ministers should do.' The comprehensive ἐν παντί, in opposition to ἐν μηδενί, comes first with emphasis; cf. vii. 11, ix. 8, xi. 9. He is glancing at the charge of self-commendation made against him, but here he uses the expression in a good sense, and therefore ἑαυτούς has not the emphatic position which is given to it in iii. 1 and v. 12. Vulg. has *sed in omnibus exhibeamus nosmet ipsos sicut Dei ministros*, which is doubly wrong, making the participle into a finite verb co-ordinate with μωμηθῇ, and making διάκονοι accusa-

* *Nihil enim magis ridiculum quam de tua apud alios existimatione vindicanda contendere quum ipse tibi flagitiosa ac turpi vita contumeliam arcessas* (Calv.).

tive, which gives a wrong turn to the meaning. Aug. is right with *commendantes*, but wrong with *ministros*. St Paul does not say 'commending ourselves as being God's ministers,' but 'as God's ministers do commend themselves,' viz. by rectitude of life. As in iv. 8–12 and xi. 23–31, he enumerates his sufferings, and in all three passages we have a lyrical balance of language which gives a triumphant tone to the whole. Both Augustine and Erasmus express detailed admiration for the beauty of this passage. The latter analyses thus ; *totus hic sermo per contraria, per membra, per comparia, per similiter desinentia, per ἀναδιπλώσεις aliaque schemata, variatur, volvitur et rotatur, ut nihil esse possit vel venustius vel ardentius.* Both critics feel the glow that underlies the words.

The Apostle leads off with one of the chief features in his ministry, ἐν ὑπομονῇ πολλῇ, and then mentions three triplets of particulars in which the ὑπομονή is exhibited. Respecting these triplets Chrys. uses his favourite metaphor of snow-showers (νιφάδες) ; they constitute, he says, a blizzard of troubles. Then come eight other leading features, still under the same preposition (ἐν), the repetition of which (18 times in all) has become monotonous, and is therefore changed to διά. Here the stream, which in the last four of the features introduced with ἐν had begun to swell, reaches its full volume and flows on in more stately clauses. After three with διά, we have a series of seven contrasts, ending with a characteristic three-fold alliteration and an equally characteristic play upon words.

ἐν ὑπομονῇ πολλῇ. See on i. 6 ; also Lightfoot on Col. i. 11 and Mayor on Jas. i. 3. The high position given by our Lord to ὑπομονή (Lk. viii. 15, xxi. 19) and to ὑπομένειν (Mk. xiii. 13 ; Mt. x. 22, xxiv. 13) accounts for the prominence given to it here and xii. 12. It not only stands first, but it is illustrated in detail ; *huc spectat tota enumeratio quae sequitur* (Calv.). The word appears in all four groups of the Pauline Epistles, chiefly in Rom. and 2 Cor., often with the meaning of fortitude and constancy under persecution. This meaning is very freq. in 4 Macc., whereas in Ecclus. and in the Canonical Books of the O.T. it commonly means patient and hopeful expectation. In 1 Thess. i. 3 ; 1 Tim. vi. 11 ; 2 Tim. iii. 10 ; Tit. ii. 2, it is placed next to ἀγάπη in lists of virtues. Like ἀγάπη, it is a word which, although not originally Biblical, has acquired fuller meaning and much more general use through the influence of the N.T. It is often treated as one of the chief among Christian virtues. Chrys. can scarcely find language strong enough to express his admiration for it. It is "a root of all the goods, mother of piety, fruit that never withers, a fortress that is never taken, a harbour that knows no storms" (*Hom.* 117). Again,

13

it is "the queen of virtues, the foundation of right actions, peace in war, calm in tempest, security in plots," which no violence of man, and no powers of the evil one, can injure (*Ep. ad Olymp.* 7). These and other quotations are given in Suicer, *s.v.* Clem. Rom. (*Cor.* 6) places this virtue at the beginning and end of his praise of the Apostle; Παῦλος ὑπομονῆς βραβεῖον ὑπέδειξειν . . . ὑπομονῆς γενόμενος μέγιστος ὑπογραμμός. Cf. xii. 12.

ἐν θλίψεσιν, ἐν ἀνάγκαις, ἐν στενοχωρίαις. This triplet consists of troubles which may be independent of human agency, and it is probably intended to form a climax; 'afflictions' (i. 4, 8, ii. 4, iv. 7), which might be avoided; 'necessities' (xii. 10), which cannot be avoided; 'straits,' *angustiae* (xii. 10), out of which there is no way of escape. Like ἀγάπη and ὑπομονή, θλίψις was a word of limited meaning and use in late Greek, which acquired great significance and frequent employment when it became a term with religious associations. In 1 Thess. iii. 7, as in Job xv. 24; Ps. cxix. 143; Zeph. i. 15, θλίψις is coupled with ἀνάγκη. In the *De Singularitate Clericorum* appended to Cyprian's works, ἐν θλίψεσιν is translated twice, *in pressuris, in tribulationibus*; see below on ἐν ἀκαταστασίαις.

It is difficult to decide between συνιστάνοντες (B P and some cursives), συνιστάντες (א* C D* F G 17), and συνιστῶντες (א³ D³ E K L). In iii. 1 the evidence is decisive for συνιστάνειν, and that gives great weight to συνιστάνοντες here. For διάκονοι, D*, f g Vulg. have διακόνους.

5. ἐν πληγαῖς, ἐν φυλακαῖς, ἐν ἀκαταστασίαις. This triplet consists of troubles inflicted by men. It is doubtful whether there is any climax; but St Paul might think 'stripes' (xi. 23) less serious than 'imprisonments' (xi. 23), which stopped his work for a time, and imprisonments less serious than 'tumults,' which might force him to abandon work altogether in the place in which the tumult occurred. Clem. Rom. (*Cor.* 6) says of St Paul, ἑπτάκις δεσμὰ φορέσας, but the only imprisonment known to us prior to 2 Cor. is the one at Philippi. Popular tumults against St Paul are freq. in Acts (xiii. 50, xiv. 5, 19, xvii. 5, xviii. 12, xix. 23–41). In 1 Cor. iv. 11, the Apostle, in describing the experiences of Apostles, says κολαφιζόμεθα, ἀστατοῦμεν, 'we are buffeted, are homeless,' and some would give the meaning of 'homelessness, vagrant life' to ἀκαταστασία here. Chrys. seems to understand it in the sense of 'being driven from pillar to post,' but in N.T. the signification of the word is 'disorder' in one of two senses, viz. 'want of order, confusion' (1 Cor. xiv. 33; Jas. iii. 16), and 'breach of order, tumult' (here and Lk. xxi. 9). In LXX only twice, in the former sense (Prov. xxvi. 28; Tob. iv. 13). In *De Singularite*

Clericorum we again have two words in the Latin for one in the Greek; *in seditionibus, in invocationibus.* It is difficult to see what the latter can mean, and one might conjecture *in concitationibus,* the *in* being accidentally repeated, or *in implicationibus,* 'in entanglements.'

ἐν κόποις, ἐν ἀγρυπνίαις, ἐν νηστείαις. This third triplet consists of those troubles which he took upon himself in the prosecution of his mission. Thdrt. groups the first two triplets together as τὰ ἔξωθεν ἐπίοντα and ἀκούσια: προστίθησι δὲ τοῖς ἀκουσίοις καὶ τοὺς αὐθαιρέτους πόνους. There is order in this triplet also, and perhaps one may call it a climax; κόποι disturb the day, ἀγρυπνίαι the night, and νηστεῖαι both. St Paul repeatedly speaks of κόποι as a prevailing feature in his own life (xi. 23, 27; 1 Thess. ii. 9, iii. 5; 2 Thess. iii. 8). While πόνος indicates the *effort* which was required, κόπος points to the *fatigue* which was incurred. Trench, § cii., suggests 'toil' for πόνος and 'weariness' for κόπος: but in the ordinary Greek of this period the difference between the two words was vanishing. Swete remarks that κόπος with its cognate κοπιᾶν is "almost a technical word for Christian work," and that in Rev. ii. 2 τὸν κόπον and τὴν ὑπομονήν are "two notes of excellence, self-denying labour and perseverance."

ἐν ἀγρυπνίαις. Here and xi. 27 only in N.T. The word covers more than sleeplessness; it includes all that prevents one from sleeping. At Troas Paul preached until midnight and yet longer (Acts xx. 7, 9). In LXX the word is almost confined to Ecclus., where it is freq. and commonly means forgoing sleep in order to work. The Apostle no doubt often taught, and travelled, and worked with his hands to maintain himself, by night.

ἐν νηστείαις. Not 'fasts' in the religious sense;* but, just as ἀγρυπνία is voluntary forgoing of sleep in order to get more work done, so νηστεῖα is voluntary forgoing of food for the same reason. St Paul often neglected his meals, having 'no leisure so much as to eat' (Mk. vi. 31). We infer from xi. 27 that νηστεῖαι are *voluntary* abstentions from food, for there they are distinguished from involuntary hunger and thirst. Here the meaning might be that he neglected the handicraft by which he earned his bread (1 Cor. iv. 11, 12), or that he refused the maintenance which he might have claimed (1 Cor. ix. 4). But omitting meals in order to gain time is simpler. These sufferings, voluntarily undertaken, form an easy transition to the virtues which are evidence that he is one of God's ambassadors and fellow-workers.

---

* St Paul would not mention as an apostolic hardship the fasts which he practised for his own spiritual good (Beet).

6. ἐν ἁγνότητι. The three triplets which state the sphere of ὑπομονή are ended, and the virtues mentioned in *vv.* 6 and 7 are co-ordinate with ὑπομονή. Ἁγνότης is mentioned again (probably) in xi. 3, but nowhere else in Bibl. Grk. While *castimonia* (Tert.) or *castitas* (Vulg.) is too narrow on the one hand, ἡ τῶν χρημάτων ὑπεροψία (Thdrt.) is too narrow on the other. It means purity of life in both senses, chastity and integrity, the delicacy of mind which makes a man careful to keep a clean heart and clean hands. The six virtues in this verse have reference to principles of action, then ἐν λόγῳ ἀληθείας characterizes preaching, and ἐν δυνάμει Θεοῦ sums up the whole of Apostolic labour.

ἐν γνώσει. Not merely practical wisdom or prudence in dealing with different men and different circumstances, *recte et scienter agendi peritia* (Calv.), but comprehensive knowledge of the principles of Christianity (viii. 7, xi. 6; 1 Cor. i. 5; Rom. xv. 14).

ἐν μακροθυμίᾳ, ἐν χρηστότητι. While ὑπομονή is the courageous fortitude which endures adversity without murmuring or losing neart, μακροθυμία is the forbearance which endures injuries and evil deeds without being provoked to anger (Jas. i. 19) or vengeance (Rom. xii. 19). It is the opposite of ὀξόθυμία, hasty temper; cf. Prov. xiv. 17, ὀξόθυμος πράσσει μετὰ ἀβουλίας. In Proverbs μακρόθυμος is uniformly applied to men, and the μακρόθυμος is highly praised (xiv. 29, xv. 18, xvi. 32, xvii. 27); in the other O.T. Books it is almost always applied to God. Μακροθυμία is late Greek and is rare, except in LXX and N.T. In N.T. it is freq. (ten times in Paul), and is used of both God (Rom. ii. 4, ix. 22; etc.) and men. It is coupled with χρηστότης both of God (Rom. ii. 4) and men (Gal. v. 22). See on 1 Cor. xiii. 4. Χρηστότης, *bonitas* (Vulg.), *benignitas* (Aug.), is 'graciousness.' It is opposed to ἀποτομία, *severitas*, of God (Rom. x. 22; cf. Tit. iii. 4). In men it is the sympathetic kindliness or sweetness of temper which puts others at their ease and shrinks from giving pain; *ut nec verbo nec opere nostro aliis generemus asperitatem amaritudinis* (Herveius).

ἐν πνεύματι ἁγίῳ. It is scarcely credible that St Paul would place the Holy Spirit in a list of human virtues and in a subordinate place, neither first to lead, nor last to sum up all the rest. We may abandon the common rendering, 'the Holy Ghost' (AV., RV.) and translate 'a spirit that is holy,' *i.e.* in the spirit of holiness which distinguishes true ministers from false. The Apostle sometimes leaves us in doubt whether he is speaking of the Divine Spirit or the spirit of man in which He dwells and works; *e.g.* ἐν ἁγιασμῷ πνεύματος (2 Thess. ii. 13); κατὰ πνεῦμα ἁγιωσύνης (Rom. i. 4). This is specially the case

with ἐν πνεύματι (Eph. ii. 22, iii. 5, v. 18, vi. 18). Westcott on
Eph. iii. 5 says. "The general idea of the phrase is that it
presents the concentration of man's powers in the highest part
of his nature by which he holds fellowship with God, so that,
when this fellowship is realised, he is himself in the Holy Spirit
and the Holy Spirit is in him." See on Rom. xii. 11. It is
worth noting that πνεῦμα ἅγιον is far more freq. in N.T. than
τὸ πνεῦμα τὸ ἅγιον or τὸ ἅγιον πνεῦμα.

ἐν ἀγάπῃ ἀνυποκρίτῳ. See on Rom. xii. 9. In 1 Tim. i. 5
and 2 Tim. i. 5, ἀνυπόκριτος is used of the πίστις which is one of
the sources of ἀγάπη: in Jas. iii. 17, of the heaven-sent σοφία: in
1 Pet. i. 22, almost as here, of φιλαδελφία, "the love like that of
brothers to those who are not brothers" (Hort). In Wisd. v. 18
it is applied to judgment which does not respect persons; and
xviii. 16, to the Divine command. This seems to be the first
appearance of the word, and St Paul may have derived it from
that Book. Hort remarks that the word is chiefly Christian, as
might be expected from the warnings of Christ against hypocrisy
and from the high standard of sincerity manifested by the
Apostles. M. Aurelius (viii. 5) has ἀνυποκρίτως, of saying what
seems to be most just, but always with kind intention, and with
modesty, and without hypocrisy.

7. ἐν λόγῳ ἀληθείας. We have the article omitted in Jas.
i. 18, as here; so also in διὰ λόγου ζῶντος Θεοῦ (1 Pet. i. 23),
a passage which perhaps was suggested by Jas. i. 18. In Eph.
i. 13; Col. i. 5; 2 Tim. ii. 15, we have the full expression,
ὁ λόγος τῆς ἀληθείας. The genitive may be of apposition, 'the
word which is the truth'; or possessive, 'the word which belongs to the truth'; or objective, 'the declaration of the truth.'
The last is best,—the teaching which told the truth of the good
tidings, the preaching of the Gospel. Some think that general
truthfulness is the meaning here; and this fits on well to 'love
unfeigned.' There was no insincerity either in the affection
which he manifested or in the statements which he uttered
(ii 17, iv. 2).

ἐν δυνάμει Θεοῦ. This Divine power was all the more conspicuous because of his personal weakness (iv. 7, xii. 9). See
on 1 Cor. ii. 4: neither there nor here is the chief reference,
if there be any at all, to the miracles wrought by St Paul. In
xii. 12, where he does mention them, ἐν πάσῃ ὑπομονῇ is
placed first among τὰ σημεῖα τοῦ ἀποστόλου, and the miracles
are secondary. Here he is referring to his missionary career
in general, the results of which showed that he must be
working in the power of God. If there is allusion to one
feature in the career more than to another, it is probably to

the exercise of the Apostolic authority in enforcing Christian discipline. The expression δύναμις Θεοῦ is chiefly Pauline in N.T. (xiii. 4; 1 Cor. i. 18, ii. 5; Rom. i. 16; 2 Tim. i. 8; cf. 2 Thess. i. 11). On ἐν δυνάμει Θεοῦ (1 Pet. i. 5) Hort remarks; " What is dwelt on is not so much that the power of God is exerted on behalf of men, as that men are uplifted and inspired by power, or by a power, proceeding from God. Ἐν is not here instrumental, but is used with its strict meaning. In one sense the power is in men; but in another and yet truer sense men are in the power, they yield to it as something greater and more comprehensive than themselves, in which their separateness is lost."

διὰ τῶν ὅπλων τῆς δικαιοσύνης. 'Through (=by) weapons of righteousness.' Here again the Book of Wisdom (v. 17–20) may have suggested the expression used: cf. 1 Thess. v. 8; Eph. vi. 13–17; and see on Rom. xiii. 12. Is. lix. 17 is another possible source. The change from ἐν to διά is made partly because the frequent repetition of ἐν has become intolerable; but the change may point to the difference between the δύναμις Θεοῦ and the ὅπλα used by the διάκονοι Θεοῦ. 'Weapons of righteousness' are those which righteousness supplies and which support the cause of righteousness (Rom. vi. 13). Whether he assailed others or defended himself, it was always with legitimate weapons and in a legitimate cause. He adds τῶν δεξιῶν καὶ ἀριστερῶν to intimate that he is thoroughly equipped; his panoply is complete. On the right hand, etc. (AV., RV.), is ambiguous; 'for the right hand,' etc., is better, i.e. 'right-hand and left-hand weapons,' offensive and defensive armour, the shield being carried on the left arm. Chrys. interprets ἀριστερά as afflictions, which not only do not cast down but fortify. So also Thdrt.; δεξιὰ δὲ καλεῖ τὰ δοκοῦντα θυμήρη, ἀριστερὰ δὲ τὰ ἐναντία. But the meaning of success and failure—ne prosperis elevemur, nec frangamur adversis—is alien to the passage and to N.T. usage.

8. διὰ δόξης καὶ ἀτιμίας. 'Through (=amid) glory and dishonour.' The meaning of διά has changed; in v. 7 it marks the instrument, in v. 8 it marks the state or condition. We must give δόξα its usual rendering; 'honour and dishonour' would be τιμῆς κ. ἀτιμίας (Rom. ix. 21; 2 Tim. ii. 20). The Apostle received δόξα from God and from those whose hearts God touched, especially from his beloved Philippians and the Galatians, who would have dug out their eyes to serve him (Gal. iv. 14). And he received plenty of ἀτιμία from both Jews and heathen. In this clause the good member of the pair comes first, in the clauses which follow the contrary order is observed,

so that the first two pairs are back to back, producing chiasmus, as in ii. 16, iv. 3, ix. 6, x. 11, xiii. 3. An open vowel after διά is avoided by this means; otherwise we should have had διὰ ἀτιμίας or διὰ εὐφημίας. In the couplets with ὡς, the order is determined by the sense; and the point of the whole series is that the combination of all these contradictions in the same persons is evidence that they stand in a special relation to God.

διὰ δυσφημίας καὶ εὐφημίας. 'Through (= amid) evil report and good report.' This is not a repetition of the preceding clause. That refers to personal treatment of the Apostle; this refers to what was said behind his back. It was during his absence from Corinth that the worst things were said of him. The next two couplets give specimens of the δυσφημία and εὐφημία.

ὡς πλάνοι. *Ut seductores*; in rendering ὡς, Vulg. varies between *ut, quasi*, and *sicut*. These clauses with ὡς look back to συνιστάνοντες ἑαυτοὺς ὡς Θεοῦ διάκονοι, and the thought behind them is, 'Our Apostleship is carried on under these conditions.' Their being called πλάνοι by their opponents told in their favour, for the calumnies of base persons are really recommendations.* The opprobrious word combines the idea of a deceiver and a tramp, an impostor who leads men astray and a vagabond who has no decent home. The idea of seducing prevails in N.T., the notion of vagrancy not appearing anywhere (1 Tim. iv. 1 ; 2 Jn. 7; Mt. xxvii. 63; cf. 1 Jn. ii. 26; Jn. vii. 12): ἀληθεῖς shows that 'deceivers' is the meaning here. Καί = 'and yet' is freq., esp. in Jn. (i. 10, 11, etc.).

9. ὡς ἀγνοούμενοι καὶ ἐπιγινωσκόμενοι. The present participles, of what is habitual and constant, continue throughout these two verses. 'As being known to none, and becoming known to all.'† Ἀγνοούμενοι does not mean 'being misunderstood, misread,' but 'being nonentities, not worth knowing,' *homines ignoti, obscuri*, without proper credentials; τοῖς μὲν γὰρ ἦσαν γνώριμοι καὶ περισπούδαστοι, οἱ δὲ οὐδὲ εἰδέναι αὐτοὺς ἠξίουν (Chrys.). This was the view that contemptuous critics took of them, while from those who could appreciate them, they got more and more recognition. See on 1 Cor. xiii. 12.

With this couplet the ἀτιμία and δυσφημία received from opponents almost passes out of view. The four remaining couplets consist, not of two contradictories, one of which is false, but of two contrasted ways of looking at facts, both of which, from different points of view, are true ; διὰ τῶν ἐναντίων τὴν μίαν ἐκέρασεν ἀρετήν (Thdrt.).

---

* "Their enemies did them service against their wills" (Chrys.).

† *Sicut qui ignoti et cogniti* (Vulg.); *ut qui ignoramur et cognoscimur* (Aug.).

ὡς ἀποθνήσκοντες καὶ ἰδοὺ ζῶμεν. He is not thinking that his enemies regarded him as a doomed man over whose desperate condition they rejoiced ; he is taking his own point of view (iv. 10, 11), ἐν θανάτοις πολλάκις (xi. 23), καθ᾽ ἡμέραν ἀποθνήσκων (1 Cor. xv. 13). He is moribund through infirmities of body, and is exposed to afflictions and dangers which may any day prove fatal. But he bears within himself 'the life of Jesus' which continues to triumph over everything, and will continue to do so (1 Cor. i. 10). The change from the participle to καὶ ἰδοὺ ζῶμεν marks the exulting and confident feeling ; ἰδού as in v. 2 and v. 17.

ὡς παιδευόμενοι καὶ μὴ θανατούμενοι.* He regards himself as requiring chastening. His enemies might regard it as a sign of Divine displeasure, but he knows that the chastening is a merciful dispensation of God. He is probably thinking of Ps. cxviii. 17, 18, οὐκ ἀποθανοῦμαι ἀλλὰ ζήσομαι . . . παιδεύων ἐπαίδευσέν με Κύριος, καὶ τῷ θανάτῳ οὐ παρέδωκέν με.

10. Here, at any rate, we may suppose that he has ceased to think of the accusations and insinuations of his adversaries, and is soaring above such distressing memories. It is somewhat far-fetched to see in these contrasts allusions to the sneer that he refused the maintenance of an Apostle, because he knew that he was not an Apostle, and that he took no pay for his teaching, because he knew that it was worthless. Yet B. Weiss thinks that Paul and his fellow-workers had been called "doleful, penniless paupers,"—*trübselige, armselige Habenichtse,*—and that he is alluding to that here. There was plenty of λύπη in his life (Rom. ix. 2 ; Phil. ii. 27), and in spite of his labouring with his hands to support himself, he was sometimes in need of help and gratefully accepted it (xi. 9 ; Phil. iv. 15).

ἀεὶ χαίροντες. Rom. v. 3–5 ; 1 Thess. v. 16 ; Phil. ii. 18, iii. 1, iv. 4. Such passages illustrate Jn. xv. 11, xvi. 33. The thought of God's goodness to him and to his converts is an inexhaustible source of joy.

πολλοὺς πλουτίζοντες.† Chrys. refers to the collections for the poor saints ; but they made no one rich, and such an explanation is almost a bathos in a pæan of so lofty a strain. It was spiritual riches which he bestowed with such profusion ; of silver and gold he had little or none. "Apart from 1 Tim. vi. 17, no instance of πλοῦτος in the sense of material wealth is to be found in St Paul's writings. On the other hand, his figurative use of the word has no parallel in the rest of the Greek

---

* *ut castigati et non mortificati* (Vulg.); *ut coërciti et non mortificati* (Aug.).

† *multos locupletantes* (Vulg.); *multos ditantes* (Aug.).

Bible. Of fourteen instances of it, five occur in Ephesians. In the use of the derivatives πλούσιος, πλουσίως, πλουτεῖν, πλουτίζειν, the same rule will be found to hold, though there are some interesting exceptions" (J. A. Robinson on Eph. iii. 8).

ὡς μηδὲν ἔχοντες. 'As having nothing'; not even himself. In becoming the bondservant of Jesus Christ, he had given both soul and body to Him, and he was no longer his own (Rom. i. 1; 1 Cor. vi. 19). The μηδέν may have its proper subjective force, but this view of the case is his own, not that of his adversaries.

καὶ πάντα κατέχοντες. The word-play between simple and compound resembles that in iii. 2 and iv. 8. The compound implies 'keeping fast hold upon, having as a secure possession.' See Milligan, Thessalonians, p. 155. Bachmann quotes Ephraim; omnia possidemus per potestatem, quam in coelis et in terris habemus. Meyer quotes Gemara Nedarim, f. 40. 2; Recipimus non esse pauperem nisi in scientia. In Occidente seu terra Israel dixerunt; in quo scientia est, is est ut ille, in quo omnia sunt; in quo illa deest, quid est in eo? What the Stoic claimed for the wise man is true of the Christian; πάντα γὰρ ὑμῶν ἐστίν (1 Cor. iii. 21). "The whole world is the wealth of the believer," says Aug. in reference to this verse (De Civ. Dei, xx. 7); and in showing that evil may have its uses in the world he says of these last four verses; "As then these oppositions of contraries lend beauty to the language, so the beauty of the course of this world is achieved by the opposition of contraries, arranged, as it were, by an eloquence not of words, but of things" (ibid. ix. 18). Jerome says on v. 10; "The believer has a whole world of wealth; the unbeliever has not a single farthing" (Ep. liii. 11, in Migne, 10).

VI. 11-VII. 16. THE RESTORATION OF CONFIDENCE BETWEEN THE APOSTLE AND THE CORINTHIANS.

Under the impulse of strong feeling the Apostle has been opening his heart with great frankness to his converts. He now asks them with great earnestness to make a similar return and to treat him with affectionate candour. The appeal is conveniently regarded as in two parts (vi. 11–vii. 4, 5–16), but the first part is rather violently interrupted by the interjection of a sudden warning against heathen modes of life which are sure to pollute the lives of the Corinthians (vi. 14–vii. 1), and would impede their reconciliation with the Apostle.

VI. 11–VII. 4. Appeal of the reconciled Apostle to the Corinthians.

Let me have some return for my affectionate frankness. Close intimacy with heathen life is impossible for you. Open your hearts to me as mine is ever open to you.

¹¹ O men of Corinth, my lips are unlocked to tell you everything about myself; my heart stands wide open to receive you and your confidences. ¹² There is no restraint in my feeling towards you ; the restraint is in your own affections. ¹³ But love should awaken love in return—I appeal to you as my children— let your hearts also be opened wide to receive me.

Warning against Intimacy with Heathen (vi. 14–vii. 1).

¹⁴ Come not into close fellowship with unbelievers who are no fit yokefellows for you. For

What partnership can righteousness have with iniquity?
Or how can light associate with darkness?
¹⁵ What concord can there be between Purity and pollution ?
Or what portion can a believer have with an unbeliever?
¹⁶ And what agreement can God's sanctuary have with idols ?

For we, yes we, are a sanctuary of the living God. This is just what was meant when God said,

I will dwell in them and move among them,
And I will be their God, and they will be My people.
¹⁷ Therefore come out from the midst of them,
And sever yourselves, saith the Lord,
And lay hold of nothing that is unclean :
And I will give you a welcome.
¹⁸ And I will be to you a Father,
And ye shall be to Me sons and daughters,
Saith the Lord Almighty.

VIII. ¹ Seeing then that the promises which we have are no less than these, beloved friends, let us cleanse ourselves from everything that can defile flesh or spirit, and secure perfect consecration by reverence for God.

² Make room for me in your hearts. Why hesitate? In no single instance have I wronged any one, ruined any one, taken advantage of any one. ³ It is not to put you in the wrong that I

am saying this. Do not think that. In pleading my own cause
I am blaming no one. I repeat what I said before; ye are in
my very heart, and you will ever be there whether I die or live.
⁴ I feel the greatest confidence in you; I take the greatest pride
in you. And so I am filled with comfort, I am overflowing with
joy, for all the affliction that I have to bear.

11. Τὸ στόμα ἡμῶν ἀνέῳγεν. 'Our mouth is open.' In late
Greek ἀνέῳγα is almost always intransitive (Jn. i. 51; 1 Cor.
xvi. 9) with the meaning of standing open. In class. Grk. the
perf. pass. is preferred (ii. 12; Rom. iii. 13). There is much
discussion as to whether these words refer to what the Apostle
has just said or to what he is about to say. The former is right,
but the latter may be to some extent included. He is himself
a little surprised at the fulness with which he has opened his
heart to them. The phrase is not a mere Hebraistic pleonasm,
used to indicate that what is said is important (Mt. v. 2, xiii. 35;
Acts viii. 35, x. 34; etc.). It is a picturesque indication that
there has been no reserve on his part. *Lata dilectio cordis nostri,
quae vos omnes complectitur, non sinit ut taceamus ea quae prosunt
vobis. Profectus enim discipulorum aperit os magistri* (Herveius).
His delight in them does not allow him to be silent.

Κορίνθιοι. Very rarely does the Apostle address his converts
by name (Gal. iii. 1; Phil. iv. 5). Nowhere else does he do so
to his Corinthians. The whole passage is affectionately tender.

ἡ καρδία ἡμῶν πεπλάτυνται. Just as his lips have been
unsealed to tell them everything about himself and his office, so
his 'heart has been set at liberty' (Ps. cxix. 32) to take all of
them in. It has been expanded and stands wide open to receive
them. Heat, as Chrysostom remarks, makes things expand, and
warm affection makes his heart expand. Their hearts are so
contracted that there is no room in them for him. *Ab ore ad cor
concludere debebant* (Beng.). In his heart their misconduct is
forgotten; their amendment and progress cancels all that, and
sorrow is turned into joy (vii. 2–4).

12. οὐ στενοχωρεῖσθε ἐν ἡμῖν. 'There is no restraint on my
side; but whatever restraint there is is in your hearts.' He had
perhaps been accused of being close and reserved. Like the
rapid changes of expression in *vv.* 14–16, the change from his
καρδία to their σπλάγχνα is made to avoid repetition of the same
word. In both cases the seat of the affections is meant.
'Bowels' is an unfortunate rendering; the word means the upper
part of the intestines, heart, liver, lungs, etc. "Theophilus (*ad
Autol.* ii. 10, 22) uses σπλάγχνα and καρδία as convertible
terms" (Lightfoot on Phil. i. 8). Many things cause the heart

to close against others, meanness, suspicion, resentment for supposed injury. Are they quite free from all these things? 1 Jn. iii. 17.

13. τὴν δὲ αὐτὴν ἀντιμισθίαν. In dictating he omits to supply a verb to govern this acc. Lit. 'But as the same requital,' *i.e.* 'In order to give me an exact equivalent for what I give you, repay open heart with open heart.' Ἀντιμισθία occurs Rom. i. 27, but nowhere else in Bibl. Grk. Various ways are suggested of explaining the irregular construction, but the meaning is the same however we regard it. The simplest explanation is that, after the affectionate parenthesis ὡς τέκνοις λέγω, he forgets the opening construction. See Cornely, *ad loc.* ; Blass, § 34. 3, 6.

ὡς τέκνοις λέγω. 'I am speaking as to my children'; not 'as to children,' implying that they are still young in the faith and need to be fed with milk (νηπίοις, 1 Cor. iii. 1); still less 'as the children *say*,' which the Greek cannot mean. In neither case would τέκνα be used, but it is St Paul's usual word in speaking of or to his spiritual children; 1 Cor. iv. 14, 17; Gal. iv. 19; 1 Tim. i. 2, 18; etc. By inserting these words he mitigates the severity of στενοχωρεῖσθε. It is not a large demand, if a father claims affection from his children.

πλατύνθητε καὶ ὑμεῖς. 'Do you also open your hearts wide'; looking back to *v.* 11. The Corinthians must surely make some response to his open-hearted statement; τὸν αὐτὸν πλατυσμὸν ὡς ἀντιμισθίαν πλατύνθητε. "He asks for the enlargement of their heart towards him; which was to be shown in separation from the world" (F. W. Robertson).

VI. 14–VII. 1. This strongly worded admonition to make no compromise with heathenism comes in so abruptly here that a number of critics suppose that it is a fragment of another letter, and some maintain that the fragment is not by St Paul. We may set aside the latter hypothesis with confidence. The fact that ἑτεροζυγέω, μετοχή, συμφώνησις, συνκάθεσις, Βελίαρ, and μολυσμός are found nowhere else in N.T. counts for very little. There are more than three dozen of such words in each of the three Epistles, Ephesians, Colossians, and Philippians, and here these unusual words are needed by the subject. There is no inconsistency between this severe injunction and 1 Cor. v. 9 f., x. 27 f. What is discouraged here is something much more intimate than accepting a heathen's invitation to dinner. And there is nothing un-Pauline in 'defilement of flesh and spirit.' It is true that he often treats the flesh as the sphere of sin, and the spirit as its opponent. But here he is using popular language, in which 'flesh and spirit' sum up the totality of human nature. What stains the whole man is an abomination to be avoided.*

There is more to be said for the hypothesis that we have here a fragment of another of the Apostle's letters, and probably the one mentioned 1 Cor. v. 9. These verses might easily form part of the one there described. Moreover, if we abstract the passage, vii. 2 fits on to vi. 13 admirably; it is obviously a continuation, either immediate or by resumption, of the same topic. Nevertheless, this attractive hypothesis is a violent one.† There is no evidence in MS., or version, or quotation, that any copy of the Epistle ever lacked this passage. If it belonged originally to another Epistle, how did it come to be inserted here, if not in the letter dictated by St Paul, in one of the earliest copies made from it? An interpolator would have chosen a more suitable place. The interpolation, if it be one, might possibly be due to accident, the careless insertion of a leaf from one MS. among the leaves of another. But we require very strong internal evidence to justify the use of such an explanation; and on this point opinions differ.‡ Some critics regard the disconnexion with the context so glaring, and the connexion of vi. 13 with vii. 2 so obvious, that the theory of insertion, either deliberate or accidental, is demonstrated. Others contend that the connexion with the context is natural and close. There is perhaps some exaggeration in both these views. It is not incredible that in the middle of his appeal for *mutual* frankness and affection, and after his declaration that the cramping constraint is all on their side, he should dart off to one main cause of that constraint, viz. their compromising attitude towards anti-Christian influences. Having relieved his mind of this distressing subject, he returns at once to his tender appeal. On the whole, this view seems better than the hypothesis of interpolation. But this is one of the many places in 2 Cor. in which our ignorance of the state of things at Corinth renders certainty unattainable. We do not know to what kind of

---

* "It is an error to suppose that Paul makes a rigorous distinction between the σάρξ and the σῶμα and its members in relation to the seat of sin" (O. Cone, *Paul*, p. 228).

† A. Sabatier, who rejects the less violent hypothesis that x.–xiii. is part of another letter, accepts this hypothesis as correct (*The Apostle Paul*, p. 177 n.).

‡ Lietzmann warns us against resorting to the hypothesis of *die von der Kritik aufgewirbelten 'fliegenden Blätter,' die sich an verschiedenen Stellen des N.T. so verwunderliche Ruheplätze ausgesucht haben sollen.* Bousset says that reasons for excising the passage are worthy of consideration but not convincing, *nicht durchschlagend.* Calvin remarks that the Apostle, having regained his hold over his converts, hastens to warn them of a perilous evil. Perhaps it was an evil which had led to the temporary breach between him and his converts.

intimacy with heathen acquaintances and customs the Apostle is alluding. But a sudden digression for a few minutes is more probable than a long pause.* In the latter case the return to *v.* 13 in vii. 2 would be less probable. See Meyer or Klöpper, *ad loc.* ; Zahn, *Intr.* i. p. 349.

14. μὴ γίνεσθε ἑτεροζυγοῦντες ἀπίστοις. Here, although perhaps not in iv. 4, we shall be right in confining ἄπιστοι to those who do not believe the Gospel, the unconverted heathen (1 Cor. vi. 6, vii. 12 ff., x. 27, xiv. 22 ff.). The false apostles are certainly not included, and the dat. does not mean '*to please* unbelievers.' And the metaphor in ἑτεροζυγοῦντες doubtless comes from Deut. xxii. 10, where, among other unnatural combinations, ploughing with an ox and an ass harnessed together is prohibited. Species are made distinct by God, and man ought not to join together what He has put asunder. Cf. Lev. xix. 19. There may also be some allusion to Deut. xi. 16, where for 'lest thy heart be deceived' LXX has μὴ πλατυνθῇ ἡ καρδία σου, and what follows is a warning against idolatry, λατρεύειν θεοῖς ἑτέροις, 'lest thy heart be enlarged so as to embrace heathenism.' But the other allusion is manifest. 'Heathen belong to one species, Christians to quite another, and it is against nature that Christians should be yokefellows with them. They will not walk as Christians do, and Christians must not walk in their ways.'† The meaning is not to be confined to mixed marriages; intimate combinations of other kinds are condemned. But with characteristic tenderness and tact St Paul does not assert that such things have taken place. He says, '*Become* not incongruously yoked with unbelievers'; such things may happen if they are not warned. Even the RV. does not preserve the important γίνεσθε. There is much softening in 'Do not let yourselves become.' Cf. μὴ οὖν γίνεσθε συνμέτοχοι αὐτῶν (Eph. v. 7). See Blass, § 37. 6, § 62. 3. The idea of ζυγός = 'balance' and of scales unfairly tipped is certainly not in the phrase, although Theophylact takes it so; 'be not too much inclined to the heathen.' St Paul had said that he himself was willing to behave as a heathen to heathen (1 Cor. ix. 21; cf. Gal. ii. 19), but not in the way of sharing or condoning their practices.

τίς γὰρ μετοχή; The absolute incongruity between Christians and pagans is emphasized by quickly delivered argumentative

* *Wir haben uns hinter v. 13 eine lange Pause im Dictieren zu denken* (Lietzmann).

† Cf. Plautus, *Aulularia*, II. ii. 51 f., *Nunc si filiam locassim meam tibi, in mentem venit, Te bovem esse, et me esse asellum: ubi tecum conjunctus siem, Ubi onus nequeam ferre pariter, jaceam ego asinus in luto ; Tu me bos haud magis respicias.* Here the dat. implies that the ἄπιστοι will dominate.

questions, as in xii. 17, 18. They are illustrations of the Apostle's rhetorical power. The first four questions are in pairs ; the last being a conclusion to the series and a premiss for what follows. The great variety of expression is no doubt studied, and it is effective. But inferior MSS. here and there spoil the effect by assimilating the constructions. ' For what partnership has righteousness with lawlessness, or what association can there be between light and darkness ?' The change from μετοχή to κοινωνία is for the sake of change, and we need not look to any important difference of meaning, as that μετοχή implies that each partner has a share, e.g. of the profits, whereas every member of a society enjoys the whole of what is κοινόν, as the use of a park or building.

Here, as in v. 8 ('honour and dishonour'), AV. makes a verbal antithesis which does not exist in the Greek. We require 'righteousness with lawlessness' (2 Thess. ii. 7 ; 1 Jn. iii. 4) or 'with iniquity' (Rom. iv. 7, vi. 19). Although μετοχή is a hapaxleg., μετέχω occurs five times in 1 Cor.

πρὸς σκότος. We have four different constructions in the five sentences, all for the sake of variety ; two datives, dat. followed by πρός, gen. followed by πρός, dat. followed by μετά. The πρός after κοινων. is late Greek ; φυσική ἐστιν ἡμῖν κοινωνία πρὸς ἀλλήλους (Epict. Dis. ii. 20) ; cf. Ecclus. xiii. 3. Light and darkness as a spiritual antithesis is freq. in N.T. and elsewhere (Rom. xiii. 12 ; Eph. v. 8 ; 1 Jn. ii. 9 ; Acts xxvi. 18 ; Is. xlii. 16 ; etc.). In N.T., σκότος is neuter.

15. τίς δὲ συμφώνησις Χριστοῦ πρὸς Βελίαρ; In the first couplet of questions we have abstract terms, in the second, concrete ; 'And what concord is there of Christ with Belial ?' The Head of the Heavenly society is opposed to the Head of the infernal kingdom, the Pattern of perfect purity to the representative of devilish abominations. But is it possible that 'Beliar' here is Antichrist ? 'What harmony can there be of Christ with Antichrist ?' The antithesis is attractive rather than probable ; but Bousset treats it as certain, and Antichrist is here represented as the devil incarnate. The Sun of righteousness and the Prince of darkness is the probable antithesis. In O.T. 'Belial' is often mentioned as meaning 'worthlessness,' 'ruin,' 'desperate wickedness.' Later, 'Belial' or 'Beliar' or 'Berial' comes to be a name for Satan or some Satanic power. In the *Book of Jubilees* (i. 20) Moses prays, "Create in Thy people an upright spirit, and let not the spirit of Beliar rule over them to accuse them before Thee." In the Testaments it is connected with various evil spirits, e.g. of impurity (*Reub.* iv. 11, vi. 3 ; *Sim.* v. 3), wrath (*Dan* i. 7, 8), and so forth. "Choose, therefore, for yourselves

either the light or the darkness, either the law of the Lord or the works of Beliar" (*Levi* xix. 1).

The interchange of λ and ρ is not uncommon ; *e.g.* κλίβανος and κρίβανος, γλώσσαλγος and γλώσσαργος. Alcibiades had a lisp which turned ρ into λ, saying ὁλᾷς for ὁρᾷς, κόλαξ for κόραξ κ.τ.λ. (Aristoph. *Vesp.* 45). 'Inferior texts here have Βελίαλ, or Βελίαν, or Βελίαβ : Vulg. *Belial.* In LXX it is translated ἀνόμημα, ἀνομία, ἀποστασία, παράνομος, and in the A text ἀσεβής. For the Beliar myth see Charles, *Ascension of Isaiah*, pp. liv f. Χριστοῦ (א B C P, d e f Copt.) is to be preferred to Χριστῷ (D E G K L, g Syrr.).   Note that d e differ from D E.

τίς μερὶς πιστῷ μετὰ ἀπίστου; Here we have a verbal antithesis, and AV. obliterates it ; 'he that *believeth* with an *infidel.*' Better, 'What portion hath a believer with an unbeliever ? ' (RV.). Comp. 1 Tim. v. 16 and Acts xvi. 1 with Jn. xx. 27. Μερίς suggests that there is a whole to be shared (Acts viii. 21). Cf. μετὰ μοιχῶν τὴν μερίδα σου ἐτίθεις (Ps. xlix. [l.] 18). It is certain that πιστῷ does not mean 'one who is faithful,' viz. God ; πιστὸς κύριος ἐν τοῖς λόγοις αὐτοῦ. *Fidelis Dominus in omnibus verbis suis* (Ps. cxliv. [v.] 13).*

16. τίς δὲ συνκατάθεσις ναῷ Θεοῦ μετὰ εἰδώλων; In this final question, which has no pair, there is no new construction; 'What agreement hath God's sanctuary with idols?' The noun is a technical term with the Stoics ; it is not found elsewhere in Bibl. Grk., but ἐκ συνκαταθέσεως, "according to agreement" occurs in papyri.   Cf. οὐ συνκαταθήσῃ μετὰ τοῦ ἀδίκου (Ex. xxiii. 1).   Manasseh had put a graven image of Ashera in the house of the Lord, and Josiah removed and burnt it (2 Kings xxi. 7, xxiii. 6).   Ezekiel tells of other abominations (viii. 3–18), for which unsparing punishments were inflicted by God.   The history of Israel had shown with terrible distinctness that God allowed no agreement between His house and idols.   This shows that ναοῦ is not to be understood before εἰδώλων, as if the opposition was between the temple of God and a *temple* of idols. The absolute incongruity is between God's sanctuary, in which not even an image of Himself might be put up, and images of false gods ; also *perhaps* between dead idols and the temple of the living God.   By the introduction of idols the temple ceases to be a temple of God.

ἡμεῖς γὰρ ναὸς Θεοῦ ἐσμὲν ζῶντος. 'The Most High dwelleth not in temples made with hands' (Acts vii. 48, xvii. 24).   The only suitable temple of the living God is the souls of living beings who can adore and love Him. 'And such are *we.*' The ἡμεῖς (see crit. note) is very emphatic.   The Christian Church,

* "There is much danger in applying this law. It is perilous when men begin to decide who are believers and who not by party badges" (F. W. Robertson).

rather than the individual Christian (1 Cor. vi. 19), is here regarded as God's sanctuary. What is it about us that is divine? asks Seneca; *Quaerendum est quod non fiat in dies deterius, cui non possit obstari. Quid hoc est? animus, sed hic rectus, bonus, magnus. Quid aliud voces hunc, quam Deum in humano corpore hospitantem? Subsilire in coelum ex angulo licet; exsurge modo, et te quoque dignum finge Deo* (*Ep.* xxxi. 9, 10). Calvin states the same fact somewhat differently; *In Leo hoc speciale est, qui quemcunque locum dignatur sua praesentia, etiam sanctificat.* As in Jn. ii. 21, ὁ ναὸς τοῦ σώματος αὐτοῦ, we have ναός rather than ἱερόν, when human beings are spoken of as shrines for God to dwell in. The ναός was the most sacred part of the ἱερόν, which included buildings for other uses than that of worship and also open spaces. Cf. 1 Cor. iii. 16, 17, vi. 19; Eph. ii. 21. Ναός is from ναίειν, 'to dwell.'

We ought certainly to read ἡμεῖς . . . ἐσμέν (א* B D* L P 17, 67**, d e Copt. Aeth.) rather than ὑμεῖς . . . ἐστε (א³ C D² E F G K, Vulg. Syrr. Arm.), which probably comes from 1 Cor. iii. 16. The confusion between ἡμεῖς and ὑμεῖς in MSS. is freq. Cf. vii. 12, viii. 8, 19; 1 Cor. vii. 15. א* has ναοί, an obvious correction.

καθὼς εἶπεν ὁ Θεός. We have first a paraphrase and then a quotation of the LXX of Lev. xxvi. 11, 12, with a mixture of other passages. Cf. Is. lii. 11; Ezek. xx. 34, xxxvii. 27; 2 Sam. vii. 14; but the remarkable ἐνοικήσω ἐν αὐτοῖς is not in any of them. It is much stronger than 'walk among them' or 'tabernacle among them.' The introductory words show in each case what passage the Apostle has in his mind. καθὼς εἶπεν ὁ Θεός points to Lev. xxvi. 12, λέγει Κύριος to Is. lii. 5 or Ezek. xx. 33 or xxxvii. 21, and λέγει Κύριος παντοκράτωρ to 2 Sam. vii. 8. Cf. Ezek. xi. 17; Zeph. iii. 20; Zech. x. 8.

καὶ ἔσομαι αὐτῶν Θεός. This privilege depends upon their willingness to accept Him; *Deus natura omnium est, voluntate paucorum* (Pseudo-Primasius).

17. διὸ ἐξέλθατε. The διό introduces the practical conclusion to be drawn from *vv.* 14–16, and to make it as impressive as possible it is expressed in language taken from the utterances of Jehovah in O.T. The withdrawal is to be moral and spiritual, not local; it is not meant that Christians are to migrate from heathen cities. And the aor. imperat. shows that the withdrawal is to be immediate and decisive, as in Rev. xviii. 4, where Swete remarks that "the cry ἔξελθε, ἐξέλθετε, rings through the Hebrew history; in the call of Abram, in the rescue of Lot, in the Exodus, in the call to depart from the neighbourhood of the tents of Dathan and Abiram, etc." Cf. Eph. v. 11; 1 Tim. v. 22. See Index IV.

ἀκαθάρτου μὴ ἄπτεσθε. In Heb. it is an unclean *person.*
Here the adj. may be masc. or neut. Luther, AV., RV. follow
Chrys. in regarding it as neut.

εἰσδέξομαι ὑμᾶς. 'Will receive you *with favour.*' The compound verb is found in LXX, esp. of God's promises, but nowhere else in N.T. St Luke, both in Gospel and Acts, often has
ἀποδέχομαι in the same sense = 'welcome.'

18. ἔσομαι ὑμῖν εἰς. This may mean 'I will *become* to you'
(Mt. xix. 5; Eph. v. 31); but more probably the εἰς means 'for,
to serve as (Heb. i. 5, viii. 10; Eph. i. 12) father.' There is to
be a family likeness and family affection between God and them.
Cf. *Jubilees* i. 24. They have been called out of their original
home, and their new one will more than compensate them. If
the friendship of the world means enmity with God (Jas. iv. 4),
the only N.T. passage in which φιλία occurs,—it is likely to be
true that separation from the world will lead to friendship with
God. The second Isaiah (xliii. 6), with characteristic insight,
penetrates to the truth that there are daughters of God as well as
sons of God. But this truth was only dimly recognized until
Christianity raised woman from the degradation into which she
had been thrust, not only in heathen cities, like Corinth, but
even among the Chosen People. With the wording comp.
2 Sam. vii. 14.

λέγει Κύριος Παντοκράτωρ. 'Saith the Lord All-Ruler' or
'All-sovereign.' See Swete on Rev. i. 8, the only other book in
N.T. in which παντοκράτωρ occurs. There and in O.T. it is
freq. It indicates One who rules over all rather than One who
is able do all things, ὁ παντοδύναμος (Wisd. vii. 23, xi. 17, xviii. 15).
The promises of such a Potentate are no mean thing, and they
are sure to be fulfilled.

VII. 1. Here again, as between i. and ii., and between iii.
and iv., and between iv. and v., and between v. and vi., the
division between the chapters is not well made. As the οὖν
shows, vii. 1 belongs closely to what precedes. It closes the
digression which warns the Corinthians against fellowship with
heathen modes of life; and then we have a resumption of the
tender appeal in which his beloved converts are implored to
make some response to the frankness with which he has opened
his heart to them.

1. Ταύτας οὖν ἔχοντες τὰς ἐπαγγελίας. Ταύτας comes first with
emphasis; 'These, then, being the promises which we have.'
They are so incalculably precious, and so sure to be fulfilled if
they are properly met.

ἀγαπητοί. With us this affectionate address has become

almost a canting expression in sermons, and it means very little.
But the Apostle is not prodigal in his use of it, and with him it
means a great deal; twice in 1 Cor. (x. 14, xv. 58), once again in
2 Cor. (xii. 19); twice in Phil. (ii. 12, iv. 1); once in Rom. (xii. 19).
καθαρίσωμεν ἑαυτούς. He again softens the severity of his
words, as in ὡς τέκνοις λέγω (v. 13); this time by including himself among those who need cleansing. Baptism cannot be
repeated, and earnest Christians would not need a repetition of
it; but all in their walk through life become soiled and need
frequent cleansing (Jn. xiii. 10). He who looks for a fulfilment
of the gracious promises must strive to be καθαρὸς ὅλος. If we
are to have God to dwell in us, we must purify the dwelling. If
we are to have Him as a Father, we must strive to acquire some
likeness to Him. The verb is not peculiar to Bibl. Grk. It
occurs in Josephus (*Ant.* XI. v. 4) and is found in inscriptions
(followed by ἀπό, as here and Heb. ix. 14) in much the same
sense as in this verse, of the necessity for purification before
entering a holy place. Deissmann, *Bib. St.* p. 216. Cf. ἀπὸ
πάσης ἁμαρτίας καθάρισον καρδίαν (Ecclus. xxxviii. 10). Index IV.

ἀπὸ παντὸς μολυσμοῦ. 'From every kind of defilement.'
The noun implies an evil stain, foul pollution; in LXX in
connexion with idolatry (1 Esdr. viii. 80 [84]; 2 Macc. v. 27;
cf. Jer. xxiii. 15). In the Testaments (*Symeon* ii. 13) we have
ἀποσχῶ ἀπὸ παντὸς μολυσμοῦ. On the date of the Testaments
see Lightfoot, *Galatians*, p. 320. Here there may be a reference
to τὴν τῶν εἰδώλων κοινωνίαν, but not to that exclusively. The
noun occurs nowhere else, but μολύνω is freq. in O.T. and N.T.
Trench, *Syn.* § xxxi.; Wetst. *ad loc.*

σαρκὸς καὶ πνεύματος. Man may be defiled in either flesh or
spirit, and in either case there must be cleansing. The two
together sum up human nature, and the intercommunion of the
parts is so close, that when either is soiled the whole is soiled.
St Paul is using popular language covering the material and
immaterial elements in man, and it is manifest that he is not
under the influence of the Gnostic doctrine that everything
material is *ipso facto* evil. He says that the flesh must be
cleansed from every kind of pollution. Gnostics maintained
that it was as impossible to cleanse flesh as to cleanse filth. In
either case the only remedy was to get rid of the unclean matter.
See P. Gardner, *Religious Experience of St Paul*, p. 165. He
quotes Reitzenstein; "All the different shades of meaning
which πνεῦμα has in Paul's writings may be found in the magic
papyri. . . . Paul has not developed for himself a peculiar
psychology, and a mystic way of speaking in accordance with
it, but speaks in the Greek of his time" (*Die Hellenistischen
Mysterienreligionen*, pp. 42, 137). Epictetus (*Dis.* ii. 3) has a

similar thought; "When you are conversing with others, know you not that you are exercising God? Unhappy man, you carry God about with you, and know it not. You carry Him within you, and perceive not that you are polluting (μολύνων) Him with unclean thoughts and filthy acts. If an image of God were present, you would not dare to do any of the things which you do. But when God Himself is present within and sees all, you are not ashamed of thinking such things and doing such things, ignorant as you are of your own nature and subject to the anger of God." Nestle's proposal to take only σαρκός with μολυσμοῦ and transfer καὶ πνεύματος to ἁγιωσύνην need not be more than mentioned.* The latter constr. is intolerable. With μολ. σαρκὸς κ. πνεύματος comp. ἁγία τῷ σώματι κ. τῷ πνεύματι (1 Cor. vii. 34). It is uncritical dogmatism to assert that St Paul would never have used such an expression as 'defilement of flesh and spirit.' See on v. 5.

ἐπιτελοῦντες ἁγιωσύνην. The mere cleansing oneself from defilement is not enough. It is right that the unclean spirit should be cast out; but the place which he has occupied must be filled with such things as will make it impossible for him to return; there must be a process of self-consecration always going on. This is the meaning of 'bringing to completeness (viii. 6, 11; Phil. i. 6) a state of holiness' (1 Thess. iii. 13; Rom. i. 4). Cf. Zech. iv. 9. In LXX, ἁγιωσύνη is used generally of God. In the Testaments (*Levi* xviii. 11) we are told that the saints who enter Paradise will eat from the tree of life, καὶ πνεῦμα ἁγιωσύνης ἔσται ἐπ' αὐτοῖς. Here it is the divine quality of ἁγιωσύνη that fits Christians to become God's sanctuary and to have Him as their Father.

ἐν φόβῳ Θεοῦ. Not in the fear or love of men. The ἐν may mark either the sphere in which the perfecting of holiness takes place or the means by which it is accomplished; cf. ἐν τῇ παρουσίᾳ, ἐν τῇ παρακλήσει (v. 7). 'The fear of God' or 'the fear of the Lord' is repeatedly given in O.T. as the principle of a good life; so esp. in Psalms (ii. 11, v. 7, etc.) and Proverbs (i. 7, 29, viii. 13, etc.). It is the whole duty of man (Eccles. xii. 13). "He who tries to do any good thing without the fear of the Lord," says Herveius, "is a proud man." Cf. v. 11; Rom. iii. 18; Acts ix. 31, x. 2, 35. In Eph. v. 21 what is said in O.T. of Jehovah is in a remarkable way transferred to Christ, ἐν φόβῳ Χριστοῦ.

2-4. The return to the affectionate appeal in vi. 11–13 is as sudden as the digression at vi. 14. He has concluded the

---

* The proposal has been anticipated by Augustine (*De Doc. Chris.* iii. 2), who points it out as possible, but does not adopt it.

warning against what would hinder complete reconciliation and gladly resumes tender language. Χωρήσατε ἡμᾶς goes back at once to πλατύνθητε καὶ ὑμεῖς. It shows still more clearly what he means by their opening wide their hearts; they are to open them to *him*.

2. Χωρήσατε ἡμᾶς. *Capite nos* (Vulg.), *Accipite nos* (Beza). The latter is better, but does not give the exact sense. 'Make room for us' in your hearts is the meaning. 'Not all men have room for the saying,' that it is not good to marry (Mt. xix. 11). Cf. Mk. ii. 2, and οὐκ ἐχώρει αὐτοὺς ἡ γῆ κατοικεῖν ἅμα (Gen. xiii. 6).* The asyndeton throughout these verses is expressive of the eagerness with which he dictates the telling sentences. He rapidly negatives reasons which might make them hesitate to open their hearts to take him in.

οὐδένα ἠδικήσαμεν. The οὐδένα comes first in each case with emphasis, and the aorists imply that there has not been a single case in which he has wronged, ruined, defrauded, any of them. Evidently he had been accused or suspected of something of the kind; but here again we are in ignorance as to the facts to which he alludes. Cf. iv. 2 and οὐκ ἐκ πλάνης οὐδὲ ἐξ ἀκαθαρσίας οὐδὲ ἐν δόλῳ (1 Thess. ii. 3). We have a similar protest in the Apostle's speech at Miletus (Acts xx. 26, 27); cf. 1 Sam. xii. 3; Num. xvi. 15. Those who think it improbable that he is alluding to charges actually made by the Corinthians take the words as playfully ironical, or as a hit at the Judaizing teachers, who *had* injured the Corinthians with their corrupt doctrine and perhaps lived in Corinth at their expense. See on iv. 2.

οὐδένα ἐφθείραμεν. 'We ruined no one,' a vague expression, which we cannot define with certainty. It may refer to money, or morals, or doctrine. Calvin is too definite: *corruptela quae fit per falsam doctrinam*, which may or may not be right. He might be said to have ruined people who had had to abandon lucrative but unchristian pursuits. The Judaizers declared that his doctrine of Christian freedom was thoroughly immoral; and some of his disciples, who misinterpreted his teaching, gave the freedom an unchristian and immoral meaning.

οὐδένα ἐπλεονεκτήσαμεν. 'We took advantage of no one.' 'Defrauded' (AV.) is too definite, as implying financial dishonesty; and we are not sure that there is any such allusion in any of the three verbs. If x.–xiii. is part of a letter written

---

* Several of the Latin commentators, misled by *Capite nos*, take this as meaning *mente capite, intelligite*, 'Consider what I say.' Others interpret, 'Consider me, take me as an example.' The Greek cannot mean this. Theophylact is right; δέξασθε ἡμᾶς πλατέως καὶ μὴ στενοχωρώμεθα ἐν ὑμῖν. Bengel expands ἡμᾶς thus; *vestri amantes, vestra causa laetantes*.

before this letter, ἐπλεονεκτήσαμεν may refer to xii. 17, 18. Excepting the difficult passage 1 Thess. iv. 6, the verb is peculiar to 2 Cor. in N.T., and in LXX it is rare; πλεονεξία is more freq. in both LXX and N.T.   See Trench, *Syn.* § xxiv.   With the rhetorical repetition of οὐδένα comp. that of κἀγώ in xi. 22, and of μὴ πάντες (seven times in all) in 1 Cor. xii. 29, 30.

3. πρὸς κατάκρισιν οὐ λέγω. ' It is not for condemnation that I am saying this.' He does not wish to find fault with any one; they must not think that; he is merely defending himself. This seems to show that in *v.* 2 he is answering accusations which had actually been made, either by some Corinthians or the false teachers. In spite of what people say of him, there is no reason why they should not open their hearts to take him in. Cf. πρὸς ἐντροπὴν ὑμῖν λέγω (1 Cor. vi. 5).

προείρηκα γάρ. He has not said these words before or anything that is exactly equivalent to them; indeed in iv. 12 he has said what is very different. But he has spoken of the bonds of affection which bind him to them, and he now speaks of these ties in a very emphatic way. Cf. xiii. 2; Gal. i. 9; 3 Macc. vi. 35.

ἐν ταῖς καρδίαις ἡμῶν ἐστε εἰς τὸ συναποθανεῖν καὶ συνζῆν. 'Ye are in our hearts to share death and to share life'; *i.e.* 'You are in our hearts, whether we die or live.' The general meaning is clear enough, but, as in Rom. viii. 39, there is a rush of emotion which does not allow the Apostle to choose his words carefully. He probably means that neither death nor any experience in life can extinguish his affection for them; but he may mean that he is ready to share either death or life with them. He will (if need be) die with them, and he cannot live without them. This is the mark of a good shepherd (Jn. x. 12). *Perfecta charitas profectum vel detrimentum aliorum credit esse suum* (Herveius). It is evident that here St Paul is including his colleagues in the ἡμῶν. In *v.* 2, as in *vv.* 11, 12, Timothy and others *may* have dropped out of sight, but here, if ἡμῶν meant himself only, he would have said ἐν τῇ καρδίᾳ. See on iii. 2, and Lightfoot on 1 Thess. ii. 4, where we have a similar case. Probably he includes others in all four verses. The interchanges between 'I' and 'we' in *vv.* 2 to 4 are quite intelligible. We cannot infer from 'dying' preceding 'living' that dying with Christ in faith in order to live with Him is meant (v. 15). The reason for putting 'dying' first is not clear; but it may point to his being ἐν θανάτοις πολλάκις (xi. 23). In Athenaeus, vi. 249 (quoted by Wetstein), the more usual order is observed; τούτους δ᾽ οἱ βασιλεῖς ἔχουσι συζῶντας καὶ συναποθνή- σκοντας.

πρὸς κατ. οὐ λέγω (‌‌א B C P) rather than οὐ πρὸς κατ. λέγω (D E F G K L), which is an obvious correction. B omits ἐστε. συνζῆν (‌א B* C D E F G) rather than συζῆν (B³ K L P).

4. πολλή μοι παρρησία πρὸς ὑμᾶς κ.τ.λ. Note the alliteration, of which St Paul is fond, esp. with the letter π. It is probable that παρρησία here means 'confidence' (1 Tim. iii. 13; Heb. x. 19), rather than 'boldness of speech' (iii. 2). 'Great is my confidence respecting you; great is my glorying on your behalf.' * The confidence is the result of their obedience and affection as reported by Titus, and this feeling of confidence manifests itself in glorying. He is very proud of them and is not afraid to say so, for they will not come short of his praise. He has told them (v. 12) that they ought to glory on behalf of their teachers, and he tells them (here and viii. 24) that he is ready to glory respecting his converts. Καύχησις (see on i. 12), παράκλησις (see on i. 3), and θλίψις (see on i. 4) are specially freq. in this Epistle, and the frequency should be marked in translation.

πεπλήρωμαι τῇ παρακλήσει. 'I am filled with the comfort'; 'I was then and I am still' (perf.). The usual constr. is with the gen. (Acts ii. 28, xiii. 52; Rom. xv. 13; etc.); but the dat. occurs in late Greek; ὁ βασιλεὺς χαρᾷ πεπληρωμένος (3 Macc. iv. 16). Cf. 2 Macc. vi. 5, vii. 21; Rom. i. 29.

ὑπερπερισσεύομαι τῇ χαρᾷ. 'I am overflowing with the joy.' A double climax; 'overflowing' is more than 'filled,' and 'joy' is more than 'comfort.' The article should probably be translated; it points to the comfort and the joy caused by the report brought by Titus. The compound verb is very rare; only here and Rom. v. 20; not in LXX. We have similar alliterations with π in viii. 22, ix. 5, 8, xiii. 2.

ἐπὶ πάσῃ τῇ θλίψει. 'Amid all my affliction.' The ἐπί does not mean that the affliction was the basis of the comfort and joy, a paradox (xii. 10) which here would have no point; but that, in all his great trouble, he was able to have abundant comfort and joy. He at once goes on to explain the cause of this happiness.

En qualiter affectos esse omnes pastores conveniat (Calvin).

VII. 5-16. The Reconciliation completed.

This part of the chapter is all of one piece; but for convenience we may divide it into three, according to the subject matter. The Apostle speaks first of his longing for the arrival of Titus, and of his relief at the tidings which he brought (5-7), especially about the great offender and the Apostle's painful

---

* Cf. Τότε στήσεται ἐν παρρησίᾳ πολλῇ ὁ δίκαιος (Wisd. v. 1): λάβετε σκῦλα καὶ μετὰ παρρησίας (1 Macc. iv. 18): also Heb. iii. 6, iv. 16, x. 35.

letter (8–12); and finally he speaks of the joy of Titus at being
able to bring such good tidings (13–16).

The close parallel with the description of Timothy's mission
to Thessalonica, and the Apostle's anxiety, followed by joy at
the happy result (1 Thess. iii. 1–9), should be noted.

5 For indeed, even after I had got as far as Macedonia, my
poor suffering frame found no relief, but at every turn I found
something to distress me; round about me were bitter conflicts
for and against me, within me were haunting fears as to how it
would all end. **6** I was almost in despair; but God, who is ever
ready to comfort the depressed, comforted me then by the
arrival and company of Titus. **7** Yes, and not only by his arrival
and company, but also by the comfort with which you comforted
him in his intercourse with you; for he gave a most welcome
report of how you longed for reconciliation with me, how you
lamented the trouble that you had caused, how eagerly you
espoused my cause; so that this still further increased my joy.

8 Because, although I know that I gave you pain by the letter
which I sent you, I cannot bring myself to regret it. When I
saw that that letter gave you pain, although only for a season,
I was inclined to regret it; **9** but now I am very glad,—not glad
because you were pained, but because your pain issued in
repentance. For you were pained in God's way and not in the
world's way, and it was His will that you should not be the worse
for anything that we did. **10** For the pain which is directed in
God's way leads to a repentance whose fruit is salvation, a
repentance which can never be regarded with regret; whereas
the pain which the heathen world inflicts on those who belong
to it works out into moral ruin. **11** For see! it was this very
thing, your being pained in God's way, and not anything else,
which did so much for you. See what earnestness it worked out
in you, how keen you were to clear yourselves from just reproach,
how indignant with the chief offender, how alarmed as to what
the consequences might be, how eager for my forgiveness and
return, how zealous in condemning evil, how stern in punishing
it. In every one of these points you put yourselves right and
purged yourselves from complicity in this distressing matter.
12 So then, although I did not let things slide but wrote severely
to you, it was not in order to get the wrong-doer punished, nor
yet to have the wronged man avenged. No, I wrote in order to

bring out clearly before you all what a genuine interest you do take in us; I wrote as in God's sight, with a full sense of responsibility. [13] It is this right conduct of yours and my own consciousness of having meant well that is such a comfort to me. But over and above our own comfort we were the more exceedingly glad at the gladness of Titus; for refreshment and repose have come to his spirit, thanks to all of you. [14] For I told him how I gloried in you, how proud I was of you, and I have had no reason to be ashamed of what I said. You have not come short of my commendation of you. Just as all that we said to you was said in truth, so all that we said before Titus in praise of you has turned out to be quite true. [15] And he feels as we do. His inmost heart goes out the more abundantly towards you, as often as he recalls the ready obedience of all of you, and how timidly and nervously anxious you were in the reception which you gave him. [16] I am indeed glad that in every particular I can be of good courage in respect of you.

5. Καὶ γὰρ ἐλθόντων ἡμῶν εἰς Μακεδονίαν. 'For indeed when we were come into Macedonia.' He is going back to ii. 13, where he tells us that even the excellent opening for preaching the Gospel which he found at Troas could not keep him there, because of his intense anxiety about Corinth, and so he crossed to Macedonia in order to meet Titus the sooner and learn how the Corinthians had taken his rebukes. So that we may regard the whole of ii. 14–vii. 4 as a digression. The fact that it exists makes the hypothesis that vi. 14–vii. 1 is a digression all the more probable. It is St Paul's way to dart off to some important side-topic and then return to what he had previously been saying. He would probably land at Philippi. But *coelum non animum mutat*; he is just as feverishly anxious in Macedonia as he had been in Troas.

οὐδεμίαν ἔσχηκεν ἄνεσιν ἡ σὰρξ ἡμῶν. In ii. 13 he says οὐκ ἔσχηκα ἄνεσιν τῷ πνεύματί μου. If there were any reason for wishing to get rid of either that passage or this, we should be told by some critics that it is impossible that St Paul, who else-where opposes σάρξ and πνεῦμα, can have written both. See above on μολυσμοῦ σαρκὸς καὶ πνεύματος (*v.* 1). Language was made for man, not man for language. The use of words in a technical sense does not bar the writer from using them else-where in a popular sense. Here ἡ σάρξ is the sphere, not of sin, but of suffering. Intense anxiety affects both flesh and spirit. In both passages we have the perf. ; cf. i. 9 ; Rom. v. 2. In all four places we might have expected the aor., and hence the reading ἔσχεν here. See on i. 9 and ii. 13. For ἄνεσιν see on ii. 13 ; also Index IV.

ἐν παντὶ θλιβόμενοι. 'In every way pressed,' as in iv. 8. He was experiencing every kind of tribulation. The participle without any verb is irregular, but intelligible and not rare ; cf. ix. 11, xi. 6, and other instances quoted in Moulton, p. 182. Here παρεκλήθημεν might be understood, but it is not required. Ἐν παντί is very freq. in 2 Cor., and often first with emphasis ; vi. 4, ix. 8, xi. 6, 9. What follows explains ἐν παντί : the pressure was both external and internal.

ἔξωθεν μάχαι. What these conflicts in Macedonia were we cannot tell ; Chrysostom thinks they were with unbelievers. The asyndeton is impressive, as in vv. 2–4.

ἔσωθεν φόβοι. The conflicts would produce fears as to the issue, but his chief fears, as the context shows, were about the state of things at Corinth. Mental perturbations, Augustine points out, are not wrong. "The citizens of the Holy City of God, who live according to God in the pilgrimage of this life, fear and desire, grieve and rejoice. . . . That fear of which the Apostle John says, 'Perfect love casteth out fear,' is not of the same kind as that which the Apostle Paul felt lest the Corinthians should be subdued by the subtlety of the serpent ; for love is susceptible of this fear, yea, love alone is capable of it' (*De Civ. Dei*, xiv. 9).

ἐσχηκεν (א C D E L P) rather than ἔσχεν (B F G K), a correction, because the perf. seemed to be out of place. C F G, Latt. Syrr. have ἐσχ. after ἄνεσιν.

6. ἀλλ' ὁ παρακαλῶν τοὺς ταπεινούς. 'But He who comforteth the downcast.' The context shows that 'the lowly' (RV.) is here not the meaning of τ. ταπεινούς. It means 'those that are cast down ' (AV.), 'the dejected, the depressed'; these rather than the lowly require to be comforted. In Ecclus. xxv. 23 a wicked woman is said to produce καρδία ταπεινὴ καὶ πρόσωπον σκυθρωπόν, which RV. renders 'abasement of heart and sadness of countenance.' The wording here (cf. i. 3) comes from Is. xlix. 13, τοὺς ταπεινοὺς τοῦ λαοῦ αὐτοῦ παρεκάλεσεν. Cf. Is. xl. 1, 11, li. 3, 12, lxi. 2, lxvi. 13.

ἐν τῇ παρουσίᾳ T. 'By the arrival and company of T.' The word implies not only the coming but the staying ; a παρουσία lasts some time. Deissmann (*Light from the Anc. East*, pp. 372, 382) has shown that it was a technical term to denote the visit of a potentate or his representative, and hence its ready transfer to the Second Advent. No such meaning attaches to it here. St Paul is not suggesting that the return of Titus to him was of an official character, but perhaps he desires to intimate that the coming meant a great deal to himself. The ἐν is instrumental rather than local, it gives the means rather than the sphere of the comforting ; cf. ἐν φόβῳ Θεοῦ (*v.* 1).

7. ἐφ᾽ ὑμῖν. The exact meaning of this is uncertain ; perhaps 'over you' is safest, indicating that the Corinthians were the basis of the comfort. Comp. the parallel passage, 1 Thess. iii. 7. **ἀναγγέλλων ἡμῖν.** 'While he told us.' The actual making of his report was a comfort to Titus. In strict grammar we ought to have ἀναγγέλλοντος, but the participle is attracted to the verb, almost inevitably.

ἐπιπόθησιν. We have to conjecture the object of this 'longing'; to be on good terms once more with the Apostle may be right, or perhaps to see him again. The noun is very rare in Bibl. Grk. (*v.* 11 ; Ezek. xxiii. 11), but ἐπιποθεῖν occurs in all groups of the Pauline Epp. and is not rare in LXX.

ὀδυρμόν. 'Lamentation' (Mt. ii. 18) for having caused so much distress.

ζῆλον. 'Zeal' (*v.* 11, ix. 2) for the Apostle against those who had attacked him, or eagerness to carry out his wishes. Trench, *Syn.* § xxvi. For the exclusively Pauline ὑμῶν between the art. and the noun (thrice in this verse) see on i. 6 and xii. 19.

ὥστε με μᾶλλον χαρῆναι. The μᾶλλον may be understood in several ways. (1) 'So that I rejoiced still more'; the meeting with Titus delighted him; the report that Titus gave of the Corinthians increased his delight. (2) 'So that I rejoiced rather than was merely comforted.' (3) 'So that I rejoiced instead of being distressed.' The first is best. The threefold ὑμῶν throws light on the meaning. It was the Corinthians' longing, the Corinthians' lamentation, the Corinthians' eagerness which inspired Titus with such joy. Previously the longing, lamentation, and eagerness had been St Paul's, and it was a delight to his emissary to find similar feelings in the Corinthians. With characteristic tact the Apostle attributes his own happiness to the comfort which the Corinthians had given to Titus and which Titus had communicated to him. He does not tell the Corinthians that he had doubted as to how they would take his letter, and how great had been his anxiety as to its possible effect. The position of μᾶλλον and the contents of *v.* 13 favour (1) rather than (2) or (3).

8. ὅτι εἰ καὶ ἐλύπησα ὑμᾶς ἐν τῇ ἐπιστολῇ, οὐ μεταμέλομαι. 'Because, though I made you sorrowful (see on ii. 2) in my letter, I do not regret it.' That he pained them by what he wrote is treated as a fact; εἰ καί rather than καὶ εἰ: see on iv. 3. The difference between μεταμέλομαι (Mt. xxi. 30, 32, xxvii. 3 ; Heb. vii. 21 from Ps. cix. [cx.] 4) and μετανοέω (xii. 21 ; Acts ii. 38, iii. 19 ; etc.) is fairly represented by the difference between 'regret' and 'repent,' but no hard and fast line can be drawn, such as that the former refers to transitory feelings respecting details, while the latter implies moral choice affecting the whole life. Either verb is used either way. But, as the derivations show, μετανοέω has the richer and more serious meaning. Trench, *Syn.* § lxix.

εἰ καὶ μετεμελόμην. See crit. note below. Whether we read βλέπω or βλέπων, we may take νῦν χαίρω as the apodosis of εἰ καὶ μετ., and treat what lies between as a parenthesis. This is somewhat awkward when written, but might easily be given in dictation. 'Though I *was* inclined to regret it—I see that that letter, though but for a time, made you sorrowful—*now* I rejoice.' We may put it more smoothly thus; 'I see that that letter gave you pain, though only for a while; *at the time* I was inclined to regret having written it, but *now* I am very glad.' 'Εκείνη puts the letter away from him; it is remote from his present attitude. It is quite clear that he had written a letter about which he had had misgivings and regrets; he could have wished that he had not written it. It is difficult to agree with those who think that he could ever have had such feelings about 1 Corinthians. Could he for a moment have regretted having written such a letter? There must have been another letter of a much more painful character. See on i. 17, ii. 3, 9. If 2 Cor. x.–xiii. is part of that letter, it is easy to point to passages which he might sometimes wish that he had never written.*

The arrangement given above is that of Tisch., WH., and the American Revisers, but RV. gives it no recognition, perhaps because of its apparent awkwardness. AV. capriciously renders ἐπιστολή first 'letter' and then 'Epistle,' and treats ἐλύπησεν as a perf., as if the pain still continued, which the Apostle certainly did not mean to imply.

πρὸς ὥραν. The pain will not last; there is nothing that need rankle; the present letter will entirely extinguish it. Gal. ii. 5 and Philem. 15 show that the expression may be used of either a short or a long time, either a few minutes or several months. The main point is that an end is certain. Cf. πρὸς καιρόν (1 Cor. vii. 5; Lk. viii. 13), πρὸς ὀλίγον (1 Tim. iv. 8), and πρὸς καιρὸν ὥρας (1 Thess. ii. 17). It is possible that εἰ καὶ πρὸς ὥραν ἐλύπησεν ὑμᾶς should be taken together, 'although it pained you for a season,' and that the sentence is left unfinished. Perhaps some such words as 'has had excellent effects' ought to have followed. However we unravel the confused constr., the general sense is clear.

* "We must remember that we have not the letter in its entirety. Are not the passages which he most repented those which have disappeared?" (Rendall, *The Epp. of St. Paul to the Corinthians*, p. 69).

After ἐν τῇ ἐπιστολῇ D* E* F G, d e f g add μου. B inserts δέ between εἰ and καί. ℵ D² E F G K L P, f g Syrr. Copt. insert γάρ after βλέπω. In all three cases we may omit. Lachmann and Hort would follow Vulg. (videns) and read βλέπων, βλεπῶ having been read as βλεπω. Videns, like the insertion of γάρ, may be an attempt to smooth the constr.

Only to those who believe in verbal inspiration in the most rigid sense could this verse cause any difficulty, other than that of reading and constr. There is no need even to ask the question, "How could an inspired Apostle ever regret what he had written?" Such questions belong to views about Holy Scripture which criticism has demonstrated to be untenable. The Apostle himself would scarcely have understood what such a question meant. If he did, he might ask, "Do you suppose that I never make a mistake?"

9. ἀλλ' ὅτι ἐλυπήθητε εἰς μετάνοιαν. With much delicacy, he makes them rather than himself the cause of his present happiness. It was not his letter, the writing of which was no pleasure to him, but their way of receiving it, which produced so much joy. He claims no credit for it.

ἐλυπήθητε γὰρ κατὰ Θεόν. 'For you were made sorrowful in God's way'; *i.e.* as God would have you sorrowful; not 'owing to the grace of God,' 'thanks to His help.' Cf. Rom. viii. 27; 4 Macc. xv. 2. 'God's way' is opposed to man's way and the devil's way.

ἵνα ἐν μηδενὶ ζημιωθῆτε ἐξ ἡμῶν. Such was God's intention; 'that in nothing ye might suffer loss (1 Cor. iii. 15; Lk. ix. 25) at our hands.' If he had not urged them to change their course, that would have been great loss to them and great blame to him. God did not will either his negligence or their loss. It is unnatural to make ἵνα depend upon ἀλλ' ὅτι ἐλ. εἰς μενάνοιαν.*

10. μετάνοιαν εἰς σωτηρίαν ἀμεταμέλητον. The adj. belongs to μετάνοιαν. There is no need to say that salvation brings no regret. To make this clear we must repeat; 'repentance unto salvation, a repentance which bringeth no regret' (RV.), or 'repentance which bringeth no regret, repentance unto salvation.' 'Repentance not to be repented of' (AV.) is a pleasing verbal antithesis, like 'righteousness with unrighteousness' (vi. 14), but neither is justified by the Greek.† Vulg. has *paenitentiam in salutem stabilem operatur*, and *stabilem* can be taken readily with *salutem* without perpetrating a truism; but *stabilis* is not an

---

* It is remarkable that μετάνοια occurs only four times in the Pauline Epistles, twice in these two verses and once in Rom. ii. 4 and 2 Tim. ii. 25, while μετανοέω occurs only in 2 Cor. xii. 21. This does not imply "the almost complete omission of the twin Rabbinic ideas of repentance and forgiveness" (C. G. Montefiore, *Judaism and St. Paul*, p. 75). These words are rare, but the thought of forgiveness, such as he himself had won, is often present as reconciliation to God.

† *Superest ne rursus provinciae, quod damnasse dicitur, placeat, agatque poenitentiam poenitentiae suae* (Plin. *Ep.* vii. 10).

accurate rendering of ἀμεταμέλητος. In Rom. xi. 29 Vulg. has *sine paenitentia* for ἀμετ. Εἰς σωτηρίαν is freq. in Paul, being found in all groups (Rom. i. 16, x. 1, 10; Phil. i. 19; 2 Thess. ii. 13; 2 Tim. iii. 15), but nowhere does he weaken σωτηρία by giving it an epithet.

ἡ δὲ τοῦ κόσμου λύπη θάνατον κατεργάζεται. 'But the sorrow of the world worketh out death.' The Revisers adopt the reading κατεργάζεται (see below), but make no difference between it and ἐργάζεται, and Vulg. has *operatur* in both places; ἡ κατὰ Θεὸν λύπη 'works' or 'promotes' σωτηρία, ἡ τ. κόσμου λ. 'works out' or 'produces' θάνατον. Cf. Rom. vii. 13.* Perhaps the reference is chiefly to sorrow for sin, and Cain, Esau, and Judas may be illustrations of the wrong kind of sorrow. But we need not confine the verse to that. Sorrow for worldly losses and troubles does not lessen them; indeed sorrow for sickness may aggravate the disease and prevent recovery; but sorrow for sin may cure the sin. Affliction which is not taken as discipline, but resented as unreasonable, hardens and deadens the soul: submission to God's will brings peace. Moreover, men regret the sorrow which they feel for worldly losses, but they do not regret the sorrow which cures sin. Cf. ἔστιν αἰσχύνη ἐπάγουσα ἁμαρτίαν, καὶ ἔστιν αἰσχύνη δόξα καὶ χάρις (Ecclus. iv. 21). In the Testaments (*Gad* v. 7) there seems to be a reminiscence of this passage; ἡ γὰρ κατὰ θεὸν ἀληθὴς μετάνοια . . . ὁδηγεῖ τὸ διαβούλιον πρὸς σωτηρίαν. See Heinrici-Meyer.

ἐργάζεται (א* B C D E P 37) after ἀμεταμέλητον is to be preferred to κατεργάζεται (א³ G K L), which is assimilation to the next clause.

11. ἰδοὺ γάρ. He wants them to see how they themselves afford an example of the right kind of λύπη and its fruits. 'For behold, this very thing, your being sorrowful in God's way, what earnestness (see on viii. 7) it worked out in you.' He looks back to what was said in *v.* 7, and in his desire to give them full credit for the excellent change in them he adds a great deal to what was said before; in *v.* 7 we have three particulars, here we have seven. He is brimming over with affectionate delight.† The repeated ἀλλά means '*but* moreover,' '*but* over and above this,' and the same effect is produced in English with either 'yea' or 'nay.' Blass, § 77. 13.

ἀλλὰ ἀπολογίαν. Not merely earnestness instead of their previous indifference; but 'self-vindication.' They were anxious to exculpate themselves and show that they had not abetted the offender or condoned his offence.

* See the Essay and the Sermon on these words by F. Paget, *The Spirit of Discipline*, pp. 1 f. and 51 f.
† A steady reformation is a more decisive test of the value of mourning than depth of grief" (F. W. Robertson).

ἀγανάκτησιν. Indignation at the shame brought upon the Church. Ἀγανακτέω occurs several times in the Synoptists, but here only does the noun occur. Cf. Thuc. II. xli. 3.

φόβον. *Ne cum virga venirem* (Beng.); but we need not restrict it to that. God's judgments may be included. Indeed it is unlikely that St Paul would put fear of himself in the foreground. 'Happy is the man that feareth alway' (Prov. xxviii. 14).

ἐπιπόθησιν. Yearning for the Apostle's favour and return. Yearning for their own improvement, *quo desideratis in melius provehi* (Herveius), is less probable.

ζῆλον. Zeal for God and the Apostle and against the evil which dishonours both.

ἐκδίκησιν. Avenging, in punishing the offender, about which there had been difficulty (ii. 6). It is placed last, possibly for that reason, or possibly because St Paul does not now regard it of great importance. Enough had been done to vindicate the authority which had been outraged. Ἐκδίκησις is from ἔκδικος (1 Thess. iv. 6; Rom. xiii. 4) through ἐκδικέω (x. 6; Rom. xii. 19). Hort (on 1 Pet. ii. 14) says, "In both LXX and N.T. ἐκδίκησις stands for both 'avenging' or 'vindication,' and, as here, for 'vengeance,' 'requital.' This sense is specially abundant in Ecclus." Bengel and Meyer arrange the last six items in pairs, dealing respectively with the shame of the Church, feeling towards the Apostle, and treatment of the offender. But the grouping is perhaps fanciful: ἀγανάκτησις may have reference to the offender, and ζῆλος to the Apostle. The grouping is probably not intended by St Paul.

ἐν παντὶ συνεστήσατε ἑαυτούς. 'In everyone of these points ye approved yourselves.' See on *v.* 5. He acquits them of all responsibility for the offence which was committed. At first they had been to blame. By not protesting against the outrage they had seemed to acquiesce in it, but all this had been put right by their reception of Titus and submission to Paul's letter.

ἁγνοὺς εἶναι τῷ πράγματι. 'To be pure in the matter,' to be purged from all complicity in it, because they no longer felt any sympathy with it. St Paul does not say γενέσθαι but εἶναι: he does not wish to hint that they had not always been ἁγνοί. Ἁγνός marks predominantly a feeling, and καθαρός a state (Westcott on 1 Jn. iii. 3). The indefinite τῷ πράγματι points to a disagreeable subject which he does not care to specify; the Corinthians know all about the unhappy business. Neither the use of this vague term (1 Thess. iv. 6) nor ἁγνούς (xi. 2) is any argument for the incredible identification of this offender (ii. 5) with the incestuous Corinthian (1 Cor. v. 1).

After λυπηθῆναι, א³ D E K L P, d e Vulg. add ὑμᾶς.   א* B C F G 17,
g omit.   κατειργάσατο (א B³ C G K L P) rather than κατηργάσατο (B*D E).
Before ὑμιν, א³ C F G P, f g Vulg. Syrr. read ἐν.   א* B D E L K omit.
א B C D*F G, f g omit the ἐν before τῷ πράγματι, which is probably an
insertion to ease the construction.

12. ἄρα εἰ καὶ ἔγραψα ὑμῖν.   'So then, although I did write to
you.'   The subject seems to be closed, and yet the Apostle does
not end here.   The excellent results of the mission of Titus and
St Paul's intense joy have been fully described, but something
more is added as a sort of explanatory appendix.   He goes on
to explain why he wrote the letter which has borne such good
fruit.   There was one point in which it had partially failed, for
the Corinthians had not treated the offender in the way in which
he had expected; they had been more lenient than he had
perhaps suggested.   But he has assured them that he is content
with what was done and does not desire anything further (ii. 5 f.);
and he now tells them that his main object in writing was not
to get the offender punished, or the person who was offended
righted, but to give them an opportunity of showing how loyal
they really were to himself.   We may regard it as almost certain
that the person offended was himself.   His whole treatment of
τὸ πρᾶγμα is in harmony with this view.   This is another allusion
to the severe letter.

> The ἄρα here is equivalent to ὥστε with a finite verb; 'so then,'
> 'accordingly,' 'consequently.'   In class. Grk. it is almost invariably sub-
> joined to another word, as in 1 Cor. vii. 14; Rom. vii. 21; Gal. iii. 7;
> etc., and is hardly ever placed first, as here; 1 Cor. xv. 18; Rom. x. 17;
> Gal. v. 11.

οὐχ ἕνεκεν τοῦ ἀδικήσαντος.   St Paul is always exhibiting
Hebrew modes of thought and language.   In Jewish literature
we often have two alternatives, one of which is negatived, without meaning that it is negatived absolutely, but only in comparison with the other alternative, which is much more important.
'I will have mercy, and not sacrifice' (Hos. vi. 6) does not
prohibit sacrifice; it affirms that mercy is much the better of
the two.   Cf. Mk. ix. 37; Lk. x. 20, xiv. 12, xxiii. 28.   Here
St Paul does not mean that he had no thought of the offender
or the offended person in writing; he means that they were not
the main cause of his doing so.   His object was to get the
Corinthian Church out of the false position in which it was in
reference to himself.   That was the thing for which he chiefly
cared, and in comparison with that all other ends were as
nothing.   Cf. 1 Cor. i. 17.   Is it possible to believe that the
letter to which allusion is here made is 1 Corinthians?
It is still less possible to believe that τοῦ ἀδικήσαντος is the
incestuous person of 1 Cor. v. 1.   St Paul would hardly have

regarded such a sin as a personal injury to an individual; it was a monstrous injury to the whole of the Corinthian Church. But there is a stronger reason than this. If ὁ ἀδικήσας is the man who had his father's wife, then ὁ ἀδικηθείς must be the man's father, who was *alive* when the son committed incest with his father's wife. Disorderly as the Corinthian Church was, it is difficult to believe that one of its members would be guilty of taking his father's wife while his father was living, and that the rest of the Church, so far from being scandalized, were as much puffed up with self-complacency as usual (see cn 1 Cor. v. 2). What is said about forgiving the offender (iv. 5 f.) is strangely worded, if he was an offender of such heinousness.

It is *possible* that ὁ ἀδικηθείς was Timothy (Hastings, *DB*. iv. p. 768), but almost certainly it was St Paul himself (*DB*. iii. p. 711).* That hypothesis satisfies all requirements, especially with regard to the reserve with which he speaks of the matter. The Corinthians would understand. Who ὁ ἀδικήσας was was known to them, but is unknown to us. He was probably a turbulent Corinthian who in some outrageous and public manner had defied the Apostle's authority. Now that the Corinthians had withdrawn all sympathy from him and had submissively sought reconciliation with St Paul, it did not matter whether the punishment inflicted by the congregation had been adequate or not.

ἀλλ' ἕνεκεν τοῦ φανερωθῆναι τὴν σπουδὴν ὑμῶν τὴν ὑπὲρ ἡμῶν πρὸς ὑμᾶς. Not for either of these ends, 'but in order that your earnestness on our behalf might be made manifest unto you.' If the same translation is to be given to ἕνεκεν in all three places, we may say, 'not in order to punish the wrong-doer, nor yet in order to avenge the wronged, but in order, etc.' The main object was to get the Corinthians to realize their true state of mind respecting the Apostle. In the friction and excitement of the recent crisis they had fancied that they could part from him with a light heart; but his letter showed them what casting him off would mean, and they found that the ties which bound them to him could not be so easily broken. They cared for him too much for that. 'Unto you' is simpler and more telling than 'among you' or 'with you' (1 Thess. iii. 4) for πρὸς ὑμᾶς. It was unto *themselves* that this revelation had to be made; they did not know the state of their own hearts till the shock of the letter came. With ὑμῶν . . . πρὸς ὑμᾶς comp. i. 11.

ἐνώπιον τοῦ Θεοῦ. Placed last with emphatic solemnity, as in iv. 2 (see the last note there). The words are to be taken with

---

* Bousset says with reason; *so gibt diese Wendung nur dann einen erträglichen Sinn, wenn man annimt, dass Paulus selbst der Betroffene sei.*

ἔγραψα : he wrote with a deep sense of responsibility. God would judge of his reason for writing and of the words which he said.

In this verse we twice have in MSS. the common confusion between ἡμεῖς and ὑμεῖς. The reading of Vulg., *sollicitudinem nostram, quam pro vobis habemus*, and of T. R., τ. σπουδὴν ἡμῶν τ. ὑπὲρ ὑμῶν, is inconsistent with the context. He did not write to manifest his zeal for them, but to bring out their zeal for him. The σπουδή in this verse is the same as in *v.* 10. B C D² E K L P, e Syrr. Copt. have τ. σπ. ὑμῶν τ. ὑπὲρ ἡμῶν.

13. **διὰ τοῦτο παρακεκλήμεθα.** 'For this cause (because our good purpose was accomplished in bringing your loyalty to light) we have been and are comforted.' These words, with a full stop after them, should have been given to *v.* 12. Chrysostom ends a Homily with them, and he begins another (xvi.) with the words which follow. A teacher is comforted by the progress of his pupils, a spiritual ruler by the loyalty of the ruled ; and spiritual rule is the highest of all arts.

Ἐπὶ δὲ τῇ παρακλήσει ἡμῶν. 'But over and above our personal comfort.' The δέ is certainly rightly placed here (see below), and it bars the rendering of Luther, Beza, and AV., which takes ἐπὶ τ. π. with the preceding παρακεκλήμεθα, reading ὑμῶν for ἡμῶν, 'we were comforted in your comfort.' This does not fit the context.

περισσοτέρως μᾶλλον ἐχάρημεν ἐπὶ τῇ χαρᾷ Τίτου. 'My own comfort was great ; in addition to it came the more abundant joy at the joy of Titus.' The strengthening of the comparative with a pleonastic μᾶλλον is not rare ; μᾶλλον περισσότερον ἐκήρυσσον (Mk. vii. 36) ; πολλῷ γὰρ μᾶλλον κρεῖσσον (Phil. i. 23). It is found in class. Grk. Blass, § 44. 5 ; Wetstein on Phil. i. 23. In xii. 9 μᾶλλον does not strengthen ἥδιστα, but belongs to καυχήσομαι.

ὅτι ἀναπέπαυται τὸ πνεῦμα αὐτοῦ ἀπὸ πάντων ὑμῶν. 'Because his spirit has been refreshed, thanks to all of you.' Cf. ἀνέπαυσαν γὰρ τὸ ἐμὸν πνεῦμα (1 Cor. xvi. 18 ; see note there). In Philem. 7, 20 we have τὰ σπλάγχνα for τὸ πνεῦμα. "The compound ἀναπαύεσθαι expresses a temporary relief, as the simple παύεσθαι a final cessation" (Lightfoot), a truce as distinct from a peace. It is refreshment and relief which Christ promises to the weary and heavy laden, not a permanent removal of their burdens, ἀναπαύσω ὑμᾶς (Mt. xi. 28). For ἀπό where ὑπό might have stood, 'at the hands of' rather than 'by,' cf. πολλὰ παθεῖν ἀπὸ τῶν πρεσβυτέρων (Mt. xvi. 21 ; also Lk. vii. 35, xvii. 25 ; Jas. i. 13). Blass, § 40. 3. This πάντων ὑμῶν is repeated in *v.* 15. The whole Corinthian Church had had a share in making this happy impression on Titus, and he was deeply grateful to them for it. The Apostle is careful to let them know this, because

Titus is to return to them to carry out the arrangements for the collection for the poor at Jerusalem (viii. 6, 16).

δέ is certainly to be retained after ἐπί, and to be omitted after περισσο-τέρως, with ℵ B C D F G K L P, Latt. Goth. The insertion after περισσ. has very little authority. A few cursives and Arm. omit δέ altogether. F K L, Copt. have τῇ παρακλήσει ὑμῶν, another confusion of the two pronouns, as in v. 12.

14. ὅτι εἴ τι αὐτῷ ὑπὲρ ὑμῶν κεκαύχημαι, οὐ κατῃσχύνθην. 'For if in anything I have gloried to him on your behalf, I was not put to shame.' This is added in explanation of the great relief which the conduct of the Corinthians had been to Titus. Titus had accepted the mission to Corinth with serious misgivings; his overtures might be rejected with contempt and violence. St Paul had praised the Corinthians to him, and had assured him that the strained situation would pass, because they were thoroughly sound at heart. St Paul is now able to tell them that his praise of them had been completely justified by their subsequent conduct. He was 'not put to shame' (RV.) by being proved to be utterly mistaken about them. Titus had found that the Apostle's high estimate of them was correct. The Corinthians were rightminded people who knew how to listen to reason and respect authority. He had told them to welcome and obey Titus, and they had done so; and this had quite won Titus' heart. For κεκαύχημαι see on ix. 2.

ὡς πάντα ἐν ἀληθείᾳ κ.τ.λ. 'As we spake all things to you in truth, so our glorying also before Titus was proved to be truth.' For ἐπί = 'in the presence of,' 'before,' cf. 1 Cor. vi. 1, 6; Mk. xiii. 9; Acts xxv. 9. The introductory ἀλλά means, 'On the contrary; so far from my being put to shame, etc.' He appeals to his own truthfulness and sincerity, which had been challenged at Corinth and had been proved to be real: ὑμῖν and ἐπὶ Τίτου balance one another, and there is a sort of chiasmus; ἐν ἀληθείᾳ ὑμῖν . . . ἐπὶ Τίτου ἀλήθεια. The first ἀλήθεια is subjective, the second is objective.

πάντα (ℵ B D E K L P, Latt.) rather than πάντοτε (C F G, g Copt.). C D E P, Latt. have ὑμῖν ἐν ἀληθείᾳ by assimilation of order to ἐπὶ Τ. ἀλ. No ἡ before ἐπὶ Τ. (ℵ* B).

15. καὶ τὰ σπλάγχνα αὐτοῦ. 'And so his heart goes out to you the more abundantly,' *i.e.* still more than before he came to you and had this happy experience.* They received him as the Galatians received St Paul (Gal. iv. 14), in spite of the stern letter which he brought. Hence his affection for them when he recalls it all. Cf. αἱ καρδίαι αὐτῶν εἰς πονηρίαν (Dan. xi. 27, Theod.).

* But it is possible that περισσοτέρως is simply 'very abundantly' and implies no comparison with any other occasion.

τὴν πάντων ὑμῶν ὑπακοήν. These words indicate that Titus had very definite demands to make, and that compliance with them was universal. There was no thought of rebellion against the Apostle or his delegate. μετὰ φόβου καὶ τρόμου. This strong expression suggests something more than that they were afraid that they could not do enough to please him. St Paul himself had confessed to having had this feeling when he first begun his work in Corinth (1 Cor. ii. 3), and in him it meant *a nervous anxiety to do his duty.** No other N.T. writer uses the phrase, and this seems to be its meaning in the four places in which it occurs. The other two are Eph. vi. 5 and Phil. ii. 12, where see Lightfoot. In Eph. vi. 5 this 'fear and trembling' is opposed to 'eye-service.' In Is. xix. 16, ἐν φόβῳ καὶ ἐν τρόμῳ means actual terror.

16. Χαίρω ὅτι ἐν παντὶ θαρρῶ ἐν ὑμῖν. A joyous conclusion to the whole section (vi. 11–vii. 16), added impressively without any connecting particle. The οὖν, 'therefore' (AV.) is one of those freq. insertions made by scribes and translators (here Goth. Arm.) for the sake of smoothness, and such smoothness generally involves weakness. It does not much matter how we take ὅτι, whether 'I rejoice *that*,' or 'I rejoice *because*.' The translation of θαρρῶ is more important; 'I am of good courage' (RV.), as in x. 1, 2, rather than 'I have confidence' (AV.). If x.–xiii. is part of the painful letter which preceded i.–ix., this verse may refer to x. 1, 2. There he is of good courage in standing out against some of them; here he is of good courage about the present obedience of all of them, and (as he hopes) about their readiness to help in raising money for the poor at Jerusalem. This verse prepares the way for the request which he is about to urge in viii. and ix. Their past good works and present loyalty give him courage in pressing this matter upon them. See on i. 23, ii. 3, 9, iv. 2, v. 13, vii. 2 for other instances in which these first nine chapters seem to refer to passages in the last four. Whatever may be the truth about this or any other possible reference, the Apostle's mood and judgment must have changed extraordinarily, if, after dictating these verses (13–16), he dictated xii. 20, 21 as part of the same letter.

ἐν ὑμῖν. 'Concerning you'; cf. ἀποροῦμαι ἐν ὑμῖν, 'I am perplexed about you' (Gal. iv. 20); lit. 'in your case.' Others explain that the *root* of the courage or the perplexity is *in* them, and translate 'through you.' The difference is not very great.

The reconciliation between the Apostle and the Corinthians is now complete; and with this verse the first main division of

---

* "In the same spirit with which a young man of character would work, who was starting in business on capital advanced by a friend" (Denney).

the Epistle (i. 12–vii. 16) ends. *Sicut sapiens medicus jam paene sanata vulnera lenissimis medicamentis curabat, ut prioris increpationis usura sanaretur* (Herveius).

Before leaving this chapter we must notice once more its exuberant and passionate tone. The Apostle " lets himself go," and can hardly find language in which to express his appreciation of the present attitude of the Corinthians towards himself and Titus, and his consequent joy over them and over the joy which they have produced in Titus. Words expressive of comfort, rejoicing, glorying, boldness, and courage occur with surprising frequency, as if he could not repeat them too often. We have παρακαλέω four times, παράκλησις thrice, χαίρω four times, χαρά twice, καύχησις twice, καυχάομαι and πορρησία and θαρρῶ once each. With regard to the good conduct of the Corinthians we have ζῆλος twice, σπουδή twice, μετάνοια twice, φόβος twice, together with ὑπακοή and other terms of approbation. And all this is within the compass of fifteen, or rather of thirteen verses. It is all the more necessary to notice this because of the very marked change of tone which is at once evident directly we leave this part of the Epistle and begin to study the next two chapters. The change of subject causes a sudden cessation of this overflowing enthusiasm and generosity of language. So far from letting himself go, the Apostle manifestly feels that he is treading on delicate ground, and that he must be cautious about what he says and the language in which he says it. The Epistle is full of rapid changes of feeling, perhaps caused in some cases by breaks in the times of dictating. Here it is the new subject that causes the change.

VIII. 1-IX. 15. THE COLLECTION FOR THE POOR CHRISTIANS AT JERUSALEM.

This is the second of the main divisions of the Epistle, and it may be divided into five sections, which, however, are made for convenience of study, without any assumption that they were intended by the Apostle. In viii. 1–7 he sets forth the Example of Liberality set by the Macedonian congregations; viii. 8–15 he points to the Example of Christ and indicates the proportion to be observed in contributing; viii. 16–24 he informs the Corinthians that this new Mission to them is to be entrusted to Titus with two others; ix. 1–5 he exhorts them to have everything ready when he comes; and ix. 6–15 he exhorts them to be liberal, for their own sakes and for the good of the Church.

The subject of this Palestine Relief Fund is mentioned in four places in N.T. ; 1 Cor. xvi. 1–3 ; these two chapters ; Rom. xv. 26, 27 ; Acts xxiv. 17. Paley (*Horae Paulinae*, ii. 1) has shown how these four passages fit into one another and explain one another, and his arguments well repay study. The fact that St Paul mentions the collection of this fund in three of his four great Epistles, and that in this one he devotes so large a portion of the letter to the subject, is evidence that he took a very keen interest in the matter and was most anxious that the collection should be a success; and there was no place in which it was more important that the collection should be a generous one than at Corinth. The distress at Jerusalem was great; that was an argument that could be urged everywhere. But it was specially fitting that it should be pressed home in Gentile Churches; for seeing that the Gentiles had been admitted to share the spiritual possessions of the Jews, it was not unreasonable that the Jews should be admitted to a share of the worldly possessions of the Gentiles. If this was freely done, the union of Jew and Gentile in Christ would be shown to be a very real and practical thing, and would be made all the more binding in future. "This collection formed the one visible expression of that brotherly unity which otherwise was rooted merely in their common faith" (Harnack, *Mission and Expansion*, i. p. 183). It was specially desirable that Corinth should come to the front in this matter. Here Judaizing teachers had been at work, claiming to have the sanction of the Mother Church at Jerusalem, and denying that St Paul had any such sanction; they said that he had no authority from the Twelve and was disowned by them. Therefore, if he succeeded in raising a good sum in Corinth for the Jerusalem poor, it would show Christians in Palestine that his authority in Corinth was an influence for good, and show his detractors that he was on good terms with the Mother Church. But perhaps his chief aim was to strengthen the ties which bound Gentile Christians and Jewish Christians together. See notes on 1 Cor. xvi. 1–4. It is there pointed out that St Paul uses seven different words in speaking of this collection. Excepting λογία, which is peculiar to 1 Cor. xvi. 1, all are found in 2 Cor., viz., χάρις (1 and 2 Cor.), κοινωνία (2 Cor. and Rom.), διακονία, ἁδρότης, εὐλογία, and λειτουργία (2 Cor. only). Theodoret notes that φιλανθρωπία is not used in this sense. What is still more remarkable, St Paul does not use ἀργύριον, or ἄργυρος, or χρυσίον, or χρυσός in this connexion: he seems to avoid the mention of money.

His thus asking the Corinthians to bring to a generous and speedy conclusion the collection which they had begun to make before their recent attitude of rebellion against the Apostle, was of course strong evidence that he regarded the old happy relation between himself and them as being completely restored. He could not easily have given them a more convincing proof of his complete confidence in them. But at the same time there was risk in doing so. After restoring friend y relations with persons who have been cherishing resentment against us, we do not think it politic to begin at once to ask favours or to remind them of their duties ; and yet this is just what the Apostle feels bound to do with the Corinthians, to whom he has only just become reconciled. One sees that he feels the difficulty of the situation. He desires to be, and to seem to be, confident of success ; confident that his beloved converts w ll do all that he wishes them to do, and all that they ought to do, in this matter. And yet he does not quite feel this confidence.* It looks as if the Corinthians were not very generous givers in this or in other things (xi. 8, 9, xii. 13 ; 1 Cor. ix. 11, 12, xvi. 4. No one from Corinth is mentioned Acts xx. 4. That may be accidental ; yet it may mean that what was subscribed at Corinth was so insignificant that it did not require a special delegate, but was entrusted to one of the others. Be this as it may, St Paul evidently feels his way cautiously, weighing his words and careful about his arguments. The thought of the malice of the Judaizing teachers is still in his mind, and he knows that he has to deal with excitable people. No word of his must give a handle to the former or provocation to the latter. It was probably owing to the Judaizing teachers that the collection had hung fire. They would oppose any scheme that St Paul advocated.

There is no good reason for suspecting that these two chapters are part of another letter, different from both the first seven chapters and the last four. They follow the seventh chapter quite naturally, and the change of tone is thoroughly intelligible. The tone is similar to that in the Epistle to Philemon. In both cases he makes a request with diffidence, delicacy, and courtesy, but at the same time with firmness, with the conviction that it ought to be granted, and the hope that it will be. And in both cases the favour which he asks is not a personal one ; he will not be the richer, if it is granted. He pleads for others, assuring those who can grant the favour that they themselves will be the better for granting it.

VIII. 1–7. *The Example of the Macedonian Churches is worthy of imitation.*

¹ Now I should like to justify this expression of the good courage which I feel respecting you all. Let me make known

---

* " *L'habilité, la souplesse de langage, la dextérité épistolaire de Paul, étaient employées tout entières à cette oeuvre. Il trouve pour la recommander aux Corinthiens les tours les plus vifs et les plus tendres* " [Renan, *Saint Paul*, p. 453).

to you, my Brothers, the grace of God which has been and still
is being exhibited very remarkably in the Churches of Macedonia.   ² In the midst of an ordeal of affliction which has served
to bring out their genuine Christianity, their overflowing happiness, combined with quite desperate poverty, has issued in a
rich stream of simpleminded generosity.   ³ For I can testify that
up to the very limits, yes, and beyond the limits of their very
slender means, they have given freely, and this without one word
of suggestion from me.   ⁴ So far from my asking them to help,
they begged us most urgently to be allowed the privilege of
taking part in the work of ministering to the necessities of their
fellow-Christians in Jerusalem.   ⁵ I should be misleading you if
I were to say that in this they acted just as we expected that
they would; one does not expect much from very poor people;
they did far more than we expected.   It was their own selves
that they gave first and foremost to the Lord and also to us,
and they made the offering in both cases because it was so willed
by God.   ⁶ The result of their double self-dedication was this.
I urged Titus that, as he had been the person to start the raising
of a relief-fund on a former visit, so he would now go once more
and complete among yourselves this gracious undertaking.
⁷ Well now, as in everything ye are found to be abundant,—in
faith, and utterance, and knowledge, and every kind of zeal, and
in the love which unites your hearts with ours,—do see to it
that in this gracious undertaking also ye are found to be abundant.   The possession of so many rich gifts may well bear this
noble fruit, and you ought not to fall short of your endowments.

1. Γνωρίζομεν δὲ ὑμῖν, ἀδελφοί. 'Now I proceed to make
known to you, brethren.' 'Moreover' (AV.) is certainly wrong.
As in Rom. xv. 14, xvi. 17; 1 Cor. i. 10, iv. 6, vii. 29, xii. 1,
etc., the δέ and the address mark a transition to something more
or less different from what has preceded, and here δέ perhaps
suggests some such connexion as 'Now do not let the joy which
I have just expressed prove vain,' or 'Now I must pass on from
the happiness which you have brought me to the happiness
which I had in Macedonia.' Γνωρίζω ὑμῖν intimates that what
he is about to communicate deserves attention (Gal. i. 11;
1 Cor. xii. 3, xv. 1, where see note). The phrase is found only in
the Epistles of this group, but the verb is freq. in N.T. See on
i. 8.
    τὴν χάριν τοῦ Θεοῦ τὴν δεδομένην ἐν τ. ἐκκλ. τ. Μακ. 'The

grace of God which has been given in the Churches of Macedonia.' God's grace has been and still is operating there, producing in the converts a marvellous degree of Christian generosity. Not 'bestowed *on* the Churches' (AV.), but 'given *in*' them (RV.). Contrast 1 Cor. i. 4. It was among the Christians there that this grace was exhibited. St Paul probably means the ancient kingdom of Macedonia, in which Philippi, Thessalonica, and Beroea were situated, rather than the Roman province, which included Thessaly and Epirus. The Romans had been very hard on these Macedonians; they had taken possession of the gold and silver mines which were rich sources of revenue, and had taxed the right of smelting copper and iron; they had also reserved to themselves the importation of salt and the felling of timber for building ships. The Macedonians said that their nation was like a lacerated and disjointed animal (Livy, xlv. 30). On the top of this had come persecution in the case of Christian converts. But God had enabled these impoverished people to do great things for their fellow-Christians; no doubt, with the grace of God, the Corinthians would do the like.

2. ὅτι ἐν πολλῇ δοκιμῇ θλίψεως. 'That in much testing of affliction.' The ὅτι depends on γνωρίζομεν, 'we make known to you that.' For δοκιμή see on ii. 9; here it seems to mean 'testing' rather than 'proof' (RV.); cf. Rom. v. 4. With the general sense comp. Jas. i. 3; 1 Thess. iii. 3. Affliction tested the Macedonians and showed what genuine Christians they were. The test was severe and prolonged (πολλῇ); οὐδὲ γὰρ ἁπλῶς ἐθλίβησαν, ἀλλ' οὕτως ὡς καὶ δόκιμοι γένεσθαι διὰ τῆς ὑπομονῆς (Chrys.). For sufferings of the Thessalonians see 1 Thess. i. 6, ii. 14.

ἡ περισσεία τῆς χαρᾶς αὐτῶν. 'The abundance of their joy'; a strange thing to be found 'in much testing of affliction.' But few things are more characteristic of the Christians of the Apostolic Age than their exuberant joy. Both substantive and verb are freq. in N.T., and there is plenty of evidence elsewhere. This abiding and conspicuous effect of 'the good tidings' was one leading cause of the Gospel's rapid success. Its missionary power was then, and is still, where it exists, very great. Those who witness great joy in people whose lives are full of trouble are led to think that such people are in possession of something which is well worth having. Περισσεία (x. 15; Rom. v. 17) is a rare word in literature, but it is found in inscriptions (Deissmann, *Light from the Anc. East*, p. 80). The repetition of αὐτῶν in this verse has rather a heavy effect; but the Apostle desires to make quite clear that the joy and the poverty and the liber-

ality are found in the very same people, and that it was the joy
and the poverty which produced the liberality. The poverty,
extreme though it was, neither extinguished the joy nor pre-
vented the liberality.

ἡ κατὰ βάθους πτωχεία αὐτῶν. 'Their down-to-depth poverty.'
Perhaps a phrase of St Paul's own coining. It does not mean
that their poverty was going deeper and deeper, but that it had
already reached the lowest stage. Strabo's ἄντρον κοῖλον κατὰ
βάθους is quoted in illustration. Cf. κατὰ κεφαλῆς (1 Cor. xi. 4).
There is an effective oxymoron in ἡ πτωχεία ἐπερίσσευσεν εἰς τὸ
πλοῦτος. Cf. The widow's two mites given out of her *want*
(Lk. xxi. 4), and one Christian having this world's good while
another has only *need* (1 Jn. iii. 17).

τὸ πλοῦτος τῆς ἁπλότητος αὐτῶν. 'The riches of their liberality.' The passage from 'single-mindedness' or 'simplicity' to
'liberality' as the meaning of ἁπλότης is not quite obvious.
In LXX it means 'innocency' (2 Sam. xv. 11 ; 1 Chron. xxix. 17 ;
Wisd. i. 1; 1 Macc. ii. 37, 60), generally, if not quite always.
In N.T. it is peculiar to Paul, and in xi. 3 it seems to mean
'innocency' or 'simplicity.' But in these two chapters (ix. 11,
13) and in Rom. xii. 8 (see note there) it seems to mean that
simplicity of purpose which is directed towards relieving the
necessities of others, and hence to denote 'generosity' or 'liberality.' * St Paul speaks of the richness, not of their gifts, which
could not have been large, but of their minds. Munificence is
measured, not by the amount given, but by the will of the giver.
Excepting 1 Tim. vi. 17, πλοῦτος is always used in the Pauline
Epp. of moral and spiritual riches; and here, as in Eph. i. 7,
ii. 7, iii. 8, 16 ; Phil. iv. 19 ; Col. i. 27, ii. 2, the best texts make
πλοῦτος neut. In Rom. ix. 23 and Eph. i. 18 it is masc., as
perhaps elsewhere in N.T.

τὸ πλοῦτος (א* B C P) rather than τὸν πλοῦτον (א³ D F G K L).

3–5. ὅτι κατὰ δύναμιν . . . διὰ θελήματος Θεοῦ. It will be
convenient to take the whole of this long sentence first, and then
examine the separate clauses; the constr. is irregular, owing to
prolonged dictation. 'For according to their power, I bear
witness, and beyond their power, of their own accord, with much
entreaty beseeching of us the favour and the fellowship of the
ministering to the saints; and [this] not in the way that we
expected, but it was their own selves that they gave first of all
to the Lord and to us, through the will of God.' Three things

---

* *Simplicitas malignitati opponitur* (Calvin). In the Testaments the
word is freq., esp. in *Issachar*, *e.g.* πάντα γὰρ πένησι καὶ θλιβομένοις παρ-
εῖχον ἐκ τῶν ἀγαθῶν τῆς γῆς ἐν ἁπλότητι καρδίας μου. But the usual meaning
is 'simplicity,' 'innocence,' rather than 'liberality.'

have been already stated with regard to the help given by the Macedonian Christians. It was rendered (1) in a time of great affliction, (2) in spite of great poverty, (3) with great joy. The Apostle now adds four more particulars. The help was rendered (4) to an extent quite beyond their small means, (5) of their own free will, (6) so much so that they begged to be permitted to take part in ministering to their fellow-Christians, (7) placing themselves at the disposal of St Paul in a way quite beyond his expectation. The long and awkward sentence requires to be broken up, and this almost necessarily involves inserting a few words. But AV. is not quite consistent in putting what is inserted in italics; for 'take upon us' (*v.* 4) and 'this' (*v.* 5) should be in italics as well as 'their,' 'they were,' and 'they did.' Moreover, 'that we should receive' (*v.* 4) is no part of the true text (see below). In RV. '*this* grace' (*v.* 4) is in excess of the Greek, which has '*the* grace.' But, in order to make the meaning clear it is almost necessary, with RV., to have 'they gave' twice, although it comes only once in the Greek.

3. μαρτυρῶ. Nowhere else is the word used absolutely, as here; cf. Gal. iv. 15; Rom. x. 2; Col. iv. 13; Rev. xxii. 18. With this parenthetical insertion of a confirmatory statement comp. ὡς τέκνοις λέγω (vi. 13), λέγω ὑμῖν (Lk. xiii. 24), and the classical οἶδα, οἶμαι, ὁρᾷς. Blass, § 79. 7.

παρὰ δύναμιν. Somewhat stronger than ὑπὲρ δύναμιν (i. 8), which K L P have here; it implies not only 'above and beyond,' but 'against, contrary to' (Heb. xi. 11). It was a sort of contradiction to their poverty to give so much. The words do not belong to αὐθαίρετοι, 'spontaneous beyond their power,' but to the belated ἔδωκαν.*

αὐθαίρετοι. The word occurs nowhere in Bibl. Grk., excepting here and *v.* 17. In Xen. *Anab.* v. vii. 29 we have it of self-elected commanders, but it is more often used of *things* which are spontaneously accepted, death, slavery, etc. (Thuc. vi. 40). Cf. αὐθαιρέτως (2 Macc. vi. 19; 3 Macc. vi. 6), in the same sense as αὐθαίρετοι here, viz. of *persons* acting spontaneously. The combination ἑκουσίως καὶ αὐθαιρέτως is freq. in papyri. Of course this excludes only the Apostle's asking; *vv.* 1 and 5 show that the Divine prompting is fully recognized.

4. δεόμενοι ἡμῶν τὴν χάριν καὶ τὴν κοινωνίαν τῆς διακονίας. 'Begging of us the favour, viz. the sharing in the ministering to the saints.' The Macedonians entreated to be allowed the privilege of fellowship in so good a work. Cf. 1 Thess. ii. 3. St Paul had possibly been unwilling to take much from people who

---

* The *supra virtutem* of Vulg. has led to needless discussion as to whether it is right to give *supra virtutem*; παρὰ δύναμιν is rather *supra vires*.

were so poor. Οὐχ ἡμεῖς αὐτῶν ἐδεήθημεν, ἀλλ᾽ αὐτοὶ ἡμῶν (Chrys.). AV. here is much astray; τὴν χάριν is not the gift for the Apostle to receive, but the favour for him to grant, viz. allowing the Macedonians to help. Cf. Acts xxiv. 27, xxv. 3. They knew that it was more blessed to give than to receive. The καί is probably epexegetic. An acc. of a substantive after δέομαι is unusual, although τοῦτο δέομαι ὑμῶν is common.

τῆς διακονίας τῆς εἰς τοὺς ἁγίους. 'The charitable ministering to the Christians.' This is a freq. meaning of διακονία (ix. 1, 12, 13; Acts vi. 1, xi. 29, xii. 25), a word which occurs more often in 2 Cor. and Acts than in all the rest of the N.T. He adds εἰς τοὺς ἁγίους to explain the motive of the Macedonians; it was because help was wanted for *Christians* that they were so urgent in asking to be allowed to contribute; sic *mavult dicere quam* '*pauperes*'; id facit ad impetrandum (Beng. on 1 Cor. xvi. 1). Deissmann (*Bib. St.* p. 117) thinks that this use of εἰς instead of the *dat. comm.* is Alexandrian rather than Hebraistic; it is found in papyri.

δέξασθαι ἡμᾶς after ἁγίους is an unintelligent gloss found in a few cursives and other inferior authorities.

5. ὃ καὶ οὐ καθὼς ἠλπίσαμεν. 'And they did this, not as we expected (but far beyond our expectations).' To confine this to their giving spontaneously is probably a mistake. What follows shows what is meant. Cf. οὐ τὰ ὑμῶν ἀλλὰ ὑμᾶς (xii. 14).

ἀλλ᾽ ἑαυτοὺς ἔδωκαν πρῶτον. The emphasis is on ἑαυτούς by position. 'On the contrary, it was their own selves that they first and foremost gave to the Lord and to us.' Cf. Ex. xiv. 31. Πρῶτον here does not mean 'before I asked them,' and probably does not mean 'before they gave money.' It means 'first in importance'; the crowning part of their generosity was their complete self-surrender. They placed themselves at the Apostle's disposal for the service of Christ. It is possible that this means no more than a general disposition to do all that was within their power; but it may refer to "personal service in the work of spreading the Gospel, such as was given by Sopater of Beroea, Aristarchus and Secundus of Thessalonica, and Epaphroditus of Philippi" (J. H. Bernard). To these we may add Jason and Gaius, who were Macedonians, and perhaps Demas. With τῷ κυρίῳ καὶ ἡμῖν comp. τῷ πνεύματι τῷ ἁγίῳ καὶ ἡμῖν (Acts xv. 28).

διὰ θελήματος Θεοῦ. Some confine this to καὶ ἡμῖν, but it belongs to the whole clause; their offering of themselves was governed by the will of God; see v. 1.

B has ἠλπίκαμεν, which may be safely rejected; the aor. is quite in place.

6. εἰς τὸ παρακαλέσαι ἡμᾶς Τίτον. We are still under the influence of the rather hard-worked ἔδωκαν, which *totam periochae structuram sustinet* (Beng.). ' It was their own selves that they gave . . . so that we entreated Titus, that, just as he started (the collection) before, so he would also complete among *you* this gracious work also.' The εἰς τό implies some such connecting thought as ' I was so encouraged by the generosity of the Macedonians that I thought I would send Titus to you.' We hardly need καί in both places, but the pleonasm would easily be made in dictating. The second καί, however, may mean that there were other things which Titus had started. The rare verb προενήρξατο implies that Titus has been at Corinth before he took the severe letter alluded to in vii. 12. This is some confirmation of the view that he, rather than Timothy, was the bearer of 1 Cor. But he *may* have been in Corinth before 1 Cor. to start the collection. In 1 Cor. xvi. 1 the λογία is mentioned as a subject already known to the Corinthians ; see note there. They may have asked about it. See on xii. 18. B here has ἐνήρξατο, a verb which occurs Gal. iii. 3 and Phil. i. 6, in both of which passages it is combined with ἐπιτελέω, and in both of them Lightfoot thinks that a sacrificial metaphor may be intended, for both verbs are sometimes used of religious ceremonials, the one of initiatory rites and the other of sacrifices and other sacred observances. See Westcott on Heb. ix. 6.* The ἵνα gives the purport rather than the purpose of the entreaty or exhortation, and ἵνα ἐπιτελέσῃ is almost equivalent to a simple infinitive ; cf. 1 Cor. iv. 3, xvi. 12.

εἰς ὑμᾶς. ' Among you '; lit. ' towards you,' ' in reference to you.'

καὶ τὴν χάριν ταύτην. ' This gracious work also.' This has no reference to τὴν χάριν τοῦ Θεοῦ (v. 1) : it is not ' the grace of God ' which Titus is to make efficacious, but the gracious efforts for the poor Christians that he is to bring to a fruitful conclusion. Nor is it likely that there is any reference to the good work done by Titus in reconciling the Corinthians to the Apostle ; that would hardly be spoken of as χάρις. It is remarkable how frequently ταύτην, ταύτῃ, or ταύτης recurs in this connexion ; vv. 7, 19, 20, ix. 5, 12, 13. In ix. 1 εἰς τοὺς ἁγίους takes its place for variety. The precise force of καί, ' as well as something else,' remains doubtful.

7. ἀλλ᾿ ὥσπερ ἐν παντὶ περισσεύετε. ' *But* there is another and a stronger consideration. What God has enabled the Macedonians to do is one incentive ; you must also remember what

---

* The meaning here might be that he treated the collection as a religious act, a sacrifice to God.

He has done for you. *You abound in everything*; do not fall short of your great powers.'

πίστει. Faith in Christ, such as every believer has. See on Rom. i. 17, pp. 31 f.

λόγῳ καὶ γνώσει. These were specially valued at Corinth ; St Paul treats both as Divine gifts, and, except in his Epistles and 2 Pet., γνῶσις is rarely so regarded in N.T. There is probably no reference to speaking with Tongues. See on 1 Cor. i. 5, which to a considerable extent is parallel to this.

σπουδῇ. The word combines the ideas of eagerness, earnestness, and carefulness. AV. employs seven different terms in translating it ; in the Epistles, 'carefulness,' 'care,' 'diligence,' 'forwardness,' 'earnest care,' and 'business'; in the Gospels, 'haste.' Even the Revisers use four ; in the Epistles, 'earnest care,' 'earnestness,' and 'diligence'; in the Gospels, 'haste.' These variations show the wide compass of the word.

τῇ ἐξ ὑμῶν ἐν ἡμῖν ἀγάπῃ. The reading is doubtful, and the meaning in either case is not quite certain, whether we read ὑμῶν ἐν ἡμῖν or ἡμῶν ἐν ὑμῖν. Neither 'the love which comes from you and dwells in us,' nor 'the love which comes from us and dwells in you,' is a phrase which has a very clear meaning. The love which wins love in return may be meant, and that may be expressed by either reading ; 'your love for us which binds us to you' seems to suit the context. The love, like the faith, etc., is in the Corinthians.

ἵνα καὶ ἐν ταύτῃ τῇ χάριτι π. This shows clearly the meaning of τὴν χάριν ταύτην in *v.* 6. The ἵνα is probably elliptical, and we may understand παρακαλῶ from *v.* 6, or a similar verb. The elliptical ἵνα is then a gentle substitute for the direct imperative, as in the letter of the Jerusalem Jews to those in Egypt, 2 Macc. i. 9 ; καὶ νῦν ἵνα ἄγητε τὰς ἡμέρας τῆς σκηνοπηγίας τοῦ Χασιλεὺ μηνός. Cf. also Gal. ii. 10 ; Eph. v. 33 ; Mk. v. 23. This use of ἵνα is found in papyri. The ἀλλά is against making ἵνα co-ordinate with the ἵνα in *v.* 6 ; and in any case this would be an awkward constr. 'Αλλά is *at* rather than *sed*; it marks, not opposition, but the transition from statement to exhortation (Mt. ix. 18 ; Mk. ix. 22 ; Lk. vii. 7). Ταύτῃ is emphatic by position ; 'in *this* gracious work also,' as in faith, utterance, knowledge, and love. He is anxious not to seem to be finding fault.

VIII. 8–15. *I give no orders. The Example of Christ need only be mentioned. Each of you must decide how much he ought to give.*

⁸ Do not think that I am issuing commands. I am not dictating to you. Not at all. I am merely calling your attention

to the enthusiasm of the Macedonians in order to prove how
genuine is your love also. (⁹ There is no need to give orders to
you. You know how gracious the Lord Jesus Christ was. He
was so rich in the glory of the Godhead ; yet all for your sake He
became so poor, in order that you, yes you, might become
spiritually rich.) ¹⁰ I say I am not giving orders ; it is just a
view of the matter that I am offering you in what I write. This
surely is the proper way in dealing with people like you, who
were first in the field, not merely in doing something but in
cherishing a desire to help, and that was as far back as last year.
¹¹ But now do carry the doing also through, so that your readiness in desiring to help may be equalled by your way of
carrying it through, so far, of course, as your means allow.
¹² For if the readiness to give is forthcoming, and to give in
proportion to one's possessions, this is very acceptable : no one
is expected to give in proportion to what he does not possess.
¹³ I do not mean that other people should be relieved at the cost
of bringing distress on you, but that there should be equality of
burdens. At the present crisis your surplus goes to meet their
deficit, ¹⁴ in order that some day their surplus may come to meet
your deficit, so that there may be equality. ¹⁵ This is just what
stands written in Scripture ;—

> ' He who gathered his much had not too much,
> And he who gathered his little had not too little.

8. Οὐ κατ' ἐπιταγὴν λέγω. ' Not by way of command am I
speaking.' Κατ' ἐπιταγήν is a Pauline phrase, and it is used
in two different senses. With a negative, as here and 1 Cor.
vii. 6 (see note), it means ' not by way of command ' ; there is
nothing dictatorial in what he says ; he is not issuing orders or
laying down rules. Without a negative and with a following gen.,
e.g. Θεοῦ, as Rom. xvi. 26 ; 1 Tim. i. 1 ; Tit. i. 3, it means ' in
accordance with God's command,' equivalent to διὰ θελήματος
Θεοῦ (i. 1, viii. 5 ; 1 Cor. i. 1 ; Eph. i. 1 ; Col. i. 1 ; 2 Tim. i. 1).
Vulg. is capricious ; here, *non quasi imperans* ; 1 Cor. vii. 6, *non
secundum imperium* ; Rom. xvi. 26, *secundum praeceptum* ; so also
1 Tim. i. 1 and Tit. i. 1. Cf. Philem. 8, 9.

ἀλλὰ . . . δοκιμάζων. ' But as proving (xiii. 5), by means of
the earnestness of others, the sincerity of your love also.' No
verb has to be supplied ; λέγω continues. The mention of the
zeal of the Macedonians will show that the Corinthians' love is
as real as theirs. Excepting Lk. xii. 56, xiv. 19 ; 1 Pet. i. 7 ;

1 Jn. iv. 1, δοκιμάζω is a Pauline word, and it is found in all four groups, 17 times in all. Whereas πειράζω is sometimes neutral, but generally means testing with the sinister object of producing failure, δοκιμάζω is sometimes neutral (as in Lk.), is never used in the sense of 'tempt,' and often as here, means 'prove' with the hope of a favourable result, or with the implied idea that the testing has had such a result. Hence it acquires the sense of 'approve' (Rom. ii. 18, xiv. 22), and is never used of the attempts of Satan to make men fail. AV. in translating uses 'examine,' 'try,' 'discern,' 'prove,' 'approve,' 'allow,' 'like'; RV. uses some of these and adds 'interpret' (Lk. xii. 56). Vulg. has *comprobo* here, but everywhere else in N.T. *probo* or *temto*. The meaning here is that St Paul is quite sure that the good example of the Macedonians will be followed at Corinth. See Trench, *Syn.* § lxxiv. ; Cremer, *Lex. s.v.*

καὶ τὸ τῆς ὑμετέρας ἀγάπης γνήσιον. 'Whatever is genuine in your love also.' St Paul is fond of the substantival adj. followed by a gen. ; τὸ μωρὸν τοῦ Θεοῦ, τὸ ὑπερέχον τῆς γνώσεως, τὸ χρηστὸν τοῦ Θεοῦ. Cf. iv. 17. We have a similar expression Jas. i. 3, τὸ δοκίμιον ὑμῶν τῆς πίστεως, and still more similar in 1 Pet. i. 7, if τὸ δόκιμον be the right reading. Deissmann (*Bib. St.* pp. 250, 259) cites an inscription of Sestos which has πρὸ πλείστου θέμενος τὸ πρὸς τὴν πατρίδα γνήσιον. See Blass, § 47. 1. Γνήσιος means 'not supposititious,' 'legitimate,' 'genuine,' and ὑμετέρας answers to ἑτέρων, both being emphatic.*

9. γινώσκετε γάρ. The γάρ introduces the reason why he issues no orders ; there is no need. The Corinthians have their own loyal affection ; they have the example of the Macedonians ; and, if that were absent, they have the far more constraining example of Christ. The γάρ in itself is almost proof that γινώσκετε is indicative, which is probable on other grounds. *Scitis enim gratiam* (Vulg.).

τοῦ κυρίου ἡμῶν Ἰησοῦ [Χριστοῦ]. B omits Χριστοῦ, but it is probably original. The full title adds to the impressiveness of the appeal ; *Domini nostri Jesu Christi* (Vulg.) ; 'the free gift of our Lord Jesus Christ.'

δι' ὑμᾶς. Placed first with great emphasis. There is not only the example of a self-sacrificing life, but of a sacrifice made on behalf of the Corinthians. Christ not only claimed obedi-

---

* Vulg. has *vestrae caritatis ingenium bonum comprobans.* If this is a corruption of *ingenuum,* the corruption must be very early, for it is found in the earliest commentators as well as in the most ancient MSS. Augustine loosely renders the words by *vestrae caritatis carissimum.* It is to the world at large that the genuineness of their love is to be proved ; St Paul needed no proof.

ence by declaring Himself to be the Legislator of a new Church and the Supreme Judge of all mankind, He also inspired intense affection and devotion by laying men under an immense obligation.   He was One whom it was impossible for men to benefit by conferring on Him earthly advantages, and yet, being so great and rich, He sacrificed for over thirty years more than men can at all comprehend, in order to do them good ; *Ecce Homo*, ch. v. *sub fin.*   The pre-existence of Christ is plainly taught here, as in Gal. iv. 4 (see Lightfoot).   See on Rom. viii. 3, 4 and Col. ii. 9 f. ; also on 1 Cor. x. 4.

ἐπτώχευσεν πλούσιος ὤν.   *Egenus factus est, cum esset dives* (Vulg.).   The ὤν is imperf. part., and the aor. points to the moment of the Incarnation.   Previous to that He was rich (Jn. xvii. 5) ; at that crisis He became poor.   That was the immeasurable impoverishment (Phil. ii. 6–8).   That for years He lived the life of a carpenter, and that when He left His Mother's house He had not where to lay His head, is of small account, and would be a very inadequate interpretation of ἐπτώχευσεν.   He was not like Moses, who renounced the luxury of the palace in order to serve his brethren ; He never had any earthly riches to renounce.   " His riches were prior to His earthly life in a pre-existent life with God.   He became poor when He entered the world, with a definite purpose to enrich His disciples, not in earthly goods, but in the same riches He Himself originally possessed in the heavenly world " (Briggs, *The Messiah of the Apostles*, p. 121).*   Here is the supreme incentive to benevolence ; to being willing, nay, eager, to give up a great deal in order to help others.   'This ineffable surrender was made for *you*.'

ἵνα ὑμεῖς τῇ ἐκείνου πτωχείᾳ πλουτήσητε.   Both pronouns are emphatic ; 'that *you*, through *His* poverty, might become rich,' viz. with the heavenly riches of union with God in Christ and the assurance of eternal life.   *Meum ergo paupertas illa patrimonium est, et infirmitas Domini mea est virtus ; maluit sibi indigere, ut omnibus abundaret* (Ambrose on Lk. ii. 41).   Perhaps the main lesson of the verse is that Christ gave *Himself*, and in all genuine liberality something of self must be given.   Cf. Jn. xvii. 22, 24 ; Rom. viii. 30 ; 2 Tim. ii. 11, 12.

This motive for liberality is remarkable as being made so incidentally, as if there was no need to do more than mention it.   It was so well known, and it was so unanswerable.   Perhaps we ought hardly to call it a parenthesis ; but such a description is only a slight exaggeration.   The Apostle at once returns to the point about which he is nervously anxious.   He is not giving

---

* This is a natural and permissible view of the Incarnation, but it is not the deepest.   See W. Temple, *Foundations*, pp. 219, 245.

16

commands as an authority who must be obeyed ; that would spoil everything. He is laying his own views before them, and they must act of their own free will.

We have again the common confusion between ἡμεῖς and ὑμεῖς. Read δι ὑμᾶς (ℵ B D F G L P, Latt. Syrr. Copt. Goth.) rather than δι ἡμᾶς (C K), which makes sense, but very inferior sense. To read ἡμετέρας (some cursives) in *v.* 8 spoils the sense.

10. καὶ γνώμην ἐν τούτῳ δίδωμι. 'And it is an opinion that I am offering you in this,' not a command. Here, as in 1 Cor. vii. 25, where γνώμη is contrasted with ἐπιταγή, Vulg. has *consilium* for the former. He has told them before (1 Cor. vii. 40) that he believes that his opinion is worth considering. Like τοῦτο in the next sentence, ἐν τούτῳ is ambiguous. It may mean either ' in what I am saying ' or ' in this matter of the relief fund.'

τοῦτο γὰρ ὑμῖν συμφέρει, οἵτινες κ.τ.λ. 'For this is expedient for people like you, who, etc.' Lit. 'for you who are of such a character as, etc.' Τοῦτο may mean simply ' *This giving liberally* which I suggest to you ' ; and in that case συμφέρει means 'is for your good morally.' But τοῦτο may also mean (and with rather more point in connexion with the preceding sentence and *v.* 8), ' *To offer an opinion, and not give a command*, is the method which is suitable to people like you, who were to the front, not only in doing something, but also in desiring to do something, as long ago as last year.' People who have not even a wish to move are the kind of people to whom one issues commands. Herveius understands τοῦτο as meaning ' *To win the riches of Christ by imitating His poverty* is well worth your doing.' This is a more elaborate form of the first interpretation. The force of οἵτινες must in any case be preserved.

But why is doing placed in this position, as if it were inferior to willing ? To say that in morals it is the will that is of value, and not what is accomplished, is not satisfying. It is not probable that St Paul had any such thought. Nor is it very satisfactory to suppose that in dictating he inadvertently transposed the two verbs. We get a better explanation if we suppose that he wished to say that the Corinthians were the very first in the field, not only in setting to work, but in intending to set to work. This explanation does not require us to give to the προ- in προενήρξασθε the meaning 'before the Macedonians,' which is perhaps too definite ; but, if that is the force of the preposition, the explanation has all the more point. The change from the aor. ποιῆσαι to the pres. θέλειν is to be noted, indicating the difference between some particular action and the continual wishing to act. This may perhaps intimate that the acting has ceased, and that only the wishing remains. They had been first in both, but now others were before them in acting. There are two other explanations, 'not only to do, but to do it willingly,' and 'not indeed with the doing, but at any rate with the willing.' Both make good sense, but neither can be got out of the Greek as we have it. There must be conjectural emendation of the text in order to justify either; and if we are to make conjectures, the simplest is the transposition of the two verbs, as is done in the Peshitto Syriac.

ἀπὸ πέρυσι. 'From last year,' *i.e.* 'as long ago as last year.' Not 'a year ago,' as AV. and RV., which implies twelve months ago. If, as is probable, 2 Cor. was written late in the year, and if St Paul is reckoning, either according to the Jewish civil year, or according to the Macedonian year, then 'last year' might mean the spring of the same year, according to our reckoning. If he is following the Olympiads, which he might do in writing to Corinthians, this way of expressing himself would be still more easy. The Macedonian year is said, like the Jewish civil year (Tisri), to have begun about October; and counting by Olympiads the year would begin in the summer. Therefore in all three cases a person writing in November might speak of the previous January–April as 'last year.' When 1 Cor. was written the collection of money at Corinth had hardly begun (1 Cor. xvi. 1 f.). On this point turns the interval between 1 Cor. and 2 Cor. Here we are told that 'last year' the collecting had begun. Does this imply an interval of much less than a year or of much more than a year? See Introduction; also K. Lake, *Earlier Letters of St Paul,* p. 140. The expression ἀπὸ πέρυσι is found in papyri, and the combination probably belongs to the language of the people; προπέρυσι and ἐκπέρυσι are also used in the like sense. Deissmann, *Bib. St.* p. 221.

προενήρξασθε (אּ B C K L P) rather than ἐνήρξασθε (D F G); cf. *v.* 6.

11. νυνὶ δὲ καὶ τὸ ποιῆσαι ἐπιτελέσατε. 'But now complete the doing also, that as there [was] the readiness to will, so there may be the completion also according to your means.' It would be a sad thing that those who were foremost in willing should be hindermost in performing; they must bring their performance into line with their willingness. There is no verb expressed with καθάπερ ἡ προθυμία τοῦ θέλειν. We may supply either 'was' or 'is.' Each Corinthian would know whether he still possessed this προθυμία. The stronger form νυνί intimates that there should be no more delay; 'precisely now and not later.' It is rare elsewhere in N.T., but freq. in Paul, generally as here in the usual temporal sense, but sometimes logical, as 1 Cor. xiii. 13; cf. Heb. ix. 29.

ἐκ τοῦ ἔχειν. Ambiguous; it might mean 'out of that which ye have' (AV.); which has little point: if they give, it must be

out of what they possess. The next verse shows that it means
'*in proportion* to what you possess.' Evidently the readiness
to give had for some time not been very great, certainly not
since the rupture between the Apostle and the Corinthians,
and now he does not wish to alarm them. He had put
before them the example of the Macedonians, who had
given 'beyond their means' (*v.* 3). He assures the Corinthians that he is not suggesting that *they* ought to give beyond
their means; but they no doubt see that they ought to give,
and he urges them to do so without further delay. Excepting Acts xvii. 11, προθυμία is peculiar to 2 Cor. (*vv.* 12, 19,
ix. 2).

12. εἰ γὰρ ἡ προθυμία πρόκειται. 'For if the readiness is there
(lit. 'lies before us'), it is acceptable according as [a man] may
have, and not according as [he] has not.' The τις is not original,
but perhaps it ought to be supplied (RV.). Otherwise ἡ προθυμία
personified is the nom. to ἔχῃ and ἔχει. Cf. Tobit iv. 8, which
is one of the offertory sentences in the English Liturgy. It
is not likely that πρόκειται here means 'precedes,' 'be first'
(AV.), *prius adsit* (Beza). The amount that a man may have
is indefinite, ἐὰν ἔχῃ: his not having is a definite fact (οὐκ
ἔχει). In Rom. xv. 31 εὐπρόσδεκτος is again used in reference
to the Palestine relief fund. See on vi. 2, and Hort on
1 Pet. ii. 5; also Index IV.*

ἐάν (B C D³ E K P) rather than ἄν (א D* F G L). א B C* D F G K P
omit τις, which C² L have after ἔχῃ and D F G after ἔχει.

13, 14. οὐ γὰρ ἵνα ἄλλοις ἄνεσις. Something is often understood before ἵνα: 'I mean' (AV.), or 'I say this' (RV.), or
'the object is' (Waite and others), etc. But the ellipse is just
as intelligible in English as in Greek, and in English no conjunction is needed; 'Not that there is to be relief for others,
pressure for you: but according to equality, etc.' For ἄνεσις
see on ii. 13; also Index IV.

ἀλλ' ἐξ ἰσότητος. These words may be taken either with
what precedes or with what follows. Although ὅπως γένηται
ἰσότης occurs at the end of the next sentence, it is perhaps best
to take ἀλλ' ἐξ ἰσότητος at the beginning of it. Place a colon at
'pressure for you' and continue; 'but according to equality—at
the present season your abundance to meet their want, that their
abundance also may meet your want, so that the result may be

* In his letter to Eustochium (*Ep.* cviii. 15) Jerome quotes thus; *Non ut
aliis refrigerium, vobis autem tribulatio, sed ex equalitate in hoc tempore, ut
vestra abundantia sit ad illorum inopiam, et illorum abundantia sit ad
vestram inopiam.*

equality.'* There is to be reciprocity, mutual give and take, so that in the end each side has rendered the same kind of service to the other. We need not bring in here the thought in Rom. xv. 27 of Gentiles giving material help in return for spiritual help. Here the help on both sides is material. The Apostle contemplates the possibility of Corinthian Christians being in distress, and of Jerusalem Christians sending money to relieve it. Vulg. supplies words which are not in the Greek; and something must be supplied; *vestra abundantia illorum inopiam suppleat; ut et illorum abundantia vestrae inopiae sit* supplementum. Beza has *suppleat* in both clauses. Ἐν τῷ νῦν καιρῷ as in Rom. iii. 26, xi. 5. τὸ ὑμῶν περίσσευμα . . . τὸ ὑμῶν ὑστέρημα. This use of ὑμῶν between the art. and the noun is freq. in Paul; see on i. 6 and cf. 1 Cor. vii. 35, ix. 12.

The δέ after ὑμῖν (ℵ³ D E G K L P, Vulg. Goth. Arm.) is probably an insertion for the sake of smoothness; ℵ* B C 17, d e, Aeth. omit. Note D E and d e.

15. The quotation hardly illustrates more than the idea of equality of some sort; not the equality which is the result of mutual give and take, which is a voluntary process, but that which is the result of the same measure being imposed on all, which is not voluntary. In LXX we have οὐκ ἐπλεόνασεν ὁ τὸ πολύ and ὁ τὸ ἔλαττον οὐκ ἠλαττόνησεν (Ex. xvi. 18). Some Israelites were eager to gather much manna; others through modesty or indifference gathered little. When they came to measure it, they all found they had exactly the prescribed amount. St Paul perhaps suggests that the equality which had to be forced upon those Israelites ought to be joyfully anticipated in the new Israel. The Corinthian Christians ought spontaneously to secure themselves against getting more than their share of this world's goods by giving to the Jerusalem Christians before there was any need to require help from them. καθὼς γέγραπται. Cf. ix. 9; 1 Cor. i. 31, ii. 9; Rom. i. 17; etc. This form of citation is in Paul confined to Corinthians and Romans, and it is very freq. in Romans.

ὁ τὸ πολὺ κ.τ.λ. *Qui multum, non abundavit, et qui modicum, non minoravit* (Vulg.). 'He who gathered his much had not too much, And he who gathered his little had not too little.' In one sense this equality holds good in the other world also (Mt. xx. 9, 10); *quia omnes habebunt vitae aeternae aequalitatem* (Herveius). But it does not follow from this that there will be no distinctions in that life.

* 'At the present season' is emphatic, and Lewin thinks that it may refer to the Sabbatic year, "during which the means of the Jews were so stinted, that even the Romans for that year remitted the tribute (Jos. *Ant.* XIV. x. 6)." More probably it refers to the prolonged poverty of the Hebrew Church.

In what follows we have the business arrangements respecting the collection for the fund. It is a kind of ἐπιστολὴ συστατική (iii. 1) for the officials.

VIII. 16–IX. 5. *Titus and two approved colleagues will help you to organize the fund. There shall be no room for suspecting underhand dealing. Give a hearty welcome to the three, and have everything ready in good time.*

¹⁶ But thanks be to God, who is putting into the heart of Titus the same eager zeal that I myself always entertain. ¹⁷ I am not speaking at random. He not only readily responds to my appeal, but being from the first full of zealous eagerness, it is of his own unprompted choice that he is setting off to go to you. ¹⁸ And I am sending with him as a colleague that brother whose services in spreading the Gospel have won him the praise of all the Churches. ¹⁹ And, what is more, this brother has been elected by the Churches to be our fellow-traveller in this work of benevolence which is being administered by us to promote the honour of the Lord Himself and increase my own readiness. ²⁰ I want to make quite sure that no one shall be able to criticize or suspect our conduct in the matter of this charity-fund which is being administered by us. ²¹ For I aim at doing what is absolutely honourable, not only in the sight of the Lord, but also in the sight of men. ²² And with Titus and the brother just mentioned I am sending another brother of whose eager zeal I have had many proofs in many particulars; and in the present matter his zeal is in a very special degree eager, by reason of the special confidence which he has been led to place in you. ²³ If anyone wishes to know about Titus, he is my intimate colleague and my fellow-labourer in all work for you; and as to the two brethren who accompany him, they are apostles of Churches, an honour to Christ. ²⁴ Give them therefore a conspicuous proof of your affection and of the good reason that I have to be proud of you; so that the Churches from which they come may know how well you have behaved.

IX. ¹ For, in the first place, with regard to the ministration to the poor Christians at Jerusalem, it is really superfluous for me to be writing to you· ² for I know your readiness, about which I am always boasting on your behalf to the Macedonians. 'Achaia,' I tell them, 'has been ready since last year.' And your zeal has been a stimulus to most of them.   ⁸ And, in the second place, I am sending Titus and his two colleagues to make sure that my boasting about you is not stultified in this matter of the relief-fund; that you might be quite ready, as I used to tell the Macedonians that you were.   ⁴ For it would be disastrous if Macedonians were to come with me and find you unprepared. That would bring utter shame to me—to say nothing of you— for having expressed this great confidence in you.   ⁵ To avoid this possible discredit I thought it absolutely necessary to entreat these three brethren to go to you before me, and get into order before I come the bounty which you promised before, so that all may be ready in good time as really a bounty and not as a grudging and niggardly contribution.

16. Χάρις δὲ τῷ Θεῷ τῷ διδόντι κ.τ.λ.   'But thanks be to God who is perpetually putting the same earnest care on your behalf in the heart of Titus.'   *Vide quam late pateat hoc officium gratias agendi* (Beng.).   Cf. ii. 14, ix. 15; 1 Cor. xv. 57; Rom. vi. 17.   We had διδόναι ἐν ταῖς καρδίαις in i. 22; cf. Jn. iii. 35; 1 Macc. ii. 7, v. 50; 3 Macc. ii. 20.   The ἐν implies that whatever is given remains where it is placed.   The changes of meaning in this chapter with regard to χάρις should be noted (*vv.* 4, 6, 7, 19 of the relief-fund; but *vv.* 1, 9, 16 quite different). 'The same earnest care' probably means 'that I have on your behalf,' rather than 'that you have for the relief-fund,' or 'that Titus had for the Thessalonians.'   There is a delicate touch in ὑπὲρ ὑμῶν.   The Corinthians might think that the zeal of Titus for the relief-fund was zeal on behalf of the Jerusalem poor; but it was really on behalf of the Corinthians.   They would be the chief losers if a suitable sum was not raised in Corinth.

διδόντι (א* B C K P, g) rather than δόντι (א³ D₁E G L, d e Vulg.).

17. ὅτι τὴν μὲν παράκλησιν ἐδέξατο.   'For, to begin with, he welcomes our appeal.'   This and the next two verbs are epistolary aorists, which must be rendered as presents in English.   Cf. ii. 3, ix. 3.

σπουδαιότερος δὲ ὑπάρχων κ.τ.λ.   'Secondly, in his character- istic earnestness, of his own accord he is going forth to you.'

18. συνεπέμψαμεν δὲ τὸν ἀδελφὸν μετ' αὐτοῦ.   'And we are sending together with him the brother, whose praise for pro- claiming the Gospel rings through all the Churches'; lit. 'whose praise in the Gospel is through all the Churches'; *der das Lob hat am Evangelio durch alle Gemeinen* (Luther).   As in Gal. ii. 12, a verb compounded with σύν is followed by μετά.   The point of a description of the two brethren who are to accompany Titus (*vv.* 18–23) is that St Paul is not sending to the Corinthians persons of no repute.* Both of them are tried men who have done good service. Lietzmann thinks that in the original letter the names must have been given, and that they were afterwards omitted, possibly because these two delegates proved to be not very acceptable at Corinth. But if the two were as yet unknown at Corinth, to mention their names would be of little use; this letter was to go with them, and Titus would introduce them. It was, however, of importance that the Corinthians should know how highly the Apostle and others thought of them.

There have been many conjectures as to the first of the two brethren; Barnabas (Chrys., Thdrt.), Luke (Origen, *Hom. 1. in Luc.*, Ephraem), and (in modern writers) Silas, Mark, Erastus, Trophimus, Aristarchus, Secundus, and Sopater of Beroea. On the whole, Luke seems to be the best guess, and it is evidently assumed in the Collect for St Luke's Day. Bachmann and G. H. Rendall strongly support it. If Luke was left at Philippi from the time when St Paul first visited it to the time of his return to it, a period of about six years, he might have become a favourite in Macedonia and be an obvious person to select to collect alms for Jerusalem in Gentile Churches. Rendall regards it as "hardly short of demonstrable that this was none other than S. Luke" (p. 79). Renan rejects it (p. 455 n.). But of course ἐν τῷ εὐαγγελίῳ cannot refer to St Luke's Gospel, which was not yet written. Souter takes τὸν ἀδελφόν in the literal sense as meaning the brother of Titus (*Exp. Times,* xviii. pp. 285, 325–336).

19. οὐ μόνον δὲ ἀλλὰ κ.τ.λ. 'And not only [is he praised through all the Churches], but he was also appointed by the Churches to be our fellow-traveller in this work of grace which is being administered by us to promote the glory of the Lord Himself and our readiness.' There are some doubtful points here. (1) To which word does πρὸς τὴν κ.τ.λ. belong? To χειροτονηθείς or to διακονουμένῃ? Was this *brother appointed* to promote the glory, etc.? Or is *the fund being administered* for this purpose? The latter seems more suitable, and is adopted in Vulg. (2) Has πρός the same sense in reference to προθυμίαν ἡμῶν as to τὴν . . . δόξαν? Both AV. and RV. make a change of meaning, which is somewhat violent, but not impossible in a dictated letter. Yet no change is necessary. We may render πρός either 'to show' or 'to promote' in both cases. 'To *show*

* St Paul often gives commendations of this kind; to Timothy and Stephanas (1 Cor. xvi. 10–15), Phoebe (Rom. xvi. 1), Tychicus, Onesimus, and Mark (Col. iv. 7–10), Zenas and Apollos (Tit. iii. 12–14).

the glory and our readiness' is simple enough ; but 'to *promote* the glory and our readiness' makes good sense and may be right, if the clause be taken with χειρονηθείς. The appointment of this efficient colleague tended to increase the glory of God and the Apostle's readiness. His enthusiasm was made still greater when the prospects of success were increased by giving Titus such a helper. The constr. of χειροτονηθείς is irregular ; we want ἐχειροτονήθη. Cf. θλιβόμενοι (vii. 5), and στελλόμενοι (*v.* 20). Blass, § 79. 10. Χειροτονέω is an interesting verb exhibiting three marked stages in its history ; (1) 'elect by show of hands' ; (2) 'elect' in any way ; (3) 'appoint,' whether by election or not. Elsewhere in N.T. Acts xiv. 23 only. It is certain that the verb is used by contemporary writers for appointment without election ; and the substantive also. Josephus has the verb of God's appointing David to be king (*Ant.* VI. xiii. 9) and of Jonathan being appointed high priest by Alexander (*Ant.* XIII. ii. 2). Philo uses χειροτονία of Pharaoh's appointment of Joseph to be governor of Egypt (*De Josepho*, § 21, Mang. p. 58). Similar usage is found in inscriptions. Neither here nor in Acts does it mean the imposition of hands in ordination, ἐπίθεσις τῶν χειρῶν, or the *stretching out* of the hands previous to imposition, which is a much later use. In Acts xiv. 23 the ordination of the presbyters is implied in προσευξάμενοι, not in χειστονή-σαντες. In Acts Vulg. has *constituo*, here *ordino* ; AV. has ' ordain ' in Acts and ' choose ' here ; RV. has 'appoint' in both.

συνέκδημος. 'To go abroad with us,' 'to be our companion in travel,' a subordinate, not a colleague, like Barnabas. Here and Acts xix. 20 only. Vulg. has *comes perigrinationis* here and *comites* without *perigrinationis* in Acts, where συνεκδήμους is used of Aristarchus and Gaius. Hence some think that it refers to Aristarchus here (Redlich, *S. Paul and his Companions*, p. 217).

ἐν τῇ χάριτι (B C P, f Vulg. Copt. Arm. Aeth.) rather than σὺν τῇ χ. (א D F G K L, d e g, Syrr.). B C D* G L, Latt. Copt. omit αὐτοῦ before τοῦ κυρίου. F and a few cursives, followed by T.R., have ὑμῶν after προθυμίαν, an obvious correction, to agree with *v.* 11 and ix. 2, where the προθυμία is in the Corinthians. Baljon conjectures κατὰ προθ. ἡμῶν.

20. στελλόμενοι τοῦτο, μή τις ἡμᾶς μωμήσηται. 'Taking precautions about this, that no man blame (vi. 3) us in the matter of this bounty which is being administered by us.' The participle explains why this colleague has been given to Titus, and in construction it belongs to συνεπέμψαμεν : διδόντες (v. 12) is somewhat similar in constr. Cf. Wisd. xiv. 1 ; 2 Macc. v. 1 ; also 2 Thess. iii. 6, the only other passage in N.T. in which στέλλομαι occurs. From meaning 'tighten,' στέλλω comes to mean ' hold back,' 'check,' and στέλλομαι means 'draw back from' ; cf. ὑποστέλλω (Gal. ii. 13), and see Westcott on Heb. x. 38. Here

Vulg. has *devitantes* and in 2 Thess. iii. 6 *subtrahatis vos* : Τὸ στέλλεσθαι ἀντὶ τοῦ χωρίζεσθαι τέθεικε (Thdrt.). τῇ ἁδρότητι. *Plenitudine* (Vulg.). From 'fulness and firmness' in the human body and speech it comes to mean any kind of 'abundance.' Wetstein says it occurs four times in Zosimus of 'munificent giving,' which is the meaning here. The Apostle assumes that the amount raised will be large, and he must secure himself against all possibility of suspicion that he administered it dishonestly.* He might have repeated ἐν τῇ χάριτι ταύτῃ (*vv.* 7, 19), but he prefers an unusual word (nowhere else in Bibl. Grk.) to show that he feels sure that the Corinthians will be bountiful.

21. προνοοῦμεν γὰρ καλά. He is quoting LXX of Prov. iii. 4, καὶ προνοοῦ καλὰ ἐνώπιον Κυρίου καὶ ἀνθρώπων, where the Heb. gives, 'And thou shalt find favour and good understanding in the sight, etc.' See Toye, *ad loc.* St Paul quotes the text again Rom. xii. 17, προνοούμενοι καλὰ ἐνώπιον πάντων ἀνθρώπων, as a reason for not being revengeful, in both cases following LXX rather than the Heb. 'For we aim at things honourable'; lit. 'we take forethought for'; cf. Wisd. vi. 8. *Caput autem est in omni procuratione negotii et muneris publici, ut avaritiae pellatur minima suspitio* (Cic. *De Off.* II. xxi. 75). *Coram Deo sufficit bona conscientia, sed coram hominibus necessaria est bona fama* (Herveius). Not to care what others think of us may be unfair to them. It would have been disastrous to his converts for them to be able to suspect the Apostle of dishonesty. *Qui fidens conscientiae suae negligit famam suam crudelis est,* says Augustine (*Serm.* 355). That St Paul was merely establishing a precedent, to protect future bearers of charitable funds from suspicion, is not probable. He knew that his critics would suspect *him.* Cf. Ep. of Polycarp, vi. 1.

προνοοῦμεν γὰρ καλά (אּ B D F G P, Latt. Syrr.) rather than προνοούμενοι καλά (K L) co-ordinate with στελλόμενοι, or than προνοούμενοι γὰρ καλά (C, Copt. Goth.).

22. συνπέμψαμεν δὲ αὐτοῖς. 'And we are sending (epistolary aor.) together with them our brother whom we have proved to be in earnest many times in many things.' 'Our brother' of course does not mean the brother of St Paul,† any more than 'the brother' in *v.* 18 means the brother of Titus. In

* Moffatt compares Byron's remark to Moore in 1822; "I doubt the accuracy of all almoners, or remitters of benevolent cash." Philo tells of the care that was taken to have trustworthy men to carry the temple-tribute (*De Monarch.* ii. § 3, Mang. 224, *sub fin.*). Schürer greatly enlarges Philo's statement (*Jewish People,* II. ii. p. 289).

† If he had a brother, he could not have made use of him as a check on himself. We know of no brother.

both cases ' brother ' means ' fellow-Christians.' Giving him a
name is pure guesswork; some conjecture Tychicus, others
Apollos. The freq. alliteration with π is conspicuous in this
verse. Cf. i. 5, vii. 4, viii. 2, ix. 8, 11, etc.
νυνὶ δὲ πολὺ σπουδαιότερον. ' But now much more in earnest
by reason of much confidence to you-ward.' In this way it is easy
to continue the alliteration. See on i. 15 for the Pauline word
πεποίθησις, which no doubt means the envoy's confidence (RV.)
rather than the Apostle's (AV.). The latter would require a
pronoun to make it clear. But this mention of the envoy's
confidence respecting them does not prove that he had been in
Corinth. What he had heard about them might make him eager
to come. See Index IV.

23. εἴτε ὑπὲρ Τίτου . . . εἴτε ἀδελφοὶ ἡμῶν. The constr. is
broken in dictating. 'Whether [anyone asks] about Titus, he is
my partner and fellow-worker to you-ward; or our brethren [be
asked about], they are apostles of Churches, a glory to Christ.'
Titus is to represent the Apostle; the two brethren are to
represent the Macedonian Churches. Cf. 1 Cor. xi. 7. He does
not say ' Apostles of Christ '; that was true of himself and the
Twelve, who had received their commission direct from our Lord,
but it was not true of these two brethren who were merely
messengers or delegates of Churches, as Epaphroditus of Philippi ;
legati, qui publico nomine pium exsequuntur officium (Beng.).
See Harnack, *Mission and Expansion*, i. pp. 319, 327. Nevertheless, to be selected by their Churches was a guarantee for their
characters and capacities. In these two verses he brings the
commendatory section to a close. For εἴτε . . . εἴτε see on
i. 6 ; cf. 1 Cor. iii. 21, xiii. 8. Its use without a verb is classical.
Blass, § 78. 2. See Hastings, *DB.* and *DCG.* art. ' Apostle.'

24. τὴν οὖν ἔνδειξιν . . . ἐνδείξασθε. See crit. note below.
' Demonstrate therefore to them the demonstration of your love
and of our glorying on your behalf to the face of the Churches.'
' Show the proof' (AV., RV.) does not preserve the repetition,
which is probably deliberate. Vulg. has *Ostensionem ergo . . .
ostendite*. It is easily preserved in English ; ' Exhibit to them
the exhibition,' ' Manifest to them the manifestation.' The
Corinthians are urged to show that their own love is genuine and
that the Apostle's pride in them is fully justified. Ἔνδειξις in
N.T. is a Pauline word (Rom. iii. 25, 26 and Phil. i. 28 only),
and it is not found in LXX. It means ' an appeal to facts,'
demonstratio rebus gestis facta.

εἰς πρόσωπον τῶν ἐκκλησιῶν. ' To the face of the Churches ';
i.e. as if the congregations to which they belong were present.
They are representative men ; delegates, who will report to the

Churches that elected them what they see and hear at Corinth, to which they are coming with high expectations; and the Corinthians must take care that there is no disappointment. This last clause is added with solemnity; it points to a host of witnesses, in whose presence the Corinthians will virtually be acting. The Apostle has suggested a variety of motives, from the example of Christ down to respect for their own reputation, for being generous.

It is not easy to decide between ἐνδείξασθε (א C D² and ³ E** K L P, f Vulg. Syrr. Copt. Arm. Aeth.) and ἐνδεικνύμενοι (B D* E* G 17, d e g Goth.). WH. prefer the former, with the latter in marg. Tisch. prefers the latter, which would be likely to be corrected to ἐνδείξασθε. The καί before εἰς πρόσωπον τ. ἐκκλ., 'and before the Churches' (AV.) has very little authority (only a few cursives).

IX. 1. Here again (see on vii. 1) the division between the chapters is not well placed. As the γάρ shows, ix. 1 is closely connected with what precedes. The Apostle continues to make arrangements respecting the collection. He has assumed all along that what has been begun will not be allowed to drop, and he has suggested reasons for a liberal contribution. He now begs them, whether they give much or little, to have all in readiness before he himself arrives.

As in the case of vi. 14–vii. 1, we have again to consider the hypothesis that a fragment of another letter has somehow or other been inserted here. It is urged that ix. 1 does not explain viii. 24, and therefore the γάρ cannot refer to viii. 24, and that in ix. we have repetitions of things which have been already said in viii. Repetitions in letters are common enough, especially when the writer is very much in earnest and has to feel his way with caution. "The tautological urgency of the appeal does not show a plurality of epistles, but a lack of certainty as to the result" (Reuss). The γάρ, as we shall see, is very intelligible. Indeed, if the division between the chapters had not been so misplaced, no one would have proposed to separate ix. 1–5 from viii. 16–24. Schmiedel divides the paragraphs between viii. 23 and 24, giving 24 to what follows.* Hypotheses of stray leaves from other documents being imbedded in N.T. writings are to be received with much scepticism, unless they are supported by strong external evidence, as in the case of Jn. vii. 53–viii. 11. Some critics suggest that it is ch. viii. that has been interpolated. But there is no evidence in any MS., or version, or series of quotations, that 2 Corinthians ever existed without viii. or without ix.

---

* Halmel insists that the omission of ταύτης and addition of εἰς τοὺς ἀγίους in ix. 1 (as in viii. 4) *proves* that in ix. 1 we begin a different and independent appeal. The inference is not strong : εἰς τοὺς ἀγίους takes the place of ταύτης.

Cyprian quotes from both, and commentators, both Greek and Latin, comment on both without betraying doubt about the genuineness of either. It will be found that ix. helps us to understand viii. See Massie, pp. 60, 61.

1. Περὶ μὲν γὰρ τῆς διακονίας εἰς τοὺς ἁγίους. The μέν anticipates δέ in v. 3; the γάρ looks back to the conclusion of viii. Cf. 1 Cor. xi. 5, xii. 8. 'I have commended the envoys to you rather than commanded you to give (viii. 8), *for*, with regard to the ministration to the saints, *in the first place* (μέν) it is superfluous for me to be writing (pres. not aor.) to you.' The similar statements in 1 Thess. iv. 9 and v. 1 should be compared; also iv. 13. For διακονία εἰς τ. ἁγ. see on viii. 4. In neither place does the εἰς limit the ministration to the transmission of the money. C, Arm. omit γάρ as unintelligible.

περισσόν μοί ἐστιν. *Ex abundanti est mihi scribere vobis* (Vulg.); better, *supervacaneum est*. We often do this; especially in cases in which we are deeply interested. We begin, 'I need not say'; and immediately we do say, perhaps at some length: σοφῶς δὲ τοῦτο ποιεῖ, ὥστε μᾶλλον αὐτοὺς ἐπισπάσασθαι (Chrys.). On the art. with γράφειν see Blass, § 71. 2, and comp. vii. 11; Phil. ii. 6, iv. 10.

2. οἶδα γὰρ τὴν προθυμίαν ὑμῶν. He has stated that he knows that they thought of doing something and began to do something in the previous year, and he assumes that they are still anxious to do something ; *solet enim se meliorem praebere ille, de quo bene sentitur ab alio* (Herveius). But we are not to suppose that St Paul deliberately gave the Corinthians praise which he knew that they did not deserve, in order to induce them to be liberal ; still less that this is a right thing to do.

ἣν ὑπὲρ ὑμῶν καυχῶμαι Μακεδόσιν. ' Of which I am continually glorying on your behalf to the Macedonians.' He is staying in Macedonia, and habitually praises the Corinthians to them. As Theodoret remarks, Διὰ μὲν Κορινθίων τοὺς Μακεδόνας, διὰ δὲ Μακεδόνων τοὺς Κορινθίους, ἐπὶ τὴν ἀγαθὴν ἐργασίαν προέτρεψεν. It would be grievous indeed, if the Corinthians now failed to imitate the Macedonians, to whom the Corinthians had been held up as a pattern. ' See that you who taught them do not fall behind your own disciples.' Καυχῶμαι with acc. of the thing gloried in is not rare (vii. 14, x. 8, xi. 30). Often in Paul καυχῶμαι is used in a good sense, not merely when the glorying is in God or in Christ (Rom. v. 11, xv. 17 ; 1 Cor. i. 31; etc.), but also when it is in men (here, vii. 14; 2 Thess. i. 4 ; Phil. ii. 16). The Apostle also glories in his own infirmities and afflictions (xii. 9 ; Rom. v. 3). Here he seems to have some misgivings as to whether he may not have praised the Corinthians to the

Macedonians somewhat too warmly. The report which Titus brought from Corinth had delighted him so greatly, that his glorying about the collection may have been somewhat in excess of the facts.

Ἀχαΐα παρεσκεύασται ἀπὸ πέρυσι. He is quoting what he says to the Macedonians ; ' Achaia has been prepared since last year' (see on viii. 10). As in i. 1, 'Achaia' probably means Corinth and the neighbouring district ; he purposely includes Christians outside Corinth, perhaps to avoid exaggeration. Corinth had done something the previous year, but apparently not very much.

τὸ ὑμῶν ζῆλος. Again we have the Pauline arrangement of ὑμῶν between art. and noun ; cf. i. 6, vii. 7, 15, viii. 13, 14, etc. In N.T., as in LXX and in class. Grk., ζῆλος is usually masc., but here and Phil. iii. 6 the neut. form is well attested. It is found also in Ign. Tral. 4. Clem. Rom. Cor. 3–6 uses both masc. and neut. indifferently. Here the meaning is uncertain, but 'your zeal' is more probable than 'emulation of you,' quae ex vobis est aemulatio (Aug.).

ἠρέθισε. 'Stimulated.' In Col. iii. 21, the only other place in N.T. in which the verb occurs, it is used in a bad sense, 'provoke,' 'irritate.' In LXX and in class. Grk. the latter sense prevails. 'Provoke' has both meanings, but commonly the bad one. Aldis Wright (Bible Word Book, p. 482) gives examples of the good meaning.

τό (א B 17) rather than ὁ (C D F G K L P).   ὑμῶν (א B C P, f Vulg Copt. Arm.) rather than ἐξ ὑμῶν (D E F G K L, d e Goth.).

3. ἔπεμψα δὲ τοὺς ἀδελφούς. 'In the second place (δέ) I am sending (epistolary aor., as in viii. 17, 18, 22) the brethren,' viz. Titus and his two colleagues.* The δέ corresponds to the μέν in v. 1. He need not urge them to give ; he is sending these three to organize their giving. D E, Copt. have ἐπέμψαμεν.

ἵνα μὴ τὸ καύχημα ἡμῶν. 'That our glorying on your behalf may not be made void in this particular.' He had praised the Corinthians for many good qualities, and he does not want his boast to be proved an empty one in the matter of the relief-fund. He is not afraid that they will refuse to give, but he is afraid that they may be dilatory for want of organization. It will pro- duce a bad impression if the money is not ready when it is wanted. He carefully limits his anxiety to 'this particular.'

ἵνα καθὼς ἔλεγον παρ. ἦτε. 'That, just as I repeatedly said (to the Macedonians) you may be prepared.' The second ἵνα is co-ordinate with the first ; cf. Gal. iii. 14.

* Possibly only the two colleagues are meant. Titus was going of his own initiative (viii. 17). Without viii. 16–24, these verses (3–5) would be rather obscure.

4. ἐὰν ἔλθωσιν σὺν ἐμοὶ Μακεδόνες. The brethren who go
with Titus may or may not have been Macedonians. Their
finding the collection not yet complete does not matter so much.
But it will look very badly, when St Paul comes to fetch the
money, if Macedonians come with him and find that very little
has been collected. There is nothing here to show that the
situation is different from that in viii.,—that there St Paul is
not coming to Corinth very soon, and that here he is coming
very soon.

ἀπαρασκευάστους. A late and rare form, here only in N.T.
The usual form is ἀπαράσκευος. Neither word occurs in LXX.

καταισχυνθῶμεν ἡμεῖς. He puts his own shame first; but of
course the disgrace would be theirs rather than his. He asks
them to spare *him*, which is a better plea than appealing to their
own interests, which are just touched parenthetically. *Multa
confusio est, si pro te qui te diligit erubescat* (Pseudo-Primasius).
'We, to say nothing of you, should be put to shame' (vii. 14;
Rom. x. 11). See Index IV.

ἐν τῇ ὑποστάσει ταύτῃ. The word has a very varied history,
but only one or two points need be noted here. From meaning
'standing ground' or 'foundation' it comes to mean 'ground of
hope or confidence' (Ruth i. 12; Ezek. xix. 5), and hence 'hope'
or 'confidence.' In LXX it represents fifteen different Hebrew
words. In Heb. iii. 14 (see Westcott) it means the resolute confidence which resists all attack. Here it means the Apostle's
confidence in the character of his converts. They must not
make people think that he has been too sure of them. Cf. xi.
17; Heb. xi. 1. In this verse St Paul makes it quite clear that
he means to visit Corinth again.

λέγωμεν (א B C² L P, f Vulg. Syrr. Copt.) rather than λέγω (C* D F G,
d e g). After ταύτῃ, א° Dᶜ E K L P, Syrr. Arm. Goth. add τῆς καυχήσεως,
from xi. 17. א* B C D* G 17, 67**, Latt. Copt. omit.

**5. προέλθωσιν . . . προκαταρτίσωσι τὴν προεπηγγελμένην
εὐλογίαν.** 'To go to you before me and get into order before I
come the bounty which was promised before (Rom. i. 2).' In
this way, or by having 'in advance' in all three places, the repetition, which is no doubt deliberate, may be preserved in English.
See on xiii. 2. It is not quite clear that the participle means
'promised long before' by the Corinthians. It might mean
'announced long before' by St Paul. With ἀναγκαῖον ἡγησάμην
comp. 2 Macc. ix. 21.

εὐλογίαν. From being used of good words it comes to mean
good deeds; from men blessing God and one another and God
blessing men it comes to mean a concrete blessing or benefit,
whether bestowed by men or by God (Judg. i. 15; Ezek. xxxiv.
26). Here it means a benefit bestowed by men on men. What

the Corinthians give will be a blessing to the Jerusalem poor
(Gen. xxxiii. 11; Josh. xv. 19). He is not hinting that liberal
giving will bring a blessing to them in this life or will be rewarded
in the next; he is thinking of the good done to the recipients.
In Rom. xvi. 18 εὐλογία has the rare sense of 'flattering speech.'
It is remarkable that St Paul, who uses so many words in connexion with this benevolence to poor Christians, κοινωνία,
διακονία, χάρις, ἁδρότης, λειτουργία and εὐλογία, nowhere speaks of
it as φιλανθρωπία : that word he uses of God's love to man (Tit.
iii. 4). Luke has it of man's love to man (Acts xxviii. 2).*

ὡς εὐλογίαν καὶ μὴ ὡς πλεονεξίαν. Here RV. makes a change
for the worse. 'As a matter of bounty, not of _covetous-
ness_' (AV.), is better than 'not of _extortion_' (RV.). In the
next verse φειδομένως as well as ἐπ᾽ εὐλογίαις applies to the
Corinthians, and φειδομένως is parallel to ὡς πλεονεξίαν as ἐπ᾽
εὐλογίαις is to ὡς εὐλογίαν. 'Not of extortion' makes πλεονεξία
apply to the Apostle and his three envoys ; 'that this might be
ready, because you are so willing to give, and not because we
force you to do so.' The meaning rather is 'that this may be
ready as a generous gift and not as a grudging contribution.'
Πλεονεξία is "The disposition which is ever ready to sacrifice
one's neighbour to oneself in all things " (Lightfoot on Rom. i.
29). It has therefore a much wider sweep than φιλαργυρία
(Trench, _Syn._ § 24), and in the case of giving it means keeping
for one's own use what one ought to bestow on others. That
is the meaning here.† But Chrysostom and Beza (_ut extortum
aliquid_) take it as RV.

εἰς ὑμᾶς (א C K L) rather than πρὸς ὑμᾶς (B D F G). προεπηγγελ
μένην (א B C D F G P) rather than προκατηγγελμένην (K L). The καί
before μὴ ὡς is probably original ; but א* F G, Latt. omit. D E have καί
although d e omit.

IX. 6–15. _Give liberally and cheerfully, for your own
sakes and for the sake of the whole Church._

⁶ Now remember this sure law; He who sows sparingly,
sparingly shall also reap, and he who sows on principles of
bounty, on principles of bounty shall also reap. ⁷ Let each man
give just what he has resolved in his mind to give, neither
impulsively, because he takes no thought, nor regretfully, because
he thinks that he cannot avoid giving. It is one who gives joyously that God loves and blesses. ⁸ Do not regard this as an
impossible standard. God can and will help you to attain to

---

* Deissmann (_Bib. St._ p. 144) proposes to read λογίαν here instead of
εὐλογίαν. There is no authority for it.
† _Wie eine Segensgabe nicht wie eine Habsuchtsgabe_ (Schmiedel).

it. He can shower earthly blessings in abundance upon you ;
and so, when you find that on all occasions you have all sufficiency in all things, you will have abundant means for accom-
plishing all kinds of good work.   ⁹ This is exactly what stands
written about the charitable man in Scripture ;

> He scattered, he gave to the needy,
> His good deeds shall never be forgotten.

God not only can do this ; He certainly will do it.   ¹⁰ He who so
bountifully supplies seed for man to sow, and thus gives bread
for him to eat, will certainly supply and multiply benefits for
you to sow, and will make the harvest which springs from your
good deeds to be a full one ; ¹¹ you will be enriched on every
side, so that all kinds of liberality will be open to you ; and this
liberality of yours, which I hope to administer, will be sure to
make the recipients very thankful to God.   ¹² For the ministration of this truly religious service of yours does a great deal more
than increase the supply of the wants of our fellow-Christians ; it
does that, but it also, through the chorus of thanksgivings which
it occasions, produces something more for God.   ¹³ This charitable ministration of yours is a proof of your Christian character, and it gives those who profit by it two grounds of thankfulness to God ; viz. the genuine loyalty with which you confess
your adherence to the Gospel of Christ, and the consequent
liberality of your contribution to themselves, which is a benefit
to the whole Church.   ¹⁴ They themselves, moreover, will respond
by offering prayers on your behalf, longing for closer union with
you, on account of the overflowing grace of God which has been
manifestly poured upon you.   ¹⁵ Thanks be to God for effecting
such brotherly love between Jew and Gentile in the Church, a
precious boon of which it is impossible to state the worth.

   The paragraph is a closely united whole and is closely connected with what precedes.   Having begged the Corinthians not
to spoil his praise of them by exhibiting unreadiness now, but
to give without further delay, he puts before them three motives
for giving liberally and joyfully.   1. Giving in a right spirit is a
sowing which is sure of a harvest.   *Dare non est amittere sed
seminare* (Herveius).   2. God is able and willing to bestow the
right spirit and the worldly wealth with which to exhibit it.   3.
What they give will not only be a relief to the recipients, but
it will fill them with gratitude to God and with affection for the

17

donors. In a few details the exact meaning is not always clear, and in several places the grammatical construction is rugged or even broken. These blemishes are due to the deep feeling with which the Apostle advocates a cause which he has greatly at heart to those who have not been very enthusiastic about it, and who quite recently have been ill-disposed to himself. We must also remember that he is dictating, and in so doing may lose the thread of the construction.

6. Τοῦτο δέ. The δέ is merely transitional; 'Now' rather than 'But.' With τοῦτο we may supply a verb which is sometimes expressed, such as, λέγω, λέγομεν, φημί, or ἴστε, νοεῖτε, λογίζεσθε, ἀναλογίσασθε: either, 'Now this I say,' or 'Now consider this.' Cf. 1 Thess. iv. 15; Gal. iii. 17; 1 Cor. vii. 29, xv. 5c; Phil. ii. 5; 2 Tim. ii. 7; etc. But τοῦτο or ἐκεῖνο without a verb is freq. in c·ass. Grk. Blass, § 81. 2; Winer, p. 746. The emphatic τοῦτο calls attention to what follows; it is a well-established and important law. Lachmann takes the τοῦτο on to ἕκαστος, 'Now let each man do this' or 'give this,' making ὁ σπείρων . . . θερίσει a parenthesis, which is an awkward and improbable construction.

ὁ σπείρων φειδομένως, φειδομένως καὶ θερίσει. The chiasmus is effective; 'He who sows sparingly, sparingly will also reap.' St Paul is fond of chiasmus; ii. 16, iv. 3, vi. 8, x. 11, 12, xiii. 3; 1 Cor. iii. 17, iv. 10, viii. 13, xiii. 2. Comp. 'One man spends, yet still increases; another withholds what is proper, but it tends only to want' (Prov. xi. 24). *Ut sementem feceris, ita metes* (Cic. *De Orat.* ii. 65). Nowhere else in N.T. or LXX does the rare adv. φειδομένως occur, but cf. δώρων δὲ ὁ φειδόμενος (Prov. xxi. 14). The harvest at which the return for the sowing will be repeated is the end of the world (Mt. xiii. 39), and the return, good or bad, is bestowed by Christ (v. 10; Gal. vi. 7; Eph. vi. 8; Col. iii. 25).

ἐπ' εὐλογίαις. 'On principles of blessing,' or 'On conditions,' or 'For purposes of blessing.' Cf. τὴν ἐκ Θεοῦ δικαιοσύνην ἐπὶ τῇ πίστει (Phil. iii. 9), and ὁ Θεὸς ἔκτισεν τὸν ἄνθρωπον ἐπ' ἀφθαρσίᾳ (Wisd. ii. 23), and πάντες ἠξίουν ἐπ' ἀγαθῷ τὴν ἐπιφανίαν γεγενῆσθαι (2 Macc. v. 4). Papyri show that ἐπ' ἀγαθῷ was a common colloquial expression, and ἐπ' ἀγαθοῖς also occurs. The plur. here indicates abundance, and the adverbial phrase may be rendered 'generously,' 'bountifully '; cf. Ecclus. xliv. 23.

The Apostle has already shown (viii. 12) that generosity does not depend upon the amount given, but upon the mind and means of the giver ; and we need not wonder that he here puts before his converts the prospect of a rich reward hereafter as a motive for being generous. Low motives, if not immoral, are admissible, esp. in dealing with those to whom high motives do not always appeal. Our Lord makes use of them (Mt. vi. 4, 6, 18 ; Lk. xiv. 14), as does St Paul elsewhere (1 Tim. vi. 17–19).

Instead of ἐπ᾽ εὐλογίαις, ἐπ᾽ εὐλογίαις, D has ἐν εὐλογίᾳ, ἐξ εὐλογίας, G has ἐν εὐλογίᾳ, ἐπ᾽ εὐλογίᾳ, Cyprian *in benedictione, de benedictione.* But it is clear from φειδομένως, φειδομένως that א B C etc. are right in having ἐπί in both places, and the plur. would be more likely to be changed to the sing. than *vice versa.*

7. ἕκαστος καθὼς προῄρηται τῇ καρδίᾳ. 'Each man just as he has determined in his heart.' As in Rom. v. 18, the ellipse of the verb makes the sentence more forcible. Each must make up his mind seriously as to what he ought to give, and then give joyously. There must be neither thoughtless nor unwilling giving. Students of Aristotle's Ethics are familiar with προαιρ-εῖσθαι of deliberate choosing, as also with αὐτάρκεια (*v.* 8); both words are freq. there, but occur nowhere else in N.T. Even if ἐπιχορηγῶν (*v.* 10) be allowed some weight, the use of such words is not very strong evidence that St Paul had acquaintance with Aristotelian philosophy. From philosophic schools these expressions had passed into the common language of the day, as Darwin's language has done among ourselves. Cf. The sluggard's hands 'deliberately refuse to do anything,' οὐ γὰρ προαιροῦνται αἱ χεῖρες αὐτοῦ ποιεῖν τι (Prov. xxi. 25); also πρὶν ἢ γνῶναι αὐτὸν ἢ προελέσθαι πονηρά (Is. vii. 15); and with τῇ καρδίᾳ cf. ὁ υἱός μου προείλατο τῇ ψυχῇ τὴν θυγατέρα ὑμῶν (Gen. xxxiv. 8).

ἐκ λύπης ἢ ἐξ ἀνάγκης. These are not alternatives, but different ways of stating the same fact. The man who gives ἐξ ἀνάγκης gives ἐκ λύπης. By public opinion or other influences he is forced to give, and therefore he gives with pain and regret. He cannot give willingly, and therefore cannot give joyfully. Cf. 'Thy heart shall not be sad (οὐ λυπηθήσῃ τῇ καρδίᾳ σου) when thou givest' (Deut. xv. 10, where see Driver).

ἱλαρὸν γὰρ δότην ἀγαπᾷ ὁ Θεός. The first word is emphatic; *hilarem, Dei similem* (Beng.). 'For it is a joyful giver that God loveth.' The quotation is from the LXX addition to Prov. xxii. 8, ἄνδρα ἱλαρὸν καὶ δότην εὐλογεῖ ὁ Θεός. St Paul is quoting from memory. He would not deliberately have changed εὐλογεῖ to ἀγαπᾷ. Nowhere else in N.T. does ἱλαρός occur, but it is fairly freq. in LXX in the Sapiential books. Wetstein quotes a Rabbinical saying, to the effect that receiving a friend with a cheerful countenance and giving him nothing is better than giving him everything with a gloomy countenance. Seneca remarks that to give with doubt and delay is almost as thankless as to refuse. *Nam quum in beneficio jucundissima sit tribuentis voluntas, qui nolentem se tribuisse ipsa cunctatione testatus est, non dedit sed adversus ducentem male retinuit. Multi autem sunt quos* *liberales facit frontis infirmitas. Optimum est, antecedere desiderium cujusque, proximum sequi (De Benef.* ii. 1). The classical form is δοτήρ or δωτήρ.

προήρηται (אּ B C P 67**) rather than προαιρεῖται (D E K L).

8. δυνατεῖ δὲ ὁ Θεός. 'Now God is *able*'; that is indisputable. To give joyfully when one has little to spare may seem difficult, but with God all things are possible. He 'is able to make every grace abound unto you.' He can give the desire to be generous and the means of being generous. It is specially the latter that is meant here. *Datur nobis, et habemus, non ut habeamus, sed ut bene faciamus. Omnia in hac vita, etiam praemia, sunt semina fidelibus, in messem futuram* (Beng.). The man with a bountiful heart finds that God supplies him with something to bestow; ὁ Θεὸς ὄψεται ἑαυτῷ πρόβατον εἰς ὁλοκάρπωσιν (Gen. xxii. 8). As in iv. 15 περισσεύω is transitive; here it must be, and there it probably is.

ἐν παντὶ πάντοτε πᾶσαν αὐτάρκειαν. '*Always* having *all* sufficiency in *all* things, may abound to *all* good works'; lit. 'to every good work,' or 'every kind of good work.' But, as in *v.* 5, vi. 3, vii. 4, viii. 22, it is worth while to keep the repetition and alliteration as far as possible. In Plato (*Menex.* 347 A) we have μηδεὶς μηδένα μηδαμοῦ ἀδικήσῃ followed by διὰ παντὸς πᾶσαν πάντως προθυμίαν πειρᾶσθε ἔχειν. Αὐτάρκεια, 'self-sufficiency,' is being independent of external circumstances, especially of the services of other people. The result is contentment, for the less a man needs or desires in the way of external goods, the easier it is for him to be contented. This does not mean the avoidance of society or the refusal of the blessings of civilization, as the Cynics taught; * these things are necessary for self-development: but it does mean being *able* to do with a small amount of these advantages. The meaning here is that the less a man requires for himself, the greater means he will have for relieving the wants of others. In 1 Tim. vi. 6 (cf. Phil. iv. 11) the meaning is, not 'sufficiency,' but 'contentment.'

δυνατεῖ (אּ B C* D* F G) rather than δυνατός (C² D² and ³ E K L P). Here, as in Rom. xiv. 4, the more usual word has been substituted for a rare one. In xiii. 3, the only other passage in N.T., δυνατεῖ is undisputed. Both in N.T. and LXX δυνατός is very freq. ; in LXX δυνατέω does not occur.

9. καθὼς γέγραπται. 'Even as it stands written.' There is exact correspondence between what has just been stated and what is said of the charitable man, 'the man who fears the Lord,'

---

* Ἀρέσκει δ' αὐτοῖς καὶ λιτῶς βιοῦν, καθάπερ Διογένης, ὃς ἔφασκε θεῶν μὲν ἴδιον εἶναι μηδενὸς δεῖσθαι, τῶν δὲ θεοῖς ὁμοίων τὸ ὀλίγων χρῄζειν (Diog. Laert. vi. 105).

in Scripture. It is possible to carry on ὁ Θεός from *v.* 8 as the subject in the quotation, and it is not fatal to this view that in Ps. cxii. 3, 9, the good man, and not God, is the subject. Quotations are often made, and with the more effect, with a complete change of application. Moreover, in Ps. cxi. 3, 'His righteousness standeth fast for ever' is said of God, and LXX is the same in both places. Nevertheless, the context here is in favour of understanding the quotation as a description of the benevolent man.

ἐσκόρπισεν, ἔδωκεν τοῖς πένησιν. 'He scattered, he gave to the needy.' 'Scattering' is the opposite of 'sowing sparingly'; it is, as Bengel says, *verbum generosum*, implying giving with a full hand. But he is less happy in adding *sine anxia cogitatione quorsum singula grana cadant*. The really charitable man takes anxious care that his benevolence is not made mischievous by being misapplied ; he gives, not to anyone who will receive, but *to the needy*. Herveius is better; *dedit non indiscrete omnibus, sed cum ratione solis pauperibus. Per hoc removetur vitium avaritiae contrarium, id est prodigalitatis.* In N.T. (Mt. xii. 30 = Lk. xi. 23 ; Jn. x. 12, xvi. 32), as in LXX, σκορπίζω commonly means 'disperse, put to flight.'

Nowhere else in N.T. does πένης occur, and therefore it is all the more necessary to distinguish it in translation from πτωχός, which is freq. in the Gospels, but is used by St Paul rarely, and only in this group of Epistles (Rom. xv. 26 ; Gal. ii. 10, iv. 9). Both words are found in conjunction, several times in Ezekiel, and more often in the Psalms, where the familiar 'poor and needy' is frequent. Yet no English Version makes any distinction here; nor does the Vulgate, which has no fixed rendering where the two words are found together. It varies between *egenus et pauper* and *pauper et inops*, and once has *mendicus et pauper*. See Index IV. Of the two words πτωχός (πτώσσω, 'I crouch') is the stronger, 'abjectly poor.' Trench, *Syn.* § xxxvi. ; Hatch, *Bibl. Grk.* p. 73. With the general sense comp. Prov. xi. 25. The righteous man does not keep for selfish use what was meant for the benefit of many.

ἡ δικαιοσύνη αὐτοῦ μένει εἰς τὸν αἰῶνα. 'His righteousness abideth for ever.' Both subject and predicate of this simple sentence are ambiguous. Ἡ δικαιοσύνη may mean either 'righteousness' in the wider sense; or 'almsgiving' as a form of righteousness, and according to Jewish notions a very important form ; or 'prosperity' as a reward for righteousness, 'blessing,' which seems to be its meaning in Ps. cxii. 9 ; cf. Ezek. xviii. 20 ; Is. lviii. 8. 'Righteousness leads to prosperity, and prosperity promotes almsgiving,' is perhaps the sequence in thought. In Mt. vi. 1 the original reading δικαιοσύνη was changed by some copyists to ἐλεημοσύνη, because they supposed that δικαιοσύνη was used there in the narrower sense. Cf. Deut. xxiv. 13.

Μένει εἰς τὸν αἰῶνα is also ambiguous, for it may refer to the life to come or be limited to this life, and the 'abiding' or 'standing fast' may be literal or may refer to perpetual remembrance by man or God. In LXX of both Psalms the expression is εἰς τὸν αἰῶνα τοῦ αἰῶνος. It is unlikely that St Paul omits τοῦ αἰῶνος in order to limit the meaning to this life, for εἰς τὸν αἰῶνα may include the life to come (Jn. viii. 51, xi. 26, xii. 34; etc.). He himself commonly uses the plur. εἰς τοὺς αἰῶνας, sometimes adding τῶν αἰώνων (Gal. i. 5; Phil. iv. 20; etc.) and sometimes not (Rom. i. 25, ix. 5; etc.).

Among possible meanings for the whole statement these merit consideration; (1) the righteous acts of the good man continue as long as he lives, for God always supplies him with the means; (2) the prosperity which rewards his righteousness continues as long as he lives; (3) his goodness will always be remembered among men; (4) his goodness will always be remembered and rewarded by God both here and hereafter; (5) the effects of his goodness will live for ever, influencing generation after generation. Wickedness will be destroyed, but righteousness can never perish. Of these five the two last are best, and of these two the last is perhaps not sufficiently obvious; the fourth is simpler and is a principle often insisted on in Scripture.

G K, fg add τοῦ αἰῶνος from LXX.

10. ὁ δὲ ἐπιχορηγῶν σπέρμα τῷ σπείροντι κ.τ.λ. He is continuing the argument that, in the long run, bounty is not ruinous to those who practise it. He has shown that God can reward it, and he now points out that we may believe that He will do so. He again resorts to Scripture, Is. lv. 10 and Hos. x. 12.

καὶ ἄρτον εἰς βρῶσιν. The clause is amphibolous, but no doubt should be taken with what precedes (RV.), not with what follows (AV.); 'Now He that bountifully supplieth seed to the sower and bread for eating, will supply and multiply what you sow.' It seems to be right to make a distinction between ἐπιχορηγέω and χορηγέω, although in late Greek compound words are often no stronger in meaning than simple ones (Bigg on 2 Pet. i. 5). Cf. Gal. iii. 5; Col. ii. 19, in both of which passages ἐπιχορηγέω means 'supply bountifully,' and ἐπιχορηγία has a similar force Eph. iv. 16 and Phil. i. 19 (Lightfoot on Gal. iii. 5). Χορηγέω, freq. in LXX, is found in N.T. here and 1 Pet. iv. 11 only. The word passed through three stages; (1) 'lead the chorus'; (2) 'supply the chorus' for a drama, a λειτουργία which cost the persons who undertook it a large outlay; (3) 'supply anything plentifully,' as here. Even the simple verb suggests generous

behaviour.   Aristotle several times uses κεχορηγημένος in the
sense of 'well furnished,' 'well fitted out' (*Eth.* i. viii. 15, x. 15,
x. vii. 4; etc.).

Rather more important than the change from ἐπιχορηγῶν to
χορηγήσει is the change from σπέρμα to σπόρον, for the former is
seed in the literal sense, whereas σπόρος is here used of the gifts
which must be scattered generously, and which God will supply
and augment. The possessions of the Corinthians are given by
God, and He augments them with a view to their being employed
benevolently.

Both external (see below) and internal evidence can show
that the three verbs are futures indicative and not optatives. A
wish does not suit the context.

St Paul does not seem to make much, if any, difference
between καύχησις (i. 12, vii. 4, 14, viii. 24, xi. 10, 17) and καύχημα
(i. 14, v. 12, ix. 3), and in late Greek the difference between -σις
and -μα in verbal substantives is not very distinct. But in the
case of βρῶσις and πόσις (1 Cor. viii. 4; Rom. xiv. 17; Col.
ii. 16) as compared with βρῶμα and πόμα (1 Cor. iii. 2, vi. 13,
x. 3, 4; Rom. xiv. 15) he appears to observe the usual difference, the former being 'eating' and 'drinking,' the latter 'food'
and 'drink.' Here βρῶσις is 'eating' rather than 'food'; *panem
ad manducandum* (Vulg.) rather than *panem ad escam* (Beza). But
elsewhere Vulg. has *esca* or *cibus* for βρῶσις as well as for βρῶμα.

αὐξήσει τὰ γενήματα τῆς δικαιοσύνης ὑμῶν.   From LXX of
Hos. x. 12; 'will make the fruits of your righteousness to grow.'
Neither LXX nor Heb. give exactly the thought which St Paul
has here, yet either might suggest the thought.   His chief
borrowing is the expression γενήματα δικαιοσύνης.   The Heb.
gives, 'Sow for yourselves righteousness; reap the fruit of love;
break up your fallow ground; since there is (still) time to seek
Jehovah, till He come and rain righteousness upon you,' or
possibly 'to the end that the fruit of righteousness may come to
you' (see Harper, *ad loc.*).   If we may take the first two commands as meaning 'Sow for yourselves righteousness and ye
shall reap in proportion to your love,' and conclude 'to the end
that the fruit of righteousness may come to you,' we come close
to what St Paul inculcates here.   LXX is very different; 'Sow
for yourselves unto righteousness; reap unto fruit of life; light
for yourselves unto light of knowledge; seek the Lord until the
produce of righteousness comes for you.'

Here, as in 1 Cor. iii. 6, 7, αὐξάνω is transitive; so always in
LXX.   Cf. x. 15; Col. i. 6, 10; 1 Pet. ii. 2.   In N.T. it is often
intransitive (Eph. ii. 21, iv. 15; Mt. vi. 28; etc.).   The change
is thought to begin with Aristotle.   Many verbs, mostly connected with motion, make this transition.   Winer, p. 314; Blass,

§ 24. Γέννημα is freq. in LXX of vegetable produce; cf. Mt. xxvi. 29 and parallels. Here of the rewards of liberality.

σπέρμα (אCD² and ³EKLP) rather than σπόρον (BD*FG), by assimilation to what follows. χορηγήσει . . . πληθυνεῖ . . . αὐξήσει (א*BCD*P, Latt. Copt.) rather than χορηγήσαι . . . πληθύναι . . . αὐξῆσαι (אᵒDᶜFGKL), γενήματα (אBCDFGKLP) rather than γεννήματα. Papyri confirm the spelling with one ν, and the derivation from γίνομαι, as coexisting with the double ν, and the derivation from γεννάω. Deissmann, *Bib. St.* pp. 109, 184. Cf. Mk. xiv. 25; Mt. xxvi. 29; Lk. xxii. 18. In Mt. iii. 7, xii. 34, xxiii. 33, and Lk. iii. 7, γέννημα is right. Blass, § 3. 10.

11. ἐν παντὶ πλουτιζόμενοι. 'Ye being enriched in everything.' The constr. is uncertain, but the meaning is clear. It is awkward to make *vv.* 9, 10 a parenthesis and connect πλουτιζόμενοι with ἔχοντες περισσεύητε in *v.* 8, for in *v.* 10 a new argument begins. Yet WH. follow Bengel in adopting this arrangement. It is less violent to connect πλουτιζόμενοι with the preceding ὑμῶν: the transition from gen. to nom. would be easily made in dictating. Cf. δοξάζοντες (*v.* 13), εἰδότες (i. 7), θλιβόμενοι (vii. 5), στελλόμενοι (viii. 20). Winer, p. 716; Blass, § 79. 10.

εἰς πᾶσαν ἁπλότητα, ἥτις κατεργάζεται κ.τ.λ. 'Unto every kind of liberality (see on viii. 2), which is such as to (viii. 10) work out (vii. 10, 11) through us thanksgiving to God.' It is difficult here to give ἁπλότης the meaning of 'simplicity,' 'singleness of mind,' which some prefer; *Biederkeit, Herzenseinfalt, Einfalt.* Here, as in viii. 2, Vulg. has *simplicitas,* Beza *benignitas.* 'Being enriched unto singleness of heart' is a strange expression, and it does not make it less strange to explain 'singleness of heart' as 'the absence of selfish motives.' The meaning is that the Corinthians will be endowed with a generosity which will enable the Apostle to excite gratitude in those who profit by it. With δι' ἡμῶν comp. τῇ διακονουμένῃ ὑφ' ἡμῶν (viii. 19, 20).* It does not make much matter whether we take τῷ Θεῷ with εὐχαριστίαν or κατεργάζεται: the former is simpler. Datives are normal after such words as εὐχαριστία, εὐχή, προσευχή, χάρις. Here B reads Θεοῦ. There is no break in the paragraph here, as if *v.* 12 was the beginning of a new point; the verse merely explains what has just been stated, that charitable work promotes devout feeling towards God. There should be no full stop at end of *v.* 11.

12. ὅτι ἡ διακονία τῆς λειτουργίας ταύτης. 'Because the ministration of this public service not only helps to fill up the wants

* Some understand δι' ἡμῶν as meaning, 'through us weak mortals'; but it probably means no more than 'through us who have to administer the bounty.'

of the saints, but it also is abounding through many thanksgivings to God.' 'The ministration of this public service' means 'the ministering which you render to others by undertaking a work of general benevolence.' The genitive is epexegetic. When Barnabas and Saul take relief from Antioch to Jerusalem in the famine-year, it is called διακονία (Acts xi. 29, xii. 25). Λειτουργία is used here in a sense closely akin to its classical meaning of the 'aids' which wealthy citizens had to render to the public in financing choruses for dramas (see on *v.* 10), fitting out triremes, training gymnasts, etc. These *publica munera* were enforced by law, but St Paul uses the word of voluntary service. The Jews gave the term a religious meaning,* 'the public ministrations of priests (Heb. viii. 6, ix. 21 ; Lk. i. 23 ; and often in Num. and Chron.) and of Levites' (Ex. xxxviii. 19) [xxxviii. 21] ; cf. 1 Chron. xvi. 4, 37. "The words λειτουργός, -εῖν, -ία, are used in the Apostolic writings of services rendered to God and to man, and that in the widest relations of social life" (Westcott, *Hebrews*, p. 231). See on Rom. xv. 27, where the verb is used of this very contribution; also Lightfoot on Phil. ii. 17, 30. The διακονία here is not the administration of the fund by St Paul (that is a subordinate detail), but the service of the Corinthians in raising the fund. What Athenian citizens who had the means were made to do, Gentile Christians will be glad to do, in order to render service to society and to God. Christians, a little later, gave these words a special religious meaning in connexion with the Eucharist, while retaining the Jewish usage respecting public worship of any kind. It is doubtful whether here any idea of 'sacrifice' ought to be included. See on *v.* 10.

προσαναπληροῦσα. 'Filling up in addition,' 'helping to fill' ; cf. xi. 9. The Corinthians were not the only contributors.

τῷ Θεῷ. As in *v.* 11, this comes at the end with special force. There it seems to belong to εὐχαριστίαν rather than to κατεργάζεται; and that is in favour of taking it with εὐχαριστιῶν here ; but there is no certainty in either case. It may belong to εὐχ. in either case or in neither. If taken with the verb, it is a *dat. comm.* 'for God,' and in that sense St Paul would perhaps rather have said εἰς τὴν δόξαν τοῦ Θεοῦ (iv. 15); see also 1 Cor. x. 31 ; Rom. xv. 7. To take τῷ Θεῷ with εὐχαριστίαν does not destroy the antithesis between προσαναπληροῦσα and περισσεύουσα, nor that between τῶν ἁγίων and -ῷ Θεῷ. B has τῷ Χριστῷ here for τῷ Θεῷ. Πολλῶν may be 'of many people,' but 'many thanksgivings' is simpler, *per multas gratiarum actiones* (Vulg.).

---

* This use, however, was not peculiar to the Jews. Papyri of 165–160 B.C. show that it was common in Egypt, esp. of the services in the Serapeum (Deissmann, *Bib. St.* p. 140).

13. διὰ τῆς δοκιμῆς τῆς διακονίας ταύτης δοξάζοντες τὸν Θεόν.
We again have an anacoluthon with a nom. participle ; see above
on πλουτιζόμενοι (v. 11), with which, however, δοξάζοντες cannot
be connected, for πλουτιζόμενοι refers to the Corinthians and
δοξάζοντες to the Christians at Jerusalem, who are the people
that offer the many thanksgivings in v. 12. The anacoluthon is
simple enough in any case, but it is rather more simple if πολλῶν
εὐχαριστίων means 'thanksgivings of many people' rather than
'many thanksgivings.' In any case this verse explains why
Palestine Christians give thanks to God ; 'seeing that through
the proof (see on ii. 9) of this ministration of yours they glorify
God.' The relief of want is one good point in benevolence, but
only one ; the glory of God is another ; and it is greatly to the
glory of God to change the spirits of others from despondency to
joyous thankfulness to Him. Affliction tested the reality of the
Macedonians' Christianity (viii. 2), benevolence will be a proof
in the case of the Corinthians.

ἐπὶ τῇ ὑποταγῇ . . . καὶ ἁπλότητι τῆς κοινωνίας. In the
fulness of his feeling the Apostle gives a compressed fulness of
expression, the general meaning of which is certain, but the exact
construction of which cannot in all particulars be disentangled
with certainty. He has just stated what would be the occasion
of the saints' thankfulness. He now states two reasons for it,
Corinthian loyalty to the Gospel, and Corinthian generosity to
themselves. They had been suspicious of Corinthian loyalty ;
many Jewish Christians had feared that converts from heathenism were turning Christian liberty into pagan licentiousness.
The brethren in Jerusalem would now see that Gentile converts
were as good Christians as Jewish converts ; and generosity was
generosity from whatever quarter it came. It does not make
much difference whether we take εἰς τὸ εὐαγγέλιον with τῇ
ὑποταγῇ or τῆς ὁμολογίας, and both Vulg. (in oboedientia confes-
sionis vestrae in evangelium Christi) and RV. ('the obedience
of your confession unto the Gospel of Christ') leave it open.
Beza (de vestra testata submissione in evangelium Christi) and AV.
('your professed subjection unto the Gospel of Christ') decide
for τῇ ὑποταγῇ. The other is better ; cf. τὴν εἰς τὸν Χριστὸν τοῦ
Θεοῦ ὁμολογίαν (Just. M. Try. xlvii. 266 D). 'Confession' needs
some further definition here. Later it was used of the confession
made at baptism ; see Suicer s.v. and ἀποτάσσομαι.

We have a similar doubt as to whether εἰς αὐτοὺς καὶ εἰς
πάντας should be taken with τῆς κοινωνίας or ἁπλότητι, and here
again connexion with the nearer noun is better (AV., RV.) ;
'and for the sincere kindness (v. 11, viii. 2) of your contribution
(viii. 4) unto them and unto all.' Cf. κοινωνίαν τινα ποιήσασθαι
εἰς τοὺς πτωχούς (Rom. xv. 26), and ἐπὶ τῇ κοινωνίᾳ ὑμῶν εἰς τὸ

εὐαγγέλιον (Phil. i. 5), where the meaning is 'your co-operation in aid of the Gospel.' See also Rom. xv. 26–31, and Hastings, *DB.* art. 'Communion.' Whether καὶ εἰς πάντας be a sudden afterthought or not, it points out to the Corinthians that a benefit conferred on the brethren at Jerusalem is a benefit to the whole body of Christians (1 Cor. xii. 26).

14. καὶ αὐτῶν δεήσει ὑπὲρ ὑμῶν ἐπιποθούντων ὑμᾶς. 'While they themselves also, with supplication on your behalf, long after you.' There is little doubt that we have here a gen. absol. (cf. iv. 18) stating the response which the Palestinian Christians will make to the generosity of their Corinthian brethren. The possibility of making δεήσει depend on ἐπί in *v.* 13, or on δοξάζοντες, or on περισσεύουσα (in which case the whole of *v.* 13 is a parenthesis), is not worth considering; the word implies "special petition for the supply of wants," and is often used of intercession. See Lightfoot on Phil. iv. 6; Trench, *Syn.* § li. The dat. here is not instrumental, nct 'by,' but 'with'; the intercession accompanies their longing. The αὐτῶν is emphatic by position. B E have ὑπὲρ ἡμῶν. For δέησις see Index IV.

διὰ τὴν ὑπερβάλλουσαν χάριν τοῦ Θεοῦ ἐφ' ὑμῖν. Note the change of constr. from διά *cum gen.* in *v.* 13; also the change of meaning in χάρις from χάριν τοῦ Θεοῦ to χάρις τῷ Θεῷ. The clause explains the reason of the longing; 'on account of the exceeding grace of God upon you.' In viii. 1 it was the grace of God which enabled the Macedonian Christians to be so generous; the Palestinians will see that a similar grace is operating strongly at Corinth. The Apostle is very generous in his praise of both parties, of the Corinthians for their great generosity, and of the Jewish Christians for their gratitude to God, not merely for the relief given to them, but also for the genuineness of the Christianity found in the donors. The praise, esp. of the Corinthians, may seem to be somewhat extravagant; but St Paul is not praising what has taken place, but what he hopes and believes will take place.* It is a glorious picture which he has before his eyes. Jewish Christians and Gentile Christians abandoning their mutual distrust and dislike, which sometimes ended in bitter hostility, and drawing close together in mutual appreciation and love.

15. Χάρις τῷ Θεῷ. This glorious picture causes him to burst out into an expression of deep thankfulness to God. He sees in it an earnest of that unity of Christendom for which he has

---

* There is evidence that it did take place. Forty years later Clement of Rome, in addressing the Corinthians (ii. 1), praises them as ἥδιον διδόντες ἢ λαμβάνοντες, which he would hardly have done had the historic collection been a failure at Corinth.

laboured so perseveringly; 'neither Jew nor Greek,' but 'all one in Christ Jesus' (Gal. iii. 28; 1 Cor. xii. 13; Col. iii. 11). The Jewish Christians thank God for the goodness of their Gentile brethren, and to this thanksgiving the Apostle utters a deep Amen in the brief but profound doxology contained in this verse. It is based on hope rather than on fact, and on the more remote rather than on the immediate and obvious results of his pleading. His intense thankfulness is not so much for the relief of the sufferings of the Jewish Christians in Palestine, as for the effect on Christendom of their being relieved by Gentile Christians in Europe. "It will disarm suspicion; it will be a practical proof of the reality and power of the Gospel, it will strengthen the sense of brotherhood, it will turn distant strangers into earnest, eager friends, who pray for their benefactors and long for a sight of their face" (McFadyen, 2 *Corinthians*, p. 375). We may compare the interjected thanksgiving 1 Cor. xv. 57, and the similar expressions of praise Gal. i. 5; Rom. ix. 5, xi. 33; 1 Tim. i. 17.

τῇ ἀνεκδιηγήτῳ αὐτοῦ δωρεᾷ. 'For His ineffable gift'; it is one which is incapable of expression by speech. The epithet is found nowhere else in LXX or N.T. Clement of Rome uses it, apparently of laws of nature; "the inscrutable (ἀνεξιχνίαστα, Rom. xi. 33) depths of the abysses and the unutterable statutes (ἀνεκδιήγητα κρίματα) of the nether regions" (*Cor.* xx. 5). It is also found in Arrian; τὴν ἀνεκδιήγητον τόλμαν (*Exp. Alex.* p. 310). Cf. ἀνεκλάλητος (1 Pet. i. 8) of joy in Christ, and ἀλάλητος (Rom. viii. 26) of the groanings of the Spirit in intercession. All three words are rare. It is rash to say that so strong a word could not be used by St Paul of anything less than God's supreme gift in sending His Son for man's redemption. A thanksgiving for that has only a very far-fetched connexion with the context. On the other hand, the thought of the complete realization of his highest hopes for the unity of Christendom as the natural fruit of mutual goodwill between Gentile and Jewish Christians is quite sufficient to account for this outburst of fervour. Chrysostom remarks; "If God's gift is indescribable, what madness it must be to raise curious questions about His Being. When what He bestows is ineffable, what must He be Himself." Of the two explanations as to what the gift was for which St Paul was so intensely thankful, Chrysostom inclines to the less probable, that it was the gift of His Son for man's salvation.

δωρεᾷ. Here, as elsewhere in N.T., the word is used of a Divine boon (Rom. v. 15, 17; Eph. iii. 7, iv. 7; Heb. vi. 4; etc.); the more freq. δῶρον is used of offerings to God (Mt. v. 23, 24, xv. 5, xxiii. 18, 19; etc.) and gifts to men (Rev. xi. 10).

א³ C² D² and ³ E K L P, Syrr. Copt. Arm. insert δέ after χάρις. א*
B C* D* F G 17, Latt. Goth. omit.   Connecting particles are often inserted by scribes and translators for smoothness, and the δέ is probably not
genuine.   If we omit it, the sentence is an exclamation of thankfulness,
closing the subject ; and thus we have an intelligible conclusion to ch. ix.
But if the δέ is genuine, the sentence looks as if it were unfinished, and the
want of connexion between ix. 15 and x. 1 becomes glaring.   This would
be a point in favour of the theory that i.–ix. is a letter of which the original
conclusion has been lost, and which has been joined to another letter of
which the original beginning has been lost.   Kennedy, *Hermathena*, XII.
xxix., 1903, p. 365.

Here the second main division of the Epistle ends.   The
whole of it (viii., ix.) is taken up with the subject of the collection
for the poor at Jerusalem.   On the interesting question whether
the remaining four chapters are part of the same letter, or
belonged originally to the severe letter which the Apostle wrote
after 1 Corinthians and before 2 Cor. i.–ix., see the Introduction,
§ IV. 5, and the note on vii. 8.   Here it may suffice to quote
the words of two recent commentators, both of whom think that
the latter hypothesis is hardly necessary.

"The most cursory reader cannot fail to perceive an abrupt
difference in tone, as he passes from ch. viii. f. to ch. x.   The
former chapters were complimentary and affectionate ; this and
the following chapters are heated, polemical, and in part ironical.
There, the Corinthians were his beloved ' brethren,' of whom he
was proud, and of whose generosity he was not afraid to boast ;
here, there are enemies in the camp—enemies who have been
challenging his authority, and detracting from his credit, and who
will therefore have to be summarily dealt with.   They will have to
be convinced, by its impact on themselves, that Paul's authority is a
very real thing, and that he is just as capable of exercising it before
their eyes as he is by means of correspondence"(McFadyen, p. 376).

The other commentator allows that there is an "abrupt
change of tone and subject at x. 1, where there is no manifest
connexion with what goes before, and after a peaceable discussion
of the fruits to be expected from the collection, we are suddenly
plunged in a piece of vehement polemical writing against adversaries, the quarrel with whom has already been adjusted in
the earlier chapters" (Menzies, p. xxxv).

It is very difficult to see how viii. and ix. "prepare for the
polemic against the Judaistic opponents" in x.–xiii.   Is asking
for money a good preparation for an incisive attack ?

X. 1–XIII. 10. ST PAUL'S VINDICATION OF HIS APOSTOLIC AUTHORITY ; THE GREAT INVECTIVE.

Whatever view may be taken of the origin of these four
chapters, it is universally admitted that the third main portion of

the Epistle, in the form in which it is found in all extant
authorities, begins here.   Having with much tenderness and
affection effected a complete reconciliation between himself and
his rebellious converts at Corinth (i.–vii.), and having felt his
way, with diffidence amounting almost to misgiving, to an urgent
request for bountiful support to the collection for the poor
Christians at Jerusalem (viii., ix.), he now, without any explanation of the change of topic and tone, suddenly begins a
vehement assertion of his Apostolic authority as superior to
that of those who oppose him, ending with something which
is almost a declaration of war against those who shall have
failed to submit when he pays his next visit to them, which will
be soon.

Like the earlier parts of the Epistle, this portion is written
under the influence of strong feeling, but, as again is universally
admitted, the feeling is of a very different kind.   Instead of
yearning affection and a desire not to seem to be straining his
Apostolic authority (i. 23, 24, ii. 4, iv. 15, v. 12, 13, vi. 11–13,
vii. 2–4, viii. 8, ix. 1, 11), he now exhibits fierce indignation and
asserts his authority to the uttermost.   Although there is no
clear evidence that in his indignation he had carefully arranged
the subject-matter of his invective, we can trace changes of
subject, and there seem to be three main divisions; 1. the
Apostle's authority and the area of his mission (x. 1–18) ; 2. the
'glorying,' a folly which has been forced upon him (xi. 1–xii. 10) ;
3. his credentials and his final warnings (xii. 11–xiii. 10).   For
convenience of investigation we can make further sub-divisions,
but this does not imply that such sub-divisions were in the
Apostle's mind when he dictated the letter.   He takes up charges
which have been brought against him and answers them as they
occur to him.

X. 1-6. Reply to the Charge of Cowardice.

*When I come to Corinth, I may be obliged to take strong
measures against those who disturb the peace of the Church.*

[1] Now this is an intensely personal matter.   I, Paul, in all
earnestness appeal to you by the meekness and unfailing fairness
of Christ,—I, whom you accuse of grovelling when face to face
with you, and of being fearlessly outspoken only when I am far
away : [2] I pray you not to drive me, when I do come to you, to
be fearlessly outspoken with the sure confidence with which I am
persuaded that I can muster courage against certain persons who
are persuaded that we think and act on worldly and carnal

principles.   ³ True that it is in the world and in the flesh that
we do think and act, but it is not on worldly and carnal principles
that we conduct our campaign.   ⁴ For the weapons of our
campaign are not those of feeble human flesh.   No, they are full
of power, in God's service and with His blessing, for the demolition of the strongholds which defy His Gospel; ⁵ seeing that we
demolish confident persuasions and every high structure that is
being lifted up to oppose the revelation which God has given of
Himself, and by making captives of every rebellious device bring
them into submissive obedience to the Christ.   ⁶ We are quite
prepared to punish all disobedience, wherever your obedience is
complete.

1. Αὐτὸς δὲ ἐγὼ Παῦλος.   It is sometimes suggested that St
Paul here takes the pen from his amanuensis and writes the rest
of the letter with his own hand, as he tells us that he did in the
case of his concluding salutations (2 Thess. iii. 17; 1 Cor.
xvi. 21; Col. iv. 18).   It is likely enough that he sometimes wrote
wrote other portions of his letters.   Gal. vi. 11 seems to imply
that the last eight verses, and possibly more, were written with
his own hand, and we may infer from Philem. 19 that in writing
that short and very intimate letter he did not employ an amanuensis at all.   But we cannot safely infer from αὐτὸς ἐγώ that
here he dismisses his amanuensis and begins to write himself;
no such inference can be drawn from Rom. vii. 25, ix. 3, or
xv. 14, in all which places αὐτὸς ἐγώ occurs.   If it means this
here, what does it mean in xii. 13?   It is possible that αὐτὸς ἐγώ
dismisses Timothy.   Hitherto Timothy has been associated with
him in writing the letter (i. 1) as being one of his colleagues in
forming the Corinthian Church; but now he is about to speak
of purely personal matters with which Timothy has nothing to
do.   It is Paul and not Timothy who has been misrepresented
and calumniated, and it is Paul alone who answers the slanders;
the responsibility and the authority are his.   It is some confirmation of this view that, whereas in the first nine chapters he
commonly uses the 1st pers. plur., while the 1st pers. sing. is
exceptional, in these four chapters the sing. is the rule, and the
plur. is exceptional.   Nevertheless, this does not carry us very
far, for in this chapter the plur. is freq.; see also xi. 12, xii. 19,
xiii. 4–7.   Moreover, this explanation gives rather a full meaning
to αὐτὸς ἐγώ.   Another possibility is that αὐτὸς ἐγώ merely prepares the way for the words which follow; 'The very Paul, who
seems to you so meek and mild when he is face to face with you,
and so resolute and brave when he is far away, this same Paul

exhorts you, etc.' For this we should perhaps have αὐτός = ὁ αὐτός.*

The best parallel to αὐτὸς ἐγώ Παῦλος is Gal. v. 2 ; Ἴδε ἐγὼ Παῦλος λέγω ὑμῖν, where ἐγὼ Παῦλος is partly an assertion of authority,† partly an indirect refutation of calumnies (see Lightfoot). Here the αὐτός makes the refutation more emphatic and perhaps somewhat scornful. St Paul rarely introduces his name in the body of a letter, and where he does it always has special emphasis (1 Thess. ii. 18 ; Eph. iii. 1 ; Col. i. 23 ; Philem. 19). In Gal. v. 2 and Eph. iii. 1 it cannot be meant to exclude those who are named in the opening salutation, for no one is coupled with the Apostle in the salutation.

Those who regard 2 Cor. as only one letter sometimes endeavour to find a connexion between ix. and x. in some such way as this ; 'I exhort you to be kind and considerate to the brethren in Jerusalem because of the gentleness and considerateness of Christ ; and I pray God that I may not be forced to do more than exhort.' But this reads into the words a good deal which is not expressed. The subject of the collection is absolutely dropped ; in these four chapters there is no further allusion to it. And it is difficult to see how "the grateful ending" of ix. "affords an easy platform of approach to the unpleasant matter" of x.–xiii. It is more reasonable to say that "the writer moves on, without indicating any connexion, to another matter " (Denney). Whatever be our view of these four chapters, it is clear that we have a fresh start. The preceding topic is now dropped and another one is begun. Three elements which are conspicuous in the four chapters find expression in these two introductory verses ; the strong personal feeling, indignation at the calumnies of his opponents, and the intimation that, if the opposition continues, he will not spare. See on 1 Cor. iv. 21, where the same question is raised.

παρακαλῶ ὑμᾶς. The extraordinary change of tone which suddenly begins here is sometimes explained by the assertion that in the first two-thirds of his letter the Apostle is addressing the loyal Corinthians, and in the last third his opponents. Of this change of address there is not the smallest intimation ; in both portions we have ὑμεῖς and ὑμᾶς throughout, and in both portions, as in 1 Cor., the whole Corinthian Church is addressed. In v. 2 the opponents are mentioned separately as τινας. The sudden change is in the Apostle's attitude towards the Corinthians. And

---

* Cassian expands thus : 'I whom you know to be an Apostle of Christ, whom you venerate with the utmost respect, whom you believe to be of the highest character and perfect, and one in whom Christ speaks.'

† Ἔμφασις τῆς ἀποστολικῆς ἀξίας (Thdrt.). There is something of defiance in the expression.

παρακαλῶ is here 'exhort' rather than 'entreat'; it has almost a minatory tone, 'I strongly advise you.' In v. 2 he lowers the tone to 'beseech.'

διὰ τῆς πραΰτητος καὶ ἐπιεικίας. This appeal has nothing to do with the collection; it refers to the warning entreaty which follows. In Aristotle πραότης is the mean between ὀργιλότης and ἀοργησία, and the opposite of χαλεπότης (*Eth. Nic.* II. vii. 10, IV. v., *Hist. An.* IX. i. 1). Plutarch (*Peric.* 39, *Sertorius,* 25, *Caes.* 57) combines it with ἐπιείκεια, as St Paul does here, and makes it the opposite of ἀποτομία. "The Scriptural πραότης is not in man's outward behaviour only; nor yet in his mere natural disposition. Rather is it an inwrought grace of the soul, and the exercises of it are chiefly towards God (Mt. xi. 29; Jas. i. 21). It is that temper of spirit in which we accept His dealings with us without disputing or resisting" (Trench, *Syn.* § xlii.). Ἐπιείκεια is that 'sweet reasonableness' (Matthew Arnold) which prevents *summum jus* from becoming *summa injuria,* by admitting limitations and making allowances for special circumstances: πραότης *virtus magis absoluta,* ἐπιείκεια *magis refertur ad alios* (Beng.). Cf. 2 Macc. x. 4. Vulg. is capricious in its renderings of both terms. Here it has *modestia* for ἐπιείκεια, but Acts xxiv. 4 *clementia.* Here and in some other places it has *mansuetudo* for πραΰτης, but Gal. vi. *lenitas,* Eph. iv. 2 and 2 Tim. ii. 25, *modestia.* In O.T. we find *reverentia* and *tranquillitas* (Wisd. ii. 19, etc.).

The appeal shows that St Paul must have instructed the Corinthians as to the character of the Redeemer, whose words and actions must therefore have been known to himself. The Gospels were not yet written, but the oral tradition was there in its fulness. That the Messiah would be πραΰς had been foretold (Zech. ix. 9), and He had proclaimed Himself to be so (Mt. xi. 29), and had declared the blessedness of those who are so (Mt. v. 5). The appeal reads somewhat strangely as a prelude to one of the most bitter and vehement paragraphs in the writings of St Paul. What follows reads rather like an echo of the wrath of the Lamb. We might have expected him to say Ἰησοῦ (iv. 10, 11; Rom. viii. 11; 1 Thess. iv. 14) when speaking of the earthly life of Christ. But Χριστοῦ may have point, because some of them professed to be in a special sense Χριστοῦ (1 Cor. i. 12).

ὃς κατὰ πρόσωπον μὲν ταπεινὸς ἐν ὑμῖν. Here ταπεινός is used in a bad sense, which is unusual. He is quoting the words of his accusers at Corinth. They had said that, when he was there, he was a Uriah Heep, very humble and cringing and artful; when he was away from them, he could pluck up his courage and be very resolute—on paper. See on vii. 6.

18

Here and throughout both LXX and N.T. we should read πραΰτης ‹א* B G P 17) rather than πραότης (א³ C D E K L). In LXX both πραΰς (Num. xii. 3 and often in Psalms) and ταπεινός (Prov. iii. 34; Zeph. ii. 3 ; Is. xi. 4) are used to translate the same Hebrew, *anav*.

2. δέομαι δὲ τὸ μὴ παρὼν θαρρῆσαι. The appeal to the meekness and gentleness of Christ influences the Apostle himself, and he drops from magisterial exhortation to earnest entreaty. RV. does not sufficiently mark this with 'intreat' and 'beseech,' nor Vulg. with *obsecro* and *rogo*, while AV. does not mark it at all, but has 'beseech' for both verbs. Δέομαι δέ takes up παρακαλῶ and repeats it in a lower key; 'I exhort, nay I beseech you, that I may not when present show courage.' Lit. 'I beg of you the not, when I am present, showing courage.' Chrys. has μή με ἀναγκάσητε. On the constr. see Blass, § 71. 1 ; παρών is attracted to the nom. of δέομαι. Cf. ἔμαθον αὐτάρκης εἶναι (Phil. iv. 11), φάσκοντες εἶναι σοφοί (Rom. i. 22). Bachmann follows Rückert and B. Weiss in thinking that δέομαι is addressed to God, which is not probable. As δέομαι must be distinguished in translation from παρακαλῶ, so also must θαρρῆσαι from τολμῆσαι, and here again AV. ignores the change. The change of word is probably neither accidental nor merely for the sake of variety, but marks the difference between the feigned courage which his critics attributed to him and the uncompromising boldness which he is confident of exhibiting if his opponents render it necessary. He beseeches them so to behave that he may be spared the distress of proving that he can be unflinching when he is face to face with them.

τῇ πεποιθήσει ᾗ λογίζομαι τολμῆσαι κ.τ.λ. 'With the confidence (i. 15) wherewith I count on being bold against certain persons who count of us as, etc.' The Corinthians of course would understand who the τινας, *quosdam*, whom he does not care to mention, are, cf. iii. 1 ; 1 Cor. xv. 12. They are a malignant coterie in the Church which he is addressing. The thought of them changes his tone once more, and he again becomes minatory. We must give the same rendering to λογίζομαι and λογιζομένους, both of which are midd. and not pass. Nevertheless there is a difference of signification, the one meaning 'I reckon' = 'I *expect*,' the other meaning 'who reckon' = 'who *suppose*.' The verb is very freq. in Paul, esp. in Rom. and 2 Cor. Vulg. here has *qua existimor audere in quosdam, qui arbitrantur nos*, etc., using two different verbs and taking λογίζομαι as passive. It uses both these verbs elsewhere, and also *cogito* (*vv.* 7, 11, iii. 5; etc.), *reputo* (v. 19; Gal. iii. 6; 2 Tim. iv. 6; etc.), *imputo* (Rom. iv. 3, 8), *cui accepto fero* (Rom. iv. 6), and *aestimo* (Rom. viii. 36, ix. 8). Rom. iv. 3 is remarkable, for in Gen. xv. 6 Vulg. has *reputo*.

ὡς κατὰ σάρκα περιπατοῦντας. 'As if our conduct were guided by carnal principles'; see on Rom. viii. 4. His opponents attributed to him unspiritual and worldly motives and conduct; that he was capricious and shuffling, verbose and vain-glorious, at once a coward and a bully, and so forth. That they accused him of unchastity is not probable; had they done so, he would have been more definite. Nor is there any reference to his physical infirmities. See on i. 17, last note; and for the Hebraistic περιπατεῖν of daily conduct see on iv. 2 and 1 Cor. iii. 3, also on ἀνεστράφημεν, 2 Cor. i. 12. The metaphor which follows suggests that κατὰ σάρκα refers, among other things, to a charge of being a coward.

3. ἐν σαρκὶ γὰρ περιπατοῦντες. 'In the flesh (emphatic) no doubt we walk, but not according to the flesh do we carry on our warfare.' The γάρ implies a tacit contradiction; 'That is not true, for, although of course we walk in, etc.' Like all human beings, he is subject to the limitations and weaknesses of humanity, such as timidity, indiscretion, love of influence; cf. iv. 7; Gal. ii. 20; Phil. i. 22. An Apostle, in his missionary work, has to reckon with these drawbacks, but they do not regulate his conduct. They constitute the condition *in* which he must labour, but they are not its *regulating principle*. Its principles are not worldly but spiritual.

That a Christian's life is warfare is often pointed out by St Paul (vi. 7; 1 Thess. v. 8; Rom. xiii. 12, 13; Eph. vi. 11–17; 1 Tim. i. 18; 2 Tim. ii. 3, 4). Cf. Wisd. v. 17–20, a book with which St Paul seems to have been familiar. The metaphor would be natural enough, even if the Apostle had not had frequent experience of Roman soldiers. Here it has special point, if he is rebutting a charge of cowardice; and he is certainly beginning to carry war into his opponents' camp. Durandus (*Rationale Divinorum Officiorum*, iv. 16), after saying that "when the Epistle is read we do not kneel but sit," adds that "*Soldiers*, however, are accustomed to stand when the Epistles of *Paul* are read, in honour of him, because he was a soldier." See V. Staley, *Studies in Ceremonial*, p. 80.

4. In form this verse is a parenthesis to confirm the truth of the preceding statement, and καθαιροῦντες in *v.* 5 goes back in grammatical constr. to στρατευόμεθα in *v.* 3. But in idea καθαιροῦντες is obviously connected with πρὸς καθαίρεσιν in *v.* 4, and the const. of *v.* 3 seems to be forgotten.

τὰ γὰρ ὅπλα τῆς στρατείας ἡμῶν. 'For the weapons of our campaign are not fleshly.' He probably refers to the artifices which his critics said that he employed in gaining converts. Adopting στρατιᾶς as the right spelling (see below), we must treat it as equivalent to στρατείας, 'campaign,' not στρατιᾶς, 'army.' "It is really superfluous to collect proofs of the fact that στρατεία could also be written στρατία" (Deissmann, *Bib. St.* p. 132). For σαρκικά see on i. 2 ; for ὅπλα, on vi. 7.

δυνατὰ τῷ Θεῷ. It is the idea of power that is wanted in opposition to the weakness of the flesh. The extraordinary effectiveness of the weapons is evidence that there is something more than mere human force in them ; and hence perhaps the use of δυνατά rather than πνευματικά, the common antithesis to σαρκικά. The force of the dat. is uncertain ; either 'for God,' 'in God's service' (*dat. com.*), or 'before God,' 'in His eyes' (RV.). From the latter the transition would be easy to the Hebraistic use for 'exceeding,' as in ἀστεῖος τῷ Θεῷ, 'exceeding fair' (Acts vii. 20). Erasmus has *afflatu Dei*, Beza *divinitus*, 'divinely powerful.'

πρὸς καθαίρεσιν ὀχυρωμάτων. 'To the demolition of strong-holds,' the fortresses which hinder the success of the campaign, *i.e.* all the prejudices and evil practices which resist the influence of the Gospel. In LXX, esp. in Maccabees (cf. 1 Macc. v. 65), ὀχύρωμα is freq., but occurs nowhere else in N.T., and possibly St Paul is thinking of Prov. xxi. 22 ; πόλεις ὀχυρὰς ἐπέβη σοφὸς καὶ καθεῖλε τὸ ὀχύρωμα ἐφ' ᾧ ἐπεποίθησαν οἱ ἀσεβεῖς. Thackeray (*St Paul and Jewish Thought*, p. 239) quotes πρός γε τὴν τοῦ ὀχυρώματος τούτου καθαίρεσιν from Philo, *De Confus. Ling.* 26. There is probably no special reference to the "fences about the Law," or the Law itself, although the Law was often a great obstacle to the success of Christian missionaries.

It is difficult to decide between στρατίας (א C D G) and στρατείας (B).

5. λογισμοὺς καθαιροῦντες. The constr. is doubtful. We can take it back to περιπατοῦντες and στρατευόμεθα, making *v.* 4 a parenthesis (AV., RV., WH.) ; but St Paul so frequently has nominative participles without any regular connexion (θλιβόμενοι, vii. 5 ; στελλόμενοι, viii. 20 ; πλουτιζόμενοι, ix. 11), that it is likely that we have a similar feature here ; 'Seeing that we demolish seducing reasonings,' *i.e.*, sophistries and plausible fallacies with which Jews and Gentiles evaded the teaching of the Apostles. Cf. Prov. xxi. 30. There is nothing personal in the warfare which the Apostles wage. They assail arguments and ideas in order to win over those who hold them. They do not attempt to destroy the reasoners in order to stop the arguments. And in demolishing reasonings St Paul did not use πιθοῖς σοφίας λόγοις, though some missionaries did according to their ability ; the spiritual power with which he was endowed sufficed. It is not likely that λογισμούς is meant to refer to λογιζομένους, and in translating the one we need not consider the other. These specious and arrogant λογισμοί belong to a class of which he goes

on to speak. Cf. Rom. ii. 15, the only other passage in which
λογισμός is found in N.T.

πᾶν ὕψωμα ἐπαιρόμενον. 'Every high thing that is lifting
itself up.' In xi. 20 ἔπαιρ. is midd., and so it probably is here.
The metaphor is from walls and towers standing defiantly, rather
than barriers hastily thrown up to check progress ; but the pass.
is possible, that is 'erected,' 'set up,' as a towering obstacle.

κατὰ τῆς γνώσεως τοῦ Θεοῦ. 'In opposition to the knowledge
of God,' that true knowledge of Him which comes through
acquaintance with One who was the image of God (iv. 4). St
Paul is sure that he possesses this. Cf. τὸ γνωστὸν τοῦ Θεοῦ
(Rom. i. 19), and πλανᾶσθαι περὶ τὴν τοῦ Θεοῦ γνῶσιν (Wisd. xiv.
22). St Paul's acquaintance with the Book of Wisdom has been
already noted. See on v. 4 and v. 1.

αἰχμαλωτίζοντες. Military metaphors still continue, and in
N.T. this metaphor of 'making prisoners' or 'taking captive' is
peculiar to St Paul (Rom. vii. 23 ; 2 Tim. iii. 6). In Lk. xxi.
24 there is no metaphor. These two military expressions are
found in conjunction 1 Macc. viii. 10 ; ᾐχμαλώτισαν τὰς γυναῖκας
αὐτῶν, . . . καὶ καθεῖλον τὰ ὀχυρώματα αὐτῶν. Cf. τὸ κάλλος
αὐτῆς ᾐχμαλώτισε ψυχὴν αὐτοῦ (Judith xvi. 9). In Eph. iv. 8 we
have αἰχμαλωτεύω, from Ezek. xii. 3. Both forms of the verb are
very freq. in LXX ; αἰχμαλωτίζω is used by Josephus, Plutarch,
Arrian, etc.

πᾶν νόημα. 'Every device'; see on ii. 11. Neither here,
where Luther's alle Vernunft has led some people astray, nor
1 Cor. iv. 4, where AV. has done the like, does St Paul express
disapproval of human reasoning, or deny the right to think for
oneself. It is those λογισμοί and νοήματα which oppose or
corrupt the truth to which he here declares hostility. But θαρρῶ
εἰς ὑμᾶς (v. 1) does not justify our taking εἰς τὴν ὑπακοήν with
πᾶν νόημα, 'every device against the obedience'; for this we
should have had κατά, as in κατὰ τῆς γνώσεως.

εἰς τὴν ὑπακοὴν τοῦ Χριστοῦ. These words go with αἰχμαλωτίζοντες, 'taking every opposing design prisoner and bringing it into
the condition of submissive obedience to the Christ.' * Cf. Lk.
xxi. 24. Submission to Christ is the new land into which they
are carried captive ; 1 Kings viii. 46 ; Judith v. 18 ; Tobit i. 10.
That the imagery of the passage was suggested by the wars of
Pompey against Mithridates and the Pirates (Stanley) is less
likely than that the wars of the Maccabees were in the Apostle's
mind. But no actual campaign is needed to suggest the
metaphors. Cf. Rom. i. 5.

* This is what Deissmann has called the "mystic genitive," where 'of
Christ' almost = 'in Christ' ; cf. 2 Thess. iii. 5 ; Eph. iii. 19, v. 21 ; Col. iii.
15 (St Paul, p. 141).

6. καὶ ἐν ἑτοίμῳ ἔχοντες ἐκδικῆσαι κ.τ.λ. 'And being quite prepared to avenge all disobedience, whenever *your* obedience shall have been completed.' This reads oddly *after* vii. 4, 16. There he is enthusiastic about them ; here their obedience is still incomplete. See also viii. 7. The ὑμῶν is emphatic; he fully expects that, after the interval which he means to allow, the Corinthian Church will be found to be obedient to Christ and submissive to His Apostle. But there may be exceptions, and with such cases he is prepared to deal severely. We have ἑτοίμως ἔχω, xii. 14, and ἐν ἑτοίμῳ ἔχω is found in Philo, Polybius, etc. See Wetstein. Such expressions, like δύναμαι, are usually followed by the aor. infin. (xii. 14; Acts xxi. 13, xxiii. 15, etc.).* The legal expression, ἐκδικῆσαι, ' to do justice,' may be compared with those in i. 22, ii. 6, 8, vii. 11, 12. The play on words between καθαιροῦντες and ἐπαιρόμενον and between ὑπακοή and παρακοή may be compared with those noted in i. 13, iii. 2, iv. 8, vi. 10, vii. 10, viii. 22. Note also the emphatic repetition in πᾶν . . . πᾶσαν, and the alliteration in ἔχοντες ἐκδικῆσαι and πᾶσαν παρακοήν. Alliteration with π. is specially freq. (ix. 8, 11). In LXX παρακοή is not found, and in N.T. it occurs only here, Rom. v. 19, and Heb. ii. 2, and St Paul would probably have used ἀπειθία (Rom. xi. 30, 32 ; Eph. ii. 2, v. 6 ; Col. iii. 6) here had he not wished to make a verbal antithesis to ὑπακοή, for παρακοή, 'failing to listen' or 'listening amiss,' implies less deliberate disobedience than ἀπειθία.†

These two verses exhibit the Apostle's severity and consideration, and his authority is manifest in both. The threat of severity anticipates xii. 20–xiii. 1, and if these four chapters are part of the lost letter which was sent before 2 Cor. i.–ix., then ii. 9 may refer to this passage. The claim to a Divine commission and to the power to decide what is contrary to the knowledge of God is conspicuous here as in ii. 14, iv. 6, v. 18. In what way he will punish those who still oppose him when he comes is not stated. He is probably thinking of the Judaistic teachers, anticipating that those whom they have misled will submit and return to their allegiance, but that these alien teachers will not do so.‡ He passes on to deal with some of the sneers which they had employed in order to undermine his authority, and some of the claims which they had made in order to establish their own.

---

* ἑτοιμότατα ἔχω and ἐξ ἑτοίμου ἔχω, followed by infin., are found in papyri.

† Lachmann's proposal to put a full stop after παρακοήν, and take ὅταν . . . ἡ ὑπακοή with what follows, is extraordinary. 'Whenever your obedience shall have been completed, look at what lies before your eyes' is scarcely sense; and the usual punctuation makes excellent sense.

‡ If this is correct, then these verses were written before iii. 1, which seems to imply that the Judaizing teachers had left Corinth.

Some of the latter may have been true enough. They came from the country of the Messiah and from the primitive Christian congregation. They had personal acquaintance with some of the Twelve and with James, the Lord's brother. That they had known Christ Himself is less probable.

X. 7–11. Reply to the Charge of Weakness.

My Apostolic Authority will be found to be as effective in fact as it looks on paper.

⁷ It is at the outward appearance of things that you look. There may be a certain person who is convinced in himself that he is Christ's man. Well then, let him, on second thoughts, be persuaded of this with himself, that just as truly as he is Christ's, so also are we. ⁸ That is no idle boast; for even supposing that I glory somewhat extravagantly about our authority, which was given me by the Lord for your upbuilding and not for your demolition, I shall not be put to shame as an impostor when I come to Corinth. ⁹ I will not say more than that, that I may not seem (as it were) to terrify you by means of my letters. ¹⁰ For I know what people say; 'Oh, yes, his letters are impressive and forcible enough; but his personal appearance is weak, and his manner of speaking is worth nothing.' ¹¹ Let the man who talks in this manner be persuaded of this, that such as we are in word by means of letters, when we are absent, just such also, when we are present, are we in act. Our words and our conduct exactly correspond.

7. Τὰ κατὰ πρόσωπον βλέπετε. It is impossible to decide with any certainty whether βλέπετε is imperative or indicative (cf. Jn. v. 39, xiv. 1; 1 Jn. ii. 27, 29, iv. 2), and, if we decide for the indicative, whether it is interrogative or categorical (cf. xii. 5, 11, 19; 1 Cor. vi. 4, 6, vii. 18, 21, 27). All three renderings, 'Ye look' (RV.), 'Do ye look?' (AV., RV. marg.), and 'Look ye' (Vulg. *videte*), make good sense. Wiclif, Tyndale, and the Genevan agree with the last, and commentators, both ancient and modern, are much divided. If βλέπετε were imperative, it would *probably* have come first; but this is not decisive. Let us follow RV. 'It is at the things which lie before your face that you are looking.' They ought to take a more comprehensive view, and also try to see a little below the surface. If self-commendation, plausibility, and adroitness suffice, then the Corinthians are quite right in accepting the Judaizers, but they ought to look to more solid things than that. One can get much the same meaning, if βλέπετε is imperative, 'Look at the facts; not what these teachers say, but what you all can see.' *Das, was vor Augen liegt—ja das fasst ins Auge* (Bachmann).

εἴ τις πέποιθεν ἑαυτῷ, 'If any man trusteth in himself that he is Christ's, let him count (*v.* 2) this again, with himself, that even as he is Christ's, so also are we.' It is 'in himself,' 'in his own mind,' that he has his confidence, and just there he ought also (πάλιν) to make his reckoning. The vague τις, like the vague τινας (*v.* 2), points to the Apostle's opponents, but the sing. τις is no proof that he is now thinking of a particular individual. Cf. xi. 4, 20. It is scarcely possible that Χριστοῦ εἶναι has any reference to the Christ party (1 Cor. i. 12). St Paul would not use language which would almost inevitably be understood to mean that he was a member of the 'Christ' party. These parties seem to have died out; for there is no mention of them in 2 Cor., not even in xii. 20, where he speaks of strifes and factions. We may conclude that the rebukes in 1 Cor. proved effectual. Χριστοῦ εἶναι here means being Christ's man, servant, or minister. With πάλιν comp. 1 Cor. xii. 21, and with ἐφ' ἑαυτοῦ, 1 Cor. vi. 1.

D* E* F G, d e f g add δοῦλος after the first Χριστοῦ. ἐφ' ἑαυτοῦ (א B L, Latt. *intra se*) rather than ἀφ' ἑαυτοῦ (C D E G K P). Χριστοῦ after ἡμεῖς (D³ E K L, Copt.) is probably not genuine; א B C D* F G P, Latt. omit.

8. ἐάν τε γὰρ . . . Confirmatory evidence that he is Christ's minister in as true a sense as his opponents are. Cf. Rom. xiv. 8. He begins with an 'if,' but he ends with a confident assertion. Even if he should use stronger language than he has done about his authority, there is not the least prospect that he will be put to shame as a convicted impostor. There will be ample justification of his claims. It is not certain that περισσότερον refers to *vv.* 3–6, 'more abundantly than I have just done': it may mean no more than 'somewhat abundantly.' In any case we notice here his abstention from denying that his opponents are in any sense Christ's ministers. All he says is that he can give ample evidence that he is a minister of Christ, invested with His authority. Contrast xi. 13–15. In this verse we have the transition from the plur. to the sing. It is still '*our* authority,' but the glorying is his own. The mixture of sing. and plur. continues for a while, and then in xi., xii., xiii. the sing. prevails.

ἧς ἔδωκεν ὁ κύριος εἰς οἰκοδομὴν καὶ οὐκ εἰς καθαίρεσιν ὑμῶν. 'Which the Lord gave me for your upbuilding and not for your demolition.' We must have the same rendering of καθαίρ. here and in *vv.* 4 and 5. Here 'building you up and not casting

you down ' seems more effective; but we talk of 'demolishing'
arguments (λογισμούς) rather than of 'casting them down.
Exactly the same expression is found again xiii. 10, and in both
places it fits the context so well that there is no need to suspect
an editorial insertion from either place to the other. The aor.
refers to the commission given at Saul's conversion (Acts ix. 6,
15, xxii. 15, xxvi. 16). The clause may intimate that his critics
said that his teaching was destructive, or that he holds that theirs
is destructive. But we cannot be sure of either; it may be a
plain statement of fact.

οὐκ αἰσχυνθήσομαι. 'I shall not be put to shame,' by being
exposed as a pretentious boaster. The change from subjunc-
tive to indicative ('shall not,' not 'should not') marks his
confidence. That will never happen. Some commentators
here add, as to be understood, 'and I do not say anything
stronger than this,' in order to account for the ἵνα which follows.
The constr., though not quite regular, is intelligible enough.

> B G 17, Syr-Pesh. Copt. omit τε after ἐάν. We may safely omit καί
> before περισσότερον with א* B C D* E* G P, Latt. Copt. Syr-Hark.
> καυχήσωμαι (B C D F K) rather than καυχήσομαι (א L P). C* P, Syr-
> Pesh. Copt. omit ἡμῶν after ἐξουσίας, perhaps as apparently out of
> harmony with the sing. verb. D³ E G K L ins. ἡμῖν after ὁ κύριος, P before
> it; א B C D* 17, d e omit. Note the divergence between E and e, which
> usually agrees with d independently of the Greek or E.

9. ἵνα μὴ δόξω κ.τ.λ. This depends on v. 8 as a whole, not
on any one clause or word. To make v. 10 a parenthesis and
carry on ἵνα to v. 11 is an intolerable constr.; 'That I may not
seem . . . let such a one, etc.' But it is perhaps in order to
ease such a connexion that Chrys. inserts δέ and Vulg. autem *
after ἵνα, for if ἵνα has no connexion with v. 8, ἵνα μὴ δόξω is
felt to be very abrupt. Ne videar without autem would be
right.

ὡς ἂν ἐκφοβεῖν ὑμᾶς. 'As it were, to terrify you.' The
compound verb has a strong meaning, 'to scare you out of your
senses,' and to tone this down ὡς ἂν is prefixed; quasi perterre-
facere vos. It is freq. in LXX (Job vii. 14, xxxii. 16; Wisd. xi.
19, xvii. 6, 19; etc.), esp. in the phrase οὐκ ἔσται ὁ ἐκφοβῶν
(Lev. xxvi. 6; Deut. xxviii. 26; Mic. iv. 4; Zech. iii. 13; Ezek.
xxxiv. 28, xxxix. 26), but is found nowhere else in N.T. It is
doubtful whether we ought to count this as a very rare instance
of ἂν c. infin. We perhaps ought to write ὡσάν, which occurs in
mod. Grk.; as also σάν, = 'as,' 'like,' or 'when.' Moulton,
p. 167.

διὰ τῶν ἐπιστολῶν. 'By my letters.' We know certainly of
two letters, 1 Cor. and its predecessor (1 Cor. v. 9). Unless

---

* Ut autem non existimer tamquam terrere vos per epistolas.

these four chapters are part of the severe letter (i. 23, ii. 3, 9, vii. 8), we know of three before these words were written, and there may have been others. But the strict injunctions about fornicators in the first letter (1 Cor. v. 9), and the severe sentence on the incestuous person in 1 Cor. (v. 3–5), would justify the expression 'terrifying by my letters,' without the addition of another severe letter.

10. φησίν. It is difficult to decide between φησίν and φασίν (see below). The τις (*v.* 7) and ὁ τοιοῦτος (*v.* 11) might cause φασίν to be corrected to φησίν. On the other hand, φησίν might be corrected to φασίν, because the context shows that this contemptuous criticism of the Apostle's letters was not confined to an individual. In either case we have interesting contemporary evidence of what some people thought of the Apostle's letters and of his personal effectiveness. Either φησίν or φασίν might be rendered 'it is said,' *on dit, man sagt.* Winer, p. 655.

βαρεῖαι καὶ ἰσχυραί. 'Weighty and powerful.'* The truth of this is seen by the description of the effect of the severe letter in vii. 8–11, a description which must be truthful, for it is sent to the Corinthians themselves, who knew the facts. His critics could not deny the solid and effective character of his letters. Βαρεῖαι probably does not mean 'burdensome,' 'grievous' (Mt. xxiii. 4; Acts xx. 29; 1 Jn. v. 3), but 'weighty,' 'impressive' (Mt. xxiii. 23 and perhaps Acts xxv. 7); yet the latter meaning is less common. Illustrations in Wetstein. Used for persons, βαρύς has commonly a bad signification, 'oppressive,' 'cross-grained'; but it sometimes means 'dignified,' 'grave,' like σεμνός. Cf. 1 Thess. ii. 6. Yet it is possible that the two epithets are not meant to be complimentary; they might mean that in his letters he was tyrannical and violent.

ἡ δὲ παρουσία τοῦ σώματος. 'Bodily presence (AV., RV.) can hardly be improved; but 'personal presence,' 'personal appearance,' 'personality' have been suggested. There is chiasmus in the contrasted epithets, ἀσθενής being the antithesis of ἰσχυραί and ἐξουθενημένος of βαρεῖαι, and each pair helps to determine the meaning of the other. It is not certain that there is here any allusion to the personal appearance of the Apostle; that he was short and insignificant, "an ugly little Jew," and that he had revolting infirmities, such as ophthalmia and epilepsy. The contrast seems rather to be between the character of his letters and the character of the man himself.

* German renderings vary considerably ; *gewichtig und gewaltig* (Bachmann) ; *schwer und wuchtig* (Bousset) ; *wuchtig und kraftvoll* (Lietzmann) ; *gewichtig und stark* (Heinrici-Meyer).

In his letters he was bold as a lion and firm as a rock ; when he
came face to face with you, he gave way at once, trying to please
everybody (1 Cor. ix. 20), and what he said was not worth
listening to (see on 1 Cor. ii. 3).* This looks like a reference to
the intermediate and unsuccessful visit.

ἐξουθενημένος. 'Despised,' 'of no account' (1 Cor. i. 28,
vi. 4; Eccles. ix. 16; Mal. ii. 9; Dan. iv. 28; 2 Macc. i. 27).
No doubt the Apostle's powers were not always the same ; his
letters show that.   At times his eloquence seemed godlike
(Acts xiv. 8–12), but he had not the brilliancy of Apollos, and
he did not keep Eutychus awake (Acts xx. 9). Ramsay, *St
Paul*, p. 84, *Church in the Roman Empire*, p. 57. "A personality of such polar contrasts made a very different impression on
different people.   Seldom perhaps has any one been at once so
ardently hated and so passionately loved as St Paul" (Deissmann,
St Paul, p. 70).   As Bousset remarks, the personality of St Paul
must have indeed been great, if, in spite of infirmities which
would be specially distasteful to Greeks, he nevertheless was to
them '*the* Apostle.'

Of the descriptions which have come down to us of the
personal appearance of the Apostle the only one which is at all
likely to be based upon early tradition is the well-known one in
the Acts of Paul and Thekla, a document which Ramsay
(*Church in Rom. Emp.* xvi.) assigns to the first century.   These
Acta exist in Syriac, Latin, Greek, and Armenian, and the
Syriac is believed to embody the earliest form of the story.   The
description in the Syriac is as follows; "A man of middling
size, and his hair was scanty, and his legs were a little crooked,
and his knees were projecting (or far apart); and he had large
eyes, and his eyebrows met, and his nose was somewhat long;
and he was full of grace and mercy; at one time he seemed like
a man, and at another he seemed like an angel." The
Armenian version says that he had blue eyes and crisp or curly
hair.   Later writers give him an aquiline nose.   See F. C.
Conybeare, *Monuments of Early Christianity*, p. 62; Smith and
Cheetham, *D. of Chr. Ant.* ii. p. 1622; Farrar, *St Paul*, exc.
xi. ; Kraus, *Real. Enc. d. Christ. Alter.* ii. pp. 608, 613.

αἱ ἐπιστολαὶ μέν (אʹ* B, r) rather than αἱ μὲν ἐπ. (א³ D F G K L P,
Latt.).   φησίν (א D E F G K L P, d e Copt.) rather than φασίν (B, f g r
Vulg. Syrr.).   Note the divergence between F and f.

11. τοῦτο λογιζέσθω. 'Count *this*.' It is worth while to have
the same rendering in *vv.* 2, 7, 11; RV. has 'count,' 'consider,'
'reckon.' Τοῦτο is emphatic, 'just this.'

τοιοῦτος. Not 'the person in question,' but 'such a one,'
ὁ λόγος would include the thought as well as the expression.

'a person of this kind.' The Apostle is not alluding to a definite individual, but quoting a current criticism.

οἷοί ἐσμεν τῷ λόγῳ. 'What we are in word by letters when we are absent, such *are we* also in act when we are present.' Menzies and Moffatt follow AV. in supplying ἐσόμεθα with τοιοῦτοι, which confines the meaning to his intended visit to Corinth. RV. is almost certainly right in supplying ἐσμεν, which makes the statement apply to his whole character and conduct. He is not one in whom the inconsistency of writing forcibly and acting feebly is found. So Alford, Bachmann, Bernard, Lietzmann, McFadyen, Schmiedel. The antithesis between λόγῳ and ἔργῳ, so freq. in Thucydides, is found Rom. xv. 18; and Acts vii. 22 we have δυνατὸς ἐν λόγοις καὶ ἔργοις αὐτοῦ. In the antithesis here, we again have chiasmus ; τῷ λόγῳ ἀπόντες, παρόντες τῷ ἔργῳ : cf. iv. 3, vi. 8, ix. 6, xiii. 3. Baljon needlessly suggests that δι' ἐπιστολῶν is a gloss.

12–18. A passage, the difficulty of which was very early felt, and hence the variations in the text, some of which are obviously the result of efforts to make things clearer. That St Paul deliberately wrote obscurely in order to avoid making definite charges against his assailants (Theodoret) is not probable.* He is satirical, and we must beware of taking his irony literally. Under cover of mock humility he shows that he is a very different kind of person from those who criticize him from a pinnacle of assumed superiority. They say that at close quarters he is a coward. Well, he must own that he has not the courage which they possess. He does not venture to put himself on a level with people who sing their own praises and try to get themselves accepted at their own valuation. Conduct of that kind is folly. His glorying has limits not of his own choosing ; they are the limits of the sphere assigned to him by God, who sent him to Corinth. And he was the first in the field there. He did not come after others had laboured there and take the credit of what they had done, although there are people who have tried to reap where he has sown. He hopes that as the Corinthians' faith increases he will be able to enlarge his sphere of influence and carry the Gospel to regions farther West, always avoiding the fields of other men's labours, so as not to seem to plume himself on work which was not his own.

The Western text (D* F G, d e f g, Ambrst.) omits οὐ συνιᾶσιν (συνιοῦσιν), ἡμεῖς δέ, and then the sentence ἀλλὰ αὐτοὶ κ.τ.λ. runs ; ' but *we* measuring ourselves by ourselves and comparing ourselves with ourselves are not going into spheres beyond our

---

* ἀσαφῶς ἅπαν τὸ χώρημα τοῦτο γέγραφεν, ἐναργῶς ἐλέγξαι τοὺς αἰτίους οὐ βουλόμενος.

measure and glorying there, etc.' This makes good sense and runs smoothly, with αὐτοί carrying on the constr. of οὐ τολμῶμεν: and it may be an instance of what WH. call "Western non-interpolations" (ii. pp. 175 ff.). But more probably the omission is an attempt to make the original text clearer. The Apostle is not likely to have declared that he made *himself* his standard of excellence. To adopt the reading συνιουσιν and make it a dat. (συνίουσιν) agreeing with ἑαυτοῖς—'compare ourselves with ourselves, unwise people, as they hold us to be'—is objectionable for the same reason, and in that case we should have τοῖς μὴ συνιοῦσιν. We must retain ἡμεῖς δέ, and then αὐτοί refers, not to the Apostle, but to his critics.* And we may safely reject the reading οὐ συνίασιν (ℵ *), which would mean that 'they compare themselves with themselves without being aware that they do so,' which is very poor sense.

X. 12-18. The Area of his Mission includes Corinth.

Self-praise is worthless; but I do claim that Corinth lies in the sphere of work which God has assigned to me.

¹² I am accused of being a coward. Well, I really cannot muster courage to pair myself or compare myself with certain persons who are distinguished by much self-commendation. They fix their own standard of excellence, and are lost in admiration of themselves and one another for conforming to it. That is really not very sagacious. ¹³ We, however, who do not fix our own standard, will not glory beyond our legitimate limits, but will keep within the limits of that sphere which God has assigned to us as a limit, and which certainly meant that we should extend our labours so as to include you. ¹⁴ For we are not, I repeat,— as would be the case if we had no commission to come as far as you,—we are not straining to exceed the limits of our province. Why, we pressed on even to you, and were the first to proclaim in Corinth the Glad-tidings of the Christ. ¹⁵ Our glorying does not go beyond legitimate limits, does not take credit for what other men have done. But we do cherish a hope that, as your faith goes on growing, we may through you get an enlargement of influence—still keeping to the sphere allotted to us—an enlargement on a great scale; ¹⁶ viz. to carry the Glad-tidings to

---

* Bousset takes the opposite view; that οὐ συνιᾶσιν· ἡμεῖς δέ is an insertion to ease the sense, *ein Notbehelf*.

the region beyond you, without glorying (as some people do) in another man's sphere of labour of things already done before we came. ¹⁷ But in any case there is only one right way of glorying ; he who glories, let him glory in the Lord who alone can make work fruitful. ¹⁸ For he who, instead of giving all glory to God, commends himself, is not the man that is accepted; the only one who wins real approval is he whom the Lord commends.

It will perhaps be as well to give a paraphrase of *vv.* 12 and 13 on the hypothesis that the Western text is correct, and it is preferred by some commentators.

¹² You may call me a coward, for I really do not possess boldness enough to pair myself or compare myself with certain persons who are distinguished by much self-commendation. On the contrary, I fix my own standard and compare myself with it, ¹³ and so my glorying will never go beyond legitimate limits, but will keep, etc.

12. Οὐ γὰρ τολμῶμεν ἐνκρῖναι ἢ συνκρῖναι ἑαυτοῖς. One suspects that for the sake of a play upon words the Apostle has used an expression which might otherwise have been clearer. 'For we have not the boldness (*v.* 2) to pair or to compare our-selves with some of those who commend themselves.' The play on words (ἐνκρῖναι ἢ συνκρῖναι) is as obvious here as in *vv.* 5, 6, and the meaning of ἐνκρῖναι seems to be 'judge amongst,' 'estimate amongst,' 'class with,' and it is stronger in meaning than συνκρῖναι, so that 'pair' and 'compare' fairly well preserves the similarity of sound and change of meaning. 'I could not venture to put myself in the same class with, or even compare myself with,' is the sarcastic declaration. Vulg. gives the sense, without preserving any play of words; *non enim audemus inserere aut comparare nos.* Beza has *nos adjungere ved conjungere,* which sacrifices the sense in order to preserve the play. Bengel's *aequiparare aut comparare* is better than either this or *inserere aut conserere.* Cf. Wisd. vii. 29; 1 Macc. x. 71. St Paul had been accused of singing his own praises (iii. 1); he here intimates that this is just what his critics are fond of doing.

ἀλλὰ αὐτοὶ ἐν ἑαυτοῖς ἑαυτοὺς μετροῦντες. If we retain ἡμεῖς δέ in *v.* 13, and it is best to do so, the αὐτοί must refer to the hostile critics; 'But they themselves measuring themselves by them-selves.' They are a "mutual admiration and self-admiration society" (Waite). They set up their own conduct as a standard of excellence, and find their conformity to it eminently satis-factory and admirable. They are a community of Pecksniffs. Calvin takes the monks of his own time as an illustration; *sibi enim intus plaudebant, non considerantes quibus virtutibus constaret vera laus.*

οὐ συνιᾶσιν.   ' Are without understanding '; they are ἄφρονες (Eph. v. 17), who are not intelligent enough to put two and two together.   These self-satisfied critics, who have no external standard, but judge everything by comparison with their own practice, come very far short of wisdom.   *Non intelligunt*, says Augustine, adding *neque quae loquuntur neque de quibus affirmant* (from 1 Tim. i. 7).   Others supply, ' how ridiculous they are,' or ' what they are talking about,' or ' what are the marks of a true Apostle.'   But οὐ συνιᾶσιν needs no supplement.   Cf. οὔπω νοεῖτε οὐδὲ συνίετε; (Mk. viii. 17).

The spelling ἐνκρι. and συνκρι. is supported by B* D*; for the former G has κρῖναι.   Naber's suspicion of dittography is not needed; the play on words is thoroughly Pauline.   D E add ἑαυτούς after the first verb, while ℵ* omits ἑαυτούς before μετροῦντες.   συνιᾶσιν (ℵ¹ B 17) rather than συνιοῦσιν (D³ E K L P) or συνίσασιν (ℵ*).   D* F G, d e f g omit οὐ συν. ἡμεῖς δέ, but the words should be retained with ℵ B D³ E K L P, r Syrr. Copt. Arm. Aeth. Goth.

13.   ἡμεῖς δὲ οὐκ εἰς τὰ ἄμετρα καυχησόμεθα.   ' But *we* will not glory beyond our measure.'   He does not fix his own standard, and he does not exceed the limits fixed for him ; moreover, he has a settled determination never to exceed these limits.   Εἰς τὰ ἄμετρα is indefinite ; it may refer to the excessive self-admiration of his opponents, or it may mean ' in respect of things beyond our scope '; but this is less probable.   Cf. εἰς τὰ μάλιστα.

ἀλλὰ κατὰ τὸ μέτρον τοῦ κανόνος κ.τ.λ.   ' But according to the measure of the length which God apportioned to us as a measure, to reach as far as even you.'   RV. and other authorities render κανών ' province,' and the rendering is so suitable to the context that we may perhaps regard it as admissible ; a specified sphere, definitely marked out, is the meaning required, and ' province ' expresses this very well.   But κανών is generally used of *length*, and τὸ μέτρον τοῦ κανόνος would mean ' the length of one's tether,' the length of the radius from one's centre.   In this case it would mean the distance which God told the Apostle to go in his missionary work.   But seeing that κανών means (1) the rod which measures, and (2) the amount which is measured, and seeing that fixing the bounds of territory may require measuring rods, it is possible that κανών may be used of the territory thus measured.   Lightfoot on Gal. vi. 16, the only other place in N.T. in which the word occurs, seems to take this as certain.   There, however, the term is used of *line*, and not of *surface*; ' all those who shall guide their steps by this rule.' *   In Judith xiii. 6 it

* We use ' line ' in a similar sense.   To be the Apostle of the Gentiles was St Paul's ' line,' and it extended to Corinth.

seems to mean a bed-pole.   More akin to the use here is 4 Macc.
vii. 21, πρὸς ὅλον τὸν τῆς φιλοσοφίας κανόνα εὐσεβῶς φιλοσοφῶν,
where κανόνα might be rendered 'sphere,' or 'province,' although
'rule' may be better.   Westcott, *Canon of N.T.*, App. A, gives
a history of the word.

οὗ ἐμέρισεν ἡμῖν ὁ Θεὸς μέτρου.   'Which *God* apportioned to
us as our measure.'   St Paul did not determine his own province
any more than his own standard of excellence.   God did that.
Cf. 1 Cor. vii. 17; Rom. xii. 3; Heb. vii. 2.   Some editors
bracket μέτρου as probably a gloss, but ἐμέρισεν μέτρου is another
alliteration, and St Paul is harping on the idea of ' measure.'
Vulg. omits; *quam mensus est nobis Deus.*   Both οὗ and μέτρου
are attracted in case to τοῦ κανόνος.

ἐφικέσθαι ἄχρι καὶ ὑμῶν.   This was what God intended; that
his line should 'reach as far as even you'; *pertingendi usque ad
vos.*   This was indisputable.   St Paul was the first to preach the
Gospel in Corinth, and it was God who had turned him from a
persecutor into a preacher.   The verb is common enough in
class. Grk., but it is found nowhere else in N.T., and perhaps
nowhere in LXX.

ουκ (א B D* G K L P) rather than οὐχι (D³ E).   εἰς τὰ ἄμετρα (א B D³
K L P) rather than εἰς τὸ ἄμετρον (D* G) *in immensum* (Latt.).   ἐφικέσθαι
(א B G K L P) rather than ἀφικέσθαι (D E F).

14.   We again have several doubtful points to consider; text,
arrangement, and punctuation are all uncertain.   At the outset
all these must be regarded as tentative.

οὐ γὰρ ὡς μή.   Adopting this reading, we will treat the verse
as not a mere parenthesis to explain *v.* 13, and will connect
v. 15 with *v.* 14; moreover, we will regard no part of *v.* 14 as
interrogative.   'For we are not overstretching ourselves, as (we
should be doing) if we did not reach unto you, for as far as even
you we were the first to come in the Gospel (viii. 18; Rom. i. 9)
of the Christ, not glorying beyond our measure, etc.'   Or, without supplying anything, we may take the first part of *v.* 14 thus;
'For we are not, as if we did not reach unto you, overstretching
ourselves.'   If the reading ὡς γὰρ μή is adopted, then the first
part must be a question; 'For are we overstretching ourselves,
as if we did not reach unto you?'   'Are we exceeding our
commission in claiming authority in Corinth?'   Facts speak for
themselves; he founded the Church there.

It is not certain that φθάνω here, as in 1 Thess. iv. 15, retains
its class. signification of 'come first,' 'precede,' 'anticipate.'   In
later Greek it commonly means simply 'come' (1 Thess. ii. 16;
Rom. ix. 31; Phil. iii. 16); so in papyri and perhaps here (RV.).
Nevertheless, the fact that he not only came as far as Corinth
with the Glad-tidings, but was the first to do so, has point.

Unless *v.* 14 is treated as a parenthetical explanation of *v.* 13 (WH.), we need only a comma at the end of it.

οὐ γὰρ ὡς μή (‭א‬ D F G K L M, Latt.) rather than ὡς γὰρ μή (B and two cursives).

15, 16. These verses are connected with *v.* 14 rather than with *v.* 13. The clumsiness of expression is due to dictation, in which the sentence has become unduly prolonged. The Judaizing teachers had intruded into his province and taken credit for what was his work, and he aims at showing that he himself has done nothing of the kind.

οὐκ εἰς τὰ ἄμετρα κ.τ.λ. 'Not glorying beyond our measure in other men's labours, but having hope that, as your faith grows, we shall be magnified in you according to our province unto still greater abundance, so as to preach the Gospel unto the regions beyond you, and not to glory in another man's province in respect of things ready to our hand.' At present Corinth is the Western limit of his sphere of missionary work. When the Corinthian Church is more firmly established, he hopes to extend his labours still farther into Europe.

15. ἐν ὑμῖν. The words are amphibolous, but they have more point if they are taken with μεγαλυνθῆναι. They are almost superfluous if taken with αὐξανομένης (Luther, Calvin); if their faith increases, it must increase in them and among them; but it is not superfluous to remind them that it lies in their power to make it quickly possible for him to extend his sphere of work. Both καυχώμενοι and ἔχοντες are *participia absoluta*, of which St Paul makes freq. use. See on viii. 20. With μεγαλυνθῆναι comp. Phil. i. 20, with περισσείαν, viii. 2.

16. εἰς τὰ ὑπερέκεινα ὑμῶν. The expression may be coined for the occasion, for ὑπερέκεινα has been found nowhere else.* It may have been a current popular word which has not found its way into literature; ἐπέκεινα (Acts vii. 43 and LXX) is classical. A little later St Paul had intentions of going to Rome and Spain (Rom. xv. 24, 28), and such ideas may have been in his mind when he wrote this letter. Regarding Antioch as his original centre, he *might* vaguely describe such regions as τὰ ὑπερέκεινα in reference to Corinth. But, *if these chapters are part of the severe letter written at Ephesus,* 'the parts beyond Corinth' would be a natural expression for Rome and Spain. See Introduction, p. xxxiii.

εὐαγγελίσασθαι. In these verses (14–16) we have εὐαγγέλιον and εὐαγγελίζομαι, expressions and ideas which are in a high degree Pauline. The former occurs in all groups of the Epistles,

* Thomas Magister condemns it as a vulgarism used only by οἱ σύρφακες.

19

60 times in all, and indeed in every Epistle, excepting that to
Titus. The latter is found chiefly in this group, but also in
1 Thess. and Eph., 20 times in all, and its usual meaning is
'preach the Gospel,' whether εὐαγγέλιον be added (xi. 7) or not;
but in a few passages it means simply 'preach,' and hardly
differs from κηρύσσω (Gal. i. 23; Eph. ii. 17, iii. 8; 1 Thess.
iii. 6). Εὐαγγέλιον more often than not has no defining adjective
or genitive, as here and viii. 18; contrast ii. 12, iv. 4, ix. 13,
xi. 7; and seeing that the verb is a technical word to indicate
the work of a Christian missionary, the noun indicates the substance or contents of mission preaching. In other words, it is
"God's plan of salvation, contained in the O.T. as a promise,
and realized through Jesus Christ" (Harnack, *Constitution and
Law of the Church*, pp. 292 f.).

εἰς τὰ ἔτοιμα καυχήσασθαι. 'To glory in respect of things
ready to our hand,' *i.e.* 'done by other persons before we came
on the scene and claimed the credit of it,' a condensed expression, the meaning of which would be obscure without the
context. The constr. καυχ. εἰς is found in Arist. *Pol.* v. x. 16.
We know that St Paul on principle avoided centres where other
missionaries had been working (Rom. xv. 20); he was commissioned to be always a pioneer, and he regarded his extraordinary success as a proof that he was commissioned by God.
It was never his desire to find things ready to his hand, still less
to claim the merit for what had been already done. Indeed
there was no merit to be claimed even when, in the province
apportioned to him, great results were produced. Therefore he
again quotes (see on 1 Cor. i. 31) an adaptation of Jer. ix. 24.

17. ὁ δὲ καυχώμενος. 'But he that glorieth, in the Lord let
him glory'; that is the only safe principle. If faith has been
planted and made to grow, it is God who gives the increase. It
is probable that ὁ κύριος here means God rather than Christ.
But it is remarkable with what readiness N.T. writers transfer
what in O.T. is said of Jehovah to Jesus Christ, and this may be
a case in point. See on 1 Cor. xv. 10; Rom. xv. 17; Eph.
iii. 7; and cf. Gal. ii. 8: in all these passages St Paul carefully
disclaims merit for what he has been enabled to accomplish.

18. οὐ γὰρ ὁ ἑαυτὸν συνιστάνων, ἐκεῖνός ἐστιν δόκιμος. 'For it
is not the man who commends himself that is the one to be
accepted' (δέχομαι) as of sterling character. See on 1 Cor.
ix. 27, xi. 19; ἐκεῖνος as in Rom. xiv. 14. St Paul had been
forced by the attacks made on him to glory about himself, but
it was not on this self-praise that he relied. The Corinthian
Church was his letter of commendation, and over and above
this there was the manifest blessing which God both in Corinth

and elsewhere bestowed upon his work. His assailants had no
such confirmation of the praise which they bestowed on themselves. Cf. ἐγκωμιαζέτω σε ὁ πέλας καὶ μὴ τὸ σὸν στόμα, ἀλλότριος
καὶ μὴ τὰ σὰ χείλη (Prov. xxvii. 2). Augustine (*in Ps.* cxliv. *n.* 7)
says, *Ecce inventum est, quomodo et te laudare possis et arrogans
non sis. Deum in te lauda, non te ; non quia tu es talis, sed quia ille
fecit te ; non quia tu aliquid potes, sed quia potest ille in te et per te.**

XI. 1–XII. 10. The Apostle continues his comparison of
himself with the Judaizing teachers who oppose him. He has
just shown that, if any question of intrusion is raised, it is not he
who has intruded into their proper area of activity, but they who
have intruded into his. He goes on to show that in other
respects he can say at least as much for himself in claiming to
be an Apostle as these teachers can do. He has worked without
payment, which he has not only not asked for but refused ; his
labours have been greater and his sufferings far greater than
theirs ; and he has received very special revelations and visita-
tions from God. But first of all he justifies himself for entering
into this comparison at all (xi. 1–6). All this glorying about
oneself is odious folly, and, seeing that he has just been
maintaining that self-praise is no recommendation, it seems
grossly inconsistent. But the boastings of his opponents have
forced him to adopt this course ; and, as the Corinthians have
shown much toleration to them, he asks them to show a little to
him, when he answers fools according to their folly. He harps
all through on the folly of it (xi. 1, 16–21, xii. 1, 11), but he is
willing to make a fool of himself to save them from disaster.
Possibly ἀνέχεσθαι ἀφρ. was a phrase used by his critics. The
difference between him and his critics is this ; that they, without
being aware of it, are fools ceaselessly, because folly has become
a second nature to them ; whereas he deliberately plays the fool
for a few minutes, because their folly can be met in no other way.

XI. 1–6. The Folly of Glorying and the Reason for it.

*Forgive my foolish boasting, which is caused by anxious
affection. I fear lest these self-asserting impostors should
seduce you from Christ.*

¹ I wish that you could bear with me in a little somewhat of
folly. (It is, of course, foolish to boast ; but you stand a good

* "Two feelings are compounded all through this passage ; an intense
sympathy with the purpose of God that the Gospel should be preached to
every creature ; and an intense scorn for the spirit that sneaks and poaches
on another's ground, and is more anxious that some men should be good
sectarians than that all men should be good disciples" (Denney, p. 309).

deal of it from other people.)   Well, I know that you do bear
with me.   ² The truth is that I am jealous over you with God's
own jealousy; for I betrothed you to one husband exclusively.
My aim was to present the Church of Corinth as a pure virgin-
bride to the Christ.   ³ But I am sadly afraid lest somehow, as
the serpent utterly deceived Eve by his craftiness, so your
thoughts should be corrupted and led astray from the single-
minded devotion and pure fidelity which should be observed
towards Christ.   ⁴ And my fear is not groundless, for if the
intruding alien (and I hear that there are such people) is
proclaiming another kind of Jesus such as we did not proclaim,
or you are receiving a different kind of spirit such as you did
not receive from us, or a different kind of Gospel such as you
did not accept at our hand,—then you bear with a person of this
kind with quite beautiful toleration !   ⁵ I ask you to be equally
tolerant towards me; for I am persuaded that in nothing have
I been inferior to those pre-eminent apostles of yours.   ⁶ Granted
that, as compared with them, I am untrained in speech, yet in
the knowledge that is worth having I am not untrained.   No;
in all things we have made that plain among all men in our
relations with you.

    1. Ὄφελον ἀνείχεσθέ μου μικρόν τι ἀφροσύνης.   'Would that
ye bore with me in a little somewhat of folly.'   The sudden
outburst looks like the beginning of a new topic, but, as has
been shown above, the connexion with what precedes is close.
He is again guarding himself against the charge of vanity and
self-praise.   The unaugmented 2nd aor. ὄφελον in late Greek is
a mere particle, hardly more than 'Oh,' expressing a wish as to
what might happen, but is almost too good to come true, as
here, or what might have been the case, but was not.   Here and
Rev. iii. 15 it is followed by imperf. indic. ; in Gal. v. 12 by fut.
indic., where, as here, there is a touch of irony ; in 1 Cor. iv. 8
by aor. indic., and there also there may be irony.   The aor.
indic. is freq. in LXX, esp. in the phrase ὄφελον ἀπεθάνομεν
(Ex. xvi. 3 ; Job xiv. 13 ; Num. xiv. 2, xx. 3).   In 2 Kings
v. 3 no verb is expressed.   In class. Grk. the augmented ὤφελον
is usually followed by the infin.   The meaning here is 'would
that ye bore,' or 'Oh that ye could bear,' not 'would that ye had
borne' (Calvin).   Blass, § 63. 5.   We have ἀφροσύνη, vv. 17, 21 ;
Mk. vii. 22 ; in 1 Cor. we have μωρία (i. 18, 21, 23, ii. 14, iii. 19).
    The constr. of the two genitives is disputed.   In Bibl. Grk.
ἀνέχομαι commonly has gen. of either person or thing, but the

acc. is sometimes found, as in class. Grk. Here the ἀνέχεσθε μου in the next clause makes it almost certain that the first μου is the gen. after ἀνείχεσθε, and then ἀφροσύνης is the gen. after μικρόν τι, which is the acc. of reference. But it is possible to take μικρόν τι as the acc. after ἀνείχεσθε and make both genitives depend upon μικόν τι.* This, however, is clumsy and improbable. ἀλλὰ καὶ ἀνέχεσθέ μου. As in x. 7, we are in doubt as to whether the verb is indicative or imperative, and most English Versions decide for the latter, as if the Apostle were repeating his wish in the form of a prayer. ‘I wish you would—nay, *do*.’ In either case the ἀλλά corrects what has just been said, while καί emphasizes what is now said, and one gets more of a correction and as much room for emphasis if one takes ἀνέχεσθε as indicative. He has just expressed a wish as if it were not very likely to be fulfilled, and then he corrects himself; ‘Well, I ought not to speak like that; you *do* bear with me’; or, ‘*But* there is no need to wish; of course you *do* bear with me.’ Blass, § 77. 13, prefers the other alternative.

ὄφελον (אּ B M P) rather than ὤφελον (D³ F G K L). ἀνείχεσθε (אּ B D F G K L M P) rather than ἠνείχεσθε (some cursives). τι ἀφροσύνης (אּ B D E M 17) rather than τῇ ἀφροσύνῃ (K L) or ἀφροσύνης without τι (P).

2. **ζηλῶ γὰρ ὑμᾶς Θεοῦ ζήλῳ.** ‘For I am jealous over you with a divine jealousy.’ The exact meaning of Θεοῦ is uncertain, but it implies that the honour of God is involved in the matter. Something will depend on the meaning which we give to ζηλῶ and ζήλῳ, whether ‘am zealous with zeal’ or ‘am jealous with jealousy.’ Such renderings as ‘zeal for God’s glory,’ or ‘zeal such as God loves,’ or ‘very great zeal’ (cf. τοῦ Θεοῦ, i. 12, and τῷ Θεῷ, x. 4) are unsatisfactory, and ‘I love you with very great love’ is impossible. Lightfoot on Gal. iv. 17 suggests that ‘I take interest in you with a divine interest’ is the meaning here; but what follows indicates that jealousy rather than zeal is meant, jealousy in the higher sense, as when we are jealous about our own or another person’s honour. St Paul assumes for himself the part of the person who has arranged the betrothal, and who watched jealously over the bride’s conduct in the interval before the marriage, which is to take place when Christ returns at the παρουσία.† In O.T. Israel is represented as the spouse of Jehovah, who is jealous of anything like unfaithfulness (Is. liv. 5, 6, lxii. 5; Jer. iii. 1; Ezek. xvi. 23–33); but there is no third person who is concerned with this relationship. In

---

* Lietzmann contends that if ἀνέχεσθε had not followed, no one would have taken the first μου with ἀνείχεσθε, and that St Paul does not mean this ; in the second sentence he has without thinking changed his construction.

† μνηστείας γάρ ἐστι καιρὸς ὁ παρὼν καιρός· ὁ δὲ τῶν παστάδων ἕτερος, ὅταν λέγωσιν, ἀνέστη ὁ νυμφίος (Chrys.).

most cases it was the parents who arranged the betrothal, and
St Paul is here regarding himself as the parent of the Corinthian
Church (xii. 14; 1 Cor. iv. 17). In Hos. ii. 19, 20 the relationship between Jehovah and Israel is represented as betrothal
rather than marriage, but again there is no third person; Jehovah
acts for Himself, just as in Eph. v. 27 Christ presents the Church
to Himself, without the intervention of any Apostle.

ἡρμοσάμην γὰρ ὑμᾶς ἑνὶ ἀνδρί. 'For I betrothed you to one
husband.' In class. Grk. the midd. would be used of the man
betrothing himself, and in Prov. xix. 14 it is used of the woman,
παρὰ δὲ κυρίου ἁρμόζεται γυνὴ ἀνδρί : the act. would be used of
betrothing another person, either ἀνδρὶ τὴν θυγατέρα (Hdt. ix.
108) or κόρᾳ ἄνδρα (Pind. Pyth. ix. 207). In the Testaments
(Iss. i. 10) Rachel says to Leah, Μὴ καυχῶ μηδὲ δόξαζε σεαυτήν,
ὅτι ἐμὲ πρότερόν σου ἡρμόσατο (Ἰακώβ), in accordance with classical
usage. But here the context fixes the meaning (Winer, p. 323),
and the midd. may indicate the Apostle's interest in the matter;
as προμνήστωρ καὶ γάμου μεσίτης (Thdrt.) he was jealously
anxious that nothing should interfere with the marriage. The
betrothed woman must devote herself exclusively to her destined
Husband, and must not allow her thoughts to be diverted to any
other. The ἑνί implies this, and is probably aimed at those
who were distracting the Corinthians from their loyalty to the
Christ preached by St Paul. Bachmann with Beza and Bengel
takes ἑνὶ ἀνδρί with παραστῆσαι, 'to present a pure virgin to one
husband, viz. the Christ'; but that leaves ἡρμοσάμην without
anything to fix its meaning, and it would inevitably mean, 'I
betrothed you to myself.' See Hastings, DB. and DCG. artt.
'Bride' and 'Bridegroom.'

παρθένον ἁγνὴν παραστῆσαι τῷ Χριστῷ. 'To present a pure
(vii. 11; Phil. iv. 8; 1 Tim. v. 22) virgin to the Christ.' Neither
AV. nor RV. put 'you' after 'present' in italics; it is not
required in English any more than in the Greek.

Here again, as in the concluding verses of x., it is clear that
St Paul is addressing the whole Church of Corinth, and not the
rebellious minority. Cf. vv. 7–11. The statement that in i.–ix.
the loyal Corinthians are addressed, and in x.–xiii. the disloyal,
and that this explains the extraordinary change of tone, is not in
harmony with the facts.

3. φοβοῦμαι δὲ μή πως. *Timeo autem ne forte.* He does not
express either complete trust or complete distrust. Cf. xii. 20;
Gal. iv. 11. He has just expressed his own share and interest
in their relationship to the Christ. Of course it must and will
be maintained; but (δέ) there are perils about which he has
misgivings.

ὡς ὁ ὄφις ἐξηπάτησεν Εὔαν. 'As the serpent deceived Eve.'
The compound verb is strong in meaning, and perhaps justifies
the insertion of 'utterly' or 'completely.' In 1 Tim. ii. 14 the
compound marks a distinction between Adam and Eve; she
was 'entirely deceived,' but he was not even 'deceived'; what
he did, he did to please himself and his wife. Nowhere else
in N.T. is Eve mentioned. In LXX the compound is very
rare, and in Gen. iii. 13 we have ὁ ὄφις ἠπάτησέν με. In N.T.
it is confined to St Paul (1 Cor. iii. 18; Rom. vii. 11, xvi. 18;
2 Thess. ii. 3; 1 Tim. ii. 14), who is fond of compounds with
ἐκ (x. 9, xi. 12, 33, xii. 15; 1 Cor. v. 7, 13, vi. 14, xv. 34; etc.).
In N.T. ἀπατάω is rare (Eph. v. 6; 1 Tim. ii. 14; Jas. i. 26).

Thackeray (*Relation of St Paul to Contemporary Jewish
Thought*, p. 55) perhaps goes too far in saying that in these
verses (3–15) we have "very strong reasons for presuming an
acquaintance on the part of St Paul with the Rabbinical legend
found in the *Apocalypse of Moses* and elsewhere, that the serpent
seduced Eve to unchastity and that Cain was their child; also
that Satan, after having first taken the form of a serpent, afterwards took that of an angel." Menzies regards it as certain that
"Paul knew a Haggadah or legend of this kind." Heinrici in
Meyer gives reasons for doubting this. Had St Paul said τῇ
ἐπιθυμίᾳ αὐτοῦ and expressed what follows with more resemblance
to the legend, his acquaintance with it would have been more
certain.* Assuming that he knew it, there is no evidence that
he believed it. He uses legends as illustrations of truth; see
on 1 Cor. x. 4.

ἐν τῇ πανουργίᾳ αὐτοῦ. 'In his craftiness' (see on iv. 2).
'Subtilty' (AV.) is no doubt meant to connect this with 'the
serpent was more subtle than any beast of the field' (Gen. iii. 1);
but there LXX has φρονιμώτατος.† The legend says that it was
because the serpent was the wisest animal that Satan took its
form. The identification of the serpent with Satan is not found
earlier than Wisd. ii. 24, and it is not certain that it is found
there. 'By the envy of the devil death entered into the world,'
may refer to Cain's envy leading him to kill Abel. Clement of
Rome (*Cor.* iii.) takes it so; as does Theophilus (*Ad Autol.* ii.
29). Cf. 1 Jn. iii. 12. See Gregg on Wisd. ii. 24.

φθαρῇ τὰ νοήματα ὑμῶν ἀπὸ τῆς ἁπλότητος. 'Your thoughts

* There is no trace of this legend in *Enoch* xxxiii. 6, lxix. 12, or *Jubilees*
iii. 18–26, or the *Apocalypse of Baruch* xlviii. 42, or 4 Esdras i. 5, 6, 21–26,
or Tobit viii. 6. See Bachmann, *ad loc.* p. 361. Is it *a priori* probable
that St Paul would allude to such legends in writing to Gentiles?

† Aquila had ὁ ὄφις ἦν πανοῦργος. It was perhaps part of the πανουργία
of the Judaizers, that in Corinth they did not attempt to enforce circumcision,
an attempt which had not been very successful in Galatia and which would
not be likely to succeed at Corinth.

(ii. 11, iii. 14, iv. 4, x. 5) should be corrupted (vii. 2 ; 1 Cor. xv. 33 ; Eph. iv. 22) from the simplicity (viii. 2, ix. 11, 13) and the purity (vi. 6 only) that is toward (viii. 22) the Christ.' Note that it is the Christian community as a whole, and not any individual Christian, that is the spouse of the Christ. The Apostle's fear that the community will be seduced is very strange *after* the satisfaction expressed in the first seven chapters. The ἀπό implies that the corruption issues in seduction and separation ; cf. Rom. vii. 2, ix. 3. If καὶ τῆς ἁγνότητος is genuine, it refers to the chaste conduct of the παρθένος ἁγνή during the interval between betrothal and marriage. Like the serpent, the false teachers were promising enlightenment as the reward of disloyalty and disobedience. See Denney, p. 323.

אB D* G P 17, d e g r, Copt. omit οὕτω before φθαρῇ, and neither οὕτω (D² and ³ E K L M, f Vulg. Syrr.) nor φθάρει (K L P) is likely to be original. καὶ τῆς ἁγνότητος after ἁπλότητος (א* B F G 17, g Goth. Aeth.) is strongly attested. But א³ D³ K L M P, f Vulg. Syrr., Clem. Alex. omit, and D* E d e have τῆς ἁγνότητος καὶ τῆς ἁπλότητος, which suggests that the words may be a gloss inserted in two different places. Note the divergence of f from F. א G M omit τόν before Χριστόν.

4. εἰ μὲν γὰρ ὁ ἐρχόμενος ἄλλον Ἰησοῦν κηρύσσει. 'For if indeed the intruder is preaching another Jesus, whom we did not preach, and ye are receiving a different spirit which ye did not receive, or a different gospel which ye did not accept, ye bear with him quite beautifully.' Cf. Mk. vii. 9. The concluding words are sarcastic, and for this the μέν at the outset prepares us. 'If indeed a person of the following description presents himself, then your toleration of his vagaries is quite lovely. Don't you think that you might show a little toleration to one who has proved to you that he is an Apostle of Christ?' The wording is obscure, because we do not know the exact character of the teaching to which St Paul alludes ; but what is suggested as rendering and meaning makes good sense. It is rash to insist on allusion to some prominent individual ; like τις and τοιοῦτος (x. 7, 10), the sing. is generic. Cf. Gal. v. 10 ; Mt. xviii. 17. 'People who act in this way' is the meaning, and in ὁ ἐρχόμενος there is probably no allusion to the familiar title of Messiah (Mt. xi. 3 ; Lk. vii. 19, 20 ; Jn. vi. 14 ; etc.). St Paul goes great lengths in his sarcasms, but he is not insinuating that the Judaizers claimed Messianic authority. By ὁ ἐρχόμενος is meant *qui suis ipsius auspiciis tamquam magister venit, quicunque ille est* (Cornely). We may reasonably conjecture that Ἰησοῦς, πνεῦμα, εὐαγγέλιον, which are a somewhat strange triplet, were leading terms in the teaching of the Judaizers. Ἰησοῦς rather than Χριστός, for Judaizers would not use Χριστός as a proper name.

The aorists, ἐκηρύξαμεν, ἐλάβετε, ἐδέξασθε, refer to the time when the Apostle converted the Corinthians, and they should be rendered as aorists. And ἐδέξασθε, 'accepted,' which is necessarily a voluntary act, should be distinguished from ἐλάβετε, 'received,' which is not necessarily such. Vulg. has *accepistis* and *recepistis*, which may serve.

It is possible that not much difference is intended by the change from ἄλλον to ἕτερον, yet the change should be marked in translation; and this neither Vulg. nor AV. does, either here or Gal. i. 6, 7, where see Lightfoot. The change here may be caused by the change from a person to what is regarded as impersonal. Thus Acts iv. 12, οὐκ ἔστιν ἐν ἄλλῳ οὐδενὶ ἡ σωτηρία· οὐδὲ γὰρ ὄνομά ἐστιν ἕτερον κ.τ.λ. There are passages, and this is one of them, in which it is not easy to decide what St Paul means by πνεῦμα. Sometimes we are not sure whether he is speaking of the human spirit or of the Divine Spirit; and when he is speaking of the Divine Spirit, it is not always clear how far he regards the Spirit as personal. A qualifying epithet or genitive often decides the first question, but not always the second; and where neither is found the first question may remain open. This is specially the case in the expression ἐν πνεύματι (Eph. ii. 22, iii. 5, v. 18, vi. 18; Col. i. 8). The distinction between personal and impersonal was less distinctly drawn than it is now, and it is safer not to make the Apostle's language more definite than he makes it himself. On the human side he has no definite scheme of psychology; on the Divine side no theological system like the *Quicunque vult.* As to the πνεῦμα ἕτερον here we may say that what he offered to the Corinthians was the spirit of freedom (iii. 17; Gal. v. 1, 15) and of joy (1 Thess. i. 6; Gal. v. 22; Rom. xiv. 17), and that what the Judaizers offered was a spirit of bondage (Gal. iv. 24; Rom. viii. 15) and of fear (Rom. viii. 15).* The general question is well handled by Headlam, *St Paul and Christianity*, pp. 95–115; Abbott, *Johannine Grammar*, p. 518.

καλῶς ἀνέχεσθε. 'You bear with him quite beautifully'; an ironical statement. Cf. Mk. vii. 9. If ἀνείχεσθε is the right reading, then we must translate, 'If he preaches . . . you *would* bear with him'; and in that case St Paul has changed his constr. in order to make the conclusion less harsh, for ἀνείχεσθε implies that εἰ ἐκήρυσσεν has preceded; and it is possible that ἀνείχεσθε has been corrected to ἀνέχεσθε to agree with εἰ κηρύσσει. But neither ἀνείχεσθε nor ἀνέχεσθε justifies 'ye might well bear with him' (AV.). Winer, p. 383. Some would make the sentence interrogative, and in that case there is no sarcasm, but the καλῶς

---

* "The same remark applies to 'theosophy,' 'spiritualism,' and other 'gospels.' It will be time to take them seriously when they utter one wise or true word on God or the soul which is not an echo of something in the old familiar Scriptures" (Denney, p. 324).

is understood literally. 'If people come and behave in this way, is it seemly that you should tolerate them? in putting up with them do you act καλῶς? You are pledged to Christ and His cause, and people come and try to disturb your fidelity; can you listen to them without dishonour?' Cf. καλῶς in 1 Cor. vii. 37, 38. This makes good sense; but there is so much irony in this part of the Epistle, that to make the sentence categorical and καλῶς sarcastic is more in harmony with the general tone of the context: *pseudoapostolis nihil non permittebant* (Calvin).

'Ιησοῦν (א B D E F K L M P and most versions) rather than Χριστόν (G, f g Vulg.). We should probably read ἀνέχεσθε (B D* 17) rather than ἀνείχεσθε (א D³ E G K L M P) or ἠνείχεσθε (some cursives).

5. λογίζομαι γὰρ μηδὲν ὑστερηκέναι τῶν ὑπερλίαν ἀποστόλων. 'For I count (x. 7, 11) that I am not a whit behind those pre-eminent apostles.' The γάρ looks back to the appeal just made; 'You tolerate these people; you surely can tolerate me; for I am at least as good as they are.' The very unusual expression οἱ ὑπερλίαν ἀπόστολοι has been explained in two very different ways, and the rendering of the rare adv. ὑπερλίαν varies according to the interpretation of the whole phrase. Baur and many others have supposed that this is a hit at the leaders among the Twelve, that such as the 'pillar-Apostles' of Gal. ii. 9 are meant, and that we have here a powerful piece of evidence in support of the theory that in the Apostolic Age there was strong opposition between Petrine and Pauline influences. On this hypothesis such renderings as 'pre-eminent,' 'very chiefest,' 'supreme,' are preferred.* Protestant controversialists have used this interpretation as an argument against the supremacy of St Peter, to whom St Paul is supposed to claim to be in every point an equal; and Romanists, instead of showing that the interpretation is erroneous, have accepted it and argued that, although St Paul claims equality in gifts, yet he says nothing about jurisdiction.

It is improbable that St Paul would use such an expression as οἱ ὑπερλίαν ἀπόστολοι of any of the Twelve. Baur's hypothesis about the conflict between Petrine and Pauline tendencies in the Apostolic Age is now almost everywhere abandoned, and there is little doubt that the phrase in question is a sarcastic description of the Judaizing leaders, who claimed to be acting with the authority of the Twelve against one who had no such authority. St Paul speaks of them as 'superlative,' 'superfine,' 'superextra,' 'overmuch' apostles. 'These precious apostles of yours' might represent the contemptuous tone of the words. It is possible

* RV. retains 'very chiefest,' which commits one to the theory that some of the Twelve are meant. The Latin renderings vary. Vulg. has simply *magni*; others have *praegrandes, qui supra modum, qui valde, qui supra quam valde, apostoli sunt*. Beza has *summi*.

that ὑπερλίαν was current in colloquial language, but the Apostle may have coined it for himself; cf. ὑπεράγαν (2 Macc. viii. 35, x. 34, xiii. 25) and the classical ὑπεράτω (Arist., Polyb.) and ὑπέρευ (εὖ).* He is fond of compounds of ὑπέρ, as this letter shows; ὑπεραίρομαι, ὑπερβάλλω, ὑπερβαλλόντως, ὑπερέκεινα, ὑπερπερισσεύω. The suggestion that he is here using a phrase coined by his opponents, and turning it against them, is not wholly incredible; but it does not seem probable that they would employ such an expression to designate any of the Twelve, or that, if they did, he would borrow it.† That he should frame it as a mock-heroic description of his unscrupulous critics is more probable. Gal. ii. 6–9 is not parallel, and is not evidence that St Paul sometimes spoke disparagingly of the Twelve. 'Preeminent' may serve as a neutral rendering, which does not at once commit one to either interpretation.

Vulg. renders ὑστερέω in a variety of ways; here *minus facio*, xii. 11 *minus sum*, elsewhere *desum, egeo, deficio* (Index IV.). The perf. here, as in Heb. iv. 1, indicates past and continuing inferiority. 'Being inferior to' and 'coming short of' must involve the idea of comparison, and hence the gen. ; cf. Rom. iii. 23.

For γάρ B has δέ, perhaps to correspond with μέν in *v.* 4. D* E, d e r add ἐν ὑμῖν after ὑστερηκέναι.

6. εἰ δὲ καὶ ἰδιώτης τῷ λόγῳ. The Apostle at once makes an admission that in one particular it may be the case that he is inferior to the Judaizing teachers. Here εἰ καί, as distinct from καὶ εἰ, represents the possibility as a fact (iv. 3, v. 16, xii. 11 ; 1 Cor. iv. 7), although it is not certain that St Paul always observes this distinction. 'But though I am untrained in oratory, yet in knowledge I am not so.' Ἰδιώτης (1 Cor. xiv. 16, 23, 24 ; Acts iv. 13) means one who confines himself to his own affairs, τὰ ἴδια, and takes no part in public life ; and such a person was regarded by Greeks as wanting in education and likely to be unpractical and *gauche*. The word also came to mean one who had no technical or professional training, with regard to some particular art or science ; unskilled, a layman or amateur, as distinct from an expert or professional. And that is the meaning here ; the Apostle admits that he is not a trained rhetorician, not a professional orator, and he perhaps implies that some of

---

* ὑπερλίαν is quoted as occurring in Eustathius, 1184, 19.

† Among the surprising things in the Bampton Lectures of 1913 is the contention that " Peter had been paying a visit of such duration to Corinth as to have created a following who boasted themselves distinctively, as being the disciples of one whom they looked upon as a 'super-eminent Apostle'" (p. 78). That St Peter had visited Corinth is assumed from 1 Cor. i. 12, ix. 5 ; and from 1 Cor. ix. 6 it is assumed that Barnabas had been there also. The evidence is not strong.

his opponents have this advantage. That any of them were *causidici*, accustomed, like Tertullus (Acts xxiv. 1), to plead in court, is not probable; but they may have pointed out to the Corinthians, who highly valued gifts of speech, that a true Apostle would be likely to possess more power in that particular than he exhibited (x. 10). See Knowling on Acts iv. 13; Wetstein on 1 Cor. xiv. 16; Suicer, *Thesaurus, s.v.*; Trench, *Syn.* § lxxix.

ἀλλ' οὐ τῇ γνώσει. He might be a poor speaker, but he knew what he was talking about. He did not profess to teach them things of which he himself was ignorant. As regards the mysteries of revelation, the essential truths of the Gospel, and their relation to human life here and hereafter, he was no self-made smatterer, but an expert and a specialist, trained and inspired by the Lord Himself. This γνῶσις is *prima dos apostoli* (Beng.). With the constr. comp. 1 Cor. iv. 15.

ἀλλ' ἐν παντὶ φανερώσαντες ἐν πᾶσιν εἰς ὑμᾶς. 'But in all things we made it manifest among all men to you-ward.' Ἐν παντί is specially freq. in the first nine chapters of this letter (iv. 8, vi. 4, vii. 5, 16, viii. 7, ix. 8, 11); elsewhere it is rare (*v.* 11, 1 Thess. v. 18). It means 'in every particular,' 'in every respect.' It is not likely that ἐν πᾶσιν is neut., which would make it a mere repetition of ἐν παντί, although some take it so; 'in all things . . . among all men' is the meaning. His teaching has been public; there has been no secrecy about it, and anyone can form an opinion of its character and of the Apostle's relation to his hearers. He has a Divine commission to manifest the truth to every man's conscience (iv. 2). In that he is no ἰδιώτης.

Here again we have a participle used absolutely, without any regular constr., as in i. 7, vii. 5, viii. 20, 24, ix. 11, 13; and it is not clear what it is that is made manifest, but probably τὴν γνῶσιν is to be understood; what has been revealed to him has been passed on to them.

D*, d e f g omit δέ between εἰ and καί. D* E d e g add εἰμι after ἰδιώτης. φανερώσαντες (אׁ B F G 17, g) rather than φανερωθέντες (אׁ³ D³ E K L P, r Syrr. Copt.) or φανερωθείς (D*, d e f). F G, f g r Vulg. Syr-Pesh. omit ἐν πᾶσιν, as superfluous, if neut. In different directions corruptions in the text are suspected. Some would omit εἰ δὲ καί . . . γνώσει as a gloss. Others would expand what follows; ἐν παντὶ πάντα φανερώσαντες ἐν πᾶσιν καὶ εἰς ὑμᾶς: cf. ix. 8, 11; 1 Cor. ix. 22, x. 33, xii. 6. The text is quite intelligible without either of these conjectural emendations. It is not quite clear what text is followed in AV.; perhaps ἀλλ' ἐν παντὶ φανερω-θέντες εἰς ὑμᾶς, but εἰς ὑμᾶς can hardly mean 'among you.' The reading φανερωθείς is an evident attempt to make the participle agree with ἰδιώτης, and the addition of ἑαυτούς after φανερώσαντες (M) is a correction of a transitive participle without an object expressed. There is no difficulty, however, in supplying τὴν γνῶσιν from the previous clause. The meaning is not intricate; ' Though I lack eloquence, I do not lack knowledge ; on the contrary, I was always able to impart knowledge publicly to you.'

**XI. 7–15. Glorying about refusing Maintenance ; the
Contrast with his Critics.**

*I had good reasons for refusing maintenance. This
was one of many points of contrast between me and the false
apostles.*

⁷ Or did I commit a sin in degrading myself by working for
my bread with my hands to raise you up from the degradation
of idolatry, in that without cost to yourselves no less a thing than
God's inestimable Gospel was preached to you by me ? ⁸ I
actually took from other Churches the cost of my maintenance—
it seemed like robbery—in order to be able to minister gratuitously to you. ⁹ And when I was staying with you at Corinth
and my resources failed, even then I 'sponged' on no one. No
Corinthian was squeezed to maintain me, for my necessities were
fully supplied by the brethren who came from Macedonia. That
was only one instance. In every emergency during my stay I
kept myself from being burdensome to you, and I mean to
continue to do so. ¹⁰ It is the truth of Christ that speaks in me
when I say that from being able to glory in preaching without
payment I will never allow myself to be barred in any region of
Achaia. ¹¹ Why have I formed this resolution ? Do you think
that it is because I care nothing about you ? God knows
whether that is true or not.

¹² But I shall persist in acting just as I am acting now about
this, in order to cut the ground from under those who desire to
have a ground for hoping that in the apostolate which they
boastfully claim they may be found working on the same terms
as we do, both of us accepting maintenance. ¹³ I will give them
no such opening, for such teachers are sham apostles, whose
whole work is a fraud, while they put on the appearance of
Apostles of Christ. ¹⁴ And no wonder ; for Satan himself, the
arch-deceiver, puts on the appearance of an angel of light. ¹⁵ It
is no amazing thing, therefore, if his ministers also put on an
appearance as being ministers of what they call righteousness.
Such professions will not profit them. Their doom will be in
accordance with their acts.

7. ῏Η ἁμαρτίαν ἐποίησα . . . ὑμῖν ; 'Or did I commit a sin in
abasing myself that you might be exalted, because I preached to

you God's Gospel for nothing?' This use of ἤ to emphasize a question is not rare (1 Cor. vi. 2; Rom. ii. 4, iii. 29, vi. 3); it introduces an alternative which those who are addressed are not likely to accept. 'If you do not admit what I have just stated, are you prepared to assert this?' The extreme expression, 'commit a sin' (found nowhere else in Paul), is, of course, ironical; it is used without irony 1 Pet. ii. 22; 1 Jn. iii. 9; see Westcott on 1 Jn. iii. 4 on the difference between ἁμαρτ. ποιέω and τὴν ἁμαρτ. ποιέω. He uses this strong language because his refusing to accept maintenance had been made a charge against him.* He states his reasons for refusing, 1 Cor. ix. 6–16 (see notes there); but his enemies may have said that the real reason was that he was too proud to do as other Apostles did, or that he refused, because he knew that he was not really an Apostle. We know from Didache xi. that the right of missionaries to maintenance for a short time was generally recognized c. A.D. 100, in accordance with Christ's directions (Mt. x. 10; Lk. x. 7). But St Paul always insisted on supporting himself by the handicraft which was so common in his Cilician home of making *cilicium*, a fabric of goats' hair, used for making tents (Acts xviii. 3) and other coverings (1 Thess. ii. 9; 2 Thess. iii. 8; 2 Cor. xii. 14–18). In his speech at Ephesus (Acts xx. 34) he may have held up 'these hands' to show how hardened they were by his habitual handiwork. We must remember that nearly all his first converts were poor (1 Cor. i. 26), and that few were in a condition to give prolonged hospitality to a missionary.

But not until he writes 2 Cor. does the Apostle intimate that anyone found fault with him for this habitual independence. At Corinth it would be easy to rouse prejudice against it. Greek sentiment would not allow a free citizen to undertake manual labour for anything less than dire necessity (Arist. *Pol.* iii. 5); and there was also a general feeling that teachers ought to be paid. The professional teachers of philosophy in Greece took large fees, and for this turning of instruction into a trade and selling wisdom for money, Socrates (Xen. *Mem.* i. vi. 1), Plato (*Gorg.* 520; *Apol.* 20), and Aristotle (*Eth. Nic.* ix. i. 5–7) condemned them. The Sophists replied that those who taught gratuitously did so because they knew that their teaching was worth nothing. It is likely enough that the Judaizers uttered similar sneers against St Paul. Hence his asking if this practice of his was a 'sin' in the eyes of the Corinthians.

ἐμαυτὸν ταπεινῶν ἵνα ὑμεῖς ὑψωθῆτε. They might think it an undignified thing for an Apostle to 'work night and day' (1 Thess. ii. 9) with his hands at a rough craft; but he was

---

* Bachmann doubts this; but why does the Apostle defend the practice, if he had not been censured for it? See Ramsay, *Cities of St Paul*, p. 231.

only following the example of the Carpenter (Mk. vi. 3), and
humbling himself in accordance with His admonitions (Mt.
xviii. 4, xxiii. 12; Lk. xiv. 11, xviii. 14). Yet he humbled
himself, not with a view to his own subsequent exaltation, but
'in order that *ye* might be exalted,' by being raised from the
death of heathen sins to the life of righteousness. Acting in
this way can hardly be stigmatized as ἁμαρτίαν ποιῶν. 'Be
exalted' means a great deal more than 'be made superior to
other Churches.'

δωρεὰν τὸ τοῦ Θεοῦ εὐαγγέλιον. Emphatic juxtaposition;
'*God's Gospel*, that most precious thing,—*for nothing*!' Elsewhere we have τὸ εὐαγγέλιον τοῦ Θεοῦ (1 Thess. ii. 2, 8, 9; Rom.
xv. 16) and τὸ εὐ. τοῦ Χριστοῦ (ii. 12, ix. 13, 14; 1 Cor. ix. 12;
etc.); but here, as in 1 Pet. iv. 17, τοῦ Θεοῦ is emphatic by
position. The Judaizers preach what is not God's Gospel, and
take maintenance for so doing; he gives God's Gospel *gratis*.
See on x. 16.

F G, f g r Vulg. (*aut numquid peccatum feci*) have ἢ μὴ ἁμαρτ. ἐπ., but
most Latin texts have *an* or *numquid*. ἐμαυτόν (א B K M) rather than
ἑαυτόν (D F G L P). *Exaltaremini* (Aug.) is preferable to *exaltemini*
(Vulg.).

8. ἄλλας ἐκκλησίας ἐσύλησα. He again uses extreme expressions; 'Other churches I *robbed*'—'you may say that it looked
like that.' It is not likely that his critics said that he plundered
Philippi, while refusing maintenance at Corinth; that would
rather have marred their argument. His crime was that he
declined to be treated as other Apostles were treated, and to
have mentioned the subsidies sent by the Philippians would have
lessened the crime (Phil. iv. 15). The verb is common enough
in class. Grk., esp. of stripping a fallen foe of his armour, but it
is very rare in Bibl. Grk.; here and Ep. Jer. 18 only.* In Rom.
ii. 22 we have ἱεροσυλεῖς, and Col. ii. 8 ὁ συλαγωγῶν. The word
may be used here in order to mark the contrast between the
conduct of the Philippians and that of the Corinthians. He
does not blame the Corinthians for allowing him to have his
way in working for nothing; but in striking language he indicates
what the Macedonian Churches did. The language is saved
from being extravagant by being immediately explained.

λαβὼν ὀψώνιον πρὸς τὴν ὑμῶν διακονίαν. (This is where the
robbery comes in;) 'by taking wages of them for my ministry
unto *you*.' The ὑμῶν, like τοῦ Θεοῦ in *v.* 7, is emphatic. The
Corinthians got his services, and he allowed other Christians to
pay him. From ὄψον, '*cooked* food,' and ὠνέομαι, 'I buy,' we get
ὀψώνιον, 'rations' or 'ration-money,' and hence pay of any kind,

---

* Aquila had it Ex. iii. 22, where LXX has σκυλεύσατε τοὺς Αἰγυπτίους.

'wages.'* See on 1 Cor. ix. 7, on Rom. vi. 23, and on Lk. iii. 14. The word occurs in 1 Macc. and often in Polybius in the sense of pay. Still earlier it is found several times, and always in the sing., in an inscription of about B.C. 265 which records an agreement between King Eumenes I. and his mercenaries. Deissmann, *Bib. St.* p. 266. The word fits well with the Apostle's description of his missionary labours as warfare, στρατευόμεθα (x. 3), and no one στρατεύεται without being furnished with the necessary supplies (1 Cor. ix. 7). He rigidly abstained from taking supplies from the Corinthians. It is possible that he brought some supplies with him from Macedonia; but these, even when supplemented by the work of his own hands, did not suffice; and then it was Macedonia that came to the rescue.

There is doubt here as to the division of the verses. Vulg., AV., RV., and other versions assign what follows to *v.* 9; but Alford, WH., and many other editors retain καὶ παρὼν . . . οὐθενός as part of *v.* 8. There is similar doubt at i. 6, 7, ii. 10, 11, ii. 12, 13, v. 14, 15.

9. καὶ παρὼν πρὸς ὑμᾶς καὶ ὑστερηθείς. 'And when I was staying with you and found myself in want'; tense and mood imply that he ran short and felt it. For the mood, comp. Phil. iv. 12; Lk. xv. 14.

οὐ κατενάρκησα οὐθενός. 'I put pressure on no man,' 'did not squeeze him till he was numb.' Verbs compounded with κατά often take a gen., as καταγελάω, καταγινώσκω, καταδυναστεύω, κατακυριεύω, καταλαλέω, κ.τ.λ. This compound is found nowhere in Greek literature, excepting here, xii. 13, 14, and once in Hippocrates (*Art.* 816 C), who uses the passive of 'being numbed,' a meaning which ναρκάω has in the active. Ναρκάω is used of the cramping or numbing of the sinew of Jacob's thigh (Gen. xxxii. 25–33), and in LXX of two other passages of doubtful reading and meaning; πλῆθος ὀστῶν αὐτοῦ ἐνάρκησεν (Job xxxiii. 19), and ὁ βραχίων αὐτοῦ ναρκήσει (Dan. xi. 6). The compound verb used here may be medical. It must have been in fairly common use, for neither Chrysostom nor Theodoret think it necessary to give any explanation. Hesychius gives ἐβάρυνα and κατεβάρησα as equivalents, which agrees with Vulg. *onorosus fui.* In his letter to the Gallic Lady Algesia (*Ep.* 121) Jerome uses *gravavi*, and he adds, *quibus et aliis multis verbis usque hodie utuntur Cilices. Nec hoc miremur in Apostolo, si utatur ejus linguae consuetudine, in qua natus est et nutritus.* It

* Both ἐσύλησα and ὀψώνιον are military words, and St Paul may be resuming the thought that missionary work is a campaign (x. 3–6). An invading army must have supplies, and sometimes has to employ strong measures to obtain them.

may have been current in the medical school at Tarsus. Galen explains νάρκη as much the same as ἀναισθησία. The meaning here seems to be 'I crippled no man by sponging on him,' *i.e.* by draining him dry.*

τὸ γὰρ ὑστέρημά μου. 'For my want the brethren, when they came from Macedonia, relieved with a further supply.' The compound, προσανεπλήρωσαν, implies something *in addition*, and this probably refers to the previous gifts of the generous Macedonians; but it might mean in addition to what St Paul earned by his handicraft. AV. obliterates the manifest connexion between ὑστερηθείς and ὑστέρημα by changing from 'wanted' to 'was lacking,' as also does Vulg. with *egerem* and *deerat*. It is probable that these brethren who came from Macedonia were Silas and Timothy (Acts xviii. 5), which would give a coincidence between this passage and i. 19. Apparently they had both joined St Paul at Athens and had thence been sent back into Macedonia, and had finally joined the Apostle at Corinth. Milligan, *Thessalonians*, p. xxx.

At first sight St Paul seems to be very inconsistent in ostentatiously refusing maintenance from the Corinthians, and yet making no secret of receiving maintenance from the Macedonians. We are nowhere told that he accepted anything for himself from the Philippians, *while he was at Philippi*, or from the Thessalonians, while he was at Thessalonica. His main object was to avoid all possibility of suspicion that in his preaching he was influenced by the thought that he must say what would please the people who housed and fed him. He must be free to rebuke and exhort, without fear or desire of losing or gaining favour, and without being open to the charge of seeking popularity for the sake of gain. His independence as a preacher must be complete and unassailable. It no way interfered with this that, while he was preaching in Corinth, he accepted supplies from Philippi.

ἐν παντὶ ἀβαρῆ ἐμαυτὸν ὑμῖν ἐτήρησα. 'In everything (see on *v.* 6) I kept myself from being burdensome.' The aor. refers to the year and a half that he stayed in Corinth, and it should be retained in translation. Cf. πρὸς τὸ μὴ ἐπιβαρῆσαί τινα ὑμῶν (1 Thess. ii. 9; 2 Thess. iii. 8); also οὐκ ἔχει τις καυχήσασθαι οὔτε λάθρα οὔτε φανερῶς, ὅτι ἐβάρησά τινα ἐν μικρῷ ἢ ἐν μεγάλῳ(Ign. *Philad.* vi.), and 2 Sam. xii. 3. Ἀβαρής seems to occur first in Arist. *De Coelo*, I. viii. 16, τὸ μὲν γὰρ ἀβαρές, τὸ δ' ἔχον βάρος. It occurs nowhere else in Bibl. Grk.

---

* The conjectural interpretation of Oecumenius and Theoplylact, οὐκ ἠμέλησα ἢ ῥαθυμότερος πρὸς τὸ κήρυγμα γέγονα, does not suit either this passage or xii. 13, 14. Beza has *non obtorpui cum cujusquam incommodo*, which is equally faulty.

20

καὶ τηρήσω. He has no misgivings as to the wisdom of this practice, and has no intention of changing it. We may assume that the Judaizing teachers claimed, or at any rate accepted, maintenance, and they wanted to taunt St Paul into following this 'Apostolic' custom. They saw that in this matter they were at a disadvantage as compared with him.

οὐθενός (אB M P 17) rather than οὐδενός (D E G K L). ἐμαυτὸν ὑμῖν (א* B M P, d e f Vulg.) rather than ὑμῖν ἐμαυτόν (א³ D E F G L); note the divergence between D E F and d e f.

10. ἔστιν ἀλήθεια Χριστοῦ ἐν ἐμοί. He elsewhere claims that the νοῦς Χριστοῦ (1 Cor. ii. 16) and the πνεῦμα Χριστοῦ (Rom. viii. 9) abides in him. This is a guarantee against conscious deceitfulness and empty boasting. Cf. ii. 17, xii. 19, xiii. 3 ; Rom. ix. 1. 'You have not my word only, but the truthfulness of Christ, to assure you that.' * With this use of ὅτι comp. ζῇ ἡ ψυχή σου ὅτι οὐ δαπανήσει ἡ δούλη σου κ.τ.λ. (Judith xii. 4). See on i. 18.

ἡ καύχησις αὕτη οὐ φραγήσεται εἰς ἐμέ. 'This glorying shall not be stopped with regard to me,' or 'so far as I am concerned.' Chrysostom derives the metaphor from the damming of rivers; ὥσπερ εἴ τις πηγὴν φράσσοι (Prov. xxv. 26), and τὸ πλῆθος αὐτῶν ἐνέφραξεν χειμάρρους (Judith xvi. 3). More probably it comes from barricading a road; φράσσω τὴν ὁδὸν αὐτῆς ἐν σκόλοψιν (Hos. ii. 6), and ἀνῳκοδόμησεν ὁδούς μου, ἐνέφραξεν τρίβους μου (Lam. iii. 9). The stopping of the mouth (Rom. iii. 19; Heb. xi. 33) might come from either, but more easily from blocking a road; and there is no personification of καύχησις in either case.

ἐν τοῖς κλίμασι τῆς Ἀχαίας. Κλίμα is rare in N.T. (Gal. i. 21 ; Rom. xv. 23), and perhaps is not found in LXX at all ; Judg. xx. 2 is doubtful. His opponents had probably not confined their operations to the city of Corinth. See on i. 1.

The σφραγίσεται of T.R. is possibly a conjecture, 'seal' in the rare sense of 'limit.' A few cursives have σφραγήσεται.

11. διὰ τί; 'Why am I so determined never to accept sustenance from you Corinthians? Is it because I care too little about you to accept anything from you or to place myself under any obligation to you?' Perhaps his enemies had suggested this.

ὁ Θεὸς οἶδεν. God knows whether he cares for them or not, and He knows what the real reason for his not accepting sustenance is. To God he has always been made manifest (v. 11). Cf. *Harum sententiarum quae vera sit, deus aliqui viderit* (Cic. *Tusc. Disp.* I. xi. 23).

---

* Calvin remarks that in these verses (10, 11) we have the equivalents of two oaths. It is fanatical to maintain that oaths may never be taken.

12. Ὁ δὲ ποιῶ καὶ ποιήσω, ἵνα ἐκκόψω τὴν ἀφορμὴν τῶν θελόντων ἀφορμήν. ' But what I do, that will I also continue to do, that I may cut off the occasion of those who wish for an occasion.' He is not going to give an opening to those who are on the look out for an opening against him; he will checkmate them by persisting in refusing remuneration from the Corinthians. His opponents pretended that his refusal showed that he was not an Apostle, and that their taking pay was evidence of their superiority. They saw that the Corinthians might have a simpler explanation, viz. that they were grasping, and that the Apostle was not; and they hoped to get him to do as they did. He means to retain his advantage.

Elsewhere in N.T. ἐκκόπτω is used of actual severing, as of branches (Rom. xi. 22, 24; Mt iii. 10, vii. 19) or limbs (Mt. v. 30, xviii. 8), and in LXX the figurative sense is rare; ἐξέκοψε ὥσπερ δένδρον τὴν ἐλπίδα μου (Job xix. 10), and thrice in 4 Macc. iii. 2–4, where we have ἐπιθυμίαν and θυμόν and κακοήθειαν after ἐκκόψαι.

ἵνα ἐν ᾧ καυχῶνται εὑρεθῶσιν καθὼς καὶ ἡμεῖς. This is one of many passages in 2 Cor. which is rendered obscure by our ignorance of the exact state of affairs in Corinth, and there has been much discussion both as to the constr. of the sentence and as to its probable meaning. To set forth all the proposals would not be repaying; the following interpretation is offered as tenable and possibly correct. The second ἵνα is not parallel with the first; it does not depend upon ποιήσω. It is improbable that St Paul's aim was to place his opponents on a level with himself, either in general, or in the matter of refusing maintenance. What advantage would it be to him to force them to equality with himself in any particular? And what likelihood was there that they would abandon the maintenance which they had accepted, and apparently claimed as an Apostolic privilege, in order to be even with St Paul? It is clear from *v.* 20, and might be conjectured from 1 Cor. ix. 12, that the Judaizing teachers did accept maintenance, and they could not have criticized St Paul for refusing it, unless they accepted it themselves. The second ἵνα depends upon τῶν θελόντων ἀφορμήν, thus; 'who wish for an occasion of being found, in the matter wherein they glory, on a level with us.' The matter in which they gloried was the dignity of being Apostolic missionaries, and it was as the possessors of this dignity that they allowed or constrained the Corinthians to support them. They saw plainly that in this particular they were at a disadvantage as compared with St Paul. In spite of all their protestations that it was a mark of Apostolic dignity to be supported by the congregation, and that Paul refused to be supported because he knew that he was not an

Apostle, yet the plain fact remained, that they were a burden to the Corinthians and that he was not. It sufficed for their purpose that he had refused maintenance; that showed that he did not believe in his own Apostleship. His accepting maintenance afterwards would not alter that evidence; but it would put an end to the damaging comparison which the Corinthians made between the generosity of St Paul in working for nothing and the greed of the Judaizers in taking all that they could get. Their aim was to get him, by some means or other, to accept maintenance; then they would be found to be no more burdensome to the community than he was.

Εὑρεθῶσιν is not a mere substitute for ὦσιν: it expresses the quality, not as it exists in itself, but as it is recognized. Cf. v. 3; 1 Cor. iv. 2; Phil. iii. 9. Lightfoot (on Gal. ii. 17) says that it "involves more or less prominently the idea of a *surprise,*" and that "its frequent use is due to the influence of Aramaic. Winer doubts the latter point (p. 769).

Other ways of taking the clause are found in Alford, Beet, Meyer, and Stanley. For ἵνα depending on a previous clause introduced by ἵνα, cf. Jn. i. 7.

13. οἱ γὰρ τοιοῦτοι ψευδαπόστολοι, ἐργάται δόλιοι. 'I must beware of allowing them any advantage, *for* persons of this kind are spurious apostles, deceitful workers.' *Nunc tandem scapham scapham dicit* (Beng.). Both the Sixtine and the Clementine Vulg. have *nam ejusmodi pseudoapostoli* sunt *operarii subdoli,* making ψευδαπόστολοι part of the subject, which is certainly wrong, and the best MSS. show that the *sunt* is an interpolation. Luther goes further into error by including ἐργάται δόλιοι in the subject; 'for such false apostles and deceitful workers fashion themselves into Apostles of Christ.' Cf. οἱ γὰρ τοιοῦτοι τῷ Κυρίῳ ἡμῶν Χριστῷ οὐ δουλεύουσιν, ἀλλὰ τῇ ἑαυτῶν κοιλίᾳ (Rom. xvi. 18), which means that, like the Judaizers at Corinth, they worked for their own advantage. Cf. τοὺς λέγοντας ἑαυτοὺς ἀποστόλους, καὶ οὐκ εἰσίν (Rev. ii. 2). In *v.* 26 we have ψευδάδελφοι, and Mk. xiii. 22 ψευδόχριστοι καὶ ψευδοπροφῆται. Such compounds are freq. in late Greek, but not in classical; ψευδόμαντις occurs in Hdt., Aesch., Soph., Eur., and ψευδοπάρθενος in Hdt. Δόλιος, freq. in LXX, esp. in Psalms and Proverbs, but found nowhere else in N.T., is in class. Grk. mostly poetical. The epithet explains ψευδαπόστολοι. Workers they certainly were, and they did an immense amount of mischief, but their devotion to the cause of Christ was a sham; what they really worked for was their own profit. See on ii. 17. *Apostolus enim ejus agit negotium a quo missus est, isti suis commodis serviunt* (Erasmus). Contrast ἐργάτην ἀνεπαίσχυντον, ὀρθοτομοῦντα τὸν λόγον τῆς ἀληθείας (2 Tim. ii. 15); also ἀπόστολοι ἐκκλησιῶν, δόξα Χριστοῦ (viii. 23), where we have a similar asyndeton.

μετασχηματιζόμενοι εἰς ἀποστόλους Χριστοῦ. ' Fashioning themselves into Apostles of Christ.' They change their appearance, they masquerade as such. In LXX the verb occurs once (4 Macc. ix. 22), in N.T. three times, all in Paul, and in each place with a different meaning; here of sham apostles fashioning themselves into genuine Apostles, as the devil fashions himself into an Angel of light; in Phil. iii. 21 of the glorious change of our body of humiliation ; and in 1 Cor. iv. 6 in quite another sense (see note there). 'Transform' implies a greater change than is meant here, and 'transfigure' should be kept for μετα-μορφόομαι (see on iii. 18), the verb used in connexion with the Transfiguration. See on Rom. xii. 2 and Phil. ii. 7 ; Trench, *Syn.* § lxx. ; Lightfoot, *Philippians*, pp. 127 f. Συνσχηματίζομαι (Rom. xii. 2 ; 1 Pet. i. 14) means 'acquire an outward form in accordance with.'

14. καὶ οὐ θαῦμα. Both this and the *v.l.* θαυμαστόν are classical in this conversational use ; τὸ μέντοι μὴ πείθεσθαι τοῖς λεγομένοις τοὺς πολλοὺς θαῦμα οὐδέν (Plato, *Rep.* 49 E D) ; ἐρᾷς· τὶ τοῦτο θαῦμα; σὺν πολλοῖς βροτῶν (Eur. *Hipp.* 439) ; also Aristoph. *Plut.* 99). *Non mirum* (Vulg.) is similarly used in Latin ; but *miraculo est*, not *miraculum*. Epictetus several times has καὶ τί θαυμαστόν ;

αὐτὸς γὰρ ὁ Σατανᾶς. "Like master, like man." If the prince of darkness can masquerade as an Angel of light, what wonder that his ministers masquerade as ministers of Christ? There is no necessity to suppose that St Paul is here alluding to some Rabbinical legend, similar to the one about Eve and the serpent, in which Satan is said to have taken the fashion of an Angel. According to some interpretations, the Angel who wrestled with Jacob was Satan. In the Prologue to the Book of Job, Satan takes no such appearance. St Paul may have known the story of our Lord's temptation in a form which might suggest this comparison. But his own experience must have taught him how specious and plausible temptations to what is known to be wrong can be made to look, so that sin may at last look meritorious. The pres. μετασχηματίζεται points to what Satan habitually does rather than to any particular occasion. This the Corinthians, very few of whom were Jews, could understand. That those of them who were Jews knew of a legend in which Satan assumed the appearance of an Angel, is unlikely ; and St Paul certainly expects to be understood in what he says here. As regards the subtlety of temptations the experience of the

Corinthians would be much the same as his own.* To say that "the reference *must* be to some apocalyptic tale" is a great deal too strong; and Schmiedel does not lay much stress on the suggestion that there may be an allusion to heathen theophanies. Would anyone regard them as instances of Satan fashioning himself as an Angel of light? For Σατανᾶς see on ii. 11 ; for ἄγγ. φωτός, cf. ἄγγ. ἐξ οὐρανοῦ (Gal. i. 8).

οὐ θαῦμα (א B D* F G P R 17) rather than οὐ θαυμαστόν (D² and ³ E K L M). Both in LXX and N.T. θαῦμα is very rare, whereas θαυμαστός is very freq. in LXX and not rare in N.T. Hence the change. D, d e m have ὡς ἄγγελος.

15. οὐ μέγα οὖν εἰ. The expression is found nowhere else in N.T. excepting 1 Cor. ix. 11. Cf. μέγα μοί ἐστιν εἰ ἔτι ὁ υἱός μου Ἰωσὴφ ζῇ (Gen. xlv. 28). 'It is no great thing therefore if his ministers (cf. Mt. xxv. 41 ; Rev. xii. 7) also fashion themselves as ministers of righteousness.' As in *v.* 13 before 'Apostles,' so here before 'ministers,' AV. inserts the article. 'Righteousness' is probably to be understood in its wider sense, as that on which Satan and his minions are ever making war. It was one of the charges brought against St Paul that his doctrine of Christian freedom was an encouragement to heathen licentiousness : the Judaizers professed to be upholders of 'righteousness' against such pestilent teaching. But, in spite of their professions, their real motive was the promotion of their own personal interests and the interests of their own party in the Church ; and they were unscrupulous in the means which they employed. We should perhaps place a colon after δικαιοσύνης (RV.) and make what follows an independent sentence. Cf. ὧν τὸ κρίμα ἔνδικόν ἐστιν (Rom. iii. 8) : ἀποδώσει αὐτῷ ὁ κύριος κατὰ τὰ ἔργα αὐτοῦ (2 Tim. iv. 14). But ὧν τὸ τέλος ἀπώλεια (Phil. iii. 19) tells the other way, and here WH. place only a comma. See on *v.* 10. At the Judgment it is not what they have looked like or what they have professed to be that will count, but what they have done. Cf. ὃς ἀποδίδωσιν ἑκάστῳ κατὰ τὰ ἔργα αὐτοῦ (Prov. xxiv. 12). Whether we regard it as an independent sentence or not, the terse statement comes at the end of the invective with considerable effect, as in Rom. iii. 8 and 2 Tim. iv. 14. But this statement tells us nothing as to St Paul's belief respecting the final condition of the wicked.

St Paul has been somewhat severely criticized for the bitter controversial style of this denunciation of his opponents, but we do not know enough about the intensity of the provocation to pronounce judgment. It is hardly more severe than συναγωγὴ

---

* It is a truism to say that, in order to tempt us, evil must be made to look attractive. The point here is that it can be made to look like innocence or like virtue.

τοῦ Σατανᾶ (Rev. ii. 9, iii. 9) and ὑμεῖς ἐκ τοῦ πατρὸς τοῦ διαβόλου ἐστέ (Jn. viii. 44). Cf. Mt. xxiii. 15, 33. We must remember not only the venomous personal attacks that had been made upon his character and antecedents, but also the widespread mischief that had been done among the converts at Corinth. Even those who do not believe in the intermediate visit can see that the mischief was great, in the unsettlement of belief and in the weakening of the Apostle's authority. But those who are convinced that such a visit was paid, and that during it St Paul was grossly insulted to such an extent that he left Corinth a defeated man, will be slow to condemn him for the fierce language which he uses in *vv.* 3-15, and especially in the concluding sentences. Bousset, who says that Paul's mode of fighting is not less passionate than that of his assailants, and that he is no saint, any more than Luther, admits that he had reason for his wrath, and that his fierce onset in the heat of the great conflict is only too intelligible. If the intruders had done nothing worse than meanly claim the credit for the crop, which he and Apollos, with the blessing of heaven, had patiently and laboriously raised, St Paul might have let a passing rebuke or sarcasm suffice for such conduct. But these new-comers had done their utmost to ruin the crop altogether, and they had employed methods which would have been hateful in any cause. We need to know more about their motives, their work, and its effects, before deciding that the severe language of the Apostle is unjustifiable.

But it is the Corinthians that he cares about. From this outburst of indignation his thoughts return to them. He must convince them, however unpleasing the work may be, that he is not inferior to these seductive teachers. That means that he must go on glorying about himself, and, like the first six verses of the chapter, the next seven are a declaration of the folly of glorying and an explanation of the reason for it. They introduce a new subject for glorying.

XI. 16-33. Glorying about his Services and Sufferings.

It seems foolish for an Apostle to be glorying, but I have no choice about it; and so I glory about my nationality, my heavy work, and my hardships.

¹⁶ I repeat what I said before; let no one think me a fool for uttering what sounds like folly: or, if you must think me one, at any rate listen to me patiently as such, that I may have my

little boast as well as other people. ¹⁷ In talking to you in this way I do not profess to be the Lord's mouthpiece; in this proud confidence of glorying I speak as a fool in his folly. ¹⁸ Seeing that many glory from their low worldly point of view, I mean to do the like. ¹⁹ For you can afford to bear with fools and do so with pleasure: you are so wise yourselves. ²⁰ Why, in your sublime tolerance you bear with any of these impostors, no matter what he does; if he makes slaves of you, if he devours your substance, if he entraps you, if he gives himself airs, if he strikes you in the face. ²¹ It may be a disgraceful confession to make, but I really have not been equal to acting in that way. Yet, wherever real courage is exhibited (remember, it is in folly that I say this), there I have courage too. ²² Let us look at nationality. Are they Hebrews, Israelites, descendants of Abraham? There we are equal, for so am I. ²³ Let us look at service. Are they ministers of Christ? (I am talking like a madman.) Let us grant that they are His ministers. I am more than their equal there, for I have suffered far more in His service;—

with labours far exceeding theirs,
with stripes far exceeding theirs,
with imprisonments beyond comparison,
with risk of life again and again;—

²⁴ from the Jews I five times received the severest scourging that is allowed,
²⁵ three times I was beaten with rods by the Romans,
once I was stoned, thrice I suffered shipwreck,
a night and a day I have drifted on the open sea.
²⁶ I have served Him in journeyings again and again;—
in perils of rivers, in perils of robbers,
in perils from my own people, in perils from the Gentiles,
in perils in the city, in perils in the wilderness,
in perils on the sea, in perils among false brethren.
²⁷ I have served Him in labour and travail;—
with watchings often, with hunger and thirst,
with fastings often, with cold and nakedness;
²⁸ besides other things which I pass over, there is that which presses on me daily,

XI. 16] SERVICES AND SUFFERINGS 313

my anxiety for all the Churches.
²⁹ What brother is weak in faith or life, and I do not feel
his weakness?
What brother is enticed into sin, and I am not in a fur-
nace of distress?
³⁰ If there must be glorying, my principle is to glory of the
things which concern my weakness, for they show my likeness
to the Lord Jesus Christ. ³¹ The God and Father of the Lord
Jesus Christ, He who is blessed for ever, knows that I am not
lying. ³² At Damascus the ethnarch of King Aretas posted
guards at the gates of the city to arrest me; ³³ but through an
opening I was let down in a basket through the city wall, and
thus clean escaped his hands.

16. Πάλιν λέγω, μή τίς με δόξῃ ἄφρονα εἶναι. The πάλιν λέγω
looks back to v. 1, where he makes a similar request; yet it is
only similar to this extent, that in both passages he begs them
not to refuse to listen to him because he is guilty of the folly of
glorying about himself. But not only is the wording different,
the meaning of the words is not the same. There he says, 'Bear
with me in my folly,' here, 'Don't think me a fool'; there he
almost retracts his request, 'I know that you do bear with me,'
here, he hardly expects it to be granted, 'At any rate give me as
much attention as you would give to a fool.' In both passages he
is anxious that the Corinthians should be aware that he recognizes the foolishness of self-praise, and that it is not his fault
that he is guilty of it. He is not indulging his own vanity; he
is sinking his self-respect in order to rescue them from the
machinations of seducing teachers. For the present all that
he asks is to be listened to with patience. It is like The-
mistocles's 'Strike, but hear me.' The Apostle says, 'Think
me a fool, but hear me.' The full constr. would be δέξασθέ με,
καὶ ἐὰν ὡς ἄφρονα δέξησθέ με. Blass, § 80. 2. In 1 Cor., St Paul
uses μωρός and μωρία repeatedly, only once ἄφρων (xv. 36),
and nowhere ἀφροσύνη: in 2 Cor. he uses ἄφρων and ἀφροσύνη
repeatedly, and nowhere either μωρός or μωρία. In speaking of
his own conduct he naturally employs the stronger term; he is
anxious to show his detestation of what he is compelled to do—
he has to act as if he were demented. He elsewhere uses ἀνόητος
(Gal. iii. 1, 3; Rom. i. 14; 1 Tim. vi. 9; Tit. iii. 3), and once
ἄσοφος (Eph. v. 15). For ἄφρων, Vulg. generally has in the
Epistles *insipiens*, but sometimes *inprudens*; in the Gospels
stultus. For μωρός Vulg. has in the Epistles *stultus*; in the
Gospels *fatuus* and *stultus*. For ἀνόητος, *insipiens*, *insensatus*,

stultus, inutilis (four different words in five places !) ; for ἄσοφος, *insipiens.*

εἰ δὲ μήγε. 'But if you do otherwise,' *i.e.* 'if you must think me a fool.' Luke is especially fond of εἰ δὲ μήγε, which Paul has nowhere else, and neither of them has the less strong εἰ δὲ μή. Burton, § 275; Blass, § 77. 4. See on Lk. v. 36. 'In any case, however, even though it be as a fool, accept me, give me a hearing.'

ἵνα κἀγὼ μικρόν τι καυχήσωμαι. 'That *I also* may glory a little.' He is anxious that they should remember that he did not start this stupid rivalry in glorying. His opponents began it, and the Corinthians listened to them ; now it is his turn, and he must go through with it. The μικρόν τι may mean that his opponents called their glorying μικρόν τι.* Everywhere in the Epistles κἀγώ, and not καὶ ἐγώ, is right, Gregory, *Prolegomena*, p. 96.

D* has εἰ δὲ μή for εἰ δὲ μήγε. κἀγὼ μικρόν τι (all uncials) rather than μικρόν τι κἀγώ (a few cursives and Syr-Hark.). καυχήσωμαι (א B F G M) rather than καυχήσομαι (D E K L P R).

17. οὐ κατὰ κύριον λαλῶ. 'I am not speaking in virtue of the Lord's command.' Christ did not send His Apostles to glory about themselves, and St Paul knows that there is nothing Apostolic in what he is now doing. He believes it to be necessary, but he does not claim Divine authority for it ; it is not official, not κατὰ τὴν πραΰτητα καὶ ἐπιείκειαν τοῦ Χριστοῦ (x. 1). Cf. μὴ κατὰ ἄνθρωπον ταῦτα λαλῶ; (1 Cor. ix. 8) and κατὰ Θεόν (vii. 9 ; Eph. iv. 24). The change from λεγῶ (*v.* 16) to λαλῶ should be marked in translation : Vulg. has *dico* and *loquor.* 'In this confidence (see on ix. 4) of glorying' he is merely giving the only effectual answer that is possible in dealing with such critics ; he must not be less confident than they are. But it is the man rather than the Apostle who is speaking. Cf. 1 Cor. vii. 12, 25, 40.

οὐ κατὰ κ. λαλῶ (א B F G K P R, fg Syr-Pesh.) rather than οὐ λ. κατὰ κ. (D E L M, d e r Vulg. Copt. Syr-Hark.).

18. κατὰ [τὴν] σάρκα. See below. Nowhere else does St Paul insert the art. in this phrase, which is very freq. in his writings ; everywhere we find κατὰ σάρκα (i. 17, v. 16, x. 2, 3 ; etc.), and this fact may have led to the omission of the art. here. If we accept the τήν as original, the difference may be that, while κατὰ σάρκα means 'from a human point of view,' κατὰ τὴν σ. may mean 'from their human point of view.' But this is precarious.

* Here, as in *v.* 1, Vulg. has *modicum quid* ; Beza has *paulisper* in *v.* 1 and *paululum quiddam* here : *aliquantulum* might be better in both places.

These Judaizers from Palestine boast of their country, of their ancestry, of their high rank as missionaries,—things which men are naturally proud of, but which do not count for much in the service of Christ. Nevertheless, whether they count for much or little, St Paul is more than their equal. But the πολλοί probably refers to people generally, and not merely to the numerous Judaizers. Many people are proud of their nation, birth, position, etc. We have a similar constr., in a much more elaborate sentence, Lk. i. 1–3, where ἔδοξε κἀμοί answers to ἐπειδήπερ πολλοί just as κἀγώ to ἐπεὶ πολλοί here.

κἀγὼ καυχήσομαι. He means not merely that he intends to glory, but to glory on the same low level as they do, κατὰ σάρκα. It is a miserable position that they have taken, but he will not shrink from contending with them on their own ground.

It is difficult to decide between κατὰ τὴν σάρκα (א B D³ E K L M P) and κατὰ σάρκα (א* D* G R 17), but the former is probably right.

19. ἡδέως γὰρ ἀνέχεσθε τῶν ἀφρόνων φρόνιμοι ὄντες. 'For *gladly* ye bear with the foolish,—you who are so wise.' The ἡδέως is emphatic, and the contrast between ἀφρόνων and φρόνιμοι is emphasized by juxtaposition. The verbal contrast might be preserved with 'senseless' and 'sensible,' but φρόνιμος means a good deal more than 'sensible' (Rom. xi. 25, xii. 16; Gen. xli. 39). Here, no doubt, φρόνιμοι ὄντες is ironical, even more so than 1 Cor. iv. 10, viii. 1; it means ' *because* ye are wise' rather than ' *although* ye are wise,' which would be very insipid in so vigorous a passage. 'You have got such a large supply of wisdom yourselves that you can even *take a pleasure* in putting up with fools.' In viii. 7, as in 1 Cor. i. 5, x. 15, he admits that the Corinthians have great intellectual gifts, and states this without any sarcasm ; but here the point is that they are content to tolerate the outrageous conduct of his opponents—no doubt because they are so serenely conscious of their own superiority.

20. ἀνέχεσθε γάρ. 'I am justified in saying that you are too magnificent to be impatient with folly, *for* you tolerate what is far worse than folly. You tolerate tyranny, extortion, craftiness, arrogance, violence, and insult. All of this, when it comes from my enemies. Can you not tolerate a little folly in me?' He would gladly always speak κατὰ κύριον (*v.* 17), as ministers of Christ should do ; but the outrageous conduct of others does not allow him to do this. What follows is a description of the way in which the Judaizing teachers treat the Corinthians. Cf. ἁρπαζόμενοι γοῦν ἀνέχεσθε, καὶ τυπτόμενοι σιωπᾶτε, καὶ τοῖς φονευομένοις οὐδὲ ἐπιστένει τις ἀναφανδόν (Joseph. *B.J.* IV. iii. 10).

καταδουλοῖ. 'Reduce to abject slavery,' as in Gal. ii. 4, the only other passage in N.T. where this compound occurs, and where, as here and Jer. xv. 14, the act. is used. Elsewhere in LXX the midd. is used, but with a different meaning. The midd. means 'enslave to oneself,' the act. means 'enslave to some other power.' This is clearly the meaning in Jer. xv. 14 and Gal. ii. 4; and in Gal. ii. 4 the power to which the false brethren would enslave the Galatians is the Mosaic Law (Acts xv. 10). This may well be the meaning here. These sham apostles wanted to impose on the Corinthians the bondage of the Law; cf. Gal. v. 1. This, however, cannot be pressed as certain, for although the midd. is commonly used of enslaving to oneself, the act. is sometimes used in this sense, which harmonizes well with the context and makes a telling contrast to the Apostle's own attitude towards the Corinthians; he is their δοῦλος (iv. 5), not they his δοῦλοι. He had no wish κυριεύειν αὐτῶν τῆς πίστεως (i. 24), or δολοῦν τὸ λόγον τοῦ θεοῦ (iv. 2): he preached God's Gospel to them without pay (xi. 7), because it was not their possessions but themselves that he desired to win (xii. 14). All this was the very opposite of what the false apostles did. They were domineering, grasping, crafty, arrogant, and violent.

κατεσθίει. 'Devour you' by claiming maintenance and accepting all that was offered them, as the Scribes did with pious widows (Mk. xii. 40; Lk. xx. 47). Cf. οἱ κατέσθοντες τὸν λαόν μου βρώσει ἄρτου (Ps. xiii. 4). Plautus and Terence use comedo in this sense; cf. καταπίνω (Pr. i. 12, xxi. 20; Is. ix. 15). The description of the false teachers in Rom. xvi. 18 and Phil. iii. 19 is similar.

λαμβάνει. 'Catch you' as birds in a snare, or fish with bait; cf. δόλῳ ὑμᾶς ἔλαβον (xii. 16); οὐδὲν ἐλάβομεν (Lk. v. 5). Field supports AV. in translating 'take of you,' and the word might mean this. Beza has si quis stipendium accipit, but it is rather a bathos after 'enslave and devour.' 'Prey upon you' combines the two ideas.

ἐπαίρεται. 'Uplift himself,' 'give himself airs'; cf. x. 5. AV. and RV. have 'exalt' for this verb and also for ὑψόω (v. 7); Vulg. has exaltemini there and extollitur here. 'Lord it over you' seems to be the meaning.

εἰς πρόσωπον ὑμᾶς δέρει. The conduct of the Sanhedrin in the case of Christ (Mk. xiv. 65) and of St Paul (Acts xxiii. 2) shows that this may possibly be understood literally; and this view is confirmed when we find St Paul directing both Timothy (1 Tim. iii. 3) and Titus (Tit. i. 7) that a bishop must not be a striker. Cf. 1 Kings xxii. 24. But it is equally possible that the expression is figurative, like 'fly in one's face'; cf. Mt. v. 39;

Job xvi. 10; Lam. iii. 30; Mic. v. 1.   'If he outrageously
insult you' would then be the meaning.   That the Judaizers
treated the Corinthians with contumely because they were
Gentiles is possible, but we cannot make any of the expressions
in this verse refer definitely to that.   For a similar repetition of
εἰ (five times in each) see 1 Tim. v. 10.

εἰς πρόσωπον ὑμᾶς (א B D* E F G P, d e f g r Vulg.) rather than ὑμᾶς
εἰς πρ. (D² K L M, Arm. Goth.).

21. κατὰ ἀτιμίαν λέγω, ὡς ὅτι ἡμεῖς ἠσθενήκαμεν. 'By way
of dishonour (vi. 8) I say it, as though we have been weak.'
The meaning of this is obscure, and the words have been
rendered in a variety of ways; but two things may be regarded
as certain.   (1) The dishonour is his own; if he had meant
'to your disgrace I say it' we should probably have had τὴν
ἀτιμίαν ὑμῶν.*   (2) The ἡμεῖς is in emphatic opposition to some
people who are not regarded as weak; and these can hardly be
any but the Judaizing teachers.   It is also highly probable that
ἠσθενήκαμεν looks back to the charge of weakness mentioned in
x. 10.   We must therefore regard the verse as a continuation of
the irony against himself, like οὐ γὰρ τολμῶμεν in x. 12.   'It is
with shame that I have to confess that with regard to behaviour
of this kind (that mentioned in v. 20) I may be stigmatized as
a weakling.' †   In ὡς ὅτι the ὡς intimates that what is introduced
by ὅτι is given as the thought of another, for the correctness of
which the speaker does not vouch.   See Lightfoot and Milligan
on 2 Thess. ii. 2.   Milligan shows that in late Greek ὡς ὅτι
hardly differs from ὅτι.   Indeed some editors write ὡσότι.   If
the MS. evidence in Xen. Hell. III. ii. 14 be rejected, then the
statement of Blass (§ 70. 2) may be accepted, that ὡς ὅτι is not
classical.   Schmiedel, ad loc. p. 287 ; Winer, pp. 771, 772.

The ironical confession of his own 'dishonour' is a real
rebuke to the Corinthians; they more than tolerate those who
trample on them, while they criticize as 'weak' one who shows
them great consideration.

ἐν ᾧ δ' ἄν τις τολμᾷ.   'But, whereinsoever any is bold.'   Yet
in whatever matter any person (whether Judaizer or not) exhibits
real courage, the Apostle does not fear comparison.   For τολμᾷ
see x. 2, 12.

ἐν ἀφροσύνῃ λέγω.   He parenthetically protests once more
that this comparing himself with others, and glorying in being

* Cf. οὐ κατ᾽ ἐπιταγὴν λέγω (viii. 8) : οὐχ ὅτι καθ᾽ ὑστέρησιν λέγω (Phil.
iv. 11).   Winer, p. 502.   'If to your disgrace' is the meaning (1 Cor. vi. 5,
xv. 34), then there is no irony.
† For ἀτιμία Vulg. has ignobilitas here, vi. 8, and 1 Cor. xv. 43, but
1 Cor. xi. 14 and Rom. i. 26 ignominia, and Rom. ix. 21 contumelia.
Ignominia would be better throughout.

their equal or superior, is folly. It is a preface to the vigorous statement of his own claims, as contrasted with those of his opponents, which follows. Chrysostom may be right in suggesting that the Apostle is anxious that this highly exceptional conduct of his should not be regarded by his converts as an example for them to follow. It is folly to be shunned. He perhaps does not also mean, 'I am fool to say this, because you will not believe me.' He expects that most of them will believe him.

ἠσθενήκαμεν (א B 17) rather than ἠσθενήσαμεν (D E G K L M P). After ἠσθ. D E, d e add ἐν τούτῳ τῷ μέρει. Sixtine and Clem. Vulg. has *in hac parte*, but the better witnesses omit. It is a gloss, but a good one, limiting the idea of 'weakness' to the contrast with his opponents' violence. 'You think me "weak." Just look at the "strong" measures of your new leaders, and is it you or I that have to feel ashamed?'

22–33. After the somewhat long prelude from x. 8 onwards, in which St Paul has stated repeatedly that he must embark on the foolish project of glorying, he at last lets himself go. He began to glory about refusing maintenance (*v.* 7), but from that he diverged to denounce those who accepted maintenance and abused him for refusing it. He returned to his prelude (*v.* 16) and again diverged to pay a sarcastic compliment to the Corinthians for their magnificent toleration of other teachers whose conduct is very different from his. But from this point to the end of the chapter, and indeed to xii. 10, there is no break; and in these twenty-one verses we have a summary of his career as an Apostle which, as an autobiographical sketch, has no equal in N.T. We have had very brief outlines in one or two places (iv. 7–10, vi. 4–10; 1 Cor. iv. 11–13) with an occasional detail (1 Thess. ii. 9), but nothing approaching to this in fulness. This autobiographical summary tells us a good deal which Luke omits in Acts, and this may help to convince us that Luke does not exaggerate in describing his friend's work. If he had liked, he could have told us a good deal more that would have been to the credit of the Apostle. Nothing that Luke tells us about him exceeds what is told us here. On the other hand, there is little ground for suspecting that the Apostle exaggerates here, for what he says about himself is told with tantalizing brevity and manifest unwillingness. Nor need we allow much for the fact that this passage, like most of 2 Corinthians, was dictated under the influence of strong feeling. There is nothing hysterical about it, and there is very little, if anything, that has the appearance of being said on the spur of the moment, and therefore inaccurately. On the contrary, it seems to have been rather carefully prepared and arranged, and even the exact wording of the clauses to have been in some cases thought out.

There were two things on which the Judaizing teachers plumed themselves, their ancestry and their dignity as Apostolic ministers. St Paul addresses himself to both these claims, devoting, as we should expect him to do, much more attention to the second than to the first, which is very quickly dismissed ; and he appeals, not to the miracles which he had wrought, or to the Churches which he had founded, but to the labours and sufferings which he had endured.

But this καυχᾶσθαι is all κατὰ σάρκα, οὐ κατὰ κύριον. It deals largely with externals which are not of the essence of the Gospel. It is faith, and not birth or exploits, which attaches men to Christ. Cf. Gal. ii. 16, v. 6, vi. 15 ; 1 Cor. vii. 19, iii. 29, iv. 10. To the opening verse (22) there is a remarkable parallel in Phil. iii. 5, where see Lightfoot.

22. Ἐβραῖοί εἰσιν; As in vi. 14–16, the Apostle rapidly asks a number of argumentative questions, all directed to the same point ; and here, as there, he keeps them from becoming monotonous by the use of synonyms. In neither passage are the questions answered, for the answer in each case is obvious ; but here he makes a rejoinder to each of the obvious answers. We may feel confident that Erasmus, Luther, Calvin, and Beza, followed by AV. and RV., are right in making these four sentences interrogative. The earlier English Versions make them categorical; 'They are Hebrews : so am I'; which is much less effective. The fact that both Wiclif and the Rhemish do so shows that the Vulg. was taken in this way; but the Latin is as ambiguous as the Greek, and is probably meant to be interrogative ; *Hebraei sunt? et ego.*

The three adjectives which refer to descent cannot be meant to be mere synonyms; in that case the questions would be tautological; and the exact meaning of the first term is clearer than those of the other two. 'Hebrew' refers to nationality and language. St Paul belongs to the same race as his opponents, and though he was born out of Palestine, he speaks the Aramaic vernacular (Acts xxi. 40, xxii. 2) as they do. In O.T. Ἐβραῖος does not seem to imply difference of race rather than of language (Gen. xxxiv. 14, 17, xl. 15, xli. 12, xliii. 31 ; etc.). 'Hebrew' denotes the offspring of Abraham as viewed by foreigners, and is used by the Hebrews themselves in dealing with foreigners, or in contrasting themselves with foreigners. In the Apocrypha the idea of difference of language is perhaps coming in (Judith x. 12, xiv. 18; 2 Macc. vii. 31, xi. 13, xv. 37 ; and several times in 4 Macc.). But in N.T. Ἐβραῖος seems generally to imply the use of the vernacular Aramaic (Acts vi. 1 ; Phil. iii. 5; cf. Jn. v. 2, xix. 13, 17, 20, xx. 16 ; Rev. ix. 11, xvi. 16) ; it means a

Jew who had not abandoned the use of Aramaic, but spoke either both Greek and Aramaic or Aramaic exclusively.   By Greek and Latin writers the term is not much used, 'Ιουδαῖος and *Judaeus* being preferred.   Hastings, *DB*. ii. p. 326; Trench, *Syn.* § xxxix.

As compared with 'Ισραελῖται and σπέρμα 'Αβραάμ, we may perhaps say that 'Εβραῖοι is the term of lowest significance, and that the three terms are meant to form a climax, σπέρμα 'Αβραάμ being the most honourable of the three.   This might be true whichever view we take of 'Εβραῖοι.   To belong to the race 'from the further side '* to which Abraham belonged was not much; nor was it much to be of those who still talked the current Aramaic. It was more to be of 'the Children of Israel,' the people of God, the nation of the Theocracy and the sacred Commonwealth (Gal. vi. 16; Eph. ii. 13); see on Rom. ix. 5.   It was perhaps most of all to be of the 'seed of Abraham,' to whom the original promises respecting the Messiah had been made.   Understood in this way, 'seed of Abraham' leads on readily to the ministers of the Messiah.   But this interpretation of the three terms cannot be regarded as certain.   If the terms are understood of the persons to whom each can be applied, they seem to be in the wrong order; we should expect 'seed of Abraham,' 'Israelites, ' Hebrews.'   For 'seed of Abraham' includes Ishmaelites and Edomites as well as Israelites, and 'Israelites' includes those Hellenists who did not speak Aramaic as well as the ' Hebrews ' who did speak it.

It may seem strange that in a Church which was composed almost entirely of Gentiles the Judaizing teachers had based their claims on the fact that they were in the fullest sense Jews. But they wished to show that they came from the original Church of Jerusalem and with the authority of the Twelve.   They questioned whether St Paul had any right to the title of Apostle, and they may have questioned whether one who was born at Tarsus in Cilicia (Acts ix. 11, 30, xi. 25, xxii. 3), and who disparaged circumcision and the whole of the Mosaic Law, was really a Jew.†   Epiphanius (*Haer.* xxx. 16) tells us that somewhat later than this the Ebionites declared that Paul was a Gentile, who had submitted to circumcision in order to marry the high-priest's daughter.

On the smooth breathing for 'Εβραῖος, 'Εβραΐς, 'Εβραιστί see WH. ii. p. 313. In English, and perhaps in Latin, the aspirate seems to be comparatively modern. Here, as well as in Phil. iii. 5 and Acts vi. 1,

---

* Cf. Gen. xiv. 13, where Abraham is called ὁ περάτης as the equivalent of ' Hebrew.'

† The statement of Jerome (*De. Vir. ill.*), that St Paul was born at Gischala in Galilee, may safely be disregarded; but his parents may have come from Gischala as emigrants or prisoners of war.

not only Wiclif but Tyndale (A.D. 1534) have 'Ebrue.' Coverdale (A.D. 1535) has 'Hebrue' in all three places; but it is not yet well established, for Cranmer (A.D. 1539) has 'Hebrue' in Acts, but 'Ebrue' in the Epistles. White (*Vulgate*, 1911) prints the aspirate in all three passages, but the fact that Wiclif omits it is evidence that his MSS. did not have it. 'Ισραελεῖται is the spelling in B* D* E* ; other witnesses have Ισραελῖται.

23. διάκονοι Χριστοῦ εἰσίν; This is a much more serious question than the first three, and as such comes last. The false teachers had claimed to be Christ's men (x. 7) and 'Apostles of Christ' (xi. 13), and διάκονος is used here as equivalent to 'Apostle': it does not of course mean that they had ministered to Jesus or had been His disciples. Nor is it likely that St Paul is now speaking, not of his opponents at Corinth, but of those whom they claimed as their supporters in Jerusalem. He still has the Judaizing teachers in view. He has just called them 'sham apostles' and 'ministers of Satan' (*vv.* 13, 15); but for the sake of argument he is willing to assume that in some sense they are what they claim to be.*

παραφρονῶν λαλῶ. 'I am talking like a madman,' a stronger expression than ἐν ἀφροσύνη λέγω (*v.* 21).† It may be understood in more ways than one. The simplest is to suppose that he means that all glorying, whether about 'knowledge' (*v.* 6) or about 'courage' (*v.* 21) is folly, but that to glory about so sacred a matter as the service of Christ is downright madness. Or he may mean that to allow that these 'ministers of Satan' may be called 'ministers of Christ,' while his own right to that honourable title is questioned, is utter madness. He ought never to consent to be put in comparison with them. Or again, that to suppose that there is anything higher than being a minister of Christ, is madness. This last assumes that ὑπὲρ ἐγώ is to be rendered as in AV., 'I am more.' Παραφρονέω occurs here only in N.T., and παραφρονία only 2 Pet. ii. 16, παράφρων nowhere. In LXX παραφρονέω (Zech. vii. 11), παραφρόνησις (Zech. xii. 4), and παράφρων (Wisd. v. 20) are found once each, παραφρονία nowhere.

ὑπὲρ ἐγώ. 'I more' (RV.) is more probably right, than 'I am more' (AV.), where 'am' ought to be in italics. It is less improbable that St Paul should allow for the sake of argument that the 'superextra apostles' may be called 'ministers of Christ,' than that he himself should claim to be 'more than a minister of Christ.' What could that mean? But if that rendering be

---

* We may compare the action of Christ, who does not challenge the confident statement of either the rich man (Mk. x. 20) or the sons of Zebedee (x. 39), but answers as if it were true.

† *Minus sapiens dico* (Vulg.) is wrong of both words; *delirans loquor* would be right, but Vulg. translates the reading λέγω.

adopted, then παραφρονῶν refers to it.   A man must be mad to make such a claim.   'I have a better claim to be called a διάκονος Χρ. than they have' is more probably right, although the *plus* (not *magis*) *ego* of the Vulg. points the other way, and Luther certainly agrees with AV., *ich bin wohl mehr.*   Augustine has *super ego.*   This adverbial use of ὑπέρ can be matched in class. Grk. (Soph. *Ant.* 518; cf. Hdt. I. xix. 3, where we have μετὰ δέ for ἔπειτα δέ), but it is unique in N.T.   Winer, p. 526; Blass, § 42. 5.

ἐν κόποις περισσοτέρως.   Here he begins the evidence that *his* claim to be a minister of Christ is well founded; he has had a large share in the sufferings of Christ (i. 5).   But we must not assume that the comparative adverb necessarily implies comparison *with his opponents*; it may mean 'more abundantly than most men' or 'than you would believe'; cf. i. 12, ii. 4, vii. 13, 15, xii. 15.   The comparative form is dropped after the repeated περισσοτέρως, and therefore only in these first two clauses is there even in form any possibility of comparison with the Judaizers. It is possible that after ὑπὲρ ἐγώ they are altogether banished from consideration, and that περισσοτέρως means 'very abundantly.'*   It is not likely that he meant that he had been put in prison more often than his opponents; they may have worked hard, but it is not likely that any of them had been imprisoned.

Just as the four questions seem to form a climax, the fourth being far more serious than the other three, so also these four clauses beginning with ἐν.   Whether or no ἐν πληγαῖς is to be regarded as worse than ἐν κόποις and ἐν φυλακαῖς, ἐν θανάτοις is much worse than the other three.   Then, just as the reply to the fourth question is developed in the clauses which follow, so the fourth clause here is explained and expanded in the sentences which follow.   The rhythm and balance of clauses continues until the exceedingly matter-of-fact statement in *vv.* 32, 33 is reached, and it is impossible to discern how much of it is premeditated and how much due to the emotion of the moment. The substance of this vigorous assertion of his claim to be a minister of Christ must have been thought over beforehand, and perhaps the Apostle, knowing how important it was that this appeal should be successful, had also considered the form in which it should be presented.   With regard to the substance it is remarkable that he does not, as elsewhere, base his claim on his relation to the Risen Lord, or on the success with which God has crowned his work, but on his sufferings and sacrifices. What he has endured is the seal of his Apostleship.

* *Ueber die Massen* (Bachmann) or *überreichlich* (Bousset) rather than *viel reichlicher* (Lietzmann).

There is no need to discuss in each case what verb is to be supplied, whether ἐγενόμην, γέγονα, εἰμί, or ἦν. The verbless clauses are thoroughly intelligible both in Greek and in English.

ἐν φυλακαῖς περισσοτέρως. The text is somewhat confused and uncertain, but περισσοτέρως is used twice, and therefore we have three different adverbs, not four, as Vulg. and AV. would lead us to suppose; *in laboribus plurimis, in carceribus abundantius, in plagis supra modum, in mortibus frequenter.* Clement of Rome (*Cor.* v.) says that St Paul was imprisoned seven times, ἑπτάκις δεσμὰ φορέσας. We know of only five; at Philippi before 2 Corinthians; Jerusalem, Caesarea, and twice at Rome after 2 Corinthians. But there may easily have been two others. See below, on *v.* 24.

ἐν πληγαῖς ὑπερβαλλόντως. 'In stripes (vi. 5) very exceedingly.' The adv. is fairly common in later Greek; μεγάλως ὑπερβαλλόντως λελάληκας (Job xv. 11); but in N.T. it is a ἅπαξ λεγόμενον. For St Paul's fondness for compounds with ὑπέρ see on *v.* 5 and xii. 7.

ἐν θανάτοις πολλάκις. On a number of occasions, and in a variety of ways, through violence, illness, and accidents, he had nearly lost his life. Cf. i. 9, 10, iv. 11; 1 Cor. xv. 32; Rom. viii. 36. A few of those are forthwith specified (*vv.* 24, 25); πολλάκις γὰρ εἰς κινδύνους παρεδόθην θάνατον ἔχοντας (Chrys.). Cf. καθ᾽ ἑκάστην ἡμέραν, μᾶλλον δὲ ὥραν, προαποθνήσκω, πολλοὺς θανάτους ὑπομένων ἀνθ᾽ ἑνὸς τοῦ τελευταίου (Philo, *In Flaccum,* § 20, 990 A, 542 Mang.). "Man feels a thousand deaths in fearing one" (Young, *Night Thoughts,* iv. 17).

λαλῶ (א B K L M P) rather than λέγω (D E G, Latt. *dico,* as in *vv.* 16 21, not *loquor,* as in *v.* 17). ἐν φυλακαῖς περισσοτέρως, ἐν πληγαῖς ὑπερβαλλόντως (B D* E 17, d e f Vulg. Goth. Aeth.) rather than ἐν φυλ. ὑπερβαλλόντως, ἐν πληγ. περισσοτέρως (P), or ἐν πληγ. περισσοτέρως, ἐν φυλ. ὑπερβαλλόντως (א F G, g), though this is followed by Tisch. with his preference for א, or ἐν πληγ. ὑπερβαλλόντως, ἐν φυλ. περισσοτέρως (א³ D² K L M, Syrr. Copt. Arm.), followed in T.R. Tertullian (*Scorp.* 13) has *in laboribus abundantius, in carceribus plurimum, in mortibus saepius.* Augustine has *in laboribus plurimum.*

24. ὑπὸ 'Ιουδαίων. He begins with sufferings which were inflicted on him by officials, Jewish and Roman, in the name of law; then, after one outrage inflicted by a lawless mob, he mentions a number which were due to the operations of nature. This use of ὑπό, 'at the hands of,' is classical and is found in papyri, but it is rare in N.T. In 1 Thess. ii. 14 and Mt. xvii. 12 we have πάσχειν ὑπό. Winer, p. 462. We expect ὑπὸ τῶν ἐθνῶν with the next statement, but in the rapid enumeration it is omitted. He naturally begins with what his own nation, which had become bitterly hostile, had done to him.

πεντάκις τεσσεράκοντα παρὰ μίαν ἔλαβον. 'Five times I

received forty save one.' *   The omission of πληγάς is idiomatic ;
see on Lk. xii. 47.   These Jewish floggings are not mentioned in
Acts or in any other Epistle.   The earliest passage in which this
kind of punishment is mentioned is Deut. xxv. 1–3, where see
Driver's notes.   More than 40 stripes could not lawfully be
inflicted, and it is said that the executioner who exceeded 40
was liable to be flogged himself; hence only 39 were inflicted for
fear of a miscount.   Some say that only 13 were given with a
whip that had three lashes, and that they counted as 39, or that
13 were given on the breast and 13 on each shoulder.   'Cause
to lie down' (Deut. xxv. 2) does not necessarily imply the
bastinado, and there seems to be no tradition that the punishment ever took this form.   It was administered in the synagogue
(Mt. x. 17), and during the infliction passages from Deut. and
the Psalms were read.   Josephus (*Ant.* IV. viii. 21) calls it
τιμωρίαν ταύτην αἰσχίστην, but he does not intimate that death
often ensued, and it is improbable that Jewish magistrates would
allow death to be risked.†   But the frail and sensitive Apostle
might feel that he had nearly died under the infliction.   This
use of παρά is found in Josephus, not in IV. viii. 21, where he
has πληγὰς μιᾷ λειπούσας τεσσεράκοντα, but in IV. viii. 1,
τεσσεράκοντα ἐτῶν παρὰ τριάκονθ' ἡμέρας, and in Herodotus
(ix. 23), παρὰ ἓν παλαίσμα ἔδραμε νικᾶν Ὀλυμπιάδα, 'he won an
Olympic victory all but one wrestling-bout.'   Cf. Ps. viii. 6,
quoted Heb. ii. 7, ἠλάττωσας αὐτὸν βραχύ τι παρ᾽ ἀγγέλους, which,
however, is not quite parallel.   See λαμβάνω, Index IV.

25. τρὶς ἐραβδίσθην.   *Ter vergis caesus sum.*   This was a
Roman, and therefore a Gentile punishment, and of the three
inflictions we know of only one, that inflicted at Philippi, in
violation of Roman Law (ὑβρισθέντες ἐν Φιλίπποις, 1 Thess. ii. 2),
by the praetors there (Acts xvi. 22, 23, 37).   Cf. Acts xxii. 25–29.
Cicero says that to beat a Roman citizen was *scelus*, but that
reckless and ruthless magistrates sometimes committed the outrage (*In Verr.* v. 62, 66).   Gessius Florus, who succeeded
Albinus as procurator of Judaea, A.D. 64 or 65, caused persons of
equestrian rank to be scourged and crucified, ignoring their

* Clement of Rome (*Cor.* v.) speaks of St Paul's sufferings thus ;
"Through jealousy and strife Paul too made attestation of the prize of steadfast endurance.   Seven times he suffered bonds, he was driven into exile, he
was stoned."   It is manifest that Clement did not know 2 Cor. xi. 24 f.
Kennedy, p. 150 ; Rendall, p. 90.

† In the Mishna, in the section called *Makkoth*, Rabbinical thoroughness
provides for such an event, which might occur from heart failure, but it cannot have been common.   Roman scourgings sometimes were fatal.   The
tractate *Makkoth* is now very accessible in two small editions, Strack,
Leipzig, 1910, and Hölscher, Tübingen, 1910.   Deissmann (*St Paul*, p. 64)
calls it "a thrilling commentary on that simple line in 2 Corinthians."

rights as Romans (Joseph. *B.J.* II. xiv. 9). The fact that
St Paul was thrice treated in this way is evidence that being
a Roman citizen was an imperfect protection when magistrates
were disposed to be brutal. We may be sure that he pro-
tested at Philippi, but there was an excited mob to hound
on the domineering praetors. Ramsay, *St Paul the Traveller*,
p. 219.

The best MSS. have ἐραβδίσθην, not ἐρραβδίσθην. "In most cases
verbs beginning with ρ do double the ρ after the initial ἐ of the augmented
tenses. Usually the evidence for the single ρ is overwhelming" (WH.
App. p. 163).

ἅπαξ ἐλιθάσθην. At Lystra, and of this we have a full account. The Apostles had a narrow escape from stoning at
Iconium. Their Jewish enemies followed them to Lystra, and
there St Paul was nearly killed (Acts xiv. 5, 6, 19). Clement of
Rome (*Cor.* v.) has λιθασθείς after ἑπτάκις δεσμὰ φορέσας,
φυγαδευθείς. Paley, *Hor. Paul.* iv. 9. In N.T. λιθοβολέω is
more freq. than λιθάζω, and in LXX it is much more freq. In
Acts we find both.

τρὶς ἐναυάγησα. We know nothing of these, for the one
recorded in Acts xxvii. took place later. The verb is classical,
but it is very rare in Bibl. Grk. Cf. 1 Tim. i. 19.

νυχθήμερον. A very rare word, meaning a complete day and
night.

πεποίηκα. The change from aorists to perfect is not casual.
The perf. shows that the dreadful experience is vividly before the
Apostle's mind, and possibly indicates that the occurrence was
recent. J. H. Moulton, p. 144.* Ποιέω occurs fairly often of
spending time; Acts xv. 33, xviii. 23, xx. 3; Jas. iv. 13; Tobit
x. 7. 'Make time' in English is not parallel.

ἐν τῷ βυθῷ. Vulg. *in profundo maris.* This translation has
helped the extraordinary idea that the Apostle had spent twenty-
four hours under water; but ἐν τῷ βυθῷ means simply 'in the
sea,' *in alto mari*, far away from land. In the other shipwrecks
he was near the shore, which he soon reached, as in Acts xxvii.;
but in this case he was tossed about, probably on a bit of
wreckage, for a night and a day. Chrysostom rejects the other
explanation as improbable, because St Paul is here speaking of
his sufferings, not of his miracles. Those who adopt the
miraculous interpretation point to Jonah as a case in point, as if
that could be regarded as history. Cf. τὰ θαυμάσια αὐτοῦ ἐν τῷ
βυθῷ (Ps. cvi. 24), which certainly does not refer to the wonderful things in the depths of the ocean. Theophylact says that there

---

* Burton § 88, Blass, § 59. 3, and Simcox, *Lang. of the N.T.* p. 104, take
other views of this perfect. If it points to a recent occurrence, we might
assign it to the intermediate and painful visit.

was an underground chamber in which St Paul lay concealed after the peril at Lystra and that this was called Βυθός. He gives this as a mere tradition; τινὲς δέ φασιν.

26. ὁδοιπορίαις πολλάκις. The ἐν of *v.* 23 is dropped here and resumed in *v.* 27, and these changes, although they make little difference to the sense, might be marked in translation; '*By* journeyings often.' Journeys of long duration were often undertaken for pleasure or profit, and lest anyone should think that this is what he means here, the Apostle proceeds to enlarge upon the dangers, of eight different kinds, which his travels involved. 'By perils of rivers, perils of robbers; perils from my countrymen, perils from Gentiles; perils in the city, perils in the wilderness; perils in the sea, perils among false brethren.' The first six of these κίνδυνοι are arranged in contrasted pairs; but there is not much contrast between the sea and false brethren. To find here a comparison between *mare infidum* (Plautus), or *insidiae mari factae* (Cicero), or *fallacior undis* (Ovid) and 'false brethren' is fanciful. From Acts we can illustrate some of these κίνδυνοι, and obviously several of them overlap; *e.g.* those ἐκ γένους, Acts ix. 23, 29, xiii. 50, xiv. 5, xxiii. 12, xxiv. 27, all of which passages would also illustrate κίνδυνοι ἐν πόλει. Cf. 1 Thess. ii. 14 f., and see Harnack, *Mission and Expansion*, i. pp. 57, 487, ii. p. 43. The changes of constr. (simple gen., ἐκ, ἐν) avoid monotony. All three are intelligible, but the simple gen. in this sense is not common; κινδ. θαλασσῶν is parallel. Rivers are often flooded, sometimes suddenly, and bridges and ferries were rare. Frederick Barbarossa was drowned in the Calycadnus in Cilicia in the third Crusade, June 1190. Brigands and pirates often made travel both by land and sea dangerous. Perils from Gentiles were found at Philippi, Acts xvi. 20, and at Ephesus, Acts xix. 23 f. 'False brethren' may be a glance at the false teachers in Corinth and in Galatia. We know least about κίνδυνοι ἐν ἐρημίᾳ, but they would overlap with rivers and robbers. Ramsay's very full article on "Roads and Travel (in N.T.)," in Hastings, *DB.* v. pp. 375 ff., does not say much about the dangers of travelling in the first century. The evidence is somewhat meagre. See Deissmann, *St Paul*, pp. 36, 37.

Excepting in the Apocrypha, κίνδυνος is surprisingly rare both in LXX (Ps. cxiv. [cxvi.] 3 only) and in N.T. (here and Rom. viii. 35 only). The rhythmic repetition of the same word is found often in literature, esp. in rhetorical passages. Cf. vii. 2, 4; 1 Cor. xiii. 4–9; Phil. ii. 2, iv. 8; 1 Jn. ii. 12–14. With the absence of the art. in ἐν πόλει and ἐν ἐρημίᾳ comp. ἐν οἴκῳ and ἐν ἀγρῷ. Perhaps ἐν πόλει, ἐν ἐρημίᾳ and ἐν θαλάσσῃ are meant to form a triplet covering the whole surface of the earth,* and then ἐν ψευδαδέλφοις is left as a climax at the end. On the omission of the art. see Blass, § 46. 5.

ἐν ψευδαδέλφοις. This was the most insidious peril of all. The other dangers threatened life and limb and property, but this one imperilled, and sometimes ruined, his work. The others often caused delay, but this one generally caused disaster. In writing to Corinthians, as to Galatians, he would mean by these 'false brethren' the Jewish Christians who wished to impose on all Christians the yoke of the Law. But they were not the only persons who could be thus described. The Epistles of St Jude and St John, the Didache and 2 Peter, together with portions of the Apocalypse, show us how seriously the Apostolic Church suffered from an evil of which Simon Magus, the Nicolaitans, the 'Jezebel' prophetess, and the libertines who preached licentiousness as the logical fruit of Christian freedom, are illustrations. That St Paul means spies, who pretended to be Christians, in order to learn all about the brethren, and then betray them, is not probable. The change from ἐκ γένους and ἐξ ἐθνῶν to ἐν ψευδαδέλφοις may be accidental, owing to the intervening ἐν . . ἐν . . ἐν. But it may be deliberate, in order to mark a difference between external foes, who were not always with him, and those of his own household, among whom he was compelled to live and work.

27. Having explained in *vv.* 24, 25 what he meant by being ἐν θανάτοις πολλάκις, and in *v.* 26 what ὁδοιπορίαις πολλάκις involved, he now adds a series of varied sufferings which continue the cumulative argument that his claim to be a minister of Christ is overwhelmingly stronger than that of his opponents. The verse consists of two evenly balanced lines, followed by a much shorter line, which is all the more effective through its being ended so abruptly. It leaves the hearer expectant.

27. κόπῳ καὶ μόχθῳ. 'By labour and travail,' or 'By toil and moil,' for it is possible that St Paul combines the two words here, as in 1 Thess. ii. 9 and 2 Thess. iii. 8, because of the similarity in sound. We have the same combination in Hermas, *Sim.* v. vi. 2, οὐδεὶς γὰρ δύναται σκαφεῦσαι ἄτερ κόπου ἢ μόχθου. Of the two words, μόχθος is active, indicating struggle and toil, while κόπος is passive, indicating the lassitude which results from prolonged exertion. Lightfoot on 1 Thess. ii. 9. The words are therefore not in logical order. In 1 and 2 Thess., Vulg. is more logical than exact with *labor et fatigatio*: here it has *labor et aerumna*. In all three places the Apostle refers to his working with his hands to maintain himself.

* Wetstein quotes from Ovid, *multa prius pelago, multaque passus humo*; and from Plutarch, πλάνας ἐν ἐρημίᾳ καὶ κινδύνους ἐν θαλάσσῃ.

ἐν ἀγρυπνίαις πολλάκις. This probably refers chiefly to voluntary 'watchings' (AV., RV.) rather than involuntary insomnia. His manual labour, his prayers and his preaching (Acts xx. 9–11, 31) often kept him from sleep. Cf. vi. 5. The word is freq. in Ecclus., elsewhere very rare in Bibl. Grk. In the prologue to Ecclus. and 2 Macc. ii. 26 it is used of sitting up at night writing a book. In Ecclus. xxxviii. 26–30 it is used repeatedly of labourers and artisans working at night. On the other hand, in xxxvi. [xxxi.] 1, 2, 20 and xlii. 9 it is used of sleeplessness caused by anxiety or discomfort.

ἐν λιμῷ καὶ δίψει. The hunger and thirst caused by inability to obtain food and drink (Deut. xxviii. 48; Is. xlix. 10). This is involuntary fasting.

ἐν νηστείαις πολλάκις. Some commentators explain this also of involuntary fasting. But this makes it a mere repetition of ἐν λιμῷ καὶ δίψει. Ἐν ἀγρυπνίαις πολλάκις is not a repetition of κόπῳ καὶ μόχθῳ. Calvin decides for *jejunia voluntaria*, because the hunger caused by want has already been mentioned; and as ἀγρυπνίαις probably refers to going without sleep in order to work, so νηστείαις probably refers to going without meals for the same reason. Fastings as a means of self-discipline (1 Cor. ix. 27) are less probable, for these would hardly be included in a list of hardships. But seeing that the Apostle is accumulating evidence that he is a true minister of Christ, it is not impossible that the work of bringing his body into subjection is included; *quin νηστείαις enim, quum λιμῷ καὶ δίψει adjungantur, jejunia voluntarie ac sine necessitate servata intelligenda sint, nemo prudens dubitat* (Cornely).* Cf. Rom. viii. 35–37.

ἐν ψύχει καὶ γυμνότητι. When he was thrown into prison, or drenched by rain, or stripped by brigands.

All this argument is in strong contrast to the comfortable doctrine of the Jews, and doubtless of the Judaizers at Corinth, that to be in easy circumstances and general prosperity was a sign of Divine favour. Chrysostom points out that St Paul says nothing about results, as to the number of converts that he had made: he counts up only what he has suffered in his missionary work. And this he does not merely out of modesty, but because his labours, even if fruitless, proved the reality of his mission.

ℵ³ K L M P, f Vulg. support ἐν before κόπῳ καὶ μόχθῳ: but we may safely omit ἐν with ℵ* B D E F G, d e g Goth. It would be more likely to be inserted as probable than dropped as unnecessary. Note the divergence of f from F.

---

* Its place in the list is against this interpretation. If that were the meaning, it should have come at the end. It is not supposed that 'cold and nakedness' refer to self-discipline.

28. χωρὶς τῶν παρεκτός. The meaning of this must remain uncertain, for the gender of τῶν is doubtful, and so also is the meaning of παρεκτός, and the different translations which these uncertainties render possible will all of them make sense in this context. But it is certain that the words are to be taken with what follows, and not as the close of the long sentence which precedes (Chrys.). We are fairly safe in assuming that τῶν is neuter; for if 'those *persons* that are without,' *i.e.* who assail me from the outside, had been the meaning, we should probably have had οἱ ἔξωθεν (1 Tim. iii. 7; cf. Joseph. *B.J.* IV. iii., where τὸ μὲν τοῖς ἔξωθεν ὑπακούειν is opposed to τὸ δὲ τοῖς οἰκείοις εἴκειν), or still more probably οἱ ἔξω (1 Cor. v. 12, 13; Col. iv. 5; 1 Thess. iv. 12), an expression which seems to be of Rabbinical origin and came to mean all who were outside the Christian Church, whether heathen or Jews; cf. Mk. iv. 11. What then does τὰ παρεκτός mean? Probably *not* 'those things which are without' (AV., RV.),* for which we should have had τὰ ἔξω or τὰ ἔξωθεν, but 'those things which are besides these,' viz. 'the things which I omit' (RV. marg. 1). Of the two halves of the compound word παρεκτός it is the παρά (*v.* 24) rather than the ἐκτός which dominates, the idea of *exception* rather than that of *externality*. But ἐκτός is used in the sense of 'except' or 'besides' (1 Cor. xv. 27; Acts xxvi. 22; Judg. viii. 26, xx. 15, 17; etc.). In LXX παρεκτός does not occur, except as a very questionable *v.l.* Lev. xxiii. 38; and Aquila has it Deut. i. 36. But the meaning in both places is 'except,' LXX πλήν. In the Testaments (*Zebulon* i. 4) we have 'I did not know that I sinned *except* in thought,' παρεκτὸς ἐννοίας. These facts justify us in adopting as the rendering of τὰ παρεκτός 'the things which I omit,'—τὰ παραλειφθέντα, as Chrysostom paraphrases the expression. The Apostle has mentioned a great many things; then he continues, 'Besides the things which I do not mention, there is, etc.' This makes good sense; but it is impossible to say how much he omits, though Chrysostom thinks that the half is not told.† The second rendering in RV. marg., 'the things which come out of course,' *i.e.* 'exceptional things,' is not probable. Such a meaning would probably have been expressed otherwise.

ἡ ἐπίστασίς μοι ἡ καθ' ἡμέραν. If μου were the right reading, this might mean, 'my daily observation,' 'my daily attentiveness.' But μοι is firmly established, and thus the other meaning of ἐπίστασις becomes necessary, 'that which presses (or rushes) upon me daily,' 'the daily onset upon me.' See crit. note below.

* There seems to be no passage in which παρεκτός means 'outside,' *extrinsecus* (Vulg.).

† πλείονα τὰ παραλειφθέντα τῶν ἀπαριθμηθέντων.

Augustine has *incursus in me*, and a *concursus in me*, which perhaps represents ἐπισύστασις μοι, although D reads ἐπίστασις μου. Ἐπισύστασις (Num. xvi. 40 [xvii. 5], xxvi. 9, of the conspiracy of Korah) means 'hostile combination,' or 'combined attack,' and in that case ἡ μέριμνα πασῶν τῶν ἐκκλησιῶν does not explain the preceding clause but states an additional cause of suffering.   But both here and Acts xxiv. 12 ἐπίστασις is the better reading, and the word occurs nowhere else in N.T. The meaning 'pressure' or 'onset' is confirmed by 2 Macc. vi. 3 δυσχερὴς ἡ ἐπίστασις τῆς κακίας, as also by such renderings as *instantia* (Vulg. here), *concursus* (Vulg. Acts xxiv. 12), and *incursus*; and with this rendering ἡ μερ. π. τ. ἐκκλ. is probably epexegetic.   But this is not certain ; by 'the daily pressure' the Apostle may mean something different from anxiety about all the Churches.   There were the criticisms and suspicions to which he was every day exposed, as also the demands that were made upon his time by unreasonable persons,—the pressing business of each day.   'The concourse of people to see me' is too definite.

ἡ μέριμνα πασῶν τῶν ἐκκλησιῶν.   'My anxiety for *all* the Churches.'   "This was the chief thing of all," says Chrysostom, "that his soul was distracted, and his thoughts divided." *   Cf. Mk. iv. 19 = Mt. xiii. 22 = Lk. viii. 14 ; also Lk. xxi. 34.   'Care' in English is ambiguous ; either that which anxious people feel, or that which considerate people bestow ; see the Greek of 1 Pet. v. 7.   Either meaning would suit this passage, and the second is often understood ; but μέριμνα means the former, the anxiety which torments him.   Therefore this does not mean that St Paul claimed jurisdiction over all Churches, whether founded by himself or not ; he is not thinking of jurisdiction at all.   But every Christian centre had claims on his thought and sympathy, those most of all of which he had intimate knowledge.   The intercourse between the chief centres was fairly constant, he was frequently receiving information which gave him plenty to think about (1 Cor. i. 11, xvi. 17), and anxiety about people generates care for them, when care is possible.   This was specially the case with so sensitive a nature as that of St Paul.   What he experienced went deep and moved him strongly.   See Index IV.

ἐπίστασις (אBDFG 17) rather than ἐπισύστασις (KLMP). μοι (א* BFG 17) rather than μου (א³ DEKLMP).

---

* Μέριμνα *significat curam sollicitam et dubiam, quae mentem in partes divisas velut dividit*, a μερίζω τὸν νοῦν.   This derivation, though probable, is not universally accepted.   Vulg. has *sollicitudo* here, Mt. xiii. 22, and 1 Pet. v. 7, *aerumna*, Mk. iv. 19, and *cura*, Lk. xxi. 34.   Other Latin texts have *cogitatio*.   See on Lk. xxi. 34, and Scrivener, *Codex Bezae*, pp. xliv f.

29. τίς ἀσθενεῖ, καὶ οὐκ ἀσθενῶ; At once he gives two examples
of the μέριμνα which distracts him ; "as though he were himself
the Church throughout the world, so was he distressed for every
member" (Chrys.). Needless scruples often troubled the weaker
brethren ; in his intense sympathy the Apostle felt the weakness,
though he did not share the scruples (1 Cor. ix. 22 ; cf. 1 Cor.
viii. 11, 12 ; Rom. iv. 19, xiv. 1, 2). But other forms of weakness
are doubtless included. Of course he does not mean, 'Who is
weak, if I am not? If anyone can be called weak, I can.' For
that, ἐγώ must have been expressed, and the wording would have
been different. Both ἀσθενῶ (v. 21, xii. 10, xiii. 3, 4, 9) and
ἀσθένεια (xi. 30, xii. 5, 9, 10, xiii. 4) are freq. in these chapters.

τίς σκανδαλίζεται καὶ οὐκ ἐγὼ πυροῦμαι; 'Who is made to
stumble (1 Cor. viii. 13) and *I* burn not' with shame and
distress? Cf. ἕνα ἕκαστον ὑμῶν ὡς πατὴρ τέκνα ἑαυτοῦ (1 Thess. ii.
11). When any Christian, and especially one of his own
converts, is seduced into sin or grievous error, the Apostle shares
his remorse ; *quanto major caritas, tanto majores plagae de peccatis
alienis* (Aug.). The exact meaning of πυροῦμαι depends in each
case on the context (see on 1 Cor. vii. 9 ; Eph. vi. 16 ; 2 Pet.
iii. 12 ; Rev. i. 15, iii. 18), and here it means feeling burning
shame with the sinner rather than hot indignation against the
seducer. In Latin we find such expressions as *flagrare pudore,
dolorum faces, dolor ardentes faces intentat,*—the last two in
Cicero. Note the emphatic ἐγώ in this question ; in the first
question the emphasis is on οὐκ, and Cyprian (*Ep.* xvii. 1) marks
the change with a change of order ; *ego non . . . non ego* ; Vulg.
has *ego non* in both places. The second question is a studied
advance on the first, for σκανδαλίζεται and πυροῦμαι express a
great deal more than ἀσθενεῖ and ἀσθενῶ, and there is the addition
of the emphatic ἐγώ : 'Who is entrapped into sin, and *my* heart
is not ablaze with pain?' In such cases there was ὀδύνη φλογί-
ζουσα τὴν ἑαυτοῦ καρδίαν, *summo dolore, quasi igne, cruciabatur ipse.*

30. τὰ τῆς ἀσθενείας μου καυχήσομαι. The future tense has
led some commentators to limit the scope of the verb to what
follows and to make a fresh paragraph begin here (xi. 30–xii. 9
or 10); so Schmiedel, Weiss, and others. But the future
indicates his general intention and guiding principle ; it covers
the whole of this foolish glorying. If it must be gone through,
it shall be about the things which concern his weakness, his
being persecuted and made a laughing-stock. They cause some
people to despise him ; but they are more glorious than the
things of which his opponents boast, for they increase his likeness
to Christ (i. 5 ; Phil. iii. 10) and his unlikeness to them : οὗτος
ἀποστολικὸς χαρακτήρ (Chrys.).

31. ὁ Θεὸς καὶ πατὴρ τοῦ κυρίου Ἰησοῦ οἶδεν. There is no reason to confine this to what follows. Like καυχήσομαι, it looks both ways. The Corinthians may be sceptical about what he has enumerated and what he has still to mention in the long series of τὰ τῆς ἀσθενείας, but in the most solemn way he assures them that there is nothing untrue in what he states; cf. i. 23; Gal. i. 20; Rom. ix. 1; 1 Tim. ii. 7; also 2 Tim. iv. 1. The strong language here and i. 23 is indirect evidence of the calumnies which were circulated about him; he said 'yes' when he meant 'no,' or said both 'yes' and 'no' in one breath (i. 17); he could not speak the truth.

D E K L M P, d e f Vulg. Copt. add Χριστοῦ. Omit with ℵ B F G 17, 37, Goth. Arm. Note the divergence of f from F.

32, 33. Here again we are confronted with difficulties through ignorance of the situation. The abrupt descent from the lofty rhetoric of a rhythmically arranged argument to the very prosaic statement of a simple matter of fact is in itself surprising, and is all the more so, when we take it in connexion with the solemn asseveration which immediately precedes it. This latter difficulty might be removed by supposing that the asseveration refers to what precedes and has no connexion with the verses which follow it; that, however, is an unsatisfactory solution, and it leaves the sudden transition unexplained.

Baljon, Hilgenfeld, Holsten, and Schmiedel find the want of connexion so surprising that they would banish these two verses, with or without all or part of xii. 1, as an interpolation, unskilfully inserted to illustrate τὰ τῆς ἀσθενείας μου.* If any such hypothesis were needed, one would have to suppose that the interpolation was made on the original letter, and possibly by the Apostle himself, for there is no evidence that the Epistle ever existed without these verses at this place. To point out that this part of the letter would read more easily if we passed straight from οὐ ψεύδομαι to xii. 1 or 2, or the middle of xii. 1, proves very little. Countless passages in letters and books would have been greatly improved if certain sentences had been omitted, and yet there is no doubt that the intrusive sentences are original. Here we are not certain that the omission of the sentences would have been an improvement. Quite possibly to those who knew what the Apostle had in his mind the abrupt transition to this (for us) not very significant incident had point and meaning. It is possible that the story of the Apostle being let down in a hamper had been employed to make him look ludicrous, or to show what a coward he was, flying in this

---

* This proposal, as Lietzmann points out, is based on the assumption that the Apostle's thoughts must proceed in a logically consecutive manner, and this they frequently do not do.

ignominious way, when there was really no danger. St Paul, therefore, after a solemn assertion that he is speaking the truth, states exactly what did take place. The danger was great; but God enabled his friends to deliver him from it. In Acts ix. 23–25, St Luke tells this story about his friend without any apparent feeling that it was from any point of view discreditable. We must be content therefore to leave the reason for the sudden mention of this incident open. To us it serves as an example of τὰ τῆς ἀσθενείας μου, and that suffices.

ἐν Δαμασκῷ ὁ ἐθνάρχης Ἀρέτα τοῦ βασιλέως κ.τ.λ. This statement raises historical questions, the answers to which are not quite simple. The Romans occupied the Nabataean territory B.C. 65, 64, and Damascus coins show that Damascus was still under the Roman Empire A.D. 33 ; but from A.D. 34 to 62 no such coins are extant, and after 62 the coins of Damascus are those of Nero. Damascene coins of Caligula and Claudius are wanting. The Nabataean king Aretas iv., whose reign extends from B.C. 9 to A.D. 39, had used some frontier-disputes as a reason for making war on Herod Antipas, who about A.D. 28 had divorced the daughter of Aretas in order to marry Herodias ; and he utterly defeated Antipas about A.D. 32. Antipas complained to Tiberius, who in a rage commanded Vitellius to capture Aretas and either bring him alive or send his head. Vitellius had no love for Antipas, and in the course of his march against Aretas went up to Jerusalem near Pentecost A.D. 37, where he heard of the death of Tiberius (16 March) and the accession of Caligula, and he at once stopped the expedition against Aretas, for Caligula liked Antipas as little as Vitellius did (Joseph. *Ant.* XVIII. v. 1–3).

In order to explain how an ethnarch of Aretas was governor of Damascus when Saul of Tarsus made his escape from the city we have these possibilities.

1. To mark his dislike for Antipas, Caligula may have given Damascus to his great enemy Aretas. In this case the escape of St Paul cannot be placed earlier than the latter part of A.D. 37, and this would give A.D. 35 or 36 as the earliest date for his conversion. On the whole, this is the most probable explanation.

2. But it is not impossible, though hardly probable, that the subtle Tiberius may have thought it worth while to secure the friendship of Aretas by letting him have Damascus. If so, this must have taken place before the complaints of Antipas reached Tiberius, and in that case the conversion of St Paul might be placed still nearer to the Crucifixion.

3. The conquest of Damascus by Aretas at any time is so improbable that it may safely be rejected from consideration.

The precise meaning of ἐθνάρχης is uncertain and not very important. The government of the Nabataean kingdom of Aretas seems to have been tribal, and ἐθνάρχης occurs in inscriptions as the head of a tribal district. Jewish governors in Palestine and Alexandria had the title, and perhaps ' viceroy ' would be the modern equivalent (1 Macc. xiv. 47, xv. 1, 2). It was applied to vassal princes, and it was under this title that the high priests governed the Jews (Joseph. *Ant.* XVII. xiii. 4 ; *B.J.* II. vi. 3).

There is no discrepancy between the statement here, that ' the *ethnarch* guarded the city to take me,' and that in Acts ix. 24, that ' the *Jews* watched the gates night and day to kill him.' It was the Jews who urged the ethnarch against Saul, and they were very numerous in Damascus (*B.J.* II. xx. 2, VII. viii. 7), and they would watch the gates along with the guards set by the ethnarch, who would not be sorry to gratify this turbulent element among his subjects by so simple a concession. Saul had already caused disturbance, and it would be an advantage to get him out of the way. But the total difference of wording, and the omission of the retirement to Arabia, show that Luke wrote quite independently of his friend's letters. See Zahn, *Intr. to N.T.* iii. pp. 121, 140.

On these various problems see Hastings, *DB.* i. pp. 145, 424, 793 ; *Enc. Bibl.* i. 296, 815 ; Herzog, *Real. Enc.* i. p. 618 (Hauck, i. p. 795); Schürer, *Jewish People in the Time of J.C.* I. ii. pp. 89, 356, II. i. p. 98 ; Lewin, *Fasti Sacri*, pp. 226, 249 ; Knowling on Acts ix. 23, 24 ; Zahn, *Intr. to N.T.* iii. p. 445 ; also Intr. to 1 Cor. p. xxviii.

32. Ἀρέτα. Note the aspirate. The original form of the name was Haritha, which in Greek would become Ἀρέθας. But the influence of ἀρετή caused inscriptions and MSS. to abolish the aspirates, and Ἀρέθας became Ἀρέτας. Deissmann, *Bib. St.* p. 183. By a converse process an aspirate was given to Ἱεροσόλυμα and Ἱερουσαλήμ through a supposed connexion with ἱερός (WH. ii. p. 313). The MSS. of N.T. have been influenced in both cases.

ἐφρούρει. In LXX the verb is mostly used in the literal sense, as here; but elsewhere in N.T. it is metaphorical. In Phil. iv. 7 we have the striking picture of ' the peace of God standing sentry over your hearts.' See also Lightfoot on Gal. iii. 23 and Hort on 1 Pet. i. 5. In dictating, St Paul seems to have forgotten that he began his sentence with ἐν Δαμασκῷ. We should have expected τὰς πύλας to follow ἐφρούρει rather than τὴν πόλιν Δαμασκηνῶν.

πιάσαι. The verb is freq. in Jn. of attempts to arrest Jesus (vii. 30, 32, 44, viii. 20, x. 39, etc.).

We should probably omit θέλων, which אC³EKLMP insert after πιάσαι με, and FG, g Copt. Syr-Hark. insert before it. BD*, def Vulg. and Syr-Pesh. omit. Note the divergence of e from E and of f from F.

33. διὰ θυρίδος. A small opening in the wall is still shown as the 'little door' through which St Paul was let down. Διὰ τῆς θυρίδος occurs Josh. ii. 15 of the escape of the spies from the city wall at Jericho, and 1 Sam. xix. 12 of the escape of David from his own house, when Saul sent men to watch him and slay him.

ἐν σαργάνῃ. Acts ix. 25 says ἐν σφυρίδι, the word always used respecting the Feeding of the 4000 (Mk. viii. 8, 20; Mt. xv. 37, xvi. 10), while κόφινος is always used of the Feeding of the 5000. The rare word σαργάνη, like σφυρίς or σπυρίς, probably means a basket made of plaited or woven material. It is said to be used in the Ληθή of the comic poet Timocles for a fish basket. As stated above, the mode of escape, for which Theodoret thinks it necessary to apologize by pointing out the greatness of the danger, had probably been in some way used to the discredit of the Apostle, and hence his abrupt and dry mention of it here. But there is nothing to show that he was then "in a state of nervous prostration" and merely "passively acquiesced in the action of his disciples" (Rackam). At any rate he himself regards it as a leading illustration of τὰ τῆς ἀσθενίας. For us it is a remarkable thing that the city to which he had set out as a persecutor was the scene of the first persecution that was directed against himself; and six centuries later it was the first Christian city that was captured by the Moslem invaders, A.D. 634. Among cities that are still inhabited, Damascus is probably the oldest in the world. It is possible that, when he began to dictate these two verses, St Paul meant to record instances of humiliating perils in other cities; but having given this one he passes on quickly to a very different subject for glorying.

It is impossible to be certain whether this escape from 'the city of the Damascenes' took place before or after the retirement into Arabia (Gal. i. 17). Luke in Acts ix. does not mention the retirement, possibly because, when he wrote, he was not aware of it, but more probably because it was not an incident on which he cared to lay stress. Some place it before *v.* 19; others refer it to the ἡμέραι ἱκαναί in *v.* 23; others again place it after *v.* 25, *i.e.* after the escape from Damascus. It is more probable that this famous incident took place after the return from Arabia,* and in that case the best position for it in Acts is in the middle of ix. 19, where both WH. and RV., and also

* Lewin, *Fasti Sacri*, pp. 254, 263.

Souter, begin a new paragraph. Ἐγένετο δέ in N.T. is peculiar to Lk. and Acts, and is freq. in both writings to mark a fresh start in the narrative. This, however, is no proof that Luke at this point was consciously passing over the Arabian interval. See A. T. Robertson, *Epochs in the Life of St Paul*, pp. 76–79; Redlich, *S. Paul and His Companions*, pp. 22, 23; Ramsay, *St Paul the Traveller*, p. 380; Emmet on Gal. i. 17.

διὰ τοῦ τείχους. Why should διὰ θυρίδος be '*through* a window' and διὰ τοῦ τείχους be '*by* the wall' (AV., RV.)? 'Through' is probably right in both cases; he was let down (Mk. ii. 4) through an opening through the wall. In Acts ix. 25 RV. has 'through the wall' for διὰ τοῦ τείχους. Epictetus (*Dis.* ii. 6 *sub init.*) says that, when he finds the door closed, he must either go away again or enter through the window (διὰ τῆς θυρίδος). It is said that the wall in which is the aperture that is now shown as the place of escape is a modern one.

ἐξέφυγον τὰς χεῖρας αὐτοῦ. This is the usual constr. after ἐκφεύγω (Rom. ii. 3; Acts xvi. 27; etc.), but we sometimes have ἐκ (Acts xix. 16) or ἀπό (Ecclus. xl. 6). Cf. οὐκ ἐκφεύξομαι τὰς χεῖρας ὑμῶν (Sus. 22). It would certainly be strange if, after so narrow an escape, he had, a year or two later, returned to Damascus again; and those who place the escape before the retirement to Arabia have to meet this difficulty. St Paul was courageous enough to risk his life again, if need required it; but he was not so fanatical as to risk it without very good reason; and what reason could there be? His return to a place that had been friendly to him is natural enough.

XII. 1-10. Glorying about Revelations to his Soul and a Thorn for his Flesh.

I have received two sublime revelations, and also, to preserve me from vanity respecting this great favour, a humiliating infirmity.

¹ This glorying is forced upon me. I have indeed nothing to gain by it, for myself or for the good of the Church; but I will pass on to a worthier subject, viz. visions and revelations granted to me by the Lord Jesus Christ. They have been called delusions or inventions, but they are sober fact. ² I can tell you of a man who was in ecstasy with Christ fourteen years ago—it was Christ's doing and no credit to the man: whether he was still in the body, I cannot tell, or whether he was in rapture away from the body. I cannot tell; that is known to

God alone : he was caught up, this man of whom I speak, even
to the third heaven. ³ I can tell you also that this man of whom
I speak, either in the body or apart from the body (God knows
which), ⁴ was caught up into the Paradise where God dwells,
and there listened to utterances unutterable, such as no human
being is allowed to repeat. ⁵ Of such a man as this, not knowing his own condition and yet so honoured, I am prepared to
glory ; but of myself personally, such as you know me, I am not
prepared to glory, except as regards what I have called my weaknesses. ⁶ I am not bound to abstain in this way, for if I choose
to glory about other things, I shall not be a fool in so doing, for
I shall only be saying what is true ; but I do abstain, because I
do not want anyone to form a higher estimate of me than that
which he can gather from what he sees me do or hears me say.
⁷ And then there is the exceeding greatness of the revelations.
Therefore, in order that I should not be exalted overmuch about
these, there was given to me a painful malady, like a stake
driven into my flesh, a messenger of Satan to buffet me, that I
should not be exalted overmuch. ⁸ About this affliction I three
times made supplication to the Lord, praying Him to remove it
from me. ⁹ And this was His reply ; " It is sufficient for thee that
thou hast received grace to become My Apostle and to convert
the nations ; for it is when man's strength fails that My power
is brought to perfection." Most gladly, therefore, I shall prefer
glorying in all my weaknesses to asking the Lord to free me from
them, so that the power of Christ may spread a sheltering cover over
me. ¹⁰ That is why I am so well pleased with weaknesses, such
as wanton injuries, dire hardships, persecutions, and desperate
straits, when they are endured for Christ's sake. For it is just
when in myself I am utterly weak that in Him I am truly
strong.

1. Καυχᾶσθαι δεῖ οὐ συμφέρον μέν, ἐλεύσομαι δὲ κ.τ.λ. Owing
probably to accidental mistakes in copying and conjectural
emendations by puzzled scribes, the text of this verse is so
confused that it is impossible to disentangle the original text
with certainty ; but on the whole this wording is likely to be
right, or nearly so ; 'I must needs glory : it is not indeed
expedient, but I will come to visions, etc.' It is however possible
that Καυχᾶσθαι δὲ οὐ συμφέρον μέν, ἐλεύσομαι δὲ κ.τ.λ. may be what
the Apostle dictated ; 'Now to glory is not indeed expedient, but
I will come to visions, etc.' The difference between these two

22

is not very important.* What is clear is that, before passing
from the great peril at Damascus to experiences of a very different
kind, he cannot refrain from remarking once more that all this
foolish glorying is forced upon him ; he knows that it is not
profitable, that it may lower his self-respect and the respect which
others have for him, but he has no choice about it ; ὑμεῖς με
ἠναγκάσατε (*v.* 11). Συμφέρον is used in a wide sense ; 'likely
to be edifying to other Christians or to myself' (viii. 10; 1 Cor.
vi. 12, vii. 35, x. 23, 33, xii. 7).

ὀπτασίας καὶ ἀποκαλύψεις Κυρίου. Seeing that Κυρίου belongs
to both substantives, the genitive is probably subjective ; 'visions
and revelations which proceed from the Lord,' rather than those
in which the Lord is seen and revealed ; cf. δι' ἀποκαλύψεως
Ἰησοῦ Χριστοῦ (Gal. i. 12). But where either objective or subjective makes good sense, it is sometimes difficult to see on
which side the balance of probability lies ; *e.g.* in the phrase τὸ
εὐαγγέλιον τοῦ Θεοῦ or Ἰησοῦ Χριστοῦ. 'Visions and revelations '
is a cross division, for some, but not all, visions reveal something,
and some, but not all, revelations are made without anything being
visible.† In *this* case, however, all the 'visions' would reveal
something, for they proceed from the Lord (Κυρίου), who sends
them for the very purpose of making something known. It is
perhaps true to say that, except in the Apocrypha (Ecclus. xliii.
2, 16 ; addition to Esther iv. 3), ὀπτασία always means a vision
that reveals something (Lk. i. 22, xxiv. 23 ; Acts xxvi. 19 ; Mal.
iii. 2 ; Dan. ix. 23, x. 1, 7, 8, 16 [Theod.], where LXX has ὅρασις
or ὅραμα). The word was probably colloquial before it became
Biblical.

The incidents to which this verse forms an introduction, like
that of the flight from Damascus, had probably been used as a
means of attacking St Paul. People may easily have said that
these ecstatic experiences, which he claimed to have had, proved
that he was a deluded enthusiast, if not actually crazy. If they
were not deliberate inventions, they were the outcome of vivid
and unrestrained imagination. He had thought about them till
he believed that they had taken place. It is possible that this
view survives here and there in the *Clementine Homilies* and
Recognitions, the Judaizing writers of which now and again, under
cover of Simon Magus, make an attack on St Paul. In particular
they deride the 'visions ' of Simon Magus. " Simon said, Visions
and dreams, being God-sent, do not speak falsely in regard to

---

* Some make the first sentence interrogative ; *Gloriari oportet? non
expedit quidem, veniam autem, etc.* Aquinas remarks ; *qui gloriatur de bono
recepto, incidit in periculum amittendi quod accepit.*

† Theophylact distinguishes the two thus ; ἡ μὲν μόνον βλέπειν δίδωσιν,
αὕτη δὲ καί τι βαθύτερον τοῦ ὁρωμένου ἀπογυμνοῖ.

those things which they have to tell.   And Peter said, You were right in saying that being God-sent they do not speak falsely. But it is uncertain whether he who sees has seen a God-sent dream" (*Clem. Hom.* xvii. 15 ; cf. *Hom.* xi. 35, ii. 17, 18 ; *Recog.* ii. 55, iii. 49, iv. 35).   See Hort, *Clem. Recog.* pp. 120 ff. ; Hastings, *DB.* iv. p. 524 ; *JTS.*, Oct. 1901, p. 53.

It is not likely that εἰ before καυχᾶσθαι (א³ 39, f Vulg.) is original. καυχᾶσθαι δεῖ (B D³ F G L P, d f g Vulg. Syrr. Goth.) is probably to be preferred to καυχᾶσθαι δέ (א D*, Copt.) or καυχ. ἐή (K M, Aeth.).   But in MSS. the confusion between ει and ε is very freq., and δέ may be original. The various readings in 1 Cor. vi. 20 illustrate the confusion between δεῖ and δή.   οὐ συμφέρον (א B G 17, 67**) rather than οὐ συμφέρει (D K L P); Gregory (*Proleg.* p. 75) shows that συμφέρον has better authority than συνφέρον.   μέν (א B G P 17, 67** f Vulg. Copt.) rather than μοι (D³ K L M, Syr-Hark., Chrys.) ; but D*, Aeth. Goth. have neither μέν nor μοι.   B 213 have ἐλευσόμαι δὲ καί.

The variations in the text of this verse do not justify its exclusion as an interpolation.   See above on xi. 32, 33.

2-5.   In solemn and subdued but rhythmical language, which reads as if it were the outcome of much meditation, and which suggests a good deal more than it states, St Paul affirms the reality of his mysterious experiences.*   Reluctantly, and only for a moment, he lifts the veil which usually covers the details of the most sacred moments of his life and allows the Corinthians to see enough to convince them that the revelations of which he has claimed to be the recipient were intensely and supremely real. He could doubt his own identity with the recipient rather than doubt the reality of the revelations, and he speaks of them as if they had been experienced by some one who during those mysterious times was other than himself.   But, whatever these experiences were, they could not be classed as 'weaknesses,' and we must admit that for the moment he has ceased to think of τὰ τῆς ἀσθενείας, for he cannot have regarded them as such, whatever his critics may have done.†

It has been suggested that these revelations are mentioned simply in order to explain the 'weakness' caused by the 'stake for the flesh' (*v.* 7), so that in reality there is no break in the catalogue of τὰ τῆς ἀσθενείας μου.   The context is against this view.   The revelations are mentioned independently of their

---

* On the rhetorical features of this and many other passages in the Pauline Epistles see the Essay on *Paulinische Rhetorik*, by J. Weiss, in *Theologische Studien*, Göttingen, 1897, esp. p. 191 ; also Farrar, *St Paul*, i., *App.* i. and ii.

† It has been thought that some of his opponents may have claimed to have had 'visions,' and that he is here pointing to experiences of his own which are superior to theirs.   This cannot be inferred from what is told us here, and no such hypothesis is required in order to make what is told us more intelligible.

consequences; and it would be more true to say that the σκόλοψ
is an appendix to the ἀποκαλύψεις than that the ἀποκαλύψεις are a
preface to the σκόλοψ. It is "because he is going to pass to
another kind of glorying, which to the many seems to set him
off in brighter colours" (Chrys.), that he writes what we have
here.

Bousset shows that among the Jews the belief in the fact of
translation to heaven was not confined to the cases of primitive
saints and heroes, such as Enoch and Elijah. Historical persons
of a much later date were believed to have had this experience.
In the Babylonian Talmud, *Chagiga*, 14b (Goldschmidt, iii.
834 ff.), we are told that four Rabbis had had this experience.
Ben Azai beheld the glory and died. Ben Soma beheld and was
stricken (went mad). Acher, who ranks as a heretic among
famous teachers, cut up the young plants (ruined the garden of
truth with his disastrous doctrine). Of R. Akiba alone is it said
that in peace he ascended and in peace he came back. The
Angels would have sent even him away, but the Holy One, who
is blessed for ever, said to them, "Suffer this old man, for he is
worthy, to enjoy My honour and glory."

But we are going beyond what this evidence warrants, if we
infer from it that a series of younger Rabbinical contemporaries
of St Paul had had ecstatic experiences similar to his, and that
he had brought this strange form of piety over from his Rabbinical past into Christianity. Granting that what is told us of these
four Rabbis is historically true,—and that may be granting a great
deal,—how can we tell that their experiences were similar to
those of St Paul, or that he knew anything of such things before
he met the Lord on the way to Damascus?

2. οἶδα ἄνθρωπον ἐν Χριστῷ πρὸ ἐτῶν δεκατεσσάρων . . . ἁρπαγέντα. '*I know* a man in Christ who fourteen years ago was
caught up.' Not, '*I knew* (AV.) such a person fourteen years
ago.' St Paul knows him intimately at the time of writing, but
not until *v.* 7 does he show that he is speaking of himself.

The meaning of ἐν Χριστῷ is not clear. It is not to be taken
with οἶδα, as if he were speaking in Christ's name; it belongs to
ἄνθρωπον ἁρπαγέντα, and it is probably inserted in order to dis-
claim all credit for the glorious experience, in which he was not
active but passive, being under Divine influence; it was 'in the
power of Christ' that he was caught up.* The mention of the
fourteen years is natural enough. In telling of a remarkable

* "*In Christ* points to spiritual contact with Christ as the source of all
that follows" (Beet). To suppose that it means no more than that it was
after he had become a Christian that he had these favours bestowed on him,
is inadequate.

incident of one's life it is natural to begin with the date, if one remembers it. The Prophets do so repeatedly with regard to their spiritual experiences, and Amos (iv. 7) does so in a manner parallel to this, πρὸ τριῶν μηνῶν τοῦ τρυγητοῦ. Cf. Hos. i. 1; Zech. i. 1, vii. 1; Is. vi. 1; Jer. i. 2, xxvi. 1, xlii. 7; Ezek. i. 1, iii. 16. The date in this case shows that it was after St Paul had been a Christian for about seven years that this event took place. But there is nothing to show that during these fourteen years he had never mentioned to any person the fact of these revelations until the Corinthians compelled him to break silence (Chrys., Thdrt., and some moderns). The context rather implies that the bare fact was known; *i.e.* it was known that he said that he had received communications direct from heaven.

There is nothing in Acts that can be identified with these experiences. The trance in xxii. 17 is very different; he is not caught up to the Lord, but the Lord comes to him, and he repeats what was said to him, as he does with regard to what was said to him on the road to Damascus. That he was caught up to heaven when he was lying apparently dead, after being stoned at Lystra (Acts xiv. 19), is a surprising hypothesis. Even more surprising is the supposition that St Paul was one of the prophets who went down from Jerusalem to Antioch and foretold the great famine (Acts xi. 27, 28), and that it was when he was in the third heaven that the coming of the famine was revealed to him! With less improbability Zahn (*Intr. to N.T.* iii. p. 462) connects this revelation with the momentous change of preaching to *Gentiles*, which was made at Antioch about A.D. 43 (Acts xi. 25, 26). But if that were correct, would not St Paul have declared that he had Divine authority for this step? Conjectural connexions of this kind are not of much value. For other visions cf. Acts xvi. 9, xviii. 9, xxiii. 11, xxvii. 23; and for ἁρπαγέντα cf. Acts viii. 39; 1 Thess. iv. 17; Rev. xii. 5. The use of ἀνελήμφθη is similar (appendix to Mk. xvi. *v.* 19; Acts i. 2, 11, 22; 1 Tim. iii. 16; 2 Kings ii. 11). Ἡρπάγην for ἡρπάσθην is late Greek.

The psychological phenomenon of ecstasy is found in other religions and philosophies, notably in Buddhism and Neo-platonism. Porphyry (*Vita Plotini*, ii. 23) tells us that, while he was with him, Plotinus four times attained to that oneness (ἐνωθῆναι) with God which was his τέλος καὶ σκοπός, and that he accomplished this ἐνεργείᾳ ἀρρήτῳ. This is very different from what the Apostle tells us about himself. In his case there is no ambitious struggle, often without success, for ecstatic union with the Deity. 'In the power of Christ' he is caught up into glory. There is another marked contrast when we compare the elaborate details given us about the experiences of Enoch and others when translated to heaven with the brief and restrained statements made by the Apostle in these few verses. He does not tell us what he saw in the third heaven, still less what he saw in the first and second, while on his way to the third.* He does not even tell us that he was conscious of passing through other celestial regions. The condensed intensity of the narrative leaves little room for the play of fancy or exaggeration.

εἴτε ἐν σώματι οὐκ οἶδα, εἴτε ἐκτὸς τοῦ σώματος οὐκ οἶδα. He is quite clear about what he knows and what he does not know. He knows that he was caught up *even* to the third heaven; about that there is no possibility of delusion. He was conscious of the transfer, and he vividly remembers that for a time he was in heaven. But he is not sure of the relation in which his spirit was to his body during this experience; about that his memory tells him nothing. His body may have been caught up to heaven, or it may have remained, bereft of consciousness, on earth. "That he was in the third heaven he was not ignorant, but the manner he knew not clearly" (Chrys.). This shows that he was alone at the time; if others had been with him, he would inevitably have solved this doubt by asking whether his body had disappeared.

Jewish beliefs respecting Enoch and Elijah, Baruch and Ezra, and perhaps also Jeremiah (Mt. xvi. 14; 2 Esdr. ii. 18; 2 Macc xv. 13, 14) had made the notion of *bodily* translation to heaven a commonplace. Such a translation may be difficult to believe, but in imagination it is easily realized, whereas disembodied spirit cannot be represented in thought. This idea of bodily translation would be familiar to St Paul, and he thought it possible that it might have taken place in his own case. With εἴτε . . . εἴτε (see on i. 6) he places the two alternatives on an equality. In the apocryphal Revelation or Vision of Paul (*Visio Pauli*) it is assumed that he was caught up *in* the body. On the other hand, in the *Assumption of Moses*, the soul is carried away *without* the body, and Philo (*De somn.* i. p. 626, Mang.) says that there was a tradition that Moses was freed from the body while he listened to the Divine utterances on the mount, ὧν ἀκροατὴν Μωϋσῆν ἀσώματον γενόμενον λόγος ἔχει. But we are not told what became of his body during the forty days on Sinai.

We may suppose that in St Paul's case the ecstasy was experienced in a form which was conditioned by his existing beliefs respecting such subjects. We do not make our dreams, and they come to us independently of our wills; but they are

---

* In any case there is no need to suspect Persian influence, or borrowing from Mazdeism, in the idea of a third heaven, as Clemen (*Primitive Christianity*, pp. 172, 368) suspects.

conditioned by the materials with which we are familiar, when we are awake (Bousset, p. 211).

Ἐν σώματι is a colloquial expression and is equivalent to an adverb. For this reason it has no art., like ἐν οἴκῳ, 'indoors, at home' (1 Cor. xi. 34, xiv. 35; Mk. ii. 1);* where it is not thus used we have ἐν τῷ σ. (iv. 10, v. 6), just as here we have ἐκτὸς τοῦ σώματος, which is not a colloquial expression. The omission of the art. before τρίτου and other ordinals is also colloquial (Acts ii. 15, xxiii. 23; Mt. xxvi. 44; Mk. xiv. 72; etc.)

ἕως τρίτου οὐρανοῦ. The ἕως does not prove that St Paul regarded the third heaven as the highest of all, but certainly 'even to the third heaven' would be more naturally used if the third heaven were the highest, than if there were four other heavens above it. We know from the Testaments of the Twelve Patriarchs (*Levi* ii. and iii.) and from the *Book of the Secrets of Enoch* that some Jews about the time of St Paul distinguished seven heavens, an idea in which they have been followed by the Valentinians and by the Mahometans. *The Secrets of Enoch* is not very clear in its account of the seven heavens, but in one place it would seem that paradise either is the third heaven or is in the third heaven (viii. 1–3, xlii. 3). In the Testaments the heavens and paradise seem to be different (*Levi* xviii. 5, 6, 10). It is by no means certain that St Paul was familiar with these ideas, and it is not probable that he is alluding to them here.† He is using language which was to be understood by the Corinthians, and it is not likely that he expected them to know about seven heavens; whereas 'even to the third heaven' might convey to any one the idea of the most sublime condition that is conceivable. Irenaeus (II. xxx. 7) has good sense on his side when, in arguing against the Valentinians, he rejects the notion that the Apostle was raised only to the third heaven in a series of seven, leaving the four highest heavens still beyond him. Bengel's suggestion may be right, that St Paul's three heavens are the heaven of the clouds, the heaven of the sun and stars, and the heaven in which God dwells; but that of Calvin seems to be preferable; *numerus ternarius κα-' ἐξοχήν positus est pro summo et perfectissimo.* Where seven heavens are counted,

---

* In the *Testament of Abraham* (Recension B. vii., viii.) σωματικῶς and ἐν σώματι are used as exact equivalents. Abraham asks to be taken up σωματικῶς, and the Lord tells Michael to take him up ἐν σώματι.

† R. H. Charles (*Book of the Secrets of Enoch*, p. xl) and Thackeray (*St Paul and Contemporary Jewish Thought*, pp. 172 f.) regard it as certain that the Apostle was familiar with these ideas and is here influenced by them. Chrysostom (*Hom. in Gen.* iv. 3) says that to teach that there are *many* heavens is to speak ἀπεναντίως τῇ θείᾳ γραφῇ. Basil (*Hexaem.* iii. 3) contends for three.

the third is a very inferior region, with somewhat earthly characteristics.

3. καὶ οἶδα τὸν τοιοῦτον ἄνθρωπον. ' I know *also* that the man of whom I speak.' We have to decide whether this is a repetition of *v.* 2 or the record of a second experience. That ἁρπάγο-μαι is used in both places is no sign that *vv.* 3, 4 simply repeat *v.* 2 with an additional fact ; in each case, if two cases are meant, he was ' caught up' from the earth. The change from 'third heaven' to 'paradise' is no evidence either way ; for 'paradise' may mean the 'third heaven' or some portion of it, and if it is a mere synonym, there may have been two occasions of rapture to the same region of heaven. Again, the plural in *v.* 1 is no evidence either way. It may mean more than one vision and revelation, or it may simply indicate a class of which one example is to be given. Moreover, even if *vv.* 3 and 4 are a repetition of *v.* 2, we still have two revelations, for the Divine communication in *v.* 9 is a revelation. See below on *v.* 7. But the καί at the beginning of *v.* 3 is rather strongly in favour of the view that we have two revelations without counting the Divine utterance in *v.* 9 ; for the καί is almost awkwardly superfluous if what follows simply repeats *v.* 2.

On the whole, patristic writers seem to be mostly in favour of either two raptures, or one rapture in two stages, first to the third heaven and thence to paradise. The language of some of them would fit either of these hypotheses (Irenaeus, II. xxx. 7 ; Tertullian, *De Praes. Haer.* 24 ; Cyril of Jerusalem, *Cat. Lect.* xiv. 26); but Clement of Alexandria (*Strom.* v. 12, p. 693, ed. Potter) is plainly for the latter ; "caught up even to the third heaven and *thence* into paradise."* In this he is followed by few moderns, who for the most part adopt the view that St Paul is speaking throughout of only one experience, and that 'paradise' is equivalent to the 'third heaven.' Bengel, however, is confident that *vv.* 3, 4 *duplex rei momentum exprimunt.* So also Bousset with somewhat less confidence ; *so werden wir schwerlich verstehen sollen, dass Paradies und dritter Himmel dasselbe seien, dass er sich also in seiner Aussage nur wiederhole* (p. 209). McFadyen finds it "hard to say, but perhaps the second statement is intended to suggest a second experience, similar but higher." The Fathers are loose in their quotations of the passage. They sometimes say that the Apostle heard unutterable words in the third heaven, which is no proof that they identify paradise with the third heaven ; and they sometimes say that he *saw* things of which it is not lawful to speak.

* With this Erasmus agrees in his paraphrase ; *raptus est in tertium usque coelum, hinc rursum in paradisum.*

χωρὶς τοῦ σώματος. '*Apart* from the body.' The change
from ἐκτός to χωρίς should be marked in translation.

Many texts in this verse read ἐκτός, and Vulg. has *extra corpus* in both
places, but χωρίς (B D* E*) is doubtless original.

4. εἰς τὸν παράδεισον. See on Lk. xxiii. 43 and Swete on
Rev. ii. 7, the only other passages in N.T. in which παράδεισος
occurs; also Hastings, *DB*. ii. pp. 668 f., *DCG*. ii. p. 318;
Salmond, *Christ. Doct. of Immortality*, pp. 346 f. The word tells
us little about the nature of the unseen world. In the O.T. it is
used either of the Garden of Eden (Gen. ii. 9, 10, 15, etc.) or of
a park or pleasure-ground (Cant. iv. 13; Eccles. ii. 5; Joel ii. 3;
etc.); but it represents three or four different Hebrew words.
We must leave open the question as to whether St Paul regards
paradise and the third heaven as identical, or as quite different,
or as one containing the other, for there is no clue to the
answer. See *Int. Journal of Apocrypha*, July 1914, pp. 74 f.

ἤκουσεν ἄρρητα ῥήματα. 'He heard unutterable utterances.'
The verbal contradiction may be accidental, but it is probably
another instance of playing upon words of which St Paul is fond
(i. 13, iii. 2, iv. 8, v. 4, vi. 10, vii. 10, x. 5, 6, 12).* Neither
'unspeakable words' (AV., RV.) nor *arcana verba* (Vulg.) exactly
reproduces the Greek. The latter might be *effata ineffabilia*.
Cf. ἀλάλους λαλεῖν (Mk vii. 37). Ἄρρητος is used in class. Grk.
of things which cannot be expressed in words (cf. στεναγμοῖς
ἀλαλήτοις, Rom. viii. 26); but more often of things which are
either too sacred or too horrible to be mentioned, *nefanda*.
What follows shows what is the meaning here, the only place in
Bibl. Grk. in which the word occurs.

ἃ οὐκ ἐξὸν ἀνθρώπῳ λαλῆσαι. No doubt ἀνθρώπῳ is to be
taken with ἐξόν rather than with λαλῆσαι: 'which it is not lawful
(Mt. xii. 4; Acts ii. 29) for a man to speak,' rather than 'not
lawful to say to a man': *non licet homini loqui* (Vulg.) will fit
either interpretation, but the difference between the two is not
very great. That he heard the voices of the heavenly choir, and
similar conjectures, are not very wise. The question, what was
the use of the revelation, if the Apostle might not make known
what was revealed? can be answered. It was a source of strength
to the Apostle himself in his overwhelming trials, and thus a
source of strength also to the millions whom he has encouraged.
Cf. Rev. x. 4, where the seer is told not to write down what he
heard. See Abbott, *Johannine Grammar*, p. 305.

5. ὑπὲρ τοῦ τοιούτου καυχήσομαι. No doubt τοῦ τοιούτου is
masc., as is shown by τ. τ. ἄνθρωπον (v. 3) and by the contrast

* We have something similar in Plato (*Sym.* 189 B); ἄρρητα ἔστω τὰ
εἰρημένα: and in Sophocles (*O.C.* 1001); ἄρρητον ἔπος.

with ἐμαυτοῦ. He speaks as if there were two Pauls, one about whom he could glory, and another about whom he would not do so. And in a sense there were two; for, as Origen remarks, "He who was caught up to the third heaven and heard unspeakable words is a different Paul from him who said, Of such a one I will glory." To a person who has been in ecstasy that experience may seem to belong to a person other than his everyday self. And it is only as having been bestowed upon a person different from his ordinary self that the Apostle will glory of the unspeakable favours bestowed in these raptures. They were not to his credit; for he was entirely passive throughout; all was 'of the Lord' and 'in Christ.' As to his own conduct, he returns to what was said in xi. 30, he will glory, not of the things which he has achieved, but of the things which he has suffered, the things in which he has been weak and the Lord strong. He returns to these in *v.* 7.

After ταῖς ἀσθενείαις ℵ D³ E G K L M P, f g Vulg. Aeth. Goth. add μου : B D* 17 67, d e Syrr. Copt. Arm. omit. Cf. xi. 30. Such insertions for completeness are common : see *vv.* 9, 10; Eph. iii. 6, v. 31; Phil. iv. 23.

6. ἐὰν γὰρ θελήσω καυχήσασθαι. 'For if I should desire to glory of revelations which I am allowed to disclose, or of things in which I was active and achieved something, I shall not be foolish in so doing (xi. 1, 16), for I shall be saying what is true' (*v.* 11). If θελήσω is fut. indic., it may imply that he does desire to do so; but it is probably aor. subjunct. Blass, § 65. 5, holds that in N.T. there is no *certain* example of ἐάν with fut. indic.; but Lk. xix. 40 and Acts viii. 31 are hardly doubtful, and ἐάνπερ ἐκπληρώσουσιν occurs in a papyrus of 2nd cent. B.C. Winer, p. 369; Burton, § 254; J. H. Moulton, p. 168. The timeless aor. infin. after such verbs as θέλω, βούλομαι, δύναμαι, ἐλπίζω is normal; ii. 7, v. 4; 1 Cor. xiv. 19, xvi. 7; etc. Burton, § 113.

φείδομαι δέ. We have this absolute use of φείδομαι again xiii. 2: cf. Is. liv. 2. In N.T. it is elsewhere followed by a gen., in LXX by a prep., ἀπό, περί, ὑπέρ, ἐπί.

μή τις εἰς ἐμὲ λογίσηται. 'Lest any man should count of me, form an estimate of me.' The constr. is unusual, but it probably does not mean 'lay to my credit,' which would almost require ἐμοί. In Hos. vii. 15 εἰς ἐμὲ ἐλογίσαντο πονηρά means 'they imagined mischief against me.'

ὑπὲρ ὃ βλέπει με ἢ ἀκούει ἐξ ἐμοῦ. 'Above that which he seeth in me or heareth from me.' He wishes to be judged, not by what he tells them respecting his exceptional privileges, but by what their own experience of him tells them, by his conduct, preaching, and letters. 'Of me' for ἐξ ἐμοῦ (AV.) is misleading: he does *not* desire to be judged by what people say *of* him; it is the words that come from him that count. In 2 Tim. i. 13, ii. 2 we have παρ' ἐμοῦ ἤκουσας.

After ἀκούει א³ D* E* K L P, d e f Vulg. Goth. Syr.-Hark. add τις : א* B D³ F G 17 67, g Copt. Arm. Aeth. omit. It is probably an interpolation. Divergence of F from f.

7. Text and punctuation of this verse are in dispute, and no certainty is attainable. There is probably some original error of dictation or of writing. But the meaning of the verse is certain and simple, however we reach it. The extraordinary revelations granted to him might have caused the Apostle to think too highly of himself ; to prevent this, severe and humiliating bodily suffering was laid upon him.

καὶ τῇ ὑπερβολῇ τῶν ἀποκαλύψεων. The plur. is some confirmation of the view that *v.* 2 and *vv.* 3, 4 give us two cases of rapture, for '*the* revelations' naturally refers to those just mentioned ; but Acts tells us of several others (xvi. 6–10, xviii. 9, xxiii. 11, xxvii. 23), and he may be including some of these here. Lachmann's proposal to take these words with the conclusion of *v.* 5 and make *v.* 6 a parenthesis, is barely possible ; ' I will not glory, save in my weaknesses (for if I should desire . . . hear from me) and in the exceeding greatness of the revelations.' WH. propose to take these words with the conclusion of *v.* 6 ; 'but I forbear, lest any man should . . ., and by reason of the greatness of the revelation.' This means that he has two reasons for forbearing, fear of being overrated and the greatness of the revelations. It is hard to believe that either arrangement was in the Apostle's mind. The best attested text comes out thus, and it is possible that something like this was the result of incoherent dictation ; 'And by reason of the exceeding greatness (iv. 7) of the revelations — wherefore, that I should not be exalted overmuch (2 Thess. ii. 4) there was given to me a stake for the flesh, a messenger of Satan to buffet me, that I should not be exalted overmuch.' St Paul begins with what is the basis of what follows,—the greatness of the revelations. Having mentioned this with emphasis, he begins a new constr. with διό and finishes with yet another constr., repeating ἵνα μὴ ὑπεραίρωμαι either through forgetfulness, or (more probably) because he wishes his readers not to forget the purpose of the σκόλοψ. For other possibilities see Meyer. To get rid of διό would be a great help, but it is indefinitely more probable that it has been omitted from some texts because of its difficulty than that it has been inserted in such good texts without authority. See ὑπερβολή, Index IV.

Ὑπεραίρομαι is found in N.T. only here and in 2 Thess. ii. 4, where it occurs in the description of ὁ ἄνθρωπος τῆς ἀνομίας. St Paul is rather fond of such compounds ; ὑπεραυξάνω, ὑπερβαίνω, ὑπερεντυγχάνω, ὑπερνικάω, ὑπερεκτείνω (x. 14), ὑπερπλεονάζω, ὑπερυψόω, all of which are ἅπαξ λεγόμενα in N.T. See also on ὑπερλίαν (xi. 5), p. 299.

ἐδόθη μοι. Of course by God, as ἵνα μὴ ὑπεραίρωμαι shows. It was sent to preserve the Apostle from spiritual pride. See Aug. *De. Nat. et Grat.* 27; also the *Reply to Faustus,* xxii. 20 This, however, does not prevent Meyer from saying that the σκόλοψ was given by Satan. Satan is regarded as an instrument for effecting the Divine purpose, as Judas in the case of the Atonement. See on 1 Cor. v. 5, also J. H. Bernard on 1 Tim. i. 20. Satan is ever ready to inflict suffering, and is sometimes made to be instrumental when suffering is needed for the discipline of souls. This idea prevails in the prologue to the Book of Job. But if St Paul had meant that it was Satan who was the agent in this case, he would have used a less gracious word than ἐδόθη which he often has of the bestowal of Divine favours; *e.g.* Gal. iii. 21; Eph. iii. 8, vi. 19; 1 Tim. iv. 14; cf. i. 22, v. 5, viii. 1, 16, x. 8, xiii. 10; etc. etc. Some such verb as ἐπιτίθημι (Lk. x. 30, xxiii. 26; Acts xvi. 23), or βάλλω (Rev. ii. 24), or ἐπιβάλλω (1 Cor. vii. 35), would have been more suitable. Gregory of Nazianzum in his *Panegyric of Basil* (*Or.* xliii. 82) speaks of a malady of his own as τὸν δεδομένον ἡμῖν παρὰ Θεοῦ σκόλοπα.

σκόλοψ τῇ σαρκί. These three words raise three questions, two of translation and one of interpretation, which have elicited a very large amount of discussion; and, when all has been said, no certain answer to any one of the three can be given. What is the exact force of the dative? What is the right translation of σκόλοψ? What form of suffering is meant by the metaphor?

1. '*For* the flesh' is on the whole more probable than 'in the flesh' (AV., RV.). Why omit ἐν if '*in* the flesh' is intended? Earlier English Versions differ. Wiclif and the Rhemish follow the ambiguous *stimulus carnis* adopted in the Vulgate from Cyprian (*Test.* iii. 6, *De Mortal.* 13) and the translator of Irenaeus (v. iii. 1); they have 'pricke of my flesh.' Between these come Tyndale 'unquyetnes of the flesshe,' Coverdale 'warynge geven unto my flesh,' Cranmer 'unquyetnes thorow the flesshe,' and the Genevan 'pricke in the fleshe.' No one now would adopt either 'of' or 'through,' but 'unto' is not very different from 'for.' See Winer, p. 276, and Waite, *ad loc.*

2. For the translation of σκόλοψ we are offered 'stake,' 'spike,' 'splinter,' and 'thorn.' The choice really lies between 'stake' and 'thorn,' *i.e.* between a very large and a comparatively small cause of bodily pain. In class. Grk. the common meaning of σκόλοψ is 'stake,' either for palisading or impaling, and a stake for impalement is a very vivid metaphor for intense physical

suffering.   Hence σκόλοψ was sometimes used of the cross (Orig. *c. Cels.* ii. 68) and ἀνασκολοπίζω of crucifixion (Eus. *H.E.* ii. 25). Tertullian twice has *sudes* as a translation (*De Fuga in Pers.* 2 ; *De Pudic.* 13).   Luther has *Pfahl ins Fleish*, Beza *surculus infixus carni.*   In his essay at the end of Gal. iv., Lightfoot interprets the expression as "a stake driven through the flesh."   Stanley (*ad loc.*) and Ramsay (*St Paul*, p. 97) decide for 'stake' rather than 'thorn'; and Beet, Emmet, Klöpper, Massie, A. T. Robertson, Waite, Way, Weymouth adopt this rendering.   But Alford, Bachmann, Bousset, Conybeare and Howson, Cornely, Field, Findlay, Heinrici, Krenkel, Lietzmann, McFadyen, Menzies, Meyer, F. W. Robertson, Schaff, and Schmiedel abide by the usual rendering, 'thorn.'   Farrar (*St Paul*, i. p. 221) tries to keep both ; "impalement . . . by this wounding splinter."

In LXX σκόλοψ occurs four times, σκόλοπες ἐν τοῖς ὀφθαλμοῖς ὑμῶν καὶ βολίδες ἐν ταῖς πλευραῖς ὑμῶν (Num. xxxiii. 55).   οὐκ ἔσονται οὐκέτι ἐν οἴκῳ τοῦ Ἰσραὴλ σκόλοψ πικρίας καὶ ἄκανθα ὀδύνης (Ezek. xxviii. 24).   ἐγὼ φράσσω τὴν ὁδὸν αὐτῆς ἐν σκόλοψιν (Hos. ii. 6).   καὶ πάχνην ὡς ἅλα ἐπὶ γῆς χέει, καὶ παγεῖσα γίνεται σκολόπων ἄκρα (Ecclus. xliii. 19).   'Thorn' or 'splinter' seems to be the meaning in all four passages, but 'stake' might be the meaning in Hos. ii. 6.   Yet we cannot be sure that one and the same rendering is right in all four places, for, in the first three, σκόλοψ represents three different Hebrew words.   It is not impossible that Num. xxxiii. 55 is the source of St Paul's expression, and in that case we have an answer to the objection urged against 'thorn,' that it is not so suitable as 'stake' to represent intense pain.*   But in all the renderings, it is the idea of acuteness that seems to be primary, and a thorn or a splinter or a spike may be sharper than a stake.

3. It is over the third question that there has been most discussion, with as much disagreement about the answer as in the other two cases.   But the attempt to answer this question raises a fourth, which can be decided with considerable probability, yet, as in the other cases, without certainty.   The σκόλοψ τῇ σαρκί is a metaphor for some kind of suffering.   Is it the same as the ἀσθένεια τῆς σαρκός and the πειρασμὸς ὑμῶν ἐν τῇ σαρκί μου of Gal. iv. 13, 14?   It is commonly assumed that it is the same, and this view has much to commend it.   But nothing approaching to proof is possible, and of the numerous conjectures as to what the form of this suffering was, one may be

---

* If Num. xxxiii. 55 was in St Paul's mind, that alone would be almost fatal to the view that the σκόλοψ was ophthalmia.   In that case he would hardly have omitted ἐν τοῖς ὀφθαλμοῖς and kept an equivalent for ἐν ταῖς πλευραῖς.

true of the σκόλοψ, while something quite different may be true of the ἀσθένεια. Unfortunately we have to confess that in neither case can we be at all certain as to what is true. Nevertheless, some negative results may be confidently maintained.

The Apostle is not referring to any individual who was a 'thorn in his side' to him, whether Alexander the coppersmith (2 Tim. iv. 14), as Ephraem Syrus thought, or anyone else, (xi. 15), as Chrysostom. That he is referring to sufferings caused by persecution is given by various Greek Fathers and one or two Latins as the explanation of the σκόλοψ. But it cannot be right. Others besides St Paul suffered greatly from persecution, and the σκόλοψ was something specially bestowed by God for his personal benefit, to counteract temptations that might be provoked by the special revelations. Moreover, he would not have prayed to be freed from persecutions. This theory continued to be held by a writer here and there, but it was at last driven from the field by an equally erroneous explanation.

When a knowledge of Greek became rare in the West, the N.T. was studied in the Vulgate, in which Jerome had left *stimulus carnis* uncorrected. He understood the σκόλοψ to mean bodily pain, but *stimulus carnis* suggested to others temptations to impurity. The explanation about persecutions may have been fostered by the fact that all Christendom had been suffering from the horrors of the Diocletian persecution ; and it is evident that the theory about carnal desires having been the Apostle's great trial spread widely at a time when monasticism accentuated the danger of temptations of the flesh. In each case men supposed that St Paul's special affliction was akin to what was a special trouble to themselves. This view of the *stimulus carnis* became almost universal in the West, until Cornelius a Lapide (d. 1637) says that it is *communis fidelium sensus*. Luther's passionate rejection of it is well known, and Calvin condemns it as ridiculous. St Paul tells us that the ἴδιον χάρισμα ἐκ Θεοῦ which he received was being able to do without marriage ; see on 1 Cor. vii. 7–9. And if it had been otherwise, he would not have regarded sexual desire as a 'weakness' in which he could glory. No Greek Father adopts this view, and it is doubtful whether any Latin writer of the first six centuries does. The statement that Jerome, Augustine, and Salvian do so is erroneous. Jerome says bodily pain, Augustine persecution, and Salvian nothing; he nowhere quotes or explains the passage.

Since the Reformation, spiritual trials, such as temptations to unbelief or despair, have been a favourite hypothesis. But they fit this passage badly, and Gal. iv. 13, 14 not at all. St

Paul nowhere hints at such difficulties, nor would he have
gloried in them from any point of view. It is those who have
themselves been tormented by such things that have imagined
them as the special trial of the Apostle.

Of these three lines of thought we may say that St Paul
would not have prayed to be freed from persecutions, and that
he would not have been told to cease to pray against evil con-
cupiscence or unbelief.

Modern writers generally go back to the earliest tradition
that the σκόλοψ was some acute malady, so painful and such a
hindrance to the spread of the Gospel as to be regarded as the
work of the devil. But it was sent by God at intervals as a
disciplinary reminder, to preserve His Apostle from spiritual
pride. It was in this aspect that Jerome compared it to the
slave behind the victorious commander in his triumphal chariot,
whispering at intervals, *Hominem te esse memento* (*Ep.* xxxix. 2).
Thus much we learn from this passage about the σκόλοψ τῇ
σαρκί. From Gal. iv. 13, 14, we gather that the ἀσθενεία τῆς
σαρκός which kept St Paul in Galatia was such as to tempt the
Galatians to regard him with contempt and disgust, a temptation
which they triumphantly overcame, treating him with the utmost
consideration and affection. Any acute and recurrent malady
will suit 2 Cor. xii. 7, but for Gal. iv. 13, 14 we require something likely to inspire those who witness it with repulsion. The
conjectures which fit Gal. iv. 13, 14 well, and might also be true
of 2 Cor. xii. 7, are epilepsy, acute ophthalmia, malarial fever,
and some forms of hysteria.* *Epilepsy* has the support of
Lightfoot, Schaff, Findlay, Bousset, Hofmann, Holsten,
Klöpper, and others. Since Max Krenkel's Essay in his
*Beiträge zur Aufhellung der Geschichte und der Briefe des
Apostels Paulus*, 1890, this conjecture of K. L. Ziegler in
Theologische Abhandlungen, 1804, has become widespread.
The objection that epilepsy commonly produces mental de-
terioration is not wholly disposed of by the cases of Julius
Caesar, Mahomet, Cromwell, and Napoleon, for we are not *certain*
that the attacks from which they occasionally suffered were
epileptic. A more serious objection is that such attacks are not
acutely painful. *Ophthalmia* is adopted by Farrar, Lewin,
Plumptre; *malarial fever* by Ramsay and Emmet; hysteria
by Lombard. When all the arguments for and against these
and other guesses have been considered, the fact remains that
we still do not know, for the evidence is insufficient. See *Enc.
Bib.* iii. 3620; Zahn, *Int. to N.T.* i. p. 171; Lietzmann,
ad loc.

---

* Other conjectures are sick headache, Malta fever, acute nervous
disorder.

ἄγγελος Σατανᾶ. 'A messenger of Satan' or 'an angel of Satan.' The σκόλοψ is here personified. Wiclif and the Rhemish have 'angel,' other English Versions, including AV. and RV., have 'messenger.' That Satan has angels was a common belief among the Jews (Rev. xii. 7–9; cf. Mt. ix. 34, xii. 24 = Lk. xi. 15), and it is not disturbed by Christ (Mt. xxv. 41). In the Ep. of Barnabas (xviii. 1) ἄγγελοι τοῦ Θεοῦ are opposed by ἄγγελοι τοῦ Σατανᾶ. Cf. *Enoch* iii. 3; *Jubilees* x. 2.

That what was the will of God for good purposes might be done by Satan for evil purposes is an idea that is also found among the Jews, as in Job i. **12**, ii. **6**, and in 2 Sam. xxiv. **1**, when compared with 1 Chron. xxi. **1**; also that Satan may be a cause of physical suffering, a belief which is not disturbed by Christ; see on Lk. xiii. **11**, **16**.*

With the reading Σατάν (see below), which is indeclinable and may be nom. or gen., some would translate 'the angel Satan,' but that would require ὁ ἄγγελος Σ. Others would translate 'a hostile angel,' which is grammatically possible, but not probable, for in N.T. Satan is always a proper name. In LXX σατάν is sometimes 'an adversary'; *e.g.* ἤγειρεν Κύριος σατὰν τῷ Σαλωμὼν τὸν Ἀδὲρ τὸν Ἰδυμαῖον (1 Kings xi. 14); but the reading σατάν here is to be rejected.

ἵνα με κολαφίζῃ. 'In order that he (the messenger) may buffet me.' The present tense, as Chrysostom and Theodoret point out, implies freq. attacks. The fact that ἄγγελος immediately precedes this clause saves us from mixture of metaphors; a stake or thorn cannot 'strike with the fist,' but a messenger can. Κόλαφος is said to be the Doric equivalent of the Attic κόνδυλος. The verb is late Greek and perhaps colloquial; see on 1 Cor. iv. **11** and cf. Mk. xiv. 65; Mt. xxvi. 67; 1 Pet. ii. 20; also Index IV.†

ἵνα μὴ ὑπεραίρωμαι. Emphatic repetition of the purpose of the σκόλοψ, which must be remembered side by side with Satan's share in the matter. In both cases we have pres. subjunct. of what was continually going on: there was freq. buffeting to counteract freq. temptation. But this does not imply that the revelations were freq. One revelation might occasion many temptations. Contrast the aorists in Rev. xviii. 4; ἵνα μή is specially freq. in 1 and 2 Cor.

* Gregory Nazianzen, who in one place speaks of a malady of his own as the σκόλοψ which was given him by God for his discipline (see above), in another says that it is possibly due to the Satan, which he, like St Paul, carries in his body for his own profit (*Or.* xlii. 26). Basil says; "The just Judge has sent me, in accordance with my works, a messenger of Satan who is buffeting me" (*Ep.* 148).

† Basil uses κατακονδυλίζω.

Baljon proposes to omit καὶ τῇ ὑπερβολῇ τῶν ἀποκαλύψεων as a gloss, but no witnesses omit the words. Nor can the perplexing διό be omitted, although D E K P L, Latt. Syrr., Iren. Aug. omit, for it is found in א A B F G 17. The omission is " a characteristic Western attempt to deal with a difficulty by excision " (WH.). There is more to be said for the excision of the second ἵνα μὴ ὑπεραίρωμαι, which א* A D E G 17, Latt. Aeth., Iren. Tert. Aug. omit ; but the omission is probably another attempt at simplifying the text. Σατανᾶ (א* A* B D* F G 17, 67**, Latt. Copt., Orig.) rather than Σατάν (א3 A** D² and ³ E K L P), which is rare in LXX and is found nowhere in N.T.

8. ὑπὲρ τούτου . . . ἵνα ἀποστῇ. 'Concerning this foe . . . that he might depart from me.' The personification still continues, as is shown by ἀποστῇ, the nom. to which is not σκόλοψ but ἄγγελος Σατανᾶ. Ἀφίστημι in N.T. is always used of *persons* ; 1 Tim. iv. 1 ; 2 Tim. ii. 19 ; Heb. iii. 12 ; and very often in Lk. and Acts. Cf. esp. ὁ διάβολος ἀπέστη ἀπ' αὐτοῦ (Lk. iv. 13), and ἀπέστη ὁ ἄγγελος ἀπ' αὐτοῦ (Acts xii. 10), and ἀπέστησαν ἀπ' αὐτοῦ οἱ μέλλοντες αὐτὸν ἀνετάζειν (Acts xxii. 29). Following the Vulg. *propter quod*, Beza *super quod*, and Luther *Dafür*, both AV. and RV. have 'this thing' for τούτου, and neither has 'thing' in italics. This use of ὑπέρ, in which the meaning 'in the interest of,' 'in behalf of' (i. 6, 11, v. 15, etc.) disappears, occurs several times in 2 Cor. (i. 8, vii. 4, 14, viii. 23, 24, ix. 2. 3, xii. 5) ; cf. 2 Thess. ii. 1. The Latin equivalent is *super* with the abl. ; *multa super Priamo rogitans, super Hectore multa* (Virg. *Aen.* i. 750), and *mitte civiles super urbe curas* (Hor. *Od.* iii. viii. 17).

τρὶς τὸν κύριον παρεκάλεσα. Such expressions as τρὶς μάκαρες καὶ τετράκις, *terque quaterque beati*, do not justify us in following Chrysostom and Calvin, who take τρίς as meaning 'often.' Why not say πολλάκις (viii. 22, xi. 23, 26, 27) ? It is more natural to understand τρίς literally, and with Bengel to compare our Lord's three prayers in Gethsemane. In each case the great trouble was not removed, but strength to bear it was given. It is fanciful to connect Acts xvi. 6, 7, 9 with these three petitions. As in the case of the 'visions and revelations,' we have no means of knowing how to fit them into the narrative in Acts. 'The Lord' no doubt means Christ, as is shown by ἡ δύναμις τοῦ Χριστοῦ (*v.* 9) ; and this use of παρακαλέω is analogous to the freq. use in the Gospels of those who besought Christ for help (Mk. i. 40, v. 18, 23, vi. 56, vii. 32, viii. 22 ; etc.). Elsewhere it is freq. of beseeching or exhorting men (ii. 8, vi. 1, viii. 6, ix. 5, etc.), but not of prayer to God, though Josephus so uses it (*Ant.* vi. ii. 2). St Paul is not intimating that Christ is man and not God, but he may be implying that on these occasions there was personal communication with the Lord (Stanley). *How* the communication was made, it is impossible to know ; *neque magnopere refert* (Calvin). Deissmann (*Light from Anc. East*, p. 311) gives an interesting parallel.

23

M. Julius Apellas states on a marble *stele* how he was several times cured at the shrine of Aesculapius in Epidaurus, and concerning one of his maladies he says, καὶ περὶ τούτου παρεκάλεσα τὸν θεόν. But it is a large inference to draw from this that St Paul " clothes " what he tells us here " in the style of the ancient texts relating to healing." Was there any fixed style in such things ? If so, did St Paul know it ? If so, did it influence him here ? The influence of the Gospel narratives is more probable.

9. καὶ εἴρηκέν μοι. 'And He *hath said* to me.' He said it then and the answer still stands, it holds good. It is frequently used of the Divine utterances ; Acts xiii. 34 ; Heb. i. 13, iv. 3, 4, x. 9, 13, xiii. 5. Cf. γέγραπται, 'it stands written.' See on ἐγήγερται, 1 Cor. xv. 4.

Ἀρκεῖ σοι ἡ χάρις μου. The thing prayed for is refused, but something much better is bestowed. See on χάρις, 1 Cor. xv. 10. This Divine gift is perpetually sufficient, good for his whole life. We have here another example of chiasmus ; cf. ii. 16, iv. 3, vi. 8, ix. 6, x. 12. In connexion with what follows see on iv. 10.

ἡ γὰρ δύναμις ἐν ἀσθενείᾳ τελεῖται. ' Where there is weakness, strength reaches completeness.' Where human strength abounds, the effects of Divine power may be overlooked. It is easy to forget Providence in reading history, but we do not obtain a more scientific view by leaving God out of the account. Where it is manifest that man was powerless, God's power becomes, not more real, but more evident ; iv. 7, xiii. 4 ; see on 1 Cor. i. 25, ii. 3, 4. Bede shows how this truth was illustrated in the cases of Ethelberga and Hilda (*H.E.* ix. 9, 21).* *Gratia esse potest, etiam ubi maximus doloris sensus est* (Beng.) ; but the χάρις does not mean the χάρισμα ἱμάτων, so that, though he was not healed himself, he was allowed the power of healing others (Chrys.). On the refusal of such requests ; *frequenter quae putamus prospera obsunt : ideo non conceduntur Deo melius providente* (Pseudo-Primasius on Rom. viii. 26). The Lord's reply convinced the Apostle that this grievous affliction would not hinder his work ; he may even have been convinced that it was a condition of success. That it was the Lord's doing, and not his, showed that he might glory in it. How the Lord conveyed this reply to him, we are not told ; but to St Paul it was real, and it is not extravagant to believe that, as on the road to Damascus, Christ conversed with him.

Here the verse should end ; see on 1 Cor. xii. 23 for a

* " You see then that none but sufferers and weak people can fight the Lord's battles, weak indeed with that weakness, founded on which that centurion of ours in the Gospel said with confidence, For when I am weak then am I strong, and again. For strength is made perfect in weakness " (Cassian).

similarly unfortunate **division.** In this Epistle most of the earlier chapters are badly divided.

Ἥδιστα οὖν μᾶλλον καυχήσομαι ἐν ταῖς ἀσθενείαις. Most gladly therefore (because of the Lord's reply) will I rather glory in my weaknesses (than pray that they may be removed). The order of the words is important. We have not got μᾶλλον ἐν ταῖς ἀσθενείαις καυχ., and we must not interpret 'will I glory in my weaknesses rather than in the revelations granted to me.' Nor must we make μᾶλλον strengthen ἥδιστα : μᾶλλον may strengthen comparatives (Phil. i. 23), but not superlatives. Blass, § 44. 5 ; Winer, p. 300.

ἵνα ἐπισκηνώσῃ ἐπ' ἐμὲ ἡ δύναμις τοῦ Χριστοῦ. A bold metaphor, which may possibly be intended to suggest the Shechinah (see on Lk. ix. 34) ; 'That the strength of the Christ may tabernacle upon me.' Κατασκηνόω is very freq. in LXX, but ἐπισκηνόω is found nowhere else in Bibl. Grk. The translations of δύναμις in this verse and of δυνατός in v. 10 should be uniform. AV. has 'strength,' 'power,' 'strong'; RV. has 'power,' 'strength,' 'strong'; better, 'strength,' 'strength,' 'strong.' Vulg. has *virtus, virtus, potens* ; Beza has *potentia, potentia, potens*.

ἡ γὰρ δύναμις (א* A* B D* G, Latt.) rather than ἡ γὰρ δύναμίς μου (א³ A² D² and 3 E K L P, Syrr. Copt.). τελεῖται (א* A B D* G) rather than τελειοῦται (א³ D³ E K L P). Both verbs are freq. in LXX and translate the same Heb. words ; both occur in Jn. xix. 28, and both are fairly common in N.T. B 67**, Syr-Hark. Copt. Arm., Iren. omit μου after ἀσθενείαις, and insertion is more probable than omission.

10. διὸ εὐδοκῶ ἐν ἀσθενείαις. 'Wherefore I am well pleased in weaknesses,' because it is precisely in them that the strength of Christ is conspicuous. Polybius and other secular authors write εὐδοκῶ τινι. In LXX and N.T. we commonly have εὐδ. ἐν, but the simple dat. occurs 2 Thess. ii. 12 (according to the best texts) ; 1 Macc. i. 43 ; 1 Esdr. iv. 39 ; cf. Rom. i. 32. See Abbott, *Johannine Grammar*, p. 387. In Mt. xii. 18 and Heb. x. 6 we have the acc. Now follow four kinds of 'weaknesses.'

ἐν ὕβρεσιν. In LXX, as in class. Grk., the word is freq. ; in N.T. only here and Acts xxvii. 10, 12. The plur. is comparatively rare ; in LXX, only Ecclus. x. 8 ; 'Sovereignty is transferred from one nation to another διὰ ὕβρεις.' The word implies wanton injury, insolent maltreatment, and therefore it is occasionally used of the apparently wanton damage done by storms, as in Acts. Josephus (*Ant.* III. vi. 4) says that the Tabernacle was protected by coverings against τὴν ἀπὸ τῶν ὄμβρων ὕβριν. For στενο ωρίαις see on vi. 4 ; in Rom. viii. 35, as here, the word is connected with διωγμός.

ὑπὲρ Χριστοῦ. It is for Christ's sake (v. 20) that he is well pleased in weaknesses. This is better than taking ὑπὲρ Χριστοῦ

with each of the four datives, although the difference in meaning
is not great. When he knows that it is not the Lord's will that
he should be freed from his afflictions, he not only does not
grieve, but for Christ's sake is well pleased.

ὅταν γὰρ ἀσθενῶ, τότε δυνατός εἰμι. ' For whenever I am weak,
then I am strong.' Cf. βοῶσα τοῖς ἐν συμφοραῖς, Μὴ ἀναπίπτετε,
τὸ ἀσθενὲς ὑμῶν δύναμίς ἐστιν (Philo, *Vita Moys*. i. 13, p. 92,
Mang.). The γάρ introduces the reason why he rejoices in his
weaknesses. In his letter to Eustochium (*Ep.* cviii. 19), Jerome
writes ; *quando infirmor tunc* fortior *sum*. With this paradoxical
outburst of triumph this paragraph closes. Experience has
taught him, and has taught those who have been witnesses of his
work, how much he can accomplish when he is apparently dis-
abled by his infirmities and afflictions ; that shows how amply the
Divine declaration is justified, Ἀρκεῖ σοι ἡ χάρις μου. To glory
in these things is to glory in the strength of Christ.

F, Vulg., but not f, insert μου after ἀσθενείαις, as these and other
authorities do in *v*. 5, and some in *v*. 9. ἐν ἀνάγκαις rather than καὶ ἀναγ.
(א, Orig.) ; but καὶ στενοχωρίαις (א* B) rather than ἐν στεν. (א³ D E G
K L P, Latt.). A omits ἐν διωγμοῖς.

XII. 11-18. The Credentials of an Apostle; exceptional Signs and exceptional Love.

*That I have become a fool by glorying is your fault;
for you have not been loyal to one whom you might know to
be an Apostle by the mighty works and the exceeding love
which he showed to you.*

11 I have been making a fool of myself by writing in this
glorying fashion ; but I am not to blame for it. It was you who
drove me to do it ; for you gave support to my opponents,
when you ought loyally to have commended me. I had a right
to expect this from you, for in no single thing was I inferior to
those pre-eminent apostles of yours, although as a matter of fact
I am nothing. 12 The signs, yes, the signs which mark the true
Apostle, were wrought out in your midst,—and the endurance
of all that they cost me never failed,—in works of significance,
works of wonder, and works of power. 13 You think that I have
treated you badly. Well, in what respect were you put in a
position of inferiority to my other Churches, except it be that I
myself did not 'sponge' on you? Of your generosity, pray forgive me this dreadful wrong !

14 Behold that I am ready to come to you now for the third

time; and you will find that, as on the two former visits, I shall
not 'sponge' on you. For what I am seeking is not your
possessions for myself, but yourselves for Christ. Do you ask
why I refuse your possessions? Because you are my children;
and there is no such obligation on children to provide for their
parents as on parents to provide for their children. ¹⁵ That is
generally admitted; but as for myself, most gladly will I spend
what I have, and be utterly spent myself, for the good of your
souls. Then, if my love for you exceeds that of fathers, am I to
be loved less? That would indeed be a strange requital. ¹⁶ But
you say, "We let that pass." You admit that I did not myself
come down on you for maintenance, but you insinuate that, like
the cunning knave that I am always supposed to be, I entrapped
you in other ways by the crafty employment of agents. ¹⁷ Did
I? By means of any of those whom I sent to you did I take
unfair advantage of you? ¹⁸ I asked Titus to visit you, and with
him I sent the brother whom you know. Did Titus take any
unfair advantage of you? No one would venture to insinuate
that. And was there any difference between his guiding principle and mine? Was there any difference between his conduct
and mine?

11. Γέγονα ἄφρων. There is a pause in the flow of impas-
sioned language. The Apostle stops a moment in his dictation
and reflects on what he has just been saying. He had warned
the Corinthians that in praising himself he would be acting like
a fool; they must make allowance for that, or at least allow him
as much consideration as they would allow to a fool (xi. 1, 16).
He now says emphatically, 'I verily *am become* a fool.' He is
not sarcastically quoting Corinthian criticism; he is seriously
making a criticism on himself. Γέγονα is emphatic, and as in
Rev. xvi. 17 (γέγονεν) and xxi. 6 (γέγοναν), means that what was
expected or predicted has come to pass. The sentence is not
a question. He admits the folly, but at once throws the
responsibility for it on the Corinthians. In the next two clauses
all the pronouns are emphatic, excepting the enclitic με.

ὑμεῖς με ἠναγκάσατε· ἐγὼ γὰρ ὤφειλον ὑφ' ὑμῶν συνίστασθαι.
'It was *you* who compelled me, for *I* ought to have been commended by *you*.' If the Corinthians had shown a decent appreciation of the Apostle's work among them, they would never
have tolerated the sneers and insinuations which the Judaizers
used in discrediting him; they would have testified strongly in
his favour. Instead of that, they commended the people who

attacked him. He was thereby compelled, greatly against his will, to commend himself, in order to free the Corinthians from the malign influence of his detractors. But for this reason, he would never have stooped to such folly. Cf. Livy, xxxviii. 29; *Mihi, quaeso, ita ignoscatis, Patres Conscripti, si longiorem orationem non cupiditas gloriandi de me, sed necessaria criminum defensio facit.*
In iii. 2 he told the Corinthians that they themselves were his commendatory letter, known and read by all men. How strange that he should now say that they had failed even to speak in his favour, when his enemies assailed him! If this severe charge was made in an earlier letter, and the high praise of iii. 2 f. was written in a later letter, after he and the Corinthians had become reconciled, all runs smoothly.

ὤφειλον . . . συνίστασθαι. 'I had a *right* to commendation; it was a *debt* owed to me by you.' Contrast δεῖ (xi. 30), 'he *must* glory,' not because it is his duty, but because circumstances force him to do so; and also *v.* 10, where 'must' depends upon Divine decree.

οὐδὲν γὰρ ὑστέρησα. 'You might have commended me with a good conscience, *for* in nothing was I inferior to your precious apostles.' The aor. refers to the time when he was living at Corinth. See on xi. 5; here it is even more clear than there that St Paul is not speaking of the Twelve, but of the Judaizing missionaries. Οὐδέν is emphatic; 'in no single thing.'

εἰ καὶ οὐδέν εἰμι. Chrysostom takes this clause as introductory to *v.* 12; so also Tyndale and Coverdale, and Hofmann among moderns. But Vulg., the Reformers, and almost all English Versions take it as the conclusion of *v.* 11. The μέν, and the very awkward asyndeton which arises if εἰ καί is prefixed to *v.* 12, are decisive against this arrangement. Chrys. seems to have had no μέν in his text. The words are an appropriate conclusion to *v.* 11. 'There is no bragging in saying that one is not inferior to such people; even a nobody may do that; and, apart from what Christ does in him, he is a nobody.' Cf. 1 Cor. iii. 7, xiii. 2, xv. 9.

L P, Syrr. Goth. add καυχώμενος after ἄφρων. ℵ A B D E G K, Latt. omit.

12. τὰ μὲν σημεῖα τοῦ ἀποστόλου κατειργάσθη ἐν ὑμῖν. 'Truly the signs of an Apostle were wrought out (iv. 17, v. 5, vii. 10, ix. 11) among you.' The change to the passive is to be noted. He does not say that he wrought them, for he was only God's instrument. The ὑπομονή (see on i. 6) was his, but the especial testimony to the reality of his Apostleship came from God. See on vi. 4 and on Lk. xxi. 19; Lightfoot on Col. i. 11, iii. 12; Westcott on Heb. vi. 12. What special form of suffering gave

the opportunity for this ὑπομονή? Did the σημεῖα provoke persecution? Or did the working of extraordinary acts of healing cause great physical exhaustion? The latter would seem to be appropriate, but discouragements and difficulties of various kinds may be in his mind. On 'the Signs of an Apostle' see Lightfoot, *Galatians*, p. 99. In English we must say '*an* Apostle,' for the art. is generic, as in Mt. xviii. 17. Winer, pp. 132, 217. In the true text there is no ἐν before σημείοις, and therefore we must not connect ἐν πάσῃ ὑπομονῇ with σημείοις.

ἐν ὑμῖν. Of all his converts the Corinthians had the best assurance that he was a true Apostle; 1 Cor. ix. 2. They knew what they had been as heathen and what his teaching had made them. Moreover, Christ had commissioned the Twelve to work miracles, and St Paul had worked miracles at Corinth.

σημείοις [τε] καὶ τέρασιν καὶ δυνάμεσιν. Evidently σημεῖα is here used with some change of meaning. In the previous clause it is a generic term, here a specific one. 'The signs of an Apostle' include the spiritual gifts with which God had richly endowed him, and which he was able to impart to many of his hearers; the effectiveness of his preaching was a very convincing sign (iii. 2; 1 Cor. ii. 4, ix. 2). They also include 'signs' in the narrow sense; χαρίσματα ἰαμάτων of an extraordinary kind. It is to the other kind of σημεῖα that St Paul commonly appeals; but elsewhere he appeals to these supernatural powers (1 Cor. xiv. 18, 19; Gal. iii. 5; Rom. xv. 19).* In Rom. xv. 19, as in 2 Thess. ii. 9 and Heb. ii. 4, we have the same threefold enumeration as here; cf. Acts ii. 22. In N.T., and especially in the Fourth Gospel, supernatural works are often called σημεῖα without τέρατα being coupled with σημεῖα, but never τέρατα without σημεῖα; they are always Divine tokens, with an instructive purpose, and they are products of Divine power (δυνάμεις); but they are never *mere* wonders, things which astonish but do not instruct.† St Paul had possibly three different kinds of miracles in his mind in this threefold enumeration, but we have no means of knowing how he classified them. See Trench, *Syn.* § xci.

It is important to notice that in none of the passages cited does St Paul write for the purpose of inducing people to believe in miracles. The mighty works are mentioned incidentally for other reasons. He appeals to them as well-known facts. He assumes that Galatians, Corinthians, and Romans know quite well that miracles *do* happen, and that he has worked many in

---

* These passages are confirmed by Acts xv. 12. 'The overmuch apostles' had nothing of the kind to show.

† The combination σημεῖα καὶ τέρατα is very freq. in LXX. The translation of both is easy; that of δυνάμεις can hardly be made uniform, but we do not need 'mighty works,' 'wonderful works,' 'mighty deeds' and 'miracles,' as in AV.

their presence. It is incredible that he should have said this, if neither he nor any other Apostle had ever done anything of the kind ; and that all were works of *healing* is an assumption.

κατειργάσθη (א A B³ K L) rather than κατηργάσθη (B* G) or κατηργάσθην (D E). But see WH. *App.* p. 161. It is difficult to decide between σημείοις τε (B א* 17, 73) and σημείοις (א¹ A D* 71, d e f). Neither ἐν σημ. (D³ E K L P) nor καὶ σημ. (G, g) is likely to be right.

13. τί γάρ ἐστιν ὃ ἡσσώθητε . . . οὐ κατενάρκησα ὑμῶν; ' For what is there wherein ye were made inferior to the rest of the Churches, except it be that I myself did not burden you by claiming maintenance?' See on xi. 9. He comes back to the subject of his refusing to take money or maintenance from them owing to the mention of ' the overmuch apostles ' in *v.* 11. It was one of the undeniable contrasts between them and him, that they claimed and took maintenance, while he refused it when offered. See on 1 Cor. ix. 12. On the form ἡσσώθητε see WH. *App.* p. 166b, and cf. Hdt. vii. 166, viii. 75. For ὑπέρ in the sense of ' beyond ' after verbs of comparison see on Lk. xvi. 8, and cf. Gal. i. 14 ; Heb. iv. 12 ; Judg. xi. 25 ; 1 Kings xix. 4. As in **x.** 1, the force of αὐτὸς ἐγώ is not clear. It may mean ' I myself,' as distinct from ' the signs of an Apostle '; his critics contended that it was the sign of an Apostle to receive mainten- ance. Or, less probably, it may mean that some of his colleagues had accepted maintenance ; see on 1 Cor. ix. 6. The Churches are local Churches (viii. 1, 18, xi. 8, 28, etc.).

χαρίσασθέ μοι τὴν ἀδικίαν ταύτην. Of course his refusing to be supported by them was an advantage to the Corinthians. With playful irony he treats it as if it were an injury, and asks them to forgive it.* Cf. ii. 10 ; Col. ii. 13 ; Lk. vii. 21, where Bengel calls ἐχαρίσατο *magnificum verbum.* In what follows he affection- ately warns them that he will have to continue to inflict this ' injury ' on them. All this shows that he is addressing the whole Corinthian Church. The change of tone in these chapters cannot be explained by the supposition that i.–ix. is addressed to the loyal members, while x.–xiii. is addressed to the rebellious, for the supposition is untenable.

ἡσσώθητε (א* B D*), after the analogy of ἐλασσόω, rather than ἡττήθητε (א³ A D³ K L P), from ἡττάω, or ἐλατώθηται (G).

14. Ἰδοὺ τρίτον τοῦτο ἑτοίμως ἔχω ἐλθεῖν πρὸς ὑμᾶς. ' Behold this is the *third* visit that I am preparing to pay you.' Or, ' See I am now in readiness to come to you for the *third* time.'

* Some hold that there is no playfulness or irony ; that he is quite serious. Corinthians think that his refusal is a reflexion on their generosity, and he asks forgiveness for seeming to treat them as niggards. Moreover, he had accepted support from other Churches.

By position τρίτον is emphatic, and τρίτον τοῦτο is acc. abs. Cf. τοῦτο ἤδη τρίτον ἐφανερώθη ὁ Ἰησοῦς (Jn. xxi. 14): τοῦτο τρίτον ἐπλάνησάς με (Judg. xvi. 15): πέπαικάς με τοῦτο τρίτον (Num. xxii. 24). So far as grammar is concerned, τρίτον τοῦτο may be taken with either ἑτοίμως ἔχω or ἐλθεῖν. We may translate, 'This is the third time that I am making preparations to come to you'; but such a meaning does not agree with the un-questioned fact that he had already paid at least one visit. If he had never visited Corinth, but had twice before made pre-parations to come, then 'This is the third time that I am making preparations to come to you' would be a very natural thing to say; but it is not a natural thing to say if he had paid one visit, had prepared to come again, and now for a *second* time was preparing to come again. The only natural meaning of xiii. 1 is that he is about to pay a *third visit*, and therefore the first trans-lation of these words is the right one. The second visit was the short one ἐν λύπῃ : see on ii. 1, Lightfoot, *Biblical Essays*, p. 274, and Conybeare and Howson, ch. xv.

The objection that ἑτοίμως ἔχω comes between τρίτον τοῦτο and ἐλθεῖν, and that therefore τρίτον τοῦτο cannot be taken with ἐλθεῖν, is baseless, as Acts xxi. 13 shows, where ἑτοίμως ἔχω comes between ἀποθανεῖν and ὑπὲρ τοῦ ὀνόματος. Krenkel (*Beiträge*, p. 185) gives numerous examples from classical and other writers. Deissmann (*Bib. St.* p. 252) says that numerous examples exist of ἑτοίμως ἔχω in the Fayyûm documents and elsewhere; but he quotes none, so that we cannot compare the position of ἑτοίμως ἔχω in the sentence with its position here.

καὶ οὐ καταναρκήσω. On this third visit he intends to be as independent as on the first and second; he will not 'sponge' on them. We must carry τρίτον τοῦτο on to οὐ καταναρκήσω in thought, if not in construction. As before, he will abstain from putting on them the benumbing pressure of having to provide for his necessities. It is possible that καταναρκάω had an invidious sound, like our 'sponge,' and that for this reason he harps on the word. His opponents did 'sponge' on the Corinthians; he must absolutely refuse to do so. The Revisers rightly omit ὑμῶν from their Greek text, but do not put 'to you' in italics.

οὐ γὰρ ζητῶ τὰ ὑμῶν ἀλλὰ ὑμᾶς. Some of them had thought that it was because he cared so little about them that he would not accept anything from them (xi. 11): he says that he cares too much about *them* to care about their *possessions*. Not that he selfishly wants them for his own glory or gratification; he seeks to present them as a spouse to Christ (xi. 2). They are quite mistaken in thinking that he will take *nothing* from them ; he wants the very best that they have to give,—themselves.

'I seek greater things; souls instead of goods, instead of gold your salvation' (Chrys.). The pres. tense indicates his habitual aim; he is always seeking to win *them.* Cf. Mt. xviii. 15 and see on 1 Cor. ix. 19. His other reasons for refusing support have been discussed xi. 7–15.

οὐ γάρ ὀφείλει τὰ τέκνα τοῖς γονεῦσιν. He appeals to nature and common sense; see on ὤφειλον (*v.* 11); ὀφείλει is not impersonal; τὰ τέκνα is the subject. As regards making provision for the needs of others, it is parents who are under an obligation to provide for their children rather than children to provide for their parents. That is the normal state of things. He does not, of course, mean that children are under no obligation to support their parents. Very often one of two alternatives is in form negatived, not in order to exclude it absolutely, but to show its inferiority to the other alternative; cf. Mk. ii. 17, vi. 4, ix. 37; Lk. x. 20, xiv. 12, xxiii. 28; Jn. xii. 44; Hos. vi. 6. Blass, § 77. 12. The Corinthians are his children (1 Cor. iv. 14, 15).

θησαυρίζειν. 'To lay up treasure,' 'to accumulate money'; 1 Cor. xvi. 2; Mt. vi. 19–21; Jas. v. 3. He does not say 'support' or 'help,' which would have been far less true, and would have run counter to Christ's teaching about Corban. For children to be under an obligation to help their parents is not uncommon; but that they should be bound to lay up money for them, though possible, is an abnormal condition of things. St Paul allowed his Macedonian children to contribute to his support (xi. 9), and he told the Corinthians to lay by money for the poor Christians in Palestine (1 Cor. xvi. 2), but he neither required nor tolerated that any converts should *raise a fund* for his support.

K L P omit τοῦτο after τρίτον, and D E, Copt. Arm. have τοῦτο before τρίτον. τρίτον τοῦτο is doubtless right (א A B F G, d e f g Vulg. Goth. Syrr. Aeth. After καταναρκήσω, D³ E K L, Latt. add ὑμῶν, and D* G add ὑμᾶς. א A B 17 omit.

15. ἐγὼ δὲ ἥδιστα δαπανήσω καὶ ἐκδαπανηθήσομαι ὑπὲρ τῶν ψυχῶν ὑμῶν. 'But *I*, I will most gladly (*v.* 9), spend and be utterly spent for the good of your souls'; ἐγὼ δὲ τῶν φύσει πατέρων καὶ πλέον τι ποιεῖν ἐπαγγέλλομαι (Thdrt.). The ἐγώ is very emphatic; he is ready to do more than a parent's duty, and to do it with delight. He will spend all he has, and exhaust all his strength, for his children; he is willing to 'be spent right out' for them. This is his answer to the question raised in xi. 11; and he intimates that his love will not be extinguished, if it meets with no response. Cf. Mk. x. 45; Jn. x. 11, 15. With the rhetorical antithesis between δαπανήσω and ἐκδαπανηθήσομαι comp. that between ἔξεστιν and ἐξουσιασθήσομαι, 'I may make free with all things, but I shall not let anything make free with me'; see on 1 Cor. vi. 12. The δέ is 'But' rather than 'And' (AV., RV.); he contrasts his own personal intentions with ordinary parental duties.

εἰ περισσοτέρως ὑμᾶς ἀγαπῶ, ἧσσον ἀγαπῶμαι; 'If I love you more abundantly, am I loved the less?' 'Are you going to let your love diminish as fast as my love increases? That would be a strange kind of return to make, a strange instance of inverse proportion!' It is not quite certain that the sentence is interrogative, but to take it as a question gives it more life and vigour. We may make it dependent on the previous sentence; 'I will most gladly be utterly spent for your souls, if the more abundantly I love you, the less I am loved.' Reading ἀγαπῶν the meaning would be, 'But I for my part will most gladly spend and be wholly spent for your salvation, if, loving you the more, I am loved the less.' Alford quotes; *animaeque magnae prodigum Paullum* (Hor. *Od.* i. xii. 38). The καί after εἰ is doubtless an interpolation, and therefore 'though' (AV.) is not admissible. There is no need to understand anything with περισσοτέρως, 'more abundantly *than I love other Churches*'; ὑμᾶς is not emphatic. And the rendering, 'If I love you more *than the false teachers do*, am I loved *less than they are*, is almost grotesque. In these intensely affectionate verses the Apostle's opponents are quite forgotten.

εἰ (א A B F G 17, Copt.) rather than εἰ καί (א³ D³ K L P, f Vulg. Syrr. Arm. Aeth.): D, d g omit both εἰ and καί. Note the divergence between F and f and between G and g. It is difficult to decide between ἀγαπῶ (א* A 17, Copt.) and ἀγαπῶν (א³ B D F G K L P, Latt.). As in 1 Cor. xi. 17, ἧσσον (א A B D*) rather than ἧττον (D³ K L) or ἔλασσον (F G).

16. Ἔστω δέ, ἐγὼ οὐ κατεβάρησα ὑμᾶς. He is quoting another charge which his detractors had made against him. It was impossible for them to deny that St Paul absolutely refused maintenance, and they are supposed to say; 'Be it so, we are agreed about that; you did not *yourself* (the ἐγώ is emphatic) burden us by coming on us for support; but you were cunning enough to catch us and our money in other ways.'* Neither this use of ἔστω nor the late verb καταβαρέω is found elsewhere in Bibl. Greek, except that καταβεβαρημένοι is a *v.l.* (א) in Mk. xiv. 4.

ἀλλὰ ὑπάρχων πανοῦργος. 'But being in character thoroughly unscrupulous.' He is, of course, quoting his critics' estimate of him; according to them, he is a born shuffler, it is his nature (ὑπάρχων) to be crafty; cf. viii. 17; Gal. i. 14, ii. 14. In such cases ὑπάρχων is almost equivalent to φύσει. Πανοῦργος is found nowhere else in N.T., but is freq. in Psalms and Ecclus.; πανουργία occurs iv. 2, xi. 3; 1 Cor. iii. 19; Eph. iv. 14; Lk. xx. 23.

* Some take ἔστω to mean 'Be it so *that I am loved the less; I* at any rate was not a burden to you'; which does not fit well with what follows.

364 SECOND EPISTLE TO THE CORINTHIANS [XII. 16-18

ἔλαβον. Like λαμβάνει (xi. 20), a metaphor from hunting or fishing; he entrapped or caught them in his wiliness. Some of his friends took maintenance (see on αὐτὸς ἐγώ, v. 13), and he shared what they got; he and his friends collected money for the poor saints, and some of it stuck to his fingers. It is hardly likely that his enemies made the accusation in such plain and blunt terms as St Paul himself uses here : but they insinuated what he states plainly, and to state such charges in plain language is to answer them. In four rapid questions he asks them whether they really believe that any of the missionaries whom he sent to them cheated them.

οὐ κατεβάρησα ὑμᾶς (A B D³ E K L P) rather than οὐκ ἐβάρησα ὑμᾶς (D*) or οὐ κατενάρκησα ὑμῶν (א F G).

17. μή τινα ὧν ἀπέσταλκα πρὸς ὑμᾶς; In his eagerness he forgets the constr. with which he started, and he leaves τινα without any verb to govern it. 'Did I, by means of any of those whom I have sent unto you, take advantage of you?' Cf. ii. 11, xii. 2; 1 Thess. iv. 6. The verb, as distinct from πέμπω, implies that those sent had a definite mission, and the tense implies that the mission was permanent. Perhaps he originally meant the question to run, 'Have I ever sent anyone to you through whom you were defrauded?' This probably means that they 'got money under false pretences,' especially in connexion with the Palestine relief fund.* See on viii. 20, 21.

18. παρεκάλεσα Τίτον καὶ συναπέστειλα τὸν ἀδελφόν. 'I exhorted Titus, and with him I sent the brother' (see on ii. 13), i.e. some Christian whom the Corinthians knew, 'the brother whom you remember.' There seem to have been three missions of Titus to Corinth; (1) the one mentioned here and in viii. 6 (καθὼς προενήρξατο), in which Titus and one colleague *started* the Palestine collection;† (2) the one alluded to in ii. 13, vii. 6, 13, in which Titus carried a severe letter from the Apostle, by means of which he succeeded in winning back the rebellious Corinthians to their allegiance; and (3) the one mentioned viii. 6, 17, 18, 22, in which Titus and two colleagues were to *finish* the Palestine collection. This last *cannot* be alluded to here; for, when ch. viii. was written, Titus and his two colleagues had not yet started for Corinth. And it is very unlikely that (2) can be the mission alluded to here. St Paul would not make so difficult a task as that of putting an end to a rebellion against his authority still more difficult by coupling with it a request for money.

* Bruce, *St Paul's Conception of Christianity*, p. 88.
† In this first mission Titus may have been the bearer of 1 Corinthians (Lightfoot, *Biblical Essays*, p. 181). He evidently made himself a *persona grata* at Corinth, and hence his success in the second mission. See on 1 Cor. xvi. 11.

Those who identify x.–xiii. with part of the severe letter *cannot* identify (2) with the mission mentioned here, for when that letter was written Titus had not started with the letter.* All the allusions fall into place, if we assume that Titus was three times sent by the Apostle to Corinth; and on other grounds there is no objection to this hypothesis.

μήτι ἐπλεκτόνησεν ὑμᾶς Τίτος; St Paul knew that the Corinthians had not suspected, and could not suspect, Titus of dishonesty. Then if Titus, the agent who worked in such perfect harmony with himself, was above suspicion, was it credible that the man for whom and with whom he laboured so loyally, was a cheat? The idea of Titus being dishonest in order to serve St Paul was ludicrous. Vulg. makes no difference between μή and μήτι, having *numquid* for both, but it marks the much more important difference between μητι interrogative and οὐ interrogative by changing from *numquid* to *nonne* as it does in Lk. vi. 39. It is possible that τι has dropped out between μή and τινα. But elsewhere Vulg. has *numquid* for μή (iii. 1; 1 Cor. i. 13, ix. 4, 5, 8, 9, x. 22, etc.) as also for μήτι.

οὐ τῷ αὐτῷ πνεύματι περιεπατήσαμεν; 'Walked we not in the same spirit' (AV.) is better than 'Walked we not by the same Spirit' (RV.), as is shown by the parallel question which follows. The two questions mean that both in mind and conduct there was absolute and manifest harmony between Titus and himself. Cf. στήκετε ἐν ἑνὶ πνεύματι (Phil. i. 27).

The fact that Timothy is not mentioned here makes it probable that he never reached Corinth. See on 1 Cor. xvi. 10, where St Paul is doubtful whether Timothy will reach Corinth. He probably remained in Macedonia, where there was plenty of work for him, until St Paul came thither from Troas (i. 1, ii. 12, 13).

XII. 19–XIII. 10. Final Warnings in view of his approaching Visit.

Think not that I am on my defence before you; it is to God that I am responsible; and it is for your good that I speak, for it is you that have to be judged by me. I pray that, through your repentance, I may have no need to punish, and you may go on to perfection.

¹⁹ Am I right in surmising that all this time you are thinking that it is to you that I am making my defence? It is before

---

* Some, however, would make παρεκάλεσα and cυναπέστειλα to be epistolary aorists, 'I am exhorting T. and am sending with him.' But this is barely possible, for ἐπλεκτόνησεν cannot be an epistolary aorist. All three verbs refer to previous missions of T. to Corinth.

God and in union with Christ that I am speaking as I do;—but every word of it, my beloved friends, with a view to your being built up in holiness. [20] And there is much need of building up, for I am afraid that perhaps in some ways the effect of my visit may be mutual disappointment,—that I should find you to be not such as I would, and that I should be found by you to be such as ye would not. I mean that I fear lest there may be among you strife and jealousy, wraths and factions, backbitings and whisperings, swellings and tumults; [21] lest, when I come back to you, my God should again, as He did before, humiliate me by showing what faulty Christians you are, and I should have to mourn over many of you who have clung to their old sins, and never repented of the impurity and fornication and lasciviousness which they practised.

XIII. [1] I am now for the third time coming to you. Remember the Scripture which says, At the mouth of two witnesses and of three shall every word be established. That implies a strict investigation. [2] I gave a warning, when I was with you a second time, to those who clung to their old sins then, and now being absent I give a warning to all the rest who may need it now,— that if I come again, as I am preparing to do, I will not spare. [3] I could not do so, seeing that you are seeking to make me give a proof that it is the Christ who is speaking in me, the Christ who in His dealings with you is not weak, but exhibits His power among you. [4] For though it is true that He was crucified through weakness, yet He is alive for evermore through the power of God. And you will find the same kind of thing in me. By union with Christ I share His weakness; yet through that same power of God and in fellowship with Christ I shall be full of life and vigour for dealing with you. [5] You seek a proof from me that Christ is in me. It is your own selves that you ought to be testing, whether you are in the faith that saves; it is your own selves that you ought to be proving. Or are you so ignorant about your state as not to know that Christ is in you? Of course He is, unless (as I will not believe) you have failed to stand this test. [6] But I trust that you will come to know that I have not failed. [7] But my prayer unto God is that you may not in any way go wrong; not in order that in this way I may be shown to have stood the test, but that you may do what is noble and right, even though I may seem to have failed.

⁸ For of course I cannot, even to secure my position as an Apostle, do anything that would be prejudicial to the Gospel; all that I do must be in furtherance of the Gospel. ⁹ Indeed, I rejoice when it is owing to your Christian strength of character that I am weakened by losing an opportunity of proving my authority; and this I not only rejoice over but pray for,—I mean the perfecting of your characters. ¹⁰ This is my reason for writing as I do while I am away from you, so that, when I am present, I may not have to act sharply, according to the authority which the Lord gave me for building up and not for demolition.

19. Πάλαι δοκεῖτε ὅτι ὑμῖν ἀπολογούμεθα; The Apostle is now rapidly drawing towards a conclusion; and this verse serves as a passage from the vigorous *apologia pro vita sua* in the last three chapters (x.–xii.) to the grave warning which reminds the Corinthians of the serious duty which he has to discharge directly he returns to them. It rests with them to decide whether this third visit shall be as painful as the second visit was (i. 23, ii. 1). A complete reformation of their evil ways is the only thing that can prevent it from being so, and for this he hopes and prays. Earlier in this part of the letter (x. 2, 6, 11) he has hinted that he may be compelled to adopt severe measures; he now speaks more fully. His vindication of himself must not mislead them as to the relation in which he and they stand to one another. 'All this time are you thinking that it is to you that we are making our defence?' Almost all English Versions follow Luther, Calvin, and Beza in making this sentence interrogative. RV. follows Wiclif in regarding it as categorical, which is more severe and less tactful. St Paul could not be sure that the Corinthians understood him in this way. Recent translators and commentators remain divided on the subject. We have found similar doubts respecting *vv.* 11 and 15 and x. 7. Πάλαι in the sense of 'for some time past' is not found elsewhere in N.T. (hence the reading πάλιν, for even if πάλαι and not ἤδη were the true reading in Mk. xv. 44, the passage would not be parallel to this; but it is found in Plato (*Phaedr.* 273 C, *Gorg.* 456 A). Excepting this passage and Rom. ii. 15, ἀπολογέομαι is confined in N.T. to Lk. and Acts; in LXX it is very rare. The plur. may include Titus, of whom he has just spoken as above suspicion; but throughout this passage the changes between 1st sing. and 1st plur. are so rapid and frequent, that we cannot safely insist on any change of meaning. See on i. 4.

κατέναντι Θεοῦ ἐν Χριστῷ λαλοῦμεν. 'It is in the sight of God in union with Christ that we are speaking.' The first four words are not to be taken together, as if they made a kind of "double oath"; they form a pair of guarantees. St Paul often appeals to the fact that he speaks and acts 'in the sight of God' and 'in Christ.' Cf. ii. 17, and see on 1 Cor. iv. 3, 4. We have similar asseverations i. 18, 23, iv. 2, v. 11, vii. 12, xi. 11, 31; Rom. i. 9, ix. 1; Phil. i. 8; 1 Thess. ii. 5, 10. See on xi. 31.

τὰ δὲ πάντα, ἀγαπητοί, ὑπὲρ τῆς ὑμῶν οἰκοδομῆς. Understand λαλοῦμεν: neither 'we do' (AV.) nor 'are' (RV.) is required: 'But every word, beloved, we speak for your edification' (see on x. 8, xiii. 10). Griesbach and Scholz put a comma between ἐν Χριστῷ and λαλοῦμεν. The affectionate ἀγαπητοί occurs here only in these last four chapters, and in vii. 1 only in the first nine chapters. It shows that St Paul is addressing the whole Church of Corinth, and not the rebellious element. We have several times had the exclusively Pauline use of ὑμῶν between the art. and the noun (see on i. 6); cf. 1 Cor. vii. 35, ix. 12. Οἰκοδομή as in x. 8.

πάλαι (א* A B F G 17, d e f Vulg.) rather than πάλιν (א³ D E K L P, g Syrr. Copt.). Note the divergence of d e g from D E G. κατέναντι (א A B G) rather than κατενώπιον (D E K L P).

20. φοβοῦμαι γὰρ μή πως ἐλθὼν οὐχ οἵους θέλω εὕρω ὑμᾶς. 'For I fear, lest by any means, when I come, I should find you not such as I would, and I should be found by you such as ye would not.' The authoritative voice of the Apostle, which begins to sound in v. 19, here increases in solemnity, yet with more tenderness than rigour. He is a father dealing with children about whom he has grave misgivings. Until he has the evidence before him, he utters no judgment, but he tells them that what he fears to find is that, instead of being peaceable and pure, as Christians must be, they indulge in the worst forms of strife and licentiousness; in short, that they have returned to their old heathen life. The γάρ explains the previous assertion that what he has been saying was spoken, not to glorify himself, but to build up them. That is the true work of an Apostle; and they are still in great need of οἰκοδομή, *for* the structure of their life seems to be utterly rotten. With a dread of this kind in his mind, the malice of the Judaizing opponents, and the outrageous conduct of ὁ ἀδικήσας (vii. 12), appear to be quite forgotten. Yet it is all put very gently; he fears, not is certain; and 'not such as I would' is a mild form of disapproval. Moreover, there is a mitigating πως here and in what follows, and in both places it is overlooked in AV. The change from active to passive, and the chiasmus which brings ὑμᾶς and ἐγώ into juxtaposition, and the shifting of the negative from the adjective to the verb, all add to the effect.

μή πως ἔρις, ζῆλος κ.τ.λ. The list of vices appears to be arranged in four pairs ; 'Lest by any means there should be found strife and jealousy (xi. 2 ; 1 Cor. iii. 3), wraths and factions (Phil. i. 7, ii. 3 ; see on Rom. ii. 8), backbitings (see on 1 Pet. ii. 1) and whisperings, swellings and tumults' (vi. 5 ; 1 Cor. xiv. 33). As in the second half of v. 19, the Apostle leaves the verb to be understood from the previous sentence, λαλοῦμεν there, εὑρεθῶσιν here. Other lists of vices should be compared, esp. 'the works of the flesh' in Gal. v. 2c, where we have ἔρις, ζῆλος, θυμοί, ἐριθίαι, as here; cf. Rom. i. 29, 30, xiii. 13 ; 1 Pet. iv. 3 ; Mk. vii. 21, 22. See on 1 Cor. vi. 10, p. 119. There is no etymological connexion between ἔρις and ἐριθεία or ἐριθία. The latter comes from ἔριθος, 'a hired labourer'; ἐριθεύεσθαι means 'to hire partisans,' and ἐριθεία means 'party spirit' or 'intrigue.' Although καταλαλεῖν (Jas. iv. 11 ; 1 Pet. ii. 12, iii. 16) is found in class. Grk., καταλαλιά (1 Pet. ii. 1) and κατάλαλος (Rom. i. 30) are not : καταλαλεῖν is freq. in LXX. For ἀκαταστασία see on 1 Cor. xiv. 33 and Lk. xxi. 9 ; the two passages show that, like 'disorder,' the word has a large range.

ἔρις (א A 17, d f g Arm., Chrys.) rather than ἔρεις (B D F G K L P, Vulg. Copt.). Note the divergence of d f g from D F G. ζῆλος (A B D* F G 17, Arm.) rather than ζῆλοι (א D³ K L P, Latt.). The two words have been made plural in assimilation to the six plurals which follow.

21. μὴ πάλιν ἐλθόντος μου ταπεινώσῃ με ὁ Θεός. Almost certainly the μή depends on φοβοῦμαι : 'lest, when I come, my God should *again* humble me.'* Πάλιν is emphatic by position, and the only way to give it emphasis is to take it, not with ἐλθόντος (AV., RV.), but with ταπεινώσῃ. He has just spoken of his return to Corinth as ἐλθών, and it is there that πάλιν would be in place, if it were used at all. But St Paul often uses ἔρχομαι, without πάλιν, for 'coming *back*' (i. 15, 23, ii. 3, viii. 17, xii. 20 ; 1 Cor. iv. 18, 19, xi. 34, xiv. 6, xvi. 2, 5, 10, 11, 12 ; etc.). It is not his *coming* again that is emphasized, but the possibility of his being *humiliated* again, as he was when he was so outraged during his second visit. Alford, Bachmann, Beet, Bernard, Bousset, Cornely, Klöpper, McFadyen, Massie, Meyer, and Waite are among those who see that to take πάλιν with ἐλθόντος is to make it superfluous rather than emphatic. St Paul took great pride in his converts (i. 14, iii. 2, vii. 4, viii. 24, ix. 2), and he felt that anything which disgraced them was a humiliation to him. But seeing that humiliation is wholesome for him, he accepts it as coming from God's hand. That fact, however, does not free the Corinthians from responsibility.

* Lachmann makes the sentence interrogative, which is possible, but harsh and abrupt.

24

πρὸς ὑμᾶς. Perhaps 'before you,' *apud vos* (Vulg.), but more probably 'in reference to you.'

καὶ πενθήσω πολλοὺς τῶν προημαρτηκότων καὶ μὴ μετανοησάντων. 'And I should mourn (as over those who are dead) for many of them who continued in sin before (during my second visit) and did not (then) repent.' * The change from perf. to aor. is intelligible. The perf. refers to the persistence in former transgression, the aor. to their refusal to repent when he came to rebuke them. Προαμαρτάνω occurs again xiii. 2 and nowhere else in Bibl. Grk. It is improbable that προ- refers to their life previous to being converted to Christianity; but those who deny the brief second visit resort to this explanation of the rare compound.

ἐπὶ τῇ ἀκαθαρσίᾳ. It is not impossible to take this after πενθήσω ('mourn over many because of the uncleanness'), but it is too awkward a constr. to be probable. If there were no πολλούς and τῶν προ. κ.τ.λ. came after ἀσελγείᾳ, πενθήσω ἐπὶ κ.τ.λ. would be easy enough, and indeed it is freq. in LXX (2 Sam. xiv. 2 ; 1 Esdr. viii. 69 (73); Is. lxvi. 10), where we have πενθέω ἐπί τινι and ἐπί τινα as well as the simple acc. Much more probably ἐπὶ τῇ ἀκ. belongs to μετανοησάντων. It is no objection to this that no such constr. is found in N.T., for nowhere else in the Epistles does μετανοέω occur, and in the Gospels and Acts it is nearly always absolute, as also is μετάνοια. In LXX, μεταν. ἐπί τινι is normal, and in English we 'repent *over*' a fault as well as '*of*' it. Cf. Wisd. xii. 19 ; 1 Chron. xxi. 15.

In Gal. v. 19 πορνεία is mentioned first of the three vices ; it is a definite form of ἀκαθαρσία, which means impurity of any kind, while ἀσέλγεια (Rom. xiii. 13 ; Gal. v. 19 ; Eph. iv. 19) adds the idea of wanton defiance of public decency.† Tertullian, Cyprian, and the translator of Irenaeus vary in their renderings of ἀσέλγεια (*vilitas* and *lascivia; immunditia* and *libido* and *incestum ; immunditia* and *libido*); and in Vulg. Jerome varies also (*impudicitia* and *luxuria*).

Neither here nor 1 Thess. ii. 3 (see Lightfoot or Milligan) can ἀκαθαρσία mean ' covetousness ' or 'impure motives in the acquisition of money.' To a Jew ἀκαθαρσία might mean 'spiritual impurity,' viz. idolatry, but not 'avarice.'

It certainly is startling to find the Apostle giving utterance to these dreadful misgivings respecting the lives of his Corinthian

---

* Contrast the Corinthians' conduct about the case of incest ; οὐχὶ μᾶλλον ἐπενθήσατε (1 Cor. v. 2). It is not likely that πενθήσω is a euphemism for 'sorrowfully *punish.*' *Veri et germani pastoris affectum nobis exprimit, quum luctu aliorum peccata se prosecuturum dicit* (Calvin).

† Originally this idea was the whole of the meaning, without any special reference to impurity.

converts *in the same letter* in which he has so frequently given them the highest praise. In the first nine chapters he says ; 'In your faith ye stand firm ' (i. 24) ; 'my joy is the joy of you *all* (ii. 3) ; 'ye are an epistle of Christ ' (iii. 3) ; 'great is my glorying on your behalf' (vii. 4) ; 'your zeal for me ' (vii. 7) ; ' in *everything* ye approved yourselves to be pure in the matter ' (vii. 11) ; 'he remembereth the obedience of you *all*' (vii. 15) ; ' in *everything* I am of good courage concerning you' (vii. 16) ; ' ye *abound in everything*, in faith, and utterance, and knowledge, and in all earnestness, and in your love to us (viii. 7) ; 'I know your readiness, of which I glory on your behalf' (ix. 2). And yet a few pages later he tells them that he fears to find them indulging in every kind of dissension and enmity, and *many* of them indulging in vile forms of impurity,—just the two forms of evil which are conspicuous in 1 Corinthians ; *e.g.* i. 11, v. 2, vi. 9–11, 13. The incongruity is so glaring that the Apostle can hardly have been unaware of it, and so tactful a teacher would see that such incompatible statements would produce little effect. What was the worth of the commendations of a man, who all the while had these black thoughts at the back of his mind?

If we suppose that these grave fears were expressed first, at a time when the condition of the Corinthian Church was alarming him, and that the generous praise followed, after the crisis had ended happily, all falls into place.

ἐλθόντος μου (א* A B G P) rather than ἐλθόντα με (א³ D K L) ; and perhaps ταπεινώσῃ (א A K) rather than ταπεινώσει (B D E G P L). But ταπεινώσῃ, like ἐλθόντα με, looks like a correction.

XIII. 1–10. The warnings connected with his approaching visit are continued, but there is not much more to be said, and he says it concisely. His concluding charges are given with Apostolic firmness and decision. He explains to them what they may expect from him (1–4), what they must do themselves (5–9), and why he writes before coming (10).

1. Τρίτον τοῦτο ἔρχομαι πρὸς ὑμᾶς. 'For the third time I am now coming to you,' or, 'This is the third time I am coming to you'; cf. xii. 14. It is possible to understand the words otherwise, for some eminent scholars do so, but the only natural meaning is that he has already paid two visits to Corinth (the long one, when he founded the Church, and the short one, when its members treated him so badly), and that he is about to pay a third. Lightfoot finds xii. 14 and xiii. 1, 2 "inexplicable under any other hypothesis." Alford says that " had not chronological theories intervened, no one would ever have thought of any other rendering." See on xii. 14.

ἐπὶ στόματος δύο μαρτύρων καὶ τριῶν. The citation is slightly abbreviated; in Deut. xix. 15 the words after καί run ἐπὶ στόματος τριῶν μαρτύρων στήσεται πᾶν ῥῆμα. In 1 Tim. v. 19 we have ἤ for καί, and some texts have ἤ here, but the sense is much the same whichever reading we adopt.* Logically 'three' should come first; 'three witnesses, and (or) two, if three are not to be had'; but it is natural to put 'two' before 'three.'

It is more important, and less easy, to decide *why* St Paul introduces this quotation. He may mean that he is going to hold a formal investigation, in which everything will be conducted according to the law which he quotes.† The accused will not be condemned unless the accusation is proved to be true on adequate testimony. He may also mean that he is not going to claim to have received revelations about the Corinthians' conduct; he will act upon human testimony, which can be sifted.

But is it likely that he was about to hold a court in which charges of misconduct could be made by one Corinthian Christian against another?‡ Would he give facilities for any such proceedings? The sins with which he is about to deal are flagrant sins, which those who committed them did not conceal, because (as they claimed) they were not sins, but acts which the emancipated Christian was free to commit, if they pleased him. There was no need of witnesses; Corinthians who gloried in their shame would be condemned out of their own mouth, and there would be no room for an Inquisition.

Again, καὶ τριῶν appears to have a definite relation to τρίτον τοῦτο, and the hypothesis of an Inquisition gives no link between the two.

To avoid these difficulties, Chrysostom and Theodoret, with Calvin and some moderns, suggest that the visits to Corinth, two paid and one about to be paid, are the three witnesses. On the previous occasions he has found much that he was obliged to condemn, and he fears that during the third visit he may find a great deal of the same kind. That will amount to threefold testimony against them. True that it is the testimony of only one witness, but it is not mere repetition of the same evidence, for he bears witness to three different groups of fact. This is not a very attractive interpretation, but St Paul's manner of using Scripture is sometimes so free that we can hardly reject this interpretation as unworthy of him. Nevertheless, if we accept it, we need not suppose with Bousset that St Paul makes the suggestion that three visits are equivalent to three witnesses

---

* Cf. Plato, *Phaedo*, 63 E, δὶς καὶ τρὶς πίνειν.

† "When he arrives, he will proceed at once to hold a judicial investigation, and will carry it through with legal stringency" (Denney).

‡ As Erasmus puts it, *quisquis delatus fuerit, is duorum aut trium hominum testimonio vel absolvetur vel damnabitur.* Cf. "Judge not alone, for none may judge alone save One" (*Pirqe Aboth*, iv. 12).

'*humorously.*' The Apostle is speaking with the utmost seriousness and gravity. Hence the impressive asyndeton of the
opening sentences. But with regard to the rival interpretations
of the Apostle's meaning we must be content to remain in doubt.
πᾶν ῥῆμα. In the original text (Deut. xix. 15) either rendering may be right, 'shall a *matter* be established' or 'shall a *word*
be confirmed,' *i.e.* regarded as valid (Num. xxx. 5). In the
quotation in Mt. xviii. 16, 'every *word* may be established'
(AV., RV.), is doubtless correct, and it may be correct here
(AV., RV.); but 'matter' or 'thing' makes equally good sense,
although there is no alternative rendering in either margin. It
is better to avoid a translation which implies that the Apostle is
about to hold a tribunal in which Corinthians will bring charges
against their fellow-Christians. He is going to pronounce
sentence on those whose conduct is notorious and is not denied.

2. προείρηκα καὶ προλέγω ὡς παρὼν τὸ δεύτερον καὶ ἀπὼν νῦν.
In order to make quite clear the balance between προείρηκα and
προλέγω, and between παρὼν τὸ δεύτερον and ἀπὼν νῦν, the
Apostle dovetails the two clauses. He says, 'I have said before,
and I do say before, as when I was present the second time, so
now being absent'; meaning, 'When I was present the second
time, I gave a warning which still holds good (perf. as in xii. 9);
and now that I am absent, I repeat the warning.' Both here and
xi. 9 παρών is imperf. participle. Those who deny the second
visit adopt the grammatically possible, but pointless and improbable
rendering, 'I have forewarned, and do now forewarn, as though
I were present the second time, although I am now absent.'
We may ask with Denney, Who would ever say 'I tell you as
if I were present with you a second time, although in point of
fact I am absent'? Such mention of the absence is so needless
as to be grotesque.

τοῖς προημαρτηκόσιν καὶ τοῖς λοιποῖς πᾶσιν. 'To those who
continued in sin before (during my second visit, as in xii. 21)
and to all the rest, viz., all those who have lapsed into sin since
that visit.' St Paul is fond of stringing together words compounded with the same preposition, esp. πρό. Cf. ix. 5; Gal.
v. 21; Rom. viii. 29; 1 Tim. i. 18, v. 24; 2 Tim. iii. 4; κατά,
xi. 20; 1 Cor. xi. 4, 5; μετά, vii. 10; παρά, 1 Tim. i. 18; ὑπέρ,
see on ὑπεραίρομαι, xii. 7.

ἐὰν ἔλθω εἰς τὸ πάλιν οὐ φείσομαι. 'If I come for the third
time, I will not spare.' Εἰς τὸ πάλιν seems to be a unique expression; but ἐς τὸ ὕστερον occurs Thuc. ii. 20. It is amphibolous here, but must be taken with what precedes. There is
no hint of hesitation in the ἐάν (cf. 1 Cor. xvi. 10; 1 Jn. ii. 1;
3 Jn. 10). In such cases 'if' is almost equivalent to 'when,'

but the possibility of an unexpected hindrance is recognized. But St Paul may be quoting what he said at the unfruitful second visit; 'If I come back again, I shall not spare.'

οὐ φείσομαι. He may have been too lenient previously; but there will be nothing of the kind now.* We have no means of knowing what manner of punishment he intends to inflict, but may conjecture public censure, degradation in public worship, and excommunication. That he would employ supernatural power to inflict bodily sickness and suffering is also possible; see on 1 Cor. v. 5 and 1 Tim. i. 20.

νῦν (‫א‬ A B D* G, Latt.) rather than νῦν γράφω (D³ E K L P, Syrr. Arm. Goth.) or νῦν λέγω (Copt. Aeth.). Some later Latin texts corrupted the *bis* after *ut praesens* into *vobis*, then *vobis* was struck out as having no authority, and thus *bis* is omitted in the Clem. Vulg.

3. ἐπεὶ δοκιμὴν ζητεῖτε. This is closely connected with what precedes, and there should be at most a semicolon (RV.) at the end of *v. 2*. He will not spare, because the Corinthians themselves have made it impossible for him to do so; 'seeing that ye are seeking a proof (ii. 9, viii. 2, ix. 13) of the Christ that speaketh in me.' They demanded that the Apostle should give some convincing sign that Christ was working in him. Christ ought to manifest His power in him. That made it necessary for St Paul to show how severely Christ condemned such sins as theirs, when there was no repentance. This seems to point to the supernatural infliction of suffering. There is perhaps something of irony in this. 'You want a proof that the power of Christ is in me. You shall have it,—in a form that will not please you.'

εἰς ὑμᾶς οὐκ ἀσθενεῖ ἀλλὰ δυνατεῖ ἐν ὑμῖν. Chiasmus once more, as in xii. 9, 20, etc.; 'Who to youward is not weak, but is powerful in you.' Δυνατέω is peculiar to Paul in Bibl. Grk., who uses it always of Divine power. When he wants a contrast to human weakness, he uses δυνατός εἰμι (*v. 9*, xii. 10); but this may be accidental. Neither towards the Corinthians nor among them had Christ shown Himself to be wanting in power. There was the amazing fact of 'saints' in such a city as Corinth. There were the spiritual gifts which had been so richly bestowed upon many members of the Church, and of which some of them had been so proud. And there were the σημεῖά τε καὶ τέρατα καὶ δυνάμεις wrought by the Apostle himself (xii. 12). Scepticism in the case of men who had had these experiences was wilful scepticism; they did not wish to be convinced. But when he comes they shall have evidence which they cannot resist.

---

* If this threat is referred to in i. 23, then this passage must have been written before that. See Rendall, p. 39.

4. καὶ γὰρ ἐσταυρώθη ἐξ ἀσθενείας. 'For it is quite true (καί) that He was crucified through weakness.' This explains *v.* 3, as *v.* 3 explains *v.* 2, and in each case there should not be more than a semicolon between the verses. To those who were on the broad way that leads to destruction the doctrine of a crucified Christ was, of course, foolishness (1 Cor. i. 18), and St Paul is here anticipating the objection that there could not be much *power* in a Christ who could not save Himself from crucifixion. He admits that in a sense it *was* through weakness that Christ was crucified; His father and He willed that He should submit to an infamous death. But that took place once for all (aor.), and now through the power of God He is alive for evermore. The ἐκ in each case marks the source; cf. xi. 26. With ἐξ ἀσθενείας cf. Phil. ii. 7, 8; Heb. v. 8; with ἐκ δυνάμεως Θεοῦ cf. Rom. vi. 4, viii. 11; Phil. ii. 9.

καὶ γὰρ ἡμεῖς ἀσθενοῦμεν ἐν αὐτῷ. Another explanation of what immediately precedes. The fact that both weakness and power have been exhibited in the case of Christ is all the more credible, because the very same surprising change is found to take place in those who have such real union with Him; 'For *we* also are weak in Him, yet we shall live with Him through the power of God toward you.' Incidentally we here see how intensely real to St Paul was his union with Christ. In this he is ever a mystic. He is again referring to vigorous action during the remainder of his life, especially to what will be manifested in his impending visit to Corinth. Even if εἰς ὑμᾶς is not original, ἡμεῖς probably means 'we Apostles' rather than 'we Christians.' The Corinthians have to deal with a Christ who was raised from death to power, and with Christ's Apostle who has been saved from many deaths to do work for Him.

St Paul uses both the classical fut. of ζάω as well as the later form ζήσομαι, but the latter occurs mostly in quotations from LXX.

The εἰ before ἐσταυρώθη (א³ A D³ E L, f Vulg. Syrr.) may be omitted with א* B D* G K P 17, d e g Memph. After ἀσθενοῦμεν it is difficult to decide between ἐν (B D E K L P, d e Vulg.) and σύν (א A F G, f g Copt.). ζήσομεν (א A B D* 17) rather than ζήσωμεν (G) or ζησόμεθα (D³ E K L). B D³ E, Arm., Chrys. (twice) omit εἰς ὑμᾶς, which Vulg. renders *in vobis*, as if we had ἐν ὑμῖν, as in *v.* 3.

5. ἑαυτοὺς πειράζετε . . . ἑαυτοὺς δοκιμάζετε. The pronouns are very emphatic; 'It is your own selves that you must continually test, . . . your own selves that you must continually prove' (pres. imperat.). The Corinthians thought that it was their business to test him, whether he was an Apostle speaking with the authority of Christ (*v.* 3). He is prepared to give them proof of this; but what they ought to be doing is testing themselves, whether they are in the faith and Christ is in them. Πειράζω here, as often, has the neutral meaning of 'test' or 'try,' without any notion of tempting to evil; see Swete on Rev. ii. 2 and Hort on 1 Pet. i. 7, and cf. Jn. vi. 6; Jas. i. 2. The testing would be self-examination in accordance with Mt. vii. 16; 'By their fruits ye shall know them'; were they living Christian lives? Δοκιμάζω is never used in the sense of tempting to evil; it may be neutral (Lk. xii. 56, xiv. 19), but it commonly means 'proving in the expectation of approving' (viii. 22; 1 Cor. xi. 28; Rom. ii. 18, xiv. 22; Eph. v. 10; 1 Thess. ii. 4). This may be the reason why St Paul adds it after πειράζετε : 'Test yourselves; and I sincerely hope that you will stand the test.' More probably he adds the word in order to prepare the way for ἀδόκιμοι and δόκιμοι. The three words give an opportunity for playing on words of similar formation, such as St Paul delights in ; cf. i. 13, iii. 2, iv. 8, etc.; also Rom. i. 28.

ἐν τῇ πίστει. An expression of comprehensive meaning, 'the principles of the new spiritual life.' On the hypothesis of the integrity of 2 Corinthians it is difficult to understand how the Apostle could tell them to test themselves as to whether they are in the faith after having assured them that τῇ πίστει ἑστήκατε (i. 24) and ἐν παντὶ περισσεύετε, πίστει, καὶ λογῳ κ.τ.λ. If he first told them to test themselves, and in a later letter assured them that he was quite satisfied, all runs quite naturally.

ἢ οὐκ ἐπιγινώσκετε ἑαυτούς ; 'Or know ye not as to your own selves, that Jesus Christ is in you?' The interrogative ἢ is not rare; 1 Cor. vi. 16; Rom. vi. 3, ix. 21; Mt. vii. 4, 9. As in 1 Cor. xiii. 12, the compound verb probably implies complete knowledge ; he thinks that they must be quite sure that Christ is in them,—unless, of course, they are leading utterly un-Christian lives.

εἰ μήτι ἀδόκιμοί ἐστε. 'Unless perhaps ye be reprobates,' i.e. are not accepted (δέχομαι) because you cannot stand the δοκιμασία. He is allowing for the distressing possibility that they may be disqualified. Both ἀδόκιμος and δόκιμος are mainly Pauline in N.T. (see on 1 Cor. ix. 27 ; Rom. i. 28), and in LXX ἀδόκιμος is very rare. Here the terms have a different meaning as applied to the Apostle and as applied to the Corinthians. Was the former a genuine Apostle ? Were all the latter genuine Christians ?

We ought perhaps to prefer Ἰησοῦς Χριστός (B D E K L, d e Syrr. Goth.) to Χρ.Ἰησ. (א A F G P, f g Vulg. Copt. Arm.); see on i. 1. B D, Aeth. omit ἐστιν after ἐν ὑμῖν.

6. ἐλπίζω δὲ ὅτι γνώσεσθε. 'But I hope that you will come to know that *we* are not reprobate.' This might mean one of two things ; 'I anticipate that experience will teach you that Christ is in *us* with power to inflict punishment' : or, 'I trust that your testing of yourselves will show that you are sound, and then you are sure to see that we are sound.' It is the spiritual who can judge with sureness of the spiritual. That ἐλπίζω may mean 'expect' rather than 'hope' is clear from viii. 5; but St Paul is not likely to have meant that he *expected* to be obliged to punish; he certainly *hoped* that no such proof of his power would be needed. The rapid changes between 1 sing. (*vv.* 2, 6) and 1 plur. (*vv.* 4, 7) should be noted. In all these cases he probably means himself only.

7. εὐχόμεθα δὲ πρὸς τὸν Θεόν. 'But we pray unto God that you may do nothing evil.' He has no desire to have any opportunity for proving his Apostolic power by inflicting punishment. He would rather that his Apostleship should be undemonstrated than that it should be demonstrated owing to their misconduct. That they should do what is noble is worth far more to him than that he should be able to give them proof of his being an Apostle of Christ. Εὔχομαι πρός occurs several times in LXX; Num. xi. 2, xxi. 7; 2 Kings xx. 2; Job xxii. 27; 2 Macc. xv. 27, which is just what we have here. The ἵνα here gives the purpose rather than the contents of his petition; the latter has been already expressed by acc. and infin.

Τὸ καλόν implies that the act is *seen* to be morally beautiful, and in Bibl. Grk. τὸ καλὸν ποιέω is peculiar to Paul (Gal. vi. 9; Rom. vii. 21). Like αὐτάρκεια, ἐπιείκεια, πραότης, προαιρέομαι, and φαῦλος, it may be evidence of St Paul's acquaintance with Greek philosophical language.

ὡς ἀδόκιμοι. The ὡς means that he would in that case seem to be disqualified. He would not have stood the test; not because he had failed when tested, but because the test had never been applied to him. He could not exhibit his power of punishing, because there was no one who deserved punishment. He would welcome such a happy state of things, however much it might tell against himself.

εὐχόμεθα (א A B D* G P 17, Latt.) is doubtless to be preferred to εὔχομαι (D³ E K L, Goth.).

8. οὐ γὰρ δυνάμεθα. He does not mean that no one can be successful in opposing the truth; *magna est veritas et praevalet*; a principle which has no special point here. He means that it would be utterly at variance with his character to take sides against the truth. Such a thing is morally impossible for him. All his life through he has been an ardent supporter of what he believed to be true, and what, since he became illuminated as a chosen Apostle of Christ, he knows to be true. This he can continue to be, and will. To rejoice in iniquity, because it gives him an advantage, is impossible for him. He cannot desire that they should be found to be doing wrong, in order that he may be proved to be right.

9. χαίρομεν γὰρ ὅταν ἡμεῖς ἀσθενῶμεν. 'For we are not merely content, we *rejoice* whenever we are weak, through not being able to manifest our power, and ye are strong, through doing nothing that requires punishment or censure.' Jonah was angry because the repentance of the Ninevites caused his prediction of their overthrow to be unfulfilled; but the Apostle is delighted whenever his Corinthians repent, or prove themselves to be in no need of repentance, and thus cause his promised demonstration of Apostolic power (*vv.* 3, 4) to be unfulfilled. The γάρ indicates that this verse is a confirmation of *v.* 8.

τοῦτο καὶ εὐχόμεθα, τὴν ὑμῶν κατάρτισιν. 'This is an additional thing that we pray for, even your perfecting.' To pray that they may go on to perfection is a great deal more than merely praying that they may do nothing evil (*v.* 7). AV. mars the effect by translating εὔχομαι first 'pray' and then 'wish.' RV. is more accurate in having 'pray' in both places, and also in rendering κατάρτισις 'perfecting' rather than 'perfection'; it is the *growth* in holiness that is meant. Cf. καταρτισμός (Eph. iv. 12). Neither noun is found elsewhere in Bibl. Grk., but the verb καταρτίζω (*v.* 11) is common enough. The original idea is that of 'fitting together,' whether of setting bones or reconciling parties, and hence in N.T. the verb is often used of setting right what has previously gone wrong, rectifying and restoring, rather than merely bringing onwards to perfection. See Lightfoot on 1 Thess. iii. 10 and J. A. Robinson on Eph. iv. 12. Such a word is admirably suited to the context; it suggests, without necessarily implying, that at present things are wrong and that a process of rectification is needed. See on i. 6 for the Pauline usage of placing ὑμῶν between the art. and the substantive.

τοῦτο καί (א* A B D* G P 17, Latt.) rather than τοῦτο δὲ καί (א³ D³ E K L).

10. Διὰ τοῦτο. 'For this cause,' as iv. 1, vii. 13 ; 1 Cor. iv. 17, etc. 'Therefore' (AV.) may be kept for οὖν (i. 17, iii. 12, v. 6, 11, 20, etc.), and 'wherefore' for διό (i. 20, ii. 8, iv. 13, etc.). It is because he desires their restoration and perfecting that he sends this letter before coming himself. But διὰ τοῦτο may possibly anticipate ἵνα and refer to what follows.

ταῦτα ἀπὼν γράφω, ἵνα παρὼν μὴ ἀποτόμως χρήσωμαι. 'When absent I write these things, that when present I may not deal sharply.' The rare adverb (Tit. i. 13 ; Wisd. v. 22) reflects its meaning upon ταῦτα: he writes sharply, that he may not have to act sharply. Ἀπότομος occurs Wisd. v. 20, vi. 5, xi. 10, xii. 9,

xviii. 15, and nowhere else in Bibl. Grk. This is further evidence (see on iv. 4, v. 1, 9, vi. 3, 6, 7, viii. 20, x. 3, 5) that St Paul knew the Book of Wisdom. Χράομαι with an adv. and no dat. occurs Job xxxiv. 20 (παρανόμως); Is. xxviii. 21 (ἀλλοτρίως); Dan. viii. 7 (διαφόρως); Esth. i. 19, ix. 27 (ἄλλως).

κατὰ τὴν ἐξουσίαν ἥν ὁ κύριος ἔδωκεν. This depends upon μὴ ἀποτόμως χρ. He desires to be able to abstain from dealing sharply 'in accordance with the authority which the Lord gave me for building up and not for casting down' (x. 4, 8). Chastisement, if needed, would, of course, be for their building up ; but at the moment it would look like demolition.

Throughout the passage the Apostle's mind hovers between hope and fear, hope that the condition of the Corinthian Church may be better than he has been led to believe, and fear that he may have to use very drastic measures. There has been wrongdoing ; of that there can be no doubt ; he witnessed it himself during his second visit. But they may have repented, and there may have been no recurrence of grievous evils. On the other hand, the wrongdoers may be still impenitent, and others may be following their bad examples. He has no prejudice against any of them, and it will be a great delight to him to find that his misgivings are now baseless. But it is fair to them to declare plainly, that there will be a thorough investigation, and that impenitent transgressors, if they exist, will be severely dealt with. That unwelcome thought is now dismissed, and with a few affectionate sentences the Apostle brings his storm-tossed letter into a haven of love and peace.

XIII. 11-13. CONCLUDING EXHORTATION, SALUTATION, AND BENEDICTION.

If we adopt the hypothesis that the last four chapters are part of a letter written and sent before the first nine chapters, we need not, as some do, stop short at xiii. 10 as the end of the earlier fragment. Beyond reasonable doubt these remaining verses are the conclusion of the earlier letter, and from x. 1 to xiii. 13 (14) is all one piece. The change to an affectionate tone here, after the vehemence and severity of x. 1–xiii. 10, is as natural and intelligible as the change in the opposite direction between chapters ix. and x. is unnatural and perplexing.* Secondly, there are fairly conspicuous links between these concluding verses and those which immediately precede them ; καταρτίζεσθε recalls τὴν ὑμῶν κατάρτισιν, while τὸ αὐτὸ φρονεῖτε, εἰρηνεύετε looks like a direct reference to his dread of finding ἔρις, ζῆλος, θυμοί

---

* There is a similar change from sternness to gentleness between 2 Thess. iii. 10-15 and 16-18.

κ.τ.λ. (xii. 20), rampant among them. There is nothing of the same kind between these concluding verses and the latter part of ix. Moreover, the hypothesis that the whole of the last portion of an earlier letter has become united with the whole of the first portion of a later one is not a violently improbable conjecture. That a section of the earlier letter has been inserted between the main portion and the conclusion of the later letter is much less easy to believe. See p. 385.

11. Λοιπόν. 'Finally'; lit. 'as to what remains' (1 Cor. i. 16, iv. 2; 1 Thess. iv. 1; 2 Tim. iv. 8). Perhaps more colloquial than τὸ λοιπόν (2 Thess. iii. 1). See Lightfoot on Phil. iii. 1, and on 1 Thess. iv. 1.

ἀδελφοί. Freq. in 1 Cor., rare in 2 Cor. i.–ix., and here only in 2 Cor. x.–xiii. They are still his brothers.

χαίρετε. "Neither 'farewell' alone, nor 'rejoice' alone" (Lightfoot on Phil. iv. 4); but here the meaning 'farewell' certainly prevails. 'Rejoice' would be rather incongruous after οὐ φείσομαι. Note the pres. imperat. in all the verbs; the good points indicated are to be lasting. 'Continue to do all these things.' There must be a considerable process day by day to bring about complete spiritual restoration.

καταρτίζεσθε. This seems clearly to refer to τὴν ὑμῶν κατάρτισιν (v. 9). 'Work your way onwards to perfection.' See on κατηρτισμένοι, 1 Cor. i. 10, which is similar in meaning, and see the illustrations in Wetstein on Mt. iv. 21. There is much that requires to be amended; many deficiencies remain to be made good, even if those who have been in sin are now penitent.

παρακαλεῖσθε. This might mean 'be of good comfort' (AV.) or 'be comforted' (RV.), but more probably it means 'be exhorted,' *exhortamini* (Vulg.), *i.e.* 'listen to my exhortations and entreaties.' For 'comfort one another' we should probably have παρακαλεῖτε ἀλλήλους, as in 1 Thess. iv. 18, v. 11, or ἑαυτούς (cf. v. 5).

τὸ αὐτὸ φρονεῖτε. 'Be of the same mind,' 'Be harmonious in thought and aim.' All Churches needed this exhortation (Rom. xii. 16, xv. 5; Phil. ii. 2, iv. 2), but no Church more than that of Corinth. This fits on well to the renderings given above; 'Farewell. Go on to perfection; follow my exhortations; be of the same mind.' But such a sequence as 'Rejoice; be perfected; be comforted; be of the same mind,' is rather disjointed.

εἰρηνεύετε. 'Live in peace' (1 Thess. v. 13; Rom. xii. 18; Mk. ix. 50). In LXX the verb is specially freq. in Job and Ecclus., but nowhere is there the exhortation εἰρηνεύετε. It is the natural result of τὸ αὐτὸ φρονεῖν. But there is a more momentous result, which is the crown of all.

καὶ ὁ Θεὸς τῆς ἀγάπης καὶ εἰρήνης ἔσται μεθ' ὑμῶν. This
corresponds to the two preceding exhortations, τῆς ἀγάπης to
τὸ αὐτὸ φρονεῖτε, and εἰρήνης to εἰρηνεύετε.   Cf. Lk. x. 6.   Vulg.
usually has *caritas* for ἀγάπη, but here, although there is no
diligo to influence the rendering, it has *dilectio*.   ' The God of
Peace ' is an expression which St Paul has elsewhere ; Rom. xv.
33, xvi. 20 ; Phil. iv. 9 ; cf. 1 Cor. xiv. 33 ; 2 Thess. iii. 16 ;
Heb. xiii. 20.   ' The God of love ' is used nowhere else.   Even
if the two preceding exhortations had not suggested the order,
St Paul would probably have put ἀγάπη before εἰρήνη (Gal. v. 22)
Some texts here change the order (D E L, d e Goth. Arm.), probably influenced by the passages in which ὁ Θεὸς τῆς εἰρήνης occurs.

12.   Ἀσπάσασθε ἀλλήλους . . . ἀσπάζονται ὑμᾶς οἱ ἅγιοι πάντες.
Salutations at the close of the letter are found in all four groups
of the Pauline Epistles ; those in 1 Cor. xvi. 19–21 are specially
full ; still more so those in Rom. xvi. 3–23.   Cf. 1 Thess. v. 26 ;
Col. iv. 10–15 ; Philem. 23 ; Tit. iii. 15 ; 2 Tim. iv. 19–21.
Papyri show that such salutations at the close of a letter were a
common feature in ordinary correspondence, and ἀσπάζομαι is
commonly the verb used.   As in 1 Cor. xvi. 20, the πάντες
comes at the end with emphasis.   The Apostle is sure that all
the Christians with whom he is in touch in Macedonia will
desire to "send their love" to their brethren in Corinth.

ἐν ἁγίῳ φιλήματι.   We must follow אB D E K P, d e in reading
thus here.   No doubt the order ἐν φιλ. ἁγίῳ has been adopted
in A F G L, f g Vulg. to make this passage agree with 1 Cor. xvi.
20 ; 1 Thess. v. 26 ; Rom. xvi. 16.   See the notes on all three
of these passages respecting the φίλημα ἅγιον, and also *Enc.
Bibl.* 4254, and *Enc. Brit.* art. 'Pax.'   The suggestion that the
'kiss of concord' was already an institution in the synagogue
has received confirmation from what seem to be Armenian quotations from Philo ; and, if that is accepted, the view that the holy
kiss in the Christian Church was never promiscuous, is confirmed.   That the kiss given to a Rabbi suggested it is less
probable.   The sexes being separated in the synagogues, the
men would kiss men, and the women would kiss women, and
Christian assemblies would follow the same practice as a security
that the φίλημα was ἅγιον.   Nowhere in N.T. is the holy kiss
connected with public worship.   Justin (*Apol.* i. 65) connects it
with the Eucharist, Tertullian (*De Orat.* 18) with all prayers,
and he seems to imply that the kiss in some cases had become
promiscuous ; thus (*Ad Uxor.* ii. 4) *Quis in carcerem ad oscu-
landa vincula martyris reptare patietur ?   Jam vero alicui fratrum
ad osculum convenire ?* and (*De virg. vel.* 14) *dum inter amplexus
et oscula assidua concalescit.*   But it is not clear that these

passages refer to the liturgical kiss. Express prohibition of the sexes kissing one another in public worship is found in the Apostolic Constitutions (ii. 57, viii. 11). In the East, the kiss seems to have taken place before the consecration of the bread and wine; in the West, after it. Cyril of Jerusalem says of it; "Think not that this kiss ranks with those given in public by common friends. It is not such: this kiss blends souls one with another, and solicits for them entire forgiveness. Therefore this kiss is the sign that our souls are mingled together and have banished all remembrance of wrong (Mt. v. 23). The kiss therefore is reconciliation, and for this reason is holy" (*Catech.* xxiii. 3). The substitution of a 'pax-bred' (pax-board), which was kissed first by the clergy and then passed round to the congregation, is said to have been introduced in England by Archbishop Walter of York in 1250 and to have spread to other Churches. Disputes about precedence caused the congregational use of these tablets to be abandoned. The British Museum possesses richly ornamented examples of them. In the Greek Church the 'holy kiss' seems to be represented by the priest's kissing 'the holy things' (paten, chalice, and table) and by the deacon's kissing his orarion, where the figure of the cross is (J. N. W. B. Robertson, *The Divine Liturgies*, pp. 290–292).

While ἁγίῳ has special point, being added in order to distinguish this kiss from the kisses of ordinary affection or respect, no special meaning is to be found in οἱ ἅγιοι, as if they were to be distinguished from other believers who were not ἅγιοι. It has the usual meaning of 'Christians,' those who by baptism had been 'consecrated' to the service of God. Cf. i. 1, viii. 4, ix. 1, 12; etc. The πάντες comes last with emphasis; but Theodoret exaggerates its meaning when he suggests that St Paul is sending a salutation from the whole of Christendom. All the converts in Macedonia who knew that the Apostle was sending a letter to Corinth wished him to include a kind message from themselves. No salutations to individuals are needed, because St Paul is so soon coming himself.

RV. and AV. follow earlier English Versions in taking ἀσπάζονται ὑμᾶς οἱ ἅγιοι πάντες as a separate verse, *v.* 13, making the benediction which follows it to be *v.* 14. Gregory (*Prolegomena*, pp. 173 ff.) has collected a number of instances in which editions differ as to the divisions between verses.

13. Ἡ χάρις τοῦ κυρίου Ἰησοῦ. The conjectures that this benediction, which is the fullest in wording and in meaning of all the benedictions in the Pauline Epistles, was written by the Apostle with his own hand (Hoffmann), and was already a formula current in the Churches which he had founded

(Lietzmann), are interesting rather than probable. If the latter were correct, we should expect to find the same formula used in the benedictions at the close of later Epistles; whereas this triple form is unique. Evidently the simple form was the one which was usual with the Apostle himself. There are slight variations in wording, as to the insertion or omission of ἡμῶν, of Χριστοῦ (as by B here), of πάντων, and of τοῦ πνεύματος before ὑμῶν, but it is only the 'Grace of the Lord Jesus' that is mentioned. In no other benediction are ἡ ἀγάπη τοῦ Θεοῦ and ἡ κοινωνία τοῦ ἀγίου πνεύματος expressed. And it is the fact that this simple form is the Apostle's usual form which accounts for the order here, 'the Lord Jesus Christ' coming before 'God' and 'the Holy Spirit.' St Paul began to write according to the type found in his earlier (1 Thess. v. 28; 2 Thess. iii. 18; Gal. vi. 18; 1 Cor. xvi. 23) and later (Phil. iv. 23; Philem. 25) letters, and then for some reason made the benediction more full. The reason may have been either a wish to show that the severe passages which he has just dictated do not mean any abatement in his affection or in his desire for their spiritual advancement, or the thought that a community in which there had been so much party-spirit and contention required an abundant outpouring of the love of God and of the fellowship of the Holy Spirit. This is a more probable explanation of the order of the Divine Names than the suggestion that it is through the grace of Christ that we come to the love of God (Bengel).* From different points of view either may be placed first. 'No man can come to Me, except the Father which sent Me draw him' (Jn. vi. 44); and 'No one cometh unto the Father but by Me' (Jn. xiv. 6). The shortest forms of benediction are found in Col. iv. 18; 1 Tim. vi. 21; 2 Tim. iv. 22; Tit. iii. 15. The only one which comes near to this in fulness is Eph. vi. 23, 24, but in that there is no mention of the Holy Spirit. Ἡ χάρις is everywhere followed by μετά: it is the Pauline amplification of the ordinary conclusion of letters, ἔρρωσο or ἔρρωσθε, ἐρρῶσθαί σε εὔχομαι or ἐρρῶσθαι ὑμᾶς εὔχομαι. Acts xv. 29 we have Ἔρρωσθε, but Acts xxiii. 30 must not be quoted for Ἔρρωσο, which is an interpolation. From 2 Thess. iii. 17 we learn that this χάρις was σημεῖον ἐν πάσῃ ἐπιστολῇ, and it is probable that he usually, if not invariably, wrote it with his own hand. See on 1 Cor. vi. 21, 23.

On the whole, it is safest to regard all three genitives as subjective; the grace which comes from the Lord Jesus Christ, the love which God inspires in the hearts of His children (cf. *v.*

---

* "It is through *the grace of Jesus* (cf. viii. 9) that Paul has learned of *the love of God*, and therefore the name of Jesus is significantly put first" (McFadyen). Cf. Eph. ii. 18, which gives some support to this.

11), the sense of membership which the Holy Spirit imparts to those who are united in one Body.   But in either the second or the third case the genitive may be objective; love towards God, communion with the Spirit.   "No exegetical skill," as Lietzmann remarks, can give us certainty as to the exact meaning of ἡ κοινωνία τοῦ ἁγίου πνεύματος.   See Bousset, *ad loc.*

μετὰ πάντων ὑμῶν.   No one is excluded.   He has had to say stern and sharp things to some of them; but to every one of them, even to those who have been his bitterest opponents, he sends his blessing.   The πάντων is exceptional in these benediction·; cf. 2 Thess. iii. 18.   See Stanley, *ad loc.*

This verse "suggests beyond a doubt that beneath the religious life of the Apostolic age there lay a profound, though as yet unformulated faith in the tripersonality of God" (Swete, *The Holy Spirit in the N.T.* p. 198); in other words, "that St Paul and the Church of his day thought of the Supreme Source of spiritual blessing as not single but threefold—threefold in essence, and not only in a manner of speech" (Sanday in Hastings, *DB.* ii. p. 213).   It is *egregium de ss. Trinitate testimonium* (Bengel), for it reveals the background of the Apostle's thought, and shows that he was able to expect that language of this kind would be understood in so young a Church as that of Corinth.   Jn 1 Cor. xii. 4–6 we have similar evidence of a sense of the threefold nature of the Source of all good; 'the same *Spirit* . . . the same *Lord* . . . the same *God.*'   But it is all undogmatic and undeveloped.   Forty years later Clement of Rome (*Cor.* xlvi. 3, lviii. 2) is more definite; "one God and one Christ and one Spirit of grace"; and "as God liveth, and the Lord Jesus Christ liveth, and the Holy Spirit."   In both places he has the usual order, whereas St Paul has it in neither.   Eph. iv. 4–6 ought not to be quoted as exactly parallel, the meaning of πνεῦμα being different.   The Apostle frequently distinguishes between Jesus Christ as Κύριος and the Father as Θεός (i. 3, xi. 31 ; 1 Thess. i. 1 ; 2 Thess. i. 1, 2, 12, ii. 16, etc.).   That he was acquainted with the tradition respecting the baptismal formula preserved in Mt. xxviii. 19 cannot be inferred from this verse.   Indeed, if he had been acquainted with it, we might here have had a nearer approach to the formula.   Cf. Eph. ii. 18, iii. 14–17 ; Heb. vi. 4–6 ; 1 Jn. iii. 23, 24, iv. 2 ; Rev. i. 4, 5 ; Jude 20, 21 ; and see Plummer, *S. Matthew*, pp. 432 ff.   The triple benediction in Num. vi. 24–26 may be compared; 'Jehovah bless thee, and guard thee; Jehovah cause His face to shine upon thee, and show thee favour; Jehovah lift up His face towards thee, and appoint thee welfare.'   But there it is only the gifts that are distinguished, the Giver being the same throughout.   See Gray, *ad loc.*

B omits Χριστοῦ, but it may be retained.　אֽ* A B C F G, 17, f g, etc., omit ᾽Αμήν, which here, as in most other places, is a liturgical addition at the end of the Epistles.

The hypothesis that the last portion cf one letter has been accidentally joined to the first portion of another letter is supported by the fact that this very thing has happened in the case of other documents belonging to primitive Christian literature. The true text of the Epistle to Diognetus ends abruptly at the tenth chapter. "The two remaining chapters belong to some different work, which has been accidentally attached to it, just as in most of the extant MSS. the latter part of the Epistle of Polycarp is attached to the former part of the Epistle of Barnabas, so as to form in appearance one work" (Lightfoot, *The Apostolic Fathers*, p. 488). These MSS. "are nine in number, and all belong to the same family, as appears from the fact that the Epistle of Polycarp runs on continuously into the Epistle of Barnabas without any break, the mutilated ending of Polycarp, § 9, ἀποθανόντα καὶ δι᾽ ἡμᾶς ὑπὸ, being followed by the mutilated beginning of Barnabas, § 5, τὸν λαὸν τὸν καινὸν κ.τ.λ." (*ibid.* pp. 166 f.).　See also Lightfoot, *S. Clement of Rome*, i. p. 5.

The subscription, πρὸς Κορινθίους δευτέρα ἐγράφη ἀπὸ Φιλίππων τῆς Μακεδονίας διὰ Τίτου καὶ Λουκᾶ, has very little authority, although it is found in K, many cursives, Syr-Hark. and Copt.　L omits 'of Macedonia'; Syr-Pesh. omits Luke; a few cursives add Barnabas.　Philippi may be pure conjecture; Titus and Luke come from viii. 18.　The best authorities, א A B 17, have simply πρὸς Κορινθίους β.

INDEXES

INDEX I. GENERAL.

387

INDEX II. GREEK.

*** Expressions peculiar to 2 Corinthians in N.T.*

INDEX III. DOUBLE COMPOUNDS.

* Words peculiar to 2 Corinthians in N.T.

26

Index IV. Variant Vulgate Renderings.

ἐκτός, *extra, praeter.*
ἔμπροσθεν, ante, coram, **in** conspectu.
ἐνοικέω, inhabito, habito.
ἐξαπορέομαι, taedet me, destituor.
ἐξέρχομαι, proficiscor, procedo, prodeo, exeo, egredior.
ἐξίστημι, mente excedo, in furorem vertor, admiror, stupeo, obstipesco.
ἔξω, *foris, extra,* foras, foras extra.
ἔξωθεν, *foris,* aforis, deforis, de foris, extrinsecus.
ἐπαίρω, extollo, *levo, elevo,* sublevo.
ἐπιβαρέω, onero, gravo.
ἐπιεικία, *modestia,* clementia.
ἐπικαλέομαι, invoco, appello.
ἐπιποθέω, cupio, desidero, concupisco.
ἐπιταγή, imperium, praeceptum.
ἐπιτελέω, *perficio, consummo* (pass.), *fio.*
ἐπιχορηγέω, administro, subministro, tribuo.
ἐριθία, dissensio, contentio.
ὁ ἔσω, qui intus est, interior.
ἕτοιμος, paratus, praeparatus.
εὐάρεστος, placeo, placens, placitus, beneplacitus.
εὐδοκέω. See the ten renderings, p. 153.
εὐπρόσδεκτος, acceptabilis, acceptus.
εὔχομαι, *oro,* opto, orationem facio.
εὐωδία, bonus odor, odor.
ζηλόω, aemulor, zelo.
ἥδιστα, libenter, libentissime.
ἡττάομαι, minus habeo, superor.
θαρρέω, audeo, confido.
θησαυρίζω, thesaurizo, recondo, repono.
θλίψις, tribulatio, *pressura.*
θυμός, animositas, ira, indignatio, furor.
ἰδιώτης, imperitus, idiota.
ἱκανόω, idoneum facio, dignum facio.
ἰσότης, aequalitas, quod aequum est.
ἰσχυρός, fortis, validus, magnus.
καθάπερ, *sicut,* tanquam, *quemadmodum.*

καθαρίζω, mundo, emundo, purifico.
καθώς, *sicut,* juxta quod, *quemadmodum,* prout.
καλῶς, recte, bene.
καταβάλλω, dejicio, projicio, jacio.
καταλύω, dissolvo, *destruo,* deverto, diverto, *solvo.*
καταισχύνομαι, *confundor, erubesco.*
καταπίνω, absorbeo, *devoro,* glutio.
καταργέω, *evacuo, destruo,* aboleo. *solvo.*
καταρτίζω, *perficio,* apto, instruo, compleo.
κατεργάζομαι, operor, *facio, perficio,* efficio, consummo.
κατεσθίω, *devoro,* comedo.
κενός, vacuus, inanis.
κενόω, *evacuo,* exinanio.
κλίματα, regiones, partes.
κοινωνία, societas, communicatio.
κοινωνός, socius, communicator, consors.
κολαφίζω, colaphizo, colaphis caedo.
κομίζομαι, refero, *percipio, recipio, accipio,* reporto.
κρίνω, *statuo, aestimo,* judico.
λαμβάνω, *accipio, capio, percipio,* consequor, sumo, *adsumo.*
λάμπω, splendesco, inluceo, luceo, fulgeo, refulgeo, resplendesco.
λαός, populus, plebs.
λειτουργία, officium, obsequium, ministerium.
λογίζομαι, existimor, *arbitror,* reputo, imputo, *aestimo,* cogito.
λογισμός, consilium, *cogitatio.*
λοιπόν, de cetero, ceterum, in reliquo, jam.
μακροθυμία, longanimitas, *patientia.*
μένω, maneo, permaneo, remaneo.
μέριμνα, sollicitudo, *aerumna,* cura.
μεταμορφόομαι, transformor, reformor, transfiguror.
μετανοέω, paenitiam ago, paeniteor.
μετασχηματίζω, transfiguro, reformo.
μηκέτι, non jam, non amplius,

non adhuc, *ultra non*, ulterius non, amplius jam non, numquam, *non*.

μόχθος, *aerumna*, fatigatio.

νηστεία, jejunium, jejunatio.

νόημα, *cogitatio*, intellectus, intelligentia, mens.

οἰκοδομή, aedificatio, structura.

οἰκτιρμός, misericordia, miseratio.

ὀλίγος, modicus, brevis, paucus, parvus, minimus, minor, pusillus.

ὅλος, universus, totus, omnis.

ὅσοι, quotquot, quicunque, qui.

οὐκέτι, non ultra, jam non, *ultra non*, amplius non, *non*.

οὕτως, ita, sic, *sicut*.

πάθημα, passio, vitium.

πάλιν, iterum, rursum, rursus.

παράπτωμα, delictum, peccatum.

παρέρχομαι, *transeo, praetereo*, praetranseo.

παρίστημι, *constituo*, exhibeo, commendo, adsigno, praeparo, *statuo*, probo.

παρουσία, praesentia, adventus.

παρών, praesens, cum essem apud, quod pervenit ad.

πενθέω, lugeo, luctum habeo.

πεποίθησις, confidentia, fiducia.

πράσσω, gero, *facio*, ago, *observo*, sector, admitto.

πραΰτης, mansuedo, lenitas, *modestia*.

προέρχομαι, *praevenio*, progredior, procedo, antecedo.

προπέμπω, deduco, praemitto.

πρόσωπον, facies, vultus.

πτωχός, egens, pauper, egenus.

πωρόω, obtundo, *excaeco*, induro.

ῥύομαι, eripio, eruo, libero.

σκῆνος, habitatio, tabernaculum.

σκοπέω, contemplor, *observo*, considero, video.

σκορπίζω, dispergo, spargo.

στέλλομαι, devito, subtraho.

στενάζω, ingemisco, gemo.

συνέχω, urgeo, coarto, comprehendo, teneo, comprimo, coangusto, contineo, insto, vexo.

συνζάω, convivo, simul vivo.

συνοχή, angustia, *pressura*.

σωφρονέω, sobrius sum, prudens sum, sana mente, sanae mentis.

τελέω, *perficio, consummo*, finio, impleo.

τέρατα, prodigia, portenta.

τηρέω, servo, custodio, conservo, *observo*, reservo.

τοὐναντίον, e contraro, e contra.

τυφλόω, obcaeco, *excaeco*, obscuro.

ὑπακοή, oboedientia, obsequium, oboeditio.

ὑπερβάλλων, excellens, eminens, supereminens, abundans.

ὑπερβολή, sublimitas, magnitudo.

ὑπομονή, tolerantia, *patientia*.

ὑποταγή, oboedientia, subjectio.

ὑστερέω, minus facio, egeo, minus sum, penuriam patior, desum, deficio.

ὑστέρημα, inopia, id quod deest.

φανερόω, manifesto, propalo (pass.), appareo, manifestus sum, patefactus sum.

φαῦλος, malus, pravus.

φθάνω, pervenio, *praevenio*.

φθείρω, *corrumpo*, disperdo.

φιλοτιμέομαι, contendo, operam do.

φράσσω, infringo, obstruo, obturo.

φρονέω, sapio, sentio.

φρόνιμος, sapiens, prudens.

χειροτονέω, ordino, *constituo*.

χορηγέω, praesto, administro.

χρηστότης, suavitas, bonitas, benignitas, bonum.

χωρέω, *capio*, revertor, emittor.

χωρίς, *praeter, extra*, sine.

ὡς, ut, quasi, *sicut*.

Latin words which translate more than one Greek word are in italics.

Printed by MORRISON & GIBB LIMITED, *Edinburgh*